THE
PERFECT
NAME

THE
PERFECT NAME

A Step-by-Step Guide to Naming Your Baby

JEANINE COX
AND THE EDITORS OF

BABYZONE®

Sterling Publishing, New York

Published by Sterling Publishing Co., Inc.
387 Park Avenue South, New York, NY 10016

© 2004 by Jeanine Cox

Distributed in Canada by Sterling Publishing
c/o Canadian Manda Group, 165 Dufferin Street
Toronto, Ontario, Canada M6K 3H6

Distributed in Great Britain by Chrysalis Books
64 Brewery Road, London N7 9NT, England

Distributed in Australia by Capricorn Link (Australia) Pty. Ltd.
P.O. Box 704, Windsor, NSW 2756, Australia

Cover and interior design by Christine Heun
Illustrations: © John Coulter/Lilla Rogers Studio

ISBN 0-7607-4295-2

Library of Congress Cataloging-in-Publication Data

Cox, Jeanine.
    The perfect name : a step-by-step guide to naming your baby / Jeanine Cox and the editors
of BabyZone.com.
      p. cm.
    ISBN 0-7607-4295-2 (pbk.)
    1. Names, Personal. I. BabyZone.com (Firm) II. Title.

CS2377.C695 2004
929.4'4—dc22
                                2004014061

  5 7 9 8 6

Manufactured in the United States of America

The quotes in this book have been drawn from many sources, and are assumed to be accurate
as quoted in their previously published forms. Although every effort has been made to verify
the quotes and sources, the publisher cannot guarantee their perfect accuracy.

To my husband Lew and
children Oliver Max and Nadia Grace

TABLE OF CONTENTS

Acknowledgments

Without the unique skills and creativity of BabyZone's editorial
and programming team, this book would not be.

Special thanks to Christine Beaudry, my long-time editor and friend. Her enthusiastic
dedication to perfection is an inspiration to all of us.
—Daughters: Erin Elizabeth and Lauren Elise

Thanks to Kathleen Finnegan whose fluency in French and German was of significant
value to the accuracy of these ethnic variant names.
—Daughter: Una; Son: Milan

Thanks to Lina Zaltsman, who created the world's best baby-names software for us
and helped us with Russian names.
—Daughter: Julia Beth

Thanks to Mariel Swiggard for her creative contributions as are evident in poems,
quotes, and interesting facts regarding names throughout the book.
—Daughter: Savannah Mae

Thanks to Pauliina Vahaama, BabyZone's community name host (visit her at
BabyZone's Name Board). Her fluency in German, Persian, and Finnish added
insight and accuracy to our database.
—Son: Saam Erick

Thanks to Claire Matze. Her expertise and fluency in Arabic and Spanish helped
pull the book together.
—Sons: Gerard and Bernard; Daughters: Laura and Sabrina

Finally, special thanks to Meredith Peters for believing in the project and helping
to bring it to perfect realization.

Other contributors:
Ayako Howard, Dr. Stanley Lieberson, Ed Lawson, David Courchane,
Kathie M. Donohue, Chikawge Windler, Jessica and John Peters,
Jim and Laura Koumarianos, Sandra Connors and all the visitors at
www.babyzone.com, Ruth Johnson, Dianna Cox, and Noel Hanlon

Contact us at Names@babyzone.com

Introduction

CONGRATULATIONS ON YOUR PREGNANCY! THIS TIME OF YOUR LIFE IS nothing short of a magical voyage that lasts (give or take) nine months. While you anxiously wait for your son or daughter, you have a very important decision to make: what will you name your precious baby?

As generations have passed, we've learned from psychological studies, case histories, and experts in onomastics—the scientific study of names—about the overwhelming evidence that names and personalities are interwoven entities, and that what you name your child will impact his or her future. Many of our own parents believed that a popular name was the most desirable choice for a child because of a flawed yet well-accepted study indicating that kids with popular names do better in school. More recently, published research says that a child should have a unique name to feel confident and special; likewise, namesakes, stereotypes, and spelling variations are often frowned upon. While this is interesting edification, what continues to be overlooked is that expectant parents have a natural and intuitive image of what their child may be and what name will suit him or her. Religious parents often choose a biblical name, creative parents may go for something more unique, while conservative parents tend toward something popular but safe. So while it can appear that the name makes the child, it seems logical that parents naming a child with certain expectations and raising a child in a particular manner potentially define or "stereotype" that name.

Fortunately, there's enough media exposure to a myriad names in our increasingly diversified culture that perceptions and stereotypes are now skewed. While it's interesting to see what impressions are associated with a name, today's society is less likely to judge people solely on their monikers. In the popular movie *There's Something About Mary*, the beautiful Cameron Diaz portrays a strong-minded and funny woman in her role as Mary Jensen Matthews. And who doesn't remember Julie Andrews as the delightfully proper Mary Poppins? So the perception of Mary as a biblical name is now mulled with a musical, magical nanny and a gorgeous blonde with unusual hair gel! Similarly, everyone knows good Johns and bad Johns, and homemaker Marthas and convicted Marthas. Love the name Hillary but fear the former First Lady has that name cornered? Think again! The teen pop star Hilary Duff is making a name for herself, and the stereotype couldn't be more different.

Despite this newfound openness in choosing a name, you still want to find a meaningful name for your child. After all, any important decision in life requires research and contemplation. But remember, only you have some inclination of what road your daughter or son may take, only you know what ideals you will set forth for your child, and only you will say, repeat, and abbreviate this given name thousands of times as you endeavor to raise your child into an exceptional person.

Here you will find facts (not opinions) gathered from various sources, as well as fun exercises, inspirational quotes, and fascinating information on the history of naming babies. What you won't find is our judgment of what makes a name cool, trendy, good, or bad. You will be provided with all the information you need to come to that conclusion on your own; after all, you are naming your child for yourselves.

When it was time for my husband and me to name our first child, we did what many parents do and bought every baby-naming book we could find. While perusing the books and forming lists, we were also busy launching and developing BabyZone.com, the popular parenting site which quickly began developing tools to help parents name babies. Nine months later, we gave birth to Nadia Grace, and two years after that her little brother Oliver Max was born. Today, seven years from my pregnancy with Nadia and the inception of BabyZone.com, my editorial staff and I have helped moms and dads name millions of babies. We've also gathered a plethora of baby-naming data from parents, experts, and public sources, and compiled stats via the Internet from millions of parents. Now, for the first time ever, we're publishing this unique factual content. Along with this data, I've added scores of lists and guides to create this all-in-one inspirational book.

So, are you ready? Let's go name your baby.

A Baby by Any Other Name...
Is Still *Your* Baby

What's in a name? Stress, pressure, disagreements…? Choosing a name for your child doesn't have to be this tough. In fact, it should be fun!

If you hope to find the ideal name for your beautiful baby, simply said, you will. As an expectant parent that has chosen this book, you are undoubtedly determined to overturn every stone until you do find the right name. Naming your child is the first of many big decisions you'll make as a parent. To guide you, we've included an easy-to-follow, step-by-step program that will inspire you to find meaningful names, followed by a guide to help you narrow down your list of potential names. But before you get started choosing a name, here are a few important points to keep in mind.

Trust Your Instincts

We've all had that deep, gut feeling that prompts us to make specific decisions, and allowing these instincts to guide you—rather than being persuaded by a barrage of opinions—offers you the best chance at picking the consummate baby name. To cultivate this skill (and yes, it is a skill), you need to get out of your own way and be open to anything. Give yourself time; you don't need to name the baby before his or her arrival. Many parents wait until they meet their baby to make a final name selection, especially if they have a couple of name favorites. Don't worry—your baby will not remain nameless because her parents were too undecided! A name will come to you, so have confidence, get informed, and enjoy the selection process. To quote Deepak Chopra, "Trust your gut and your heart and your toes too." Your baby's name could come from a person, place, thing, or idea, and it can be popular or unusual—it can be anything you want it to be, because it's not the name that makes the person, it's the person that makes the name. Your child's name, personality, and beliefs will be interwoven and mixed into a combination that is truly unique.

Name Dilemmas

While our handy lists and methods help add order to your naming process, there is no way to address every possible name dilemma expectant couples encounter. The most frequent predicament is that parents can't agree on a name. While some couples are so like-minded they easily agree on name choices, others agonize over this decision. Here are a few guidelines to help you overcome naming problems.

- See if you can begin the journey on common ground. Try agreeing on a strategy or process as opposed to a specific name. Think about what naming style you both do agree on—whether you're looking for a unique name, a biblical name, or a traditional family name, for example.

- Keep baby naming between you and your mate. Unless you have a very secure relationship with your parents or in-laws, it's usually best to keep their opinions out of the mix. The same goes for other well-meaning relatives and friends. One of the most common naming problems is that a relative or friend may feel she has ownership over a name you're choosing. What they don't know won't hurt them.

- Establish that both parents have the right to veto any name they absolutely do not like. After all, you want your mate to feel like an equal partner in this decision as well as many future decisions to come. Begin on common ground and name your child together.

- Think compromise. You have a first name and a middle name to work with, and if you're planning on having more children after this baby, you'll have additional opportunities for baby naming. If all else fails, try the "if it's a boy/girl—the mother/father picks the name" process. (However, avoid having one parent select the first name, while the other selects the middle name. Here the *compromise* tends to become the priority, when the *best name combination* for your child should receive precedence.)

A Word to the Mothers If you're pregnant, you are naturally hormonal! The father-to-be may have an opposing opinion about your favorite baby-name selection, but remember, this is not a personal attack on you or your choices. Keep in mind, you're carrying this child, and Dad doesn't have much say in the whole pregnancy experience. Naming your child is one of the most meaningful decisions concerning your unborn baby that requires his input.

As desperate as you may be to choose baby's name, it is imperative that you and the baby's dad move into the realm of parenthood as partners. If this is his first child, be sensitive to the metamorphosis of the man becoming a father. Contrarily if your partner seems ambivalent about the chosen name, consider that he is over-whelmed with the concept and still in "acceptance stage," or he may simply trust that you will do a wonderful job and is choosing to focus his time on your baby's college tuition fund! Whether he's opinionated or ambivalent, you *are* hormonal, so take it in stride!

A Word to the Fathers Some women begin dreaming of names for their unborn children as early as age three and grow up with favorite names or ideas of how they will name their babies. The expectant mom is also hormonal (I can't stress this enough!), and that means she is particularly sensitive to everything—especially conflict. While you may have some very strong opinions about baby's name, try to be sensitive to the mom-to-be. Often men want to avoid unique names for boys, but keep in mind that more unusual names didn't hinder Emeril (Lagasse), Stone (Phillips), Ashton (Kutcher), Tiger (Woods), and Kelsey (Grammer). Try to keep an open mind, Dad.

> *My husband and I thought it was most important that we agreed on names for our children. We did not reveal the names we had chosen until after the births. For us, unwanted feedback about something so personal would have added unneeded stress.*
>
> —Amy W., BabyZone.com member

A Word about Siblings There's a balancing act between keeping an older child involved in the pregnancy and not setting him up for disappointment because you didn't choose his name for the baby. If babies' siblings chose their names, there would be plenty of Barbies, Shreks, Doras, and Nemos being born—not to mention children's wonderfully creative invented name choices! Undoubtedly, kids will hear you discussing names amongst yourselves and will naturally have "suggestions," but make it clear from the beginning that naming baby is big business (tell them their own baby-naming story), and is a decision ultimately made by Mommy and Daddy. Do be sure to listen to your child though, because you never do know where that perfect name might originate—and if it does happen to come from a sibling, it can be all the more meaningful.

A Word about Grandparents (and Other Well-Meaning Friends and Relatives) Your well-intentioned parents and in-laws will inevitably have opinions about your child's name, whether it's concerning a namesake or a style of naming they find comfortable. Assess how much pressure they are capable of putting on you and make a decision to put the "rules" in place before discussing names with them. The rule may be that you are going to keep your name choices confidential until your baby is born, thus not allowing any outside influences. You will inevitably get unsolicited name suggestions from relatives and friends, which you can politely respond to with, "thanks for the suggestion, we'll keep that in mind" (whether you like the name or not!).

Naming a child after a beloved and possibly deceased relative is certainly a strong and sentimental desire, and something you may consider. Many parents who choose to incorporate a namesake do it in baby's middle name or find a variation of the namesake that suits their taste. If that compromise is not possible, keep in mind that no matter what name you choose, Grandma and Grandpa will fall in love with your little one at first sight and most likely forget there was ever an issue with the baby's name.

How to Use This Book: The Name Selection Process

To begin, all you need is a pencil, an eraser, and an open mind. Throughout the following chapters, you'll find various baby-naming exercises. Use these exercises with the corresponding workbook in the back of the book (see page 399). This workbook will keep you on track and communicating effectively with your partner. If you're single and pregnant, you can choose a close friend or relative to partner with or simply ignore instances where we ask your partner to step in and find a name solo. There are a total of ten exercises to be done as you go through the chapters and intermittently browse our name dictionary. If you're expecting twins or multiples, copy the exercises to a notebook to allow enough space for all your name ideas.

Feel free to return to the exercises or lists at any time throughout the process to add or remove names. The first exercise—which will most likely generate your longest list and the one you return to the most—is also where you can add names that "sound nice" if they don't fit into the other list categories. Keep in mind that the process is just that—a process, not to be rushed or forced, but to be enjoyed either on your own or as a couple.

Exercise One: Visualization

As you fantasize about your baby, take it a step further, and visualize who your child might be, what she might look like, and what her genetic code is. You have a sense for this child along with a special innate knowledge available only to you as parents. Now visualize the same person as a young adult, and then reach a little further and imagine her in a career or family setting. Begin thinking of names for this person, and as these names come to you, write them in the corresponding workbook space in back of the book, on page 401. We recommend doing this for both boy and girl names, but if you're certain of the sex and want to focus all of your attention on a specific gender that is, of course, your prerogative.

Over time, feel free to add or remove names. This will be your primary ongoing collection, to which you may refer as you complete the rest of the exercises in the book. We encourage both parents to work on this and all the exercises as a team, but at this stage, only the parent that added a name to the list can remove that name.

CHAPTER 2

Let the Names Begin

What to Consider When Choosing a Name

"A signature always reveals a man's character—and sometimes even his name."
—*Evan Esar (1899–1995)*

First Things First! Last Names

Good, bad, or just plain funny—your child's surname is the name you have the least control over, yet it is the most important consideration in choosing the right-sounding first and middle names. As your child grows and enters the workforce, his identity will no longer be as simple as a first name. He will be referred to by first and last or, if he chooses, first, middle, and last. When considering names, keep in mind that a lengthy, difficult-to-spell last name would be compounded by a difficult first name;

likewise, a plain last name might be further diluted with a common or short first name. An easily picked-on last name (Cox) could be toned down or up with the right or wrong first name. It could also fade into a complementary first name—Courteney Bass Cox—becoming a memorable identity. A quick study in alliteration (the repetition of initial consonant sounds in two or more neighboring words) can inspire some rhythmic name ideas.

BabyZone.com poll:
How did you choose
your child's name?

Parents' Favorite Choice 31%
Family Name 22%
Religion 13%
Nationality 10%
Geographic Location 2%
None of the Above 18%

Count Your Syllables According to some experts, an important naming rule is to have an odd number of syllables between the first and last names. So Meredith (three syllables) could go with Ruskin (two syllables), and Grace (one) might link nicely to Connors (two), but there are so many exceptions to the rule, perhaps it shouldn't be a rule at all. Some general guidelines to find compatible names include not picking a first name with many syllables if your last name also is multi-syllabic. And while you want your child's name to sing, you don't necessarily want it to rhyme. Although, I bet no one forgets Peter Streeter once they've heard his name! On the other hand, Kate Mates is definitely a questionable choice. Your child's name should be memorable but pleasant sounding.

> ### Exercise Two: "A" Is for Alliteration
>
> Use this exercise to discover complementary first names based on your last name. (You may even take it a step further and brainstorm ideas for middle names in this style.) Flip through the alphabetical listings of names that have a similar initial sound as your last name; for example, Smith should look at S and the soft-sounding C. If any names in these sections appeal to you, add them to your list on page 402.

Acronyms and Initials When creating your lists, always consider the entire name including the surname. Look at the initials, ensuring that nothing offensive is spelled. Peter Isaiah Gunther (PIG) or even more subtle initials like Phillip Ike Nathanson (PIN) could prove tortuous to a child with a particularly nasty bully in the classroom.

In 1998, Dr. Nicholas Christenfeld at the University of California studied death certificates from 1969 to 1995 and determined that men whose initials form nasty acronyms, such as ASS or UGH, die an average of 2.8 years sooner than those with meaningless initials. Men blessed with positive initials such as ACE, JOY, or GOD were apt to live around 4.48 years longer. Mysteriously, negative initials had no impact on women's longevity. Perhaps, that's because they can change their initials upon marriage?

> ### Exercise Three: The Acronym Game
>
> Try using initials to spell a desirable acronym. Take the first letter of the baby's last name, and place it at the end of your acronym. Then spell desirable words with the first letters of first and middle names you like. For example, if your last name is Parker, use the P as the last letter to spell POP. Add a first name beginning with a P and a middle beginning with an O: Paul Oz Parker. (Note that you can use phonetic, instead of actual spellings, if that's easier for you. ROK and ROL work just as well as ROCK and ROLL!) See page 403 in the workbook.

Another obvious, but noted consideration is the first and last initials. Victoria Daniels (VD) could expose your child to teasing, while Brandon Browne could end up with the nickname "BB" or Jeffery Russell with "JR." While you do have some control over what your child may be tagged as a nickname, no naming strategy is foolproof. An ancient Hungarian proverb states, "A child with many names is a loved child." With that in mind, consider possible pet names or nicknames before the rest of the world does, because assuredly, your child will be loved!

So what if your favorite baby name spells something less than desirable? As caring, thoughtful parents we don't want to expose our children to unnecessary ridicule. If your "perfect" name creates an unpleasant acronym or initials you're not thrilled with, make sure you think through your decision and evaluate all of your priorities and options. Look at a spelling variation as an option, as well as using the mother's maiden name hyphenated with the last name. Also, keep in mind that while bullies do still exist in the classroom, it's much less common in today's society for it to go on unnoticed. For every problem, there is a solution. An answer will come to you.

What about the Middle?

Consider the middle name your "insurance"—a name your child can default to or use with her first name to achieve a desired effect. It is also where you can go light if you have a formal first name or vice versa. Legally, you are not required to give your child a middle name, but we can't think of one good reason not to. It can be an ambiguous world, but a middle name helps add to your child's identity. There may be plenty of Emily Wilsons in the world,

> "Any child can tell you that the sole purpose of a middle name is so he can tell when he's really in trouble."
> –Dennis Frakes

but how many Emily René Wilsons are there? An interesting trend in choosing a middle name is to use the mother's maiden name. So a David Nielson might become a David Howell Nielson. Since surnames are increasingly being used as first names, this option often works well and is especially meaningful if the mother doesn't have siblings to carry on her last name.

To Peek or Not to Peek: That Is the Question

At around the twentieth week of pregnancy, many expectant parents are offered a sonogram to check in on the well-being of their cute little fetus. At the same time, the questioned is raised: "Do you want to know the sex of your child?" This is a very personal decision that mother and father may or may not agree on. Couples that wish to wait appreciate the nostalgia of times gone by when ultrasound technology wasn't available

Chinese Lunar Calendar

Will you have a handsome baby boy or a beautiful baby girl? Try consulting the Chinese Lunar Calendar. A Chinese scientist discovered and drew this chart which was buried in a royal tomb about 700 years ago. The original is kept in the Institute of Science of Peking. The accuracy of the chart has been proven by thousands of people—in fact, it's believed to be ninety-nine percent accurate!

If you're a mother, look across the top of the table and find your lunar age (add nine months to your actual age) at the date of conception. Next, find the month of conception, located along the left side of the calendar. Follow the column and row, and see where the two intersect. If the box is blue, the calendar predicts you'll have a boy; white, you'll have a girl. For instance, a thirty-year-old-woman who conceived in January will give birth to a boy, according to the Chinese Lunar Calendar.

Mother's Lunar Age at Conception

Month of Conception	18	19	20	21	22	23	24	25	26	27	28	29	30	31	32	33	34	35	36	37	38	39	40	41	42	43	44	45
Jan.																												
Feb.																												
Mar.																												
Apr.																												
May																												
Jun.																												
Jul.																												
Aug.																												
Sep.																												
Oct.																												
Nov.																												
Dec.																												

Boy = [   ]   Girl = [   ]

and enjoy the anticipation leading up to the big surprise, thus creating "the moment." Many of these couples do not have a gender preference or are first-time parents.

Parents—and parents of children with a strong preference concerning their new sibling's gender—often choose to learn baby's sex, finding time to prepare themselves or their potentially "disappointed" children. After all, it wouldn't be very pleasant if your three-year-old daughter's whole baby-sister fantasy world came to a screeching halt at the sight of her newborn brother. Childbirth and temper tantrums do not mix!

Finding out your child's sex has many other advantages from choosing paint color and making clothing purchases to focusing on a particular gender in the name selection process. Keep in mind, that while it is very rare, there are instances of boys playing hide and seek or being late bloomers, leading to a false gender prediction. In a world where all goods are exchangeable and walls can easily be repainted, your only real concern may be making sure you are covered in the name arena. So, even if you're expecting a girl, you may want to consider choosing a backup boy's name, and vice versa, just in case.

Unique vs. Popular Names

Once upon a time, not so long ago, there were a plethora of Lindas, Jennifers, Jasons, and Michaels in a classroom. Naming your child a popular name was so common that a child with an unusual name may have stood out negatively. The resulting confusion in the classroom (Stephanie "C" please!) prompted many parents to give more conspicuous names to their children, adopting a belief that offering a child an unusual moniker inherently sets a premise of creative and unique expectations.

On the other hand, kids naturally want to fit in with their peers, and bestowing an easy to remember, familiar name has many advantages. "Contrary to the 'Boy Named Sue' idea that a nonstandard name will strengthen a child in adulthood, the more unusual a person's name, the harder it is for them to adjust," says Dr. Albert Mehrabian, a doctor of psychology and the author of *The Name Game*. However, looking at current trends, it may just be that "fitting in" means having an uncommon name. With more parents choosing "nonstandard" names in general, all names—previously popular, familiar, and even "old fashioned"—have more room to be chosen and still considered fresh without being trendy or too popular.

> *"I sometimes think I was born to live up to my name. How could I be anything else but what I am having been named Madonna? I would either have ended up a nun or this."*
>
> – Madonna

Naming a Boy vs. Naming a Girl

In our society, parents tend to choose more unique or exotic-sounding names for girls. But our culture has had stricter rules for boys—strapping boys require strong, familiar names. Even parents inclined to choose a more unusual name for their son may ultimately opt to name him something "safe." While good, common sense is important in the process of naming any child regardless of sex, parents should keep in mind that this is a new age of naming. Ethnic names are infusing our society, and parents are searching for something beyond tradition, looking to be more daring with boys' names; however, if you just love the time-tested and popular name Matthew, then by all means add it to your list.

> Picabo Street was Baby Girl Street until age two, when officials questioned her hippie parents about the blank on her birth certificate during a vacation to Mexico. The name has been explained in press accounts as being her favorite baby game and the name of a town near her Idaho home meaning "shining waters."

Another trend that has taken shape over the last couple of decades is giving unisex or traditionally male names to daughters with an underlying intention of helping them succeed professionally "in a man's world." If this is something you are pondering, also consider that young children are very gender specific and may not necessarily appreciate sharing their name with another child of the opposite sex.

If you're naming a girl and are undecided, there are names like Samantha ("Sam"), Alexandra ("Alex"), and Andrea ("Andy") that can double under any circumstances. On the other hand, many of the androgynous names are very appealing. We have a nice list of unisex names on page 76 for you to peruse, but also let your imagination work; as girls continue to dip into the pool of boy names, there are many more options available to those expecting daughters. If you're expecting a son, not to worry! Boys can still use names that have been given to the opposite sex. Think Jordan, Cameron, and Riley.

> ### Exercise Four: Get Descriptive
>
> Write down adjectives that define personal characteristics most important to you. Now, take these virtues and check synonyms in a thesaurus for possible boy and girl name options, or search our name dictionary for names with those meanings. (See our lists of virtue names on pages 89, 171, 236, and 311 for ideas.) For example, "honest" could lead to the name Candid for a girl. If you can't find anything in the thesaurus or dictionary, try just listing names that you naturally associate with a characteristic. See page 404 in the workbook.

Exercise Five:
The Family Name Quiz

Looking to your family can provide an abundance of name ideas. Try answering the following questions for inspiration:

1. Which relative(s) has inspired you the most throughout life?

2. What is your mother's maiden name?

3. Is there a relative that has passed away that should be remembered?

4. Any other special family names? Add them to your list on page 405.

Family Names

Keeping a name in the family has strong sentimental appeal. Turning to a beloved family member or digging deeper into your genealogy can open the door to desirable and extremely meaningful possibilities. Surnames are making a splash as good first name options today, which expands your possibilities further. Popular names from the past have hit the scene again, so open your mind to all those vintage varieties. Do you have a Great Aunt Matilda but fear her name is too dated? "Tilly" makes a cute familiar variant, and you're still using a family name. Or look to your mother's maiden name for a special name for your child. I found Relyea, Connor, Zive, Hanlon, and Carston amongst my immediate list of family names that could become first names.

Name Histories and Trends
1900—(Early) 1960: The Brits and the Bible

At the turn of the century in North America, many names were inspired by the Bible or by British customs. At the time, very few name books were published, and those available were mostly etymological studies—not advice to help parents name their babies. In 1857, William Arthur's *An Etymological Dictionary of Family and Christian Names* was published in the United States, making it easy to see how biblical names such as Mary, Elizabeth, Sarah, Joseph, and John were so consistently popular they remained in the top ten throughout World War II and up until 1965. Other names such as Frank, meaning "free," William "the Conqueror," Henry, Margaret, Emma, and Alice were all borrowed from the British, while the Brits borrowed many of them from neighboring European languages.

Most Popular Names 1900-1910

Courtesy of the US Social Security Administration

RANK	MALE NAME	FEMALE NAME
1	John	Mary
2	William	Helen
3	James	Margaret
4	George	Anna
5	Joseph	Ruth
6	Charles	Elizabeth
7	Robert	Dorothy
8	Frank	Marie
9	Edward	Mildred
10	Henry	Alice

1960—1979: A Time for Change In 1965, Mary was officially bumped from its number one spot by Lisa. In fact, by 1972 Mary had dropped out of the top ten names completely and Jennifer hit the scene. About this time, John was seeing competition with David and Michael, and names like Jason were appearing on the boys' list. Jennifer remained number one throughout the '70s and well into the '80s, with other less traditional names entering the mix such as Heather, Angela, Amy, and Jessica. Meanwhile, the boys danced around their biblical conservative mix while slowly adding a few additional biblical varieties such as Daniel and Joshua.

Most Popular Names 1970-1980

Courtesy of the US Social Security Administration

RANK	MALE NAME	FEMALE NAME
1	Michael	Jennifer
2	Christopher	Amy
3	Jason	Melissa
4	David	Michelle
5	James	Kimberly
6	John	Lisa
7	Robert	Angela
8	Brian	Heather
9	William	Stephanie
10	Matthew	Jessica

1980—2000: Invented and Place Names Brandon and Tyler became two of the favorites for boys of the '90s. Jessica and Ashley replaced Jennifer in 1985 and were accompanied by up-and-coming names such as Sara and Brittney (Britney Spears was born in 1981). Then in 1992 we saw Emily, a name that has remained on the top with other antique names such as Olivia and Emma. At the same time, place names like Austin and Savannah entered the scene, opening a whole new look at geography and a much wider range of name possibilities.

While looking to geography for names seems to be a relatively new trend, naming a child after a place is not an entirely modern concept. Medieval crusaders often took water from the Jordan River to baptize their children, and often these children (both boys and girls) would be dubbed Jordan. Later in history, Kimberley was first bestowed as a baby name soon after the town of Kimberley, South Africa, was besieged during the Boer War (1899–1902). Names of religious shrines like Loreto or Lourdes were commonly given to Catholic children—a tradition that continues today. Affluent English-speaking parents often named their children after the city in which they were born; Florence Nightingale is a prime example.

BabyZone's Most Popular Names of 2004

RANK	MALE NAME	FEMALE NAME
1	Ethan	Madison
2	Jacob	Emma
3	Aidan	Emily
4	Ryan	Kaitlyn
5	Tyler	Olivia
6	Matthew	Hailey
7	Joshua	Sarah
8	Nicholas	Isabella
9	Michael	Alexis
10	Andrew	Hannah

The Present The dichotomy between "old-fashioned" names and unique and place name trends creates a wonderful world of naming possibilities for parents. Current statistics confirm what we've seen with names like Isabella, Hannah, and Madison all in our top ten for 2004, and on the boys' list, Jacob shares the spotlight with Aidan and Ethan. (For a complete list of the top 100 baby names according to the Social Security Administration, see pages 396-397.)

In general, all names, even our most popular, are now less popular per capita because of our vast name pool and increasing population. In 2003, one of the most popular boys' names, Jacob, was chosen for roughly 1.5 percent of the approximate two million boys born that year. Translation: if you name your son Jacob or Aidan, he may still be the only one in his classroom. Girls' names are even more eclectic, and with so many to choose from, popular vs. unique is no longer much of an issue.

Name Perceptions and Associations

Often when you hear a name an image will flash in your head, or it reminds you of an event, song, or time in history. You don't want to stereotype a person based solely on hearing her name but you often can't help yourself. Some names carry a stronger stereotype than others, usually because there is a famous person we identify with that name.

Though you may want to discover how people perceive your favorite name, avoid being influenced by others' perceptions. Concerning

Exercise Six: Place Names

Find out if a place important to you could work as a name for your child. Try answering the following questions (see page 406 in the workbook):

1. Where did you meet your partner?

2. Where were you when you got engaged?

3. Where did you go on your honeymoon?

4. Where were you when you conceived your child?

5. What do you think is the most beautiful place on earth?

6. Do any special places or moments come to mind? Add them to this list.

yourself only with the stereotype you and your partner associate with a name is critical in choosing your perfect name; keep in mind that your child will define the name you choose! With the barrage of media in our culture, everyone is likely to have some perception of the name you select. The world is simply too big and too creative to concern yourself with others' opinions of your baby-name choice.

While you don't need to concern yourself with what others think, you should pay close attention to the perceptions you and your partner have. If your husband dated a Celeste that he never quite forgot, you most likely don't want to name your daughter Celeste! After you hear the name Jeremiah, do you sing "was a bullfrog"? That could get annoying. Even though your child will ultimately define his or her name, certain names may always carry a derogatory association for you or your partner. Also keep in mind that if you have a strong perception of or association with a name because of someone famous or infamous, you're likely not to be alone and others will potentially make the same association. Have you ever wondered how many little Adolfs have been named since World War II?

CHAPTER 3

A World of Ideas

Baby-Naming Traditions around the World

 How did our ancestors and neighbors around the world find and celebrate their babies' names? Ethnic and religious customs can lead you to a strong, ethnically rooted, meaningful name.

Europe

If you were born in Elizabethan England (1558–1603), you may have been named by your parents just a few days after birth, at your baptism. Like many other newborns of the time, you were named after one of your godparents, carefully chosen for their higher socioeconomic stature. The pool of names considered acceptable during this time was significantly smaller than what we are used to today. Elizabeth, Anne, Joan, Margaret, Alice, Mary, and Agnes accounted for approximately sixty-five percent of all girls' names. Likewise, John, Thomas, William, Richard, and Robert accounted for approximately sixty percent of male names. When it came to naming baby in old England, life was comparatively simple but somewhat boring. Naming options broadened during the classical revival period which brought in French and Italian imports, opening the door for more creativity.

Today, throughout predominately Christian Europe, you find similar baptismal ceremonies but various customs in adopting namesakes—that is, who your child will be named after. Orthodox

Exercise Seven: The Ethnic Challenge

Wouldn't it be nice to fall in love with a name that creates a connection between your child and his or her own heritage? Peruse the name dictionary for names specific to your or your partner's ethnic background. If you find something you like (even a little), add it to the list on page 407; it may just be a fit as a middle name.

Greeks have customarily named their babies after the fathers' parents. The French often use a child's middle name to pay homage to a set of grandparents, using both grandmothers' first names for a girl and both grandfathers' names for a boy. The Spanish, known for their traditionalism, have rigid rules even for today; the first-born daughter is named after the father's mother, whereas the first son is named after the father's father. Younger siblings are named after the mother's parents, and even younger siblings after aunts and uncles on the paternal side followed by the maternal aunts and uncles. Many other European countries also have customs of naming after the parents. In the common, patronymic style, the "Jr." wears his father's moniker. Likewise, but much less common, a girl may become her own mother's namesake.

The Americas

In the Americas, the earliest naming traditions we find are from Mesoamerican communities where a child may be named after the day on which she was born—a common tradition throughout many aboriginal communities around the world.

Native American Native American naming traditions, some of which are still followed today, vary greatly from tribe to tribe and were often inspired by natural conditions, animals, and virtues. This is especially apparent in the Miwok tribe's use of water names, often chosen by the way the stream looked when the baby was born. The Southwest Hopis had a mystic tradition of placing an ear of corn, representing Mother Earth, next to the newborn. Twenty days after baby's birth, the corn was rubbed over his body while the baby, held to face the rising sun, was named when the first ray of sun hit his forehead. The Navajos attribute great powers to their names. A Navajo name is considered so precious it's only used during ceremonies, meaning a day-to-day conversation in a Navajo family may go something like "Mother, go get Son." The Salish tribe follows a "naming trail" in which the name given to a baby by his parents at birth (usually a virtue or trait the parents hope for the baby) is eventually replaced at adolescence with another name that is given by the tribal leader at a ceremony called the Jump Dances. This name usually represents a talent or strength for which the child is

"My name, Apv-whilt-tin-toom, was given me by my adoptive Indian mother, Ella McCarty. Her Native American name was Am-toola (One Who Sits in the Circle). My name is a remembrance of a warm moment between us, when I said to her, 'You are like a mother to me.' She said, 'Apv-whilt-tin-toom, that will be your name, Like a Mother to Me.' So, she adopted me and sent me on the Naming Trail...."
—Kathie M. Donohue, Native American Genealogy Foundation

known. Likewise, as an adult, yet another name might be granted, but this name would reflect expectations or something for the person to live up to.

The Puritans While biblical names satisfied most Puritan American colonists in New England, some families of the Mayflower age chose to bestow their own virtuous names such as Charity, Joy, Mercy, Grace, Prudence, and Hope. In more extreme examples, parents derived slogans to send a very direct message through their child's name: "Fear-God," "Jesus-Christ-came-into-the-world-to-save," and "No-Merit," to name a few. One has to wonder about the conscience of a young lad named "If-Christ-had-not-died-for-thee-thou-hadst-been-damned." And what do you think "Sin-deny" did when he was caught dozing in church?

In many cultures, a name is chosen for a specific attribute the parents or society consider desirable. Ada (Hebrew), Alika (Nigerian), Anabelle (Latin), Belinda (English), Calista (Greek), Jolie (French), Jameelah (Arabic), Keely (Irish), Meili (Chinese), Nazneen (Persian), Omorose (Egyptian), and Wyanet (American Indian) are just a handful of examples that all carry the same meaning—beautiful.

Hawaii If you're of Hawaiian descent, your "Inoa" (name) is your most prized possession. Traditionally, Hawaiians believed that an ancestral god will mystically send a name to a member of the unborn child's family. They look for this name in signs, visions, and dreams, and believe that if the specified name is not used, it will cripple the child. If a name is not chosen through the god, there are many different types of names—such as those given to trick evil spirits or known only in secret—and more than one name may be given to a child. Christian names are also used in Hawaii and have been altered to fit with the Hawaiian language, which doesn't pronounce many English sounds.

African American African Americans have their own unique naming history and culture. In the days of slavery, a slave owner often renamed his slaves something not generally used by whites; Greek mythology names were commonly used (Daphne, Apollo, Nessus, or Diana) or a slave's full name was converted into a diminutive cognate of another white-owned name (Tom, Cas, Lil, Bo). Slave owners also granted biblical names in their attempt to convert slaves to Christianity. However, in an attempt to preserve their heritage, slaves often gave their children ethnically based names, which they used secretly in their communities. It wasn't until the Civil War that most African Americans had complete control in naming their children; with newfound freedom, slaves immediately bestowed previously prohibited names on their children (Moses, Abraham) and also changed their shortened names to the formal versions (Thomas, Cassandra, Lillian, and Robert).

African Americans also adopted the style of creating unique names, which took off even further during the 1960s as individual names, distinct from the white community, surfaced. Traditionalism and pride inspired them to look to their Muslim and African roots, to names like Muhammad, Hassan, and Ali for boys, and Shawana, Naajila, and Malaika for girls.

Mormons Similarly, Utah Mormons are known to create unique or uncommon names in a variety of ways, often combining parents' or grandparents' first names. So, Lewis and Amanda might result in Le'Anda. They also appreciate extremely unusual spelling variations, such as Kellee, Katlynn, Leee, and Alysoon. Could it be the Mormons that started the surname as first name trend? It seems they've been doing this for decades; we found Bowden, Doerr, and Rainey amongst surnames used for males. Mormons also love French sound prefixes ("La" or "De") and wouldn't hesitate to completely concoct a name: LaJune or DeBekka. Creativity is the name of the game for Mormon parents.

Muslim Following tradition, Muslim parents may name their child on his or her birthday or at an "Aqeeqah." Held on the seventh day after baby's birth, this ceremony entails a sacrifice of a goat or sheep (two for a boy, one for a girl). The infant's head is then shaved and covered with saffron. It is important to Muslims to give their child a good name, determined by its meanings, which should be beautiful.

Jewish A Jewish boy is given his Hebrew (as opposed to his secular) name at his "Bris" eight days after his birth, at which time he is also circumcised by a trusted Mohel. A Jewish baby girl receives a naming ceremony eight to fifteen days after birth that includes a public reading of the Torah. During the reading, the special "Mi Sheberach" blessing is said. The blessing begins with a prayer for the mother's health and continues with the giving of the baby's name—and a prayer that this new daughter should grow to be a wise and understanding person of goodness. Jewish people believe that you should name an infant after someone who was righteous in hopes that the child will emulate that person. The Eastern European, Yiddish-speaking Ashkenazic tradition is to name after a beloved departed relative, while the Sephardic Jews may name their offspring after a living person.

From Asia

China　What do a name and an egg have to do with each other? If you're in China, you might be invited to a "Red Egg and Ginger" baby-naming party—a celebration held after baby's first month of life. The egg, considered a delicacy in ancient China, represents fertility and is dyed the color red for good luck. At the ceremonial feast, the baby's hair is shaved and gifts are presented to the new life. Today, modern Chinese families use brightly colored eggs as party favors at their adapted ceremonies.

> In the Chinese capital of Beijing, the word "Shu" (kind and gentle) is the favorite name for women.

Superstitious as they are, the Chinese wouldn't dare name a child before he is born! Instead they will give him a fake or "milk" name—something very undesirable, such as "mud face" or "excrement," that is meant to disgust evil spirits and trick them to stay away from the child. These names may stay with children throughout childhood. On the heels of the many childbirth practices they follow, the Chinese believe that each child is unique and should carry an individual moniker; however, this is becoming increasingly difficult for them to follow as the most populous country in the world.

Japan　In Japan, on the "Oshichiya" (baby's seventh day), family and friends congregate for a celebratory feast. Traditionally, the baby may be clothed exclusively in white, and an elegant "Shodo" (name plaque) with the child's name eloquently inscribed in Japanese characters on a special Japanese paper is hung on the wall. The festivities continue with laughter and eating—certainly a pleasurable celebration for new parents and a visual welcome to the world for their new baby.

India　There are many variations of the "Namakarana" naming ceremony in India. In the state of Maharashtra, you will walk in on a beautiful image of a baby in the cradle, decorated with flower garlands and surrounded by women singing hymns and gently rocking the cradle. The mother or a grandmother will then enter the room with a lit silver lamp and a small gold jewel for the child. Afterwards, the baby is blessed with rice and a small dot of vermilion is placed on her forehead. Blessings are once again said, and the ceremony ends with the mother whispering the gods' names and then whispering the child's name in her ear. Finally, the name is announced to the guests.

Buddhists have their own Namakarana within the first three months of life or when it's thought that the baby can hear. During the event, a mother writes the baby's name on a banana leaf, which is then covered with handfuls of uncooked rice. The mother lays the baby on the banana leaf and whispers the child's name three times in his ear, after which the other relatives and guests do the same. A frequent practice among Hindus is to name their children after sages, saints, holy persons, deities, and the names of the incarnation of God. It is believed that by repeatedly calling such names, one is reminded of God.

Out of Africa

In many regions of Africa, naming ceremonies are extensive and elaborate, with special prayers recited by an appointed religious teacher. Usually, animals are sacrificed during these proceedings. Africans mostly choose names that denote the time ("Abena"—born on Thursday), something that represents the times ("Iniko"—born during troubled times), a physical characteristic ("Hassain"—handsome), or possibly the child's position within the family ("Delu"—the only girl).

As a Muslim African newborn, you will be told of God's greatness before you are shown the sun. Afterwards your father will whisper "God is Great" immediately followed by your given name.

"Omoro then walked out before all of the assembled people of the village. Moving to his wife's side, he lifted up the infant and, as all watched, whispered three times into his son's ear the name he had chosen for him. It was the first time the name had ever been spoken as this child's name, for Omoro's people felt that each human being should be the first to know who he was."
—Alex Haley, *Roots*

If you are an Egyptian, you may learn of a special naming ceremony called the "Sebooh," held on the child's seventh day of life. As a guest of this event, you will find the baby dressed in white and placed in a sieve. The parents will slowly rock the sieve to symbolize acquainting their child with the motions of life. Guests chant, sing, and laugh as the child is placed on a white cloth on the floor with everyone surrounding her and scattering grains around her—symbolic of the earth's bounty. At this time, gifts are presented to the infant. The baby's mother may then sidestep the baby's body seven times to ward off evil spirits. Everyone's focus is on the mother's motions, as a knife is momentarily laid across the baby's body to ward off more evil spirits. The ceremony ends with the lighting of candles, which are given to attending children to bear in a procession led by the mother, who is carrying the baby throughout the home. She is followed by the incense bearer shaking a lantern-like incense burner releasing cleansing scents.

This time-honored custom dates back to the Pharaohs but is still used throughout Egypt in Christian and Muslim homes alike.

Creating Traditions Today

It is a strong human force to mark life's mileposts through ceremony or festivity. Good decisions and achievements should be celebrated, and surely, you're reaching far and wide to find the perfect baby name, so certainly a celebration of the naming of your child is in order! This is especially true since for most American parents today, the closest thing to a name tradition is a mailed birth announcement.

While we hope these customs throughout history and around the world have inspired you to add more names to your list, you may also want to consider creating a naming tradition within your own family. Christian families, for example, may choose to announce their baby's name at his baptism or christening on the seventh day of life. While we don't recommend sacrificing animals or shaving the baby's head, you may want to look to the Japanese and have a calligrapher create a special name plaque for your son or daughter, or simply have the baby's closest relatives whisper her name in her ear (babies can hear at birth) in a peaceful and gentle setting. Likewise, the Chinese "Red Egg and Ginger" custom could be the theme of a welcoming party for your new baby. A naming ceremony can be performed by anyone and can offer a place for mothers and fathers to declare their commitment to being good parents within their circle of friends and family.

But, first we need to choose a name, so let's carry on....

CHAPTER 4

Suiting Your Style
Meaningful Lists
....

 By now your workbook section should be coming together with several lists of possible baby names. Throughout this book, we've empowered you to form your own naming style with self-confidence. Now, with both confidence and experience you're ready for the less structured exercise of choosing names by categories.

Biblical Names

If the idea of a biblical name with a sense of tradition appeals to you, closely analyze the following list for possible name choices. Many of these namesakes, whether from the Old or New Testament, have incredible character and qualities parents find favorable for their children. You may wish to further research the figures behind the names (and some of their fasci-nating stories) or revisit your favorite scripture for a name choice.

Exercise Eight: Choose Your Lists

Select one or more of the following name types that have significance to you: Biblical, Nature, New Age, Shakespearean, Musical, Place, and Surnames as First Names. After you have decided which of these lists have meaning to you, browse those lists for more naming ideas; if you find any possibilities, add them to your workbook on page 408.

Biblical Names

BOYS' NAMES			
Aaron	Elijah	Jesus	Nicholas
Abel	Elisha	Jhon	Noah
Abner	Elliot	Joash	Obadiah
Abraham	Emmanuel	Joel	Oren
Abram	Ephraim	John	Paul
Achan	Esau	Jonah	Peter
Adam	Eshton	Jonas	Philip
Ahio	Ethan	Jonathan	Reuben/Ruben
Alexander	Ethnan	Jordan	Salomon
Ammon	Ezekiel	Joseph	Samson
Amnon	Ezequiel	Joshua	Samuel
Amon	Ezra	Josiah	Saul
Amos	Felix	Josias	Seth
Andrew	Gabriel	Judas	Sidon
Aner	Gideon	Jude	Silas
Anslem	Ira	Kanan	Simeon
Asa	Isaac	Kenan	Simon
Asher	Isaiah	Kirk	Simri
Bartholmew	Israel	Lazarus	Solomon
Becher	Jabin	Levi	Stephen
Benaiah/Benayah	Jacob	Liam	Thaddeus
Benjamin	Jadon	Lucas	Thomas
Cain	Jalon	Luke	Tilon
Cainan	James	Mahlon	Timothy
Caleb	Jamin/Jaymin	Malachi/Malachy	Tobias
Canaan	Jared	Marcus	Zacariah/
Chislon	Jaroah	Mattaniah	Zachariah
Cyrus	Jashen	Matthew	Zaccheus/
Damian	Jason	Matthias	Zacchaeus
Daniel	Javan	Micah	Zachariah
Dathan	Jedediah/Jedidiah	Michael	Zebediah
David	Jeremiah	Moses	Zebulon
Eden	Jeremy	Naamon	Zephan
Eleazar	Jeriah	Nathan	Zion
Eli	Jericho	Nathaniel	
Elias	Jesiah/Jesse	Nehemiah	

GIRLS' NAMES			
Abigail	Beraiah	Hannah	Merari
Adalia	Bethany	Hazael	Micaiah/Michaiah
Adeil	Carmel	Hazaiah	/Mykayah
Adina	Celeste	Haziel	Michaela
Adriel	Cheran	Irijah	Michal
Ahira	Chloe	Izri	Milalai
Ahlai	Claudia	Jael	Naomi
Aiah	Dalaiah	Jane	Natalie
Aliah	Dana	Jannah	Rachel
Amzi	Danielle	Japhia	Ramiah
Anaiah	Deborah	Jemima	Reaia
Angela	Delaiah	Jesaiah	Reaiah
Anna	Delilah	Jesse	Rebekah
Annabel	Dinah	Jessica	Rhea
Ara	Easter	Jezliah	Ruth
Areli	Eden	Joanna	Sala
Arisai	Elasa	Judith	Salah
Asahiah	Elhanan	Kelaiah	Salome
Asaiah	Eliah	Kezia/Keziah	Sarah/Serah
Ashbel	Elika	Kirsten	Seraiah
Asriel	Elisabeth/Elizabeth	Leah	Shelah
Atarah	Elisha	Lydia	Shiloh
Athaiah	Esther	Lysias	Susannah
Athalia	Eve	Madaleine	Tabitha
Athena	Ezri	Magdalena/	Talia/Thalia
Azaliah	Faith	Magdelena	Tamar
Azaniah	Freya	Mahalah	Tamara
Azarael	Gabrielle	Mara	Tarah
Azaria	Grace	Mary/Maria	Tarea
Azriel	Gwyneth	Maryam	Trinity
Bela	Halliday	Melea	Zipporah
Belah	Hanani	Meraiah	

Nature Names

Is the great outdoors where you and your baby will spend time? What natural elements represent who you are—and who your child may be? If you're looking for something feminine, browse through the flower names for some fragrant female name choices.

Sun Names

GIRLS

Alaine (French)
Asia (Arabic)
Dawn (English)
Helia (Greek)
Kalinda (Hindi)
Lian (Chinese)
Solana (Latin)
Talayeh (Persian)

BOYS

Arun (Hindi)
Ciro (Spanish)
Dinesh (Sanskrit)
Etu (Native American)
Helios (Greek)
Sampson (Hebrew)
Sol (Latin)

Earth Names

GIRLS

Adda (Welsh)
Ertha (German)
Kaia (Greek)
Meadow (English)
Tellus (Latin)
Tuwa (American Indian)

BOYS

Adam (Hebrew)
Blair (Gaelic)
Clay (English)

Ezebo (Egyptian)
Forrest (French)
Damek (Czech)
Mahkah (American Indian)

Water Names

GIRLS

Assana (Irish)
Brooke (English)
Coral (English)
Dalis (Hebrew)
Eathelyn (English)
Edlin (English)
Fontaine (French)
Kallan (Scandinavian)
Lana (Hawaiian)
Lynn (English)
Oceana (Greek)
Sarila (Turkish)
Talulla (Native American)

BOYS

Assan (Irish)
Cain (Welsh)
Calder (Scottish)
Callan (Scandinavian)
Dallas (Scottish)
Evian (English)
Kelsey (Teutonic)
Moses (Hebrew)
River (French)
Wade (English)

Fire Names

GIRLS

Adan (Irish)

Barbara (Greek)

Brande (English)

Bridget (Irish)

Edna (Celtic)

Fia (Italian)

Kai (Scottish

Sarafina (Hebrew)

BOYS

Aidan (Irish)

Ash (Hebrew)

Azar (Persian)

Edan (Celtic)

Eth (Irish)

Flint (English)

Ignazio (Spanish)

Air, Wind, and Sky Names

GIRLS

Ambar (Hindi)

Aura (Greek)

Avira (Hebrew)

Ilma (Finnish)

Lani (Hawaiian)

Loni (Greek)

BOYS

Avirit (Hebrew)

Shu (Egyptian)

Dyaus (Hindi)

Nasim (Persian)

Rodor (Anglo-Saxon)

Uranus (Greek)

Girl Flower Power Names

Azalea (Greek)

Aziel (Hebrew)

Brionna (English)

Calla (Greek)

Camilia (Latin)

Daffodil (Greek)

Daisy (English)

Dalia (Arabic)

Fern (English)

Ginger (Latin)

Heather (English)

Holly (English)

Iris (Greek)

Ivy (English)

Jasmine (French)

Laurel (Latin)

Leia (Hawaiian)

Lilly (English)

Linnae (Scandinavian)

Magnolia (French)

Pansy (French)

Peony (French)

Petunia (Native American)

Rose (Latin)

Violet (French)

Zahara (African)

New Age Names

If your eyes are focused on the stars, research your child's zodiac sign based on your intended due date. Obviously, this can be somewhat risky given that babies are rarely punctual, so you may want to include an alternate sign as well. Look to your child's zodiacal element and go back to nature names (page 38) for compatible name ideas. Gems and flowers offer additional interesting possibilities, while lucky Hindi name sounds might inspire phonetically harmonious selections.

	ZODIAC SIGN	ELEMENT	FLOWER
	Aries (March 21–April 19)	Fire	Daisy
	Taurus (April 20–May 20)	Earth	Lily of the Valley
	Gemini (May 21–June 20)	Air	Rose
	Cancer (June 21–July 22)	Water	Water Lily
	Leo (July 23–August 22)	Fire	Gladiolus
	Virgo (August 23–September 22)	Earth	Aster
	Libra (September 23–October 22)	Air	Cosmos
	Scorpio (October 23–November 21)	Water	Mum
	Sagittarius (November 22–December 21)	Fire	Narcissus
	Capricorn (December 22–January 19)	Earth	Carnation
	Aquarius (January 20–February 18)	Air	Violet
	Pisces (February 19–March 20)	Water	Daffodil

GEMS	LUCKY HINDI NAME SOUNDS
diamond, ruby, bloodstone, amethyst, jasper	chu, che, cho, la, lee, lu, le, lo, aa
emerald, sapphire, quartz, diamond , agate	chu, che, cho, la, lee, lu, le, lo, aa
agate, alexandrite, tourmaline, pearl	ee, oo, ae, o, va, vi, vu, ve, vo, ba, bi, bu, be,bo
pearl, moonstone, ruby, beryl, emerald	hi, hu, he, ho, da, di, du, de, do
ruby, amber, peridot, topaz, diamond	ma, mi, mu, me, mo, ta, ti, tu, te
agate, carnelian, sapphire, peridot, jade	to, pa, pu, kh, tha, pe, pi, pi
opal, sapphire, aquamarine, tourmaline, blue topaz	ra, ri, ru, re, ro, ta, ti, tu, te
topaz, tourmaline, bloodstone, opal, black pearl	to, na, ni, nu, ne, no, ya, ya, ye, yu
turquoise, lapis lazuli, topaz, obsidian	ye, yo, bh, bhi, bhu, gh, ph, dh, bhe
garnet, onyx, black pearl, turquoise	bho, ja, ji, ju, je, jo, kh, khi, khu, khe, khoo, ga, gi
aquamarine, hematite, jet, garnet	gu, ge, go, s, sh, si, su, se, so, da
amethyst, sugilite, aquamarine, bloodstone	di, du, tha, jh, ja, de, do, ch, chee

Shakespearean Names

Literature buffs, this list is for you! Peruse your favorite Shakespearean works for some unusual name choices used (and even created) by one of history's greatest and most prolific writers. Or, recall your favorite book, poem, or play for potential name choices.

A Midsummer Night's Dream
  Lysander
  Theseus
  Titania

All's Well That Ends Well
  Lafeu
  Rinaldo

As You Like It
  Adam
  Audrey
  Jaques
  Oliver
  Orlando
  Phoebe
  Rosalind
  Silvius

Barbara Pym: Less Than Angels
  Aleric

Comedy of Errors
  Adriano
  Aegeon
  Aemilia
  Balthazar
  Luce
  Luciana
  Nell

Cymbeline
  Belarius
  Pisanio

Hamlet
  Barnardo
  Marcellus
  Ophelia
  Reynaldo

Henry IV
  Thomas

Henry V
  Alice
  Michael

Henry VI
  Peter
  Thomas

King John
  Arthur
  Peter

King Lear
  Oswald
  Regan

Love's Labour's Lost
  Jaquenetta
  Katharine
  Maria
  Mercade
  Rosaline

Macbeth
  Angus
  Lennox
  Malcolm
  Ross
  Seyton

Measure for Measure
  Isabella
  Juliet
  Lucio
  Peter
  Pompey

Merchant of Venice
Antonio
Jessica
Lancelot
Leonardo
Lorenzo
Portia
Merry Wives of Windsor
Robin
Much Ado About Nothing
Antonio
Beatrice
Ursula
Othello
Montano
Othello
Roderigo
Richard II
Thomas
Richard III
Anne
Thomas
Romeo and Juliet
Abraham
Juliet
Paris
Peter
Romeo
Rosaline
Sampson
Taming of the Shrew
Katharine
Mariana

Nathaniel
Philip
The Tempest
Adrian
Ariel
Iris
Juno
Miranda
Sebastian
Stephano
Timon of Athens
Timandra
Timon
Titus
Aaron
Andronicus
Marcus
Twelfth Night
Maria
Olivia
Sebastian
Toby
Valentine
Viola
Two Gentlemen of Verona
Antonio
Julia
Launce
Silvia
Valentine
Winter's Tale
Paulina

Musical Names

Musically inclined? Relax to the sound of your favorite CD while you look through these names with melodious meanings. Or reflect on your favorite band, orchestra, or musician for other noted name ideas.

GIRLS' NAMES

Alima	Understands dance and music
Aria	Melody
Cadence	Rhythmic flow of sounds
Cannia	Song
Carmen	Crimson song
Carol	Melody
Celia	St. Cecilie was a talented musician and patron saint of music
Chantal	Singer
Gala	Lovely voice
Harmony	Harmonious
Jazmine	A play on the musical style of jazz
Lyria	Variation of *Lyric*
Lyric	Words to a song
Melody	Melodious
Rena	Joyous song
Shira	Tune
Taraneh	Song
Viola	Instrument in the violin family
Yarona	Sing

BOYS' NAMES

Amadeus	The name of Wolfgang Amadeus Mozart, an Austrian composer considered one of history's best and most creative musical geniuses
Baird	Minstrel; a medieval musical entertainer
Hototo	The whistler
Leron	The song is mine
Rani	My song
Ron	My song
Shiron	Songfest

Place Names

In chapter two, we discussed how place names have become fun, common options for parents. The name of a place can also have very meaningful associations or a potential destination for a trip shared with your child. Browse our collections for a place name that might be perfect for your baby.

BOYS' NAMES		GIRLS' NAMES	
Aspen	Kent	Abilene	Italia
Athens	Kerry	Alabama	Jamaica
Bergen	Leicester	Albany	Jordan
Berlin	Leith	Alma	Kerry
Boston	Lester	America	Kimberley
Brighton	Lincoln	Ashanti	Libya
Brooklyn	London	Asia	Loraine
Cairo	Maldon	Aspen	Loreto
Camden	Marlow	Bali	Lourdes
Carlyle	Milan	Bethany	Lucerne
Cayman	Nazareth	Bethel	Madison
Chester	Nevada	Beverly	Marseilles
Cleveland	Phoenix	Britney	Martinique
Cyprus	Rhodes	Capri	Normandy
Dakota	Ross	Chelsea	Odessa
Dallas	Rudyard	Cheyenne	Paloma
Dane	Rugby	China	Paris
Darien	Selby	Clare	Rhodesia
Dayton	Sheffield	Dakota	Sahara
Denver	Siam	Devon	Savannah
Denzel	Skipton	Dixie	Selby
Devon	Spaulding	Eden	Seville
Everest	Sterling	Florence	Shannon
Eyton	Tennessee	Florida	Shelby
Holland	Texas	Geneva	Sinai
Houston	Tyrone	Georgia	Valencia
Israel	Welsh	Guadalupe	Venice
Jericho	Whitby	Gwyneth	Wyoming
Jordan	Zaire	India	Zamora

Surnames as First Names

Appropriately, we have saved surnames for last! Surnames are a great way to find a unique name.

Bestowing last names as first names has become increasingly popular for children of either sex—take for example the recent use of Irish surnames for children: Braden, Keegan, Kennedy, and Riley. Parents seeking to combine originality with a sense of familiarity can find good options with surnames. Here are a few of our favorites.

Abram	Brice	Dane	Evens
Adler	Bronte	Darwin	Everet
Albee	Bryce	Dedrick	Ewing
Alden	Byron	Devlin	Fairley
Alston	Cadby	Devon	Falkner
Anson	Caddell	Dewey	Farley
Archer	Cade/Caide/Cayd	Dexter	Farris
Arlo	Caidan	Dickins	Fenton
Arman	Calbert	Digby	Fielding
Ash	Calder	Dillon	Fischer
Ashton	Calvert	Dixon	Fitz
Aubrey	Calvin	Donnelly	Fletcher
Austin	Camden	Donovan	Flynn
Avery	Carsen	Doogan	Forrest
Baird	Carsten	Doran	Foster
Bartley	Carver	Dorsett	Frantz
Barton	Casper	Drake	Frasier
Basel	Chet	Drew	Frisbee
Baxley	Clemens	Drexel	Frye
Baxter	Clement	Duke	Gaige
Beaudry	Cole	Duncan	Galvin
Benson	Conan	Dunlap	Garland
Bernard	Conlan	Durwin	Garner
Blaine	Cortlan	Duval	Garrett
Blair	Cortland	Eames	Garvin
Blake	Costa	Eden	Gerard
Blane	Daine	Elias	Gibson
Boston	Dale	Elmer	Gillean
Bowden	Dallas	Elton	Gilmore
Bowen	Dalton	Ernest	Gleason
Brandeis	Damon	Erving	Glenn

Grafton
Graham
Grant
Grear
Greig
Grey
Grier
Griffin
Gulbert
Gunther
Gustin
Guthrie
Hadley
Hagen/
    Haygen
Halston
Halton
Hanley
Hanlon
Harley
Harmon
Harper
Hartley
Hayden
Heath
Heyden
Hogan
Holden
Holland
Hudson
Humphrey
Hunter
Irving
Irwin
Ives
Jackson
Jaegar
Jansen/Janson
Jarvis
Jensen

Kallen
Kameron
Karsen
Keane
Keaton
Keegan
Kelsey
Kendall
Kimball
Kipley
Kipling
Lamar
Lane
Langley
Larkin/Larkyn
Larsen
Lennon
Lesher
Lincoln
Logan
Loren
Lucas
Lyndon
Macaulay
Maccoy
Maddock
Maguire
Mallorey
Manning
Markham
Marlin
Marlow
Marques
Marshall
Milan
Milton
Mitchum
Nelson
Neumann
Nielsen

Norton
Odar
Ohnstad
Oldham
Olsen
Otis
Owen
Palmer
Parker
Percy
Peyton
Phillip
Piper
Presley
Preston
Quinne
Radcliff/Radcliffe
Raleigh
Randolph
Reese
Riley
Rosen
Ross
Rowan
Royce
Sanborne
Sanders
Sawyer
Sergent
Seth
Shay
Sheldon
Sidney
Skyler
Spencer
Sterling
Stetson
Steward
Stryker
Sullivan

Taft
Taggart
Talbot
Talon
Tanner
Teagan
Thatcher
Tobias
Tomlin
Torrance
Travais
Trent
Truman
Tucker
Vance
Wade
Wallis
Ward
Warren
Webster
Wesleyan
Wessley
Whitney
Willis
Wilson
Wrenn
Wyatt
Zale/Zaile/Zayle
Zive

Drumroll, Please...

Making Your Final Selection and Loving It

 So here you are, closing in on the baby-naming journey. While I am sure you've enjoyed your trip, the vacation is nearly over and a decision must be made—it's finally time to choose that perfect name. By now you may have a good idea of what your decision is, but even if you do, you will find the final phases of this guide are fun and enlightening while empowering you to make that selection with confidence.

Making Your Lists, Checking Them Twice

Before moving to the next phase, review your name lists, being careful not to have missed an opportunity to find another contender for a name. While this book aims to inspire, there is no exact formula to selecting your child's name. At this point, you want to feel that you've thoroughly explored all your options and you're excited by your collection of name choices—enthusiastically ready to begin the process of filtering down and discovering the right name.

On the hit TV series *Mad About You*, Jamie and Paul chose the name Mabel for their infant daughter—an acronym for Mothers Always Bring Extra Love.

Eliminating the Fear Factor

During this final phase, you should also keep in mind that many parents choose a name simply because of the way it sounds—especially with their surname and even middle name choice. So, if at the end of your nine-month journey, you "just love the way it sounds," then be secure in your decision because you've truly set all other issues aside and simply chosen what you feel is the most suitable name possible for your new family member.

You might also worry that your child will hate his name. Well fear no more! In a study conducted through Mindworks—a forum for children in grades 1–12 to express their opinions—most kids said they liked their names and felt that their efforts and life decisions—not their names—would shape them. Even the few that didn't like their names said they appreciated the sentiment behind their names and would never consider changing them. So that takes a load off, right? Your young to school-aged child will most likely love his name as much as you love his name, but all bets are off once he hits the teen scene, during which everything will be "your" fault anyway! But we don't need to go there yet, and chances are your child will go full circle and eventually return to loving his name just as he did before.

☑ Exercises: completed
☑ Thoroughness: checked
☑ Fear factor: eliminated

As a caution to new parents: don't be concerned if you find you're uncomfortable calling your child by her carefully selected moniker. For some parents, especially those that have waited until the last minute to decide on their baby's name, there is a very normal period of adjustment that shouldn't be interpreted as you having chosen the wrong name. You will see—after a few short days, the name and child truly do become one.

The Process of Elimination

Up until now, you have been asked to work side-by-side with your partner compiling your lists; but now it's time to divide and conquer! So turn on your internal dialogues, pull out your pencils and lists, and let's get started.

Exercise Nine: Mom and Dad's Lists of Favorites

Both Mom and Dad should now spend alone time with the lists you've created together. Each of you should form "your personal list"—individually selecting first names that you compiled together during the various exercises. (You'll find a separate list for each of you in the workbook section.) You can also look up new names if you think the perfect moniker is still out there. As you copy the names, try rating each one. Absolutely Love the Name gets a 10, and Can Live with It a 1, 2, or 3. Your lists should not exceed your top ten choices. You will also want to include notes on why you like the names on your list. You may love one name because it sounds great with your surname, or it is a family name or—better yet—it is a family name and it sounds great with your surname. Whatever meaning it is a family name and it sounds great with your surname. Whatever meaning your name choices have should be written in the allocated space in your workbook on page 410.

Now Mom and Dad (doesn't that sound nice?), it's time to take a break. There's actually no rush unless you're eight centimeters dilated, and even if that's the case, remember to relish this time and enjoy your pregnancy and the process of naming your child. With that in mind, you may want to spend some time with your personal lists paying close attention to the reasons you chose the names. You might be surprised to see that this process can also be revealing to your priorities and parenting style. Did you find yourself giving higher rankings to religious or family names than you had expected? Now would be a good time to reopen the discussion of baby-naming priorities with your partner, reevaluating what's important to each of you. This is also a nice time to get intimate with your partner and even peek in on his or her list, because the fun will soon begin, and your "final cut" is next!

Exercise Ten: The Final Cut

If you haven't done so already, it's time to compare lists and, once again, combine efforts in the selection process. After comparing the lists you created in Exercise Nine, consider it "hitting the lottery" if a name shows up on both lists and immediately bring that name down to the "final cut" section of your workbook, on page 412. (If you're doing this alone, you can simply select your highest-rated names.) Follow up these agreed-upon first names with complementary middle names. Keep in mind, while the middle can be a good compromise, your priority is choosing the right names (both first and middle) for your child's last name. See page 19 for important considerations in choosing a middle name.

Next, Mom and Dad should now each choose their favorite first names from the opposite parent's list, and write these names in the allotted workbook space. For those first names that Dad chose, Mom gets to select her favorite complementary middle names, and vice versa.

You now have your final list of potential names for your baby. Whenever you're ready, choose your favorite first-and-middle name combination for each gender. A good trick to play on yourself when you're at this point is to think about how you will feel calling your child with these various names at a playground. Visualize your child coming when you call—does the name turn heads? And if so, does it matter? Does her name roll off your tongue? Does his name make you grin?

The Last Word on Baby's First Name

If this isn't smooth sailing so far, try re-reading the section on working through name dilemmas in chapter one. As we've mentioned, naming your baby is not an exact science, and bending and flexing are absolutely in order. Because of your union, we hope you will glide through this process effortlessly and that by now congratulations are in order as you have both methodically and carefully chosen a meaningful name for your baby, but if you still have a few options in the mix, wait.... Meet your little one and let him tell you which name to choose. Maybe he looks more like an Owen than a Rohan, or she more like an Erin than a Lauren. Generally, you have a window of a few days after giving birth before you're required to fill out the baby's birth certificate form. (This paperwork is typically provided by the hospital and begins the process of making the name official.)

And just for the record, if you've made it to the end of this process and put this much time and effort into naming your child, you will undoubtedly be the "perfect" parents to a young Master or Misses (fill in the blank).

HELLO
my name is

Chel...

Cheyenne

Jam...

Jo...

...ia

China

K...

Clare

...rica

Dakota

...anti

Devon

...ia

Dixie

...pen

Eden

Florence

...Bali

Florida

Bethany

Bethel

Geneva

Beverly

Georgia

Guadal...

Britney

...ri.

Gwyne...

Girls'
Names

AASE Norse: Tree-covered mountain

ABAN Persian: Eighth month of the Iranian calendar

ABAYOMI African: Bring great joy (Nigeria)

ABBASEH Persian: Lioness

ABBY American: Nickname for Abigail
Abbie, Abbey, Abhy

ABDERA Greek: Place name of a town in Greece

ABEBE African: Asked for (Nigerian)
Abebi

ABEDABUN Native American: Sight of day (Cheyenne)

ABELLA French: Variation of Ahelia
Abelia, Abelina

ABENA African: Born on Thursday
Abenaa, Abbena

ABEO African: Her birth brings happiness

ABEQUA Native American: Stays at home (Cheyenne)

ABERFA Welsh: From the mouth of the river

ABHIRATI Hindi: Mother of five hundred children; a mother goddess

ABIA Arabic: Great
Abeya; **Famous Namesakes:** *French author Elisabet Abeya*

ABIGAIL Hebrew: Gives joy, my father rejoices; Abigail was the third wife of the biblical King David and was described as discreet and beautiful in form.
(Spanish) *Abegail;* (Gaelic) *Abaigeal;* (Irish)
Abiageal, Gobinet, Gobnait; Abaigael, Abegayle, Abhy, Abichail, Avagail, Avichayil, Avigail, Abagail, Abbigail, Abigale, Abbigale, Abbigayle, Abbigaile; **Nicknames:** *Abbey, Abbie, Abby, Gael, Gail, Gaila, Gayla;*
Famous Namesakes: *Advice columnist Abigail Van Buren, First Lady Abigail Adams;*
Star Babies: *Daughter of Anthony Perkins*

ABILENE American: City in Texas

ABIR Arabic: Fragrant or numerous
Abeer

ABIRA Hebrew: My strength

ABRA Hebrew, Italian: Mother of many nations; a feminine form of Abraham. Arabic: Lesson
Abarrane, Abree, Abri, Abriana, Abrianna, Abrielle, Abrienne

ACACIA Greek: Thorny; in Greek mythology, the acacia tree symbolizes immortality and resurrection. Acacia wood was used in the Bible to build the tabernacle in the wilderness.
Acantha; Akantha; **Nicknames:** *Cacia, Casey*

ACCALIA Latin: Meaning uncertain; possibly derived from Acca Larentia, the mythological she-wolf who nursed the twins Remus and Romulus

ACELINE French: Noble

ADA Hebrew: Beautiful, adorned. African: First daughter. English: Prosperous, happy
(Finnish) *Aada; Adah, Adda*

ADABEL Teutonic: Lovely or happy

ADAIN Welsh: Winged

ADAIR Scottish: From the oak tree ford; surname
Adaira, Adairia

ADALINA Teutonic: Diminutive form of Adele

ADAMINA Hebrew: Of the red earth; feminine form of Adam
Admina

ADANYA African: Her father's daughter (Nigerian)
Adanna

ADARA Greek: Beauty. Welsh: Catches birds. Hebrew: Darkened. Irish: From the ford at the oak tree. Arabic: Virgin, unblemished pearl, untrodden sand

The young man waited impatiently for the lady to finish with the drugstore telephone directory. After she had turned page after page he said, "Madam, can I help you find the number you want?"

"Oh, I don't want a number," she replied, "I'm looking for a pretty name for my baby."
—Bell Telephone News

ADDIE French: Nickname for Adelaide

ADDIENA Welsh: Beautiful
Addien

ADDISON English: Of Adam; this surname was traditionally a male name but is growing in popularity for girls.
Addeson, Adison, Adisson, Addisyn; **Nicknames:** *Ad, Addie, Addy*

ADE Arthurian Legend: A mistress of Lancelot

ADELA Latin: Variation of Adelaide

ADELAIDE German, French: Of the nobility; the wife of Emperor Otto the Great and the name of an Australian city
(Latin) *Adela;* (French) *Adele;* (Spanish) *Adalia, Adelaida, Alita;* (Dutch) *Aaltje, Aleta;* (Polish) *Adelajda; Adalene, Adaliz, Adalyn, Adelia, Adelle, Adelynn, Adilene;* **Old Forms:** *Adelheid, Adelheide;* **Nicknames:** *Ada, Addie, Heida, Heide, Heidi, Addy, Del, Della, Delle, Lady*

ADELE German: Of the nobility, a noble wolf; feminine form of Adolph
(English) *Adalbrechta;* (German) *Adalicia, Adalie, Adaliz, Adalwolfa, Adelinda;* (Teutonic) *Adal, Adaline, Adelicia; Adali, Adel, Adelle, Edelle, Adela, Adelia;* **Old Forms:** *Adellinde;* **Diminutive Forms:** *Adalina, Adelita, Adette*

ADELINA French: Of the nobility; variant of Adelaide
Adeline; **Nicknames:** *Adele, Lina*

ADELITA Spanish: Of the nobility, noble; a diminutive form of Adela. During the Mexican Revolution in the early twentieth century, adelitas were "soldaderas" or female soldiers who cooked for and washed up after the armies, cared for their wounded men, and fought bravely in battles alongside the soldiers. A vital force in the war effort, these women are memorialized in the famous Mexican song "La Adelita."

ADELPHA Greek: Dear sister
Adelphe, Adelphie

ADENA Hebrew: Noble, delicate
Adina, Adinah, Adine; **Old Forms:** *Adinam*

ADERYN Welsh: Bird

ADHELLE Teutonic: Lovely or happy

ADIA English: Wealthy

ADIBA Arabic: Polite, learned, honest; Adiba stems from Adab, meaning manners and synonymous with culture and literature.
Adeeba, Adeebah, Adibah

ADILA Arabic: Similar, bundle, equivalent; feminine form of Adil

ADIRA Arabic: Strong, powerful, wealthy

ADITI Hindi: Free

ADMETA Greek: From a tale of Hercules

ADOETTE Native American: Large tree (Omaha)

ADOLPHINE Teutonic: Noble wolf; feminine form of Adolph
Adolpha

ADONIA Greek: Beautiful lady

ADORABELLA Latin: Adored beauty
Adorabelle

ADOREE French: Adored

ADORIA Latin: Glory
Adora

ADRASTEIA Latin: Unyielding

ADRIAN Latin, English: Dark; from the Adriatic Sea region
(French) *Adreanna, Adrienne*; (Italian) *Adreana*; (Dutch) *Adrie*; *Adra, Adrea, Adria, Adriana, Adrielle, Adrienna, Adrina*; **Star Babies:** *Daughter of Harry Belafonte*

ADSILA Native American: Blossom (Cherokee)

ADYA Hindi: Born on Sunday

AEDON Greek: Daughter of Pandareos

AEGERIA Latin: From the Aegean Sea
Aegaea, Aegates

AEGINA Latin: Mother of Aeacus, who, in Greek mythology, was the first king of Aegina. Aeacus was known for his piety and became a judge in Hades after his death.
Aeginae

AELDRA English: Noble

AEOLIA Latin: Daughter of mythological chariot-warrior Amythaon

AERLENE Anglo-Saxon: Elfin

AERONA Welsh: Berry

AERWYNA English: Friend of the sea

AETHRA Greek: Mother of Theseus, the hero and king of Athens who slew the Minotaur

AETNA Greek: From Aetna

AFARIN Persian: Praise
Afareen

AFRA Latin: Roman nickname for African woman; the name of two early saints

AFREDA English: Friend of the elves
Aelfraed, Aethelwine, Aethelwyne; **Old Forms:** *Aelfwine*

AFRICA Celtic: Pleasant, agreeable, a large continent; Africa is the Anglicized form of Aifric, an Irish name popular since medieval times. Some parents may choose Africa as a name symbolic of the continent of their heritage.
Affrica, Aifric, Aphria, Apirka, Affricah, Affrika, Affrikah, Africah, Afrika, Afrikah, Aifrica, Aphfrica, Apirkah; **Nicknames:** *Afric*

AFRODILLE French: Daffodil

AFSOON Persian: Spell

AFTAB Persian: Sun

AFTON English: From the Afton River

AGALIA Greek: Splendor
Agalaia

AGATHA Greek: Good, kind; Saint Agatha was a third-century Sicilian martyr (Greek) *Agathi*; (French) *Agathe*; (Spanish) *Agacia*; (Irish) *Agate*; (Swedish) *Agda*; (Russian) *Agafiya*; (Hungarian) *Aggie, Agi, Agotha, Agoti*; *Agaue, Agave, Agna, Agata, Agueda*; **Famous Namesakes:** *English mystery writer Dame Agatha Christie*

AGATON Swedish: Pure

AGHAVNI Armenian: Dove

AGLAIA Greek: Goddess of grace

AGLAUROS Greek: Mythological woman who was turned into stone by Hermes

AGNES Greek: Pure, chaste, innocent; a popular Roman martyr of the Middle Ages. See also *Ina* (English) *Anessa, Anisha, Anissa, Annice, Annis*; (French) *Ynes, Ynez*; (Spanish) *Agnese, Ines, Inesa, Inez*; (Gaelic) *Aigneis*; (Irish) *Aghna, Una*; (Danish) *Agneta*; (Russian) *Agnessa, Agnia, Inessa*; (Czech) *Anezka*; (Finnish) *Anneetta, Aune*; *Agnella, Annissa, Anyssa*

AGRAFINA Latin: Born feet first (Russian) *Agrafena*; *Agrafine*; **Nicknames:** *Fenya*

AGRIPPINA Latin: Colonist
Agrippinae

AHALYA Hindi: Night

AHANA Irish: From the little ford

AHANG Persian: Harmony

AHAVA Hebrew: Dearly loved
Ahave, Ahuda, Ahuva

AHELIA Hebrew: Breath
(French) *Abella*; *Ahelie*

AHELLONA Greek: Masculine

AHISMA Hindi: Gentle

AIDA Italian, English: Reward, happy, helper; Aida is one who brings benefits and advantages, and was the Prophet Mohammed's favorite wife. Verdi's opera bears the same name and is an epic classic tale of love, loyalty, betrayal, and courage. It tells of the love triangle between Aida, Amneris, and the soldier they both love.
Aidia

AIDAN Irish: Little, fiery; Aidan is a modern English spelling of the early medieval Gaelic name Áedán.
Adan, Adeen, Eideann, Etney; **Star Babies:** *Daughter of Faith Daniels*

AIDEEN Irish: Spelling variation of Etain

AIDOIOS Greek: Honored

AIFE Celtic: A great female warrior of myth

AILA Scottish: From the strong place

AILANI Hawaiian: High chief

AILEEN Scottish, Irish: Light, from the green meadow; also see *Eileen* and *Helen* (Greek) *Alina*; (Irish) *Aileene*; *Aileana*; **Nicknames:** *Ailey, Aili, Ailia, Lina, Leena*

AILI German: Sweet

AILIN Irish: Noble
Ailinn, Ailan, Ailyn, Ailynn, Aelin, Aelinn, Aelyn, Aelynn, Aelan

AILIS German: Sweet

AILSIE Hebrew: Devoted to God

AIMÉE French: Variation of Amy
Famous Namesakes: *Singer Aimee Mann*

AINA Celtic, Swedish: Joy. Finnish: Forever

AINSLEY English: My own meadow
Ansley, Ainsleigh, Ainslee, Ainslea, Ainslie

AIRIC Celtic: Agreeable

AIRLEAS Gaelic, Irish: Oath

AISHA Arabic: Lively; Aish means food, wheat, or bread; it is symbolic of the sustenance of life. See also *Asha*
Ashia, Iesha, Myesha, Myeshia, Aishah, Ayeisha, Ayesha, Ayisha, Aysha, Eisha, Ieshea;
Star Babies: *Daughter of Stevie Wonder*

AISLEY Anglo-Saxon: Spelling variation of Ashley

AISLIN Irish: Vision; may also be a variant of Ashlyn
Aisling, Aislinn, Ashling, Isleen

AITHNE Celtic: Fire

AIYA Hebrew: Bird

AIYANA Native American: Eternal blossom

AJAYA Hindi: Invincible

AKAKIA Greek: Guileless

AKELA Hawaiian: Noble

AKIKO Japanese: Iris; light and bright

AKILI African: Bright, smart (Tanzanian)

AKILINA Latin: Eagle-like

AKIRA Scottish: Anchor

AKIVA Hebrew: Protected
Akiha

ALAIDA Latin: Winged

ALAINA Irish: Fair, good-looking; feminine form of Alan or variant of Helen
(Swedish) *Gala; Alain; Alana, Alane, Alani, Alanna, Alannah, Alayna, Alayne, Allana, Allene*

ALALEH Persian: Buttercup

ALAMEA Hawaiian: Ripe, precious

ALAMEDA Spanish: Promenade. Native American: Grove of cottonwood

ALANA Hawaiian: An offering

ALANE Celtic: Fair

ALANZA Spanish: Ready for battle

ALAQUA Native American: Sweet gum tree

ALARICE German: Rules all; feminine form of Alaric
(Teutonic) *Alaricia; Alarica, Allaryce*

ALASTRINA Celtic, Irish: Defends mankind; feminine form of Alastair and a variant of Alexandra
Alastrine, Alastriona

ALATHEA Greek: Mythological goddess of truth

ALAULA Hawaiian: Light of daybreak

ALAWA Native American: Pea (Arapaho)

ALAZNE Basque, Spanish: Miracle

ALBA Latin: White
(Italian) *Albinia*; (Arthurian Legend) *Albiona*; *Albina, Alvinia*

ALBERTA German, Teutonic: Bright, noble; This feminine form of Albert is also related to the name Bertha.
(English) *Alberteen*; (French) *Albertina*; (Spanish) *Albertine, Elbertina*; *Albertyna, Alhertine, Auberta, Elbertine, Alberthine, Auberte, Aubertha, Auberthe, Aubine, Elbertha, Elberthina, Elberthine*; **Nicknames:** *Ali, Alli, Allie, Ally, Berrie, Berry, Bert, Berta, Bertie, Berty*; **Famous Namesakes:** *Singer Alberta Hunter*

ALCAMENE Latin: Mother of Hercules

ALCESTIS Greek: In Greek mythology, the name of a woman who gave her life to save her husband

ALCHEMY American: A power or process of transforming something common into something special
Star Babies: *Daughter of Lance Henrikson and Jane Pollack*

ALCINA Greek: Feminine of Alcinous, a mythical character that helped Odysseus return home. Alcina is also the name of a mistress of alluring enchantments and sensual pleasures in the Orlando poems.
(Italian) *Alcee, Alcinia*; *Alcine*

ALCIPPE Greek: In mythology, Alcippe is the daughter of Aglaurus and Ares, and mother of Daedalus by Eupalamus.

ALCMENE Greek: Mother of Hercules
(Latin) *Alcmena*

ALCYONE Greek: In mythology, daughter of King Aeolus

ALCYONEUS Greek: Alcyoneus fought against Athena in Greek mythology

ALDA German: Wise, elder, sometimes wealthy; variant of Aldo. See also *Aldys, Aleda* (German) *Aldona*; *Aldea, Aldis*

ALDENE Italian, Spanish: Wise, elder; variant of Aldo

ALDERCY English: Chief

ALDONA German: Variation of Alda

ALDONZA Spanish: Nice, sweet
Aldonsa

ALDORA Greek: Winged gift. English: Noble

ALDYS English: From the old house

ALEANA Hebrew: Spelling variation of Alena

ALEANDRA Russian: Defender of man

ALECTA Greek: Honesty

ALEDA English: Winged

ALEEN Celtic: Fair, good-looking; variant of Helen or Eileen

ALENA Greek: Light; variant of Aileen
Aleana, Alyna, Aleena, Alenna, Alenah

ALENE Celtic: Fair, good-looking; feminine variant of Alan. Dutch: Alone

ALERA Latin: Eagle
Aleria

ALESANDESE Greek, Basque: Helper of man; feminine form of Alesander

ALETHEA Greek: Truthful; mythological goddess of truth
(Spanish) *Aletea, Aletia*; *Aletha, Aletheia,*

Alethia, Alithea, Alithia, Olethe, Olethea, Olethia, Olithia

ALEV Turkish: Flame

ALEX Greek: Defender of mankind; a familiar form of Alexandra
Alyx; **Famous Namesakes:** *Actress Alex Kingston*

ALEXANDRA Greek: Defender of mankind; feminine form of Alexander
(English) *Alexandrea*; (French) *Alexandrina, Alexandrine*; (Italian) *Alessandra, Alessia*; (Spanish) *Alandra, Alejandra, Alejandrina, Alondra*; (Russian) *Aleksandra*; (Czech) *Olexa*; (Polish) *Olka*; (Ukrainian) *Olesya*; (Hungarian) *Alexa*; *Alexandina, Alexandria, Alexandriana, Alexine, Alixandra, Alyssandra, Lexandra, Oleisia*; **Nicknames:** *Aleka, Alex, Alexia, Alexis, Alix, Drina, Lexann, Lexi, Lexie, Lexina, Lexine, Sandra, Sandrine, Sasha, Shura, Xandra, Zandra, Zondra*; **Diminutive Forms:** *Sashenka, Shurochka, Sondra*; **Famous Namesakes:** *Actress Alexandra Paul, Educator Alexa Canady*; **Star Babies:** *Daughter of Mikhail Baryshnikov and Jessica Lange, Barry Gibb, Whoopi Goldberg, Dustin Hoffman, Christopher Reeve, Keith Richards*

ALEXIS English: Nickname for Alexandra
Alexus; **Nicknames:** *Lexi, Lexie, Lexy*; **Famous Namesakes:** *Actress Alexis Smith*; **Star Babies:** *Daughter of Ted Danson, Dennis Rodman and Annie Banks, Martha Stewart*

ALFONSA Spanish: Noble and ready, or battle ready; this was the name of six kings of Portugal and kings of several ancient regions of Spain.
(German) *Alfonsine*; (Italian) *Alonza*; (Teutonic) *Alphonsa*; *Alonsa, Alphonsine, Alphonza, Alphosina*

ALFREDA English: Elf counselor; feminine form of Alfred. Teutonic: Oracle
Alfrida

ALGIANA Teutonic: Elf-spear, spearman; feminine variant of Alger or possibly Algernon
Algiane

ALGOMA Native American: Valley of flowers (tribe unknown)

ALHERTINE French: Spelling variation of Alberta

ALI Arabic: Greatest; a variant of Allah, the Supreme Being in the Muslim faith; feminine form of same name
Alli, Allie, Aly; **Famous Namesakes:** *Actress Ali McGraw*; **Star Babies:** *Daughter of Robert Plant, daughter of Ruth Pointer*

> *"Must a name mean something?"*
> Alice asked doubtfully.
> *"Of course it must,"* Humpty
> Dumpty said with a short laugh:
> *"My name means the shape I
> am—and a good handsome shape
> it is, too. With a name like yours,
> you might be any shape, almost."*
> —Lewis Carroll,
> *Through the Looking-Glass*

ALICE German, English: Noble, of the nobility; Alice is a variant of the old French name Adeliz, a form of Adelaide. Children of all ages know Alice as Lewis Carroll's heroine in *Alice's Adventures in Wonderland*.
(Hebrew) *Alisa*; (Latin) *Alisia, Alycia, Alysha*; (German) *Alison*; (French) *Alisanne, Alyson*; (Spanish) *Allyce, Alyce*; (Gaelic) *Ailis, Ailse*; (Irish) *Ailise, Allison, Allsun*; (Hungarian) *Alisz, Aliz*; *Ailisa, Alicea, Alise, Alissa, Alisse, Allyse, Allyson, Alys, Alyse, Alyssa, Alysse, Alyssia*; **Old Forms:** *Allis*; **Famous Namesakes:** *Author Alice Walker*

ALICIA Spanish: Noble; variant of Alice and Adelaide
Alecia, Alesia, Alycia, Alysha; **Diminutive Forms:** *Lecia, Licia, Lisha*

ALIDA Latin, Dutch: Small winged one; (German) archaic
(English) *Alita, Elida, Elita, Oleda, Olita*; (French) *Allete; Aletta, Oleta*

ALIKA African: Most beautiful (Nigerian)

ALIMA Arabic: Knows dance and music, sea maiden, knowledgeable, delicate, a well yielding much water; stems from "eilm," meaning knowledge; feminine form of Alim or Al Alim

ALINA Latin: Of the nobility; variant of Eileen and feminine form of Alan. Celtic: Fair
(Latin) *Alyna; Aline*

ALISON German: Variation of Alice
Allison, Allyson, Alyson; **Nicknames:** *Ali, Allie, Ally*; **Famous Namesakes:** *Author Alison Lurie, Actress Alison Eastwood*; **Star Babies:** *Daughter of Tom Berenger, daughter of Heather Menzies and Robert Urich*

ALISSA English: Spelling variation of Alice
Alisa, Alysa, Alyssa

ALITA English: Variation of Alida

ALIYAH Hebrew: To ascend, to rise up
Aaliyah, Alea, Aleah, Alia, Aliya, Aliah, Aliye, Allia, Alliah; **Famous Namesakes:** *Singer and actress Aaliyah Haughton*

ALIYN Gaelic: Beautiful; feminine form of Alan
(Teutonic) *Allys*

ALIZ German: Sweet

ALIZA Hebrew: Joy, joyous one
Aleeza, Aleezah, Alitza, Alizah

ALKA Polish: Intelligent. Hindi: Long hair

ALLA Russian: The goddess; from Allat, name of pre-Islamic Arabic goddess of fertility
Nicknames: *Alka, Allochka*; **Famous Namesakes:** *Russian singer Alla Pugacheva*

ALLAIRE French: Cheerful, glad; variant of Hilary
Alair

ALLEFFRA French: Cheerful

ALLEGRA Latin, English: Joyous
Alegra, Alegria, Allegria; **Nicknames:** *Allie*

ALLINA Latin: Of the nobility; variant of Adelina. See also *Aleen*
(Celtic) *Allena; Aleena*

ALLURA English: To allure

ALMA Latin, Spanish: Nourishing, soul. Persian: Apple. Celtic: Good. Swedish: Loving

ALMAS Arabic, Persian: Diamond, adamant
Almaz

ALMETA Latin: Driven. Danish: Pearl

ALMIRA Arabic: Stores, provisions, wheat; the food assembled for travel or for a reunion

ALMUDENA Spanish: The city; the Virgin of Almudena is the patron saint of Madrid.

ALODIA Anglo-Saxon: Rich
Alodie

ALOISA German: Famous warrior; feminine form of Alois
Aloise, Aloisia

ALONA Hebrew: Strong as an oak tree
Allona, Allonia, Alonna

ALONSA German: Spelling variation of Alfonsa

ALOYSIA German: Famous fighting. Teutonic: Famous in battle

ALPHA Greek: Firstborn; the first letter of the Greek alphabet

ALSATIA French: From Alsace, a region in France

ALSOOMSE Native American: Independent (Algonquin)

ALTA Latin, Spanish: Lofty

ALTAGRACIA Spanish: High grace; given in honor of Mary, mother of Jesus
Nicknames: *Alta*

ALTAIR Arabic: Bird, poultry; Altair is the name of the main star in the constellation Aquila, which is known as Orion in the western world.
Altaira

ALTHA English: Healer

ALTHEA Greek: Pure, wholesome
Althaea, Althaia, Altheda, Althia; **Famous Namesakes:** *Tennis star Althea Gibson*

ALULA (Al Oola) Arabic: The first, number one; refers to firstborn child

ALUMA Hebrew: Girl, maiden, or hidden secret
Alumit

ALURA English: Divine counselor
Alurea

ALVA Hebrew: Exalted one; an Old Testament descendant of Esau

ALVAR English, German: Army of elves (Latin) *Alvita*; (Spanish) *Alvara, Alvarita*; *Alvarie, Alvera*; **Nicknames:** *Alvie*

ALVERA Spanish: Speaker of truth; feminine form of Alvaro

ALYDA German: Archaic

ALYNA Latin: Variation of Alina

ALYSSA Greek: Rational
Alissa

ALZINA Arabic: Adornment, feast, illumination; when used in a name, these attributes refer to Woman.
Alzena

AMA Norse: Eagle. African: Born on Saturday (Ghanaian)
Ami, Amma

AMABELLE Latin, French: Lovable; beautiful or loving
Amabel, Amabilis

AMADA Latin: To love
(Spanish) *Amata; Amare*

AMADAHY Native American: Forest water (Cherokee)

AMADEA Latin: Loves God; feminine form of Amadaeus
Amadis

AMADÉE French: Variation of Amanda

AMADI Arabic: My pillar. African: Rejoicing (Nigerian)

AMADINA Latin: Worthy of God

AMAIA Basque: The end

AMAL Arabic: Hope, trust, expectation
Amala

AMALIA Latin: Original form of Emily
Nicknames: *Lia, Maya*

AMALTHEA Greek: Woman who nursed Zeus

AMALUR Spanish: Homeland
Amalure

AMANDA Latin, English: Worthy of being loved; poets and playwrights brought this name into popular usage in the seventeenth century.
(French) *Amadée*; **Nicknames:** *Manda, Mandalyn, Mandi, Mandie, Mandy;* **Famous Namesakes:** *Actress Amanda Plummer;* **Star Babies:** *Daughter of George Lucas, Donna Summer, Billy Bob Thornton*

AMARA Greek: Eternal; a form of Amarantha

Amarantha sweet and fair,

Ah, braid no more that shining hair!

As my curious hand or eye

Hovering round thee, let it fly!

—Richard Lovelace
"To Amarantha, that she would dishevel her Hair"

AMARANTHA Greek: Unfading; refers to the Amaranth plant with dense bulbous green and red flowers. The plant is so named because the flowers retain their color even when dried.
(French) *Amarante*; (Spanish) *Amaranta*; *Amaranda, Amarande*; **Nicknames:** *Amara*

AMARIAH Hebrew: Yahweh; name of several Old Testament characters
Amarisa, Amarise

AMARIS Hebrew: Given by God. Spanish: Child of the moon

AMARYLLIS Greek: Flower; poetically used to mean a simple shepherdess or country girl in *I Care Not For Those Ladies* by Thomas Campion (1567–1620)
Nicknames: *Marilis*

AMBA Hindi: Mother. See also *Umayma Amhi, Amhika*

AMBAR Hindi: Sky, horizon

AMBER English: A jewel-quality fossilized resin; derived via Old French and Latin from Arabic ambar; as a color, the name refers to a warm honey shade and was popularized by Kathleen Winsor's novel *Forever Amber*
(French) *Ambre*; *Amberlee, Amberly, Amberlyn, Amberlynn, Ambra*; **Star Babies:** *Daughter of Simon LeBon, daughter of Neil Young*

AMBIKA Hindi: Goddess of the moon

AMBROSIA Greek: Immortal; in mythology, Ambrosia is a food delicacy of the gods and immortal beings
Ambrotosa, Amhrosine

AMEENA African: Trustworthy (Swahili)

AMELIA Latin: Industrious, hard working; Amelia is the heroine of Henry Fielding's 1751 novel *Amelia*.
Famous Namesakes: *Aviation pioneer Amelia Earhart*

A Matter of Fact

Roscellinus of Amorica (1050–1121) was the founder of nominalism in the Middle Ages and instigated another approach to universals. According to Dr. C. George Boeree in his essay on the Middle Ages, Roscellinus was quoted as saying that the universe is just a vocal sound, or a word: "Only individuals actually exist. Words, and the ideas they represent, refer to nothing."

AMETHYST Greek: A purple or violet gemstone; according to ancient Greek superstition, an amethyst protected its owner against the effects of strong drink.

AMIA English: Spelling variation of Amy

AMINA Arabic, African: Trustworthy or faithful
(Persian) *Amineh*; *Ameena, Ameenah, Aminah*

AMIRA Arabic: Princess; feminine form of Amir. Hebrew: One who speaks
Ameerah, Amirah; **Famous Namesakes:** *Actress Amira Casar*

AMITA Hebrew: Truth

AMITOLA Native American: Rainbow
(Unknown tribal origin)

AMITY Latin: Friendship
(French) *Amité*; *Amitée*

AMMA Norse: Grandmother

AMOR Spanish: Love
Amora

AMORICA English: Ancient name for Britain; in the Middle Ages, the Celtic nation of Brittany became known as Amorica, and was considered a center of Celtic culture in Europe.

AMORITA Latin: Little loved one
Amoretta, Amorette

AMPHITRITE Greek, Latin: A sea goddess; aunt of Achilles

AMREI German: A blend of Anne and Marie

AMRITHA Hindi: Precious

AMSER Welsh: Time

AMY French: Dearly loved
(French) *Aimée*; *Amia, Amie, Ami*; **Famous Namesakes:** *Actress Amy Irving, Singer Aimee Mann*; **Star Babies:** *Daughter of Robert Redford, daughter of Julie Andrews and Blake Edwards*

AMYMONE Greek: The mythological daughter of Danaiis

AMYNTA Latin: Protector

ANABEL Latin: Spelling variation of Annabel

ANAHITA Persian, Hindi: Immaculate, undefiled; this was the name of the Persian goddess of fertility and water. She was sometimes identified with Artemis, Aphrodite, and Athena.
(Armenian) *Anahid*

ANAIS French: Variation of Ann
Famous Namesakes: *French author Anaïs Nin*; **Star Babies:** *Daughter of Noel Gallagher and Meg Mathews*

ANALA Hindi: Fiery

ANALENA Spanish: Grace, favor; variant of Anna

ANALISA English: Blend of Anna and Lisa (Latin) *Analiese, Analisia*; (Swedish) *Annalina*; *Analicia, Analise, Annalisa, Annalise, Annalissa*

ANAMARI Hebrew: A hybrid of Anna and Marie

ANANDA Hindi: Bliss

ANANTA Hindi: Name of a serpent

ANAROSA Spanish: Grace, favor; variant of Anna

ANASTASIA Russian, Greek: Resurrection; the daughter of the last tsar of Russia, she was killed with the rest of her family and small dog by the Bolsheviks in 1918. In 1920, a Polish peasant girl with a striking resemblance to Anastasia claimed her identity. It wasn't until her death and subsequent DNA testing that she was identified accurately as an imposter. Disney pictures animated this true story in the film *Anastasia* in 1997. (Greek) *Anastacia, Anastasha*; (Russian) *Nastasia*; (Czech) *Anastazie*; (Polish) *Anastazja*; (Hungarian) *Anasztaizia*; *Anastashia, Anastassia, Anastazia, Annastasia, Anstice*; **Nicknames:** *Asya, Nastia, Stacie, Stacy, Tasya, Tazia, Ana*; **Famous Namesakes:** *Russian ballerina Anastasia Volochova*

ANASUYA Hindi: Charitable

ANAT Hebrew: To sing. Egyptian: A wife of Seth
Anata, Anate

ANATOLA Greek: From the east
Anatolia

ANAXARETE Greek: Unfeeling woman turned to stone by Aphrodite

ANCE Hebrew: Grace

ANCELIN French: Handmaiden
Ancelina

ANCYRA Latin: From Ankara

ANDEANA Spanish: Leaving

ANDELA Czech: Variation of Angela

ANDENA English: A man's woman; variant of Andrea

ANDIE English: Nickname for Andrea
Andee, Andi, Andy; **Famous Namesakes:** *Actress Andie MacDowell*

ANDISHEH Persian: Thought

ANDRAS Norse: Breath

ANDRASTE Celtic: Victory

ANDREA Greek, French: A man's woman; feminine form of Andrew; This name may be considered particularly appropriate for Andrea Verrocchio, a Renaissance sculptor who taught Leonardo da Vinci and Perugino (Latin) *Andranetta, Andrena*; (Greek) *Andreas*; (French) *Andrée*; (Spanish) *Andere*; (Danish) *Anndrea*; *Andena, Andreana, Andreanna, Andreya, Andria, Andriana, Andrianne, Andrienne, Andrina, Aundrea*; **Nicknames:** *Anda, Andee, Andes, Andi, Andie, Andra*

ANDROMEDA Greek: In Greek mythology, Andromeda was the daughter of Cassiopeia and the wife of Perseus. This is also the name of a northern constellation named after the mythological figure.

ANE Hebrew: Prayer

ANEISHA English: Variant of Ann or Agnes

ANEKO Japanese: Older sister

ANELMA Finnish: Variant of Unelma

ANESSA English: Variation of Agnes

ANEVAY Native American: Superior
Anevy

ANEZKA Greek: Gentle

ANFISA Russian: Blossoming

ANGA Hindi: From Anga

ANGELA Latin, Italian: Messenger of God;
feminine form of Angelus
(Hebrew) *Erela, Erelah*; (Latin) *Angel*;
(Greek) *Angeliki, Angelina, Angelique*;
(Anglo-Saxon) *Engel*; (French) *Ange,
Angelette, Angeline, Angilia*; (Spanish)
Angelia, Angelita; (Gaelic) *Aingealag*; (Celtic)
Aingeal; (Czech) *Andela*; (Persian) *Fereshteh*;
Angelena; *Angele, Angelee, Angelene, Angeli,
Angelisa, Angell, Angelle, Angelyn, Anjali*;
Nicknames: *Angie*; **Famous Namesakes:**
Actress Angela Lansbury

ANGELICA Latin: Angelic; derived from
Angelicus
(German) *Angelika*; (Spanish) *Anjelica*;
Famous Namesakes: *Actress Anjelica Huston*

ANGELINA Greek: Variation of Angela
Famous Namesakes: *Actress Angelina Jolie*

ANGENI Native American: Spirited angel
(Tribal origin unknown)

ANGERONA Latin: In mythology, goddess
who relieved men from pain and sorrow
(Arthurian Legend) *Angharad, Angharat*

ANGIE Latin: Nickname for Angela
Famous Namesakes: *Actress Angie
Dickinson*

ANICE Scottish: Variation of Ann

ANICHKA Russian, Ukrainian: Grace
(Hebrew) *Aniki*; (Dutch) *Anika*; (Slavic)
Anica; (Finnish) *Annikki*; (Hungarian) *Aniko*;

Annikka, Annikke; **Famous Namesakes:**
Swedish golfer Annika Sorenstam

ANIELI Polish: Masculine

ANISA Arabic, Persian: Friendly, social
Anysia; **Famous Namesakes:** *Hard rock
artist Anisa Murphy*

ANITA Hebrew: Grace; variant of Ann
(Hebrew) *Anitra*; *Aneta, Anetta*

ANJEANETTE English: Gift of God's favor;
blend of Anne and Janet
Anjanette, Anjanique, Annjeanette

ANJOLIE English: Blend of Anne and Jolie

ANKARA Latin: From Ankara

ANKINE Armenian: Valuable

ANKTI Native American: Repeat dance
(Hopi)

*I am in a delight with you,
Music Man.*

*Your name is Dr. Y. My
name is Anne.*

—Anne Sexton,
"Letters to Dr. Y"

ANN English: Graceful; a variant of Hannah
introduced to Britain in the thirteenth century
(Hebrew) *Ayn*; (German) *Antje*; (French)
Anais, Anne; (Scottish) *Anice*; (Swedish)
Annika, Annike; (Dutch) *Anke, Anki*;
(Russian) *Anna*; (Polish) *Ania*; (Finnish)
Anniina, Annukka, Anu; (Hungarian) *Anci;
Ana*; **Nicknames:** *Anni, Annie, Anya*;
Diminutive Forms: *Anechka*; **Famous
Namesakes:** *Fashion designer Anne Klein,
Actress Anne Bancroft, Writer Anne Frank,*

*Author Anne Morrow Lindbergh, Advice
columnist Ann Landers*

ANNA Russian: Variation of Ann. Native
American: Mother (Algonquin)
Famous Namesakes: *Tennis player Anna
Kournikova;* **Star Babies:** *Daughter of Bob
Dylan, Peter Gabriel, Kirk Cameron, Tom
Petty*

ANNA CRISTINA Swedish: Graceful
Christian

ANNABEL Latin: Beautiful, beloved;
considered an elaboration of Anna and
Belle or a variation of Amabel
(Irish) *Annabla; Anabel, Anabelle, Annabella,
Annabelle*

*And the stars never rise
but I feel the bright eyes
Of the beautiful Annabel
Lee*

—Edgar Allan Poe,
"Annabel Lee"

ANNABETH English, Latin: Blend of Ann
and Beth; in the Bible, a devout woman who
saw infant Jesus presented at the temple in
Jerusalem.

ANNALIE Swedish: Graceful meadow
(German) *Annalena;* (Spanish) *Analee,
Analeigh; Annalee, Annali*

ANNAMARIA Hebrew: Grace or bitter;
blend of Anna and Maria
(Spanish) *Anamarie, Yanamaria, Yanamarie*

ANNASTIINA Finnish: Blend of Anna and
the Swedish name Stina, which is a short
form of Kristina
Annastina

ANNBRITT German: Blend of Ann and
Brigitte

ANNEGRET German: Blend of Ann and
Margaret

ANNEKE Scandinavian: Favor, grace:
variant of Hebrew Hannah

ANNELI Swedish, Finnish: Graceful meadow;
a pet form of Anna

ANNELIESE Hebrew: Grace or devoted
to God; a blend of Anne and Lisa
Annaliese, Annelisa, Annelise; **Star Babies:**
Daughter of Kelly LeBrock and Steven Seagal

ANNEROSE German: Blend of Anne
and Rose

ANNETTE French: Little Ann
Famous Namesakes: *Actress Annette
Funicello*

ANNIE Hebrew: Nickname for Ann
Star Babies: *Daughter of Kevin Costner,
Jamie Lee Curtis, Glenn Close*

ANNIS Greek, Anglo-Saxon: Whole

ANNORA Latin: Variant of Honora
Annorah

ANNYS Greek: Whole

ANOOSHEH Persian: Happy

ANORA Hebrew: Grace. English: Light

ANOUK Hebrew: Grace
Annouk

ANOUSH Armenian: Sweet-tempered

ANSA Latin: Opportunity. Finnish: Constant, also "trap" in the traditional Finnish meaning of the word
Anse

ANSTACE Greek: One who will be reborn; derived from Anistemi, meaning to stand up, to raise up

ANTANDRA Latin: From the Amazon

ANTEA Greek: Feminine form of Antaeus, son of Poseidon

ANTHEA Greek: Flower; Lady of flowers
Antea, Anthia; **Nicknames:** *Thia, Thea*

ANTICLEA Greek: In mythology, mother of Odysseus

ANTIGONE Greek: The mythological daughter of Oedipus and sister of Priam

ANTIOPE Greek: In mythology, daughter of Asopus

ANTOINETTE French: Variation of Antonia
Famous Namesakes: *French Queen Marie Antoinette*

ANTONIA Latin, Italian: Praiseworthy; feminine form of Anthony
(German) *Antonie*; (French) *Antoinette*; (Italian) *Antonella, Antonietta*; (Russian) *Antonina; Antoinetta, Antonette, Antonique*; **Nicknames:** *Nella, Toinette, Toini, Toni, Tony, Tonya*; **Famous Namesakes:** *British author Lady Antonia Fraser*; **Star Babies:** *Daughter of Anthony Quinn, daughter of John Wayne*

ANUNCIACION Spanish: Of the Annunciation

ANWEN Welsh: Very beautiful

ANYA Russian: Nickname for Ann
Star Babies: *Daughter of Stanley Kubrick*

AOLANI Hawaiian: A heavenly cloud

APALA Hindi: Endearing, beautiful; name of a legendary Hindu wise woman

APHRAH Hebrew: Biblical place name meaning dust or of the earth
Afra, Afrah, Aphra; **Famous Namesakes:** *Writer Aphra Behn*

APHRIA Celtic: Pleasant; variant of Africa

APHRODITE Greek: Foam-born; the Greek goddess of love, Aphrodite was born from the sea foam, married to the smith god Hephaestus, and became the mother of Eros (Cupid) among others.

APOLLONIA Greek: Belonging to Apollo; Apollo was the Greek god of sun, light, music, and poetry.
(Latin) *Apollonis*; (French) *Apolline*; (Scandinavian) *Abelone*; (Danish) *Abellona*; *Abellone, Apollina, Apollinaris*

APONI Native American: Butterfly
Aponee

APRIL Latin, English: Opening up, evocative of the opening of flower buds in the spring; born in or belonging to the month April
(French) *Avril*; (Spanish) *Abril*; *Aprille, Apryl, Apryll, Averil, Averill, Averyl, Avriel, Avrill, Avryl, Aipril, Aprill, Averel, Averell, Averyll, Averylle*

APSARAS Hindi: In Hindu mythology, Apsaras are female spirits of nature akin to water or forest nymphs. They are considered beautiful creatures who are also talented artists and performers.

APULIA Latin: Place name for the south-eastern-most region of Italy and the river Apulia

AQUANETTA English: The exact origin is unclear, but this is most likely a recently created name based on a feminization of the blue-green color aqua.
Aquanette

AQUENE Native American: Peace

AQUILINA Spanish: Eagle
Aquiline

AQUITANIA Latin: Place name referring to a region in southwestern France or people from that region; the name of a transatlantic ship of the Cunard line so beloved that it earned the name Ship Beautiful

ARA Latin: Altar or place of prayer; the name of a star constellation south of Scorpius. Arabic: Brings rain. Teutonic: Eagle's wisdom

ARABELLA Latin, English, Dutch: Answered prayer; almost any female name ending in "bella" will remind people of the Latin meaning beautiful. See also *Orabella* (English) *Orabel*; *Arabelle, Arabel, Arabela, Arabele, Arbela, Arbell, Arbella, Arbelle, Orabelle*; **Nicknames:** *Ara, Bel, Belle, Bella, Ora, Orra*

ARABIA Latin: Place name referring to ancient country to the southwest of Mesopotamia, which in modern geography would include the Middle East and might reflect a family or cultural connection to that part of the world

ARACELI Latin, Spanish: Altar of heaven
Aracelia, Aracelis, Arcilla, Aricela, Aracely, Ariceli, Aricelly

ARACHNE Greek: In Greek mythology, Arachne was a young girl whose pride in her weaving skills and attitude during a weaving contest prompted Athena to turn her into a spider. In Latin mythology, it is Minerva who transForms Arachne.

ARAMA Spanish: Reference to the Virgin Mary

ARAMINTA English: Unclear origin and meaning; possibly invented by playwright William Concreve for his heroine in the 1693 play, *The Old Bachelor*; possibly a variant or blend of Amynta or Arabella
Araminte

ARCADIA Greek, Latin: A mountainous region of Greece that became a symbol of, and endowed this name with, the virtues of the simplicity and joy found in pastoral life
Arcadie

ARCELIA Spanish: Treasure, altar of heaven

ARDA Hebrew: Bronze, strong metal
Ardah, Ardath

ARDALA Irish: High honor; feminine form of Ardal, from the old name Ardghal

ARDEA Latin: From Ardea, an ancient town of the Rutuli people and now a modern village in west-central Italy

ARDEN Latin, English, Celtic: Burning with enthusiasm, passionate and eager; Shakespeare set the romantic comedy *As You Like It* in the magical forest called Arden. The name also evokes the image of glamorous actress Eve Arden.
(French) *Ardella, Ardelle*; (Celtic) *Ardena, Ardene, Ardra*; *Arda, Ardeen, Ardel, Ardelia, Ardelis, Ardina, Ardine, Ardinia, Ardis, Ardyne, Ardys*; **Nicknames:** *Ardi*

ARELLA Hebrew: Messenger of God, an
angel
(Latin) *Arela*; *Arelle*

ARENA Greek: Holy one

ARETE Greek: Virtue, the Greek concept of
striving for excellence in all aspects of one's
life; unforgettably linked to singer Aretha
Franklin
Areta, Aretha, Aretina, Oretha, Oretta, Orette;
Nicknames: *Retha*

ARETHUSA Greek, Latin: In mythology,
Arethusa was pursued by the river god
Alpheus, who had fallen in love with her.
Rather than give in to him, she begged
Artemis to save her, which she did by turning
her into a spring. Not to be defeated, Alpheus
turned himself to water and united with her.

AREVIG Armenian: Like the sun

AREZOO Persian: Wish

ARGANTE Arthurian Legend: Name of
a queen

ARGEL Welsh: Refuge

ARGENTA Latin, Spanish: Silvery; the
country Argentina was named after the
precious metal explorers hoped to find there.
Argentia, Argentina

ARIA Italian, Greek, English: Melody, generally
referring to an elaborately done and beautiful
song sung by a soloist in an opera; possible
familiar form of Greek name Ariadne.
Teutonic: Eagle, eagle's wisdom. See Ara
(English) *Ariette*; *Arietta*

ARIADNE Greek, Latin: Holy one; in Greek
mythology, Ariadne is the daughter of King
Minos who saves Thesus by helping him
navigate the prison maze known as the
Labyrinth.

(French) *Ariane*; (Persian) *Aryana*; *Arene,
Ariadna, Ariana, Arianna, Arianne, Arriana,
Ariagna, Arianie, Aryane, Aryanie, Aryanna,
Aryanne*

ARIANA Welsh: Like silver; also a variant
of Ariadne
*Arian, Ariane, Arianna, Aryanie, Aryanna,
Aryanne*

ARICIA Latin: From Aricia

ARIEL Hebrew: Lioness of God, a biblical
name for Jerusalem; Ariel is also
Shakespeare's name for a mischievous spirit
in *The Tempest* and Disney's lovable character in *The Little Mermaid*.
(French) *Arielle*; (Spanish) *Ariela*; *Areille,
Arial, Ariele, Ariellel*

ARIETTA Italian: Small melody sung by
a soloist; variant of Aria
Ariette

ARILDE Teutonic: Hearth maiden
Arilda

ARISHA Russian: Diminutive form of Arina

ARISTA Greek: The best; Arista is the name
of a star in the Virgo constellation and of a
major recording company known for making
musical stars. Latin: Ear of corn
(Persian) *Arissa*; *Aristella, Aristelle*

ARJEAN French: Silvery
Arcene

ARLAIS Welsh: From the temple

ARLEIGH English: Variation of Harley

ARLENE English, Irish: Pledge or oath;
variant of names ending in "arlene," such
as Carlene and Charlene. Arlene may also be
a feminine form of Arlen or Charles
Arlyne, Arlana, Arleana, Arleen, Arleena,

Arleene, Arlena, Arlenna, Arleta, Arlette, Arlina, Arline, Arlyn, Arlyne; **Diminutive Forms:** *Arla;* **Famous Namesakes:** *Actress Arlene Francis*

ARLETTE French: A medieval given name; derived from a feminine diminutive of Charles
Arleta, Arletta

ARLEY English: Unisex name, meaning bowman
Arlee, Arlie

ARLINDA English: Origins unclear, but probably a modern blend of Arlene and Linda

ARLISE Hebrew: Pledge, probably related to the name Arlene; feminine variant of Arliss
Arlyss

ARMENIA Latin: Place name of country located in southwestern Asia, east of Turkey

ARMES Welsh: Prophetess

ARMIDA Latin: Little armed one, little warrior

ARMILLA Latin: Bracelet, armlets

ARMINA German: Warrior maiden; feminine variant of Armand or Herman
Armilda, Armilde

ARNE German: Eagle
Diminutive Forms: *Arnette*

ARNELLE English: Eagle strength; feminine form of Arnold
Arnalda, Arnolda

ARROSA Latin, Basque: Of the rose or of the rosary; variant of Rose
Arrose

ARSENIA Greek: Strong; feminine form of Arsenio
Arcenia, Arsania, Arsemia

ARTEMIS Greek: Huntress and virgin goddess of the moon in Greek mythology, the equivalent of the Roman goddess Diana

ARTEMISIA Greek: Gift from Artemis, perfection
Artemia, Aretmasia, Artemesia

ARTHES Welsh: Bear; a name related to Arthur

ARTHURINE English: Noble, courageous; a modern feminine variant of Arthur, which would confer meanings of stone and bear as well
Artheia, Arthelia, Arthene, Arthurene, Arthurette, Arthurina, Artia, Artice, Artina, Artis, Artlette, Artrice

ARTURA Spanish: Noble or courageous; feminine form of Arturo

ARUNA Hindi: Radiant morning star

ARVADA Danish: Eagle

ARVANEH Persian: Wild violet

ARWEN English: In J.R.R. Tolkien's *The Lord of the Rings*, Arwen is the daughter of Elrond and marries Aragorn to become queen of elves and men. She is called Evening Star.

ARYA Hindi: Noble goddess

ASA Hebrew: Healer; traditionally a male name. Japanese: Born in the morning. Norse: Goddess

ASAL Persian: Honey

ASDIS Norse: Divine spirit; Asdis was a character in Grettir's Saga

ASE Norse: Goddess
Asa

ASELMA Gaelic: Fair, divine

ASENATH Egyptian: Gift of the sun god; in
the Bible, Asenath is Joseph's Egyptian wife and
mother of his sons Manasseh and Ephraim.
Acenath

ASGRE Welsh: Heart

ASHA African: Lively, woman, life; variant
of Aisha
Ashia

ASHILDE Norse: God fighting
Ashild, Ashilda

ASHIRA Hebrew: Wealthy or I will sing
Asheera, Ashirah

ASHLEY Anglo-Saxon: From the ash tree
meadow; a surname and an increasingly
popular girls' name in recent years
*Aisley, Aisly, Ashla, Ashleah, Ashlee, Ashleen,
Ashleena, Ashleigh, Ashlen, Ashlie, Ashly*;
Famous Namesakes: *Actress Ashley Judd,
Actress Ashley Olsen;* **Star Babies:** *Daughter
of Howard Stern*

ASHLYNN English: Possible variant of either
Ashley or Aisling; possible blend of Ashley
and Lynn
Ashlin, Ashlinn, Ashlyn, Ashlynne

ASHTON English: Town of the ash trees;
surname
Ashten, Ashtyn, Ashtin, Ashtynn

ASIA Greek, Latin: The rising sun; a Greek
sea-nymph, daughter of Oceanus and Tethys,
for whom the continent was named
Aja, Asiah, Azhah

ASIANNE Arabic: Plait, tress, braid; stems
from El Assina

ASIMA (Aasema) Arabic: Capital of a country, town; also someone that one turns to for
protection or help
Aasema

ASLI Turkish: Genuine, real

ASPASIA Greek: Welcoming, inviting;
history remembers the fifth-century bearer
of this name as the mistress of famed Greek
statesman Pericles and as one of the most
beautiful and educated women of her time.

ASPEN American: Type of tree noted for
heart-shaped leaves which flutter in the
slightest breeze; Aspen is also a place name
of a ski resort town in Colorado.
Star Babies: *Daughter of Tyler England and
Shanna*

ASSANA Irish: Waterfall
(Irish) *Assane*

ASTA Greek, Latin, Swedish, Finnish: Like
a star, of the stars; possible diminutive for
Augusta, Anastasia, or Astrid
Nicknames: *Asteria*

ASTARTE Latin: Phoenician predecessor to
the Greek Aphrodite, mythology places her as
goddess of war, passionate love, and fertility.
Egyptian: Goddess of Syrian origin introduced
into Egypt during the eighteenth dynasty.

ASTERIA Latin: Like a star; variant of Asta.
In Greek mythology, Asteria hurled herself
into the sea after being abducted by Zeus.
She became the island of the same name.

ASTHORE Irish: Loved one

ASTOLAT Arthurian Legend: In Arthurian
Legend, Astolat is the home of Elaine, who
falls in love with Lancelot, but whose love
is unrequited.

ASTRAEA Greek: Star maiden; Astraea was the daughter of Zeus and Themis, and a goddess of justice. When the gods abandoned earth, Astraea was the last to leave, becoming the constellation Virgo when she finally did. *Astrea*

ASTRID Norse, Scandinavian: Divine strength; popular since the Viking age, this name was borne by Astrid Lindgren, Swedish author of *Pippi Longstocking*. (Teutonic) *Astred*; *Astlyr, Astrud, Astryd*; **Old Forms:** *Astrithr*

ASTYNOME Latin: In Greek mythology, she is a daughter of Chryses, probably fathered by Agamemnon, although her mother claimed Apollo was the father.

ASUNCION Spanish: Assumption; refers to the assumption of the Virgin Mary into heaven

ASVOR Norse: Wife of Asrod from Grettir's Saga *Asvora, Asvoria*

ATALANTA Greek, Latin: Immovable; the name of a female athlete and huntress in Greek mythology who vowed never to marry a man unless he beat her in a race. See also *Atlanta* *Atalante, Atlante*

ATALAYA Spanish: Guard tower

ATARA Hebrew: Crown, coronet, related to the word tiara *Atarah, Atera, Ateret*; **Nicknames:** *Tara*

ATE Greek: Blindness; she was the Greek goddess of rash decisions and irrationality

ATELLA Italian: From Atella

ATEPA Native American: Wigwam (Choctaw)

ATHALEYAH Hebrew: Lioness of God

ATHANASIA Greek: Immortal *Atanasia, Atanasya, Athenasia*

ATHDARA Irish, Scottish: From the oak tree ford

ATHELAS English: From J.R.R. Tolkien's *Lord of the Rings*, a miraculously nourishing bread

ATHENA Greek: Mythological goddess of wisdom and war, Athena is the daughter of Zeus but has no mother. She sprang forth from his head, fully grown and fully armed. Her symbol is the owl, and the city of Athens is named for her. (Latin) *Athene*; **Famous Namesakes:** *Journalist Athena Desai*

ATILDA English: At the elder tree *Athilda*

ATIYA Arabic: Gift, present, allowance; feminine form of Atteya *Ateya, Atteya, Atteyah*

ATLANTA American: Immovable; variant of Atalanta and the capital city of the state of Georgia

ATOOSA Persian: Name of a princess

ATROPOS Greek: In Greek mythology, Atropos was one of the three Fates or Moirae, female deities who supervised rather than determined outcomes. Atropos was the fate who cut the thread or web of life. *Atropes*

ATTHIS Greek: Mythical Greek princess for whom the city of Attica was named

ATTICA Greek: From Attica in Greece, a town in the vicinity of Athens

Thirty Uncommon Unisex Names

Interested in a gender-free moniker?
Here are a few of our favorite not-so-common
recommendations:

Avery	Reece/Reese
Bryce	Rohan/Rowan/Rowen
Chaney	Royce
Channing	Rumor/Rumer
Chauncey	Satchel
Janson/Jansen	Sawyer
Kai	Scout
Kalen	Sean/Shawn
Layne	Skylar
Luca/Luka	Sloane/Sloan
Merrill/Meryl	Tate/Tait
Peyton/Payton	Tayler/Taylor
Piper	Teague
Presley	Tegan/Teagan/Teigan
Quinn	
Raleigh	

ATTRACTA Latin: Drawn to, attracted. Irish: Name of a saint, healer, and co-worker with Saint Patrick in Ireland, also called Araght or Taraghta

AUBINA Latin: White
Aubine

AUBREY French, English: Elf ruler, implying leadership with supernatural wisdom; Aubrey was originally a male name, only recently becoming popular for girls.
Aubree, Aubrie, Aubry, Avery, Aubary, Aubery, Aubreigh, Aubrette, Aubury; **Star Babies:** *Daughter of Jimmy Connors, Bob Saget*

AUBRIANNE French, English: Modern blend of the names Aubrey and Ann, possibly an attempt to endow the originally male name Aubrey with a more feminine sound
Aubriana, Aubrianna

AUBRIELLE English: Blend of Aubrey and Gabrielle

AUDE French: Old or wealthy
(Norse) *Aud, Auda*

AUDHILDA Norse: Rich warrior woman
Audhild, Audhilde

AUDNEY Norse: Prosperity, wealth
Audny

AUDREY Anglo-Saxon: Noble strength; Saint Audrey, one-time queen of Northumbria, was known for wearing fancy lace necklaces, which supposedly helped cause her death.
(French) *Audra, Audree, Audrielle; Audelia, Audene, Audre, Audrea, Audreana, Audreanna, Audria, Audriana, Audrianna, Audrie, Audrina, Audris, Audreen, Audry, Audrye*; **Nicknames:** *Audie, Audri, Audi, Audy*; **Famous Namesakes:** *Actress Audrey Hepburn*

AUDRIS Teutonic: Lucky, wealthy
Audfis, Audrisa, Audriss

AUDUNA Norse: Friend of wealth; feminine form of Audun, the Westfjorder from Grettir's Saga

AUGUSTA Latin: Majestic; feminine form of Augustine
(English) *Austine*; (Irish) *Augusteen; Agustina, Augustina, Austen, Austina*; **Nicknames:** *Gussie*

AULIS Greek: Small port of ancient Greece where the Greek fleet sailed against Troy after the sacrifice of Iphigenia

AURA Latin: Gold, subtle light or glow surrounding a subject, also a variant of Aurelia. Greek: Gentle breeze
Aure, Aurea, Ora

AUREAR English: Gentle to hear, music
Auriar

AURELIA Latin, Spanish: Golden; originally a Roman clan name
(French) *Aurelie, Aurielle, Orane*; (Italian) *Oria*; (Spanish) *Aureliana*; (Hungarian) *Aranka; Aureline, Aurene, Auriel, Orali, Oralia, Oralie, Orelia, Orlene, Orlina*; **Nicknames:** *Aura, Ora*

AURKENA Spanish: Present
Aurkene

AURNIA Irish: Golden lady

AURORA Latin: Dawn; Aurora was the Roman goddess of the dawn and the equivalent of the Greek goddess Eos. Aurora is also the name of the beautiful princess in many versions of *Sleeping Beauty*.
(French) *Aurore; Zorah*

AUSET Egyptian: Another name for Isis; most powerful of the female Egyptian goddesses, she was consort and sister to Osirus, mother of Horus, and is usually depicted as a motherly woman with arms wide open.
Aset

AUSTEN English: Spelling variation of Augusta

AUTONOE Greek, Latin: With a mind of her own; in Greek mythology, she was the daughter of Cadmus and Harmonia and the mother of Actaeon. In Roman lore, she is the mother of Palaemon by Hercules.

AUTUMN English: Born in the fall, seasonal name
Star Babies: *Daughter of Jermaine Jackson*

AVA Hebrew, English: Like a bird; possibly related to the names Aya and Aveline. Persian: Voice
Avah, Avis; **Famous Namesakes:** *Actress Ava Gardner*

AVALON Celtic: Celtic for island of the apples, Avalon is the magical island where the old and the new religions of England meet and overlap in legend. Legends of the island as a paradise probably pre-date Arthur, but the island is most famous as King Arthur's burial place and the place where he will return to earth.
Avaron, Avarona, Avilon

AVASA Hindi: Independent

AVATARA Hindi: Descending

AVELINE French, English: Nut, hazelnut, akin to Hazel
(English) *Avalee, Avelyn, Avlynn*; *Avelaine, Avelina*

AVENA Latin: From the oat field
Avina

AVERA Hebrew: Crossing over, transgression

AVERNA Latin: Roman goddess and queen of the underworld

AVERY English: Elf ruler, implying leadership with supernatural wisdom; also a variant of Aubrey

AVIANA English: Origin unclear; possible variant or blend of Ava, Anna, or Aviva
Avia, Avianna

AVIANCE English: Bearer of good news; modern blend of Ava and Ana

AVICE French: Warlike

AVIRA Hebrew: Air

AVIS Latin: Bird; variant of Ava and Aya. English: Refuge in battle

AVISA Persian: Clear water

AVITA Latin: Youthful

AVIVA Hebrew, Latin: Springlike, dewy and fresh, implies innocence and youth; feminine variant of Aviv
Avivah, Avivi, Avivit, Auvit; **Nicknames:** *Viv, Viva*

AVONLEA English: River meadow

AVONMORA Irish: From the great river

AVRIL French: Variation of April
Averel, Averell, Averil, Averill, Averyl, Avrill

AWEL Welsh: Breeze
Awell

AWENASA Native American: My home
(Cherokee)

AWENDELA Native American: Morning

AWENITA Native American: Fawn
Awinita

AXELLE German: Of peace; feminine
variant of Axel

AYA Hebrew: Bird; possibly related
to the name Avis
Ayla

AYALA Hebrew: Gazelle or hind (female roe
deer), suggestive of a graceful, shy animal
Ayalah; **Nicknames:** *Aya*

AYANNA Hebrew: He answers

AYASHA Native American: Little one
(Chippewa)
Ayashe

AYITA Native American: Worker
(Cherokee), first to dance (Cheyenne)

AYLA Hebrew: Oak tree; possible variant
of Aya. In literature, Ayla is the heroine of
Jean Auel's *Clan of the Cave Bear*. Persian:
Halo around the moon
(Persian) *Aylin*; *Aila*

AYN Hebrew: Variation of Ann
Famous Namesakes: *Philosopher Ayn Rand*

AYSEL Turkish: Like the moon, like
the moonlight

AZADEH Persian: Free

AZALEA Latin: The dry earth; a beautiful
flowering shrub closely related to the
rhododendron
(Greek) *Azalia*

AZAM Persian: Greatest, supreme
Aazam

AZAR Persian: Fire, also September

AZARA Persian: Scarlet

AZARIN Persian: Chamomile
Azareen

AZELIA Hebrew: Aided by God; feminine
form of Azriel
Azelie, Azriela

AZHAR Arabic: Flower, blossom, appear;
El Azhar University is the world's oldest
university and Sunni Islam's foremost seat
of learning.

AZIMA Arabic: Resolute, steady, determined
Azeema, Azeemah

AZIZA Arabic, African, Egyptian: Cherished,
beloved
Azizah, Azizeh

AZRIELA Hebrew: God is my strength,
God helps me; feminine variant of Aziel
and Azriel

AZURA Persian: Sky-blue
(English) *Azurine*; (French) *Azure*; *Azur*

BABETTE French: Diminutive form of Barbara

BADRA Persian: Full moon
Nicknames: *Badri*

BAHA Persian: Price, value

BAHAR Persian: Spring

BAHATI African: Lucky, fortunate (Swahili)

BAHIRA Arabic: Dazzling, brilliant, splendid, dazzled by sunlight; feminine form of Bahir
Baheera

BAHITI African: Fortunate (Swahili)

BAHRAMAN Persian: Ruby

BAILEY English: Steward or law enforcer from occupation of bailiff; surname adapted to first name use
Bailee, Baylee, Bayley, Baylie, Baileigh, Bailie, Bayleigh; **Star Babies:** *Daughter of Melissa Etheridge*

BAKA Hindi: Crane

BALARA Latin: Strong; variant of Valerie

BALI Contemporary: A country in Indonesia

BALLARD German: Bold or strong

BAMBI Italian: Pet name for Bambino, meaning little child; Bambi is the fawn of Walt Disney's famous children's storybook and movie.

BANAFSHEH Persian: Violet

BAPTISTA Greek: Baptizer; feminine form of Baptiste
(Italian) *Baptiste, Battista, Bautista*

BARANEH Persian: Rain; possibly used as a feminine variant of Baran
Baran

BARBARA Latin: Foreign woman, exotic; Barbara stems from *barbus*, meaning stranger. In Catholic custom, Saint Barbara is a protectress against fire and lightning. Barbie dolls are a household name throughout the world.
(Spanish) *Barvara;* (Gaelic) *Baibin, Bairbre, Barabal, Barabell;* (Swedish) *Barbro;* (Slavic) *Varvara;* (Russian) *Varushka;* (Czech) *Barbora, Baruna, Barunka, Baruska, Varina;* (Polish) *Basha;* (Hungarian) *Borbala, Borhala, Boriska, Borsala, Brosca, Broska; Babara, Vavara, Babarra, Barbera, Varvera;*
Nicknames: *Babita, Barbie, Basia, Bora, Borka, Vara, Varya, Wava, Bab, Babe, Babs, Bar, Bara, Barb, Barbs;* **Diminutive Forms:** *Babette, Barbarina, Barbina, Varinka;*
Famous Namesakes: *Journalist Barbara Walters, Singer Barbra Streisand, Author Barbara De Angelis, First Lady Barbara Bush*

> *"A baby is a blank cheque made payable to the human race."*
> –Barbara Christine Seifert

BARRAN Irish: Top, summit

BARSIN Persian: Clover

BASILIA Greek: Regal, royal; feminine form of Basileios
Basilea, Basila

BASIMAH Arabic: Nickname for Ibtesam

BASTET Egyptian: In Egyptian mythology, Bastet was a cat-goddess whose cult-center was at Bubastis in the Nile Delta. In the Late Period she was regarded as a beneficent deity.

BATHILDA German, Teutonic: Warrior woman, commanding, heroic
Bathild, Bathilde, Bertild, Bertilda, Bertilde

BATHSHEBA Hebrew: Daughter of the oath; Bathsheba was the beautiful wife of King David, whom she married after David had her husband Uriah killed in battle. She was the mother of Solomon.
Bethsheba; **Nicknames:** *Sheba*

BATTZION Hebrew: Daughter of Zion
Battseeyon

BATULA Arabic: Virgin; feminine form of Batul
Batoula

BATYA Hebrew: God's daughter
Bitya, Basha

BAUCIS Greek: In mythology, she was the wife of Philemon. Though poor, they were a happy couple and, when tested by the gods, they were found to be generous and giving people.

BEA Latin: Nickname for Beatrice
Famous Namesakes: *Actress Bea Arthur*

BEATA Latin: Blessed, happy
Beate

BEATE Polish: Blesses; variant of Beatty

BEATHA Celtic: Life
Betha

BEATRICE Latin, Italian: Bringer of joy; author Beatrix Potter is well remembered for the joy she brought countless children with her Peter Rabbit and other classic characters. Beatrice is the name of literary heroines ranging from Dante's idyllic heroine in his *Divine Comedy* to Shakespeare's spunky protagonist in *Much Ado About Nothing*. (Spanish) *Beatrisa, Beatriz; Beatricia, Beatrix*;

Nicknames: *Bea, Trixie, Trixy*; **Famous Namesakes:** *French actress Béatrice Dalle;* **Star Babies:** *Daughter of Prince Andrew and Sarah Ferguson, Paul McCartney and Heather Mills*

But Nature never framed a woman's heart

Of prouder stuff than that of Beatrice.

William Shakespeare,
Much Ado About Nothing

BECCA English: Captivating, beautiful; variant of Rebecca

BECKY Hebrew: Captivating, beautiful, desirable, to tie or bind; variant of Rebecca

BEDA English: Battle maiden, female warrior

BEDEGRAINE Arthurian Legend: A surname; castle and forest where Arthur fought his infamous battle against eleven kings
Bedegrayne

BEHNOUSH Persian: Pleasant

BELDA French: Fair maiden

BELEN Spanish: Bethlehem

BELGIN Turkish: Dear

BELINDA Latin, Spanish: Beautiful. Italian: Serpentine
Bellinda; **Nicknames:** *Bel, Bella, Belle, Linda*; **Famous Namesakes:** *Musician Belinda Carlisle*

BELKA Russian: Squirrel; also Russian nickname for Bella

BELLAMY French: Handsome friend; possible variant of Isabella

BELLANCE Italian: White, strong, karmic or predestined; variant of Blanca, meaning white

BELLE French: Beautiful, fair, lovely one; an abbreviation of Isabelle; in the fairytale, *Beauty and the Beast,* Belle is a young woman who teaches the enchanted Beast how to love and is rewarded handsomely for learning herself to see beyond appearances and trust her heart. **Star Babies:** *Daughter of Donna Dixon and Dan Aykroyd*

BELLISSA Italian: Fair; lovely one

BELLONA Latin: Goddess of war

BENEDICTA Latin: Blessed; feminine form of Benedict. See also *Benita* (Italian) *Benedetta*; (Swedish) *Bengta*; (Czech) *Benedikta*; *Benecia, Benetta, Benicia, Bente, Benedictine, Benoite*; **Nicknames:** *Bennie, Benny, Binnie, Binny, Dixie*; **Famous Namesakes:** *Opera singer Benita Valente*

BENITA Spanish: Blessed; common variant of Benedicta

BENTLEY English: From the meadow of coarse or bent grass; Bentley also evokes images of the luxury vehicle. This surname is traditionally used for boys. However, as with many male monikers ending in "ley," this name is becoming more popular for girls. *Bentlea, Bentleah, Bentlee, Bentleigh*

BERDINA German: Glorious. Greek: Intelligent maid *Berdine, Berdeena, Berdinna*

BERENICE Greek, French: One who brings victory; spelling variant Bernice is referred to in the New Testament of the Bible (Spanish) *Bernicia*; *Bernice, Bernyce, Berynice, Berrenice*; **Nicknames:** *Berny*; **Famous Namesakes:** *Writer Edgar Allan Poe wrote* Berenice.

BERJOUHI Armenian: Elegant lady

BERKELEY English: From the birch tree meadow; Berkeley is also a well-known university in California. Originally a surname and traditionally a boys' name, Berkeley is increasingly used for girls. *Berklea, Berkleigh, Berkley*

BERNA Turkish: Young

BERNADETTE French: Courage of a bear; feminine form of Bernard. Saint Bernadette was a French peasant girl who was visited by the Virgin Mary at a grotto near Lourdes. (Irish) *Berneen*; *Berdine, Bernadea, Bernadina, Bernadine, Bernarda, Bernardina, Bernelle, Bernetta, Bernette, Bernita*; **Nicknames:** *Nadetta, Nadette*; **Famous Namesakes:** *Actress Bernadette Peters*

BERTHA Teutonic, German: Sparkling, bright, splendid (French) *Berthe*; (Swedish) *Berta*; (Hungarian) *Bertuska*

BERTILDA Teutonic: Warrior woman, commanding, heroic; variant of Bathilda

BERYL Greek, English: Beryl stones have been historically associated with good luck, eternal youth, and strength. Traditionally pale green, including emeralds and aquamarines, beryl gemstones may also be red or colorless. This birthstone is associated with the astrological sign of Gemini. *Beryla, Beryle*; **Nicknames:** *Berri, Bery*

BESS English: Nickname for Elizabeth
Bessie; **Famous Namesakes:** *Singer Bessie
Smith*

BETH Hebrew: House; a diminutive of
Elizabeth and Bethany. Beth is remembered
fondly by generations of readers as the gen-
tle, loving sister in Louisa May Alcott's *Little
Women.*
Betsey

BETHAN Welsh: Consecrated to God

BETHANY Hebrew, Aramaic: A village near
Jerusalem where Jesus raised Lazarus from
the dead; a possible variant of Beth and Ann
(Spanish) *Bethania*; *Bethanee, Bethani,
Bethanie, Bethann, Bethaney, Bethannie,
Bethenny, Betheney, Betheny*

BETHEA Hebrew: Maid-servant of Jehovah

BETHELL Hebrew: House of God
Bethel, Betheli, Bethelle, Bethuel, Bethuna

BETHIA Hebrew: Daughter, follower of
Jehovah
(English) *Betia*; *Bitia*

BETJE Hebrew: Devoted to God

BETSY English: God is my oath; a nickname
of Elizabeth. Students of American history
remember Betsy Ross, a seamstress and flag
maker during the American Revolution who
is often, and with little evidence, credited
with sewing the first Stars and Stripes.

BETTE French: God is my oath; a familiar
form of Elizabeth
Famous Namesakes: *Actress and singer
Bette Midler, Actress Bette Davis*

BETTINA German: Nickname for Elizabeth

BETTY English: God is my oath; a variant
of Elizabeth
Famous Namesakes: *Actress Betty White,
Activist Betty Friedan, First Lady Betty Ford,
Cookbook author Betty Crocker*

BEULAH Hebrew: To marry, claimed as a
wife; in the Bible, Beulah is a name symbolic
of the heavenly Zion.
Beula

BEVERLY English: From the beaver stream
or meadow; a surname and place name of
Beverly Hills, California. Traditionally a boys'
name, Beverly is now more commonly used
for girls.
*Beverlee, Beverley, Beverle, Beverlie, Beverlye,
Bevlyn*; **Nicknames:** *Bev, Buffy, Verlee, Verlie,
Verly, Verlye*; **Famous Namesakes:** *Singer
Beverly Sills*; **Star Babies:** *Daughter of Sidney
Poitier*

BEVIN Irish: Fair lady, melodious one;
an Anglicized variant of Bebhinn
Bebhinn

BHADRA Hindi: Auspiciousness unto thee

BHAGIRATHA Hindi: Having a glorious
chariot

BHARATI Hindi: India, being maintained;
feminine form of Bharat

BHUDEVI Hindi: Lord of the earth

BHUMA Hindi: Earth

BIANCA Italian: White, shining; variant
of Blanche
Bianka; **Star Babies:** *Daughter of
Jean-Claude Van Damme*

BIBIANA Latin: Animated. Persian: Lady
Nicknames: *Bibi*

BIBSBEBE African: Lady of the house

BIENVENIDA Spanish: Welcome

BIJOU French: Jewelry
Star Babies: Daughter of John Phillips

BILGE Turkish: Wise, intelligent

BILLIE English: Nickname for Wilhelmina
Famous Namesakes: *Singer Billie Holiday,*
Tennis star Billie Jean King; **Star Babies:**
Daughter of Carrie Fisher

BINAH African: Dancer

BINTA African: With God

BIRDIE English: Bird, like a bird; contemporary name referring to our fine feathered
friends and their characteristics and talents
Birdena, Birdine, Birdy, Byrdene

BISA African: Greatly loved

BITA Persian: Unique

BITYA Hebrew: God's daughter; variant
of Batya

BLAKELEY Anglo-Saxon: From the dark or
pale meadow; surname traditionally used for
boys but, like many English names ending in
"ley," is increasingly popular for girls
Blakelee, Blakely, Blaknee, Blakeney, Blakeny;
Nicknames: *Blake*

BLANCHE French: White
(Czech) *Blanka*; *Blanch*; **Famous**
Namesakes: *Publisher Blanch Knopf*

BLANCHEFLEUR French: White flower

BLANDINA Latin: Mild, fair-haired, blond
(French) *Blondell, Blondelle, Blondene;*
Nicknames: *Blondie*

BLESSING English: Consecration
Bletsung

BLISS Anglo-Saxon, English: Intense joy;
a name used since medieval times
Blisse, Bliths, Blyss, Blysse

BLITHE English: Cheerful, lighthearted
Blythe; **Famous Namesakes:** *Actress Blythe*
Danner

BLODWEN Welsh: White flower
Blodwyn

BLOSSOM English: Blossom, flower

BO English: A name made popular by
actress Bo Derek. Scandinavian:
Commanding. Chinese: Precious

BOADICEA Anglo-Saxon: Victorious; a
queen of the Iceni when the Romans invaded
Britain, Boadicea was beaten in an attempt
to intimidate her people. She became a fierce
enemy of the Romans until their more
organized forces finally captured her.
Bodiccea, Bodicea, Bodicia, Boudicea

BOBBI English: Modern diminutive
of Roberta and Barbara
Famous Namesakes: *Family therapist,*
author, and personal historian Bobbi Fischer;
Star Babies: *Daughter of Whitney Houston*
and Bobby Brown

BODIL Norse, Danish: Commanding battle
Bodile, Bothild, Botilda

BOGDANA Polish: God's gift; feminine
form of Bogdan
Bohdana; **Nicknames:** *Bogna*

BOHUSLAVA Czech, Ukrainian: God's
glory; feminine form of Boguslaw

BOLANLE African: Finds wealth at home

BOLBE Latin: A mythical nymph

BOLIVIA American: Place name for a country in South America

BOLOUR Persian: Crystal

BONITA Spanish: Pretty little one

BONNIE Scottish, English: Pretty, charming, beautiful; this Scottish term is likely a derivation of the French word "bon," meaning good or nice.
Bonni, Bonny; **Famous Namesakes:** *Singer Bonnie Raitt, Speed skater Bonnie Blair*

BOUSSEH Persian: Kiss

BRADLEIGH English: From the broad meadow; this surname has been adapted to widespread first-name use.
Bradlea, Bradlie, Bradly, Bradney

BRANDY English: A type of alcoholic beverage used as a given name; possibly a variant of Brandeis or Brendan
Branda, Brande, Brandee, Brandi, Brandice, Brandie, Brandilyn, Brandyce, Brandyn, Brandais, Brandea, Brandess, Brandye, Branndais, Brannde, Branndea, Branndi; **Famous Namesakes:** *Actress Brandy Ledford*

BREANDAN Gaelic: Little raven

BREENA Gaelic: Fairy palace; also variant of Brianna and Sabrina
Nicknames: *Breen*

BRENDA Teutonic: Sword; a feminine form of Brendan. Gaelic: Little raven
Famous Namesakes: *Actress Brenda Vaccaro*

BRENNA Celtic, Irish: Raven, black-haired; also used as a variant of Brenda
(English) *Brynna*

BRETT English: A person from Britain or Brittany; Brett is derived from a French surname and was co-opted by the English as a first name for both girls and boys. Lady Brett Ashley is the heroine of Hemingway's *The Sun Also Rises.*
Bret

BRIALLEN Welsh: Primrose
Briallan

BRIANNA Celtic, English, Irish: Strong or ascends; feminine form of Brian
Breana, Breanna, Breanne, Briana, Briann, Briannah, Brianne, Briannon, Brielle, Brienna, Brienne, Brina, Bryana, Bryann, Bryanna, Bryanne, Bryna; **Diminutive Forms:** *Brea, Bree*;
Famous Namesakes: *Journalist Bree Walker*

BRICELYN English: Spelling variation of Bryce
Bricelynn, Brycelyn, Brycelynn, Bricelin, Bricelinn, Brycelin, Brycelinn

BRIDGET Irish: Strength, power; Brighid is an ancient name borne by the mythological Irish goddess of poetry, wisdom, and song, as well as Ireland's fifth-century patron Saint Brighid. See also *Zytka*
(German) *Brigitta*; (French) *Brigitte*; (Italian) *Brigida*; (Spanish) *Brigidita*; (Portuguese) *Brites*; (Celtic) *Brigid*; (Irish) *Brighid*; (Welsh) *Ffraid*; (Scandinavian) *Birgit, Britt, Britta*; (Swedish) *Birget, Birgitta*; (Polish) *Brygida*; (Finnish) *Pirjo*; *Brigetta, Bridgett, Bridgette, Brietta, Brigette*; **Nicknames:** *Biddy, Bidelia, Brid, Bride, Brit*; **Diminutive Forms:** *Gitta*; **Famous Namesakes:** *Actress Bridget Fonda, Model Bridget Hall, French actress Brigitte Bardot*

BRIELLA English: Exalted beauty

BRIGANTIA Celtic: Bright light; Celtic goddess representing healing, awakening, and rebirth

BRIGHTON English: From the bright town; Brighton is a seaside town in southern England. A surname traditionally used for boys, Brighton name may become more gender neutral in the future.
Bryton

BRINLEY American: Virtuous, princess
Brinleigh, Brinlee, Brinlea, Brinlie, Brynley, Brynleigh, Brynlee, Brynlea, Brynlie, Brynnley, Brynnleigh, Brynnlee, Brynnlea, Brynnlie

BRIONY English: Botanical name, a flowering perennial vine with heart-shaped leaves and a root used in some folk medicine; variant of Bryony

BRISEIS Greek: Captive maiden given to Achilles
(Spanish) *Brisa, Brisha, Brisia, Briza*

BRIT Celtic: A person from Britain or Brittany; Brit was derived from a French surname. In recent history, the name Brittany has become so popular that many do not realize that Brit was the original, not a nickname.

BRITANNIA Latin: A poetic name for Great Britain; also variant of names Brit/Brittany
Britania, Brittannia

BRITTANY English, Celtic: A native of Brittany (originally the ancient duchy of Bretagne in France) or Britain. The surname Brit became a given name, Brett, in the English language and in recent history has given rise to longer and more feminine-sounding variants.
(Norse) *Brit*; *Brettany, Britani, Britney, Brittaney, Brittani, Brittania, Brittanie, Brittanya, Brittnee, Brittney, Brittni*; **Nicknames:** *Bret, Brett, Bretta, Brette, Brite, Britta*; **Famous Namesakes:** *Singer Britney Spears*

BRONISLAVA Czech: Protecting glory; feminine form of Bronislaw
Branislava; **Nicknames:** *Bronya*

BRONTE English: Surname, probably derived from the Gaelic word meaning bestower
Famous Namesakes: *Authors Emily, Anne, and Charlotte Brontë*

BRONWYN Welsh: Fair raven or white-breasted; according to Welsh myth, Branwen is the sister of Bran and wife of Irish king Matholwych.
Brangwen, Branwen, Branwenn, Branwyn, Bronwen, Bronwin

BROOKE English: Near the small stream; a surname originally used for boys, Brooke is now used often for girls as well, especially when spelled with an "e" at the end.
Brook, Brooklyn, Brooklynn, Brooklynne

BROOKLYN English: Small stream, bringing forth, and a borough of New York City; variant of Brooke
Brookelyn, Brooklynn; **Star Babies:** *Daughter of Donna Summer*

BRUCIE French: Feminine form of Bruce, a surname since medieval times

BRUNA German: Brown, dark-haired; feminine form of Bruno
Brune, Brunetta

BRUNELLE French: Dark-haired
Brunella

BRUNHILDA German, Teutonic, Norse: Armor-wearing warrior maiden; the mythological Brunhilda is one of the Valkyries.
Brunhild, Brunhilde, Brunnehilde, Brynhild, Brynhilde; **Nicknames:** *Hilda, Hilde, Hildie, Hildy*

BRYCE Latin: Son of a nobleman, though child of nobleman makes more sense for girls with this given name, which was once reserved for boys but is now used for both genders
Bricelyn, Brice; **Star Babies:** *Daughter of Ron Howard*

BRYLEE American: Noble, strong, meadow
Bryley, Bryleigh, Brylea, Brylie

BRYNNA English: Variation of Brenna

BRYONY English: Botanical name for a flowering perennial vine with heart-shaped leaves and a root used in some folk medicine
Brione, Brioni, Brionna, Brionne, Briony, Bryani, Bryoney, Bryonie

BUENA Spanish: Good

BUFFY American: Nickname for Elizabeth

BUNME African: My gift
Bunmi

BURCU Turkish: Sweet scent

BURGUNDY American: A region in France famous for its wine; also a color name, referring to a deep red

BYHALIA Native American: White oak standing (Choctaw)

CACA Latin: In Roman mythology, Caca was the sister of the Giant Cacus. She was originally a goddess of the hearth, but was later demoted to a minor part in one tale of Hercules.
Star Babies: *Daughter of Vukan*

CACEY Irish: Vigilant; spelling variation of Casey

CADENCE Latin: Rhythmic flow of sounds (Italian) *Cadenza; Cadena, Cadencia, Cadyna;* **Nicknames:** *Cadee, Cadi, Cadie, Cady, Kady*

CADHA Scottish: From the steep place

CADHLA Irish: Beautiful

CADIE English: Nickname for Cadence
Cadee, Cady

CAELA Gaelic: Slender; feminine form of Keelan

CAIETA Latin: In Roman mythology, the wet nurse of Aeneas

CAILIN Irish: Girl; variant of Colleen
Caelan, Caileen, Cailyn, Caylin

CAIRO English: Cairo is a place name for the capital of Egypt.
Star Babies: *Daughter of Beverly Peele*

CAITLIN Irish: Pure, innocent; variant of Catherine
Caitilin, Caitlyn, Caitlan, Caitland, Caitlinn, Caitlyn, Caitlynn, Catelyn, Catlin, Catline, Catlyn, Kaitlan, Kaitleen, Kaitlin, Kaitlyn, Kaitlynn, Katelin, Kateline, Katelinn, Katelyn, Katelynn, Katlin, Katlyn, Katlynn, Katlynne; **Nicknames:** *Cait, Caitie;* **Famous Namesakes:** *Musician Caitlin Cary*

CALANDRA Greek: Beautiful one or name given to a lark
(French) *Calandre*; (Spanish) *Calandria*; *Calyndra*; **Nicknames:** *Calla, Calli*

CALANTHA Greek: Lovely blossom
(French) *Calanthe*

CALEDONIA Latin: From Scotland
Star Babies: Daughter of Shawn Colvin

CALIANA Arabic: A castle or tower; Caliana was a Moorish princess for whom a splendid palace was built in Spain.
Kaliana

CALIDA Latin: Ardent, warm, or loving. Greek: The most beautiful
Callida; **Nicknames:** *Calla, Calli*

CALINA Russian: Snowball tree

CALINDA Hindi: The sun; variant of Kalinda. English: Most likely a modern blend of names such as Carolyn, Calandra, and Cassandra with Linda

CALLAGHAN Irish: Strife
Callahan, Ceallach

CALLEN Gaelic: Powerful in battle
Calynn

CALLIA Greek: Beautiful voice

CALLIE Greek, Gaelic: Most beautiful; pet form of Callista and other names beginning with "Cal"
Kahli, Kalli, Kallie, Kallita, Kally, Cahli, Calli, Cally

CALLIGENIA Greek: Born of beauty

CALLIOPE Greek: Beautiful voice; describes a mythological muse for epic poetry and a musical instrument filled with steam whistles
Kalliope

CALLISTA Greek: Most beautiful; in mythology, Callista was tricked by Zeus and as a result gave birth to a son, Arcas. Hera transformed Callista into a bear, and when she was almost killed by her hunting son, both were transformed into constellations, creating Ursa Major and Ursa Minor. Callisto is also a moon of Jupiter.
Calissa, Calista, Calisto, Calliste, Callisto, Calysta, Kallista; **Nicknames:** *Cali, Calla, Calli, Kallie*; **Famous Namesakes:** Actress Calista Flockhart

CALLULA Latin: Beautiful

CALVINA Latin: Bald; feminine form of Calvin
Calvinna

CALYBE Latin: A mythical nymph, small hut

CALYCE Latin: In Greek mythology, Calyce was the mother of King Cycnus.

CALYPSO Greek: Hidden; the mythological sea nymph and daughter of Atlas who beguiled Odysseus for seven years. Calypso is also a West Indies style of singing.

CAMBRIA English: Place name originating from the Latin word for Wales
Kambria, Cambrya, Kambrya; **Nicknames:** *Cambrie*

CAMDEN Scottish: From the winding valley; a surname adapted to first-name use and a place name of a section of London.
Camdyn, Kamden, Kamdyn

CAMELIA Latin, English: Evergreen tree or bush with white or red roselike blossoms known for their beauty and fragrance
Camella, Camellia, Kamelia, Kamella

The Way of the Warrior

Want to arm your child with a name
he or she can take into life's daily battles?
Here are some names meaning "brave" or "strong."

Boys' Names

Aitan (Hebrew)

Albern (English)

André (French)

Andreas (Swedish)

Armstrong (English)

Arnold (Teutonic)

Arseni (Russian)

Artur (Celtic)

Baldwin (Teutonic)

Balen (Latin)

Beamard (Irish)

Bern (Scandinavian)

Bernhard (German)

Cathal (Irish)

Durango (Spanish)

Emory (English)

Ethan (Hebrew)

Everett (English)

Farrel (Celtic)

Garet (English)

Gifford (English)

Harding (English)

Hartman (German)

Helmut (German)

Honovi (Native American)

Jabari (African)

Karl (German)

Ken (Japanese)

Maynard (Anglo-Saxon)

Merrick (Teutonic)

Oz (Hebrew)

Prewitt (French)

Reginald (Teutonic)

Reinhard (German)

Riley (Gaelic)

Songaa (Native American)

Tracey (Anglo-Saxon)

Urho (Finnish)

Valiant (English)

Zytka (Polish)

Girls' Names

Adira (Hebrew)

Allona (Hebrew)

Arthurine (English)

Artura (Spanish)

Bernadette (French)

Briana (Celtic)

Bridget (Irish)

Caci (Gaelic)

Carla (German)

Caroline (Latin)

Fermina (Spanish)

Isa (German)

Karel (Czech)

Kemina (Spanish)

Magnilda (German)

Mathilda (French)

Maude (French)

Melicent (Teutonic)

Millicent (German)

Nadette (German)

Nadina (German)

Naja (African)

Nalda (Spanish)

Nina (Native American)

Orva (English)

Raina (Teutonic)

Ricarda (Spanish)

Tarsha (Native American)

Tyra (Scandinavian)

Valentina (Russian)

Valerie (Latin)

Yanaha (Native American)

CAMEO Latin, English: Portrait, usually of an elegant woman, carved on a shell or jewel
Cammeo, Kameo; **Nicknames:** *Cami*

CAMERON Gaelic: Crooked nose; the name of a great Highland clan
Kameron, Kamren, Kamron, Kamryn, Camryn; **Famous Namesakes:** *Actress Cameron Diaz, Actress Camryn Manheim*

CAMILLA Latin: Possibly indicates the beautiful ceremonial girl who assisted in ancient pagan rites. See also *Kamila, Milla* (French) *Camille*; (Polish) *Kamilka, Kamilla*; (Egyptian) *Kamilah*; *Camile, Cammi, Kamille, Kamlyn*; **Nicknames:** *Milja*; **Famous Namesakes:** *Prince Charles' companion Camilla Parker-Bowles*

CAMPBELL Scottish: Crooked mouth; name of a famous Highland clan

CANAN Turkish: Beloved

CANDACE Latin: Dazzling white; Candace was also an ancient hereditary title used by Ethiopian queens.
(Greek) *Candance*; (French) *Candide*; *Candice, Candida, Candiss, Candyce, Kandace, Kandice, Kandis, Kandiss, Kandyce*; **Nicknames:** *Candi, Candie, Candy, Kandee, Kandi, Kandy, Kandie*; **Famous Namesakes:** *Actress Candice Bergen*

CANEADEA Native American: Where the heavens lay upon the earth, the horizon (Iroquois). The country name, Canada, is derived from this name.
Canada

CANENS Latin: A mythological nymph, Canens was the wife of King Picus and the personification of song.

CANIAD Welsh: Song
(Latin) *Cantilena*

CANNIA Latin: Song

CANTARA Arabic: Bridge

CAOILFHIONN Gaelic: Slender and fair

CAOIMHE (KEE-va) Irish: Beautiful

CAPRICE Italian: Fanciful, whimsical; derived from the Italian word capriccio
Kaprice, Kapricia, Kaprisha; **Nicknames:** *Kapri*

CAPUCINE French: Cape, hood
Capucina

CARA Italian: Beloved, darling. Celtic: Friend
(Spanish) *Carisa*; *Carissima, Carita, Carrissa, Carah*; **Nicknames:** *Cari, Carina, Carinna*

CARALISA Latin: Beloved

CARDEA Latin: The mythological goddess of thresholds and protectress of hinges

CARELLA Latin: Beloved
Caralea, Caralee; **Nicknames:** *Cari*

CAREN English: Spelling variation of Karen

CARESSE French: Endearing, tender touch
Caress, Caressa, Carressa

CAREY Welsh: Near the castle
Cary, Karee, Kary

CARI Turkish: Flows like water; also familiar form of many names beginning with C

CARIDAD Spanish: Variation of Charity
Nicknames: *Cari*

CARILLIE Latin: Beloved

CARINA Latin: Keel; one of the five stars in the Orion constellation. Italian: Little darling
Carena, Cariana, Carine, Carinna, Carrina, Caryna, Karina

CARISSA Greek, Italian: Beloved; very dear person
Karessa, Karisa, Karissa

CARLA German: Strong; also a familiar form of Carolyn
(German) *Karla*; (Irish) *Carleen*; (Scandinavian) *Karlee, Karlin*; (Contemporary) *Karlesha*; *Karleen, Karleigh, Karlen, Karlene, Karlyn*; **Nicknames:** *Carlie, Carly, Karley, Karli, Karlie, Karly*; **Diminutive Forms:** *Carlita*; **Famous Namesakes:** *Actress Carla Gugino, Singer Carly Simon*

CARLEEN Irish: Variation of Carla
Carlene

CARLIN Irish: Little champion
Carlinn, Carlyn, Carlynn, Karlin, Karlinn, Karlyn, Karlynn

CARLOTTA Italian: Variation of Charlotte

CARMELA Hebrew: Garden, orchard, vineyard; Mount Carmel in Israel is considered a paradise.
(Italian) *Carmelina, Carmeline*; (Spanish) *Carmelita, Carmina*; *Carmella, Carmelle, Karmel, Karmelit, Karmelita, Karmelle, Karmit*; **Nicknames:** *Carmel, Carmencita, Melita*

CARMEN Latin: Song; Carmen is well known as the main character in Bizet's opera, *Carmen*, based on a short novel by the French author Prosper Merimee. A beautiful gypsy, Carmen becomes entangled in love affairs that lead her to a tragic ending.
(Spanish) *Carmita*; *Carmia, Carmin, Carmina, Carmine, Karmen, Karmia, Karmina*; **Famous Namesakes:** *Singer Carmen Miranda*; **Star Babies:** *Daughter of Robert Plant*

CARNA Latin: The name of at least two figures in Roman mythology: the goddess of bodily organs and a nymph with power over door handles

CARO English: Nickname for Caroline

CAROL Gaelic, English: Melody, song; feminine form of Carl
(English) *Carolan*; (German) *Carola, Karola*; (French) *Carole*; (Spanish) *Carrola*; *Carolanne, Carroll, Caryl, Karol, Karole*; **Famous Namesakes:** *Comedienne Carol Burnett, Singer Carole King, Actress Carole Lombard*

CAROLA German: Variation of Carol
Karola

CAROLANN English: A blend of Carol (song) and Ann (graceful)

CAROLINE Latin: Strong; Caroline is the feminine form of Carolus (manly), which is the Latin form of Charles. See related names Carla and Carol
(German) *Karolina*; (Italian) *Carolina*; (Scandinavian) *Karoline*; (Finnish) *Karoliina*; *Caraleen, Caraleena, Caraline, Caralyn, Carilyn, Carilynne, Caroliana, Carolyne, Carolynn, Karlin, Karlina, Karline*; **Nicknames:** *Caro*; **Famous Namesakes:** *First daughter Caroline Kennedy Schlossberg, Princess Caroline of Monaco*; **Star Babies:** *Daughter of Katie Couric*

CAROLYN English: Little woman; variant of Caroline
Karalyn, Karalynn

CARONA Spanish: Crowned

CARRIE English: Familar variant of Carol, Carla, and Caroline
Caree, Carree; **Star Babies:** *Daughter of Dick Van Dyke*

CARRINGTON English: Origin is not entirely clear, but it refers to a town; English surname
Carington

CARSON English: Child of Carr; a name originally for boys, now used for both genders
Carsyn, Carsynn, Carsen, Karson, Karsyn, Karsen, Karcyn, Karcen; **Famous Namesakes:** *Writer Carson McCullers*

CARYS Welsh: Love
Karis

CASEY Irish: Vigilant. Greek: Familiar form of Acacia
(English) *K.C.*; *Cacey, Caci, Cacia, Casee, Caycee, Kacee, Kacey, Kaci, Kacia, Kacie, Kacy, Kasey, Kasie, Kayce, Kaycee, Kayci, Kaycie*

CASPERIA Latin: Second wife of Rhoetus

CASSANDAN Persian: Meaning unknown; name of Kourosh the Great's wife

CASSANDRA Greek: Helper of men; in Homer's epic poem *The Iliad*, King Priam's daughter Cassandra foretold the ending of the Trojan war, but her warnings were tragically ignored.
(Spanish) *Casandra, Kasandra*; *Cassandrea, Cassaundra, Cassondra, Kasondra, Kassandra, Kassondra*; **Nicknames:** *Casey, Cassi, Cassie, Cassy, Kassi, Kassie*; **Star Babies:** *Daughter of Charlie Sheen*

CASSIA Greek: Cinnamon; Hebrew variant Keziah was one of Job's daughters in the Bible
(Hebrew) *Keziah*; *Kassia*

CASSIDY Irish, Gaelic: Clever or curly-headed
Caiside, Kassidy; **Star Babies:** *Daughter of Kathie Lee and Frank Gifford*

CASSIE English: Familiar form of Cassandra, Cassiopeia, Cassidy, and similar names
Cassi, Cassy, Kassi, Kassie, Kassy

CASSIOPEIA Greek: In Greek mythology, Cassiopeia was the mother of Andromeda. According to legend, both women are now constellations.

CASTA Latin, Spanish: Pure, modest one

CASTALIA Greek: According to Greek mythology, Castalia was a nymph loved by Apollo. A spring of water was named after her as the sacred fountain of the Muses.

CAT Irish: Nickname for Catherine

CATALINA Spanish: Variation of Catherine

CATARINA Italian: Variation of Catherine

CATH Welsh: Cat

CATHERINE Greek: Pure, innocent; a traditional female name having variations in many languages and used since the third century A.D. Early Latin Forms: Katerina and Caterina became Katharine and Catherine.
(German) *Katharina, Katrin*; (Italian) *Catarina*; (Spanish) *Catalina*; (Portuguese) *Catrina*; (Gaelic) *Caitrin, Catriona*; (Welsh) *Catrin*; (Norse) *Trine*; (Scandinavian) *Katrina*; (Swedish) *Katarina*; (Danish) *Katrine*; (Dutch) *Tryn*; (Basque) *Catalin*; (Russian) *Ekaterina*; (Czech) *Katerina*; (Polish) *Katanyna*; (Finnish) *Katariina, Katri, Katriina*; (Hungarian) *Katakin, Katalin*; *Caitriona, Catalyn, Catarine, Cateline, Catharina, Catharine, Catherin, Catheryn, Catheryna, Cathlyn, Cathrine,*

Cathryn, Katalina, Katalyn, Katarin, Katarzyna, Katerine, Kati, Katilyn, Katina, Katine, Katlyn, Katriana, Katriane; **Nicknames:** *Cat, Cate, Cathi, Cathia, Cathie, Cathy, Catia, Catlee, Cattee, Karen, Kat, Kate, Katica, Katie, Katiya, Katja, Katy, Katya, Kaysa, Kit, Kitty, Riina, Trina;* **Diminutive Forms:** *Catrinetta, Catrinette, Kätchen, Katyenka, Katyushka;* **Famous Namesakes:** *Russian Empress Catherine the Great, French actress Catherine Deneuve*

CATHLEEN Irish: Spelling variation of Kathleen

CATRICE English: Modern blend of Catrina and Patrice; derived from the Latin word catarata, meaning waterfall

CATRIONA Gaelic: Variation of Catherine

CAYENNE English: Biting; the name of a very hot pepper

CEARA Anglo-Saxon: Dark, sorrowful; likely a variant of Ciara

CECILIA Latin: Dim-sighted, blind; Saint Cecilia, the patron saint of music, was blind and a talented musician. See also *Sheila* (English) *Cecily, Cicely, Cicily;* (German) *Silke;* (French) *Cecile, Cecille;* (Gaelic) *Sighle;* (Scandinavian) *Silje;* (Czech) *Cilka;* (Finnish) *Silja;* (Hungarian) *Cili; Cecelia, Cecilee, Cecilie, Cicilia, Zezili, Zezilia;* **Nicknames:** *Cece, Ceil, Cele, Celia, Celie;* **Famous Namesakes:** *Model Cecilia Chancellor;* **Star Babies:** *Daughter of Vera Wang*

CEDRICA English: Chief, battle chieftain; feminine variant of Cedric, a name of Celtic origin
Cedrina; **Nicknames:** *Cedra*

CELANDINE Greek: A swallow
Celandina

CELESTE French: Heavenly; from the Latin name Celestia
(French) *Celesse, Celestiel, Celestine;* (Spanish) *Celesta, Celestina; Celestia; Celestyna*

CELIA Latin: Of the heavens; familiar form of Cecilia

CELINE French: A beautiful name of Greek origin, meaning Greek goddess of the moon; one of seven mythological daughters of Atlas transformed by Zeus into stars of the Pleiades constellation
(Greek) *Zelena;* (English) *Zelene;* (Spanish) *Selena; Celena, Celene, Celenne, Celicia, Celina, Celinda, Celinna, Salena, Salina, Selene, Selia, Selina, Xalina;* **Famous Namesakes:** *Singer Celine Dion*

CELLA Italian: Nickname for Marcella

CELOSIA Greek: Burning

CENDRILLON French: Of the ashes
Cinderella

CENOBIA Spanish: Variation of Zenobia

CERDWIN Celtic: The mother goddess

CERELIA Latin, English: Of the spring, fertile; possible variant of Cyril, which means lady
Cerella, Cirilla, Sarelia, Sarilia

CEREN Turkish: Young gazelle

CERES Latin: Goddess of the harvest and love for children in Roman mythology, equivalent to the Greek goddess Demeter

CERI Italian: Nickname for Cyrilla

CERIA Italian: Form of Cyrilla

CERIDWEN Welsh: Blessed poetry; the name of a Celtic mythological poetry goddess

CERISE French: Variation of Cherry

CESARINA Latin: Long-haired; feminine form of Caesar
Kesare

CHABA Hebrew: Life, a primitive root

CHALINA Spanish: Form of Rosa

CHALIPA Persian: Cross

CHANAH Hebrew: Spelling variation of Hannah

CHANDRA Sanskrit: Of the moon
Candra, Chanda, Chandaa, Chandara, Chandi, Chaundra

CHANEL French: Surname used as first name; popularized through the fame of French haute couture designer Gabrielle "Coco" Chanel
Chanell, Chanelle, Channelle, Chenelle, Shanel, Shanelle

CHANNA Hindi: Chickpea

CHANNING English, French: Of uncertain origin, possibly related to French meaning canal or indicating a church official; the spelling is suggestive of a paternal meaning such as Chan or Cana's child.

CHANTAL French: Song, singer
Chantae, Chantalle, Chantay, Chante, Chantel, Chantell, Chantelle, Chantrell, Chaunte, Chauntel

CHARDAE French: Nickname for Charlotte

CHARIS Greek: Grace and beauty
Carrissa, Charissa, Karis

CHARISH English: Held dearly, beloved

CHARITY Latin, English: Benevolent goodwill and love; a theological virtue
(Spanish) *Caridad; Chariety*

CHARLA English: Nickname for Charlotte

CHARLAINE French: Variation of Charlotte

CHARLENE English: Variation of Charlotte

CHARLISA French: Manly; feminine form of Charles

CHARLIZE French: Variation of Charlotte
Famous Namesakes: *Actress Charlize Theron*

CHARLOTTE French: Strong, a feminine form of Charles and the name of many queens throughout history, including the wife of King George III of England, after whom a major city in North Carolina is named. It is also the name of the clever and kind-hearted arachnid heroine of E.B. White's *Charlotte's Web*.
(English) *Charlene;* (German) *Karlotta;* (French) *Charlaine, Charlize;* (Italian) *Carlotta;* (Spanish) *Carlota;* (Irish) *Searlait;* (Russian) *Sharlotta; Charlayne, Charleen, Charleena, Charlena, Charlette, Charline, Charlyn, Charlynn;* **Nicknames:** *Chardae, Charla, Charlee, Charli, Charlisa, Charly, Lotta, Lotte, Lotye, Sharlene;* **Diminutive Forms:** *Charlita;* **Famous Namesakes:** *French actress Charlotte Gainsbourg, Welsh singer Charlotte Church, Author Charlotte Brontë;* **Star Babies:** *Daughter of Pierce Brosnan and Cassandra Harris, Sigourney Weaver, Amy Brenneman*

CHARMAINE French, English: Feminine form of Charles; Charmain was one of Cleopatra's attendants in Shakespeare's *Antony and Cleopatra.*
Charmae, Charmain, Charmayne, Charmine

CHARO Spanish: Nickname for Rosario

CHARUMATI Hindi: A beautiful mind, one who is wise

CHASTITY Latin: Purity; a virtue name *Chasity, Chastina, Chastine*; **Nicknames:** *Chasta*; **Star Babies:** *Daughter of Cher and Sonny Bono*

CHASYA Hebrew: Sheltered by God *Chasye*

CHAVA Hebrew: Life *Chabah, Chaka, Chaya, Chayka*; **Famous Namesakes:** *Singer Chaka Khan*

CHAVIVA Hebrew: Dearly loved *Chavive*

CHELINDA Arthurian Legend: Tristan's grandmother *Chelinde*

CHELSEA English: Seaport; the word itself is derived from an Old English expression meaning landing place for limestone, which likely refers to the docks in the Chelsea district of London. *Chelsa, Chelsee, Chelsey, Chelsi, Chelsie, Chelsy, Kelsey*; **Famous Namesakes:** First daughter Chelsea Clinton; **Star Babies:** *Daughter of Tom Berenger, Steven Tyler, Rosie O'Donnell*

CHENOA Native American: Variation of Columba

CHER French: Spelling variation of Cherie **Famous Namesakes:** *Singer and actress Cher*

CHERELL French: Spelling variation of Cherie

CHERICE French, English: Dear one, beloved; variant of Charish, Cher, and Cherie *Cherese, Cheresse, Cherisa, Cherise, Cherisse*

CHERIE French: Dear one; darling (French) *Cherise, Cherrelle*; *Charee, Cher, Chere, Cheree, Chereen, Cherell, Cherelle, Cheri, Cherina, Cherine, Cherree*; **Nicknames:** *Cherita*

CHERILYN English: Modern blend of Cheryl and Lynn *Cherilynn*

CHERINE French: Spelling variation of Cherie

CHERRY Latin, French: Variant of Charity. English: Cherry fruit, bright red (French) *Cerise*; *Cherri, Cherrie*

CHERYL English: Modern English variant of the French name Cherie (dear one); possibly a blend of Cherie with Beryl or Meryl *Cherrell, Cherrill, Cheryll, Sheryl, Sherill*; **Nicknames:** *Sherri, Sherry*; **Famous Namesakes:** *Actress Cheryl Ladd*

CHEYENNE Native American: A name given to a tribe of the Algonquians by the Sioux, Cheyenne is derived from a word meaning unintelligible speakers, but a truer meaning might be strangers or foreigners. *Cheyanna, Cheyanne, Chiana, Chianna*

CHICA Spanish: Pet name meaning little girl

CHIKA African: God is supreme (Nigerian)

CHIKAGE Japanese: Thousands of views or vistas **Famous Namesakes:** *Japanese actress Awashima Chikage*

CHIKO Japanese: Close child

CHINA English: Asian country; fine, delicate porcelain *Chyna, Chynna*; **Famous Namesakes:** *Singer Chynna Phillips*

CHIQUITA Spanish: Pet name meaning little girl

CHIYO Japanese: Thousand or intellect, generation, or lifetime

CHLOE Greek: A young green shoot *Cloe, Khloe, Kloe*; **Star Babies:** *Daughter of Candice Bergen and Louis Malle, Tom Berenger, Olivia Newton-John*

CHLORIS Greek: Blooming, greenish; a mythological goddess of flowers or spring *Cloris*; **Famous Namesakes:** *Actress Cloris Leachman*

CHRISTABEL Latin: Beautiful Christian; see Christina *Christabella, Cristabel, Cristabell*

CHRISTAL Scottish: Variation of Crystal

CHRISTINA Greek: Christian, follower of Christ; feminine form of Christian (German) *Kristin*; (French) *Christine*; (Spanish) *Crista, Cristina, Cristine*; (Gaelic) *Cairistiona*; (Irish) *Cristin, Cristiona*; (Scandinavian) *Stina*; (Swedish) *Kerstin, Kristina*; (Polish) *Krysia, Krysta, Krystka, Krystyna, Krystynka*; (Finnish) *Kirsi, Kirsikka, Kristiina*; (Hungarian) *Kriska, Kriszta, Krisztina*; *Christan, Christana, Christanne, Christeen, Christeena, Christen, Christena, Christene, Christiana, Christiane, Christianna, Christyn, Chrystina, Cristen, Cristyn, Kristen*; **Nicknames:** *Chrissa, Chrissie, Chrissy, Christa, Christi, Christie, Christy, Chryssa, Chrysta, Chrystie, Crissa, Crissie, Crissy, Cristie, Cristy, Crysta, Krista, Tiina, Tina*; **Famous Namesakes:** *Poet Christina Rossetti, Actress Christina Ricci, Tennis star Chris Evert*; **Star Babies:** *Daughter of Maria Shriver and Arnold Schwarzenegger*

CHRYSANTHE Greek: Golden flower; feminine form of Chrysanthos (Spanish) *Chrysann, Crisann*

CHYNA English: Spelling variation of China

CIANA Italian: Variation of Jane

CIARA Irish: Dark-haired one; feminine form of Ciaran *Ceara, Chiara, Kiara, Kiera, Cierra, Sierra*

CIBIL Greek: Seer; variant of Sibyl

CICELY English: Variation of Cecilia **Famous Namesakes:** *Actress Cicily Tyson*; **Star Babies:** *Daughter of Sandra Bernhard*

CILLA Latin: Daughter of Laomedon

CIMBERLEIGH English: Spelling variation of Kimberly

CINDERELLA English: Of the ashes; Cinderella is a beloved fairy tale told in more than 3,000 versions around the world.

CINDY English: Familiar form of Cynthia and Lucinda *Cinda, Cindel, Cindi, Cindia, Cindee*

CINNAMON Greek: Sweet reddish-brown, aromatic spice *Cinamon, Sinamon*

CIRCE Greek, Latin: The mythological sorceress who tempted Perseus and changed Odysseus' men to swine; derived from the Greek word kirke, meaning bird

CIVIA Hebrew: Spelling variation of Tzviya

CIYMENE Greek: Famous one; the name of several women in Greek mythology, including the mother of Atalanta and the daughter of Oceanus and mother of Atlas *Ciymena*

CLADY Danish: Variation of Claudia

CLAIRE French: Clear, bright; variant of Clara
Famous Namesakes: *Actress Claire Danes;*
Star Babies: *Daughter of Oliver Platt*

CLARA Latin, English, German: Clear, bright, from the Latin word "clarus." See also *Claire*
(Latin) *Clarine*; (Greek) *Clarrisa*; (English) *Claressa*; (German) *Clarinde*; (French) *Clarinda, Clarisse*; (Italian) *Chiara, Clariee*; (Spanish) *Clarisa, Clarita*; (Swedish) *Klara*; *Clair, Clare, Clarice, Clariss, Clarissa, Clarissant, Klarissa*; **Nicknames:** *Clarette*;
Famous Namesakes: *Actress Clara Bow, Red Cross founder Clara Barton, Politician Clare Booth Luce*; **Star Babies:** *Daughter of Ewan McGregor*

CLARABELLE English: Bright and beautiful; a blend of Clara (bright) and Belle (beautiful)
(French) *Claribel, Claribelle*

CLARETA Latin: Clarity, distinguished

CLARICE English: Spelling variation of Clara
Claris, Clarise, Clarisse, Claryce, Klarice, Klaryce

CLARIMOND German: Brilliant protectress
Clarimonda, Clarimonde

CLARISSA English: Spelling variation of Clara

CLAUDIA Latin: Lame; feminine form of Claudius. In the Bible, the name is mentioned in one of Paul's letters to Timothy.
(English) *Claudelle, Claudine*; (French) *Claude, Claudette*; (Italian) *Claudina*; (Danish) *Clady*; *Klaudia*; **Famous Namesakes:** *German model Claudia Schiffer, Actress Claudette Colbert*

CLEANTHA English: Glorious woman; derived from the Greek "kleo," meaning fame or glory

CLEMATIS Greek: A climby floral vine

CLEMENCE Latin, French: Clemency, mercy; Clemence was the mythological Roman goddess of pity.
(French) *Clementine*; (Spanish) *Clementina*

CLEMENTINE French: Variation of Clemence
Star Babies: *Daughter of Cybill Shepherd*

CLEONE Greek: The mythological daughter of a river god
(Irish) *Gliona*

CLEOPATRA Greek, Egyptian: Of a famous father or glory of the father; Cleopatra was a queen of ancient Egypt and mistress to Julius Caesar and Mark Antony, two great Roman leaders. Her story has been immortalized in several works, including *Antony and Cleopatra* by William Shakespeare.
Nicknames: *Cleo*

CLEVA English: Lives near the hills, cliffs; feminine form of Cliff, Clive, and Clifford

CLIANTHA Greek: Glory
Clianthe, Clyantha, Cleanthea

CLODAGH Irish: Name of a river in Tipperary, Ireland

CLODOVEA Spanish: Famous warrior; feminine form of Clodoveo

CLORINDA Latin: Renowned
Clorynda, Klorinda, Klorynda; **Nicknames:** *Clory*

CLOTAIRE French: Glory, power

CLOTHO Greek: A goddess of Greek mythology and the youngest of the three fates

CLOTILDA German: Renowned battle
Clotilde

CLOVER English: Clover, a wild flower
Old Forms: *Claefer*

CLYTIA Greek: Lovely; in Greek mythology, Clytia was a sea nymph who was in love with the sun god. Upon her death, she became a sunflower and now always turns her face toward the sun.
Clytie

COAHOMA Native American: Panther, cat (Choctaw)

COCHETA Native American: Stranger

COCO French: Made popular by French haute couture designer Gabrielle "Coco" Chanel
Star Babies: *Daughter of Sting, daughter of Kim Gordon and Thurston Moore*

CODY English: Pillow
Codea, Codee, Codey, Codi, Kodee, Kodie, Kodey, Kody

COLBY English: Dark-skinned or from a coal town
Kolby

COLETTE French: Dark; a diminutive form of the masculine name Cole
Collette, Kolette; **Famous Namesakes:** *French actress Colette;* **Star Babies:** *Daughter of Dylan McDermott*

COLLEEN Irish: Girl, derived from the Gaelic name Cailin; curiously, Colleen has been commonly used for many years in the United States and England, but is not at all common in Ireland.

Coleen, Colene, Collena, Collene; **Famous Namesakes:** *Actress Colleen Dewhurst, Australian author Colleen McCullough*

COLUMBA Latin: Dove; Saint Columba was an Irish missionary who reintroduced Christianity to Scotland. Two female saints also had this name. See also *Columbine* (Native American) *Chenoa;* **Famous Namesakes:** *Third-century martyr Saint Columba of Sens*

COLUMBINE Italian: Dove; also a beautiful plant known for its unusually shaped flower and its medicinal properties

CONCEPCION Spanish: Common reference in Latin American countries to the Virgin Mary and the Immaculate Conception (Italian) *Concetta, Conchetta*

CONNELLY Irish: Love, friendship; a popular surname

CONNEMARA Irish: Place name of a scenic region in Ireland

CONNIE English: Nickname for Constance
Famous Namesakes: Journalist Connie Chung, Entertainer Connie Francis

CONSOLACION Spanish: Consolation

CONSTANCE Latin: Constancy, steadfastness (Italian) *Constantia, Constantina, Constanza; Constanze, Konstanza, Konstanze;* **Old Forms:** *Constancia;* **Nicknames:** *Con, Connie;* **Famous Namesakes:** *Actress Constance Zimmer*

CONSTANCIA Latin: Original form of Constance

CONSUELO Spanish: Consolation
Consuela; **Nicknames:** *Chela, Consolata*

CORA Greek: Maiden, from the coral of the sea. See also *Corinne* (Latin) *Coraline*; (Greek) *Coralin, Coralina*; (French) *Coralie, Corette*; *Coralia, Coralyn, Coreen, Coreene, Coretta, Corisa, Corissa, Correen, Correena, Corrissa*; **Nicknames:** *Corri*; **Famous Namesakes:** *Activist Coretta Scott King*

CORAL Greek, English: Sea coral

CORALIN Greek: Variation of Cora

CORAZON Spanish: Heart
Famous Namesakes: Philippines President Corazon Aquino

CORDELIA Latin: Warm-hearted, loving; in Shakespeare's *King Lear*, Cordelia is a princess noted for her unwavering honesty and her undying devotion to her father. Welsh: Jewel of the sea
Nicknames: *Delia*

CORELLA Greek: Maiden

COREY Irish: From the hollow
Cori, Corie, Corrie, Corry, Cory

CORIANDER English: Spice

CORIANNE English: Modern blend of Cori (Cory) and Ann
Coriann, Corianna, Corrianna, Corrianne

CORINNE French: Maiden
Corine, Korine, Korinne

CORINTHIA Greek: Woman of Corinth

CORISSA English: Spelling variation of Cora

CORNELIA Latin: Horn; feminine form of Cornelius
Cornella, Kornelia, Kornelie; **Nicknames:** *Nelia, Nella, Nellie, Nelida, Nelly*

CORONIS Greek: Crow; the mythological mother of Asclepius

CORRINA Latin, Greek: Maiden; variant of Corinne
Corina, Kor; **Star Babies:** *Daughter of Amy Grant and Vince Gill*

COSETTE French: Victorious; the name of one of the main characters in Victor Hugo's *Les Misérables*. The beleaguered ï and romantic Cosette is the daughter of infamous refugee, Jean Valjean.

COSMA Greek: Universe, order; feminine form of Cosmo
Kosma, Kosmo

COUNTESS English: Title name; the feminine equivalent of Count

COURTNEY French, English: Courteous or from the court
Cortney, Courtlyn, Courtlynn; **Famous Namesakes:** *Actress Courteney Cox Arquette*

CRESCENT French: Increasing, growing
Creissant

CRIMSON English: A shade of red

CRISANNA Spanish: Variant of Chrysantus

CRYSTAL Greek: Ice; a brilliant clear glass of high quality
(Greek) *Kristel, Kristell*; (Scottish) *Christal, Christel*; *Khrystalline, Kristabelle, Kristalena, Kristalyn, Krystabelle, Krystal, Krystalyn, Krystalynn*; **Famous Namesakes:** *Singer Crystal Gayle*

CYAN English: Greenish-blue color

CYBELE Greek: An Asian mythological nature goddess worshipped as the Great Mother of the Gods, Cybele was later identified with Rhea by the Greeks, and with Maia and Ceres by the Romans.

CYDNEY English: Spelling variation of Sydney
Star Babies: *Daughter of Chevy Chase*

CYMA Greek: Flourish

CYNTHIA Greek: Woman from Cynthos; Cynthia was a name of the mythological moon goddess Artemis, referring to her birth on Mount Cynthos.
(Italian) *Cinzia*; *Cinthia, Kynthia*;
Nicknames: *Cyndee, Cyndi, Cyndy*

CYPRESS Latin: A coniferous tree, usually evergreen and known for durability

CYPRIS Greek: From Cyprus; feminine form of Cyprian
(Italian) *Cipriana*; *Cyprien, Cyprienne*

CYRA Persian: Sun or enthroned, feminine variant of Cyrus

CYRENE Greek: In Greek myth, Cyrene wrestled with a lion, which endeared her to Apollo. He took her away to Africa and built a city for her that now bears her name.
Cyrena, Kyrene

CYRILLA Greek, Latin: Lordly; feminine form of Cyril
(Italian) *Ciri*; (Spanish) *Ceri, Ceria*; *Cyrillia*

CYTHEREA Greek: From the island of Cythera; another name for Aphrodite, who rose from the sea near Cythera and was worshipped there
Cytheria

DACIA Latin: From Dacia (near Rome)

DAERE Welsh: Friend
Dera

DAFFODIL Greek: Springtime yellow flower with a trumpet-shaped central crown

DAGANYA Hebrew: Ceremonial grain
Old Forms: *Daganyah*

DAGMAR German: Glorious day
Dagna; **Old Forms:** *Dagomar*

DAHLIA Norse: From the valley; the flower Dahlia was named in honor of Swedish botanist Anders Dahl.
Daliah, Dalyah, Dallia

DAHNA Italian: Variation of Dana

DAINA Lithuanian: Song

A Matter of Fact

British television chef Jamie Oliver chose two delectable names for his daughters: Poppy and Daisy.

DAISY English: Day's eye; a flower name; a slang term for someone who is deemed excellent or notable; in F. Scott Fitzgerald's *The Great Gatsby*, the title character is hopelessly in love with Daisy Buchanan.
Daisey, Daisi, Daisie, Daizy, Daysi, Deysi;
Star Babies: Daughter of Markie Post, daughter of Lucy Lawless

DAKOTA Native American: To be considered a friend, ally; name of a group of tribes more familiarly known as the Sioux
Dakoda, Dakotah; **Famous Namesakes:** *Actress Dakota Fanning*; **Star Babies:** *Daughter of Melanie Griffith and Don Johnson*

DAKSHINA Hindi: Competent

DALE English: Lives in the dell or valley; originally a surname
(Norse) *Dalr*; (Dutch) *Dael; Daelyn, Dalena, Dalene, Dalenna, Dayle*; **Nicknames:** *Daly*; **Famous Namesakes:** *Actress Dale Evans*

DALIAH Hebrew: Tree branch, gentle
(Arabic) *Dalia; Daliyah*

DALILA Hebrew: Desired or languishing. Spanish: Delicate. African: Gentle (Tanzanian and Swahili)

DALIS Hebrew: Drawing water
Dalit

DALLAS Scottish: From the field with the waterfall; a village in Scotland and a major city in Texas
Dallis, Dalles

DAMARA Greek: Gentle; in Biblical reference, Damaris was the educated woman who heard Paul speak at the open-air supreme court of Athens.
(Latin) *Damaress; Damaris, Damariss*

DAMAYANTI Hindi: Subduing; in Hindu legend, the name of a beautiful princess

DAMIANA Greek: One who tames or subdues; feminine form of Damian
(French) *Damia, Damiane, Damien*

DAMITA Spanish: Little noblewoman

DANA English: From Denmark; variant of Daniel or Donna. Persian: Wise
(Italian) *Dahna, Dahnya; Daena, Daina, Danah, Danna, Dannah, Dayna*; **Nicknames:** *Daney, Dania, Dannalee, Dannia, Danya*; **Famous Namesakes:** *Actress Dana Delany*

DANAE Greek: Mythological daughter of Acrisius who became the mother of Perseus when Zeus appeared to her as a shower of gold; also a variant of Danielle
Danay, Danaye, Danea, Danee, Denae, Denay

DANICE English: Spelling variation of Danielle

DANIELLE Hebrew: God is my judge; feminine form of Daniel
(Italian) *Daniella*; (Basque) *Danele; Danelle, Danetta, Danice, Daniela, Danila, Danita, Dany*; **Nicknames:** *Dani, Danise, Danit, Danitza, Dannee, Dannell, Dannelle, Danni, Dannon, Danya, Danylynn*; **Diminutive Forms:** *Danette*; **Famous Namesakes:** *Author Danielle Steele*; **Star Babies:** *Daughter of Jerry Lewis, daughter of Donna Dixon and Dan Aykroyd*

DANIKA Slavic: Morning star
Danica, Dannica, Dannika; **Famous Namesakes:** *Actress Danica McKellar*

DANNON English: God is my judge; variant of Daniel and Danielle

DANTINA English: God is my judge; a blend of Danielle and Tina

DAPHNE Greek: Bay tree or laurel tree; the mythological and virtuous Daphne was transformed into a laurel tree to protect her from Apollo.
Dafne, Daphney

DARA Hebrew: Wisdom; the biblical Dara was a male descendant of Judah and was known for his wisdom. Gaelic: Oak tree
Darah, Dareen, Darissa, Darra, Darrah

DARACHA Scottish: From the oak

DARBY Norse: From the deer estate. Irish: Free man

DARCY Irish: Dark. French: From the Arcy (Oise River) which flows into the Seine (French) *D'arcy*; *Darcel, Darcell, Darcelle, Darcey, Darchelle, Darci, Darcia, Darcie*; **Famous Namesakes:** *Ballerina Darci Kistler*

DARDA Hungarian: Dart

DAREEN Hebrew: Spelling variation of Dara

DARERCA Irish: Name of a saint

DARIA Persian: Rich; feminine form of Darius. Saint Daria was martyred with her husband Chrysanthus under the Roman emperor Numerian.
(Russian) *Darya, Dasha*; *Darian, Darianna, Dariele, Darielle, Darienne, Darrelle*; **Star Babies:** *Daughter of Gregory Hines, daughter of Brian Wilson*

DARISSA Hebrew: Spelling variation of Dara

DARLA English: Nickname for Darlene

DARLENE English, Anglo-Saxon: Darling; from the Old English dearling, possibly used on occasion as a variant of the male name Darryl
Darel, Darelene, Darelle, Darleane, Darleen, Darleena, Darlena, Darlina, Darline, Darolyn, Darrellyn, Darylene, Daryll, Darylyn; **Nicknames:** *Darla*

DARNELL English: From the hidden place **Nicknames:** *Darnetta, Darnisha*

DARU Hindi: Pine

DARYL English: From a French surname and place name, D'Arel (from Arielle in Calvados) *Darrill, Darryll, Daryll*; **Famous Namesakes:** *Actress Daryl Hannah*

DARYN Greek: Spelling variation of Dora

DASHA Russian: Variation of Daria

DAVENEY French: Name of a town and castle in Flanders; also a rhyming variant of Daphne

DAVINA Hebrew: Cherished, beloved; feminine form of David
Daveen, Davia, Davianna, Davida, Davinah, Davine, Davinia, Davita, Davitah, Davite, Davonna, Davynn; **Nicknames:** *Davi, Davy, Vida*

DAWN English: The first appearance of daylight; daybreak
Dawne, Dawnika; **Nicknames:** *Dawna*; **Diminutive Forms:** *Dawnelle, Dawnetta, Dawnette, Dawnielle*

DAYO African: Joy arrives

DEARBHAIL Irish: True desire
Derval, Dervilia, Dervla; **Famous Namesakes:** *Irish harpist Dearbhail Finnegan*

DEBORAH Hebrew: Bee; Deborah was a biblical prophetess and heroine of Israel. Her victory song is in the Book of Judges.
Debora, Debra, Debrah, Debralee, Devery, Devora, Devorah, Devoria, Devra, Devri; **Nicknames:** *Deb, Debbie, Debby, Debi, Devi*; **Famous Namesakes:** *Actresses Debbie Reynolds and Debra Winger, Journalist Deborah Norville, Musician Deborah Gibson*

DECIMA Latin: Born tenth
Famous Namesakes: *British opera singer Decima Moore*

DECLA Irish: Full of goodness; feminine form of Declan

DEE English: Abbreviation of names beginning with the letter "D"

DEEANNA English: Valley; feminine form of Dean or possible variant for Diana
Deana, Deane, Deann, Deanna, Deanne, Deeana, Deeann, Dene, Deneen, Denia, Denni

DEFENA English: From Devonshire

DEHEUNE Celtic: Divine one

DEINA Spanish: Religious holiday
Deiene

DEIRDRE Celtic: Melancholy; in Celtic legend, Deirdre died of a broken heart.
Dedre, Deedra, Deidra, Deidre, Deirdra;
Nicknames: *Dee*; **Famous Namesakes:**
Actress Deidre Hall

DEKA African: Pleasing (Somali)
Dekah

DELANEY Irish: Descendant of the challenger; Delaney could also be derived from the Norman surname De l'aunaie meaning from the alder grove in French.
Famous Namesakes: *Actress Kim Delaney;*
Star Babies: *Daughter of John and Martina McBride*

DELARAM Persian: Quiet-hearted

DELBINA Greek: Flower
Delbin, Delbine

DELICIA Latin: Delightful, gives pleasure
(English) *Delight*; (French) *Delice; Delicea, Deliciae, Delisa, Delisha, Delissa, Delit, Deliza, Delyssa*

DELILAH Hebrew: Desired, seductive; the biblical Delilah tempted Samson into revealing the secret of his strength.
Delila; **Star Babies:** *Daughter of Lisa Rinna and Harry Hamlin*

DELLA German, English: Bright, noble; Della is a short form of Adelle, Adeline, and Adelaide, and is today seen as a name in its own right.
Dell, Delle; **Famous Namesakes:** *Singer Della Reese*

DELMA German, Spanish: Noble protector
Delmi, Delmira, Delmy

DELMARA Spanish: Of the sea
Delmar, Delmare

DELPHINA Greek: From Delphi, dolphin; thirteenth-century French Saint Delphine is the patron saint of brides.
(French) *Delphine; Delfina, Delfine, Delphia*;
Famous Namesakes: *French actress Delphine Delage*

DELTA Greek: Born fourth, fourth letter of the Greek alphabet

DELU African: The only girl

DEMAS Greek: Popular
Demos

DEMETRIA Greek: Of Demeter; the Greek goddess of the harvest and fertility, and mother of Persephone
Demeter, Demetra, Demitra, Demitras, Dimetria, Dimitra; **Nicknames:** *Deetra, Deitra, Demi, Detria*; **Famous Namesakes:**
Actress Demi Moore

DENA Native American: Valley

DENDERA Egyptian: From Dendera

DENICA English: Avenged; a blend of Deana (divine) and Dina (from the valley)

DENISE French: Derivative of the Greek name Dionysus (the god of wine and revelry); also feminine form of Denis (Spanish) *Denisa*; *Denice, Deniece, Denissa, Denisse, Dennise, Denyse*

DENISHA African: Wild

DENIZ Turkish: Sea

DEOCH Celtic: Mythical princess of Munster

DERBY English: Deer town

DEREKA English: Gifted ruler; modern feminine variant of Derek, derived from Theodoric
Derica, Dericka, Derrica

DERORICE Hebrew: Free
Derora, Derorit

DERRICA English: Spelling variation of Dereka

DERYA Turkish: Ocean

Those that do teach young babes

Do it with gentle means and easy tasks.

—Desdemona,
in Shakespeare's *Othello*

DESDEMONA Greek: Unlucky; Shakespeare's leading lady in *Othello*, Desdemona is a faithful, loving wife who dies for her love. A satellite of Uranus is named for her.

DESIREE French: The one desired (English) *Desire*; (Spanish) *Desideria*; *Desarae, Desaree, Desirae, Desirat, Dezirae*; **Old Forms:** *Desirata*

DESMA Greek: Oath

DESTINY English, French: Fate, fortune *Destanee, Destine, Destinee, Destini, Destinie, Destiney*; **Star Babies:** *Daughter of Billy Ray Cyrus*

DESTRY American: Feminine variant of a French surname usually used for boys **Star Babies:** *Daughter of Kate Capshaw and Steven Spielberg*

DEVA Hindi: Superior

DEVAKI Hindi: Black

DEVAMATAR Hindi: Mother of the gods

DEVAN English: Spelling variation of Devin

DEVERA Spanish: Task

DEVERRA Latin: Goddess of birthing

DEVI Sanskrit: Divine; Devi is a mythological Hindu title relating to Shiva's wife who is known by different names according to her exercise of power for good or ill.

DEVIKA Sanskrit: Little goddess; from the mythological Hindu Devi

DEVIN English: Poet, poetic; possibly related to the Latin word for divine. The variant Devon is a county in England noted for beautiful farmland.
Devan, Devana, Devanna, Devon, Devona, Devondra, Devonna, Devonne, Devyn, Devyna, Devynn

DEVONY Irish: Dark-haired
Devinee

DEVORIA Hebrew: Spelling variation
of Deborah

DEVOTA Latin: Devoted

DEXTRA Latin: Adroit, skillful

DHANA Sanskrit: Wealthy
Dhanna

DHARANI Hindi: Earth

DHARMA Hindi: Ultimate law of all things;
in certain religions, such as Buddhism and
Hinduism, dharma is the essential nature
of all that is, of the cosmos, and of each of
us. Dharma is closely linked to the concept
of karma.

DIAMOND English: Of high value, brilliant;
can refer to the precious stone
(French) *Diamante*; *Diamanda, Diamonique,
Diamontina*

DIANA Latin: Divine; ancient Roman
goddess of the moon, Diana was noted
for her beauty and swiftness.
(French) *Diane*; (Hawaiian) *Kiana*; *Deona,
Deonna, Deonne, Di, Diahann, Diahna, Dian,
Dianna, Diannah, Dianne, Dyana, Dyann,
Dyanna*; **Famous Namesakes:** *Princess of
Wales Diana Windsor, Actress Diane Keaton,
Journalist Diane Sawyer*; **Star Babies:**
Daughter of Veronica Lake and Andre De Toth

DIANDRA Greek: Flower of God; also a
botanical term for flower with two stamens
Deandra, Deondra

DIANTHA Greek: Heavenly flower
Dianthe

DICE Greek: Justice, to slice; numbered
cubes used in board games

DIDO Greek: The legendary founder and
queen of Carthage; Dido was the subject
of Henry Purcell's opera *Dido and Aeneas*.
Famous Namesakes: *British musician Dido*

DIEGA Spanish: Supplanter; feminine form
of Diego

DIGNA Latin: Worthy
Digne

DILYS Welsh: Perfect, true

DINAH Hebrew: Judged; the biblical Dinah
was Jacob and Leah's only daughter.
(Spanish) *Dinora*; *Deena, Dena, Dina,
Dinorah, Dynah*; **Famous Namesakes:**
Entertainer Dinah Shore

DINARA Russian: Breath
Famous Namesakes: Russian tennis player
Dinara Safina

DIONE Greek, English: Divine queen; in
Greek mythology, Dione was Zeus's mate
and the mother of Aphrodite.
Diona, Diondra, Dionna, Dionne; **Famous
Namesakes:** *Singer Dionne Warwick*

DIONYSIA Latin, Greek: Named for
Dionysus, God of wine
(Spanish) *Dionisa*; *Dionysie*

DIORBHALL Gaelic: Variation of Dorothy

DIRCE Greek, Latin: Mythical mother
of Lycus

DISA Greek: Twice or double. Norse:
Spirited

DITA Spanish: Variation of Edith

DITI Hindi: Daughter of Daksha

DIVINA Latin: Divine one
(Celtic) *Divone*; *Devina, Devona*;
Nicknames: *Deva, Diva*

DIVSHA Hebrew: Honey
Divshah

DIVYA Hindi: Divine

DIXIE English: Refers to the French word
for ten; Dixie is also a term for the southern
states below the Mason-Dixon Line.
Famous Namesakes: *Actress Dixie Carter*

DOANNA English: American compound
of Dorothy and Anna

DOCILLA Latin: Calm

DOLI Native American: Bluebird (Navajo)

DOLLY English: A vision, gift of God; pet
form of Dorothy
Famous Namesakes: *Singer Dolly Parton,
First Lady Dolly Madison*

DOLORES Spanish: Sorrows
Delora, Deloras, Delores, Deloris, Deloros;
Nicknames: *Dee, Dee Dee, Lola, Loleta,
Lolita, Lolitta;* **Diminutive Forms:** *Dolorita*;
Famous Namesakes: *Actress Dolores Fuller,
Actress Delores Del Rio*

DOMELA Latin: Mistress of the home
(Gaelic) *Domhnulla; Domele*

DOMIDUCA Latin: Mythical surname
of Juno, a goddess in astrology

DOMINA Latin: Spelling variation of Donna

DOMINIQUE Latin, French: Of the Lord,
belongs to God; a feminine variant of
Dominic, this French spelling is used
primarily for girls.

(Spanish) *Domenica, Dominga; Domenique,
Dominica, Domitiana, Domitiane;* **Famous
Namesakes:** *Gymnast Dominique Dawes,
Jazz Singer Dominique Eade;* **Star Babies:**
Daughter of Michael Caine

DONALDA Gaelic: Ruler of all; feminine
form of Donald

DONATA Italian, Latin: To give

DONELLA Italian: Variation of Donna

DONNA Italian, Latin: Lady, a respectful title
and female equivalent of Don
(Italian) *Donella*; (Spanish) *Dona*; (Gaelic)
*Donia; Damina, Domina, Donetta, Donica,
Donielle, Donisha, Donnalee, Donnalyn,
Donya*; **Nicknames:** *Don, Donni, Donnie*;
Famous Namesakes: *Singer Donna
Summer, Actresses Donna Mills and Donna
Reed*

DONOMA Native American: The sun is
there (Omaha)

DONYA Persian: World
Dunya

DORA Greek: Gift; familiar form of
Dorothy, Doris, and Theodora
(French) *Dorine; Daryn, Darynn, Darynne,
Doralia, Doralice, Doralie, Doralis, Dordei,
Dorelia, Doretta, Dorinda, Doryne*;
Nicknames: *Dorie*

DORALICE Greek: Heroine of a Russian
fairy tale by Straparola

DORBETA Spanish: Reference to the Virgin
Mary

DORCAS Greek: Gazelle; the biblical woman who abounded in good deeds and gifts of mercy
Dorkas

DORE African: Gift

DORÉE French: Golden
D'or, Dior

DOREEN Irish: Moody, sullen; variant of Dora
(Greek) *Dorienne; Dorene;* **Old Forms:** *Doireann;* **Nicknames:** *Doire, Dory;* **Famous Namesakes:** *German actress Doreen Jacobi*

DORIAN Greek: Of the sea, descendant of Dorus of Greek myth and a variant of Doris
Dorea, Doria, Doriana, Dorianna, Dorianne, Dorien, Dorrian

DORICE Greek: Spelling variation of Doris

DORIS Greek: Gift; Doris was the mythological daughter of the sea god Oceanus and mother of fifty sea nymphs.
Doree, Dorice, Dorisa, Dorris; **Nicknames:** *Dori, Dorri, Dorrie, Dorry, Dory;* **Famous Namesakes:** *Actress Doris Day, Author Doris Lessing, Actress Doris Roberts*

DOROTHY Greek: A vision, gift of God; the character of Dorothy in Frank Baum's *The Wonderful Wizard of Oz* learned that there was no place like home.
(English) *Dorit, Dortha;* (German) *Dorothea;* (Spanish) *Dorotea;* (Gaelic) *Diorbhall;* (Russian) *Doroteya;* (Polish) *Doroata;* (Hungarian) *Dorika, Dorottya, Duci; Dorita, Dorlisa, Dorote, Dorothee;* **Nicknames:** *Doll, Dollie, Dolly, Doro, Dorte, Dottie, Dot, Thea, Tea;* **Famous Namesakes:** Figure skater Dorothy Hamill, Author Dorothy Parker, Activist Dorothea Dix

DORY English: Nickname for Doris
Dori, Dorri, Dorrie, Dorry; **Famous Namesakes:** *Singer Dory Previn*

DOTTIE English: Gift of God; pet form of Dorothy

DRAGOMIRA Slavic: Precious, peaceful

DREW Scottish: Brave; the feminine of the familiar form of Andrew
Famous Namesakes: *Actress Drew Barrymore*

DRISANA Hindi: Daughter of the sun

DRUCILLA Latin: Strong; feminine form of the Roman family name Drusus
Drusilla; **Nicknames:** *Dru*

DUANA Irish: Dark; feminine form of Duane
Duayna, Dubhain, Duvessa; **Old Forms:** *Dubheasa;* **Nicknames:** *Du*

DUENA Spanish: Chaperone

DULCIE Latin: Sweet, sweetness; Dulcinea was the name created by Cervantes' literary character Don Quixote for his idealized lady.
(Spanish) *Delcine, Dukine, Dulce, Dulcina, Dulcinea; Dulcea, Dulcine, Dulcy;* **Old Forms:** *Dulcia*

DURGA Hindi: Unattainable; in Hindu mythology, this is the name of a fierce goddess.

DUSANA Czech: A spirit or soul; feminine form of Dusan
Dusan

DUSTY English: Fighter; a pet form of the male name Dustin
Dustee, Dusti

DYANI Native American: Deer

DYLLIS Welsh: Sincere, genuine
Dylis

DYMPHNA Irish, Gaelic: Bard, poet
Old Forms: *Damhnait*

EABHA Irish: Breath of life

EADA English: Wealthy
Eadda, Ead

EADAN Irish: Jealous

EADIGNES Anglo-Saxon: Bliss

EADLIN Anglo-Saxon: Princess

EADWINE English: Wealthy friend; an Old English name compounded from "ead," meaning rich or happy, and "wine," meaning friend

EALASAID Gaelic: Devoted to God; Gaelic variant of Elizabeth
Elasayd

EALGA Irish: Noble; Ireland is sometimes referred to as Inis Ealga, "the Noble Isle," which is the source of this unusual name.

EARIE Scottish: From the east
Eara

EARLENE English: Noble woman, shield; feminine form of Earl
(Spanish) *Erlene; Earla, Earlena, Earline, Earleen*

EARNA English: Eagle

EARTHA English, German: Earth, the planet, soil in which to grow
Ertha; **Famous Namesakes:** *Singer Eartha Kitt*

EASTER Anglo-Saxon: Goddess of the dawn; a fitting name for a little girl born on Easter
Eastre

EAVAN Irish: Fair, beautiful; an Anglicized variant of Aoibheann, the name of Saint Enda's mother
Aoibheann, Aoibhin

EBBE Swedish: Strong, flowing tide; variant of Esbjorn
Ebba

EBERTA Teutonic: Intelligent
Ebertta; **Nicknames:** *Ebe*

EBONY Greek, English: Black or a dark hardwood
Ebonee, Eboni, Ebonique

EBRILL Welsh: Born in April
Ebril

ECE Turkish: Queen

ECHO Greek: Sound; Echo was a mythological nymph who faded away until only her voice was left.
Ekko

EDANA Irish: Fire; feminine form of Aidan
Edelina, Ediline; **Nicknames:** *Edee*

EDDA German: Pleasant; refuge from battle
Eda; **Old Forms:** *Hedda*

EDEE English: Nickname for Edana

EDEEN Scottish: From Edinburgh

EDEN Hebrew: Pleasure, delight; the biblical paradise home of Adam and Eve
Eaden, Eadin, Edin

EDINA English: Wealthy; possibly a variant of Edwina. Scottish: From Edinburgh
Edine

EDITH English: Prosperity, goodness and wealth; Edith was a fashionable name in the nineteenth century.

(Anglo-Saxon) *Edit*; (Italian) *Edita, Editta*;
(Spanish) *Dita*; (Teutonic) *Edyte*; *Edyt,
Edyta, Edyth, Edythe*; **Famous Namesakes:**
*British writer Edith Sitwell, Author Edith
Wharton, French singer Edith Piaf*

EDLYN English: Noble or princess
Edlen, Edlin, Edlynn, Edlynne; **Nicknames:**
Edla

EDMUNDA German: Wealthy defender
(English) *Edmanda*; (Anglo-Saxon)
Edmonda; *Edmee*

EDNA Hebrew, Celtic: Pleasure, delight;
derived from the same word as the biblical
Garden of Eden
Edra, Edrea

EDOLIE Teutonic: Good humor
Edolia

EDUARDA English: Rich benefactress

EDULICA Latin: Mythical protectress
of children

EDURNE Basque: Snows

EDWINA English: Rich in friendship;
feminine form of Edwin
Edwinna; **Nicknames:** *Winnie*

EFFIE Greek: Fair flame; abbreviation
of Greek name Euphemia

EGBERTA English: Shining sword
Egbertina, Egbertine, Egbertyne

EGERIA Latin: A water nymph

EGUSKINA Basque: Sunshine
Eguskine

EIDEANN Gaelic: Spelling variation
of Aidan

EILA Irish: Nickname for Evelyn

EILEEN Irish: Shining light; variant
of Aileen
Eileene, Eilena, Eilene; **Old Forms:** *Eibhlhin,
Eibhlin*

EILWEN Welsh: White, fair

EILY Irish: Light
Old Forms: *Eilidh*

EIRA Welsh: Snow

EIRICA Scottish: Ruler

EIRLYS Welsh: Snowdrop

EITHNA Irish: Fire; form of Aidan

EKATERINA Russian: Variation of
Catherine
Katerina; **Nicknames:** *Katia, Katusha, Katya*;
Famous Namesakes: *Rumanian gymnast
Ecaterina Szabo, Russian skater Ekaterina
Gordeeva*

ELAHEH Persian: Goddess

ELAINE French: Shining light; Old French
variant of Helen. In Arthurian Legend,
Elaine was a young maiden who was in
love with Lancelot. She was also the sister
of Sir Percival and mother of Sir Galahad.
(Irish) *Elan*; *Elaina, Elayne, Ellaine, Ellayne*;
Star Babies: *Daughter of Veronica Lake and
John Detlie*

ELAN Irish: Variation of Elaine

ELANA Hebrew: Oak tree
Elanah, Elanie, Elanna

ELATA Latin: Glorified

ELBERTE English: Noble or glorious; variant of Alberta
Elberta, Elbertyna

ELDORA Spanish: Gilded, golden
Eldoris, Eldreda, Eldrida, Eldride;
Nicknames: *Elda, Elde*

ELDRID Norse: Fiery spirit; also a variant of Aldred

ELEADORA Greek: Gift of the sun

ELEANA Latin, Greek: Daughter of the sun. See also *Elena*
(Spanish) *Iliana; Elayna*

> "Women are like tea bags; put them in hot water and they get stronger."
> —Eleanor Roosevelt

ELEANOR Greek: Shining light; variant of Helen
(French) *Eleonore*; (Italian) *Eleanora, Elenora, Elenore*; (Gaelic) *Eilionoir*; (Irish) *Eilinora*; (Swedish) *Ellinor*; (Finnish) *Eleonoora; Eleanore, Eleonora, Elienor, Elinor, Elinore, Elnora*; **Nicknames:** *Ella, Ellie, Leora, Nora*; **Famous Namesakes:** *First Lady Eleanor Roosevelt*; **Star Babies:** *Daughter of Diane Lane and Christopher Lambert*

ELECTRA Greek: The fiery sun; Electra was the mythological daughter of Agamemnon and a central character in three Greek tragedies.
Elektra

ELENA Greek: Light; variant of Helen
Star Babies: *Daughter of Sam Neill*

ELETA Latin: Chosen
Electa, Elekta

ELETHEA English: Healer
Elethia, Elthia

ELFREDA English: Of or related to elves (English) *Elfrieda*; (Teutonic) *Elfrida*;
Nicknames: *Elfie*

ELGA Teutonic: Spelling variation of Helga

ELHAM Persian: Inspiration

ELIANA Hebrew: My God has answered. Latin, Greek: Daughter of the sun
(Greek) *Elianne*; (German) *Eliane; Elianna, Lianna*

ELICA German: Noble; a variant of the old German name Alice

ELIDA English: Variation of Alida

ELIKAPEKA Hawaiian: Variation of Elizabeth

ELINA Spanish, Finnish: Shining light; variant of Helen

ELIORA Hebrew: God is light; feminine form of Elior

ELISAMARIE French: Blend of Elise and Marie

ELISE French: Consecrated to God; abbreviation of Elisabeth
(English) *Ilyssa*; (German) *Ilyse*; (Spanish) *Elisa; Elicia, Elisha, Elishia, Ellesse, Ellyce, Elyce*

ELISKA Czech: Truthful

ELISSA Greek: Devoted to God, from the blessed isles; Elissa is another name for the mythological Dido who was Queen of Carthage. English: Variation of Elizabeth
(German) *Elyse; Elysa, Elysha, Elysia, Elyssa, Elysse*

ELITA Latin: Chosen one; familiar form of Carmelita

ELIVINA English: Good elf

ELIZA English: Nickname for Elizabeth *Elyza*

ELIZABETH Hebrew, English: God is my oath; Elizabeth was the mother of John the Baptist in the Bible. Today, Elizabeth is one of the most frequently used names in England. Royal namesakes include Queen Elizabeth I and Queen Elizabeth II. (French) *Elisabeth*; (Italian) *Elisabetta, Elizabetta*; (Scottish) *Elsbeth*; (Scandinavian) *Elisabet, Elizabet*; (Danish) *Ailsa, Lisbet*; (Dutch) *Liesbeth*; (Russian) *Elisaveta, Lizaveta*; (Czech) *Alzbeta*; (Polish) *Elzbieta*; (Ukrainian) *Yelysaveta*; (Hungarian) *Erzsebet, Orzsebet*; (Hawaiian) *Elikapeka*; *Elizaveta, Elsa, Lisabet, Lisabeth, Lizabeth, Lyzbeth*; **Old Forms:** *Elisheva, Elspeth*; **Nicknames:** *Bess, Bessie, Bessy, Beta, Beth, Betsey, Bette, Betti, Bettina, Bettine, Betty, Buffy, Eliza, Elli, Els, Elyza, Elzira, Ilsa, Ilse, Libby, Lilibet, Lilibeth, Lise, Liz, Liza, Lizbet, Lizbeth, Lizzie, Lyza, Sissy, Telsa*; **Diminutive Forms:** *Liesl, Liezel, Lizette*; **Famous Namesakes:** *Queen Elizabeth of England, Actress Elizabeth Taylor, Cosmetics executive Elizabeth Arden, Entertainer Liza Minnelli*

ELKA Hebrew: God has created; feminine form of Elkanah

ELKE German: Noble; variant of Alice **Famous Namesakes:** *German actress Elke Sommer*

ELLA German: All, complete; also familiar form of Eleanor and Ellen. English: A beautiful fairy woman *Elle*; **Famous Namesakes:** *Singer Ella Fitzgerald*; **Star Babies:** *Daughter of Kelly Preston and John Travolta, Annette Bening and Warren Beatty, Gary Sinise*

ELLAMAE English: Blend of Ella and Mae

ELLECIA English: Variant of Elias

ELLEN English: Light; a variant of Helen (Greek) *Eleni*; (Italian) *Elene*; (Irish) *Elleen*; (Welsh) *Elen*; (Norse) *Elin*; *Ellena, Ellene, Ellyn*; **Nicknames:** *Ellee, Ellia*; **Diminutive Forms:** *Ellette*; **Famous Namesakes:** *Actresses Ellen Burstyn and Ellen Barkin, Actress and comedienne Ellen DeGeneres*

ELLERY English: Joyful, happy; surname *Ellary, Ellerie, Ellarie*

ELLICE Hebrew: The Lord is my God; the Tuvalu Islands were formerly known as Ellice Islands. *Ellis, Ellisha*; **Famous Namesakes:** *Painter and sculptor Ellice Endicott*

ELLISON English: Variant of Elias, the Greek form of Elijah *Ellisyn*

ELLORA Hindi: The name given to the cave temples of India

ELLY English: An abbreviated form of Eleanor and Ellen *Elli, Ellie*

ELMA German: God's protection. Greek: Friendly

ELMAS Turkish: Diamond

ELMINA Teutonic: Intimidating fame *Elmine*

ELMIRA English: Noble

ELOINA Latin: Worthy

ELOISE French: Renowned in battle; French variant of Louise (see also *Heloise*) (Italian) *Eloisa*; *Eloisee, Heloise*; **Famous Namesakes:** *Actress Eloise Howe*

ELSE German, Scandinavian: Noble maid; also a familiar form of Elizabeth (Spanish) *Elsa*; *Ilse*; **Old Forms:** *Elsje*; **Nicknames:** *Elsie*

ELSHA German: Noble

ELVA English: Nickname for Elvira

ELVIRA Spanish: Truth, white, or beautiful. See also *Wira* (English) *Elvyne*; (Anglo-Saxon) *Elwine*; (Irish) *Elvinia*; (Polish) *Elwira*; *Elvena, Elvera, Elvia, Elvine, Elwyna*; **Nicknames:** *Elva, Elvie, Elvin*

ELVITA Spanish: Truth

ELZIRA Hebrew: Nickname for Elizabeth

EMBER English: Anniversary; Ember day is a day in Lent devoted to fasting and prayer. Ember can also be used as a rhyming variant of Amber. *Emberly, Emberlyn, Emberlee, Emberley, Emberleigh, Emberlie, Emberlea, Emberlynn, Emberlin, Emberlinn*

EMBLA Norse: From an elm

EMELIA Latin: Industrious, striving; variant of Amelia (Teutonic) *Emiline*; *Emelin, Emelina, Emilia*

EMELINE French: Variation of Emily

EMERALD English: Green gemstone; the birthstone for May (French) *Emeraude*; (Spanish) *Esmeralda, Esmerelda, Ezmeralda*; *Esma*; *Esmeraude*; **Nicknames:** *Esme, Meralda*

EMERSON German: Surname; son of Emery *Emersyn, Emercyn*; **Star Babies:** *Daughter of Teri Hatcher*

EMESTA Spanish: Serious (English) *Earnestyna*; (German) *Emestine*; *Enerstina, Enerstyne*

EMILIA Latin: Spelling variation of Emelia

EMILY Latin: Industrious, striving; Emily is one of the most popular names in America and England. (German) *Amalasand, Amalasanda, Emilie, Emmeline*; (French) *Amalie, Amelie, Emeline, Emmaline*; (Italian) *Amalia, Emilia*; (Teutonic) *Aimiliana, Aimilionia, Amialiona*; (Gaelic) *Aimil*; (Finnish) *Emmi*; *Amalija, Amelinda, Amelita, Amilia, Emalee, Emely, Emilee, Emmalee, Emmalei, Emmalyn, Emiley, Emmaleigh*; **Old Forms:** *Amalea*; **Nicknames:** *Emmy, Em*; **Famous Namesakes:** *Poet Emily Dickinson, Etiquette expert Emily Post, Author Emily Brontë*; **Star Babies:** *Daughter of Tatum O'Neal and John McEnroe, Chevy Chase, Beau Bridges, Alex Trebek*

"Emma Woodhouse, handsome, clever, and rich, with a comfortable home and happy disposition seemed to unite some of the best blessings of existence..."
—Jane Austen

EMMA German: Complete, whole, universal; can also mean nanny (Spanish) *Ema*; **Famous Namesakes:** *British actress Emma Thompson, Poet Emma Lazarus*; **Star Babies:** *Daughter of Julie Andrews and Tony Walton, Wayne Gretzky and Janet Jones, Christine Lahti*

EMMALINE French: Variation of Emily

EMMANUELLA Hebrew: God is with us; feminine form of Emmanuel, a name used throughout the Bible for Jesus
(Spanish) *Manuela*; *Emmanuelle*

EMOGENE Latin: Spelling variation of Imogene

EMUNAH Hebrew: Faith

ENCARNACION Spanish: Reference to the Incarnation of Christ

ENDORA Greek: Fountain

ENFYS Welsh: Rainbow

ENGEL Anglo-Saxon: Variation of Angela

ENGELBERTHA German: Bright angel
(German) *Engelbertine*; *Engelbertina*, *Engleberta*; **Nicknames:** *Engl*

ENID Welsh, Celtic: Soul; Enid is a heroine in Arthurian Legend as the immaculate wife of Geriant, a knight of the Round Table.
Enit, Enite, Enyd

ENNEA Greek: Born ninth

ENNIS Irish: From Ennis

ENOLA Native American: Solitary

ENRIQUA Spanish: Keeper of the hearth, rules her household; feminine form of Enrique, popular Spanish form of Henry
Henriqua

ENYA Irish: Spelling variation of Ethna
Famous Namesakes: *Irish musician and composer Enya*

ENYO Greek: A mythological goddess of war
Nicknames: *Eny*

EOSTRE Anglo-Saxon: Goddess of the dawn

EPHYRA Latin: Daughter of Oceanus

ERELA Hebrew: Variation of Angela

ERENDIRA Spanish: She who smiles; an Aztec name

ERIANTHA Greek: Sweet
Erianthe, Erianthia

ERICA Norse, Scandinavian: Eternal ruler, forever strong; feminine form of Eric. The spelling variation Erika is popular in numerous European countries.
(Finnish) *Eerika*; *Ericka, Erika, Erikka*

ERIENNE Gaelic: Spelling variation of Erin

ERIKO Japanese: Inlet, cove, child

ERIN Gaelic, Irish: Peace; a poetic name for Ireland
Erienne, Erina, Erinn, Erinna, Erinne, Eryn, Erynn

ERIPHYLE Greek: Wife of Amphiaraus

ERIS Greek: Goddess of discord

ERITH Hebrew: Flower
Eritha

ERLINA Gaelic: Girl from Ireland
Erleen, Erlene, Erline

ERNESTINE English: Serious, determined; feminine form of Ernest
(Latin) *Ernestina*; (Spanish) *Ernesta*; (Hungarian) *Ernesztina*; *Ernesha*; **Nicknames:** *Erna*

ERRITA Greek: Pearl

ERWINA English: Friend of the sea
Earwyn, Earwyna, Erwyna; **Old Forms:**
Earwine

ESHE African: Life, energy (Swahili)

ESIN Turkish: Inspiration

ESMA Anglo-Saxon: Kind defender

ESMÉE French: Esteemed
Esma; **Famous Namesakes:** *Dutch actress
Esmée de la Bretonière*

ESMERALDA Spanish: Variation
of Emerald
Esmerelda; **Nicknames:** *Esme, Meralda*

ESPERANZA Spanish: Hope
(French) *Esperance*; **Nicknames:** *Espe,
Speranza*; **Star Babies:** Daughter of Bob
and Anna Sellers

ESTA Italian: From the east

ESTEBANA Spanish: Crowned with laurels;
feminine form of Esteban, a popular Spanish
form of Stephen
Estefana, Estefania, Esteva; **Nicknames:**
Estefani, Estefany, Estefanita

ESTÉE French: Star; variant of Estelle
Famous Namesakes: *Cosmetics executive
Estée Lauder*

ESTELLE French: Variation of Stella

ESTHER Hebrew, Persian: Of debated origin
and meaning, possibly star or myrtle leaf; in
the Old Testament Book of Esther, a beautiful
young Hebrew woman named Esther marries
the Persian King Xerxes. As queen, she then
risks her life to save the Jews from persecution.
(Hebrew) *Estrela*; (Spanish) *Ester, Izar,
Izarra, Izarre*; (Irish) *Eistir*; (Finnish) *Esteri*;
(Hungarian) *Eszter, Eszti*; **Nicknames:** *Essie,
Hester*

ETAIN Irish, Celtic: Little fire; in Irish
mythology, Etain was a sungoddess and
the lover of Midhir.
Aideen

ETHEL Anglo-Saxon, Hebrew, English:
Noble
(English) *Ethelreda*; (German) *Ethelinda*;
(Hungarian) *Etel*; *Eathelin, Eathelyn, Ethelda*;
Famous Namesakes: *Actress Ethel
Barrymore, Entertainer Ethel Merman*

ETHETE Native American: Good quality
(Arapaho)

ETHNA Irish: Kernel; Saint Eithne was the
daughter of a king and one of Saint Patrick's
followers. The name variant Enya is likely
best known in America for the modern Irish
musician and composer.
Ena, Enya, Ethne; **Old Forms:** *Eithne*

ÉTIENNETTE French: Variation of
Stephanie

ETNEY Irish: Spelling variation of Aidan

ETTIE English: Pet form of Etta, which is
an abbreviation of Henrietta

EUDOKIA Greek: To seem well
(Latin) *Eudocia*; *Eudosia, Eudosis, Eudoxia*;
Nicknames: *Dunya, Dusya*

EUGENIA Greek: Well-born, noble;
feminine form of Eugene
(French) *Eugenie*; (Czech) *Evzenie*; *Eugena,
Eugina*; **Nicknames:** *Zhenya*; **Famous
Namesakes:** *Actress Eugenia Silva, Artist
Mary Eugenia Surratt*; **Star Babies:** *Daughter
of Prince Andrew and Sarah Ferguson*

EULA Greek: Nickname for Eulalie

EULALIE Greek: Sweet-spoken
(French) *Aulaire*; (Spanish) *Lala, Lali, Lalla*;
(Hawaiian) *Iulalia, Ulalia*; **Nicknames:** *Eula,
Eulah, Eulia, Lelia, Ula*

EUNICE Greek: Joyous victory, she con-
quers; in the Bible, Eunice was the daughter
of Lois and the mother of Timothy, to whom
Paul addressed two of his Epistles: Timothy I
and Timothy II. She was a woman noted for
being without hypocrisy.

EUPHEMIA Greek: Well-spoken; Saint
Euphemia was a virgin martyr
(Spanish) *Eufemia*; *Euphemie*; **Nicknames:**
Effie, Phemie

EURYDICE Greek, Latin: Wife of Orpheus
in Greek mythology; this name is derived
from the blend of two root words: "eury"
(broad or wide) and "dice" (woodworm).

EUSTACIA Greek: Fruitful, productive;
feminine form of Eustace

EUSTELLA Greek: Fair star

EVA Latin: Form of Evelyn
Star Babies: *Daughter of Susan Sarandon*

EVANGELINA Greek: Bearer of good news
Evangela, Evangelia, Evangeline, Evangelyn

EVANIA Greek: God has been gracious;
feminine form of Evan
Evanee, Evanna, Evin

EVANNA English: Spelling variation
of Evania

EVANTHE Greek: Flower

EVE Hebrew: Life; in the Bible, Eve was
Adam's wife and the first woman. Eva is a
name used in many countries throughout
the world.
(Hebrew) *Evika, Evike, Ewa*; (Spanish) *Evita*;
(Irish) *Aoife*; (Welsh) *Efa*; (Russian) *Yeva*;
(Ukrainian) *Yevtsye*; (Persian) *Havva*; *Evia,
Eviana*; **Nicknames:** *Evie*; **Famous
Namesakes:** *Argentine First Lady Eva (Evita)
Peron, Performance artist Eve Ensler, Actresses
Eve Arden and Eva Marie Saint*

EVELYN English: Life; originally a surname
and masculine name, but became popular as a
feminine name in the late nineteenth century
(French) *Evelyne*; (Italian) *Evelina*; (Finnish)
Eeva, Eevi, Eveliina; *Eva*; *Evaleen, Evalina,
Evaline, Evalyn, Eveleen, Evelin, Eveline,
Evelynn, Evelynne*; **Nicknames:** *Eila*

EVERAINE English: Modern blend of a
word name with a nature name

EVERLYN English: Modern blend of a word
name with the feminine suffix "-lyn"
Everlynn

EVETTE Latin, Hebrew: Living one; variant
of Eve or Ivette
Evetta

EVIANA Hebrew: Spelling variation of Eve

EVIN English: Spelling variation of Evania

EVINA Scottish: Right-handed

EVONNA German: Variation of Yvonne
Evon, Evony

EYOTA Native American: The greatest
(Sioux)

FABIA Latin: Bean farmer; feminine variant of Fabian, from the Roman family name Fabius
(French) *Fabienne*; (Italian) *Fabiana*; *Fabianna, Fabianne, Fabiola, Fabra, Favianna, Faviola*

FADILAH Arabic: Virtuous, distinguished, superior; feminine form of Fadil
(African) *Fadhila*; *Fadila, Fadileh*

FAE English: Form of Faith

FAELYN English: Beautiful fairy
Faelynn, Failyn, Failynn

FAINA Russian: Bright

FAIREN American: Beautiful
Fairyn, Fayre, Fairynn, Fayryn, Fayrynn, Faeryn, Faerynn

FAIRLY English: From the bull's or sheep's meadow; a surname and variant of Farley, with a more feminine spelling for girls
Fairlee, Fairleigh, Fairlea, Fairlie

FAIRUZA Turkish: Turquoise

FAITH English: Enduring belief that does not require proof; Faith is a virtue name that was commonly used by the Puritans.
(Spanish) *Fe*; *Faithe, Fayanna, Fayth, Faythe*; **Nicknames:** *Fae, Fay, Faye*; **Diminutive Forms:** *Fayette*; **Famous Namesakes:** *Singer Faith Hill*

FAKHRI Persian: Glory

FALA Native American: Crow (Choctaw)

FALALA African: Born in abundance

FALLON Irish: In charge; surname used as a first name
Faline, Fallyn, Falon

FANCHON French: Free; a common name in Brittany
Fanchone; **Nicknames:** *Fanny*

FANNY English: Nickname for Frances

FANTINE Latin: Childlike
Fantina; **Nicknames:** *Fanny*

FAQUEZA Spanish: Weakness

FARAH English: Traveler, fair-haired. Persian: Happy
Famous Namesakes: *Actress Farrah Fawcett*

FARICA Teutonic: Spelling variation of Frederica

FARIDA Arabic, Egyptian: Unique, peerless; feminine form of Farid
(Persian) *Farideh*; *Fareeda, Fareedah, Faridah*

FARKHONDEH Persian: Happy

FARREN Irish: Adventurous; some spelling variants are also surnames
Farin, Farrin, Farron, Farryn, Faryn, Ferran, Ferryn

FARVA Persian: Precious

FARZANEH Persian: Wise; feminine form of Farzan

FATIMA Arabic: Captivating, sea fowl; Fatima was the daughter of the Prophet Mohammed and one of four perfect women mentioned in the Koran.
(Persian) *Fatemeh*; *Fatimah*

FAUNE French: Young deer; Fauna was the mythological Roman goddess of fertility and nature.
(English) *Fawn*; *Fauna, Faunia, Fawna, Fawne, Fawnia*

FAUSTINE Latin: Fortunate one; feminine form of Faust
(Italian) *Fausta*; (Spanish) *Faustina*; *Faust*

FAVOR English: Approval

FAWN English: Variation of Faune

FAYDELL English: Valley fairy
Faydelle, Faedelle

FAYE English: Nickname for Faith
Famous Namesakes: *Actress Faye Dunaway*

FAYLINN English: Fairy kingdom
Faylyn, Faylynn, Faylin, Faelinn, Faelin, Faelyn, Faelynn

FAYME French: Held in high esteem, famous

FAYOLA African: Walks with honor

FEALTY French: Fidelity

FEDELMA Irish: Great beauty

FEE German: Fairy

FEECHI African: Worship God

FELDA German: From the field

FELICIA Latin: Spelling variation of Felicity
Felisha, Phylicia; **Famous Namesakes:**
Actress Phylicia Rashad

FELICITY Latin: Happy; feminine form of Felix
(French) *Felicia, Felicienne*; (Spanish)
Felicita, Felicitas, Felisa; (Polish) *Fela, Felka*;
Falisha, Felecia, Feleta, Felice, Feliciona, Felise, Felisha, Felita, Filicia; **Famous Namesakes:**
Actress Felicity Huffman

FEMI African: Adore me (Nigeria)

FENNELLA Celtic: White shoulder

FERESHTEH Persian: Variation of Angela

FERMINA Spanish: Strong

FERN English: Botanical name for a green plant that loves shade; also a short form of Fernanda
Ferne

FERNANDA Spanish: Adventurer, traveler; feminine form of Fernando
Nicknames: *Anda, Nan, Nanda*

FERNLEY English: Fern meadow
Fernlea, Fernleigh, Fernlee, Fernlie

FIA Scottish: Dark of peace

FIACHINA Irish: Raven
Fiachra

FIAMMETTA Italian: Little fiery one
Nicknames: *Fia*

FIANAIT Irish: Deer

FIANNA Celtic: Comes from a legendary tale about Irish hero Fionn Mac Cool; Fianna was the name of his Celtic army of warriors.

FIDELITY Latin: Faithful
Fidela, Fidelia, Fidelina, Fidelita

FIDELMA Irish: Anglicized spelling of Feidhelm, an old name of uncertain origin; Fidelma and her sister Eithne were early converts of Saint Patrick.
Feidhelm

FIFI French: Diminutive form of Josephine
Star Babies: *Daughter of Paula Yates and Bob Geldof*

FILA Persian: Lover

FILBERTA English: Extraordinarily brilliant; feminine form of Filbert
Philiberta, Filiberta, Philberta, Philberthe

FILIA Greek: Daughter; represents love between a parent and child

FILOMENA Spanish: Variation of Philomena

FINEENA Irish: Fair at birth; feminine form of Fineen

FINNEA Irish: Wood of the ford; also an Irish village
Finea

FINOLA Irish: White shoulders; an Anglicized variation of Fionnghuala
Fenella, Finella, Finnguala, Fionnuala, Finoula; **Nicknames:** *Nola, Nuala, Nualla*; **Famous Namesakes:** *Actress Finola Hughes*

FIONA Irish, Gaelic: Fair; feminine form of Fionn
Finna, Fionn, Fionna

FIROUZEH Persian: Turquoise

FIRTHA Scottish: Narrow inlet of the sea

FISSEHA African: Happiness

FLAIR English: Style, verve

FLAMINIA Latin: Priest
Flamina

FLANNA Irish: Red-haired
Nicknames: *Flannery*

FLANNERY Irish: Nickname for Flanna
Famous Namesakes: *Author Flannery O'Connor*

FLAVIA Latin: Golden or blond; from the Roman family name Flavius

FLETA English: Swift
Fleda, Flede, Flita, Flyta

FLEURETTE French: Little flower

FLORA Latin: Flower; the mythological Roman goddess of flowers and spring
(French) *Fleur, Flore*; (Spanish) *Flor, Florida, Florita*; (Gaelic) *Floraigh*; (Hungarian) *Florka*; *Floressa, Flori, Floria, Floriana, Florinda*; **Nicknames:** *Florrie*; **Diminutive Forms:** *Fleurette, Floretta*; **Famous Namesakes:** *Chinese actress Flora Chan*

FLORENCE Latin, English: Blooming, flourishing; Florence is often thought of in reference to a beautiful city in Italy that is considered a cultural art center. Renowned nurse Florence Nightingale was named for this city of her birth.
(Italian) *Florentina, Florenza*; (Spanish) *Florencia, Florinia*; (Irish) *Blathnaid*; *Florella, Florentine, Florentyna, Florice, Floris*; **Nicknames:** *Flo*; **Famous Namesakes:** *Athlete Florence (Flo Jo) Griffith Joyner, Actress Florence Henderson*

FLORIANA French: Spelling variation of Flora

FLORIDA Spanish: Variation of Flora

FLORINDA French: Spelling variation of Flora

FONTAINE French: Fountain, spring
Fontanne; **Famous Namesakes:** *Actress Joan Fontaine*

FORBA Scottish: Headstrong. Celtic: Fields
Forbia

FOROUNZANDEH Persian: Shining

FORTUNE Latin: Fortune, good fate; Fortuna was the Roman goddess of happiness.
Fortuna, Fortunata

FRANCE French: Free one; also a place name for the country of France
Francia; **Diminutive Forms:** *Francena, Francene, Francine*; **Famous Namesakes:** *French singer France Gall*

FRANCES Latin: From France, free one; feminine form of Francis
(German) *Franziska*; (French) *Françoise*; (Italian) *Francesca*; (Spanish) *Francisca, Paquita*; (Teutonic) *Ziska, Ziske, Zissi*; (Slavic) *Fanya*; (Czech) *Frantiska*; (Polish) *Franciszka*; (Hungarian) *Franciska; Fanceen, Francille, Francina, Francique, Franze*; **Nicknames:** *Fani, Fania, Fanni, Fannia, Fannie, Fanny, Fran, Franci, Francie, Franki, Frankie, Franny, Franky*; **Famous Namesakes:** *Actresses Frances McDormand, Francis Conroy, Fran Drescher*; **Star Babies:** *Daughter of Kurt Cobain and Courtney Love*

FRANCESCA Italian: Variation of Frances
Star Babies: *Daughter of Martin Scorsese, Erik Estrada, Frances Fisher and Clint Eastwood*

FRANCINE French: From France, free one
Famous Namesakes: *British television personality Francine Lewis*

FRANZISKA German: Variation of Frances

FREDA German: Nickname for Frederica

FREDERICA German: Tranquil leader, peaceful ruler; feminine form of Frederick. Three years after founding Georgia in 1733, General James Edward Oglethorpe established Fort Frederica to defend the fledgling colony against Spanish attack from Florida. (German) *Friederika*; (French) *Frédérique*; (Swedish) *Frederika, Frideborg; Farica, Farika, Fredrika, Friederike*; **Old Forms:** *Friedegard, Friedegarde*; **Nicknames:** *Freda, Fredda, Freddi, Frici, Frida, Frieda, Frika, Frikka, Fritjof, Fritzi, Fritzie, Fryda*; **Famous Namesakes:** *Opera singer Frederica von Stade*

> *"My aunt goes to church with a family who has seven kids. They named the youngest one Enuff, as in 'enough.' She's about eight now and they call her Nuffy."*
> —from BabyZone.com's Message Boards

FREIRA Spanish: Sister

FRESCURA Spanish: Freshness

FREYA Norse: A noble woman; Freya was the Norse goddess of love and fertility for whom Friday is named, said to be the most beautiful of the goddesses.
Freja, Freyja, Froja

FRICI Hungarian: Nickname for Frederica

FRIEDA German: Peaceful ruler; feminine form of Frederick
Frida; **Famous Namesakes:** *Mexican artist Frida Kahlo*

FRIGG Norse: Beloved; in Norse mythology, Odin's wife Frigg was mother of the gods and the goddess of the earth, fertility, and love.
Frigga, Nerthus

FRITZI German: Nickname for Frederica

FRONDA Latin: Leafy branch
Fronde

FUKAYNA Egyptian: Knowledgeable, intelligent

FULLA Norse: A name from Norse mythology of uncertain meaning; Fulla was one of the goddess Frigg's attendants.

FULVIA Latin: Blond

GABRIANNA English: Modern blend of Gabrielle and Anna

GABRIELA Hebrew: Variation of Gabrielle
Famous Namesakes: *Argentine tennis player Gabriela Sabatini, Writer Gabriela Mistal*

GABRIELLE Hebrew, French: God is my strength; feminine form of Gabriel
(Hebrew) *Gabriela*; (Italian) *Gabriella*; (Slavic) *Gabinka*; *Gabriele, Gabriell, Gavra, Gavriella, Gavrila, Gavrilla*; **Nicknames:** *Gabi, Gaby*; **Famous Namesakes:** *Volleyball player and model Gabrielle Reece*

GADAR Armenian: Summit
Gadara, Gadarine

GAEA Greek: Variation of Kaia

GAEL English: Joyful; Gael is an abbreviation of Abigail and a term for descendants of the ancient Celts in Scotland, Ireland, and the Isle of Man.
Gail, Gale

GAERWEN Welsh: White fort

GAETANA Italian: From Gaete
(French) *Gaetane*; **Famous Namesakes:** *Italian mathematician Maria Gaetana Agnesi*

GAHO Native American: Mother

GAIA Greek: The earth; mythological female personification of the earth and mother of the Titans
Star Babies: *Daughter of Emma Thompson and Greg Wise*

GAILA English: Joyful; abbreviation of Abigail and a variant of Gael or Gail

GAIRA Scottish: Small one
Gara, Garia

GALA Norse: Lovely voice, singer

GALATIA Greek: White as milk; in mythology, Pygmalion fell in love with the statue Galatia and Aphrodite brought her to life for him.
(French) *Galatée*; *Galatea*

GALE English, Norse: Joyful; abbreviation of Abigail
Gayle, Gaylen, Gaylene, Gael, Gail; **Famous Namesakes:** *Actress Gale Sondergaard*

GALIANA German: Haughty
Galiena, Galiene

GALICE Hebrew: Fountain, spring
Galit; **Nicknames:** *Gali*

GALILAH Hebrew: God shall redeem
Galila; **Nicknames:** *Galia*

GALILAHI Native American: Attractive
(Cherokee)

GALINA Russian: Calm, tranquil; feminine form of Galen
Nicknames: *Galka, Galya*; **Diminutive Forms:** *Galenka, Galochka*

GALKA Russian: Jackdaw; also a nickname for Galina

GALLIA French: From Gaul
Galla

GAMADA African: Glad

GAMILA Egyptian: Beautiful
Jamila

GAMMA Greek: Third letter in Greek alphabet

GANDHARI Hindi: Mythological Hindu princess known as just and a fearless speaker

GANESA Hindi: Hindu god who removes obstacles

GANIEDA Arthurian Legend: Merlin's sister

GANIT Hebrew: Garden
Gana, Ganet, Ganice, Ganya

GARABI Latin: Clear
Garbi

GARABINA Spanish: Purification
Garabine, Garbina, Garbine

GARAITZ Basque, Spanish: Victory

GARAN Welsh: Stork

GARCELLE French: Tomboy; probably
derived from the French word *garçon*,
meaning boy
Famous Namesakes: *Haitian actress
Garcelle Beauvais*

GARDE German: Guarded
Garda

GARDENIA English: Sweet flower blossom
Gardenya; **Famous Namesakes:**
Capeverdean singer Gardenia

GARIN Armenian: Name of an ancient city

GARNET English: A dark-red gemstone
named for the pomegranate because of its
color; from Old French *grenat*
Garnett

GARUDA Hindi: Sacred bird that carries
Vishnu

GARUDI Hindi: Bird of prey

GASPARA Spanish: Treasure; feminine form
of Gaspar

GAURI Hindi: Yellow or pale; name of
a Hindu goddess

GAVINA Scottish: White hawk; feminine
form of Gavin
Gavenia

GAY French: Joyful, light-hearted; variant
of Gail
Gae, Gaie, Gaye

GAYATRI Hindi: A singer

GAYLA English: Nickname for Abigail

GECHINA Basque, Spanish: Graceful

GEIRBJORG Norse: Sister of Bersi the
Godless

GELASIA Greek: Inclined to laughter

GELLA Hebrew: Golden-haired

GELSEY English: A variety of jasmine
Gelsi, Gelsy; **Famous Namesakes:** *Ballerina
Gelsey Kirkland*

GEMMA Latin: Gem, a jewel
Gemmalyn, Gemmalynn, Jemma;
Nicknames: *Gem*

GENAYA English: White wave; variant
of Jenny

GENEROSA Spanish: Generous

GENESEE Native American: Beautiful,
shining valley (Iroquois)
Gennisheyo

GENESIS Hebrew: Origin; Genesis is the
name of the first book in the Bible.
Genessa, Genisa, Genisia, Genisis

GENEVA English: Place name for a historic
city in southwestern Switzerland

GENEVIÈVE French: Name of unclear origin and meaning; possibly means juniper, white shoulders, or the race of women (Italian) *Genevra, Ginevra*; (Spanish) *Genoveva, Ginebra, Ginessa*; (Russian) *Zenevieva*; *Geneve, Genevie, Genevre, Genivee, Jenavieve, Jeneva, Jenevieve, Jennavieve, Jenneva*; **Nicknames:** *Genny, Gen*; **Famous Namesakes:** *Canadian actress Genevieve Bujold*

GENISTA English: Broom plant

GENNA English: Spelling variation of Jennifer

GEONA Hebrew: Glorify

GEORGETTE French: Variation of Georgia *Georgetta, Jorjette*

GEORGIA Greek: Farmer; Georgia is a feminine form of George and the name of a southern state (French) *Georgette*; (Italian) *Giorgia, Giorgina*; (Spanish) *Jorgelina*; (Finnish) *Irja*; *Georgeanne, Georgegina, Georgiana, Georgianna, Georgina, Georgine, Jeorjia, Jorja*; **Nicknames:** *Gia, Gigi*; **Famous Namesakes:** *Painter Georgia O'Keeffe*; **Star Babies:** *Daughter of Jerry Hall and Mick Jagger, Harry Connick Jr., Harrison Ford*

GEOVANA Italian: Variation of Jane

GERALDINE German: Rules by the spear; feminine form of Gerald *Geralda, Geraldina, Geralyn, Geralynn, Geriann, Gerianne, Gerica, Gericka, Gerika, Gerilyn, Gerilynn, Gerrilyn, Jeraldine*; **Nicknames:** *Geri, Gerri, Jeralyn, Jerelyn, Jeri, Jerilyn, Jerilynn, Jerri, Jerrilyn, Deena, Dina*; **Famous Namesakes:** *Politician Geraldine Ferraro, Actress Geraldine Page, Opera singer Geraldine Farrar*

GERARDA German, Spanish: Mighty with a spear; feminine form of Gerard *Gerhardina, Gerhardine, Gerwalt*

GERD Norse: Enclosure, protection; in Norse mythology, Gerd was a fertility goddess. (German) *Gerde*; (Swedish) *Gerda*; (Danish) *Gjerta*; *Gerta, Gerte*; **Nicknames:** *Gerdie*

GERMAINE French: Brotherly; derived from the Latin word germen, meaning a sprout or bud; feminine form of Germain *Germane, Germayne*; **Famous Namesakes:** *Australian feminist author Germaine Greer*

> *"Everybody has a name anybody has a name and everybody anybody does what he does with his name feels what he feels about his name, likes or dislikes what he has to have with having his name, in short it is his name unless he changes his name unless he does what he likes what he likes with his name."*
> —Gertrude Stein

GERTRUDE German: Spear of strength (Spanish) *Gertrudes, Gertrudis*; (Swedish) *Gertrud*; *Gertruda, Gertrut, Gesine, Truda, Trudchen, Trude*; **Old Forms:** *Gertraud, Gertraude*; **Nicknames:** *Gesa, Trudie, Trudy, Trula, Gert, Gertie*; **Famous Namesakes:** *Author Gertrude Stein, Actress Gertrude Berg*

GETHSEMANE Hebrew: Oil vat; the name of a garden on the Mount of Olives where Jesus prayed just before his arrest and crucifixion

GEVA Hebrew: Hill

GHADA Armenian: Young girl

GHALYELA African: Precious

GHASSEDAK Persian: Dandelion

GIA Italian: Nickname for Georgia

GIANA Italian: God is gracious; variant of Jane
Geonna, Gianara

GIGI French: Nickname for Georgia

GILBERTA German: Brilliant, pledge, trustworthy
Gilbarta, Gilberte; **Old Forms:** *Gisilberhta*

GILDA English: Golden; also an abbreviation of Germanic names containing "gilde."Celtic: Serves God
Gildan, Gildas, Gylda, Gyldan; **Famous Namesakes:** *Comedienne Gilda Radner*

GILIA Hebrew: Eternal joy
Geela, Gila, Gilah, Gilal, Gilala, Gilana, Gilat, Gilit; **Nicknames:** *Gili*

GILLIAN English: Spelling variation of Jillian
Jillian; **Star Babies:** *Daughter of Patty Hearst*

GINA Greek: Well born
Famous Namesakes: *Actress Geena Davis, Actress Gina Lollabrigida*; **Star Babies:** *Daughter of Tony Danza, daughter of Sidney Poitier*

GINATA Hawaiian: Flower

GINGER English: Pep, liveliness; Ginger is also a nickname for Virginia. The pungent ginger root is used as a spice.
Famous Namesakes: *Dancer Ginger Rogers*

GINNY English: Nickname for Virginia
Giney, Ginnee, Ginni, Ginnie, Jinnee, Jinney, Jinni, Jinnie, Jinny

GIORDANA Italian: Variation of Jordan

GIOVANA Italian: Variation of Jane

GIOVANNA Italian: Variation of Jane
Jeovana; **Nicknames:** *Gian, Gianina, Gianna, Giannina*

GISELLE German: Pledge, oath
(German) *Gisela, Gisella*; (Polish) *Gizela*; (Hungarian) *Gizella*; *Ghislaine, Gisel, Gisele, Guilaine, Jiselle*; **Nicknames:** *Gilla, Gisa, Gizi, Gizike, Gizus*; **Famous Namesakes:** *Brazilian model and actress Giselle Bundchen*

GITA Hindi: Song

GITANA Spanish: Gypsy

GITHA English: Gift

GIULIANA Italian: Variation of Juliana
Star Babies: *Daughter of Luciano Pavarotti*

GIZA Hebrew: Cut stone
Gazit, Gisa

GLADYS Welsh: An old name of uncertain meaning; possibly a derivation of the Latin name Claudia, meaning lame
Gladis, Gwladys; **Nicknames:** *Glad*; **Famous Namesakes:** *Singer Gladys Knight*

> *"Sure he (Fred Astaire) was great, but don't forget that Ginger Rogers did everything he did—backwards and in high heels."*
> —originally from a *Frank and Ernest* cartoon, famous from its use by Governor Ann Richards

GLAFIRA Russian: Elegant, slim
Nicknames: *Glasha*

GLAN Welsh: From the shore

GLAW Welsh: Rain

GLEDA English: Happy

GLENDA Welsh: Fair, good, or from the glen
Glinda, Glynda; **Famous Namesakes:**
Actress Glenda Jackson

GLENNA Gaelic, Irish: From the glen
(Welsh) *Glynnis, Ghleanna, Glen, Glenn,
Glenne, Glennis, Glenys, Glyn, Glynae, Glynis,
Glynn, Glynna, Glynnes, Glynnis*; **Famous
Namesakes:** *Actress Glenn Close*

GLIONA Irish: Variation of Cleone

GLORIA Latin: Glory, renown, and respect
*Gloriana, Gloriane, Glorianna, Gloribel,
Gloriosa*; **Famous Namesakes:** *Musician
Gloria Estefan, Feminist Gloria Steinem,
Fashion designer Gloria Vanderbilt*

GLORIANN English: Glorious grace;
modern blend of Gloria and Ann

GLYNNIS Welsh: Variation of Glenna

GOBNAIT Irish: Variation of Abigail

GODIVA English: Gift from God; Lady
Godiva is the subject of a legend where she
rode through the town of Coventry naked,
covered only by her long, flowing hair.

GOEWIN Welsh: Legendary daughter
of Pebin

GOLBAHR Persian: Spring flower

GOLDA English, Hebrew: Golden, bright,
and precious
Nicknames: *Goldie, Golds, Goldy*; **Famous
Namesakes:** *Prime Minister of Israel Golda
Meir, Actress Goldie Hawn*

GOLEUDDYDD Welsh: Bright day

GOLNAZ Persian: Cute like a flower

GOLSHAN Persian: Flower garden

GONCA Turkish: Rosebud

GORAWEN Welsh: Joy

GORDANA Scottish: From the wedge-shaped
or three-cornered town or settlement, heroic;
feminine form of Gordon
Gordania

GOTILDA Swedish: Strong
Nicknames: *Gota, Gote*

GRACA Latin: Spelling variation of Grace

GRACE Latin, English: Lovely or graceful,
a virtue; the three mythological graces,
or charities, were nature goddesses: Aglaia
(brilliance), Thalia (flowering), and
Euphrosyne (joy). See also *Ance*
(German) *Gratia*; (Italian) *Grazia, Graziosa*;
(Spanish) *Engracia, Gracia, Graciana,
Graciela*; (Polish) *Grazyna*; (Hawaiian)
Kalake; *Gracella, Gracelynne*; *Graca, Graciene,
Gracinha, Grata*; **Nicknames:** *Gracelyn,
Gracie*; **Famous Namesakes:** *Princess Grace
Kelly, Singer Grace Jones;* **Star Babies:**
*Daughter of Meryl Streep and Don Gummer,
daughter of Wynonna Judd*

GRACELYN English: Graceful; a blend
of Grace and Lynn
Gracelynn, Gracelin, Gracelinn, Gracelynne

GRACIE English: Nickname for Grace
Famous Namesakes: *Comedienne Gracie
Allen*; **Star Babies:** *Daughter of Danny
DeVito and Rhea Perlman, daughter of Faith
Hill*

GRÁINNE Irish: Possibly derived from the
Gaelic word *grán*, meaning grain; name of
an ancient Irish grain goddess and often
associated with *gráidh*, meaning love
Graina, Graine, Grania, Granya

GRANIA Celtic: Spelling variation of Gráinne

GREENLEIGH American: Green meadow; possibly a varaint of Greeley, but more likely a modern blend of the color green and the English ending "leigh" (meadow)
Greenley, Greenlie, Greenlea

GREER Scottish: Variation of Gregoria
Famous Namesakes: *Actress Greer Garson*;
Star Babies: *Daughter of Kelsey Grammer*

GREGORIA Latin: Watchful; feminine form of Gregory
(Scottish) *Greer*; *Gregoriana*

GRETA Swedish: Nickname for Margaret
Gretal, Grete, Gretel, Gretta, Grette, Griet, Grietje; **Famous Namesakes:** *Swedish actress Greta Garbo;* **Star Babies:** *Daughter of David Caruso, Phoebe Cates and Kevin Kline*

GRETCHEN German: Diminutive form of Margaret

GRISELDA German: Gray battle maiden; Italian author Giovanni Boccaccio used the name for an exceptionally patient wife—thus the expression "patience of Griselda."
(French) *Griselle*; (Gaelic) *Giorsal*; (Scottish) *Grizel, Grizela*; (Dutch) *Griseldis, Grishilde*; *Gricelda, Griselde, Grisella, Grissel, Grizelda, Gryselda;* **Nicknames:** *Zelda, Zelde*

GUADALUPE Spanish: This name of a Spanish city also refers to a chain of mountains in Spain and a city in Mexico. The Virgin Mary is Mexico's Lady of Guadalupe. Christopher Columbus signed his contract to go to the New World at the Royal Monastery of Our Lady of Guadalupe in Spain, now a popular destination for pilgrims. Arabic: Valley of the wolf
Guadaloupe, Guadaloupa, Guadolupe; **Nicknames:** *Lupe, Lupita, Guada, Lopina, Lupeta, Lupina*

GUDA Swedish: Supreme

GUDNY Swedish: Unspoiled

GUDRUN Norse: Divinely inspired wisdom; derived from the Old Norse roots "guð" (God) and "run" (secret wisdom); Gudrun was the wife of Sigurd in Norse legend.
Gudrid, Gudruna

GUENNOLA Celtic: White

GUIDA Italian: Guide

GUIDITTA Italian: Variation of Judith

GUILLELMINA Italian: Variation of Wilhelmina

GUINEVERE Welsh, Arthurian Legend: White and smooth, or fair lady; Guinevere was King Arthur's beautiful queen in Arthurian Legend. Jennifer derives from this name.
Guenevere, Gwenevere, Gwenhwyfar, Gwenhwyvar, Gwenyver; **Old Forms:** *Gaenor, Gaynor;* **Nicknames:** *Gwen*

GUISEPPINA Italian: Variation of Josephine

GULLVEIG Norse: Refers to Goldbranch, a sorceress of Norse mythology who had a great lust for gold

GUNHILDA Norse: Battle maiden
(Swedish) *Gunilla, Gunnef, Gunhilde, Gunnel, Gunnhild, Gunnhilde*

GUNNA Scottish: White

GURI Hindi: Hindu goddess of plenty

GURICE Hebrew: Cub
Gurit

GURO Norse: Divinely inspired wisdom

GUSTAVA Swedish: Staff of the Goths; feminine form of Gustav
(Dutch) *Gust, Gusta, Gustaafa*; **Nicknames:** *Gustha, Gussie, Gussy*; **Diminutive Forms:** *Gustel*

GWANWYN Welsh: Spring

GWEN Welsh: Nickname for Gwendolyn
Star Babies: *Daughter of Tammy Wynette*

GWENDA Welsh: Spelling variation of Gwynn
Gwynda

GWENDOLYN Welsh: Fair bow, a blend of the elements "gwen" (white, fair, or blessed) and "dolen" (bow or ring)
Guendolen, Gwendelyn, Gwendolen, Gwendolin, Gwendoline, Gwendoloena, Gwyndolen, Gwyndolin, Gwyndolyn;
Nicknames: *Gwen, Gwendi, Gwyn, Wendi, Wendie, Wendy, Wynne*; **Famous Namesakes:** *Poet Gwendolyn Brooks*

GWENER Welsh: Variant of Venus, goddess of love

GWYNETH Welsh: White, fair, or blessed
Gweneth, Gwenith, Gwenneth, Gwenyth, Gwynedd, Gwynith; **Famous Namesakes:** *Actress Gwyneth Paltrow*

GWYNN Welsh: Fair, blessed
Gwen, Gwenda, Gwenn, Gwenna, Gwyn, Gwynne

GYPSY English: Wanderer; derived from Egyptian to describe tribes of nomads who migrated from India to Europe
Gipsy

HABIBAH Egyptian: My sweetheart, my beloved
Habiba

HABIKA African: Dearest

HADA African: Nickname for Hadassah

HADAR Hebrew: Beautiful, honored
Hadara, Hadarah

HADASSAH Hebrew: Myrtle tree; also the biblical Queen Esther's Hebrew name
Nicknames: *Hada*

HADEYA Arabic: Gift, offering; also a spelling variant of Hadya, meaning quiet, well-behaved
(African) *Hadiya*; *Hedeya, Hadeyya, Hadya*

HADLEY English: From the heath or heather-covered meadow; a surname now used as a given name
Hadlee, Hadleigh, Hadlea, Hadlie

HADREA Latin: Dark; from the Adriatic Sea region; feminine variant of Adrian and Hadrian
Hadria

HADYA Arabic: Well-behaved, quiet; feminine variant of Hadi
Hadyah, Hadia, Hadiah

HAGAR Hebrew: Flight; in the Old Testament, Hagar was Sarah's Egyptian serving-maid who became the concubine to Abraham and mother of Ishmael, considered to be the founder of the Arab people.

HAIBA African: Charm

HAIDEE Greek: Haidee was created by Byron for a character in his poem *Don Juan*. He may have taken it from the Greek "aidos," meaning modesty.
Haydee

HAILEY English: Spelling variation of Hayley

HAIMATI Hindi: Snow queen

HAIMI Hawaiian: Seeker

HAJNAL Hungarian: Dawn

HAKAN Norse: Of the chosen, traditionally used as a male name. Swedish: Highborn child

HAKIDONMUYA Native American: Time of waiting moon (Hopi)

HALAG German: Variation of Helga

HALCYONE Greek: Time of peace, kingfisher; in Greek mythology, Halcyone threw herself into the sea after the death of her husband. Out of pity, the gods changed the pair into kingfishers, or halcyons, and caused the winds to cease blowing during the kingfisher's mating season. The expression "halcyon days" is derived from this myth and means a time of tranquillity.

HALDIS Teutonic: Spirit of stone
Halldis; **Nicknames:** *Haldisa, Halldora*

HALEH Persian: Halo

HALEY Scandinavian: Heroine, brave one. English: Variant of Halley and Hayley

HALFRID German: Peaceful heroine (English) *Halfrith, Halfryta, Hallfrita*; *Halfrida*; **Nicknames:** *Halifrid*

HALFRIDA German: Peaceful heroine; variant of Halfrid

HALIA Hawaiian: Remembrance of a loved one

HALIMA Arabic: Gentle, patient; a fitting name for the woman who cared for the young prophet Mohammed after his mother's death *Halimah*

HALIMEDA Greek: Thinking of the sea

HALLA Norse: Rock, stone

HALLDORA Norse: Spirit of stone; variant of Haldis

> *"My mom went to high school with a girl named Baby. She said her parents couldn't think of a name and called her Baby until they came up with one. But by then she wouldn't respond to the new name, only Baby. So they put that on her birth certificate."*
> —from BabyZone.com's Message Boards

HALLE English: Variant of Halley or Hayley *Hallie, Halley*; **Famous Namesakes:** *Actress Halle Berry*

HALLEY English: From the meadow near the hall (implying large estate or home); a surname also used as a variant of Hayley *Haley, Halie, Halle, Hallie*

HALLIE English: Variant of Halley and Hayley *Halle, Halley*

HALONA Native American: Fortunate

HAMIDEH Persian: Praiseworthy, glorified; feminine form of Hamid, derived from hamd (giving thanks, usually to God) *Hamida*

HANA Arabic: Bliss. Persian: Shrub henna *Hanaa*; **Star Babies:** *Daughter of Muhammad Ali*

HANITA Hindi: Divine grace

HANNAH Hebrew: Favor, grace; Hannah was the biblical mother of the prophet Samuel.
(English) *Hannalee*; (Danish) *Hanne*; (Finnish) *Hanna, Hannele, Henna, Henni*; (Hungarian) *Hajna*; *Chana, Chanah, Hanah*; **Nicknames:** *Hana, Hannela*; **Famous Namesakes:** *Philosopher Hannah Arendt, Sportscaster Hannah Storm*; **Star Babies:** *Daughter of Jilly Mack and Tom Selleck, Jessica Lange and Sam Shepard, Mel Gibson, Pat Benatar*

HANNELA Hebrew: Nickname for Hannah

HANNELE Hebrew: Nickname for Hannah

HANZILA African: Road, path

HARA Hindi: Another name for the Hindu deity Shiva

HARIMANNA German: Warrior maiden
Harimanne

HARIPRIYA Hindi: Another name for Lakshmi, the goddess of prosperity and wife of Vishnu

HARLEY Anglo-Saxon, English: From the hare's meadow; Harley is a surname associated with the famous Harley-Davidson motorcycles. While traditionally a name for boys, it is now increasingly being used for both genders.
(English) *Arleigh*; *Harlea, Harlee, Harleen, Harleigh, Harlie*

HARLOW English: From the hill of the hares, from the army hill; traditionally a boy's name, Harlow is now being used increasingly for both genders.
Harlowe; **Famous Namesakes:** *Actress Jean Harlow*

HARMONY Latin: Unity, concord, musically in tune; Harmonia was the mythological daughter of Aphrodite.
(French) *Harmonie*; *Harmonee, Harmonia*

HAROLDA Teutonic: Commander; feminine variant of Harold
Haralda, Harelda, Harelde, Harolde

HARPER English: Minstrel; harpers were more than entertainers when this name was created. They were a primary source of news and keepers of the historical record.

HARPINNA Latin: Mare of Oenomaus

HARRIET English: Nickname for Henrietta
Famous Namesakes: *Abolitionist Harriet Tubman*

HASINA African: Good (Swahili)

HATSHEPSUT Egyptian: Princess Hatshepsut was the daughter of Thutmose I and Queen Ahmes

HATTIE English: Nickname for Henrietta
Famous Namesakes: *Politician Hattie Wyatt Caraway*

HAUKEA Hawaiian: White snow

HAUSIS Native American: Old woman (Algonquin)
Nicknames: *Hausisse*

HAVEN English, Dutch: Place of safety, shelter

HAVVA Persian: Variation of Eve

HAYA Hebrew: To be, to live

HAYLEY English: From the hay meadow; an adapted surname traditionally used as a boy's name, now more common for girls
Hailey, Haleigh, Hallie, Haylie, Halley, Haley, Haylee, Hayleigh, Haileigh, Hailee, Haeley,

Haelie, Haely, Hailea, Haily, Haylea;
Nicknames: *Halle;* **Famous Namesakes:**
Actress Hayley Mills; **Star Babies:** *Daughter of Stephen Baldwin, David Hasselhoff, Jeff Bridges*

HAZAN Turkish: Autumn

HAZEL English: The hazel tree
Hazell

HEATHER English: A flowering evergreen plant that thrives on peaty, barren lands such as those found in Scotland
Famous Namesakes: *Actress Heather Locklear;* **Star Babies:** *Daughter of Paul McCartney and Linda Eastman, daughter of Jerry Garcia*

HECUBA Latin: Wife of King Priam of Troy; Hecuba was the mother of Paris and Hector in Greek mythology.

HEDDA Teutonic: Pleasant, refuge from battle; a variant of Edda
Famous Namesakes: *Writer Hedda Hopper*

HEDIA Greek: Pleasant
Nicknames: *Hedy, Hedyla*

HEDWIG German: Struggle, strife; the fictional Harry Potter named his owl Hedwig. (French) *Hedvige;* (Czech) *Hedvika; Hedvig;* **Old Forms:** *Haduwig, Hadwig;* **Nicknames:** *Hedy, Heddy;* **Diminutive Forms:** *Hadu*

HEHET Egyptian: Goddess of the immeasurable

HEIDI German: Sweet or noble; a short form of Adelaide and Adelheid
Heida, Heide; **Star Babies:** *Daughter of Larry Hagman*

HEIDRUN Norse: In the Edda Saga of Norse mythology, Heidrun is the name of the goat that stands on the roof of Valhall. Instead of milk she produces mead for the warriors of Odin.

HEKUBA Greek: Mother of Paris and Hector in Greek mythology

HELA Norse: Goddess of the underworld in Norse mythology

HELEN Latin: Nickname for Helena
Famous Namesakes: *Singer Helen Reddy*

HELENA Greek: Light; in Greek mythology, Helen was the daughter of Zeus by Leda and the most beautiful woman in the world. By abducting her, Paris began the Trojan War. In Christopher Marlowe's play *Doctor Faustus*, the devil taunts Faustus with the image of Helen, whom he describes as "the face that launched a thousand ships," in reference to the entire Greek fleet that set sail to bring her home.
(French) *Helene;* (Spanish) *Ileanna;* (Russian) *Alyona, Yelena;* (Czech) *Helenka;* (Polish) *Halina;* (Ukrainian) *Olena;* (Finnish) *Ilona;* (Hungarian) *Ili, Ilka, Ilke, Ilon, Ilonka, Iluska, Onella; Elynn, Helaine, Ileana, Ilena, Ilene, Iliana, Yalena, Yalene;* **Nicknames:** *Helen, Lena;* **Diminutive Forms:** *Yalenchka;* **Famous Namesakes:** *Cosmetics entrepreneur Helena Rubinstein, Author Helen Keller*

HELENE Greek: Spelling variation of Helena

HELGA Scandinavian, German: Blessed, holy
(German) *Halag; Elga, Helge, Olga*

HELGE Norse: Spelling variation of Helga

HELIA Greek: Sun; feminine form of Helios

HELIKE Greek: Helike was an ancient Greek city that was destroyed by a massive earthquake and tidal wave. The entire city and all its inhabitants were lost beneath the sea. Helike is also the name of a nymph.
Helice

HELLÄ Finnish: Gentle, tender

HELMI Finnish: Pearl

HELOISE French: Spelling variation of Eloise
Famous Namesakes: *Self-help queen Heloise*

HELSA Hebrew: Devoted to God

HELSIN Arthurian Legend: Mother of Lancelot

HEMERA Greek: Goddess of the day

HENGAMEH Persian: Uproar, wonder

HENICEA Greek: Daughter of Priam

HENLEY Irish: High field; surname

HENNA Finnish: Variation of Hannah

HENRIETTA German: Keeper of the hearth, rules her household; feminine form of Henry. See also *Enriqua*
(French) *Harriette, Henriette*; (Teutonic) *Enrika, Henuita*; (Swedish) *Henrika*; (Dutch) *Hendrika*; (Polish) *Henka, Henrieta*; (Finnish) *Riikka*; *Enrica, Enriqueta*; *Hanrietta, Hanriette, Harriett, Harrietta, Hatty, Henuite*; **Nicknames:** *Etta, Ettie, Etty, Harriet, Hattie, Heike, Hen, Henia, Henie, Hennie, Henny, Hettie*; **Famous Namesakes:** *English cookbook author Henrietta Green*

HEPSIBA Hebrew: She is my delight; Hepzibeth is another variant of this name. *Hephzibah*; **Nicknames:** *Hepzibeth*

HEQET Egyptian: Mythical frog-headed goddess of Antinoopolis where she was associated with Khnum, a helper of women in childbirth.

HERA Greek: Hera is the mythological wife of Zeus and was mainly worshipped as a goddess of marriage and birth.

HERLINDE German: Shield
(Spanish) *Erlina*; **Famous Namesakes:** *Photographer Herlinde Koelbl*

HERMANDINA Greek: Well-born; variant of Hermione

HERMIONE Greek: Well-born, earthly; feminine form of Hermes and, in Greek mythology, the daughter of Menelaus and Helen. Kids and adults alike are sure to recognize the name as a character in J.K. Rowling's *Harry Potter* series.
Hermia; **Nicknames:** *Hermandina, Hermandine, Herminia*

HERMOSA Spanish: Beautiful

HERO Greek: Hero; in Greek mythology, Hero was the lover of Leander, who would swim across the Hellespont each night to meet her. Hero is also the name of a character in Shakespeare's play *Much Ado About Nothing.*

HEROPHILE Latin: Daughter of Lamia and Poseidon, priestess of Apollo

HERSILIA Latin: A name from Roman mythology, Hersilia married a follower of Romulus.

HERTHA English: Of the earth
(German) *Herta*; (Teutonic) *Heartha, Herthe*;
(Finnish) *Hertta*

HERZELOYDE Arthurian Legend: Percival's
mother

HESIONE Greek: Daughter of Laomedon

HESPER Greek: Evening star
(Latin) *Hesperie*; **Nicknames:** *Hespera,
Hesperia*

HESPERIA Greek: Nickname for Hesper

HESTER Greek: Nickname for Esther.
Persian: Star, myrtle leaf; Esther was a young
Hebrew woman in the Bible who married
the Persian ruler Xerxes and risked her life
to save her people.
(Persian) *Hetty*

HESTIA Greek, Persian: Goddess of hearth
and home

HETTY Persian: Variation of Hester

HIALEAH Native American: Pretty prairie
(Seminole)

HIBERNIA Latin: An old name for Ireland

HIBISCUS Latin: Flower; the hibiscus is
the state flower of Hawaii.
Hibiskus

HIJA African: Daughter

HILA Hebrew: Praise; feminine form of
Hillel. Persian: Sparrow-hawk

HILARY Latin: Cheerful, joyful; derived
from the Latin word hilarius
(French) *Hilaire*; (Irish) *Hiolair*; *Hilaeira,
Hillary*; **Old Forms:** *Hilaria*; **Famous
Namesakes:** *Senator and Former First Lady
Hillary Rodham Clinton, Actress Hilary Duff,
Actress Hilary Swank*

HILDA German: Defending battle maiden;
nickname for Hildegard
Hilde, Hildy

HILDEGARD German: Defending battle
maiden; in Scandinavian mythology,
Hildegard was a Valkyrie sent by Odin to
escort battle heroes to Valhalla. Hildegard
gained popularity in Germany in Medieval
times through Saint Hildegard of Bingen.
Nicknames: *Hilda, Hildagarde, Hilde*

HILDUR Norse: Battle maiden

HILLA Finnish: Cloudberry

HILMA German: Nickname for Wilhelmina

HIPPODAMIA Greek: In Greek mythology,
she was the wife of Pirithous. The battle
between Centaurs and Lapiths began at their
wedding.
(Latin) *Hippodameia*

HIPPOLYTE Greek: Greek mythological
queen of the Amazons, a tribe of women
warriors
Nicknames: *Hippolyta*

HISOLDA Irish: Fair; variant of Isolde

HJORDIS Norse: Sword goddess
Hjördis

HOLDA German: Merciful; Holda was a Germanic goddess whose cult survived in the folklore of Germany, Austria, and Switzerland. She was considered the patron of the spinner.

Hope is the thing with feathers that perches in the soul and sings the tune without words and never stops at all.
—Emily Dickinson

HOLLAND English: Place name in the Netherlands; English surname
Famous Namesakes: *Actress Holland Taylor*

HOLLIS English: Holy or holly tree; variant of Holly

HOLLY English: Holy or holly tree; a beautiful seasonal name for girls born at Christmas, and the name of Audrey Hepburn's memorable character Holly Golightly in *Breakfast at Tiffany's*
Hollee, Hollie, Holley; **Nicknames:** *Hollis, Hollyn*; **Famous Namesakes:** *Actress Holly Hunter*; **Star Babies:** *Daughter of Michael Bolton*

HOMA Persian: Phoenix

HONEY English: Sweet

HONORA Latin: Honor; feminine form of Honorius
(Spanish) *Honoratas*; *Honorata, Honoria, Honorina, Honorine, Honour, Onora*;
Nicknames: *Honor*

HONOVI Native American: Strong deer (Hopi)

HOPE English: The feeling that a desire will be fulfilled, one of the three Christian virtues; a name first commonly used by the Puritans

HORATIA Latin: Keeper of the hours

HORTENSE Latin: From the Roman family name Hortentius, which is derived from hortus, the Latin word for garden
(Spanish) *Hortencia*; (Polish) *Hortenspa*; *Ortensia, Ortensiana, Ortensie*; **Nicknames:** *Hortendana*

HOURI Persian: Fairy

HOURIG Armenian: Small fire

HUBERTA German: Bright in spirit; feminine form of Hubert
Huberte

HUETTE German: Intelligent, thoughtful; feminine form of Hugh
(French) *Hugette*; *Huetts, Hughetta, Hughette, Hugiet, Hugolina, Huguetta, Ugolina*

HULDA Norse: Sweet, beloved
(German) *Hulde*

HUMILITY English: Humble, without false price; a virtue name

HUMITA Native American: Shelled corn (Hopi)

HUNTER English: To hunt; an occupational name
Famous Namesakes: *Actress Holly Hunter*

HURIT Native American: Beautiful (Algonquin)

HYACINTH Greek: A flower known for its beautiful scent and color; in Greek mythology, Hyacinthus was beloved and accidentally killed by Apollo. In tribute, Apollo had the flower that bears his name spring from his blood.
(French) *Hyacinthe, Jacinthe*; (Spanish) *Jacinta, Jakinda; Giancinta, Giancinte, Jacenia, Jacinda, Jacintha*; **Nicknames:** *Jaxine*

HYPATE Greek: Exceptional
Hypatia

...*What men*

Unborn shall read o'er ocean wide

And find Ianthe's name again

—Walter Landor,
"Well I Remember How You Smiled"

HYPERMNESTRA Greek: One of the Danaides, fifty daughters of Danaus

HYPSIPYLE Greek: Mythical Queen of Lemnos

HYRIA Greek: Mythical daughter of Amphinomus

IAERA Latin: Dryad nymph, mother of Bitias and Pandarus

IANTHE Greek: Violet flower; mythological sea nymph and daughter of Oceanus
Iolantha, Iolanthe

ICA Greek: Light

IDA German: Diligent, hard working. Hindi: Hindu goddess of prayer and devotion. Greek: Name of a mountain in Asia Minor and a Greek nymph, mother of Teucer, Troy's first king. English: Properous. See also *Idella Idaia*; **Star Babies:** *Daughter of Dolph Lundgren*

IDABELLE English: Modern blend of Ida and Belle
Idabella

IDAIA German: Spelling variation of Ida

IDALIA Greek: Glorious sun; (German) elaboration of Ida, diligent
Idalie, Idaliah

IDALINA Teutonic: Possibly a variant of Ida or a blend of Ida and Lina
Idaline

IDALIS English: Origins are unclear, but Idalis may be either a variant of Adelle or Alise, or possibly a blend of Ida and Alise
Idalise, Idelis

IDEASHIA English: Modern blend of Ida and Aisha
Ideashiah

IDELISA Celtic: A modern blend of Ida and Lisa

IDELLA Welsh: Bountiful

IDETTA German: Hard working; variant of Ida using a feminine French suffix
Idette

IDOIA Spanish: From the Spanish place name Idoia, an important place of worship of the Virgin Mary
Idoya

IDOLINA Spanish: Idol, worshipped image

IDONA German: Variant of either Ida (diligent worker) or Idony (renewed)
Idone

IDONIA Spanish: Happy, good girl

IDONY Scandinavian: Renewed, rejuvenated; in Norse mythology, she was the goddess of spring and immortality charged with guarding the gods' apples of youth.
Idun, Iduna, Idunn

IDURRE Basque: Reference to the Virgin Mary

IEKIKA Hawaiian: Variation of Jessica

IESHA English: Spelling variation of Aisha
Ieshea

IFE African: Love (Nigeria)

IGNACIA Latin, Spanish: Fiery, passionate
Ignatia, Ignaci, Ignaciah, Ignacie, Ignacya, Ignasha, Ignashia; **Nicknames:** *Ignia, Nacha*

IGONE Basque, Spanish: Refers to Christ's Ascension

IGRAINE English: Graceful; the legendary King Arthur's mother over whom a war was fought between her first husband, Gorlois, and her second, Arthur's father, Uther Pendragon
Igrayne, Ygraine

IKERNE Basque: Visitation

ILANA Hebrew: Tree
Ilane; **Nicknames:** *Ilanit*

ILDIKO Hungarian: Warrior

ILEANA Greek: Spelling variation of Helena

ILIA Latin: Mythical vestal virgin who broke her vow of celibacy and became the mother, by the god Mars, of the twin boys Romulus and Remus

ILIANA Greek: Light; variant of Helena

ILMA Finnish: Air
Ilmatar

ILONA Finnish: Variation of Helena

ILORI African: Special treasure

ILSE German: Spelling variation of Else

ILUMINADA Spanish: Illuminated

ILYSE German: Variation of Elise

ILYSSA English: Variation of Elise

IMALA Native American: Strong-willed, independent
Imalah

IMBER Polish: Ginger

IMELDA Spanish: Powerful fighter; the name of a fourteenth-century Spanish saint
Famous Namesakes: *Former First Lady of the Philippines Imelda Marcos*

IMENA African: Dream

IMMACULATA Latin: Immaculate or without stain; given to commemorate the Virgin Mary's Immaculate Conception as Maria Immacolata
(Spanish) *Immaculada*

IMOGENE Latin: Image, likeness; there is evidence that Imogen as a name is not derived from the Latin, but simply resulted from a mistake in the use of the Gaelic Inghean, meaning maiden.
Emogene, Imogen, Imogenia

IMPERIA Latin: Imperious, commanding

INA Irish: Pure or virginal; variant of Agnes

INARA Arabic: Heaven sent, enlightened
Enara

INARI Finnish: Place name for Lake Inari in Finland

INCA Scandinavian: Ing's abundance (Ing was the Norse mythological god of the earth's fertility); Inca also refers to Quechuan people living in the Cuzco valley in Peru.

INDIA English: From the Sanskrit for river; India is a country in southern Asia. Fictional India Wilkes was Ashleigh's sister in Margaret Mitchell's *Gone with the Wind*.
Inda, Indee, Indi; **Star Babies:** *Daughter of Marianne Williamson, Catherine Oxenberg, Philip Michael Thomas*

INDIANA English: Place name for Indiana, one of the United States fondly known as the Hoosier State

INDIGO English: Deep blue-violet

INDIRA Sanskrit: Splendid. Hindi: Mythological wife of Vishnu

INDRAJIT Hindi: Conqueror of Indra

INDRANI Hindi: Mythological Indra's wife and consort, in some accounts called the goddess of wrath

INEZ Spanish: Variation of Agnes
Ines

INGE Scandinavian, German: One who is foremost; an independent name and a short form of several Scandinavian and German names having "Ing" as their first element. In Norse mythology, Ing was another name for the fertility and agriculture god Frey.
Inga

INGEBORG Scandinavian: Ing's protection, fortress of Ing; refers to the Norse god of fertility and agriculture
Ingaborg

INGELISE Scandinavian: Combination name pairing Inga and Liese

INGRID Scandinavian: Beautiful; feminine version of the Norse fertility god Ing's name
(Finnish) *Inka, Inkeri; Inger, Inga, Inge*;
Famous Namesakes: *Swedish actress Ingrid Bergman*

INIGA Latin: Fiery, passionate

INIKO African: Born during troubled times

INIS Irish: Island

INKERI Finnish: Variation of Ingrid
Nicknames: *Inka*

INO Greek: Greek mythical daughter of Cadmus, foster mother of Dionysis, and stepmother of Prixes; it was from Ino that Prixes fled on the ram with the golden fleece. Zeus saved Ino from a tragic fate by turning her into Leucotha, the white sea goddess.

INOCENCIA Spanish: Innocence
Inocenta

INOLA Native American: Black fox
(Cherokee)

INTISARA Arabic: Triumphant
Intisar, Intesara, Entesara

IOKE Hawaiian: Variation of Joyce

IOLA Greek: Violet, dawn; in Greek mythology, the hero Hercules loved Iola. Welsh:
Deemed worthy, valued by God
Iole

IOLANA Hawaiian: To soar like the hawk;
also the Hawaiian for Yolanda, a variant
of Violet
Iolani

IONA Greek, English: Amethyst, violet
flower. Scottish: Place name for an island off
the west coast of Scotland, likely derived
from Gaelic *ioua*.
Ionanna, Ione, Ionessa, Ionia, Ionna; **Famous
Namesakes:** *Archeologist Ione Mylonas Shear*

IRAN Persian: Place name for Iran, an
ancient Middle Eastern country in Asia

IRAN-DOKHT Persian: Daughter of Iran

IRATZE Basque: Reference to the Virgin Mary

IRELAND English: Place name for Ireland,
a small country in northwestern Europe
Irelyn; **Star Babies:** *Daughter of Kim
Basinger and Alec Baldwin*

IRENE Greek: Peace; Irene was the Greek
goddess of peace. Another famous bearer was
an eighth-century Byzantine empress, the
first woman to lead the Empire. She originally
served as regent for her son but later had
him killed and ruled alone.
(Russian) *Arina, Irina*; (Hungarian) *Irenke*;
Eirene, Irayna, Irena, Iriana, Irinia, Iryna;
Nicknames: *Irini, Rena, Rina*

IRIS Greek, Hebrew: Rainbow; Iris was the
Greek mythological goddess of the rainbow.
This name can also be given in reference to the
English word (which derives from the same
Greek source) for the name of the iris flower
or the colored part of the eye. See also *Irsia*
(Finnish) *Iiris; Irisa*

IRMA German: Strength, universal or complete; a short form of many names beginning
with the element Irm or Erm, probably
derived from irm, the root of the name
Irmin, a German mythological god of war
(Latin) *Ermina; Erma, Ermelinda, Ermelinde,
Irmgard, Irmina, Irmine*; **Nicknames:**
Irmuska; **Famous Namesakes:** *Humorist
Erma Bombeck*

> *"When my kids become wild and
> unruly, I use a nice, safe playpen.
> When they're finished, I climb out."*
> —Erma Bombeck

IRSIA Persian: Rainbow; variant of Iris

IRUNE Spanish: Reference to the Holy
Trinity

IRVETTE English: Sea friend; (Irish) attractive. Welsh: White river
Irvetta, Irveta, Irvetah

ISA German: Nickname for Isabel
Star Babies: *Daughter of Michael Bolton*

ISABEL Spanish: Devoted to God; Isabel
is generally considered a medieval Spanish
form of Elizabeth, though some sources
suggest Isabel actually derives from an old
Semitic name meaning daughter of Baal.
It is a royal name in Spain and Portugal.
(Hebrew) *Isibeal*; (French) *Isabelle*; (Italian)
Isabella; (Scottish) *Iseabail, Isobel*;
(Armenian) *Zabel; Isabela, Izabella, Ysabel,
Ysabelle*; **Nicknames:** *Bel, Bella, Belle,*

Chavela, Chavelle, Isa; **Star Babies:** *Daughter of Annette Bening and Warren Beatty*

ISABELLA Italian: Variation of Isabel **Nicknames:** *Isa, Iza, Belicia, Belita*; **Star Babies:** *Daughter of Nicole Kidman and Tom Cruise*

ISABIS African: Something that is beautiful

ISADORA Greek: Gift of Isis; derived from the name of the Egyptian fertility goddess and the Greek doron, meaning gift (Spanish) *Isidora*; *Isadore*; **Famous Namesakes:** *Dancer Isadora Duncan*

ISAURA Greek: From Isaurus, an ancient Asian country *Isaure*

ISEUT French: Variation of Isolde

ISHA Hebrew: Protector

ISI Native American: Deer (Choctaw)

ISIS Egyptian: Most powerful of the female Egyptian goddesses, she was consort and sister to Osirus, mother of Horus, and is usually depicted as a motherly woman with arms wide open. Isis was worshipped at the Island of Philae, and was later worshipped over the entire Roman Empire. *Auset, Aset*

ISLA Scottish: From Islay, a name of an island off the Scottish coast

ISMENE Greek: Accounted wise, Greek mythical daughter of Oedipus and Jocasta and sister of Antigone *Ismini*

ISOKE African: Gift from God

ISOLDE Celtic, German: Fair one; legendary Isolde of the White Hands (Iseut aux Blanches Mains) fell in love with the knight Tristan after drinking a love potion. Her story is the subject of Wagner's opera *Tristan und Isolde*. (German) *Yseult*; (French) *Iseut*; (Irish) *Iseult*; *Hisolda, Isold, Isolda, Isole, Isotta, Isoud, Isoude, Ysolde*

ITA Gaelic: Thirsty *Itah*

ITSASO Basque: The sea

ITXARO Spanish: Hope

IULALIA Hawaiian: Variation of Eulalie

IVALYN English: A name of unclear origins; possibly a variant of Ivana or Evelyn, possibly a blend of Ivy and Lynn

IVANA Czech: God has been gracious; feminine form of Ivan (Russian) *Ivanna*; **Nicknames:** *Iva, Ivah, Vania, Vanya*; **Diminutive Forms:** *Ivanka*; **Famous Namesakes:** *Socialite Ivana Trump*

IVONNE French: Spelling variation of Yvonne

IVORY English: White, pure; a reference to the creamy-white color of ivory or to the hard tusk used for carving fine art and jewelry

IVY English: Botanical name for any one of a large number of climbing or creeping ornamental plants or vines (Spanish) *Ivette*; *Ivey, Ivie*

IVYANNE English: Variant of Ivana or a modern blend of Ivy and Anne *Ivyanna*

IZASKUN Basque: Reference to the Virgin Mary

IZUSA Native American: White stone *Izusah*

JACELYN English: Modern blend of Jaye or Jacey and Lynn

JACENIA Greek: Spelling variation of Hyacinth

JACEY English: Modern name, possibly based simply on the initials J.C. or a variation of Jacinda
Jacee, Jaci, Jacy, Jaicee, Jaycee, Jaycie, Jacie, Jayci

JACINDA English: Spelling variation of Hyacinth

JACINTHE French: Variation of Hyacinth

JACKIE English: Nickname for Jacqueline
Jacki, Jacqui

JACOBA Hebrew: Supplanter or seizing by the heel; feminine form of Jacob
Jakoba, Jakobe

JACQUELINE French: Supplanter; feminine form of Jacques, Jacob, and James
(Hebrew) *Jakobah; Jacalyn, Jackleen, Jacklynn, Jaclyn, Jacqualine, Jacqueleen, Jacquelyn, Jacquelyne, Jacquelynne, Jaklyn, Jaquelin, Jaquelina, Jaqueline, Jaquetta;* **Nicknames:** *Jackie, Jacqui;* **Diminutive Forms:** *Jacquenetta, Jacquenette, Jaquenette;* **Famous Namesakes:** *First Lady Jacqueline Bouvier Kennedy, English actress Jacqueline Bisset*

JADE Spanish: Jewel, a green gemstone (English) *Jadira; Jaida, Jayde;* **Nicknames:** *Jady;* **Star Babies:** *Daughter of Mick Jagger, daughter of Jesse Ventura*

JADEN American: Unisex name; originally a male biblical name meaning God has heard
Jaiden, Jayden, Jadyn, Jadynn, Jaidyn, Jaidynn, Jaydyn, Jaydynn

JAE English: Spelling variation of Jayna

JAEDA Arabic: Goodness, long-necked beauty
Jada, Jawda, Jaydra, Jayeda, Jaide; **Famous Namesakes:** *Actress Jada Pinkett Smith*

JAELEAH English: Spelling variation of Jayna

JAFFA Hebrew: Beautiful
Jafit, Jafita, Yaffa, Jafa, Yafa, Yafit

JAGODA Slavic: Strawberry

JAHIA African: Prominent
Jahiah

JAIDA English: Spelling variation of Jade

JAIME Spanish: Supplanter; feminine form of James
(Scottish) *Jaimie; Jaimee, Jaimelynn, Jaimi, Jamee, Jamey, Jami, Jamia, Jamie, Jamilyn, Jaymee, Jaymie*

JAIMELYNN Scottish: Blend of names Jaime and Lynn

JAINA Hebrew: Spelling variation of Jane

JAIONE Basque: Reference to the nativity

JALA Arabic: High, great, imposing, illustrious
Jalaa

JALEH Persian: Rain

JALEN American: Variant of Jalena
Jaylen, Jaylin, Jaylinn, Jaylyn, Jaylynn, Jalyn, Jalynn, Jailen

JAMILA Arabic, African: Beautiful
(African) *Jameelah, Jamelia, Jamille; Jamilah, Jamilia, Jamilla, Jemila, Jamilieh, Jamile;* **Star Babies:** *Daughter of Muhammad Ali*

JAN Hebrew, Slavic: Gift from God; Jan is a feminine form of John and a variant of Jane. In Roman mythology, Jana was the wife of Janus.
(Hebrew) *Jana*

JANA Irish: Variation of Jane
Jannah; **Nicknames:** *Janie, Janey*

JANAI English: God has answered; variant of Jane or Jean
Jenae, Jenai, Jenay, Jenaya, Jennae, Jennay; **Nicknames:** *Jenee*

JANAIS English: God has answered; modern variant of Jane
Janae

JANALEE Polish: Feminine form of John and a variant of Jane; Jana was the wife of Janus in Roman mythology.

JANALYN Polish: Feminine form of John and a variant of Jane
Jannalynn

JANAYA English: God has answered; modern variant of Jane
Janaye

JANE Hebrew: God is gracious; feminine form of John and a variant of Joan. See also *Shona*
(Hebrew) *Jans*; (Latin) *Joana*; (English) *Johnelle, Johnetta, Johnette*; (French) *Jeena, Jehane*; (Italian) *Ciana, Geovana, Gianina, Gianna, Giannina, Giovana, Giovanna*; (Spanish) *Yoana, Zaina, Zanetta, Zanita*; (Gaelic) *Sheena, Sine, Siobhan*; (Irish) *Jana, Sinead*; (Welsh) *Sian*; (Russian) *Zhanna*; (Polish) *Janah, Janceena, Janica, Janka, Janna, Jannah, Jannalee, Jasia*; (Finnish) *Jaana*; *Jaina, Jaine, Janiece, Janis, Jannae, Janne, Jayne, Jenice, Jeniece, Jenise, Jeovana, Jeovanna, Joan, Johnna, Johnnie, Jonalyn, Jonalynn, Jonay, Jonell, Jonna, Zanna*; **Old Forms:** *Janita, Jansje*; **Nicknames:** *Janee,*

Janey, Janicia, Janie, Jayni, Jaynie, Joanie, Joeanna, Joeanne, Joni, Jonni, Juanetta, Juanisha, Juanita; **Diminutive Forms:** *Jenette, Jonetta, Jonette, Jonnelle*; **Famous Namesakes:** *Actress Jane Fonda, Author Jane Austen, Journalist Jane Pauley, Naturalist Jane Goodall, Singer Janis Joplin*; **Star Babies:** *Daughter of Jim Carrey and Melissa Womer*

> *"It's giving girls names like that,"* said Buggins, *"that nine times out of ten makes 'em go wrong. It unsettles 'em. If ever I was to have a girl, if ever I was to have a dozen girls, I'd call 'em all Jane."*
> —H.G. Wells, referring to the name Euphemia

JANELL English: God is gracious; variant of Jane
Janella, Janelle

JANET Hebrew: Gift from God; originally a diminutive of Jane, from the French variant Jeanette
(Scottish) *Janneth*; (Welsh) *Sioned*; (Russian) *Zaneta; Jannet*; **Diminutive Forms:** *Janetta, Janette*; **Famous Namesakes:** *Singer Janet Jackson, Attorney General Janet Reno*

JANETTE Hebrew: Diminutive form of Janet

JANICA Polish: Variation of Jane

JANICE Hebrew: God is gracious; variant of Jane
Janise, Jannis, Janiece, Janis, Jenice, Jeniece, Jenise; **Famous Namesakes:** Singer Janis Joplin

JANICIA English: God is gracious; variant of Jane

JANNA Hindi: Paradise
(Persian) *Jannat*

JANNAH Polish: Variation of Jane

JARA Slavic: Spring

JARITA Hindi: Mythical bird

JASLYNN English: Modern variant of
Jasmine; blend of Jocelyn and the musical
term jazz

JASMINE Persian: Flower known for its
sweet fragrance
(Arabic) *Yasmina*; (French) *Jasmin*; (Danish)
Gelsomina; (Hindi) *Yasiman*; (Turkish)
Yasemin; *Jasmeen, Jasmyne, Jazmaine,
Jazmina, Jazmine, Jazzmine, Jazzmyn,
Jessamina, Jessamine, Jessamyn, Yasmia,
Yasmin, Yasmine, Yazmin*; **Famous
Namesakes:** *Actress Jasmine Guy*; **Star
Babies:** *Daughter of Michael Jordan, daughter
of Martin Lawrence*

JASONE Spanish: Assumption

JAVANEH Persian: Young

JAVIERA Spanish: Spelling variation of
Xaviera

JAXINE English: Variant of Jacinta, which is
a Spanish form of Hyacinth; also a contemporary blend of Jack and Maxine

JAYA Hindi: Victory
Old Forms: *Jayanti*

JAYANE Sanskrit: Victorious

JAYLYNN English: Blend of Jay and Lynn;
feminine variant of Jay
Jaylene

JAYNA English: God has been gracious;
variant of Jane that has become an independent name in much the same way the
name Jay became independent from its
origin, Jacob
Jae, Jaeleah, Jaena, Jaenette

JAZLYN English: Modern variant of
Jasmine; blend of Jocelyn and the musical
term jazz
Jazlynn; **Nicknames:** *Jazzy*

JEAN Scottish: Variation of Jeanne

JEANETTE French: Diminutive form
of Jeanne
Jenette; **Famous Namesakes:**
Congresswoman Jeanette Rankin

JEANINE French: Gift from God; diminu-
tive form of Jeanne, which is the French
form of Jane or Joan
(Hebrew) *Janina*; *Janene, Janine, Jannina,
Jeannine, Jeneen, Jenina, Jenine, Jennine,
Jineen, Ganeen*

JEANNE French: Gift from God; variant
of John, Jean, or Jane
(Scottish) *Jean*; *Jeana, Jeanae, Jeanay, Jeane,
Jeanee, Jeanna*; **Nicknames:** *Jeanie, Jeannie,
Jenelle*; **Diminutive Forms:** *Jeanelle, Jeanetta,
Jeanette, Jeanice, Jeanina, Jeannell, Jeannette,
Jenella*; **Star Babies:** *Daughter of William
Hurt and Sandrine Bonnaire*

JEMIMA Hebrew: Little dove; in the Bible,
one of Job's three daughters, who were
known as the most beautiful women of their
time (the other two were Keziah and Keren)
Jemimah

JEMINA Hebrew, Finnish: Listened to

JEN English: Nickname for Jennifer

JENAE English: God has answered; modern
variant of Jane or Jean, and a variation of
Janai

Jeannine, I dream of lilac time.

Your eyes, they beam in lilac time.

Your winning smile, and cheeks blushing like the rose,

Yet, all the while, you sigh when nobody knows.

—from the motion picture
Lilac Time (1928)

JENAYA English: Spelling variation of Janai

JENDAYI African: Grateful, thankful (Zimbabwe)

JENELLE English: Gift from God; variant of Jeanne
Jenella

JENICA Romanian: God is gracious; a contemporary Romanian form of Jane

JENNA English: Modern variant of Jenny and Jennifer
Jena, Jennah; **Star Babies:** *Daughter of Dustin Hoffman and Anne Byrne*

JENNALEE English: Spelling variation of Jennifer

JENNALYN English: Spelling variation of Jennifer

JENNARAE English: Spelling variation of Jennifer

JENNIFER Welsh: Fair one; variant of Guinevere
(English) *Jenita*; (Finnish) *Jenna*; *Genna, Jenalee, Jenalyn, Jenalynn, Jenarae, Jenifer, Jennabel, Jennady, Jennalee, Jennalyn, Jennarae, Jennasee, Jennessa, Jennika, Jennilee, Jennilyn, Jennyfer*; **Nicknames:** *Jen, Jena, Jeni, Jenilynn, Jennah, Jenni, Jennie, Jennis, Jenny, Jennyann, Jennylee, Jinni, Jinny*; **Diminutive Forms:** *Jenetta, Jennelle*; **Famous Namesakes:** *Tennis player Jennifer Capriati, Actress Jennifer Aniston*; **Star Babies:** *Daughter of Jack Nicholson and Sandra Knight, David Lynch, Billy Crystal, Bill Gates*

JENNY English: Nickname for Jennifer
Jenni, Jennie; **Famous Namesakes:** *Diet guru Jenny Craig*; **Star Babies:** *Daughter of Tony Orlando*

JENSINE Danish: God is generous

JERI English: Nickname for Geraldine

JERILYNN English: Rules by the spear. Blend of Jeri, which is a diminutive form of Geraldine, and the suffix -lyn.

JERSEY English: A place name for the Channel Isle of Jersey in England, and a familiar abbreviation for New Jersey

JERUSHA Hebrew: Inheritance

JESARA English: Rich, God beholds; a modern variation of Jessica

JESSAMINE French: Jasmine flower known for its sweet fragrance

JESSICA Hebrew: Rich, God beholds
(Hawaiian) *Iekika*; **Famous Namesakes:** *Actress Jessica Lange, Actress Jessica Tandy*; **Star Babies:** *Daughter of Robert and Kate Capshaw, Bruce Springsteen, Jeff Bridges*

JESUSA Spanish: Derived from Mary de Jesus, mother of Jesus Christ and a name for the Virgin Mary

JETTA Latin: Jet black
Jette

JEWEL Latin: Precious gem
Famous Namesakes: *Singer Jewel*

JILL English: Youthful; familar form of Jillian or Gillian
Gill, Jilly, Jyl, Jyll; **Famous Namesakes:** *Actress Jill St. John, Actress Jill Eikenberry*

JILLIAN English: Youthful; derived from the Latin name Julian
Gillian, Gillien, Jilian, Jillanne, Jillayne, Jillene, Jillesa, Jilliane, Jilliann, Jillianna, Jillianne, Jyllina; **Nicknames:** *Gill, Jill, Jilly, Jyl, Jyll;* **Famous Namesakes:** *Actress Jillian Bach;* **Star Babies:** *Daughter of Vanessa Williams and Ramon Hervey*

JIMENA Spanish: Heard

JIMI English: Modern feminine form of Jimmy, a familar form of James
Jimmi

JINA African: Named child (Swahili)

JINX Latin: Spell
Jinxx, Jynx

JO English: A familiar form of Joanna and other names beginning with "Jo"

JOAN Hebrew: Spelling variation of Jane

JOANNA Hebrew: Gift from God; variant of Joan, a feminine form of John
(Hebrew) *Johanna;* (German) *Johannah;* (Polish) *Joanka; Joann, Joanne, Ohanna;* **Nicknames:** *Jo;* **Star Babies:** *Daughter of Julie Andrews and Blake Edwards*

JOBINA Hebrew: Persecuted; feminine form of Job

JOCELYN French: Originally a boy's name, derived from the Germanic name Gautelen
(English) *Joceline; Jocelin, Jocelina, Jocelyne, Jocelynn, Josalind, Josalyn, Josalynn, Joscelin, Josceline, Joscelyn, Joscelyne, Josilyn, Joslin, Joslyn, Jozlyn;* **Famous Namesakes:** *Australian film director Jocelyn Moorhouse*

JOCHEBED Hebrew: God's glory

JODY English: Nickname for Judith
Jodi, Jodee, Jodie; **Famous Namesakes:** *Actress Jodie Foster*

JOELLE Hebrew, French: Lord is God; feminine form of Joel
Joeliyn, Joell, Joella, Joellen, Joelliana, Joelliane; **Famous Namesakes:** *Actress Joelle Carter*

JOELLEN French: Spelling variation of Joelle
Joeliyn, Joellyn

JOHANNAH Hebrew: Original form of Joanna

JOHNELLE English: Variation of Jane

JOHNETTA English: Variation of Jane

JOHNNA English: Spelling variation of Jane

JOHNNIE English: Spelling variation of Jane
Joni, Jonni, Jonnie, Johnny; **Famous Namesakes:** *Artist and author Joni Eareckson Tada*

JOLA Hebrew: God is willing

JOLENE English: Beautiful; variant of Jolie
Joleen, Jolina, Joline

JOLIE French: Beautiful
Jolee, Joleen, Joleigh, Joli, Jolien; **Nicknames:**
Jolena, Jolene, Jolina, Joline, Jolleen, Jollene;
Famous Namesakes: *Actress Angelina Jolie;*
Star Babies: *Daughter of Quincy Jones*

JONALYN English: Spelling variation of
Jane

JONATI Hebrew: Dove

JONELL English: Spelling variation of Jane
Jonelle, Jonnelle

JONETTA English: Diminutive form of Jane
Jonette

JONI English: Nickname for Jane
Famous Namesakes: *Singer Joni Mitchell*

JONNA English: Spelling variation of Jane

JORCINA English: Farmer; variant of
Georgia and Georgina
Jorcine

JORDAN Hebrew: To flow downward;
Jordan, the river in Palestine where Jesus was
baptized, has been used as a given name
since the Crusades.
(French) *Jordane;* (Italian) *Giordana;*
(Spanish) *Jordana; Jordanna, Jordanne,
Yardena, Yordana, Jordyn, Jordynn;*
Diminutive Forms: *Jori;* **Star Babies:**
*Daughter of Bono, Leeza Gibbons, Cheryl
Ladd*

JOSEPHINE Hebrew: May God give
increase; feminine form of Joseph
(Italian) *Guiseppina;* (Spanish) *Josefa, Josefina;*
(Irish) *Seosaimhthin;* (Hungarian) *Jozsefa;*
*Josebe, Josepha, Josephina, Josetta, Yosebe,
Yosepha, Yosephina;* **Nicknames:** *Fifna, Fifne,
Fina, Josee, Josie, Josina;* **Diminutive Forms:**
Fifi, Fifine, Josette; **Famous Namesakes:**
Singer Josephine Baker; **Star Babies:** *Daughter
of Linda Hamilton and James Cameron*

JOSETTE French: Diminutive form of
Josephine

JOSIE English: Nickname for Josephine

JOSLIN French: Spelling variation of
Jocelyn

JOSUNE Spanish: Named for Jesus

JOURNEY American: Travel

JOVENA Spanish: Feminine form of the
Roman name Jove, another name for Jupiter,
king of the gods and ruler of the universe in
Roman mythology
Jovana, Jovina; **Nicknames:** *Jovita*

*I have no name.
I am but two days old.
What shall I call thee?
I happy am,
Joy is my name.
Sweet joy befall thee!*
—William Blake,
from *Songs of Innocence*

JOY English, French: Joyous, merry; derived
from "joie," a word with Middle English and
Old French lineage. Joy is also used as a
familiar form of Jocelyn and Joyce.
(Latin) *Joya; Joi, Joia, Joie*

JOYANN English: Blend of the names Joy
(rejoicing) and Ann (graceful)
Joyanna, Joyanne, Joyceanne

JOYCE English: Joyous, merry; derived
from Latin word jocosa, meaning joyous; a
possible variant of Jocelyn
(Hawaiian) *Ioke; Joycelyn, Joycelynn*

JOYELLE French, English: Rejoicing

JUANA Spanish: God's gift; feminine form of Juan, the popular Spanish form of John

JUDAH Hebrew: Praised
Nicknames: *Jude*

JUDE Latin: Nickname for Judah

JUDITH Hebrew: Woman of Judea, praised one; Judith is a feminine form of Judah. Judea was the name of an ancient country in southern Palestine.
(French) *Judithe*; (Italian) *Guiditta*; (Scandinavian) *Judit*; (Hungarian) *Juci, Jucika*; *Yehudit*; **Nicknames:** *Joda, Jodee, Jodi, Jodie, Jody, Judi, Judie, Judy*; **Famous Namesakes:** *Dancer and choreographer Judith Jamison, Actress Judith Ivey*

JUDY Hebrew: Nickname for Judith
Judee, Judi, Judie; **Famous Namesakes:** *Actress Judy Garland, Singer Judy Collins, Actress Dame Judi Dench, Author Judy Blume*

JULIA Latin: Youthful, Jove's child; feminine form of Julian or Julius
(Italian) *Giulia, Guilia*; (Spanish) *Julina*; (Russian) *Ulyana, Yulia, Yuliya*; (Hungarian) *Juliska; Guilie, Iulia, Iulius, Julee, Juleen, Julene, Julesa, Juli, Julita*; **Nicknames:** *Ulya, Yulya*; **Diminutive Forms:** *Yulenka*; **Famous Namesakes:** *Actresses Julia Ormond and Julia Roberts, British chef Julia Child*; **Star Babies:** *Daughter of Shaun Cassidy, daughter of Tony Randall*

JULIANA Latin: Youthful; feminine form of Julian
(Italian) *Giuliana; Julianna, Julianne, Julieann, Julieanna, Julieanne, Julienne*;
Famous Namesakes: Musician Juliana Hatfield, Actress Julianna Margulies; **Star Babies:** *Daughter of Shelley Long*

JULIET French: Youthful, Jove's child; variant of Julia. Juliet is the star-crossed lover in the Shakespearean tragedy *Romeo and Juliet*.
(French) *Juliette*; (Italian) *Julietta*; (Spanish) *Julieta*; **Famous Namesakes:** *Actress Juliette Binoche*; **Star Babies:** *Daughter of Janine Turner*

JUNE Latin: Young; in Roman mythology, Juno was a protectress of women and marriage. In modern times, June is known as the bridal month.
Junae, Junel, Junia, Juno; **Diminutive Forms:** *Junelle, Junette*; **Famous Namesakes:** *Actress June Allyson*

JUSTINE Latin: Fair, just, upright; feminine form of Justin
Jestina, Jestine, Justa, Justeen, Justeene, Justene, Justina, Justyne; **Famous Namesakes:** *Actress Justine Bateman*; **Star Babies:** *Daughter of Louis Malle and Alexandra Stewart*

KABIRA African: Powerful

KACEY English: Alert, vigorous; a phonetic form of the initials K.C. or variant of the Irish name Casey
K.C., Kacee, Kaci, Kacie, Kacy, Kasey, Kayce, Kaycee, Kayci, Kaycie

KACIA English: Alert, vigorous; variant of Casey

KADIA English: Rhyming variant of Katy or Cady
Kadee, Kadi, Kadian, Kadie, Kadienne

KAESHA English: Modern form of Kacie

KAFI African: Quiet

KAI Native American: Willow tree, graceful (Navajo). Hawaiian: The sea

KAIA Greek: From the earth; mythological womanly personification of the earth and mother of the Titans; (Hawaiian) the sea (Greek) *Gaea*; (Finnish) *Kaija*

KAILA Hawaiian: Style

KAILANI Hawaiian: Sea and sky
Kalanie

KAILASA Hindi: Silver mountain

KAINDA African: Hunter's daughter

KAIRA Scandinavian: Nickname for Katherine

KAISA Greek, Finnish: Pure
Nicknames: *Kaisu*

KAISLA Finnish: Reed

KAITLYN Irish: Spelling variation of Caitlin
Kaitlan, Kaitleen, Kaitlin, Kaitlynn, Katelin, Kateline, Katelinn, Katelyn, Katelynn, Katlin, Katlyn, Katlynn, Katlynne

KAKALINA Hawaiian: Variation of Katherine

KALA Hawaiian: Variation of Sarah. Hindi: Black

KALAMA Hawaiian: Flaming torch

KALANI Hawaiian: Form of Kalani

KALANIT Hebrew: Flower

KALARA Latin: Shines
Kalate

KALEA Hawaiian: Bright
Kaleah

KALEI Hawaiian: The flower wreath

Why are there so many Hawaiian names beginning with K?

The Hawaiian alphabet, known as the piapa, contains only twelve letters: five vowels (a, e, i, o, u) and seven consonants (h, k, l, m, n, p, w). To "Hawaiinize" an English name containing consonants not found in the Hawaiian alphabet, trying using the below table. As you can see, more of the English consonants translate to K than to any other letter.

English:	Hawaiian:
B, F, P	P
C, D, G, J, K, Q, S, T, X, Z	K
H	H
L, R	L
M	M
N	N
V, W	W
Y	I

KALENA Hawaiian: Variation of Katherine

KALI Hawaiian: Hesitation. Hindi: In mythology, Kali is the wife of Shiva and a Hindu goddess symbolizing the essence of destruction.

KALIFA African: Chaste, holy (Somali)

KALIKA Greek: Rosebud
(African) *Kali*; *Kalyca*; **Nicknames:** *Kalie, Kaly*

KALINA Polish: A flower

KALINDA Hindi: The sun; a Hindu mythological reference to the mountains of Kalinda
Kalindi, Kalynda, Calinda

KALLAN Scandinavian: Flowing water, a stream. Gaelic: Powerful in battle

KALLISTA Greek: Spelling variation of Callista
Kalista, Kallysta; **Nicknames:** *Kallie*

KAMALA Hindi: One who is like a lotus

KAMEA Hawaiian: The one and only
Kameo

KAMEKO Japanese: Child of the tortoise

KAMI Japanese: Divine aura

KAMILA Arabic: Spelling variation of Camila. Czech: A Roman family name, possibly meaning noble
Kamilah, Kamilla, Kamille, Camila

KANELI Finnish: Cinnamon

KANERVA Finnish: Heather

KANIKA Egyptian: Black

KANYA Hindi: Virgin; the younger daughter

KARA Greek: Pure. Latin: Beloved, darling; variant of Cara

KARAMIE Arabic: Hospitable

KAREN Danish, English: Pure, innocent; variant of Katherine
(German) *Karin*; (Scandinavian) *Kariana, Karianna, Karianne*; (Finnish) *Kaarina*; *Caren, Carin, Caryn, Carynn, Karan, Karena, Kariann, Karina, Karon, Karrah, Karren, Karrin, Karyn*; **Nicknames:** *Kari, Karie, Karri, Karrie*; **Famous Namesakes:** *Musician Karen Carpenter, Actress Karen Allen*

KARIANNE Dutch: Blend of Katharina and Johanna
Carianne

KARIMA Arabic: Generous, noble-born lady or daughter; feminine variant of Karim
Karimah

KARINA Arabic: Companion or accomplice. English: Pure; abbreviation of Katherine
Kareen, Kareena, Karin, Qareen, Qareena, Qarin

KARINTHA English: Beauty

> *"Karintha is a woman. She who carries beauty, perfect as dusk when the sun goes down."*
> —Jean Toomer, *Cane*

KARISMA English: Divinely favored

KARLA German: Variation of Carla
Star Babies: *Daughter of Otis Redding*

KARLESHA Contemporary: Variation of Carla

KARLINA German: Spelling variation of Caroline

KARLOTTA German: Variation of Charlotte

KARLY German: Nickname for Carla

KARMA Sanskrit: Fate, destiny; Buddhist and Hindu concept of the inevitable effect of one's life actions
Carma

KAROLINA German: Variation of Caroline

KASEY Irish: Spelling variation of Casey

KASMIRA Slavic: Commanding peace

KASSIA Greek: Spelling variation of Cassia

KASTANJA Finnish: Chestnut

KASTEL American: Dew
(Finnish) *Kastehelmi*; *Kastelle*

KAT English: Nickname for Catherine

KATHERINE Greek: Pure, innocent; Katherine is a traditional name for women. It has variations in many languages and has been used since the third century A.D. Early Latin Forms Katerina and Caterina evolved into Katharine, Katherine, Catharine, and Catherine. Katherine is also a royal name: in England, it was borne by the formidable and popular Katherine of Aragon (1485–1536), first wife of Henry VIII, as well as by the wives of Henry V and Charles II. See also *Karina*
(Greek) *Kasienka, Kolena, Kolina*; (French) *Carine*; (Scandinavian) *Karielle*; (Danish) *Kasen*; (Polish) *Kaska*; (Finnish) *Katja*; (Hawaiian) *Kakalina, Kalena*; (Yiddish) *Reina*; *Katheryn*; *Karalee, Karalie, Katharine, Katharyn, Kathelyn, Katherina, Kathrina, Kathrine, Kathryn, Kathryne, Kathrynn, Kethryn, Kathrin, Katherin, Katharin, Katrine*;

Nicknames: *Kaira, Karah, Kathe, Käthe, Kathy, Kay, Kath, Kathye, Kat, Katie, Katy, Kate*; **Famous Namesakes:** *Actress Katharine Hepburn, Actress Katharine Ross;* **Star Babies:** *Daughter of Sting, daughter of Tony Danza*

KATHLEEN Irish: Pure or innocent; variant of Catherine. Bing Crosby crooned the famous ballad, "I'll Take You Home Again, Kathleen."
Cathleen, Cathlin, Kathleena, Kathlene, Kathlynn; **Nicknames:** *Kathy, Kathye, Kath, Leen*; **Famous Namesakes:** *Actress Kathleen Turner, Hollywood producer Kathleen Kennedy*

KATHY English: Nickname for Katherine
Cathy, Kathye; **Nicknames:** *Kath*; **Famous Namesakes:** *Actress Kathy Bates*

KATICA Greek: Nickname for Catherine
Nicknames: *Katy*

KATIE English: Pure, innocent; a familiar form of Catherine, Katherine, and their spelling variants that can stand as an independent name as well
Katy; **Nicknames:** *Kat, Kate*; **Famous Namesakes:** *News anchor Katie Couric, Lifestyle guru Katie Brown, Actress Kate Hudson;* **Star Babies:** *Daughter of George Lucas*

KATRINA Scandinavian: Variation of Catherine

KATYA Russian: Nickname for Catherine
Katia; **Star Babies:** *Daughter of Hunter Tylo*

KAY Scandinavian, Greek: Pure, keeper of the keys; an abbreviation of Katherine and other names beginning with K. Sir Kay was one of King Arthur's knights.
Kaye

KAYA Native American: My elder sister (Hopi)

KAYANA English: Blend of Kay and Anna (English) *Kayanna*

KAYLA English: The laurel crown. See also *Kaila*
Kailah; Caila, Cayla, Kaela, Kaelah, Caylah, Caela, Caelah

KAYLEY English: Uncertain meaning; Kayley could likely derive from a Gaelic word meaning slender, but may also be a variant of Kay.
Caileigh, Cailley, Caleigh, Callee, Calli, Caylee, Cayley, Caylie, Kaelee, Kaeleigh, Kaeley, Kaeli, Kaelie, Kailee, Kailey, Kalee, Kaleigh, Kaley, Kalie, Kaylea, Kaylee, Kaylei, Kayleigh, Kayli, Kaylie; **Nicknames:** *Kaelene, Kaelin, Kaelyn, Kaelynn, Kailan, Kailene, Kailin, Kailyn, Kailynne, Kalan, Kalen, Kalin, Kalyn, Kalynn, Kaylan, Kayleen, Kaylen, Kaylene, Kaylin, Kaylyn, Kaylynn*

KAYSA Swedish: Nickname for Catherine

KEALA Hawaiian: The pathway

KEANNA Irish: Ancient; feminine form of Kian or Keane

KEARA Irish: Dark-haired; feminine form of Kieran
Keira, Kera, Keriam, Keriana, Keriann, Kerianna, Kerianne, Kerilyn, Kerra, Kerri, Kerrianne, Kerrie

KEARNEY Irish: Victorious

KEARY Celtic: Father's dark child

KEELY Celtic: Beautiful
Famous Namesakes: *Actress Keely Shaye Smith*

KEELYN Irish: Lively, aggressive; variant of Kelly
Keelia, Keelin

KEESHA English: Nickname for Lakeisha

KEIKI Hawaiian: Child

KEILANI Hawaiian: Glorious chief

KEISHA English: Nickname for Lakeisha
Famous Namesakes: *Actress Keisha Castle-Hughes, Actress Keisha Knight-Pulliam*

KELBY Norse: Farm near the spring

KELDA Norse: Fountain or from the ship's island

KELILAH Hebrew: Laurel crown
Kelula, Kelila

KELLAN Gaelic: Blend of Kelly and Ellen

KELLSEY Irish: Brave

KELLY Irish: Warrior or bright-minded; originally a boy's name
Keeley, Keilah, Kelleigh, Kellen, Kelley, Kelli, Kellie, Kellye, Kellyn; **Famous Namesakes:** *Actress Kelly Ripa, Actress Kelly McGillis;* **Star Babies:** *Daughter of Larry King*

KELLYANNE Gaelic: Blend of Kelly and Anne. Irish: Lively, aggressive

KELSEY Scottish: From the island, possibly from the island of ships. English: Spelling variant of Chelsea. See also *Kellsey*
Kelcey, Kelcie, Kelcy, Kellsie, Kelsee, Kelsi, Kelsie, Kelsy; **Nicknames:** *Kelsa;* **Star Babies:** *Daughter of Kelly McGillis, daughter of Gabrielle Carteris*

KEMINA Spanish: Strong
Kemena

KENDALL English: Valley of the Kent; this surname has become a unisex name and likely refers to a river in England.
Kendal, Kendyl, Kyndall; **Star Babies:** *Daughter of Bruce Jenner*

KENDRA English: Blend of Ken (royal obligation, clear water) and Sandra (protector of man) or Andrea (manly or masculine); also feminine form of Kendrick (fearless leader). Anglo-Saxon: Water baby

KENISHA English: Modern creation, possible blend of Kenya and Aisha

KENNA English: Born of fire, good-looking; feminine form of Kenneth
Kenina

KENNEDY Irish: Helmet-head; a traditionally male name now used for either gender
Kennadi, Kennady, Kennedi

KENYA English: A country in Africa
Star Babies: *Daughter of Nastassja Kinski and Quincy Jones*

KENZINGTON English: Handsome, fiery; surname

KEREN Hebrew: Ray, beam, light, glory, horn, beauty; abbreviation of Kerenhappuch. In the Bible, Keren was one of Job's three daughters.
Kelyn, Keran, Kerrin, Keryn

KERI Irish: Spelling variation of Kerry

KERIANA Irish: Spelling variation of Keara

KERRY Gaelic, Irish: Dark haired; a country in Ireland
Keri, Carrie, Cari, Kari, Karrie, Kerrie

KERSTIN Swedish: Variation of Christina

KESARA Spanish: Long-haired; feminine form of Caesar

KESAVA Hindi: She of the beautiful hair

KEVIA English: Beautiful child; feminine form of Kevin
Kevina, Kevya; **Nicknames:** *Keva*

KHALILA Arabic: Dearly beloved, darling, sweetheart, friend; feminine form of Khalil
Kalila, Khaleela, Khaleelah

KHANDAN Persian: Smiling

KHEPRI Egyptian: The scarab-beetle god identified with Re (Ra) as a creator god; often represented as a beetle within the sun-disk

KHINA Persian: Sweet voice, song

KIANA Hawaiian: Variation of Diana

KIANDRA Irish: Spelling variation of Keana

KIELO Finnish: Lily of the valley

KIKKA German: Mistress of all

KILIWA Hawaiian: Variation of Sylvia

KIMBERLY English: English surname with an original meaning now unknown, but which almost certainly refers to a meadow. Some speculation exists that it is derived from a word referring to a royal meadow camp. Traditionally a boys' name, Kimberly is now more popularly used for girls.
Cimberleigh, Cymberly, Cynburleigh, Cyneburhleah, Kimberlee, Kimberleigh, Kimberley, Kimberli, Kimberlie, Kimberlyn, Kimblyn, Kymberleigh, Kymberley, Kymmberly, Kymbra, Kymbrely; **Nicknames:** *Kim, Kimber, Kimbra, Kimm, Kimmi, Kimmy, Kym*

KIMI Native American: Secret (Algonquin)

KIMIA Persian: Alchemy

KIMIMELA Native American: Butterfly (Sioux)

KIRA Latin: Spelling variation of Kyra

KIRBY English: Church village, Teutonic residence; the Kirby coat of arms came into existence centuries ago. The process of creating coats of arms (often called family crests) began in the eighth and ninth centuries.

KIRIE Latin: Light

KIRSTEN Scandinavian, English: Christian **Nicknames:** *Kirstie, Kirsty*

KIRSTIE Greek: Nickname for Kirsten *Kirsty*; **Famous Namesakes:** *Actress Kirstie Alley*

KIT English: Nickname for Catherine

KITTY English: Nickname for Catherine **Famous Namesakes:** *Singer and actress Kitty Carlisle Hart*

KIVI Hebrew: Protected

KLARA Swedish: Variation of Clara

KLARIKA Latin: Clear *Klarisza*; **Nicknames:** *Klari*

KOBRA Persian: Major

KOKO Native American: Night (Blackfoot)

KOLETE Greek: People's victory

KOLETTE Greek: Spelling variation of Colette

KONA Hawaiian: Lady

KRISTIN German: Variation of Christina

KRISTINE Latin, Danish: Follower of Christ; variant of Christine (Polish) *Krystyn*; *Kristeena, Kristena, Kristian, Kristiana, Kristiane, Kristianna, Kristianne, Kristyne, Krystiana, Krystianna, Krystine*; **Nicknames:** *Kris, Krissie, Krissy, Kristie, Kristy*

KUKKA Finnish: Flower

KYLA Gaelic, Hebrew: Victorious; a narrow strait or channel *Kylah, Kylea, Kyleen, Kyley, Kyli, Kylianne, Kylin*

KYLIE Gaelic, Celtic: Victorious; a narrow strait or channel *Kylee, Kyleigh, Kiley*; **Star Babies:** *Singer Kylie Minogue*

KYNA Gaelic: Intelligent

KYOKO Japanese: Capital city

KYRA Latin, Greek: Light; feminine form of Cyrus and variant of Cyra *Kira*; **Famous Namesakes:** *Actress Kyra Sedgwick*

KYRABEL English: Modern blend of Kyra and Belle

LACEY French: Derived from a French nobleman's surname brought to the British Isles after the Norman conquest
Lacee, Lacene, Laci, Laciann, Lacie, Lacina, Lacy, Lacyann, Laycie; **Nicknames:** *Lace*; **Famous Namesakes:** *Actress Lacey Chabert*; **Star Babies:** *Daughter of Jackie Zeman*

LACHESIS Greek: In Greek mythology, Lachesis was the second of the three fates. Her job was to measure the thread of life spun by Clotho.

LADA Russian: An Eastern European goddess of spring and love, Lada was worshipped throughout Lithuania, Poland, and Russia.

LADAN Persian: A flower

LAHJA Finnish: Gift

LAILA Arabic, Finnish, Persian: Born at night, nightfall; Qays, a seventh-century Arab poet, named the central character in his poems Laila.
Laylah, Leilah, Leyla, Leila, Lailah; **Star Babies:** *Daughter of Muhammad Ali*

LAJILA Hindi: Shy, modest

LAKEISHA American: Popular modern name, possibly an elaboration of Aisha (woman) using "La" as a prefix, but may also be a variant of Letitia (joyful)
Lakesha, Lakeshia, Lakiesha, Lakisha, Laquisha, LaKisha, LaKeesha, LaKysha; **Nicknames:** *Kecia, Keesha, Keisha, Kisha*

LAKEN American: Nature name, taken from lake, a body of water
Laiken, Layken, Laikyn

LAKSHMI Hindi: A good sign; a goddess of good fortune and wife of Vishnu

LALA Slavic: Tulip

LALASA Hindi: Love
Lalassa, Lallasa

LALEH Persian: Tulip

LALIA Greek: Talkative, chatterer
Lalage

LALITA Sanskrit: Pleasant, playful; in Hindu mythology, Lalita is playmate to the god Krishna.

LAMPETO Latin: Amazon leader mentioned in mythology

LANA Latin: Woolly, soft wool. English: Abbreviation for names such as Helen, Alana, and Svetlana. Irish: Content, pretty and peaceful. Hawaiian: Floating, frequently a part of Hawaiian names as well as a name itself
Lanna; **Famous Namesakes:** *Actress Lana Turner*

LANAI Hawaiian: Terrace

LANDA Spanish: Reference to the Virgin Mary

LANDRADA Spanish: Counselor
Nicknames: *Landra*

LANDRY English: Ruler of the place

LANE English: Path or small roadway
Laina, Laine, Lainie, Laney, Lanie; **Famous Namesakes:** *Actress Diane Lane, Fictional reporter Lois Lane*

LANGLEY English: From the long meadow; a surname and traditionally a boy's name, now being used for both genders. Langley, Virginia, is the famous home of the CIA.
Langlea, Langleah, Langly; **Star Babies:** *Daughter of Mariel Hemingway*

LANKA Hindi: From Lanka

LAODAMIA Greek: In Greek mythology, she was the wife of Protesilaus, the first Greek to be slain by the Trojans. Granted the chance for one last meeting with her dead husband, she decided she could not live without him and followed him.

LAPIS Egyptian: A beautiful azure-blue stone that has been used in jewelry and for its medicinal value since ancient times

LARA Latin: Famous, shining; Lara was a mythological Roman nymph who betrayed the love affair of Jupiter and Juturna, and was struck speechless as a result. Greek: Cheerful, happy; variant of Larissa, Laura, and Laraine
(Hawaiian) *Lala*; *Larae, Lari, Laria, Larah, Lariah, Larra, Larya, Laryah*; **Famous Namesakes:** *Actress Lara Flynn Boyle*; **Star Babies:** *Daughter of Bob Saget*

LARALAINE Latin: Modern blend of Lara/Laura and Elaine

LARAMAE Latin: Modern blend of Lara/Laura and Mae/May

LAREINA Spanish: The queen

LARENTIA Latin: She-wolf who nursed Remus and Romulus; variant of Laurentia

LARINA Greek: Sea gull. Danish: Feminine form of Lars
(Danish) *Larine*

LARINDA Latin: Protection; derived from lares, individual Roman household gods who were protectors of home and fields.

LARISSA Greek: Cheerful; in Greek mythology, Larissa was the mother of Pelasgus. Larissa is also the name of a city in Greece and is a moon of the planet Neptune. See also Lara.

(Spanish) *Larisa*; (Russian) *Laryssa*; *Larisse*; **Nicknames:** *Lara, Risa*

LARK English: Lark, a songbird
Larke; **Star Babies:** *Daughter of Mia Farrow and Andre Previn*

LARKIN English: Songbird; also an adapted surname meaning belonging to Laurence

LASSIE Scottish: Little girl; the name of the beloved and brave canine heroine of Eric Knight's classic, *Lassie Come Home.*
Lassey, Lassi, Lassy; **Nicknames:** *Lass*

> *"Lassie wi' the lint-white locks,*
> *Bonie lassie, artless lassie,*
> *Wilt thou wi' me tent the flocks,*
> *Wilt thou be my Dearie, O?"*
> —Robert Burns,
> "Lassie wi' the Lint-white Locks"

LATASHA English: Joyful, glad; modern variant of Letitia

LATONIA Latin: Feminine form of Anthony

LATOYA Spanish: Victorious one; possibly derived from Victoria
Famous Namesakes: *Singer LaToya Jackson*

LATRICE African: Noble woman
Latricia

LAURA Latin: The laurel or sweet bay tree, symbolic of honor and victory; old name with many variants
(German) *Lorita*; (French) *Laure, Laurie*; (Spanish) *Laurinda, Laurita, Lora*; (Scottish) *Lorna*; (Russian) *Lavra*; *Lauica, Laurissa, Lorah, Loria, Lorinda, Loris*; **Nicknames:** *Lori*; **Famous Namesakes:** *Author Laura Ingalls Wilder, Actress Laura Linney, Actress Laura Dern*

LAURALEE English: Spelling variation of Lorelei

LAUREL Latin, English, French: The laurel tree or sweet bay tree is symbolic of honor and victory. This is an old name with many variants.
Laural, Lauralyn, Laurella, Laurelle, Lauriel

LAUREN Latin: Laurel, symbolic of honor and victory; Lauren is also a feminine form of Laurence, meaning from Laurentium, a city in ancient Italy.
Laureen, Laurena, Laurene, Laurenne, Laurina, Lauryn, Loreen, Loreene, Loren, Lorena, Lorene, Lorenia, Lorenna, Lorin, Lorren, Lorrin, Lorrina, Loryn; **Famous Namesakes:** *Actress Lauren Bacall, Model Lauren Hutton*

LAURENA English: Spelling variation of Lauren

LAURENTIA Latin: Crowned with laurel or from Laurentium, a city in ancient Italy known for its laurel trees
(Italian) *Lorenza*; (Spanish) *Laurencia*; *Larentia*

LAVEDA Latin: Purified
Lavare, Lavetta, Lavette

LAVERNE Latin: Spring, springlike
La Vergne, La Verne, Lavern, Laverna, Verna; **Diminutive Forms:** *Vernita*

LAVINIA Latin: Women of Rome; in Roman legend, Lavinia was the daughter of King Latinus and the wife of Aeneas, a Trojan hero in Greek and Roman mythology. According to legend, Aeneas founded the city of Lavinium and named it in honor of his wife.
(Spanish) *Levina, Luvenia, Luvina*; *Lavena, Lavina*

LEA Hawaiian: Mythological goddess of canoe builders

LEAH Hebrew: Weary; in the Bible's Old Testament, Leah was the first wife of Jacob, and ancestress to the twelve tribes of Israel. Leah and her sister Rachel were considered symbols of the active (Leah) and the contemplative (Rachel) lives.
(French) *Léa*; **Famous Namesakes:** *Actress Lea Thompson, Chef Leah Chase*

> *"If anyone should want to know my name, I am called Leah. And I spend all my time weaving garlands of flowers with my fair hands."*
> —Dante Alighieri,
> *The Divine Comedy*

LEAL African: Faithful

LEALA French: Spelling variation of Lela

LEANDRA Greek: Lioness; feminine form of Leander
Leodora, Leoine, Leoline, Leona, Leonelle, Leonette, Leonice

LEANN English: Origin unclear, possibly a variant of Liana, which is a short form of Juliana (young), or a modern blend of the names Lee and Ann.
Leana, Leanna, Leianna, Leanne, Leeann, Leeanne; **Famous Namesakes:** *Singer LeAnn Rimes*

LECHSINSKA Polish: A woodland spirit of legend

LEDA Greek: Mythological queen of Sparta and mother of Castor and Pollux, Leda was seduced by Zeus who came to her in the form of a swan. That union resulted in the birth of her daughter, Helen of Troy.
Leta, Leyda, Lyda

LEE English: Meadow; an adapted surname now used as a given name for girls and boys
Lea, Leia, Leigh, Ley; **Famous Namesakes:** *Actress Lee Merriweather, Actress Lee Remick*

LEELA Sanskrit: Playful
Lila

LEGARRE Spanish: Reference to the Virgin Mary

LEHANA African: One who refuses

LEIGH English: Spelling variation of Lee

LEIGHTON English: From the meadow town or settlement; surname

LEILA Arabic: Born at night; music fans will surely recognize Layla from the popular Eric Clapton song.
Laila, Laili, Lailie, Layla, Laylie; **Star Babies:** *Daughter of Greta Sacchi and Vincent D´Onofrio, Deborah Roberts and Al Roker*

LEILANI Hawaiian: Child of heaven, heavenly flowers
Nicknames: *Lani, Leia*

LEIRIA Spanish: Reference to the Virgin Mary

LELIA Latin: A Roman clan name of uncertain meaning. Greek: Well-spoken; a variant of Eulalia
Laelia, Lelah

LEMMIKKI Finnish: Sweetheart

LEMPI Finnish: Love

LENA Latin: A common pet form in several languages for names like Helena, Elena, Caroline, Magdalena, and Marlene
Leena, Lina; **Famous Namesakes:** *Actress Lena Olin, Singer Lena Horne*

LENAE English: Light; blend of Lena and Renee

LENIS Latin: Mild
Lenet, Leneta, Lenita

LENORA English: Light; variant of Leonora

LEOCADIA Spanish: Name of an island in Greece and a fourth-century Spanish saint
(French) *Léocadie*

LEODA German: Of the people
Leota

LEONA Latin: Lioness; feminine form of Leon
(French) *Leone, Leonie*; (Spanish) *Leonita*; *Leoine, Leoline, Leonce, Leonda, Leondra, Leondrea, Leonela, Leonelle, Leonlina, Lonna*; **Nicknames:** *Loni, Lonnie*

LEONARDA French: Lion; feminine form of Leonard

LEONORA Greek: Light; a variant of Helena. See also *Lenora*
(German) *Leonore*; (French) *Léonore*; (Spanish) *Leonor*; *Lenore*; **Nicknames:** *Leola, Nora, Norah*

LEONTYNE English: Like a lioness
Leontin, Leontina, Leontine; **Famous Namesakes:** *Opera diva Leontyne Price*

LEOPOLDA German: Of the people
Leopoldina, Leopoldine

LEORA Greek: Light; a nickname for Eleanor
Liora

LEPEKA Hawaiian: Variation of Rebecca

LERA Spanish: Reference to the Virgin Mary

LESLIE Scottish, Gaelic: From the gray fortress, smaller meadow, or garden of hollies; Leslie was derived from a Scottish place name, became a surname, and is now used as a first name for both sexes.
Leslee, Lesley, Lezlie

LETA Latin: Joyful
Lita

LETHE Greek: Forgetfulness; in Greek mythology, Lethe was the River of Oblivion that caused the dead to forget about their past lives.
Leitha, Letha, Lethia

LETITIA Latin: Joyful, glad
(Italian) *Letizia*; (Spanish) *Leticia*; *Laetitia, Lateisha, Latesha, Laticia, Latisha, Letisha*; **Nicknames:** *Latasha, Lettie, Letty*

LEUCIPPE Greek: A mythological nymph

LEUCOTHEA Greek: This mythological sea nymph was known as the White Goddess after she followed her son into the sea. Dionysus rescued her and she became Leucothea.
Leucothia

LEVANA Latin: To rise; Levana was a Roman mythological goddess and protectress of newborns.

LEVENE English: Nickname for Levina

LEVIA Hebrew: Lioness of the Lord
Leviah

LEVINA English: Flash, lightning
Levyna; **Nicknames:** *Levene*

LEXIE English: Nickname for Alexandra
Lexi, Lexina, Lexine, Lexy

LEYA Hindi: Lion. Spanish: The law

LIA Greek: Bringer of good news; also an abbreviation of names like Amalia and Rosalia

LIADAN Irish: Gray lady

LIAN Chinese: Graceful willow

LIANA French, Spanish: Lily
(French) *Liane*; *Leana, Leann*

LIANNA English: Spelling variation of Eliana

LIBBY English: Consecrated one, my God is bountiful, God of plenty; used alone or as a pet form or variant of Elizabeth

LIBERTY English: Freedom
(Latin) *Libera, Libertas*; (French) *Liberté*; **Star Babies:** *Daughter of Jean and Casey Kasem*

LIEALIA French: Spelling variation of Lela

LIGIA Greek: Clear voice
Liegia

LIL Irish: Nickname for Lilian

LILA English: A pet form of Lilian or Delilah. Persian: Lilac. Sanskrit: Playful
Lyla, Lilah

LILAC Persian: Lilac

LILIAN Latin: Lily; symbolic of innocence, purity, and beauty
(Hebrew) *Lilah*; (Greek) *Lilika, Lilis*; (German) *Lilli*; (French) *Liliane*; (Italian) *Liliana*; (Finnish) *Lilja*; *Lila, Lilch, Lilia, Lilianna, Lilianne, Lilith, Lilla, Lillian, Lilliana, Lilliane, Lilliann, Lillianna, Lillis*; **Old Forms:** *Lillium*; **Nicknames:** *Lil, Lili, Lilie, Lillie, Lilly, Lily*; **Famous Namesakes:** *Author Lillian Hellman*

LILO Hawaiian: Generous one; Lilo was the tiny heroine in the Disney film *Lilo and Stitch.*

LILY English: The lily is a flower symbolic of innocence, purity, and beauty.
Nicknames: *Lil, Lili, Lilie, Lillie, Lilly, Lilli;*
Famous Namesakes: *Actress Lily Tomlin;*
Star Babies: *Daughter of Chris O'Donnell and Caroline Fentriss, Amy Madigan and Ed Harris, Kathy Ireland, Meredith Vieira*

LILYBETH English: Blend of Lily and Elizabeth
Lilybet, Lilibeth

LIMA Latin: Mythological goddess of the threshold
Limentina

LIN English: Waterfall or lake; spelling variation of Lynn; (Chinese) forest or beautiful jade

LINA Latin: A popular variant in several languages of names ending with "-line" or "-lina." Arabic, Persian: Tender
Leena, Lena

LINDA Spanish, English: Pretty; may also refer to the linden, an ornamental shade tree also used for medicinal purposes
Lynda, Lyndall, Lyndee; **Nicknames:** *Lindi, Lindie, Lindy, Lyndi;* **Famous Namesakes:** *Actress Lynda Carter, Journalist Linda Ellerbee*

LINDEN English: The linden tree; this name describes a group of beautiful and often ornamental shade trees

LINDSAY English, Scottish: Island of linden trees
Lindsey, Linsey, Lyndsay, Lyndsey, Lyndsie, Lynsey, Lynzee, Lynzie; **Star Babies:** *Daughter of Billy Crystal*

LINKA Hungarian: Mannish

LINNEA Scandinavian: Lime tree or small mountain flower
Linna, Linnae, Lynae; **Nicknames:** *Nea*

LIOR Hebrew: The light is with me, God's gift of light to me
Liora

LIRIT Hebrew: Lyrical, poetic, musical
Lirita

LISA English: My God is bountiful; variation of Elizabeth
(Finnish) *Liisa; Lesa;* **Famous Namesakes:** *Actress Lisa Kudrow*

LISETTE German: Devoted to God
Lysette, Lizette, Lizete

LISSA English: Honey; Lissa is an abbreviation of Melissa, Lissandra, and Alyssa. Lissa is also the name of a mother goddess in African mythology.
Lyssa

LITONYA Native American: Darting hummingbird (Miwok)

LIV Norse: Life; also a familiar form for names like Olivia or Livana
Famous Namesakes: *Actress Liv Tyler, Actress Liv Ullmann*

LIVANA Hebrew: White or the moon
Levana; **Nicknames:** *Leva, Liv, Liva*

LIZ English: Nickname for Elizabeth

LOANE Celtic: Light

LODEMA English: Guide
Lodima, Lodyma

LOGAN American: From the Gaelic name meaning from the hollow; Logan has become a unisex name in addition to being a surname.

LOIS English: Uncertain meaning, possibly a variant of Louise or from a Greek word meaning better. The biblical Lois was a grandmother of Timothy.
Loes

LOKELANI Hawaiian: Small red rose

LOLA Spanish: Nickname for Dolores
Famous Namesakes: *Singer Lola Falana;*
Star Babies: *Daughter of Annie Lennox*

LONDON English: Place name for the capital of the United Kingdom
Londyn, Londynn, Loundyn, Loundynn

LONI English: Lioness; a variant of Leona; (Hawaiian) sky
Lonnie; **Famous Namesakes:** *Actress Loni Anderson*

LORANNA German: Variation of Loriann

LOREA Spanish: Flower

LOREEN English: Spelling variation of Lauren

LORELEI German: Temptress whose singing lures men to destruction; also a rocky cliff on the Rhine River dangerous to boat passage
Lauralee, Lauralie, Loralei

LORELLE Latin: Little laurel
Lorella, Lorilla

LORENA English: Spelling variation of Lauren

LORETTA Latin: Little laurel; diminutive form of Laura
(French) *Laurette; Lauretta, Loreta, Lorette;*
Famous Namesakes: *Singer Loretta Lynn, Actress Loretta Young*

LORI English: Nickname for Laura
Famous Namesakes: *Actress Lori Loughlin, Actress Lori Singer*

LORIA English: Spelling variation of Laura

LORIANN English: Refers to the laurel tree or sweet bay tree, symbolic of honor and victory; modern variant of Lora and Laurie
(German) *Loranna;* (Spanish) *Laurana; Lorian, Loriana, Lorianne*

LORIEL English: Modern variant of Lora and Laurie, referring to the laurel tree or sweet bay tree symbolic of honor and victory

LORILLA Latin: Spelling variation of Lorelle

LORILYNN English: Modern variant of Lora and Laurie, referring to the laurel tree or sweet bay tree symbolic of honor and victory

LORIN French: Spelling variation of Lauren

LORNA Scottish: Variation of Laura

LORRAINE French: From Lorraine, the name of a province in France and a French royal family
(English) *Lareina; Laraine, Larraine, Lauraine, Loraina, Loraine, Lorayne, Lorraina, Lorine;* **Nicknames:** *Lori, Lors, Lora;* **Famous Namesakes:** *Author Lorraine Hansberry, Actress Laraine Newman;* **Star Babies:** *Daughter of Rebecca Broussard and Jack Nicholson*

LORRELLA Teutonic: Form of Laurel

LOTTE German: Nickname for Charlotte

LOTUS Greek: The lotus flower

LOU German: Nickname for Louise

LOUELLA English: Blend of names Louise (renowned warrior) and Ella (all) (Spanish) *Luella*

LOUISE German, French: Renowned warrior; feminine form of Louis (German) *Louisa, Luise*; (Italian) *Luigina, Luisa*; (Spanish) *Luiza*; (Gaelic) *Liusaidh*; (Irish) *Labhaoise*; (Scandinavian) *Lovisa*; (Finnish) *Loviisa*; (Hungarian) *Lujza; Louisane*; **Nicknames:** *Lou, Loulou;* **Famous Namesakes:** *Actress Mary-Louise Parker, Author Louisa Mae Alcott;* **Star Babies:** *Daughter of Prince Edward and Sophie Wessex*

LOURDES Spanish: Reference to the Virgin Mary; taken from a town in France that became famous as a shrine for Catholic pilgrims after a peasant girl was said to have had visions of the Virgin Mary at a grotto there *Louredes*; **Nicknames:** *Lorda, Lola;* **Star Babies:** *Daughter of Madonna*

LOVE English: Love, affection
Nicknames: *Lovelyn*

LOVELYN English: Variant of Love

LUANA German: A blend of Louise and Ann *Luane, Louann, Louanna, Louanne, Luann*

LUBA Russian: Nickname for Lubov
Lyuba

LUBOV Russian: Love
Lubava; **Nicknames:** *Luba;* **Diminutive Forms:** *Lyubochka;* **Famous Namesakes:** *Russian actress Lubov Orlova*

LUCERIA Latin: Circle of light
(Russian) *Lukeriya, Lusha*

LUCERNE Latin: Circle of light, lamp; also a city in Switzerland
Lucerna

LUCIANNA Italian: Graceful, light, illumination

LUCILLE French: Variation of Lucy
Lucila, Lucile, Lucilla; **Nicknames:** *Luci, Lucie, Lucy;* **Famous Namesakes:** *Actress Lucille Ball*

LUCINA Latin: Illumination; Lucina was a mythological Roman goddess of childbirth and giver of first light to newborns.
(Spanish) *Lucena; Lucinna*

LUCINDA Latin: Spelling variation of Lucy
Nicknames: *Cyndee, Cyndi, Cyndy*

LUCINE Armenian: Moon

LUCJA Polish: Bright; Polish form of Lucille

LUCRECE French: From the Latin name Lucretia; Lucrece goes back to the Renaissance era (Lucrezia Borgia was sister to Cesare Borgia).

LUCRETIA Latin: Unknown meaning; feminine form of the clan name Lucretius. See also *Lucrece*
(Italian) *Lucrezia*; (Spanish) *Lucrecia;* **Famous Namesakes:** *Antislavery and women's rights leader Lucretia Mott*

LUCY Latin: Light; a vernacular form of Lucia, the feminine form of Lucius
(French) *Lucette, Lucie, Lucienne, Lucile, Lucille*; (Italian) *Lucia, Luciana, Lucilla*; (Spanish) *Lucila, Lucita; Luci, Lucinda;* **Nicknames:** *Lou, Lu, Lulu;* **Famous Namesakes:** *Actress Lucille Ball, Actress Lucy Liu;* **Star Babies:** *Daughter of Mimi Rogers*

LUCYNA Polish: Bright; Polish form of Lucille

LUDMILA Russian: Loved by people
Lyudmila; **Nicknames:** *Luda*

LUISA Spanish: Variation of Louise

LUJZA Hungarian: Variation of Louise
Famous Namesakes: *Hungarian actress Lujza Blaha*

LULU English: Pet form of names such as Louise, Louella, or even Lucy. African: Pearl. Native American: Rabbit
Star Babies: *Daughter of Edie Brickell and Paul Simon*

LUMI Finnish: Snow

LUNA Latin: Moon
Lunetta

LUNDI French: Monday

LUPERCA Latin: In mythology, the goddess of herds and fruitfulness; Luperca, the wife of Lupercus, changed into the she-wolf who nursed Romulus and Remus.

LUR Spanish: Earth

LURLEEN German: Temptress; a modern variant of Lorelei
Lurlene, Lurlina, Lurline

LUSHA Russian: Variation of Luceria

LUZ Spanish: Light; Maria de la Luz (Mary of the Light) is another name for the Virgin Mary

LYCORIAS Greek: A mythological sea nymph

LYDIA Greek, Swedish: From Lydia (Russian) *Lidia, Lidija, Lidiya; Lydea;*
Nicknames: *Liddie, Liddy;* **Star Babies:** *Daughter of Bill Paxton*

LYNAE Scandinavian: Spelling variation of Linnea

LYNETTE English, Welsh: Variant of ancient Welsh name Eiluned (shape or form) or Lynn (waterfall); in Arthurian legend, Lynette accompanied Sir Gareth on a knightly quest.
Lanette, Linette, Linnette, Luned, Lynelle, Lynessa, Lynet, Lynley, Lynnet, Lynnette;
Nicknames: *Lynna, Lynne, Lyn, Lynn*

LYNN English: Waterfall or lake
Linn, Linne, Lyn, Lynna, Lynne, Lin

LYRA Greek: Of the lyre or song; lyrical
Lyric, Lyrica, Lyris

LYRIC English: Nickname for Lyra
Star Babies: *Daughter of Kenny and Tami Anderson*

LYS French: Lily

LYSANDRA Greek: Liberator; feminine form of Lysander, and sometimes used as a variant of Alexandra
Lisandra, Lisanne, Lissandra, Lizandra, Lizann

LYSIPPE Latin: Lets loose the horses; in Greek mythology, Lysippe was an Amazon queen revered for her intelligence and bravery. She was killed in battle, a heroine of her people.

MAARIT Finnish: Variation of Margaret

MAAT Egyptian: Mythical goddess of orderly conduct, order, truth and justice, she was represented as a woman with an ostrich feather on her head.

MAB Irish: Happiness; Mab was known as the fairies' midwife, but she delivered dreams, not children.

MABEL English: Lovable; abbreviation of Amabel
(Welsh) *Mabli*; *Mabelle, Mable*; **Famous Namesakes:** *Actress Mabel Albertson;* **Star Babies:** *Daughter of Tracey Ullman and Allan McKeown*

"O, then, I see Queen Mab hath been with you.

She is the fairies' midwife, and she comes

In shape no bigger than an agate-stone

On the fore-finger of an alderman"

William Shakespeare, *Romeo and Juliet*

MABINA Celtic: Nimble
Mabbina

MACHA Irish: In Irish mythology, Macha was one of the three aspects of the goddess of war and destruction, along with Bodb and Morrigan.

MACHARA Scottish: Plain

MACKENNA Scottish: Child of the handsome one
Makenna, Mckenna; **Nicknames:** *Kenna, Mac*

MACKENZIE Scottish: Child of the fair or wise one
Mckenzie, MacKenzie, McKenzie, Makenzie; **Nicknames:** *Kenzie*; **Famous Namesakes:** *Actress Mackenzie Phillips*

MACY French: Possibly from an Old French word meaning Matthew's estate, though the name may also derive from a surname Mace, a medieval English personal name of unknown meaning, or a similar Gaelic place name meaning long, low hill.
Macee, Macey, Maci, Macie; **Famous Namesakes:** *Singer Macy Gray*

MADA Arabic: The end of the path

MADDIE English: A familiar form of Madeleine and Madison
Maddi, Maddy

MADEIRA Spanish: Sweet wine; wine production is the principal industry of the Madeira Islands in the Atlantic Ocean off Africa's coast.

MADELEINE French: High tower or woman from Magdala, a village on the Sea of Galilee and home to the biblical Mary Magdalene
(Hebrew) *Madalen, Madalyn, Madelaine*; (English) *Madelina*; (German) *Maddalen, Maddalena, Maddalene, Maddalyn*; (Italian) *Maddelena*; (Spanish) *Madalynn, Madena, Madia, Madina*; (Irish) *Madailein, Maighdlin*; (Scandinavian) *Malena*; (Swedish) *Malin*; (Slavic) *Madlenka*; *Madalene, Madeleina, Madelena, Madelene, Madeline, Madelon, Madelynn*; **Nicknames:** *Maddie, Maddy, Madie, Mady*; **Famous Namesakes:** *Actress Madeleine Stowe, Author Madeleine L'Engle, Actress Madeline Kahn*

MADGE Greek: Nickname for Margaret

MADISON English: This surname derived from Matthew or Matilda has become a popular name for girls
Madisyn; **Nicknames:** *Maddi, Maddie, Maddy*; **Star Babies:** *Daughter of Sissy Spacek*

MADONNA Latin: My lady; Madonna is a respectful form of address similar to the French madame, also used in reference to the Virgin Mary, mother of Jesus Christ, especially in art depicting her as a mother with infant Jesus in her arms.
Famous Namesakes: *Singer Madonna Ciccone*

MADORA Greek: Variant of Medea

MADRE Spanish: Mother
Madra, Yadra

MADRI Hindi: Name from Indian mythology, wife of Pandu

MADZEIJA Polish: Hope

MAE French: Spelling variation of May
Famous Namesakes: *Actress Mae West*

MAERTISA English: Famous

MAERYN Welsh: Variation of Mary

MAESEN English: Stone worker; feminine form of Mason
Mason, Maesyn

MAEVE Irish: Intoxicating; the name of a great Irish warrior queen
Meadhbh

MAFUANE Egyptian: Soil

MAGDA Hebrew: Nickname for Magdalene

MAGDALENE Hebrew: Woman from Magdala; the biblical Mary Magdalene came from Magdala, a village on the sea of Galilee whose name meant "tower" in Hebrew. She was healed by Jesus and remained with him during his ministry and the crucifixion, and was a witness to his resurrection.
(French) *Magdalène*; (Spanish) *Magdalena*; (Finnish) *Matleena*; *Magdala, Magdalen*; **Nicknames:** *Alena, Leena, Magda*

MAGENA Native American: Moon

MAGGIE Scottish: Pearl; a familiar form of Margaret
Maggy; **Star Babies:** *Daughter of Faith Hill and Tim McGraw, Pat Sajak*

MAGNA Norse: Great; feminine form of Magnus

MAGNILDA German: Strong battle maiden
Magnhilda, Magnild, Magnilde

MAGNOLIA French: Flower known for its sweet scent, can be used as a reference to girls from the American South

MAHADEVI Hindi: Great goddess

MAHALA Hebrew: Tender, loving. Arabic: Powerful, slowly, gently, progresses in good works. Native American: Woman
Nicknames: *Mahalia*; **Famous Namesakes:** *Singer Mahalia Jackson*

MAHIN Persian: Greatest

MAHINA Hawaiian: Moon, moonlight

MAHLA Persian: Friendly

MAHOGANY English: Dark wood of the mahogany tree

MAHTA Persian: Moonlight
Mahtab

MAHUBEH Persian: A flower

MAHWAH Native American: Beautiful (Algonquian)

MAIA Greek: Meaning unknown; in Greek and Roman mythology she was the goddess of spring and growth. Maia was the eldest of the Pleiades, the group of seven stars in the constellation Taurus, who were the daughters of Atlas and Pleione. She and Zeus had a son Hermes, a god of fertility. Hebrew: Close to God
Maya

MAIBE Egyptian: Grave; also means juices of quinces prepared into medicine

MAIDA English: Maiden
Mayda, Mayde

MAILE Hawaiian: Derived from the name of a type of vine that grows in Hawaii

MAILLE Irish: Variation of Molly

MAIRA Scottish: Variation of Mary

MAISIE Scottish: Pearl; abbreviation of Margaret

MAITANE English: Dearly loved
Nicknames: *Maitena*

MAITE Spanish: Lovable; blend of Maria and Teresa

MAITI Irish: Strong battle maiden; variant of Matilda and Maitilda

MAITLAND English: From the meadow land, possibly from Matthew's land; surname

MAIZAH African: Discerning

MAJA Swedish: Nickname for Margaret

MAJELLA Irish: Surname of Saint Gerard Majella; commonly used as a first name for girls in Ireland

MAJESTAS Latin: Royal bearing, dignity; Majestas was a Roman goddess of honor.
Nicknames: *Majesta*

MAKALA Hawaiian: Myrtle

MAKAWEE Native American: Generous, abundant, freely giving and motherly (Sioux)
Macawi, Macawee

MAKENNA Scottish: Spelling variation of MacKenna

MALAK Arabic, Hebrew: Angel, messenger
Malaika

MALANA Hawaiian: Buoyant

MALCAH Hebrew: Queen
Malkah

MALIA Hawaiian: Variation of Maria

MALIKA Arabic, African: Queen; feminine form of Malek, meaning king. Hungarian: Industrious

MALINA Hebrew: From the tower; variant of Magdalene. Hawaiian: Peace

MALLORY French: Unfortunate, ill-fated; this surname became popular as a girl's name due to the female character Mallory on the popular TV series *Family Ties*, and as a tribute to Mallory Square, the location of Key West's famous Sunset Celebration.
Star Babies: *Daughter of Rick Derringer*

MALMUIRA Scottish: Dark-skinned
Nicknames: *Malmuirie*

MALVA Greek: Soft
Nicknames: *Malvina, Malvine, Malvinia*

MAMIE English: Bitter; familiar form of Mary and Miriam
Famous Namesakes: *Actress Mamie Van Doren*

MANAR Arabic: Light; derived from Nour, meaning light
Manara

MANDALYN English: Nickname for Amanda

MANDANA Persian: Name of a Persian princess

MANDARA Hindi: From Mandara

MANDISA African: Sweetness
Star Babies: *Daughter of Danny Glover*

MANDY English: Familiar form of Amanda, worthy of love
Mandi, Mandie; **Famous Namesakes:** *Actress Mandy Moore*

MANNING English: Son of a hero; surname

MANON French: Bitter; diminutive form of Marie

MANOUSH Persian: Sweet sun

MANSI Native American: Plucked flower (Hopi)

MANTO Latin: Roman mythological nymph and prophetess, Manto was the mother of Ocnus, founder of the city of Mantua

MANUELA Spanish: Variation of Emmanuella

MAOLA Irish: Handmaiden
Nicknames: *Maoli*

MAOLMIN Gaelic: Polished chief

MARA Hebrew: Bitter; the biblical Naomi claimed the name Mara as an expression of grief after the deaths of her husband and sons. Mara is also a variant of Mary and abbreviation of Tamara.

MARAL Armenian: Deer

MARALAH Native American: Born during an earthquake

MARCAIL Scottish: Variation of Margaret

MARCELLA Latin: Warring; feminine form of Marcellus, a name believed to have its root in Mars, the name of the mythological Roman god of war; also related to the name Mark
(French) *Marcelle, Marcellia, Marchelle;* (Spanish) *Marcela, Maricel, Maricela, Maricelia, Maricella, Marisela; Marcelina, Marcelinda, Marcellina, Marcelline, Marcelyn, Marcena, Marcine, Marsila, Marsile, Marsilla;* **Nicknames:** *Cella, Marci, Marcia, Marcy, Marsha, Marsil;* **Famous Namesakes:** *Tennis player Marcella Mesker*

MARCIA Latin: Nickname for Marcella
Marsha, Marsia, Martia; **Famous Namesakes:** *Actress Marcia Gay Harden*

MARCY Latin: Nickname for Marcella
Marci, Marcie

MARDEA African: Last

MARELDA German: Famous battle maiden
Old Forms: *Maganhildi*

MAREN German: From the sea, though also a possible variant of Mara and Mary
(Italian) *Marea*

MARGARET Greek: Pearl; medieval virgin Saint Margaret was beloved in many cultures.
(German) *Margit;* (French) *Margaux, Margeaux, Margot, Marguerite;* (Italian)

Margherita; (Spanish) *Margarita*; (Gaelic) *Mairearad, Mairghread, Marsali*; (Irish) *Mairead*; (Scottish) *Marcail*; (Welsh) *Marged, Margred, Mererid*; (Scandinavian) *Margareta*; (Danish) *Margarethe, Mettalise*; (Czech) *Marjeta, Marketa*; (Polish) *Margisia, Margita*; (Finnish) *Maarit, Maija, Marketta*; (Armenian) *Margaid, Margarid*; *Margaretta, Margeret, Margerie, Margery, Margrit, Marjory*; **Nicknames:** *Ghita, Gitta, Greta, Gretal, Grete, Gryta, Madge, Maggi, Maggie, Maggy, Mai, Maiju, Maikki, Maj, Maja, Majori, Majorie, Margalo, Margo, Margolo, Marji, Marjo, Meg, Meta, Peg, Pegeen, Peggy, Peigi, Rita, Marge*; **Diminutive Forms:** *Gretchen, Gretel, Margosha*; **Famous Namesakes:** *Prime Minister Margaret Thatcher, Author Margaret Mead, Actress Meg Ryan, Author Margaret Atwood*

MARGHERITA Italian: Variation of Margaret

MARGO French: Nickname for Margaret *Margaux*

MARI Welsh: Bitter; a variant of Mary and favored prefix for blending with other names

MARIA Latin, Italian, Spanish: Bitter; variant of Mary and the most popular Spanish name in the world. This name is often given in honor of the Virgin Mary, Christ's mother. See also *Manon* (French) *Marie*; (Spanish) *Malita, Mariquita*; (Scandinavian) *Mia*; (Slavic) *Marika*; (Finnish) *Maaria, Marita, Marja, Miia, Riia*; (Hungarian) *Mariska*; (Hawaiian) *Malia*; **Nicknames:** *Maree, Mimi*; **Diminutive Forms:** *Manette*; **Famous Namesakes:** *Journalist and California first lady Maria Shriver, Opera singer Maria Callas, Educator Marie Montessori*

MARIAH English: Bitter; a variant of Mary **Famous Namesakes:** *Singer Mariah Carey*; **Star Babies:** *Daughter of Kerry Kennedy and Andrew Cuomo*

MARIAMNE Hebrew: Rebellious; variant of Miriam and the name of biblical King Herod's wife

MARIAN Latin: Bitter; derived from Mary (English) *Maryann*; (French) *Marianne*; (Dutch) *Marien*; (Hungarian) *Marianna*; *Mariana, Marianda, Mariane, Mariann, Marion, Maryan, Maryanna*

MARIANA Latin: Spelling variation of Marian *Marianna*

MARIANNE French: Variation of Marian

MARIBELL Latin: Beautiful Marie; a blend of the names Mary or Marie and Belle *Maribel, Maribella, Maribelle, Marybell, Marybelle*

MARICA Latin: A nymph

MARICRUZ Spanish: Mary of the Cross

MARIE French: Variation of Maria **Famous Namesakes:** *Singer Marie Osmond*

MARIELLE French: Diminutive of Maria (English) *Mariel*; (Italian) *Mariella*; *Mariela, Mariele*; **Famous Namesakes:** *Actress Mariel Hemingway*

MARIETTE French: Bitter; pet form of Marie *Marietta*; **Famous Namesakes:** *Actress Mariette Hartley*

MARIGOLD English: Mary's gold; also the name of a small golden, yellow, or orange flower **Nicknames:** *Mari*

MARIKO Japanese: True or straight and benefit or reason

MARILIS Greek: Flower; an abbreviation of Amaryllis

MARILLA Celtic: Shining sea; a variant of Muriel and possible variant of the names Amaryllis or Amarilla

MARILYN English: Blend of Marie or Mary and Lyn.
Maralyn, Marilynn, Marylin, Marylyn, Marylynn; **Nicknames:** *Marlyn, Marlynn*; **Famous Namesakes:** *Actress Marilyn Monroe*

MARINA Latin: Of the sea
(Russian) *Marinochka*; *Marnee, Marnell, Marni, Marnie*; **Old Forms:** *Marnisha*; **Nicknames:** *Marinda, Marinella*

MARIPOSA Spanish: Butterfly

MARISA Latin, English: Of the sea; variant of Maris or Maria
Mareesa, Marissa; **Nicknames:** *Marise*; **Famous Namesakes:** *Actress Marisa Tomei*; **Star Babies:** *Daughter of John Wayne*

MARISHA Hindi: Dew; (Russian) diminutive form of Maria

MARISOL Spanish: Bitter sun; a blend of Mary and Sol

MARJA Finnish: Variation of Maria

MARJAANA Finnish: A blend of the names Marja and Jaana

MARJAN Polish: Bitter, a variant of Mary. Persian: Coral
Marjaneh

MARJETA Czech: Variation of Margaret

MARJOLAINA French: Flower

MARKA African: Rebel

MARLA English: Nickname for Marlene

MARLENE German, English: Blend of Maria and Magdalene referring to Mary Magdalene of the Bible; the name was first used by the German actress and singer Marlene Dietrich, whose real name was Maria Magdalene von Losch.
Marlenne, Marlin, Marline; **Nicknames:** *Marla, Marlaina, Marlayne, Marleena, Marleene, Marleina, Marlena, Marlina, Marlinda, Marlisa, Marliss, Marlys, Marlyssa*

MARLEY English: Near the meadow by the lake; surname; also a variant of Marlene, woman from Magdala
Marleigh, Marlea, Marleah, Marlee, Marly; **Famous Namesakes:** *Actress Marlee Matlin*

MARLINDA German: Nickname for Marlene

MARLISA English: Nickname for Marlene
Marlissa

MARLOWE English: Marshy; from the hill by the lake
Marlow, Marlo; **Famous Namesakes:** *Actress Marlo Thomas*

MARMAR Persian: Marble

MARNIE Hebrew: Rejoicing; variant of Marina
Marnee, Marnell, Marni

MARPESIA Greek: Snatcher; Amazon Queen who ruled with Lampedo, and together they excelled at building the Amazon empire. The Caucasus Mountains were once called The Marpesians after her.

MARQUISE French: Royalty; a French royalty title
Marquisa, Marquisha

MARSALI Gaelic: Variation of Margaret

MARSHA Latin: Nickname for Marcella
Marcia, Marsia, Marsita, Martia; **Famous Namesakes:** *Actress Marsha Mason*

MARTHA Aramaic: Lady; the biblical Martha was sister to Lazarus and Mary.
(French) *Marthe*; (Spanish) *Marta*; (Russian) *Marfa*; (Czech) *Marticka*; (Polish) *Masia*; (Finnish) *Martta*; *Marit*; **Nicknames:** *Marti, Mattie, Mart, Martie, Marty, Pat, Patti, Patty*; **Famous Namesakes:** *Dancer Martha Graham, First Lady Martha Washington*

MARTINA Latin, Spanish, Swedish: Warlike; feminine form of Martin
(French) *Martine*; *Marteena, Martella*;
Famous Namesakes: *Czech tennis stars Martina Navratilova and Martina Hingis*

MARVINA Celtic: Friend of the sea; feminine form of Marvin

MARY Hebrew, English: Bitter; anglicized variant of Miriam; the mortal mother of Jesus Christ, generally known as the Virgin or Mother Mary, also the name of other important biblical characters, including Mary Magdalene.
(Gaelic) *Mairi*; (Irish) *Maire, Mayra*; (Scottish) *Maira*; (Welsh) *Maeryn*; (Russian) *Maruska*; **Diminutive Forms:** *Mamie*;
Famous Namesakes: *Philosopher Mary Wollstonecraft, Author Mary Shelley (Wollstonecraft's daughter), Queen Mary (known as Queen of Scots), Artist Mary Eugenia Surratt*; **Star Babies:** *Daughter of Meryl Streep and Don Gummer*

MARYANN English: Variation of Marian

MARYVONNE French: Blend of Marie and Yvonne

MASIA Polish: Variation of Martha

MASIKA Egyptian: Born during the rain

MASTANEH Persian: Joyful

MATILDA German: Mighty battle maiden
(German) *Mathilda*; (French) *Mathilde*; (Czech) *Matylda*; *Mathild, Matilde*;
Nicknames: *Maiti, Tilda, Tilde, Tille, Tilly*;
Famous Namesakes: *English actress Tilda Swinton, French actress Mathilda May*; **Star Babies:** *Daughter of Elizabeth Perkins*

> *"Who'll come a-waltzing Matilda my darling,*
> *Who'll come a-waltzing Matilda with me?"*
> —Traditional Australian folk song

MATRIKA Hindi: Divine Mother

MATRYONA Russian: Lady; derived from the Latin word matrona
Nicknames: *Matryosha, Matryoshka*

MATSUKO Japanese: Pine tree and child

MATTHEA Hebrew: Gift of God; feminine form of Matthew
Matea, Mathea, Mathia, Mattea, Matthia

MATUTA Latin: Derived from *Matuta Mater*, the Roman goddess of dawn

MAUDE French, Irish: Strong in war; variant of Mathilda
Maud; **Famous Namesakes:** *Actress Maude Adams*

MAURA Irish: Bitter; variant of Mary. Also a feminine variant of the Latin *Maurus* and English *Maurice*, meaning dark-skinned
(Spanish) *Mora, Morisa, Morissa*; *Morah*;
Famous Namesakes: *Actress Maura Tierney*

MAUREEN Irish: Bitter; a variant of Mary
Maurine, Maura, Maurene, Maurisa,
Maurita, Moreen, Morene, Morine;
Nicknames: *Mo;* **Famous Namesakes:**
Actresses Maureen O'Hara and Maureen
O'Sullivan, Tennis star Maureen "Little Mo"
Connolly

MAURISA Latin: Moorish, dark-skinned;
feminine form of Maurice
(Italian) *Maurizia; Maurissa, Morisa, Morissa*

MAVA Hebrew: Pleasant

MAVIE Celtic: Variation of Mavis

MAVIS English: From the name of the type
of bird, also called the song thrush, ultimately derived from Old French.
(Celtic) *Mavelle, Mavie*

MAVRA Latin: Moorish, dark-skinned

MAXINE Latin: Greatest; feminine form
of Max
(Italian) *Massima; Maxime, Maxina;*
Nicknames: *Maxie*

MAY Latin: In Roman mythology, Maia was
goddess of spring growth. The name of the
month May comes from Maia. See also *Maia*
(Hebrew) *Mayah;* (French) *Mai;* (Spanish)
Maya; Mae, Maelee, Maelynn; **Nicknames:**
Maylee, Mayleen, Maylene, Maylin; **Star**
Babies: *Daughter of Madeline Stowe and*
Brian Benben

MAYA Sanskrit: Illusion, fantasy or God's
power; also a variant of Maia
Famous Namesakes: *Poet Maya Angelou*

MAYLEA Hawaiian: Wildflower

MAZEL Hebrew: Luck

MEADOW English: An open, uncultivated
field

MEDA Native American: Prophetess

MEDB Celtic: A mythical queen

MEDEA Greek: In Greek mythology, Medea
was one of the great sorceresses, and helped
Jason win the Golden Fleece. She fled her
home to be with him, but he deserted her.
Nicknames: *Madora, Medora*

MEDESICASTE Greek: Mythical daughter
of Priam, she was taken captive by the
Achaeans after the sack of Troy.

MEDITRINA Latin: Healer; mythical goddess of wine and health

MEDUSA Greek: Sovereign female wisdom;
Medusa was imported into Greece from
Libya where she was worshipped by the
Libyan Amazons as their Serpent-Goddess.
Medusa (Metis) was the destroyer aspect of
the Great Triple Goddess also called Neith,
Anath, Athene, or Athenna in North Africa.

MEEDA Irish: Thirsty; an Anglicized variant
of Mide
Ide, Mide

MEENA Sanskrit: Precious stone
Mena; **Famous Namesakes:** *Actress Mena*
Suvari

MEGAN Welsh: Pearl; a variant of Marged,
Megan is now commonly used as an inde-
pendent name
Maegan, Meegan, Meeghan, Meggan, Meghan,
Maygan, Maygen, Meaghan; **Nicknames:**
Meg, Meggie; **Famous Namesakes:** *Actress*
Meg Ryan

MEGARA Greek: Mythological wife of
Hercules
Nicknames: *Magaere*

MEHADI Hindi: Flower

MEHETABEL Hebrew: God's best, God's favor

MEIRA Hebrew: Light

MELANIE Greek: Dark; the name of a Roman saint who became a great religious philanthropist
(French) *Melaina*; (Polish) *Mela, Melka*; *Melana, Melanee, Melania, Melanne*; **Famous Namesakes:** *Actress Melanie Griffith*; **Star Babies:** *Daughter of Peter Gabriel, Vanessa Williams and Ramon Hervey*

MELANIPPE Greek: Sister of Hippolyte and daughter of Ares. Heracles captured her and demanded Hippolyte's girdle in exchange for her freedom.

MELANTHA Greek: Dark flower
Melanthe, Melantho

MELE Hawaiian: Song

MELEK Turkish: Form of Malak

MELIA Greek: Greek mythological nymph of clouds and rain, daughter of Oceanus. Hawaiian: Plumeria

MELIKA Persian: A plant, melic grass

MELINA Greek: Honey

MELINDA English, Greek: Modern blend of Melissa or Melanie and Linda, this name may also derive from the Latin word *melitus*, meaning sweet.
Malinda, Melynda; **Nicknames:** *Mindi, Mindie, Mindy*; **Star Babies:** *Daughter of John Wayne*

MELISSA Greek: Honeybee; a mythological Greek nymph who fed honey to the infant god Zeus and was later transformed into a bee
(French) *Melisande*; (Spanish) *Melisenda*, *Meliza; Melisa, Melise, Melisha, Melisse, Mellisa*; **Nicknames:** *Lissa, Lyssa, Missy, Mel*; **Famous Namesakes:** *Singer Melissa Manchester, Singer Missy Elliott*

MELITA Greek: Honey

MELLONA Latin: Roman goddess, patroness of bees and beekeeping

MELODY Greek: Melody, song
(French) *Melodie*; *Melodee, Melodi*

MELOSA Spanish: Honey, sweet
Nicknames: *Melosia*

MELPOMENE Greek: Mythical muse of tragedy

MELVINA Irish, English: Chieftan; feminine form of Melvin
Melva

MEMDI Native American: Henna

MENACHEMA Hebrew: Consolation
Menachemah

MENDIA Spanish: Reference to the Virgin Mary

MENGLAD Norse: A Norse goddess sometimes identified with Freya

MEOQUANEE Native American: Wears red (Chippewa)

MERCEDES Spanish: Mercies; given in honor of the Virgin Mary
(French) *Mercède*; (Italian) *Mercede*; *Mercedez, Mercia, Mercie, Mercilla, Mercina*; **Star Babies:** *Daughter of Joanne Whalley and Val Kilmer*

MERCER English: Merchant; a name used for both genders

MERCY English: Merciful; virtue name
Mercie

MEREDITH Welsh: Magnificent chief
or protector
Meridith; **Old Forms:** *Maredud, Meredydd*;
Nicknames: *Mer, Meri, Merry*; **Famous
Namesakes:** *Actress Meredith Baxter*

MERI Finnish: Sea. English: Mirthful, joyous; variant of Merry, Meredith, Merilee, and
similar names

MERIDEL English: Mirthful, joyous; variant
of Merry and possibly Meredith

MERLA French: Blackbird; feminine form
of Merle
Merlina

MEROPE Greek: Daughter of Oenopion,
king of Chios; Orion fell in love with her, but
Oenopion refused to give her up and blinded
Orion.

MERRILEE English: Modern blend of
Merry and Lee
Merilee

MERRILL English: Shining sea; also a feminine variant of Merle, meaning blackbird
Merrille

MERRY English: Cheerful, happy; also a
variant of Mary, Mercy, Meredith, and
similar names
Merri, Merrie, Meri

MERULA Latin: Blackbird

MERVEILLE French: Miracle
Marvel, Marvella, Marvelle

MERYL Celtic: Spelling variation of Muriel
Famous Namesakes: *Actress Meryl Streep*

MESSINA Latin: Middle child; Messina is
also a city in Italy.

MI-NA Native American: Firstborn daughter
(Sioux)

MIA Scandinavian: Variation of Maria
Famous Namesakes: *Actress Mia Farrow*;
Star Babies: *Daughter of Kate Winslet and
James Threapleton*

MIAKODA Native American: Power of the
moon

MICA Hebrew: Who is like the Lord; a
diminutive of Michaela. Mica is also a type
of mineral known for its ability to be separated into thin, even transparent, leaves.
Meeca, Meica, Michah, Mika, Myka, Mykah

MICHAELA Hebrew, Latin, English: Who is
like the Lord; feminine variant of Michael;
Though the popular perception is that
Michaela is a relatively new name, and a ver-
sion of Michelle, the exact opposite is true
and Michaela is the original. Michaela has
a long history, and many spellings are well
grounded in various ethnic traditions. One
of the first was the biblical Michal: King
Saul's daughter and the first wife of David.
(Latin) *Micaela, Mikayla, Mikella, Mikelle,
Mikki, Mychaela*; (English) *Mikaela*; (French)
*Michela, Michele, Michèle, Micheline,
Michelle, Mychele, Mychelle*; (Spanish)
Micaella, Miguela, Miguelita, Miquela, Quela;
(Slavic) *Miesha, Mischa, Misha*; (African)
Machelle; (Hawaiian) *Makelina*; *Mical,
Michaelina, Michaeline, Michaelyn, Michalin,
Michella, Mikele, Macaela, Macaila, Macayla,
MacKayla, Mahalya, Makaila, Makayla,
Makyla, Mckaila, Mckayla, Mechaela,
Meeskaela, Mekea, Micaila, Micayla, Michael,
Michell, Mihaila, Mihaliya, Mikaila,
Mikhaila, Mikhala, Mishaela, Mishaila,
Miskaela, Myshell, Myshelle*; **Nicknames:**
*Chelle, Chelly, Meeca, Meica, Mia, Mica,
Micah, Michal, Micole, Mika, Mickey, Micki,*

Mickie, Micky, Myka, Mykah, Schelley, Shellee, Shelley, Shellie, Shelly; **Famous Namesakes:** *Cinematographer Michaela Denis;* **Star Babies:** *Daughter of Kerry Kennedy and Andrew Cuomo*

MICHELLE French: Variation of Michaela *Michele, Michella, Michell, Mychele, Mychelle, Myshell, Myshelle*; **Nicknames:** *Chelle, Chelly, Meecha, Micha, Misha, Schelley, Shellee, Shelley, Shelli, Shellie, Shelly*; **Famous Namesakes:** *Actress Michelle Pfeiffer, Olympic Skater Michelle Kwan;* **Star Babies:** *Daughter of Anne Rice, Deborah Norville, Kate Capshaw and Steven Spielberg*

MICHIE Japanese: Gateway; gracefully drooping flower

MICHIKO Japanese: Child of beauty

MIDORI Japanese: Green
Famous Namesakes: *Figure skater Midori Ito*

MIEKO Japanese: Beautiful, blessed child

MIGISI Native American: Eagle (Chippewa)

MIGNON French: Cute, attractive
Diminutive Forms: *Mignonette;* **Famous Namesakes:** *Opera singer Mignon Dunne*

MIKA Native American: Intelligent raccoon (Hokan)

MIKIL Hawaiian: Quick, nimble

MIKKI English: Variation of Michaela *Micki, Mickie, Mickey, Micky*

MILA Russian: Favor of the people; a short form of Ludmila. Persian: Stork

MILAGROS Spanish: Miracle; taken from the Virgin Mary's title *Nuestra Senora de los*

Milagros, Our Lady of Miracles
Milagritos, Milagrosa; **Nicknames:** *Mila*

MILCAH Hebrew: Counsel

MILDRED English: Gentle counselor; Saint Mildred was a seventh-century abbess known for her generosity to the poor. *Mildraed, Mildrid, Mildryd*

MILENA Czech: Gracious

MILIANA Latin: Industrious; a feminine form of Emiliano

MILILANI Hawaiian: Praise, exalt; also a town in Hawaii

MILJA Finnish: Freeborn, noble; variant of Milla

MILKA Slavic: Industrious

MILLA Finnish: Freeborn, noble; a pet form of Camilla

MILLICENT German: Noble, strong (German) *Milicent;* (French) *Mélisande; Melicent;* **Nicknames:** *Millie;* **Famous Namesakes:** *Congresswoman Millicent Fenwick*

MILOSLAVA Slavic: Lover of glory

MIMI French: Nickname for Wilhelmina
Famous Namesakes: *Actress Mimi Rogers;* **Star Babies:** *Daughter of Donna Summer*

MINA German: Nickname for Wilhelmina. Persian: The gemstone, lapis lazuli *Minna*

MINDEL Yiddish: Bitter

MINDY English: Nickname for Melinda *Mindee, Mindi, Mindie*

Virtue Names

Looking for a name that represents a quality important
to you and your partner? Browse the below list
for some virtuous monikers.
(For more virtue names, see pages 89, 236, and 311.)

Names Meaning "Fair" or "Just"

BOYS

Adel (Arabic)
Justin (Latin)
Nemesio (Spanish)
Zadok (Hebrew)

GIRLS

Adeleh (Persian)
Dice (Greek)
Justine (Latin)
Mackenzie (Scottish)

Names Meaning "Honest" or "Trustworthy"

BOYS

Achates (Greek)
Adib (Arabic)
Amin (Arabic)
Hemen (Hebrew)
Renjiro (Japanese)
Truman (English)

GIRLS

Alecta (Greek)
Amina (Arabic)
Ruth (Hebrew)
Vera (Latin)
Veronica (Latin)

Names Meaning "Loyal" or "Faithful"

BOYS

Amnon (Hebrew)
Dillon (Gaelic)
Fidel (Latin)
Fido (Spanish)
Leal (English)
Loyal (French)

GIRLS

Faith (English)
Fidelity (Latin)
Iman (Arabic)
Sadiki (Egyptian)
Usko (Finnish)
Wafa (African)

Names Meaning "Kind" or "Generous"

BOYS

Corliss (English)
Declan (Irish)
Elden (English)
Fen (English)
Generoso (Spanish)
Karim (Arabic)
Maher (Irish)
Terence (Latin)

GIRLS

Adette (German)
Agatha (Greek)
Esma (Anglo-Saxon)
Cordelia (Latin)
Generosa (Spanish)
Lilo (Hawaiin)
Lina (Arabic)
Yetta (English)

MINERVA Latin: Goddess of wisdom

MINKA Teutonic: Resolute

MINNEHAHA Native American: Laughing water (Sioux); the name of the girl Hiawatha loved

MINNIE French: Nickname for Wilhelmina **Famous Namesakes:** *Disney's beloved cartoon Minnie Mouse, Comedienne Minnie Pearl*

MINOU Persian: Paradise

MINTA Greek: Mint (Finnish) *Minttu*; *Mintha*

MIRA Latin: Wonderful; derived from the Latin word mirandus; (Hindi) prosperous; a name born by India's Saint Mira Bai, a poet and devotee of Krishna **Nicknames:** *Myrelle, Myrilla*; **Famous Namesakes:** *Actress Mira Sorvino*

MIRABELLE French: Wonderful *Mirabella*

MIRANDA Latin: Wonderful; derived from the Latin word "mirandus." Miranda is the young girl in Shakespeare's *The Tempest*, raised and educated on an isolated island by her magician father Prospero. (Spanish) *Mireya*; (Slavic) *Miriana*; *Mirande*; **Nicknames:** *Randa, Randi, Randie, Randy*; **Famous Namesakes:** *Actress Miranda Richardson*

MIRARI Spanish: Miracle

MIREILLE French: Variation of Miriam

MIRIAM Hebrew: Rebellious; an original variant of Mary (French) *Mireille*; (Finnish) *Mirjami*; (Yiddish) *Mirel*; *Mariam*; **Nicknames:** *Mariamne, Mirit, Mitzi*; **Famous Namesakes:** *Singer Miriam Makeba*

MIRKA Slavic: Peaceful

MISAE Native American: White sun (Osage)

MISCHA Russian: Who is like the Lord; variant of Michaela *Meecha, Micha, Misha*

MISTY English: Misty *Misti, Mistie, Mystee, Mysti*

MITENA Native American: Born at the new moon (Omaha)

MITRA Persian: Name of a deity worshipped by ancient Iranians (goddess of loving kindness)

MITSU Japanese: Shine

MITZI German: Nickname for Miriam **Famous Namesakes:** *Actress Mitzi Gaynor*

MIYA Japanese: Beauty **Star Babies:** *Daughter of Muhammad Ali*

MNEMOSYNE Greek: Goddess of memory

MOANA Hawaiian: Ocean, sea

MODESTA Latin: Modest, a virtue (English) *Modesty*

MODRON Celtic: Divine mother; a Celtic goddess by this name was linked with legendary Morgan Le Fay, sister to King Arthur. Both women were closely associated with the mythical island of Avalon.

MOERAE Greek: Fate, destiny
Moirae

MOIRA Irish: Bitter; a variant of Maire, an Irish form of Mary
Moire; **Famous Namesakes:** *Actress Moira Kelly*

MOLARA Basque: Reference to the Virgin Mary

MOLLY Irish, English: Bitter; from the Gaelic Maili or Maille, which is a pet form of Mary
(Irish) *Maille, Mallaidh*; *Molli, Mollie*;
Famous Namesakes: *Actress Molly Ringwald*

MONA Irish: Little noble one, also used in several languages as a short form of Monica; the *Mona Lisa* painting by Leonardo da Vinci may be the most famous portrait in the history of art. The name *Mona Lisa* is a shortened form of *Madonna Lisa* (my lady, Lisa). Native American: Gathered of the seed of a jimson weed
Moina, Moyna

MONAHAN Irish: Monk; a surname adaptation traditionally used for boys
Monaghan

MONCA Irish: Wise

MONCHA Irish: Alone; possibly derived from the name of a Celtic goddess

MONICA Latin: Advisor, counselor; fourth-century saint known mainly by the writings of her son, Saint Augustine
(German) *Monika*; (French) *Monique*;
Moniqua; **Famous Namesakes:** *Actress Monica Potter, Italian actress Monica Bellucci*

MONIFA Egyptian: Lucky

MONIR Persian: Shining
Moneer

MONTANA Latin: Mountain; a northwestern American state
Star Babies: *Daughter of Judd Hirsch*

MONTSERRAT Latin: Jagged mountain; Montserrat is the name of a mountain near Barcelona, Spain.
Famous Namesakes: *Spanish soprano Montserrat Caballe*

MOR Gaelic: Great
Nicknames: *Morag, Morella*

MORELA Polish: Apricot

MORGAN Welsh: Circling sea; a traditionally Welsh male name, used in legend by the powerful sorceress sister or stepsister of King Arthur
Morgen; **Nicknames:** *Morgaine, Morgana, Morgandy*; **Famous Namesakes:** *Actress Morgan Fairchild*; **Star Babies:** *Daughter of Clint Eastwood and Dina Ruiz*

MORGAUSE Welsh: Queen, half-sister of legendary King Arthur and Morgan le Fay, wife of King Lot, mother of the important knights Agravaine, Gawain, Gareth, and Gaheris, she also was said to have raised Arthur's son, Mordred, and in some versions was his mother.
Margawse, Morgawse

MORIAH Hebrew: God teaches, seen by Yahweh; biblical name of the mount of the Jerusalem's Temple of Solomon
Moriel, Morit

MORNA Celtic: Dearly loved
Merna

MORRIGAN Celtic: A war goddess in Irish mythology

MORRIN Irish: Long-haired

MORVARID Persian: Pearl
Morvareed

MORWEN Welsh: Young girl
Nicknames: *Morwenna*

MOSELLE Hebrew: From the water

MOSWEN Egyptian: Light-colored skin

MOYA Celtic: Bitter; a variant of Mary

MUIRE Irish: From the moor; a surname adapted to given name use

MUNA Arabic: Desire, aspiration. Native American: Overflowing spring (Hopi)
Mona

MURIEL Irish: Shining sea; also a variant of Mary. Arabic: Myrrh
(Irish) *Muireall; Merryl, Meryl, Myrla, Meriel;*
Old Forms: *Muirgheal*

MUSADORA Greek: Gift of the Muses
Musidora

MUSETTE French: A song
Musetta

MUT Egyptian: Mythical mother, ancient Egyptian war goddess, consort of Amon and part of the Theban Triad group of gods. Mut was worshipped at Thebes.

MUTA Latin: Roman personification and goddess of silence

MYESHA Arabic: Spelling variation of Aisha
Myeshia

MYFANWY Welsh: My woman

MYRA English: Derived from the Latin word for myrrh, and possibly a variant of the name Myrna; Myra may also have been invented by the English poet Fulke Grenville.
Nicknames: *Myrina*

MYRINA English: Myrrh; a variant of Myra

MYRNA Arabic: Myrrh, an aromatic gum resin obtained from several Asian or African trees and shrubs, used in making perfume and incense; Considered very precious in ancient times, it was a kingly gift for one of the Magi to give to the the newborn Jesus.
Famous Namesakes: *Actress Myrna Loy*

MYRTLE English: A botanical name for an evergreen shrub; myrtle was considered sacred to the Roman goddess of love, Venus, who used it as one of her symbols.
(Latin) *Myrta;* (Greek) *Myrtia, Myrtisa;*
Nicknames: *Myrtice, Myrtis*

MYSTIQUE French: Air of mystery; Betty Friedan's bestselling book, *The Feminine Mystique*, is credited with launching the second wave of the feminist movement.
Mistique

NABILA Arabic: Born into nobility

NABIRYE Egyptian: Mother of twins

NADA Arabic: Dew, giving
(Persian) *Nadia*; *Nadya, Nadah*

NADIA Russian, Slavic: Hope
(Slavic) *Nadege*; (Polish) *Nadzia, Nata, Natia*;
Nadya; **Old Forms:** *Nadezda, Nadezhda*;
Nicknames: *Nadusha*; **Diminutive Forms:**
Nadenka, Nadyenka, Nadyuiska; **Famous
Namesakes:** *Romanian Gymnast Nadia
Comaneci*

*"Loving a child doesn't mean giving
in to all his whims; to love him is
to bring out the best in him, to
teach him to love what is difficult."*
—Nadia Boulanger, first woman to conduct
the Boston Symphony Orchestra

NADIE Native American: Wise (Algonquin)

NADINE French, Latin: Hope; diminutive of
Nadia and a familiar form of Bernadette
(German) *Nadina*; *Nadeen*

NAEEMAH Egyptian: Benevolent

NAHEED Persian: Immaculate

NAHLAH Arabic: Drink of water, to quench
Nahla

NAIA Hawaiian: Dolphin

NAIARA Spanish, Basque: Of the Virgin
Mary
Naiaria

NAIDA Greek: Water nymph
Naia, Naiadia

NAILAH African, Egyptian: Successful
Nala

NAIMA African: Graceful

NAIRI Armenian: Country of rivers

NAIRNA Scottish: Dwells at the alder tree
river
Nairne

NAJA African: Strong

NAJILA Arabic: Brilliant eyes
Nicknames: *Najla*

NAJLA Arabic: Star; variation of the word
Najee which means star

NAKEISHA African: Her life

NALANI Hawaiian: Silence of the heavens

NALDA Spanish: Strong

NALIN Native American: Young maiden
(Apache)

NAMID Native American: Star dancer
(Chippewa)

NAMPEYO Native American: Snake girl
(Hopi); the name of one of the most
celebrated of Hopi potters in the twentieth
century

NANA Hawaiian: Name of a spring month,
name of a star

NANCY English, French: Grace; variant of
Ann often regarded as an independent name
(Irish) *Nainsi*; (Hungarian) *Nancsi, Nusa,
Nusi*; *Nancey, Nanci, Nancie*; **Nicknames:**
Nannie, Nan; **Famous Namesakes:** *First
Lady Nancy Reagan, Figure skater Nancy
Kerrigan*; **Star Babies:** *Daughter of Robert
Duvall*

NANETTE French, Hebrew: Favor, grace; variant of Anne
(French) *Nanine, Nynette; Nanelia, Nanelle, Nanetta, Nannette, Nanon, Ninette;*
Nicknames: *Nan, Nana, Nann, Nanny*

NANI Hawaiian: Beauty

NANNA Norse: Wife of Balder

NAOMI Hebrew: Pleasant; in the Old Testament, Naomi was the mother-in-law of Ruth. After the death of her husband and sons and upon her return to Bethlehem, Naomi took the name Mara, meaning bitter.
(French) *Noemie;* (Spanish) *Noemi; Naamah, Neomi, Nyomi;* **Famous Namesakes:** *Actress Naomi Watts;* **Star Babies:** *Daughter of Stephen King and Tabitha Spruce*

NAPIA Latin: Of the valley
Napea

NARA Greek: Contented, happy. Japanese: Oak
Narra

NARCISSA Greek: Daffodil; feminine form of Narcissus, the beautiful boy of Greek mythology who fell in love with his own reflection in a pool and, unable to find consolation, died of sorrow
(Spanish) *Narcisa;* (Russian) *Narkissa;* (Turkish) *Nergis*

NARDA Latin: Fragrant. Persian: Anointed
Nardia

NAREEN Celtic: Contented
Nareena, Nareene

NARISSA Greek: Sea nymph, daughter of Nereus; in Greek mythology the Nereids were mermaids and deities of the seas.

NARMADA Hindi: Gives us pleasure

NASCIO Latin: Goddess of childbirth

NASHA Native American: Owl (Navajo)

NASHOTA Native American: Twin

NASIMA Arabic: Breeze, fresh air; feminine form of Nasim. Sham el Nasim, or "smell the breeze," is an Egyptian spring festival that takes place the day after Easter in commemoration of Pharaonic spring and Nile festivals, and is celebrated by Muslims and Christians alike.
Naseema, Naseemah, Nessima, Nesima, Nesimah, Nessimah, Nesime, Nesimeh

NASRIN Persian: Wild rose
Nasreen

NASTASIA Russian: Variation of Anastasia
Nastasiya, Nastassja; **Nicknames:** *Nastya, Nastia, Nastiya;* **Diminutive Forms:** *Nastunya;* **Famous Namesakes:** *German actress Nastassja Kinski*

NATA Russian: Nickname for Natalia and Renata; (Native American) speaker

NATALIE French: Born on Christmas; popular name from the Latin Natalia. See also *Natasha*
(Italian) *Natala, Natale;* (Spanish) *Natalia;* (Russian) *Natalya; Natalee, Natassia, Nathalee, Nathalia, Nathalie;* **Nicknames:** *Nat, Tasha, Nata, Natty;* **Diminutive Forms:** *Natashenka, Tashia, Tassa, Tosha;* **Famous Namesakes:** *Actress Natalie Wood, Actress Natalie Portman;* **Star Babies:** *Daughter of George Foreman*

NATANE Native American: Daughter (Arapaho)

NATASHA Russian: Nickname for Natalya; Natasha Rostova is one of the main characters in Leo Tolstoy's novel *War and Peace.*
Natascha; **Nicknames:** *Tasha;* **Famous**

Namesakes: *Canadian actress Natasha Henstridge, British actress Natasha Richardson;* **Star Babies:** *Daughter of Candace Cameron and Valeri Bure, Vanessa Redgrave, Michael Caine*

NATESA Hindi: Dancer

NATHAIRA Scottish: Snake
Nathara

NATHANIA Hebrew: God's gift; feminine form of Nathaniel

NATI Hindi: Humble, bowing

NATIVIDAD Spanish: Birth; reference to the nativity
Navidad; **Nicknames:** *Nati*

NAUNET Egyptian: Mythical goddess of the ocean

NAUSICAA Greek: Princess who finds Odysseus shipwrecked on Scheria; she is one of the most charming figures in *The Odyssey.*

NAUTIA Latin: From the sea

NAVEENA Native American: New

NAVIT Hebrew: Pleasant

NAWA Egyptian: Storm; those storms that recur roughly at the same time each year have names taken from the historic Coptic language.
Nawah, Nawwah

NAZNEEN Persian: Exquisitely beautiful, charming; a name used for a beloved woman or child

NAZY Persian: Cute
Nazilla; **Nicknames:** *Nazneen*

NEA Swedish: Nickname for Linnea

NEBULA Latin: Misty

NECEDAH Native American: Yellow (Winnebago)

NEDA English: Wealthy protector, feminine form of Ned. Slavic, African: Born on Sunday
Nedda

NEDIVAH Hebrew: Giving
Nediva

NEEJA Hindi: Lily

NEEMA African: Born in prosperity (Swahili)

NEENAH Native American: Running water (Winnebago)

NEHAMA Hebrew: Comfort; also a surname
Nechama

NEILA Gaelic: Champion; feminine variant of Neil
Neala, Neelie, Nielsine, Neela; **Nicknames:**
Nealie, Neely, Nia

NEILIKKA Finnish: Clove

NEITH Egyptian: The divine mother, great creator-goddess; in ancient Egyptian mythology, Neith is shown wearing a red crown, her emblem is a shield with two crossed arrows worn on her head. Neith was later associated with Athena by the Greeks. See also *Athena, Matrika*
(Latin) *Athene;* **Old Forms:** *Mut, Net*

NEJMA Arabic: Star
(Egyptian) *Negma*

NELDA English: One who lives by the alder tree

NELIDA Spanish: A diminutive form of Cornelia, Elena, and Reinalda

NELKE German: Carnation; flower name

NELL Greek, English: Light; familiar form of Eleanor, Cornelia, Prunella, and similar names
(Russian) *Nelya*; *Nella, Nelma*; **Nicknames:** *Nelli, Nellie, Nelly*; **Famous Namesakes:** *Actress and singer Nell Carter*

NELWIN English: Bright friend, Nell's friend
Nellwyn, Nelwina, Nelwyna

NEMESIS Greek: Retribution; the Greek goddess of vengeance

NEOLA Greek: Youthful

NEOMA Greek: New moon
Neomea, Neomenia, Neomia

NEORAH Hebrew: Enlightened
Neira, Nera

NEPHTHYS Egyptian: Mythical nature goddess; sister of Isis
Old Forms: *Nebt het*

NEREA Spanish, Basque: Mine
Neria

NERIDA Greek: Sea nymph, mermaid; in Greek mythology the Nereids were the fifty daughters of Nereus and Doris who dwelled in the Mediterranean Sea.
Nereida, Nereyda, Nerice, Neried, Nerina, Nerine, Neris, Nerita

NERISSA Greek: From the sea; also a character in Shakespeare's *Merchant of Venice*

NERYS Welsh: Lady

NESSIA Greek: Pure. Scottish: From the headland
Nessa, Neysa

NET Egyptian: Original form of Neith

NETA Hebrew, Spanish: Plant or shrub

NETTIE French: Familiar form for names such as Annette, Antoinette, Nanette, and others
Netty

NEVAEH American: Heaven spelled backwards

NEVE Irish: Anglicized spelling of Niamh
Famous Namesakes: *Canadian actress Neve Campbell*

NEYLAN Turkish: Fulfilled wish

NIA English: Nickname for Neila

NIABI Native American: Young deer, fawn
(Osage)

NIAMH Irish: Radiance, brightness; the daughter of the sea god Manannan, she was known as "Niamh of the Golden Hair," a beautiful princess riding on a white horse.
Neve; **Famous Namesakes:** *Irish Actress Niamh Cusack, Canadian actress Neve Campbell*

NICHELE English: Modern blend of Nicole and Michelle
Nichel, Nichelle

NICOLE Greek, French: Victorious; feminine form of Nicholas
(French) *Nicolette*; (Italian) *Colletta, Nicola*; (Spanish) *Coleta, Coletta, Nicanora, Nicolasa*; *Nichole, Nikolia*; **Nicknames:** *Nicci, Nicea, Nicia, Nicki, Nickie, Niki, Nikki, Nikkie*; **Famous Namesakes:** *Actress Nicole Kidman*; **Star Babies:** *Daughter of Lionel Richie*

NIDRA Hindi: Goddess of sleep

NIEVES Spanish: Snows; a name given in honor of Nuestra Señora de las Nieves (Our Lady of the Snows)
Nieva; **Nicknames:** *Neva, Nevada*

NIJLON Native American: Mistress (Algonquin)

NIKE Greek: Mythological personification of victory; also a major brand of athletic shoes and sports equipment

NIKI Greek: Nickname for Nicole

NIKITA Russian: Masculine name used as feminine; popularized by the film *La Femme Nikita*

NILIA Latin: From the Nile
Nila, Nile, Nilea

NILOUFER Hindi: From the heavens
Nicknames: *Nilou*

NIMAH Arabic: Blessing, grace
Neima, Neimah, Nima

NINA Russian: Dreamer, possibly from old Slavonic word *ninati* that means to dream. Spanish: Little girl. Native American: Strong (Finnish) *Niina*; **Diminutive Forms:** *Ninacska, Ninochka*; **Famous Namesakes:** *Jazz singer Nina Simone*; **Star Babies:** *Daughter of Robert DeNiro and Helena Springs*

NINEL Russian: Inversion of the name Lenin, the name of the first Soviet prime minister
Nicknames: *Nelya*

NINON French: Diminutive form of Anne

NIOBE Greek: Fern; Niobe was the daughter of Tantalus in Greek mythology.

NIPA Hindi: Stream

NIRA Hebrew: Plow or God's field
Niria

NIRETA Greek: From the sea

NIRVELI Hindi: From the water

NISSE Scandinavian: Friendly elf
Nissa, Nysse

NITA Hebrew: To plant. Native American: Bear (Choctaw)

NITSA Greek: Peace

NITUNA Native American: Daughter

NITZANAH Hebrew: Blossom
Nizana; **Nicknames:** *Nitza*

NIXI Latin: Goddess of childbirth

NOA Hebrew: Motion; in the Old Testament, Noa was the daughter of Zelophehad; feminine form of Noah
Famous Namesakes: *Israeli actress Noa Tishby*

NOE Hawaiian: Mist, misty

NOELANI Hawaiian: Mist of heaven

NOELLE French: Christmas; feminine variant of Noel
Noel, Noele, Noell, Noella; **Famous Namesakes:** *Actress Noelle Evans*

NOKOMIS Native American: Grandmother (Chippewa)

A Celebrity by Any Other Name...

Are you a die-hard fan of Shelton Lee flicks?
Turn up the radio every time a
Gloria Maria Fajardo tune comes on?
Here's a surprising list of celebrity name-changers.

Star Name	*Birth Name*
Kareem Abdul-Jabbar:	Ferdinand Lewis Alcindor, Jr.
Muhammad Ali:	Cassius Marcellus Clay, Jr.
Woody Allen:	Allen Stewart Konigsberg
Julie Andrews:	Julia Elizabeth Wells
Fred Astaire:	Frederick Austerlitz
Babyface:	Kenneth Brian Edmonds
Lauren Bacall:	Betty Joan Perske
Tony Bennett:	Antonio Dominic Benedetto
Milton Berle:	Milton Berlinger
Sonny Bono:	Salvatore Phillip Bono
David Bowie:	David Robert Hayward-Jones
George Burns:	Nathan Brinbaum
Nicolas Cage:	Nicholas Coppola
Michael Caine:	Maurice J. Micklewhite
Truman Capote:	Truman Streckfus Persons
Chevy Chase:	Cornelius Crane Chase
Chubby Checker:	Ernest Evans
Cher:	Cherilyn Sarkisian
Eric Clapton:	Eric Clapp
Andrew Dice Clay:	Andrew Silverstein
Alice Cooper:	Vincent Damon Furnier
David Copperfield:	David Kotkin
Elvis Costello:	Decian Patrick McManus
Joan Crawford:	Lucille LeSueur
Tom Cruise:	Thomas Cruise Mapother IV
Rodney Dangerfield:	Jacob Cohen
Ted Danson:	Edward Bridge Danson III
Tony Danza:	Anthony Iadanza
Bo Diddley:	Elias Bates
Kirk Douglas:	Issur Danielovitch Demsky
Michael Douglas:	Michael Delaney Dowd, Jr.
Bob Dylan:	Robert Zimmerman

Gloria Estefan:	Gloria Maria Fajardo
Whoopi Goldberg:	Caryn Johnson
Pee Wee Herman:	Paul Rubenfeld
Hulk Hogan:	Terry Jean Bollette
Engelbert Humperdinck:	Arnold Gerry Dorsey
Elton John:	Reginald Kenneth Dwight
Michael Keaton:	Michael Douglas
B.B. King:	Riley B. King
Larry King	Larry Zieger
Spike Lee:	Shelton Lee
Little Richard:	Richard Penniman
Madonna:	Madonna Louise Ciccone
Lee Majors:	Harvey Lee Yeary
Malcolm X:	Malcolm Little
Meat Loaf:	Marvin Lee Adair
Marilyn Monroe:	Norma Jean Mortensen
Demi Moore:	Demi Gynes
Nancy Reagan:	Anne Frances Robbins
Robert Redford:	Charles Robert Redford, Jr.
Roy Rogers:	Leonard Slye
Mickey Rooney:	Joe Yule, Jr.
Winona Ryder:	Winona Horowitz
Soupy Sales:	Milton Supman
Susan Sarandon:	Susan Abigail Tomalin
Charlie Sheen:	Carlos Irwin Estevez
Martin Sheen:	Ramon Estevez
Sinbad:	David Atkins
Sting:	Gordon Matthew Sumner
Donna Summer:	La Donna Andrea Gaines
Tina Turner:	Annie Mae Bullock
Christopher Walken:	Ronald Walken
John Wayne:	Marion Michael Morrison
Stevie Wonder:	Steveland Judkins

NOLA Celtic: Nickname for Finola
Nuala

NOLANA Gaelic: Noble and renowned; feminine form of Nolan
Nolene

NOLITA Latin: Unwilling; also name of hip Manhattan neighborhood north of Little Italy
Noleta

NOMA Norse: Fate. Hawaiian: Example
Norn

NONA Latin: Ninth, born ninth
Nonna

NORA Greek: Light; diminutive of Eleanor. Irish: Honor; familiar form of Honora (Irish) *Noreen, Noreena*; (Finnish) *Noora*; *Norah, Norina, Norine*; **Famous Namesakes:** *Singer Norah Jones*

NORABEL English: Beautiful light; a modern blend of Nora and Belle

NORBERTA German: Bright heroine; feminine form of Norbert
Norberte; **Old Forms:** *Norberaht*

NORDICA German: From the north
Norda, Nordika

NOREEN Irish: Variation of Nora

NORMA Latin: From the north; feminine form of Norman

NOVA Latin: New. Native American: Chases butterfly (Hopi)
Novea, Novia

NOX Latin: Night
Nyx

NUBIA Egyptian: From Nubia (ancient name for Ethiopia)

NUDARA Arabic: Pure gold or silver; feminine variant of Nudar

NUMEES Native American: Sister (Algonquin)

NUMERIA Latin: Goddess of childbirth

NUNA Native American: Land

NUNZIA Italian: Announces
Nunciata

NURAY Turkish: Bright moon

NURIT Hebrew: Plant
Nirit, Nureet, Nurita

NURU Egyptian: Born during the day

NUTTAH Native American: My heart (Algonquin)

NYCHELLE Contemporary: Compound name of Nicole and Michelle
Nichelle

NYLA Arabic: Winner

NYMPHA Greek: Nymph, bride

NYOMI Hebrew: Spelling variation of Naomi

NYSSA Greek: Goal
Nysa, Nyse

OAKLEY English: From the oak tree meadow; a surname and variant of Ackerley
Oaklea, Oaklee, Oakleigh, Oaklie, Oakly

OANA Romanian: God is gracious

OBA African: River goddess

OBELIA Greek: Pointed, from the Greek *obeliskos*, a pointed pillar
Obelie

OCEANA Greek: Feminine form of Oceanus; in Greek mythology, Oceanus was a Titan father of rivers and water nymphs.

OCTAVIA Latin: Eighth, traditionally given to the eighth child born into a family; the feminine form of Octavius
Octaviana, Octavie, Ottavia, Octaviacia, Octiana, Otavita, Ottava, Ottaviana;
Nicknames: *Tava, Tavia*

ODA Norse: Pointed; familiar form of any of the names with the roots of *aud* or *odd*

ODANDA Spanish: Famous land

ODDVEIG Norse: Woman of the spear; derived from *oddr* pointed and *veig* woman, this name has been used for many centuries

ODE African: Born on the road, during travel (Nigeria)

ODEDA Hebrew: Stands strong, brave
Odede, Odeada

ODELETTE Greek, French: Little spring, little singer or ode
Odelet, Odeletta, Odelina, Odelle

ODELIA Greek, French: Melody, ode. Hebrew: Praise God. German: Prosperous battle, Odila is the more common spelling for this German name. See also *Odette, Otylia*
(German) *Ordella, Otthild, Otthilda, Otthilde*; (French) *Odile*; (Czech) *Othili, Ottilie*; *Odele, Odelina, Odelinda, Odiana, Odiane, Odila, Odilia, Otilie, Ottila, Ottilia, Ottillia*

ODELLA Anglo-Saxon: Woods on the hill
Odelyn, Odelyna

ODESSA Greek: Wrathful; Odessa is the feminine version of Odysseus, which has taken on the connotative meaning of wandering, traveling adventure in honor of the famous voyage in Homer's epic *The Odyssey*.

ODETTE French: Variant of Odelia and Odile, the name of the bewitched heroine and love of Prince Siegfried in Tchaikovsky's classic ballet *Swan Lake*

ODIANA German: Spelling variation of Odelia

ODINA Native American: Mountain (Algonquian)

OENONE Greek: In Greek mythology, daughter of the river-god Cebren, she was abducted by Paris and became his first wife and mother of Corythus.

OGIN Native American: Wild rose
Ogina, Ogyna

OHANNA Hebrew: Spelling variation of Joanna
Ohana, Ohannah

OIHANE Spanish: From the forest

OKALANI Hawaiian: Heaven, heavenly
Okalana, Okalanah

OKSANA Ukrainian: Variation of Xenia
Oksanna, Oxana; **Diminutive Forms:** *Ksanochka, Oksanka*; **Famous Namesakes:** Skater Oksana Baiul

OLA Scandinavian: Ancestor's relic, related to the masculine name Olaf; (Greek) possibly a familiar form of Olesia
Olah

OLABISI African: Joy multiplied (Nigeria)

OLALLA Greek: Spoken sweetly

OLATHE Native American: Beautiful (Shawnee)

OLAUG Norse: Dedicated to our ancestors

OLDWIN English: Special friend
Oldwyn; **Nicknames:** *Oldwina*

OLEANDER English: Botanical name from an evergreen shrub known for its fragrant white, lavender, or pink flowers and its poison. See also *Oliana*

OLENA Ukrainian: Variation of Helena

OLETHA Scandinavian: Nimble, light-footed
Yaletha, Oleta

OLETHEA Latin: Honest, truthful; variant of Alethea

OLGA Russian, Romanian, Hungarian: Blessed, holy; feminine form of Oleg and variant of Helga. Saint Olga was a princess of Kiev who introduced her subjects to Christianity.
Olenka; **Nicknames:** *Olya, Olina*; **Famous Namesakes:** *Soviet gymnast Olga Korbut*

OLIANA Hawaiian: Variant of Oleander

OLINA Hawaiian: Joyous. Czech: Familiar form of Olga

OLINDA Latin: Fragrant, perfumed. Spanish: Guardian of the property. Greek: Possible variant of Yolanda, violet flower

OLITA English: Variation of Alida

OLITHIA Latin: Spelling variation of Alethea

OLIVIA Latin, Spanish, Swedish: Olive tree (Irish) *Alvy, Oilbhe, Olive*; **Nicknames:** *Livia, Livie, Lyvia, Olivie*; **Famous Namesakes:** *British actress Olivia de Havilland, Australian singer and actress Olivia Newton-John*; **Star Babies:** *Daughter of Reggie Arrizu and Sheila Arrizu, Denzel Washington, Lori Loughlin and Massimo Giannulli*

OLKA Polish: Variation of Alexandra
Ola

OLWEN Welsh: White footprint, white tracks; Olwen was the Celtic mythological daughter of Ysbaddaden and wife of Culwch, who saved her from her monstrous father.
Olwina, Olwyn, Olwyna

OLYMPIA Greek: From Mount Olympus, home to the gods
(French) *Olympe*; (Italian) *Olimpia*;
Nicknames: *Pia*; **Famous Namesakes:** *Actress Olympia Dukakis*

OMA Hebrew: Reverent, devoted. German: Grandmother, probably derived from the Latin meaning; Latin: Mother and another name for the Roman fertility goddess Bona Dea. Arabic: Mother, people, nation
Omah

OMENA Finnish: Apple

OMPHALE Greek: Legendary queen of Lydia

ONEIDA Native American: Standing rock; one who is a member of the Oneida tribe

ONELLA Hungarian: Variation of Helena

ONI African: Born on holy ground, blessed place (Yorba)

ONNELI Finnish: Happiness

ONORA Irish: Spelling variation of Honora

OONA Irish: Unity; Gaelic form of Agnes
Una, Oonagh; **Famous Namesakes:** *Actress Oona O'Neill Chaplin (daughter of Eugene O'Neill, wife of Charlie Chaplin)*

OPAL English: A jewel; a semiprecious stone known for its beautiful iridescent colors (Hindi) *Upala*; *Opalina, Opaline, Opel*

OPHELIA Greek: Help; likely the most famous Ophelia is Polonius' daughter in Shakespeare's *Hamlet*
(French) *Ophelie*; (Spanish) *Ofelia*

OPS Latin: Another name for the Roman Sabine, goddess of the earth and of abundance and wealth

ORA Latin, Spanish: Golden, variant of Aura and Aurelia. Greek: Gentle breeze. Hebrew: Light
Orah

ORABELLA English: Answered prayer; variant of Arabella
Orabel, Orabelle; **Nicknames:** *Bel, Belle, Bella, Ora, Orra*

ORALEE Hebrew: The Lord is my light; also a variant of Aurelia

ORANE French: Variation of Aurelia

ORBONA Latin: Roman goddess invoked by parents to grant them children

OREA Greek: From the mountains
Oreah, Oria, Oriah

ORELLA Latin: Message from the gods, delivered from the oracle, a name for the oracle herself
Orela

ORIANA Latin, Italian: Golden

ORIDA Native American: Expected one

ORIEL French: Bird; related to the Oriole, known for its brilliant orange-gold markings

ORKIDEH Persian: Orchid

ORLENA French: Gold
Orlene

"We don't know when our name came into being or how some distant ancestor acquired it. We don't understand our name at all, we don't know its history and yet we bear it with exalted fidelity, we merge with it, we like it, we are ridiculously proud of it as if we had thought it up ourselves in a moment of brilliant inspiration."
—Milan Kundera

ORMA African: Free

ORNA Irish: Little green one
(Gaelic) *Odharnait*; *Ornat*

ORPAH Hebrew: Fawn; Oprah Winfrey's name is actually a misspelling of this uncommon Old Testament name.
Ofra, Ophrah, Oprah; **Famous Namesakes:** *Canadian cellist Ofra Harnoy*

ORQUIDEA Spanish: Orchid
Orquidia

ORTENSIA Latin: Spelling variation of Hortense

ORTYGIA Greek: Island known from Greek mythology as the birthplace of Apollo and Artemis

ORVA English: Brave friend. French: Golden

OSANE Basque: Health

OSANNA Latin: Praise God
Osana, Oksanna

OSEYE Egyptian: Happy
Osey

OSYKA Native American: Eagle (Choctaw)

OTRERA Latin: Queen of the Amazons and
mother of Penthesilea and Hippolyta in
Greek mythology

OTYLIA Polish: Rich, prosperous, variant
of Odelia

> *"Change it to what? Tiffany?*
> *It's been an advantage. It's*
> *unforgettable. I'm the only one."*
> —Swoosie Kurtz

OVIA Latin: Egg
Oviah

OWENA Welsh: Noble-born, young fighter

OZLEM Turkish: Yearning

PADMA Hindi: Lotus

PAIGE French: Page, attendant
Page; **Famous Namesakes:** *Actress Paige
Moss*; **Star Babies:** *Daughter of Sinbad*

PAISLEY Scottish: A particularly patterned,
usually colorful fabric first produced in
Paisely, Scotland
Paislee, Paisleigh, Paislie

PÄIVI Finnish: Day

PALES Latin: A goddess of shepherds and
flocks in Roman mythology

PALLAS Greek: Another name for Athena,
goddess of wisdom

PALMA Latin: Palm tree; also a place name
(Spanish) *Palmira*; *Palmyra*

PALOMA Spanish: Dove
Nicknames: *Aloma*; **Famous Namesakes:**
Jewelry designer Paloma Picasso; **Star Babies:**
Daughter of Emilio Estevez and Carey Salley

PAMELA English: Invented by the sixteenth-
century poet Sir Philip Sidney, Pamela is
possibly derived from the Greek words "pan"
meaning all and "meli" meaning honey.
Pamelina, Pameline, Pamella, Pammeli;
Nicknames: *Pam*; **Famous Namesakes:**
*Actress Pam Dawber, Actress Pamela Anderson
Lee*

PAMINA Italian: Meaning unknown; a character from Mozart's opera *Die Zauberflöte*

PAMUY Native American: Water moon
(Hopi)

PANDARA Hindi: Wife

PANDITA Hindi: Studious

PANDORA Greek: All gifted; according to mythology Pandora was the first woman endowed with gifts from the gods. Pandora's box contained all the evils of the world.

PANPHILA Greek: All-loving

PANSY English: Flower name from the French word *pensée* meaning thought (Finnish) *Orvokki*; *Pansie, Pansey*; **Old Forms:** *Pensée*

PANTEHA Persian: Name of a princess

PANTHEA Greek: All the gods; related to the Greek word *pantheon* which means temple to all gods
Panthia, Pantheya

PAOLA Italian: Variation of Paula

PAPINA Native American: Vine which grows on oak tree (Miwok)

PARAND Persian: Silk

PARCA Latin: Named for the furies; myth name for the jewel

PARIS English: Original meaning uncertain, though the modern meaning refers to the French capital
Star Babies: *Daughter of Michael Jackson*

PARISA Persian: Like a fairy

PARKER English: Park keeper
Famous Namesakes: *Actress Parker Posey*

PARTHENIA Greek: Chaste
Parthenie

PARVANEH Persian: Butterfly

PASCALE French: Born at Easter (Greek) *Pesha*; (Spanish) *Pascuala*; (Russian) *Parasha, Pasha, Praskovia*; *Pascala, Pascaline, Pasclina*; **Famous Namesakes:** *French actress Pascale Bussières*

PASTORA Spanish: Shepherdess
Pastore

PATIENCE Latin, French: Patient; a virtue name similiar to Hope and Prudence (Spanish) *Paciencia*; *Patiencia, Patientia*

PATRICIA Latin: Noble, patrician; feminine form of Patrick
(French) *Patrice*; (Italian) *Patrizia*; (Irish) *Padraigin*; **Nicknames:** *Pati, Trisa, Trish, Trisha, Pat, Patsy, Patti, Patty*; **Famous Namesakes:** *Singers Patti LaBelle and Patsy Cline, Actress Patty Duke, First Lady Pat Nixon*

PAULA Latin, Spanish, Swedish: Small; feminine form of Paul
(French) *Paulette, Pauline*; (Italian) *Paola*; (Swedish) *Paulina*; (Russian) *Pavlina, Polina*; (Ukrainian) *Pavla*; (Finnish) *Pauliina*; (Hungarian) *Palika*; **Nicknames:** *Pauleta*; **Diminutive Forms:** *Pauletta, Paulita*; **Famous Namesakes:** *Singer Paula Abdul, Czech model Paulina Porizkova*

PAULINE French: Variation of Paula
Famous Namesakes: *British actress Pauline Collins*; **Star Babies:** *Daughter of Princess Stephanie of Monaco*

PAVATI Native American: Clear water (Hopi)

PAX Latin: Peace; a Roman goddess of mythology

PAZ Hebrew: Golden. Spanish: Peace
Paza; **Nicknames:** *Pazia, Pazit*

PEACE English: Peace, tranquillity, contentment

PEARL English: Pearl; birthstone for the month of June that is said to impart health and wealth
Pearla, Pearle, Pearlina, Pearline; **Famous Namesakes:** *Singer Pearl Bailey*

PEDRA Spanish: Rock; feminine form of Pedro, a popular Spanish form of Peter

PEG Greek: Nickname for Margaret

PEGAH Persian: Dawn

PELAGIA Greek: Dweller by the sea

PELICIA Greek: Weaver

PELLKITA Latin: Happy
Pellikita

PEMBE Turkish: Pink

PENELOPE Greek: Bobbin worker, weaver; faithful wife of Odysseus during the Trojan War
Penelopa, Pennelope; **Nicknames:** *Penny, Pennie*; **Famous Namesakes:** *Parenting expert Penelope Leach, Actress Penelope Ann Miller*

PENINAH Hebrew: Pearl
Penina, Penine

PENTHESILEA Greek: A queen of the Amazons

PENTHIA Greek: Born fifth
Penthea

PEONY Greek: Flower known for its medicinal powers; from Greek "paionia" and Paion, the physician of the gods

PEPITA Spanish: He shall add; dimunitive of Jose, popular Spanish form of Joseph

PERDITA Latin: Lost; Perdita was the mother to ninety-nine dalmatians in Disney film *101 Dalmatians*

PEREGRINE Latin: Wanderer, voyager; the peregrine is a favored bird in the ancient sport of falconry.
Peregrina; **Nicknames:** *Perry*

PERFECTA Spanish: Perfect

PERO Greek: The beautiful daughter of Neleus and Chloris and mother of Asopus

PERPETUA Latin: Continual

PERSEPHONE Greek: Goddess of the underworld, daughter of Zeus and Demeter
Persephonie

PERSIA Contemporary: Place name of a country now known as Iran
Persis

PERZSIKE Hebrew: Devoted to God
Nicknames: *Perzsi*

PETA Native American: Golden eagle (Blackfoot)

PETRA Greek: Rock; a feminine variant of Peter
(French) *Pierrette*; (Italian) *Pietra*; (Swedish) *Petronella*; (Danish) *Pedrine, Petrine*; (Polish) *Petronela*; *Parnella, Petrina, Petronelle, Petronia, Petronilla, Petronille, Pierretta*

PETUNIA English: Lovely trumpet-shaped flower

PEYTON English: Warrior's village; a name used for both genders. *Peyton Place* was the name of a popular TV show from the 1960s.
Payton, Payten, Payden, Paiden, Paydyn, Paidyn

PHAEDRA Greek: Bright; daughter of Minos

PHEDORA Greek: Supreme gift
Pheodora

PHIALA Irish: Fifth-century Irish saint

PHILIPPA Greek: Lover of horses; feminine form of Philip
(Spanish) *Felepita, Felipa*; (Polish) *Filipa, Filipina*; *Philipa, Philippine, Phillipa*; **Nicknames:** *Pippa*

PHILLINA Greek: Loving
Phila, Philida, Philina, Phillida

PHILOMELA Greek: Nightingale
Philomel

PHILOMENA Greek: Greatly loved
(French) *Philomène*; (Italian) *Filomena*; *Filomenia, Filomina, Philomina*

PHOEBE Greek: Sparkling, the shining one; in Greek mythology Phoebe was goddess of the moon, daughter of Leda, and mother of Leto.
(Greek) *Pheobe*; *Phebe*; **Famous Namesakes:** *Actress Phoebe Cates*

PHOENIX Greek: Dark red; in mythology, the phoenix was a beautiful bird that built its own pyre and then was reborn from the ashes.
Star Babies: *Daughter of Melanie Brown and Jimmy Gulzar*

PHYLLIS Greek: Green bough
Philis, Phillis, Phylis; **Famous Namesakes:** *Comedian Phyllis Diller*

PIA Latin, Italian, Spanish, Swedish: Pious
Famous Namesakes: *Actress and singer Pia Zadora, Journalist Pia Lindstrom*; **Star Babies:** *Daughter of Ingrid Bergman*

PIEDAD Spanish: Mercy

PIERRETTE French: Variation of Petra

PILAR Spanish: Pillar
Pelar, Peleria, Piliar, Pillar; **Nicknames:** *Pili, Piluca, Pilucha*

PILI Egyptian: Born second

PILUMNUS Latin: Goddess of birthing

PINGA Hindi: Tawny

PINJA Finnish: Pine tree

PIPER English: A surname that was originally given to a person who played on a pipe (flute)
Famous Namesakes: *Actress Piper Laurie*; **Star Babies:** *Daughter of Gillian Anderson and Clyde Klotz*

PIPPA English: Nickname for Philippa

PLACIDA Spanish: Tranquil; feminine form of Placido
Old Forms: *Placidia*

POCAHONTAS Native American: Playful; Chief Powhatan's daughter who successfully argued for the life and release of Captain John Smith. Pocahontas was later held for ransom by Jamestown, Virginia, settlers, and eventually married one of them.

POLLY English: Bitter; variant of Molly, diminutive of Mary
Famous Namesakes: *Actress Polly Bergen, British actress Polly Walker*

POMONA Latin: Apple; Roman goddess of fruit trees and fertility

POPPY Latin, English: Flower name popular in the southern United States
Famous Namesakes: *Author Poppy Z. Brite*; **Star Babies:** *Daughter of Jamie Oliver*

PORTIA Latin: From a Roman family name of obscure meaning; name of a character in Shakespeare's *The Merchant of Venice* who disguises herself as a man in order to defend her husband Antonio in court
Famous Namesakes: *Australian actress Portia de Rossi*

POTINA Latin: The Roman goddess who blessed mothers' milk.

PRABHA Hindi: Light

PRESLEY English: From the priest's meadow; surname
Preslea, Preslee, Presleigh, Preslie; **Famous Namesakes:** *Singer Lisa Marie Presley;* **Star Babies:** *Daughter of Tanya Tucker*

PRIMA Latin: First
Primalia; **Star Babies:** *Daughter of Connie Seleccha and John Tesh*

PRIMAVERA Italian, Spanish: Spring

PRIMROSE Latin, English: Flower name derived from the Latin phrase *prima rosa* meaning first rose.

PRISCILLA Latin: Archaic, ancient, she was banished; feminine variant of the Roman name Priscus
(Hungarian) *Piri, Piroska;* **Diminutive Forms:** *Prisca;* **Famous Namesakes:** *Actress Priscilla Kinsler, Singer and songwriter Priscilla Ederly, Actress Priscilla Presley*

PROSPERA Latin: Prosper
Prosperia

PRUDENCE English: Derived from the Latin word "prudens" meaning good judgement; virtue name
(Spanish) *Prudencia;* **Old Forms:** *Prudentia;* **Famous Namesakes:** *Author Prudence Foster*

PRUNELLA Greek: Plum
(French) *Prune; Prunelle, Prunellia;* **Famous Namesakes:** *British actress Prunella Scales*

PUEBLA Spanish: The town; a state in Mexico

PURA Spanish: Pure
Nicknames: *Pureza, Purisima*

PURIFICACION Spanish: Purification; refers to the ritual purification of the Virgin Mary after the birth of Christ
Purificasion; **Nicknames:** *Puro*

PYRENA Greek: Ardent, burning
Pyrene, Pyrenie

QETURAH Hebrew: Incense

QIANRU Chinese: Pretty smile

QUEEN English: Highest royal title for a woman
Queena, Queenie, Queeny; **Old Forms:** *Cwen, Cwene*; **Famous Namesakes:** *Singer and actress Queen Latifah*

QUENBY Scandinavian: Womanly, from the woman's estate
Quinby

QUERIDA Spanish: Beloved

QUESTA Latin: Seeker

QUIANA English: Divine
Quianna

QUIBILAH Egyptian: Peaceful
Star Babies: *Daughter of Malcolm X*

QUIES Latin: Tranquil, restful; from Latin word *quiescere* meaning to rest

QUILLAN Gaelic: Cub

QUINLAN Gaelic: Graceful, strong, well made; also a variant of Quinn
Quinnlan, Quinlyn, Quinnlyn, Quinnlynn

QUINN Irish: Intelligent, wise; surname
Famous Namesakes: *Actress Quinn Cummings*

QUINTA Spanish: Born fifth
Quintina

QUITERIE Basque: Calm, tranquil
Quiteira

RAANANA Hebrew: Unspoiled, beautiful
Raananah

RABIA African: Spring

RACHEL Hebrew: Ewe; in the Bible's Old Testament, Rachel was the favorite wife of Jacob and mother of Joseph and Benjamin. See also *Rahele*
(Spanish) *Raquel*; (Gaelic) *Raonaid*; (Scottish) *Raoghnailt*; (Swedish) *Rakel*; (Russian) *Rahil*; (Polish) *Rahel*; (Finnish) *Raakel, Rachele, Rachelle*; **Nicknames:** *Rae*; **Famous Namesakes:** *British actress/model Rachel Ward*; **Star Babies:** *Daughter of Kathleen Turner and Jay Weiss*

RADELLA English: Elfin counselor

RADINKA Slavic: Lively

RAE English: Doe; familiar form of Rachel or feminine form of Ray
Famous Namesakes: *Actress Rae Dawn Chong*

RAFA Arabic: Happy, lightening, to shine, to flutter (as in bird fluttering)

RAFIYA African: Dignified

RAHA Persian: Free

RAHELE Persian: Traveler

RAHIMA Arabic: Grace, merciful

RAIMUNDA Spanish: Wise defender

RAINEY English: Familiar form of Regina; Rainey is sometimes also is used in reference to wet weather.
Raini, Rainie, Rainy

RAISA Russian: Easy, light
Famous Namesakes: *Soviet First Lady Raisa Gorbachev*

RAJA Arabic: Hope
Rajaa, Ragaa

RAMIRA Spanish: Judicious

RAMLA African: Prophetess

RAMONA Spanish: Wise defender; feminine form of Ramon
Nicknames: *Mona, Ramonia*; **Star Babies:** *Daughter of Jonathan Demme*

RANA Arabic: Behold, attractive, beauty. Persian: Elegant

RANIA Egyptian: Delightful
Ranya

RANICA Hebrew: Lovely tune
Ranice, Ranit, Ranita

RAPHAELLA Hebrew: God has healed
Rafela, Rafaella, Rafaela, Raphaela

RAQUEL Spanish: Variation of Rachel
Famous Namesakes: *Actress Raquel Welch*

RASHA Arabic: Gazelle

RASHIDA Egyptian: Righteous
Rasheeda

RAUHA Finnish: Peace

RAVAN Persian: Spirit, soul

RAVEN English: Raven, black bird
Ravyn

RAYKA Persian: Beloved
Ryka

RAYNA Czech: Pure, clean; variant of Catherine
Raina, Raine; **Star Babies:** *Daughter of Mike Tyson and Monica Turner*

RAYSEL Yiddish: Rose

REAGAN Irish: Little ruler
Reaghan, Regan, Raygen

REBA Hebrew: Fourth born, a square, one that lies or stoops down
Famous Namesakes: *Singer Reba McEntire*

REBECCA Hebrew: Captivating, to tie, beautiful, desirable; Rebecca is the Latin form of the Hebrew name Rivka. The biblical Rebecca was the wife of Isaac and mother of Jacob and Esau.
(Hawaiian) *Lepeka*; *Rebekah*; **Nicknames:** *Becca, Becki, Becky*; **Famous Namesakes:** *Actress Rebecca De Mornay, Author Rebecca West*; **Star Babies:** *Daughter of Dustin Hoffman and Lisa Gottsegen*

REESE English: Passionate, enthusiastic
Reece, Rice; **Famous Namesakes:** *Actress Reese Witherspoon*

REGINA Latin: Queen
(French) *Reine*; (Spanish) *Reina*; (Norse) *Rana, Rania*; (Hindi) *Rani*; *Regine, Reginy*; **Nicknames:** *Rainey, Rainy, Reg, Reggie, Gina*; **Famous Namesakes:** *Actress Regina Taylor*

Mother of heaven, Regina of the clouds,

O sceptre of the sun, crown of the moon,

There is not nothing, no, no, never nothing,

Like the clashed edges of two words that kill.

—Wallace Stevens

REIJA Finnish: Vigilant, watchful

REINA Spanish: Variation of Regina

REMEDIOS Spanish: Remedies

RENATA Latin: Reborn
Renatta, Rennatta; **Nicknames:** *Renny*

RENÉE French: Reborn, to rise again
(German) *Renate*; *Rene, Renee, Renella,
Renelle*; **Nicknames:** *Rena*; **Famous
Namesakes:** *Actress Renée Zellweger, opera
singer Renée Fleming*; **Star Babies:** *Daughter
of Rachel Hunter and Rod Stewart*

RENITA Latin: Dignified
Renyta, Renetta, Renitah

RETA Greek: Speaker. African: Shaken

RETTA English: Unknown meaning; this
uncommon name likely began as a nickname
for Henrietta, Margareta, or Loretta.
Reta, Rheta, Rhetta

REVA Hebrew: Rain or one quarter, a fourth

REZ Hungarian: Copper-haired

RHEA Greek: A brook or stream; in mythology, the mother of Zeus
Famous Namesakes: *Actress Rhea Perlman*

RHEDA Anglo-Saxon: Anglo-Saxon goddess
known because of a mention by Bede the
Venerable that the third month of the year
was named for her

RHIANNON Welsh: Great queen; in Welsh
mythology, Rhiannon was the goddess of fertility and the moon. Stevie Nicks of the band
Fleetwood Mac was inspired by the ethereal
sound of Rhiannon when she wrote her
smash hit of the same name.
Nicknames: *Rhianna*

RHODA Greek: Rose

RHODOS Latin: Daughter of Poseidon
Nicknames: *Rhode*

RHONWEN Welsh: Slender, fair

RIA Spanish: From the river's mouth

RICA Spanish: Rich

RICARDA Spanish, Italian: Strong ruler;
feminine form of Ricardo, a popular Spanish
and Italian form of Richard

RICHAEL Irish: Saint

RIDHAA African: Goodwill

RIGMORA Swedish: Name of a queen
Rigmor

RIINA Finnish: Nickname for Catherine

RILEY Irish: Brave; originally a boy's name,
Riley has become increasingly popular as a
name for girls
Rylie, Rylee, Ryleigh, Reilly; **Star Babies:**
Daughter of Howie Mandel

RILLA German: Brook
Rille, Rillia, Rillie

RIMA Arabic: White antelope

RIMONA Hebrew: Pomegranate

RINA Hebrew: Song
Rena, Rinna, Rinnah

RIO Spanish: River

RIONA Irish: Royal

RIPLEY English: From the shouter's meadow
Star Babies: *Daughter of Thandie Newton*

RITA Greek: Pearl; a popular form of Margaret or Margarita
Famous Namesakes: *Actress Rita Moreno, Actress Rita Hayworth*

RIVA Latin: Regain strength

RIVE French: From the shore

ROBERTA English: Famous
Nicknames: *Bobbi, Robertia;* **Famous Namesakes:** *Singer Roberta Flack*

ROBIN English: Bright with fame; an abbreviation of Robert that has become a unisex name, also the name of a bird
(Scottish) *Robena, Robina; Robyn;* **Diminutive Forms:** *Robinetta, Robinette;* **Famous Namesakes:** *Actress Robin Givens, Actress Robin Wright Penn*

ROCIO Spanish: Dew drops

RODERICA German: Famous ruler; feminine form of Roderick
(Spanish) *Roderiga*

ROHINI Hindi: Red

ROLANDA German: Renowned in the land; feminine form of Roland
(Spanish) *Roldana; Orlanda, Rahlaunda*

ROMA Latin, Italian: From Rome, the capital of Italy
Famous Namesakes: *Irish actress Roma Downey*

ROMAINE French: From Rome
Romana

ROMIA Italian: From Rome

ROMY German: Bitter rose
Famous Namesakes: *Actress Romy Schneider;* **Star Babies:** *Daughter of Ellen Barkin and Gabriel Byrne*

RONA Norse: Mighty strength

RONIYA Hebrew: Joy of the Lord
Ron, Rona, Ronela, Ronella, Ronia, Ronit

RONJA Scandinavian, Finnish: A character from a children's book by Astrid Lindgren

RONLI Hebrew: Joy is mine
Ronili

ROSABELLE Latin: Beautiful rose

ROSALBA Latin: White rose

ROSALIE Italian: Rose
Rosalee, Rosalia

ROSALIND Spanish: Beautiful rose
Rosaleen, Rosalina, Rosalinda, Rosalinde, Rosaline, Rosalyn

Jaques. Rosalind is your love's name?
Orlando. Yes, just.
Jaques. I do not like her name.
Orlando. There was no thought of pleasing you when she was christened.
—William Shakespeare,
As You Like It

ROSAMARIA Spanish: Compound name of Rosa and Maria

ROSAMUND German: Noted protector or guardian
Rosamonde, Rosamunde, Rosemond, Rosemonde, Rosemunda

ROSANNA English: Blend of Rose and Anna
Rosana, Rosanne; **Famous Namesakes:** *Actress Rosanna Arquette*

ROSARIO Spanish: Rosary; refers to devotional prayers honoring the Virgin Mary
Nicknames: *Charo*

ROSE English, French: The rose is a flower known not only for its exceptional beauty and fragrance, but also as an enduring symbol of love. See also *Rozenn*
(Italian) *Rosa*; (Polish) *Rozalia*; (Finnish) *Roosa*; (Hungarian) *Rozsa*; *Roesia, Rohais*;
Nicknames: *Rosie*; **Diminutive Forms:** *Rosetta*; **Famous Namesakes:** *Actress and model Rose McGowan*

ROSEMARY English, Latin: Blend of Rose and Mary; also refers to the herb
(French) *Rosemarie*; *Rosemaria*

ROSHANAK Persian: Small light

ROWAN English: Little red-haired one; can also refer to the flowering Rowan tree
Rowen; **Nicknames:** *Ro*

ROWENA English: Famous friend. Celtic: Fair-haired
Rowynna

ROXANNE Persian, French: Dawn; in Edmund Rostand's play *Cyrano de Bergerac*, Cyrano and Christian court the beautiful Roxanne.
Roxane; **Old Forms:** *Roxana*; **Nicknames:** *Roxie, Roxy*; **Famous Namesakes:** *Actress Roxanne Hart*

ROYA Persian: Dream, vision

ROYALE French: Regal

ROZENN French: Rose; a name from Brittany, a region of France

RUBY Latin: A deep red, translucent precious stone; the name is derived from the Latin word "rubeus," and can also be used as a pet name for Roberta and Robin.
Rubie; **Famous Namesakes:** *Actress Ruby Dee*;
Star Babies: *Daughter of Rod Stewart and Kelly Emberg, Suzanne Vega, Matthew Modine*

"I looked on child rearing not only as a work of love and duty but as a profession that was fully as interesting and challenging as any honorable profession in the world and one that demanded the best that I could bring to it."
—Rose Kennedy

RUFINA Latin, Italian, Spanish: Red-haired
(Spanish) *Rufa*

RUNO Finnish: Poem

RUTH Hebrew: Friend; the Old Testament Book of Ruth centers on a young, loyal Moabite woman who refused to desert her mother-in-law even after her husband's death. She became an ancestor of King David.
(Gaelic) *Rut*; *Ruti*

RYBA Czech: Fish, girl

SAADA African: Helper

SABA Greek: From Sheba; Muslim origin means eastern wind

SABAH Arabic, Egyptian: Morning
Saba

SABIA Irish: Sweet

SABINA Latin: The Sabines were an ancient people of central Italy. Parents may recall the romantic *Griffin & Sabine Trilogy* by Nick Bantock.
(German) *Sabine*; *Savina*; **Nicknames:** *Bine, Bina*; **Famous Namesakes:** *Dutch actress Sabine Koning*

SABRA Hebrew: Unclear meaning, possibly to rest or cactus. African: Patience

SABRINA Latin: From the border; Sabrina is the Latin word for the Severn River in Wales. In Celtic legend, Sabrina was the name of a princess who was drowned in the Severn.
Sabria, Xabrina; **Nicknames:** *Zabrina, Zavrina*

SACAJAWEA Native American: Bird woman; the famous Sacajawea was a Shoshone woman named Boinaiv (grass maiden), who was renamed after Crow warriors captured her as an adolescent and sold her to a French-Canadian fur trader. The trader, Charbonneau, was hired as a guide for the Lewis and Clark expedition but it was Sacajawea, traveling with her newborn son, who was an invaluable asset on the journey.
Sacagawea

SACHIKO Japanese: Good fortune, happiness
Nicknames: *Sachi*

SADBH Irish: Good, sweet; this is the name of several Irish princesses, including the daughters of Conn of the Hundred Battles, Queen Medb of Connacht, and King Brian Boru.
Sadhbh

SÄDE Finnish: Ray of light

SADIE Hebrew: Nickname for Sarah
Sada; **Famous Namesakes:** *Actress Sada Thompson*

SADIRA Arabic, Persian: Prominent point of a valley

SAETH Welsh: Arrow

SAFARA African: Her place

SAFFRON English: A spice
Star Babies: *Daughter of Simon Le Bon*

SAFIYA Egyptian: Pure

SAGA Norse: Legend, myth

SAGE Latin: Wise one
Saige; **Star Babies:** *Daughter of Lance Henriksen and Jane Pollack*

SAGIRA Egyptian: Little

SAHKYO Native American: Mink (Navajo)

SAIDA Arabic, Persian: Happy, fortunate; feminine variant of Said
Saidah

SAILOR English: Sailor; an occupational name
Sayler, Saylor, Sailer; **Star Babies:** *Daughter of Christie Brinkley and Peter Cook*

SAKARI Hindi: Sweet

SAKHMET Egyptian: A lion-headed goddess worshipped in Memphis, wife of Ra

SAKINAH Arabic: God-inspired peace of mind; Sakinah stems from the word *sekoon*, meaning tranquillity.
(Persian) *Sakineh; Sekina*

SAKRA Hindi: From India

SAKURA Japanese: Cherry blossom

SALACIA Latin: Goddess of salt water

SALALI Native American: Squirrel (Cherokee)

SALIHAH Egyptian: Agreeable

SALIMA Arabic: Peaceful, safe; feminine form of Salim and a spelling variant of Salama
Saleema, Zulima, Selima

SALLA Finnish: Place name of a mountain in Lapland

SALLY Hebrew: Nickname for Sarah
Sallee, Salli, Sallie, Salley; **Nicknames:** *Sal*; **Famous Namesakes:** *Actresses Sally Field and Sally Struthers, Astronaut Sally Ride*; **Star Babies:** *Daughter of Carly Simon and James Taylor*

SALMA Arabic: Peaceful; stems from *salam*, meaning peace. Persian: Sweetheart
Famous Namesakes: *Mexican actress Salma Hayek*

SALOME Hebrew: Peaceful
Saloma, Selima; **Star Babies:** *Daughter of Alex Kingston*

SALVADORA Spanish: Savior; refers to Christ
Salbatora, Salvatora, Xalbadora, Xalvadora

SALVIA Latin: Whole, safe; Latin name indicating the medical value of the herb sage
Salva, Salvina, Salvinia

SAMANTHA Hebrew: Told by God; possibly a feminine form of Samuel. Aramaic: Listener
(Greek) *Amantha; Xamantha*; **Nicknames:** *Sam, Sami, Sammi, Sammie, Sammy*; **Famous Namesakes:** *Singer Samantha Fox*

SAMARA Hebrew: Under God's rule

SAMIA Arabic: Elevated; feminine form of Sami

SAMINA Arabic: Healthy, plump, and voluptuous; in certain parts of the Middle East, a woman's weight is symbolic of her social status, wealth, and health, and in that regard, "more" is considered better.
Saminah

SAMIRAH Arabic: Companion, one who is entertaining

SAMUELA Hebrew: Told by God; feminine form of Samuel

SANAM Persian: Idol

SANAZ Persian: A flower

SANCIA Latin: Sacred
(Spanish) *Sancha*

SANCTA Latin: Sacred, a feminine variant of Archard

SANDHYA Hindi: Twilight

SANDRA Italian: Nickname for Alexandra
Sandie, Sandy; **Famous Namesakes:** *Actress Sandra Bullock*

SANNA Finnish: Variation of Susan
Sanni

SANURA African: Kitten (Swahili)

SANY Hindi: Born on Sunday

SAOIRSE Irish: Freedom

SAPPHIRA Hebrew, Greek: Beautiful;
Sapphira was the biblical wife of Ananias
who conspired to deceive others and died
after lying. Variant of Saphire
Sapphire

SARAH Hebrew: Princess; Sarah was the wife
of Abraham in the Old Testament. Originally
named Sarai, God changed her name after he
told Abraham of Sarah's pregnancy.
(Spanish) *Sarita*; (Irish) *Saraid, Zaira*;
(Finnish) *Saara, Sari*; (Hungarian) *Sarika,
Sasa*; (Hawaiian) *Kala; Sara, Zara, Zarah*; **Old
Forms:** *Sarai*; **Nicknames:** *Sadie, Sallie, Sally*;
Famous Namesakes: *Actress Sarah Jessica
Parker, Duchess of York Sarah Ferguson*; **Star
Babies:** *Daughter of Jimmy Buffett, Kiefer
Sutherland, Andie MacDowell*

SARAMA African: Nice

SARANNA English: Princess; a modern
blend of Sarah and Anna

SARDA African: Hurried

SARELIA Latin: Of the spring, fertile; variant of Cerelia and possibly a variant of Cyril,
in which case it will mean lady
Sarilia

SARILA Turkish: Waterfall

SARINA Persian: Pure

SARISHA Hindi: Sophisticated

SASHA Russian: Nickname for Alexandra
Sacha; **Star Babies:** *Daughter of Kate
Capshaw and Steven Spielberg, Vanessa
Williams and Rick Fox*

SASSANDRA African: Name of a river
located on the Ivory Coast

SATINE English: Smooth fabric

SATU Finnish: Fairytale

SATURNINA Spanish: Gift of Saturn;
derived from the name of the Roman god

SAURA Hindi: Of the Saura; sun worshipper

SAVANNAH American: From the open
plain; this well-known spelling variation of
the Spanish *Savanna* is especially recognizable in the United States as a city in Georgia.
(Spanish) *Savanna; Sabana*; **Star Babies:**
Daughter of Steven Seagal and Arissa Wolf,
Jimmy Buffett

SAWNI Native American: Echo (Seminole)
Suwannee

SAXONA English: Swordsman; feminine
form of Saxon
Saxonia

SCARLETT English: Red; recognizable for
Scarlett O'Hara, the strong-minded heroine
of Margaret Mitchell's epic *Gone With the
Wind*
Scarlet; **Famous Namesakes:** *Actress Scarlett
Johansson*

SCHLOMIT Hebrew: Tranquil

SCHOLASTICA Latin: Scholar; based upon
centuries of tradition, Saint Scholastica is
considered the twin sister of Saint Benedict
of Nursia, founder of monastic communities
and compiler of the Rule of Saint Benedict.

SCHUYLER Dutch: Scholar
Skyla; **Diminutive Forms:** *Skye*

SCOTLYNN English: Variation of a place
name, Scotland

SCOTTI English: From Scotland
Scota, Scottee, Scottie, Scotty

SCOUT American: To listen; name of the
young heroine in *To Kill a Mockingbird*
Star Babies: *Daughter of Demi Moore and
Bruce Willis*

SEBASTIANE Latin: Revered or the Roman
term for a person from the ancient city of
Sebastia; feminine form of Sebastian
(French) *Sebastienne*; (Italian) *Sebastiana*;
Nicknames: *Bastiana*

SEBILLE Arthurian Legend: A fairy

SEGULAH Hebrew: Precious; treasure

SEGUNDA Spanish: Born second
(Latin) *Secuba*

SEINA Spanish: Innocent

SELA Hebrew: Rock; Sela was the biblical
capital of Edom. Its variant Selah is found
several times in the Book of Psalms, possibly
indicating a pause.
Selah, Sele, Seleta; **Famous Namesakes:**
Actress Sela Ward

SELAS African: Trinity

SELENA Spanish: Variation of Celine
Selina; **Famous Namesakes:** *Tejana singer
Selena Quintanilla Perez*

SELMA Teutonic: God's protection; a
feminine contraction of Anselm
Zelma; **Old Forms:** *Anselma*

SEMADAR Hebrew: Berry

SEMELE Greek: In Greek myth, the mother
of Dionysus

SEMIRA Hebrew: Height of heavens

SENALDA Spanish: Sign

SENECA Latin: Discipline; the name of a
Roman philosopher and statesman. Seneca
also refers to a Native American tribe in
New York.

SENOBIA Spanish: Variation of Zenobia

SENONA Spanish: Lively

SEPTEMBER English: The ninth month,
born in the ninth month

SEPTIMA Latin: Born seventh

SERAPHINA Hebrew: Fiery; Seraphim are
angels of heaven, each with three pairs of
wings and known for their strong love.
(Italian) *Serafina*; *Seraphine*

SEREN Welsh: Star

SERENA Latin: Tranquil, serene
Serene, Serina; **Famous Namesakes:** *Tennis
player Serena Williams*

SERIHILDE German: Armored battle maiden
*Serhild, Serhilda, Serihilda, Serilda, Serilde,
Zereld, Zerelda, Zerelde*

SERLINA Latin: Beautiful dawn; variant
of Zerlina

SETAREH Persian: Star

SEVAN Armenian: Name of a lake, exact
meaning unknown

SEVILLA Spanish: Place name of a city
in Spain

SHABAHANG Persian: Evening star

SHABNAN Persian: Raindrop
Shabnam

SHADA Native American: Pelican

SHADI Persian: Happiness
Shadee; **Nicknames:** *Shadan*

SHAELAN Irish: A surname of unknown meaning, Shaelan may be a variant of Shea meaning hawklike, majestic.
Shaelyn, Shaelynn, Shealan, Shealyn, Shealynn, Shaylan, Shaylyn, Shaylynn, Shaelin, Shaelinn, Shealin, Shealinn, Shaylin, Shaylinn

SHAHLA Persian: Dark-eyed woman

SHAHNAZ Persian: King's pride

SHAIBYA Hindi: Faithful wife

SHAKIRA Arabic: Grateful; feminine variant of Shakir
Shakeera, Shakeerah, Shakirah

SHALOM Hebrew: Peace

SHANATA Hindi: Tranquil

SHANESSA Irish: God is gracious

SHANI African: Wonderful

SHANIECE African: Gift of God

SHANNON Irish: Old and wise; from the Shannon, the longest river and chief waterway of Ireland
Shanahan, Shannen; **Famous Namesakes:** *Astronaut Shannon Lucid, Gymnast Shannon Miller, Actress Shannen Doherty*

SHANTI Hindi: Peaceful

SHAQUANA African: Truth in life

SHARADA Hindi: Lute; goddess or learning

SHARIFAH Arabic: Illustrious, noble, honorable, respectable, honest; feminine form of Sherif
Sharifa, Sherifa, Cherifa, Charifa, Cherifah, Charifah

SHARLENE English: Spelling variation of Charlene; variant of Charlotte

SHARON Hebrew: A plain; an area of ancient Palestine where many roses grew
Shareen, Sharelle, Sharin, Sharona, Sharoni, Sharyn; **Nicknames:** *Shari, Sherri, Sherrie, Sherry*; **Famous Namesakes:** *Actress Sharon Stone*

SHASA African: Precious water

SHASTI Hindi: Goddess of childbirth

SHAWN Irish: God has been gracious; feminine variant of Sean, a popular Irish cognate of John
Seana, Shauna, Sina; **Famous Namesakes:** *Musician Shawn Colvin, Actress Sean Young*

SHAWNEE Native American: Southern people, a tribal name (Algonquian)

SHAZIA Persian: Princess

SHEA Irish: Hawklike or majestic; an Irish family name that has become a popular name for girls
Shayla, Shae, Shay, Shaye; **Nicknames:** *Shaylee*

SHEILA Irish: Blind; an Irish variant of Cecilia, also an affectionate Australian slang term for a woman or girl
Sheela, Sheelagh, Sheelah, Sheilagh, Sheilah; **Famous Namesakes:** *Singer Sheila E., Actress Sheila Kelley*

SHEINA Yiddish: Beautiful
Shaine, Shayne

SHEIRAMOTH Hebrew: From heaven

SHELBY English: From the village or estate on the ledge; a surname that is more often used as a given name for girls than for boys. *Shelbey*

Shelby figures in Marie Osmond's fairytale collection *Tail!* as a beautiful mermaid with long, flowing locks.

SHELLEY English, Anglo-Saxon: From the ledge meadow; traditionally a boy's name, Shelley is now used for both genders and is a popular nickname for Michelle *Shelly, Shellea, Shelleah, Shelleigh, Shellie*; **Nicknames:** *Shell;* **Famous Namesakes:** *Actress Shelley Long, Actress Shelley Winters*

SHEMARIAH Hebrew: Protected by God

SHENANDOAH Native American: Beautiful daughter of the stars (Algonquian); the name of a river and valley in the Blue Ridge Mountains of Virginia, renowned for its pristine beauty

SHERIDAN Irish: Untamed *Sheriden, Sheridon*; **Nicknames:** *Sheri*

SHERRY English: Variant of Cheryl, Cher, and Sharon *Shari, Sherri, Sherrie*; **Famous Namesakes:** *Puppeteer Shari Lewis*

SHEYDA Persian: Lovesick *Shayda*

SHIFRA Hebrew: Beautiful

SHILOH Hebrew: The peaceful one, he who is to be sent; in the Bible, Shiloh is a prophetic name for the Messiah. Shiloh is also significant as the site of a crucial battle in the American Civil War. *Shilo*; **Star Babies:** *Daughter of Tom Berenger*

SHIRA Hebrew: Song *Shiri, Shirah*

SHIRIN Persian: Sweet *Shireen*

SHIRLEY English: From the bright meadow; surname *Sherlee, Sheri, Sherlie, Sherrlie, Sheryl, Shirely, Shirlea, Shirlee, Shirleen, Shirleigh, Shirlene, Shirlindam Shirline, Shirlley, Shirly, Shirlyn, Shurlee*; **Nicknames:** *Shirl;* **Famous Namesakes:** *Actress Shirley MacLaine*

SHOHREH Persian: Famous

SHOLEH Persian: Flame

SHONA Gaelic: God is gracious; a variant of Jane and Joan

SHOSHANA Hebrew: Lily (Armenian) *Shousnan*

SIAN Welsh: Variation of Jane *Shan*; **Nicknames:** *Shanee, Siani*; **Star Babies:** *Daughter of Dave Evans*

SIANY Irish: Good health

SIBLEY Greek: Nickname for Sybil

SIDDALEE American: Meaning unknown, but possibly related to Siddel, an Old English male name meaning from the wide valley; Siddalee is a character in books by Rebecca Wells. Sidda is also a school of yoga meditation.

SIDERA Latin: Luminous; the stars **Nicknames:** *Sidra*

SIDONIA Latin: From Sidonia
(French) *Sidonie*

SIEGFRIEDA German: Victorious peace;
feminine form of Siegfried

SIENA Italian: A city in the Tuscany region
of Italy
Sienna

SIERRA Spanish: Saw-toothed; also a
spelling variation of the Irish name Ciara
Cierra, Siera; **Star Babies:** *Daughter of James
Worthy*

SIGNY Norse: New victory
(Swedish) *Signe*

SIGRID Norse: Beautiful victory

SIGUN Norse: Daughter of Volsung
Sigune, Sigyn

SIKA African: Money

SILE Gaelic: Youthful
Sileas

SILVER English: Precious metal, white metal

SIMA Scottish: Listener. Persian: Face

SIMBRA African: Lioness

SIMCHA Hebrew: Joy

SIMI Native American: Valley of the wind
(Chumash); a place name in California,
known for its fine wine production

SIMIN Persian: Silver

SIMONE Hebrew, French: Hearkening, lis-
tening; feminine form of Simon
(Italian) *Simona*; *Shimona, Simeona*; **Famous
Namesakes:** *Scottish actress Simone Lahbib*

SINA Irish: God has been gracious; a variant
of Shawn and Seana
Famous Namesakes: *German track star Sina
Schielke*

SINCLAIR English: Saint Claire

SINEAD Irish: Variation of Jane
Sineaid; **Famous Namesakes:** *Singer Sinead
O'Connor*

SINI Finnish: Blue
Nicknames: *Sinikka*

SINOBIA Greek: Stranger
Sinovia

SINOPA Native American: Young fox
(Blackfoot)

SIOBHAN Irish: God has been gracious
(English) *Chevonne*; (Scottish) *Siubhan*;
Diminutive Forms: *Siobhainin*

SIPPORA Hebrew: Bird

SIRAN Armenian: Beautiful

SIRENA Greek: A siren; the mythological
sirens of Greek mythology lived on islands
and lured sailors to destruction on the rocks
with their sweet singing.

SISIKA Native American: Bird

SISKO Finnish: Sister

SISSY German: Nickname for Elizabeth
Famous Namesakes: *Actress Sissy Spacek*

SISTINE Italian: Refers to the Sistine Chapel
in the Vatican

SITA Hindi: Goddess of the harvest

SITALA Native American: One who
remembers (Miwok)

SITARA Hindi: The morning star

SIV Norse: Wife of Thor in Norse mythology

SIVE Irish: Goodness

SIYANDA African: We are growing.

SKENA Scottish: From Skene

SKYE English: Sky; also a short form of Schuyler

SKYLA English: Sky; also variant of Schuyler

SLANIA French: Health

SLOAN Scottish: Warrior, fighter; surname *Sloane*

SNOW English: Snow

SOCORRO Spanish: Help **Nicknames:** *Coco*

SOFIA Greek: Spelling variation of Sophia **Famous Namesakes:** *Colombian actress Sofia Vergara;* **Star Babies:** *Daughter of Lionel Richie, daughter of Mikhail Baryshnikov*

SOHA Persian: Star

SOINTU Finnish: Sound

SOKANON Native American: Rain (Algonquin)

SOLANA Spanish: Sunlight

SOLANGE French: Dignified, religious

SOLEDAD Spanish: Solitude *Soledada*

SOLITA Latin: Accustomed *Solyta;* **Nicknames:** *Sol*

SOLVEIG Norse: Compound of the old Norse words for house and strength **Famous Namesakes:** *Actress Solveig Dommartin*

SONIA Russian: Variation of Sophia *Sonja, Sonje, Sonya;* **Famous Namesakes:** *Skater Sonja Henie;* **Star Babies:** *Daughter of Nastassja Kinski and Ibrahim Moussa*

SONNET Italian: A lyric poem **Star Babies:** Daughter of Forest Whitaker

SOPHIA Greek: Wisdom (Greek) *Zsofie;* (Spanish) *Sofia;* (Scandinavian) *Sonje;* (Dutch) *Sofie;* (Russian) *Sonia, Sonya;* (Hungarian) *Zsofia, Zsofika; Zofia, Zofie;* **Nicknames:** *Sofi, Sophie;* **Famous Namesakes:** *Actress Sophia Loren;* **Star Babies:** *Daughter of Rebecca DeMornay and Patrick O'Neal, Jennifer Flavin and Sylvester Stallone*

SOPHRONIA Greek: Wise, sensible; feminine form of Sophronius *Sofronia;* **Nicknames:** *Fronia*

SORAYA Persian: Name of a constellation **Famous Namesakes:** *Wife of Reza Pahlewi, Shah of Iran*

SORCHA Irish: Shining bright

SORINA Danish: Strict; feminine form of Soren

SORJA Finnish: Slender

SOROUSHI Persian: Messenger

SORREL English: An herb

SOUZAN Persian: Fire

SOYALA Native American: The winter solstice (Hopi)

STAR English: Star
Starla, Starr; **Famous Namesakes:** *TV commentator Star Jones*

STELLA Latin: Star. See also *Estée* (French) *Estelle*; (Spanish) *Estela, Estella, Estrella, Estrellita, Trella*; **Diminutive Forms:** *Estelita*; **Famous Namesakes:** *Drama instructor Stella Adler, Actress Stella Stevens;* **Star Babies:** *Daughter of Elisabeth Shue, Harvey Keitel, Melanie Griffith and Antonio Banderas*

That Stella (o dear name)
that Stella is

That virtuous soul, sure
heir of heavenly bliss
—Sir Philip Sidney,
"Astrophil and Stella"

STEPHANIE Greek: Crowned in victory; feminine form of Stephen
(German) *Stefanie*; (French) *Étiennette*; (Russian) *Panya, Stepanida, Stesha*; (Czech) *Stepanka*; (Hawaiian) *Kekepania*; *Stefana, Stefania, Stephana, Stephania*; **Nicknames:** *Fanetta, Fanette, Stef, Steffi, Steffie, Steph, Stephie, Stevie*; **Famous Namesakes:** *Actress Stefanie Powers, Tennis player Steffi Graf, Singer Stevie Nicks;* **Star Babies:** *Daughter of Jon Bon Jovi*

STOCKARD English: Origins unclear, but this name may refer to a hardy tree or lumber. This unusual name has become recognizable with the popularity of actress Stockard Channing.
Stockhard, Stockhart, Stokkard

STORM English: Tempest
Storme; **Nicknames:** *Stormie, Stormy*; **Star Babies:** *Daughter of Nikki Sixx*

SUE English: Nickname for Susan

SUEANNE English: Lily; blend of the names Sue and Anne

SUELLEN English: Lily; blend of the name Sue and Ellen

SUMA Hindi: Flower

SUMMER English: Born in summer
Sommer; **Famous Namesakes:** *Swimmer Summer Sanders*

SUNNIVA Irish: Gift of the sun; Saint Sunniva was the daughter of a tenth-century Irish king and fled her homeland to avoid marriage to a pagan king.
(Swedish) *Synnove*; **Old Forms:** *Sunngifu*; **Nicknames:** *Sunn, Synne*

SUNNY English: Sunny, cheerful
Sunni, Sunnie

SUNSHINE English: Light from the sun

SUOMA Finnish: Finland

SURI Persian: Red rose

SUSAN Hebrew: Lily; short form of Susannah and commonly used as an independent name. See also *Zuzu* (German) *Susanne*; (French) *Suzanne*; (Italian) *Susanna*; (Spanish) *Suelita, Susana*; (Irish) *Sosanna*; (Scottish) *Siusan*; (Slavic) *Suzan*; (Czech) *Zusa, Zuza, Zuzana*; (Polish) *Zuzanny*; (Finnish) *Sanna, Sanni*; (Hungarian) *Zsuska, Zsuzsanna, Zsuzsi*; *Suzanna, Suzannah, Suzetta*; **Old Forms:** *Susannah*; **Nicknames:** *Sue, Sueanne, Suellen,*

Susie, Susy, Suzy, Zsa Zsa; **Diminutive Forms:**
Suzette; **Famous Namesakes:** *Activist Susan
B. Anthony, Actress Susan Sarandon, Actress
Susan Dey*

SUVI Finnish: Summer

SUZANNE French: Variation of Susan

SUZU Japanese: Bell

SVETLANA Russian: Luminescent
Nicknames: *Sveta*; **Famous Namesakes:**
*Russian gymnast Svetlana Boguinskaia, Opera
singer Svetlana Strezeva*

SWANHILDA Teutonic, Norse: Battle swan;
in Norse mythology, Svanhild was the
daughter of Sigurd and Gudrun.
*Svanhild, Svenhilda, Svenhilde, Swanhild,
Swanhilde*; **Nicknames:** *Sunhild*

SYBIL Greek: Prophetess; in Greek and
Roman legend, Sibyl was a name given
to female prophets or fortunetellers.
(Irish) *Sibeal*; (Scandinavian) *Sibella, Sibylla*;
Cibil, Cybil, Cybill, Sibyl, Sibyll, Sybilla, Sybyl;
Nicknames: *Sibley, Sib, Sibbie, Sibby*;
Famous Namesakes: *Actress Cybill Shepherd*

SYDNEY French, English: The meaning of
this name is uncertain and may derive from
a French place name for Saint Denis.
Another theory states that this name comes
from Old English for wide island. Sydney is
easily recognized as the name of Australia's
oldest and largest city.
Cidney, Cydnee, Cydney, Sidney, Sydnee

SYLVIA Latin: From the forest; Rhea Silvia
was the mother of the twins Romulus and
Remus in Roman mythology.
(French) *Sylvie*; (Italian) *Silvia, Sylvana*;
(Polish) *Sylwia*; (Hawaiian) *Kiliwa*; *Silva,
Sylva, Sylvania, Sylvina, Sylvonna*; **Famous
Namesakes:** *Poet Sylvia Plath, Journalist
Sylvia Poggioli*

TABIA Egyptian: Talented

TABITHA Aramaic: Gazelle
Tabita, Tabatha, Tabetha; **Nicknames:** *Tab,
Tabi, Tabbi, Tabbie, Tabby*; **Famous
Namesakes:** *Journalist Tabitha Soren*

TABLITA Native American: Tiara (Hopi)

TABORRI Native American: Voice that carries

TACINCALA Native American: Deer

TACITA Latin: Silent
Nicknames: *Tacy*

TADEWI Native American: Wind (Omaha)

TAFFY Welsh: Loved one
Famous Namesakes: *Folk singer Taffy Nivert*

TAHIRAH Arabic, Egyptian: Virginal;
feminine form of Tahir

TAHKI Native American: Cold (Algonquin)

TÄHTI Finnish: Star

TAIFA African: Nation, tribe

TAIKA Finnish: Magic, spell

TAIMA Native American: Thunderclap

TAIMI Finnish: Young tree

TAINI Native American: New moon
(Omaha)
Tainee

TAITHLEACH Gaelic: Quiet; also a surname

TAJA African: To mention

TAKALA Native American: Corn tassel
(Hopi)
Takalah

TAKIYAH African: Righteous

TAKOUHI Armenian: Queen

TALA Persian: Gold. Native American: Wolf

TALAR Welsh: From the headland in the field

TALAYEH Persian: Golden ray of sun

TALE African: Green

TALIAH Hebrew: Dew of heaven; may be an abbreviation of Natalia
Tahlia, Tal, Talia, Talya; **Famous Namesakes:** *Actress Talia Shire*

TALIBAH Egyptian: Seeks knowledge

TALIHAH Arabic: Scholar, knowledgeable person; a term used to describe an avant-garde researcher in a particular field

TALISE Native American: Beautiful water

TALITHA Aramaic: Young girl
Taletha

TALOR Hebrew: Morning dew
Talora, Talori

TALULA Native American: Leaping water (Choctaw)
Tallulah, Tallula, Talulah, Talulla; **Famous Namesakes:** *Actress Tallulah Bankhead*

TAMA Native American: Beautiful or fox

TAMAE Japanese: Ball

TAMALA African: Dark tree

TAMARA Hebrew: Palm tree; a variant of Tamar, this name is used as a symbolic name due to the beauty and fruitfulness of the tree.
Tamar, Tamarah, Tamra, Tamryn;

Nicknames: *Tami, Tammie, Tammy, Toma, Tomka*; **Famous Namesakes:** *Olympic skier Tamara McKinney*

TAMASHA African: Pageant

TAMIKA Japanese: People
Tami

TAMMY English: Nickname for Tamara
Tami, Tammi, Tammie; **Famous Namesakes:** *Singer Tammy Wynette*

TAMSIN English: Twin; variant of Thomasina

TANA Greek: Fire or star goddess

TANDY Native American: Flower

TANESHA African: Born on Monday
Tanishia

TANGERINE English: From Tangiers; also a type of fruit known for its deep orange color
Tangerina

TANGINIKA African: Lake goddess

TANIS Spanish: Camp of glory, military glory; feminine abbreviation of Estanislao, the Spanish variant of Stanislaus
Tannis

TANYA Russian: Uncertain meaning, though some suggest praiseworthy; Tanya is a popular pet name for Tatiana, feminine form of the Roman family clan name Tatius, and easily stands on its own as an independent name.
Tahnya, Tania, Tonnya, Tonya, Tonyah; **Famous Namesakes:** *Musician Tanya Tucker*

TAPANGA African: Sweet

TAPATI Hindi: Daughter of the sun god

TARA Irish, Gaelic: Rocky hill; place name of an Irish hill that served as an ancient seat of kingship. Tara is widely recognized as the name of the O'Hara's plantation in Margaret Mitchell's *Gone With the Wind*. Sanskrit: Star; a goddess of Hindu and Buddhist mythology (English) *Taralynn, Tarin*; (Gaelic) *Teamhair*; *Tarrah*; **Famous Namesakes:** *Olympic figure skater Tara Lipinski*; **Star Babies:** *Daughter of Oliver Stone and Chong Son Chong, daughter of Johnny Cash*

TARANEH Persian: Song

TAREN Greek: Innocent

TARIAN Welsh: Shield

TARINA Finnish: Story

TARISAI African: Look, behold

TARSHA Native American: Brave

TARU Finnish: Legend

TARUH Arabic: Happy, remote, forsaken; one who examines things carefully then offers them up for discussion

TARYN Contemporary: Rocky hill
Taren, Tarin, Tarren, Tarynn

TASINA SAPEWIN Native American: Black blanket (Ogala); the wife of Crazy Horse

TATE English: Cheerful
Tait, Taite, Tayte; **Nicknames:** *Tatelyn, Tayten*

TATELYN English: Cheerful; a variant of Tate
Tatelynn, Taytelyn, Taytelynn

TATIANA Russian: Feminine form of Tatius, an ancient Roman clan name of uncertain meaning
(Scandinavian) *Taina; Tatianna*; **Nicknames:** *Tanya, Tania*; **Diminutive Forms:** *Tiahna, Tiane, Tianna, Tiauna, Tionna*; **Famous Namesakes:** *Opera singer Tatiana Troyanos*; **Star Babies:** *Daughter of Caroline Kennedy and Ed Schlossberg*

TATUM English: Light-hearted
Famous Namesakes: *Actress Tatum O'Neal*

TAURA English: Bull; feminine form of Taurus, an astrological name
Taurina

TAURET Egyptian: Mythical goddess of pregnant women

TAVIA Latin: Nickname for Octavia

TAWNY English: Golden brown; the warm sandy color of a lion's coat
Tawnee, Tawney, Tawni, Tawnia, Tawnie

TAYA Japanese: Young

TAYANITA Native American: Young beaver (Cherokee)

TAYEN Native American: New moon

TAYLA African: She has been seen

TAYLOR English: Tailor; once a surname and boy's name, Taylor and its variants are growing in popularity as names for daughters.
Tailor, Tayler; **Famous Namesakes:** *Singer Taylor Dayne*; **Star Babies:** *Daughter of Michael Crichton, David Hasselhoff, Garth Brooks*

TAYSIR Arabic: Makes easier, simplifies

TEAGAN Irish: Little poet
Tegan, Teige

TEAL English: The bird teal; also the blue-green color.
Nicknames: *Teela*

TEFNUT Egyptian: God of atmospheric moisture; with Shu, Tefnut formed the first pair of the Heliopolitan Ennead.

TEHYA Native American: Precious

TELLUS Latin: Earth

TELYN Welsh: Harp

TEMIMA Hebrew: Whole, honest
Teme

TEMIRA Hebrew: Tall

TEMPEST English: Turbulent, stormy
Tempeste; **Famous Namesakes:** *Actress Tempestt Bledsoe*

TEMPLA Latin: Sanctuary, temple
Temple

TENDAI African: Be thankful to God

TERCEIRA Spanish: Born third

TERENTIA Latin: Tender, good; feminine form of the Roman clan name Terentius, Terentia was the name of Cicero's first wife

TERESA Spanish: Variation of Theresa
Nicknames: *Tere, Teresita*

TERIANN English: Modern blend of the familiar form of Theresa and Ann
Teriana

TERIKA English: Modern blend of the familiar form of Theresa and Erica

TERILYNN English: Modern blend of the familiar form of Theresa and Lynn

TERPSICHORE Greek: Delight of dance; a mythological muse of dance and lyric poetry

TERRA Latin: The planet earth; in mythology, Terra is the Roman earth goddess equivalent to the Greek Gaia.
Teralyn, Terrah

TERRENE Latin: Smooth
Terrin, Terryn, Teryn

TERRY English: Nickname for Theresa
Teri, Terri; **Famous Namesakes:** *Author Terry McMillan, Actress Teri Garr*

TERTIA Latin: Third
(Italian) *Terza*

TESS English: Nickname for Theresa
Famous Namesakes: *British TV host Tess Daly*

TETHYS Greek: The mythical Tethys and her husband Oceanus had thousands of children who became the world's lakes and rivers.

THADDEA Greek: Meaning uncertain, possibly brave or wise; feminine form of Thaddeus
Thaddia

THADINA Hebrew: Given praise
Thadine

THAIS Greek: Beloved; Saint Thais is the famous Egyptian courtesan portrayed in Massenet's opera *Thaïs*. According to the legend she was a reputed sinner in Egypt who was converted to Christianity by Saint Paphnutius, brought to a convent, and lived out the rest of her days in seclusion.
(Russian) *Taisiya*; *Thaisia, Thaisis*

THALASSA Greek: The sea, a mythological woman of the sea
Famous Namesakes: *Author Thalassa Ali*

THALIA Greek: To bloom; in Greek mythology, Thalia was the joyous muse of comedy. *Talia, Thaleia;* **Famous Namesakes:** *Actress Talia Shire*

THANDIWE African: Loving

THEA Greek: Goddess, godly; also abbreviation of names like Althea and Dorothea. The mythological Thea was the Greek goddess of light and mother of the sun, moon, and dawn.
Teah, Tia, Tiah, Tea; **Famous Namesakes:** *British musician Thea Gilmore*

THEKLA Greek: Divine fame; name borne by an early martyr
(Polish) *Tekli; Tecla, Tekla, Thecla*

THELMA Greek: Nursing
Telma; **Famous Namesakes:** *Actress Thelma Ritter*

THEMA Greek: Goddess of justice, often portrayed holding scales
Themis

THEODORA Greek: Gift of God; feminine form of Theodore
(Italian) *Teodora;* (Russian) *Fedora, Fedosia, Feodora;* (Polish) *Teodory; Theadora;*
Nicknames: *Dora, Teddi, Tedra, Tedre, Thea, Theda*

THEODOSIA Greek: Gift of God; feminine form of Theodosios
(Polish) *Teodozji*

THEOLA Greek: Divine

THEOPHILIA Greek: Loved by God

THERESA Greek: Reaper; Saint Theresa of Avila is one of the principal and most beloved saints of the Catholic Church, known for her simple goodness and nature of her love for God.

(German) *Tresa;* (French) *Therese;* (Italian) *Teresa;* (Spanish) *Teresita;* (Irish) *Toireasa;* (Scandinavian) *Terese;* (Swedish) *Teresia;* (Romanian) *Tereza;* (Hungarian) *Teca, Terezia, Treszka; Tassos, Teresina, Terisita, Thera;* **Nicknames:** *Teri, Terri, Terrie, Terry, Tess, Tessa, Tessia, Tessie, Tosia, Tracee, Traci, Tracy, Zyta;* **Famous Namesakes:** *Albanian Missionary Mother Teresa of Calcutta, Actress Theresa Russell;* **Star Babies:** *Daughter of Jerry Garcia*

THETIS Greek: Thetis is the mother of Achilles in Greek mythology. She held her son by the heel and dipped him into the river Styx in an attempt to make him immortal. Because his heel did not touch water, it was his one vulnerable spot.

THIRZA Hebrew: Delightful

THISBE Greek: Where the doves live; Thisbe was considered the fairest maiden in all of Babylon, and was the lover of Pyramus, the most handsome youth.

THOMASINA Hebrew: Twin; feminine form of Thomas
Thoma, Thomasin, Thomsina, Tomasina, Tomasine; **Nicknames:** *Tommie*

THORA Norse: Thunder goddess; feminine form of Thor
Thyra, Tora, Tyra

THURAYYA Arabic: Star; refers to the Pleiades

TIA Spanish: Aunt
Famous Namesakes: *Actress Tia Carrere*

TIBERIA Latin, Italian: From the Tiber River

TIERNEY Irish: Regal, lordly; surname
Famous Namesakes: *Actress Maura Tierney*

TIERRA Spanish: Earth

TIESHA African: Life. English: Variant of Leticia or Latisha. Latin: Variant of Tisha

TIFFANY Greek: God's appearance; a common English variant of the Greek name Theophania
Theophaneia, Theophania, Theophanie, Tifany, Tiffani, Tiffanie, Tiffeny, Tiffney, Tiphanie; **Nicknames:** *Tiff, Tiffi, Tiffy*

TIKVA Hebrew: Hope

TILLY English: Nickname for Matilda

TIMEA Hungarian: Honor

TIMOTHEA Greek: One who honors God; feminine form of Timothy
Timothia; **Nicknames:** *Thea, Timmie, Timmy*

TINA Persian: Clay; Tina is also an English familiar form of Christina or Christine
Famous Namesakes: *Singer Tina Turner*

TIOMBE African: Shy

TIPONI Native American: Child of importance (Hopi)

TIPPER Irish: Water wall; nickname and variant of the Irish surname Tabar
Famous Namesakes: Second Lady Tipper Gore

TIRA Hebrew: Encampment, enclosure

TIRTHA Hindi: Ford

TIVA Native American: Dance (Hopi); Hopi dances are not just beautiful, but an integral part of the culture.

TIVONA Hebrew: Love's nature

TOIBE Hebrew: Goodly; the Yiddish form of the name means dove

TONI English: Nickname for Antonia
Tony; **Famous Namesakes:** *Author Toni Morrison*

TONIA Latin, English: Praiseworthy; an abbreviation of Antonia
Nicknames: *Tonisha*

TONISHA English: Praiseworthy; a variant of Tonia, which is a short form of Antonia

TOPAZ Latin: Yellow or pale-blue precious stone

TORI English: Nickname for Victoria
Torey, Torie, Torree, Torrey, Torri; **Famous Namesakes:** *Actress Tori Spelling, Musician Tori Amos*

TOURMALINE Singhalese: Green or blue gemstone

TOVA Hebrew: Good
Toba, Tovah, Tove; **Nicknames:** *Tobi, Tobey, Tobelle*

TRACY Greek: Nickname for Theresa
Tracee, Tracey, Traci, Tracie, Trasey, Trasy; **Nicknames:** *Trace*; **Famous Namesakes:** *Actress Tracey Gold, Entertainer Tracey Ullman, Tennis player Tracy Austin, Singer Tracy Chapman*

TREASA Irish: Strong
Treise

TREVA Celtic: Prudent

TRILBY Italian: One who sings musical trills, a soft hat; early editions of George Du Maurier's novel *Trilby* showed a character wearing a felt hat with a narrow brim. The runaway success of the novel and stage production of the story created an immediate demand for the hat.

TRINA Scandinavian: Nickname for Catherine

TRINITY Latin: Three beings in one

TRISHA Hindi: Thirst

TRISNA Hindi: Desired
Trishna

TRISTANA Welsh: Full of sorrows; feminine form of Tristan
Triste, Tristen, Tristina, Tristyn; **Old Forms:** *Trista*

TRIXIE Latin: Nickname for Beatrice
Star Babies: *Daughter of Damon Wayans*

TRUDY German: Spear of strength; diminutive of Gertrude commonly used as an independent name
Famous Namesakes: *Producer (and wife of Sting) Trudy Styler*

TSIFIRA Hebrew: Crown

TUCCIA Latin: One of the six Vestal Virgins

TUESDAY English: The third day of the week, born on a Tuesday
Old Forms: *Tiwesdaeg*

TUIJA Finnish: Cedar

TULA Native American: Mountain peak (Choctaw)

TULIA Latin: Bound for glory
Tulla, Tullia

TULLY Celtic: Peaceful

TUSA Native American: Prairie dog (Zuni)

TUULI Finnish: Wind; the variant Tuulikki is a Finnish forest goddess
Tuulikki; **Nicknames:** *Tuulia*

> *"A good name is better than precious ointment."*
> –Hebrew Ecclesiastes, 7:1

TUWA Native American: Earth (Hopi)

TWYLA English: Woven
Twila; **Famous Namesakes:** *Choreographer Twyla Tharp*

TYNE English: River
Tyna; **Famous Namesakes:** *Actress Tyne Daly*

TYRA Scandinavian: Spelling variation of Thora
Famous Namesakes: *Model and actress Tyra Banks*

TYTTI Finnish: Girl

TZIGANA Hungarian: Gypsy
Tzigane, Zigana

TZURIA Hebrew: God is strength
Tzuriya, Zuria

TZVIYA Hebrew: Doe, female gazelle
Civia, Tzivia, Zibia, Zibiah, Zivia

UALANI Hawaiian: Heavenly rain
Ualana, Ualaney, Ualania, Ualanie

UDELE Anglo-Saxon: Wealthy, successful
Udela, Udella, Yudelle; **Nicknames:** *Uda,*
Udah

ULA Celtic: Jewel of the sea. Spanish: Sweet
spoken; a pet form of the Greek name
Eulalie. Scandinavian: Wealthy

ULALIA Hawaiian: Variation of Eulalie

ULLA German, Swedish: Strong willed, from
the Norse *ullr*, willful, determined. Latin:
Familiar form of Ursula

ULRIKE German: Noble ruler, feminine
form of Ulrich
Ulrica, Ulrika; **Nicknames:** *Uli*

ULTIMA Latin: Final, the last one

ULU African: Second daughter (Nigeria)

ULULANI Hawaiian: Divine inspiration

ULYANA Russian: Variation of Julia
Nicknames: *Ulya*

UMA Hindi: Mother; another name for
the Hindu goddess Devi
Famous Namesakes: *Actress Uma Thurman*

UMAYMA Egyptian: Little mother

UNA Latin: One, unity, together; in Edmund
Spenser's epic poem *The Faerie Queene*, Una
is the knight Redcrosse's virtuous lady fair
whose parents are held captive by a dragon.
Native American: Remember (Hopi). Welsh:
White wave. See also *Oona*
Ona; **Famous Namesakes:** *Actress Una*
Merkl

UNDINE Latin: Little waves, ripple, mermaid;
in German mythology, undines were female
water-spirits created without a soul, but if
one married a mortal man and bore him a
child, she was granted a soul and made
human.
Undina, Undinia, Ondine, Ondina

> *"I want to have children while my*
> *parents are still young enough to*
> *take care of them."*
> —Rita Rudner

UNELMA Finnish: Dream, fantasy

UNIQUE Latin: Only one, special, undupli-
cated

UNITY English: Standing together, acting
as one
Unita

UNN Norse: Beloved girl
Unne

UPALA Hindi: Variation of Opal

URANIA Greek: Heavenly, mythological
muse of the astronomy
Urainia

URBANA Latin: Urban, lives in and belongs
to the city; implies sophistication
Urbania, Urbanah

URBI African: Princess (Nigeria)

URENNA African: Father's pride (Nigeria)

URI Hebrew: My light

URIANA Greek: Heaven, from the same
root as the name Urania
Urianna, Uriannah

URIKA Native American: Useful to the tribe (Omaha)
Ureka, Urica

URIT Hebrew: Bright, light
Urice, Urita

URITH German: Deemed worthy
Uritha

URSULA Latin: Little bear; Saint Ursula was a British princess who was martyred for her faith during her return from a pilgrimage to Rome.
(French) *Ursule*; (Spanish) *Ursulina*; (Polish) *Urszula, Urszuli*; *Urseline, Ursola, Urzula, Vorsila*; **Nicknames:** *Sula, Ursa, Ulla*; **Famous Namesakes:** *Swiss actress Ursula Andress*

USHA Sanskrit, Hindi: Dawn, mythological daughter of heaven and sister of night
Ushas

UTE German: Wealthy
Uta; **Famous Namesakes:** *German cabaret singer Ute Lemper, German actress Uta Hagen*

UTINA Native American: Member of my tribe, kin

UZZIA Hebrew: God is my strength
Uzia, Uziah, Uzziah

VACH Hindi: Well-spoken
Vac

VADIT Hebrew: Rose
Varda, Vardit, Vared

VALA Welsh: Chosen

VALDA Norse: Renowned ruler. Teutonic: Spirited in war
Valdis, Velda

VALENCIA Latin, Spanish: Brave, strong; place name of a Spanish city
Star Babies: *Daughter of Marlon Jackson*

VALENTINA Latin, Italian: Brave, strong; feminine form of Valentinus
(Slavic) *Valeska*; *Valentia*; **Nicknames:** *Valen, Valene, Valyn*; **Diminutive Forms:** *Valechka*; **Famous Namesakes:** *First Russian female cosmonaut Valentina Tereshkova;* **Star Babies:** *Daughter of Angelica Bridges and Sheldon Souray*

VALERIE Latin, French: Strong; derived from ancient Roman family name Valerius
(Italian) *Valeria*; *Balara, Balera, Balere, Valari, Valeraine, Valere, Valora, Valery, Valarie*; **Nicknames:** *Val*; **Famous Namesakes:** *Actress Valerie Perrin, Actress Valerie Harper*

VALMA Finnish: Variation of Wilhelmina

VANAMO Finnish: A flower

VANESSA Greek: Butterfly; from Phanessa, the mystic goddess of an ancient Greek brotherhood. Latin: Named for Venus
(Spanish) *Vanesa*; *Venessa*; **Old Forms:** *Phanessa*; **Nicknames:** *Vania, Vanna, Vanny*; **Famous Namesakes:** *British actress Vanessa Redgrave, Singer and actress Vanessa Williams*

VANORA Welsh: White wave

VAPPU Finnish: The first of May

VAROUNA Hindi: Infinite

VARSHA Hindi: Rain

VARTOUGHI Armenian: Rose lady
Vartouhi

VARUNANI Hindi: Goddess of the sea

VASHTI Persian: Beautiful

VASILISA Russian: Royal; feminine form
of Basil
Nicknames: *Vassa*

VAYU Hindi: Vital force

VEDA Sanskrit: Understanding

VEDAS Hindi: Eternal laws

VEDETTA Italian: Guardian, scout
Vedette

VEGA Latin, Swedish: One of the brightest
stars in the sky; also a surname. Arabic:
Falling star, messenger
Famous Namesakes: *Musician Suzanne Vega*

VELEDA Teutonic: Inspired intelligence;
the historical Veleda was a first-century
Germanic prophetess regarded as divine.

VELIKA Slavic: Great, famous

VELLAMO Finnish: Protector

VELVET English: Soft, rich fabric; velvet has
become an adjective to describe almost anything which has a soft, rich feel or texture.

VENETIA Italian: Place name for a northern
Italian city
Venita, Venice

VENICE Italian: Place name for a town in
Italy and also an area in southern California

VENTURA Spanish: Good fortune

VENUS Latin: Goddess of love and beauty
and the equivalent of the Greek goddess
Aphrodite; from the ancient Greek "Venus de
Milo" statue to Sandro Botticelli's "Birth of
Venus," and even to a 1980s pop music song,
Venus is an enduring symbol in the art and
music of the world. The second planet from
the sun is named for her.
(Russian) *Venera*; **Famous Namesakes:**
Tennis player Venus Williams

VERA Latin: True. Russian: Faith
(Latin) *Veradis, Veradisia*; (Spanish) *Verdad*;
(Russian) *Verochka*; (Czech) *Viera*; (Finnish)
Veera; *Verena*; **Nicknames:** *Vreni*; **Diminutive**
Forms: *Verushka*; **Famous Namesakes:**
Fashion designer Vera Wang

VERBENA Latin: Sacred herb with fragrant
flowers and leaves
Verbana, Verbenia

VERDA Latin: Unspoiled

VERENA German: Sacred wisdom; also
a variation of Vera, meaning true
Verene, Verina

VERNA Latin: Spelling variation of Laverne
Famous Namesakes: *Actress Verna Bloom*

VERONA Italian: Place name of a town
in Italy; also a variation of Verena

VERONICA Latin, Greek: Honest image; this name stems from a legend of a maiden who handed Christ her handkerchief on the way to Calvary, whereupon his likeness miraculously appeared on the cloth. (German) *Veronika*; (French) *Veronique*; (Polish) *Weronikia*; *Veronicha*; **Famous Namesakes:** *Actress Veronica Lake, French singer Veronique Sansone;* **Star Babies:** *Daughter of Rebecca DeMornay and Patrick O'Neal*

VESPERA Latin: Evening star
Vesperia, Vespira

VESTA Latin: Goddess of the hearth

VETA Latin, Spanish: Life

VEVINA Irish: Sweet lady; Vevina was used by Scottish poet James MacPherson in his Ossianic poetry.

VIANNE French: Blend of Vivian and Anne; Juliette Binoche played a character with this name in the film *Chocolat.*

VICENTA Spanish: Victor, conquering; feminine form of Vicente

VICTORIA Latin: Triumphant; feminine form of Victor. During the reign of England's Queen Victoria, Britain reached new heights in industrial and colonial power and diplomatic influence. The term Victorian today recalls her strong position on personal moral issues. (Spanish) *Vittoria*; (Swedish) *Viktoria*; (Polish) *Wikitoria, Wikta, Wiktorja*; (Hawaiian) *Wikolia*; *Victoriana, Victorina, Victorine, Victriva*; **Nicknames:** *Torey, Tori, Toriana, Torree, Torrey, Torri, Torrie, Tory, Vic, Vicky, Vickie*; **Famous Namesakes:** *Actress Victoria Principal, Singer Victoria "Posh" Adams;* **Star Babies:** *Daughter of Tommy Lee Jones and Kimberlea Cloughley*

VIDA Hebrew: Nickname for Davina

VIDONIA Portuguese: Vine branch

VIENNA Latin: Place name for the capital city of Austria

VIGILIA Latin: Alert, vigilant

VIJAYA Hindi: Victory

VIKA Scottish: From the creek

VILJA Finnish: Grain

VIMALA Hindi: Pure

VINA Spanish: From the vineyard

VINCENTIA Latin: Triumphant

VINEETA Hindi: Simple, humble

VINODINI Hindi: Happy girl

VIOLA Latin, Swedish: Violet, the name of a purple flower and also for that shade of purple; Viola is also an instrument in the violin family and the name of Shakespeare's heroine in *Twelfth Night.*
(French) *Yolande*; (Polish) *Jolanta*

VIOLET English: Lovely purple flower (French) *Violette, Yolanthe*; (Italian) *Violetta*; (Spanish) *Yolanda*; **Nicknames:** *Vi*; **Famous Namesakes:** *Ugandan author Violet Barungi*

VIRAG Hungarian: Flower

VIRDISIA Latin: Young and budding
Virdia, Virdis, Virdisa, Viridianai

VIRGINIA Latin, English: Virginal, chaste; also refers to Queen Elizabeth of England, the "Virgin Queen," who did not marry and for whom the state of Virginia is named. See also *Gina*
Verginia, Verginya, Virgena, Virgene, Virgenya, Virginee, Virginya; **Old forms:** *Virgina;* **Nicknames:** *Ginna, Ginnie, Ginny, Gigi, Ginger, Ginia, Ginya, Virge, Virgie, Virgy;* **Diminutive Forms:** *Ginnette;* **Famous Namesakes:** Author Virginia Woolf

VIRTUS Latin: Virtue
Virtua

VITA Latin: Life
(Hungarian) *Vicuska; Vitia*

VIVECA Scandinavian: With living voice, from Middle Latin phrase *viva voce;* life, alive. Teutonic: War castle, a place of refuge (Danish) *Vibeke; Vivica;* **Famous Namesakes:** *Actress Vivica Fox*

VIVIAN Latin, English: Full of life, lively; in Arthurian legend, Vivian was the Lady of the Lake and enchantress of Merlin.
(French) *Viviane, Vivienne;* (Italian) *Viviana;* (Spanish) *Bibiana;* (Finnish) *Viivi; Vivianne, Vivien;* **Nicknames:** *Bibi, Vavay;* **Famous Namesakes:** *British actress Vivien Leigh;* **Star Babies:** *Daughter of Debbie Allen*

VLADA Russian: To rule; feminine form of Vlad
Diminutive Forms: *Vladka*

VOLVA Norse: A prophetess

VOR Norse: An omniscient goddess

VORSILA Greek: Spelling variation of Ursula

VOSHKIE Armenian: Golden
Vosgi

WACHIWI Native American: Dancing girl (Sioux)

WADAN English: Old English, meaning to go

WAFA African: Form of Wafaa

WAKANDA Native American: Inner, magical power

WALBURGA Teutonic: Strong defender; Saint Walburga was an eighth-century English missionary to Germany.
Walburgha, Walpurga, Walpurgis

WALDA German: Divine power; feminine form of Waldo and Oswald
Welda, Waldah, Waldina, Wellda

WALLIS English: From Wales; feminine form of Wallace
Waleis

WANDA German: Wanderer
(Polish) *Vanda, Wandy; Vande, Wande, Wandis, Wende, Wendelin, Wendelina, Wendeline;* **Famous Namesakes:** *Singer Wanda Jackson*

WANETA Native American: Charger
Wanita

WANETTA English: Pale, fair-faced; could also be given as a phonetic spelling of the Spanish name Juanita
Waneta, Wanita; **Nicknames:** *Wann*

WANGARI African: Leopard

WARDA English: Guard; feminine form of Ward

WASHTA Native American: Good (Sioux)

WATSEKA Native American: Pretty woman (Potawatomi)

WAUNA Native American: Call of the snow geese flying (Miwok)

WAVERLY English: Quaking aspen
Waverley, Waverlee, Waverlie, Waverlea, Waverleigh

WAYLAHSKISE Native American: Graceful (Shawnee)

WAYNOKA Native American: Sweet water (Cheyenne)

WEAYAYA Native American: Sunset (Sioux)

WELCOME English: Received gladly, happily greeted

WENDA English, Welsh: Wanderer, stranger; variant of Wendy, Gwyneth, Guenevere, and Wanda

WENDELLE English: Wanderer, stranger; see also *Wenda*

WENDY English: A literary name that first appeared in James Barrie's *Peter Pan*. He took it from his childhood nickname *fwendy*, meaning friend. Some think it may also be a diminutive of the Welsh name Gwendolyn.
Nicknames: *Wendi*

WENONA Native American: Spelling variation of Winona

WESLEE English: From the western meadow; surname
Weslie, Weslia, Weslea, Wesleigh

WESLIA English: From the western meadow; a variant of Wesley
Weslie, Weslea, Wesleigh, Weslee, Wesley

WESTLEY English: From the western meadow; surname
Weslyn, Westlyn, Weslea, Weslee, Wesleigh, Westlea, Westleah, Westleigh

WHITLEY English: From the white meadow
Whitlea, Whitleigh, Whitlee

WHITNEY English, Anglo-Saxon: From the white island
Famous Namesakes: *Singer Whitney Houston*

WICAHPI Native American: Star (Sioux)
Wicapi

WICAPI WAKAN Native American: Holy star (Sioux)
Wicahpi Wakan

WIEBKE German: War

WIHAKAYDA Native American: Youngest daughter (Sioux)

WIKOLIA Hawaiian: Variation of Victoria

WILDA Anglo-Saxon: Willow. German: Untamed, wild
Wildah, Willda, Wylda

WILEEN English: Variation of Wilhelmina

WILHELMINA German: Resolute protector; feminine variant of Wilhelm
(English) *Wileen*; (Italian) *Guillelmina, Gulielma*; (Spanish) *Guillermina*; (Swedish) *Vilhelmina*; (Danish) *Wilhelmine*; (Finnish) *Miina, Valma*; *Wilhemina*; **Old Forms:** *Wilhelma*; **Nicknames:** *Billie, Hilma, Mimi, Mina, Minetta, Minna, Minnie, Minny, Vilma, Willa, Wilma, Wilna*; **Diminutive Forms:** *Minette, Willette*

WILLA English: Nickname for Wilhelmina
Famous Namesakes: *Author Willa Cather*

WILLOW English: Slender, graceful; from the willow tree noted for graceful branches and leaves
Star Babies: *Daughter of Will Smith and Jada Pinkett Smith*

WILMA German: Nickname for Wilhelmina

WILONA Anglo-Saxon: Desired, longed for
Wilone, Wylona

WINEMA Native American: Female chief (Miwok)

WINIFRED Welsh, German, Teutonic: Reconciled, blessed; Winifred was a martyred Welsh princess and traditionally considered the patron saint of virgins.
Nicknames: *Winnie*

> *"Native Americans regard their names not as mere labels, but as essential parts of their personalities. A native person's name is as vital to his or her identity as the eyes or the teeth."*
> —Wilma Mankiller, first female elected as chief to the Cherokee Nation

WINIFRID German: Peaceful friend. Welsh: Variant of Guenievere
(Welsh) *Winnifred; Winfreda, Winifreda, Winifride, Wynfreda, Wynifred, Wynnifred*

WINNIE Welsh: Nickname for Winifred; few children will hear the name Winnie without thinking of the beloved bear Winnie the Pooh and his friends in the Enchanted Forest.

WINOLA German: Gracious friend
Winolah, Wynola

WINONA Native American: Firstborn daughter, eldest (Sioux)
Wenona

WINTER English: Seasonal name, born in the winter
Wynter

WIRA Polish: White; variant of Elvira
Wyra

WITASHNAH Native American: Pure, untouched (Sioux)

WYANET Native American: Legendary, beautiful

WYNNE Celtic: White or fair, light-skinned; also a familiar form of Guinevere, Gweneth, and similar names
Wyn; **Nicknames:** *Wynnie*

XABRINA Latin: Spelling variation of Sabrina

XALINA French: Solemn, dignified; variant of Salina

XAMANTHA Hebrew: Spelling variation of Samantha

XANDRA Spanish: Nickname for Alexandra

XANTHE Greek: Blond, yellow, golden
Xantha, Xanthia, Zanthe

XAVIERA Spanish: Owns a new house; feminine form of Xavier. Arabic: Bright
Javiera, Xavierre, Xevera, Xeveria

XENIA Greek: Welcoming, hospitable; pop culture character Xena, warrior princess, will cause many to associate this name with strength and independence.
(Russian) *Aksiniya, Ksenia, Oksanochka*;
(Ukrainian) *Oksana*; *Xena, Zena, Zenda, Zene, Zenia, Zenina, Zenna*; **Nicknames:** *Xia, Zina*; **Diminutive Forms:** *Oksanka*

XHOSA African: Sweet

XYLEENA Greek: Lives in the forest, loves the forest
Xylia, Xyliana, Xylina, Xylinia, Xylona, Zylina

YAAKOVA Hebrew: Supplants

YAEL Hebrew: Mountain goat; in the Old Testament, the name of a woman who killed the captain of the Canaanite army
Jael, Yaela, Yaella

YAFFA Hebrew: Spelling variation of Jaffa
Jafa, Jafit, Yafa, Yafit

YALETHA Scandinavian: Spelling variation of Oletha

YAMKA Native American: Blossom (Hopi)

YANAHA Native American: She meets the enemy, brave (Navajo)

YARA Arabic, Persian: Courage, strength

YARDENA Hebrew: Spelling variation of Jordan

YARKONA Hebrew: Green

YARONA Hebrew: Sing

YASMINE Hindi: Spelling variation of Jasmine

YEDDA English: Beautiful voice; possible variant of Yetta

YEDIDA Hebrew: Friend
Jedidah, Yedidah

YESENIA Spanish: Meaning unknown; gained popularity in the 1970s as a title character of a Spanish-language soap opera
Llesenia

YETTA English: Generous, giving; possible diminutive of Henrietta

YNES French: Variation of Agnes

YOCHEVED Hebrew: God's glory
Yochebed

YOKI Native American: Rain (Hopi)

YOLANDA Spanish: Variation of Violet

YONA Hebrew: Dove; feminine variant of Jonah
Jonina, Jonita, Yonina, Yonita, Yonah

YOSEBE Hebrew: Spelling variation of Josephine

YSEULT French: Fair one; variant of Iseut and Isolde

YSOLDE Arthurian Legend: Spelling variation of Isolde

YULE Norse: Born during Yuletide

YULIA Russian: Variation of Julia

YURIKO Japanese: Lily child or village of birth

YVETTE French: Diminutive form of Yvonne

YVONNE French: Archer; feminine variant of Yves
(German) *Evon, Evonna, Evonne*; (Polish) *Iwona; Evony, Ivonne*; **Diminutive Forms:** *Yvette*; **Famous Namesakes:** *Actress Yvonne Craig*

ZABANA Native American: Meadow; variation of Savannah (Taino)

ZADA Arabic: Huntress, fortunate

ZAHAR Hebrew: Dawn
Zaher, Zahir

ZAHAVAH Hebrew: Gold or golden; variant of Zehava
Zahava

ZAHRA Arabic: White, flowering, beauty. African: Flowering (Swahili)
(African) *Zahara; Zara, Zahraa, Zahrah*;
Famous Namesakes: *Maltese children's author and illustrator Trevor Zahra, Journalist Zahra Kazemi*

ZAIDA Arabic: Lucky, bountiful; also used in auction language, meaning to outbid another
Zayda

ZAIDEE Arabic: Wealthy; see also *Zada*
Zaidi

ZAINA Spanish: Variation of Jane

ZAINABU African: Beautiful (Swahili)

ZALIKA African, Egyptian: Well-born, noble (Swahili)
Zaliki

ZALTANA Native American: High mountain
Zaltanah

ZAMORA Spanish: Place name of a Spanish city

ZANDRA Spanish: Nickname for Alexandra

ZANETA Russian: Variation of Janet

ZANNA Hebrew: God is gracious; variant of Jane and possibly a variant of Susanna

ZANOBIA Arabic: Father's ornament, petite and voluptuous
Zanouba, Zanoubia

ZANTA African: Beautiful girl

ZARA Hebrew: Spelling variation of Sarah
Star Babies: *Daughter of Princess Anne and Mark Phillips*

ZARAHLINDA Hebrew: Beautiful princess; spelling variant of names Sarah and Linda

ZARIA Arabic: Rose, visitor

ZAYNA Arabic: Beauty, ornament

ZDENKA Czech: Follower of Saint Denis, martyred Bishop of Paris; variant of Zdenek

ZEHAVA Hebrew: Gold or golden
Zahavah, Zehave, Zehavi, Zehavit, Zahava, Zehovit, Zehuvit

ZEHIRA Hebrew: Careful, protective

ZELDA Teutonic: Nickname for Griselda
Famous Namesakes: *Author Zelda Fitzgerald (wife of F. Scott Fitzgerald);* **Star Babies:** *Daughter of Robin Williams and Marsha Garces*

ZELENA Greek: Variation of Celine

ZELENE English: Variation of Celine

ZELENKA Czech: Green, new, fresh, innocent

ZELIA Spanish: Sunshine, daylight

ZELLA African: One who knows the way (Bobangi)

ZELMA English: Spelling variation of Selma

ZEMIRAH Hebrew: Joyous melody, song of praise
Zemira, Zimra, Zimria, Zymirah

ZEMORA Hebrew: Branch, extension
Zemorah

ZENA African: News, but predominantly when the name is used, it is a variant of Xenia, meaning welcoming

ZENAIDA Greek: White dove, symbol of purity and adoration; also related to Zeus
(Russian) *Zinaida; Zenaide;* **Nicknames:** *Zina;* **Diminutive Forms:** *Zinochka*

ZENDA Persian: Womanly; also Greek variant of Xenia, meaning welcoming

ZENOBE Greek: Born of Zeus; originally a male name, after the Greek mythological youngest son of Cronus and Rhea.

ZENOBIA Greek: Sign; Queen Zenobia was third-century ruler of the wealthy Arabian Desert city of Palmyra.
(Spanish) *Cenobia, Senobia;* (Russian) *Zinovia;* **Nicknames:** *Zena*

A Matter of Fact

Zenobia, the Queen of Palmyra, lived in the third century and was known as the "warrior queen." She led her people in a war against Rome, much like Boudica did in England. Zenobia claimed to be a descendent of Cleopatra (of Egypt) and, indeed, came from a long history of Syrian and Abyssinian queens, including the Queen of Sheba.

ZEPHYR Greek: West wind, the gentle wind (Greek) *Zephira*; (English) *Zephrine*; (Polish) *Zefiryn*; *Zephyra, Zyphire*; **Nicknames:** *Zephan*

ZERA Hebrew: Seeds, beginnings
Zerah

ZERLINA Latin: Beautiful dawn; Zerlina is a young girl pursued by the Don in Mozart's opera *Don Giovanni*.
Serlina

ZETA Greek: Born last, the last letter of the Greek alphabet. English: Rose

ZEUXIPPE Latin: Greek mythological queen of Athens, she was the mother of Erechtheus, Butes, Procne, and Philomela

ZHANNA Russian: Variation of Jane

ZIA Arabic: Light, splendor, beautifully adorned

ZIBA Persian: Beautiful

ZIBIA Hebrew: Spelling variation of Tzviya
Zibiah

ZIGANA Hungarian: Spelling variation of Tzigana

ZIHNA Native American: Spins, spinning (Hopi)

ZILLAH Hebrew: Shadow; an Old Testament name
Zilla

ZIMRA Hebrew: Spelling variation of Zemirah

ZINA English: Welcoming, hospitable; variant of Xenia

ZINERVA Italian: Fair, light-skinned

ZINNIA English: A flower

ZIPPORAH Hebrew: Bird; the name of Moses' wife in the Old Testament
Tzippa, Tzzipporah, Zippora

ZITA Arabic: Mistress; also the diminutive form for names ending in sita or zita, such as Rosita

ZITKALA Native American: Bird (Sioux)
Famous Namesakes: *Sioux teacher and writer Zitkala Si*

ZIVA Hebrew: Brilliant, radiant
Zivah

ZIVIA Hebrew: Spelling variation of Tzviya

ZLATA Slavic: Golden, guilded

ZOE Greek: Life, energy
(Russian) *Zoyechka, Zoyenka*; *Zoel, Zoelle, Zoey, Zoia, Zoya, Zoie, Zoyee, Zowy*; **Old Forms:** *Zoelie*; **Famous Namesakes:** *Actress Zoe Caldwell*; **Star Babies:** *Daughter of Lisa Bonet and Lenny Kravitz, Woody Harrelson, Rosanna Arquette*

ZOFIA Greek: Spelling variation of Sophia
Zofie

ZOHAR Hebrew: Sparkling, shining
Zoheret, Zohara, Zohera

ZOHREH Persian: The planet Venus

ZOLA Italian: Piece of the earth
Zoela, Zolah, Zoila

ZONA Latin: Sash or belt, mark of distinction
Zonah, Zonia

ZORA Slavic: Dawn; variant of Aurora.
African: A bargain (Hausa)
Famous Namesakes: *Author Zora Neale Hurston*

ZORINA Slavic: Golden
Sorina, Zorana

ZOYA Greek: Spelling variation of Zoe

ZSA ZSA Hungarian: Familiar name for Susan; many people will think immediately of glamorous actress Zsa Zsa Gabor

ZSOFIA Hungarian: Variation of Sophia
Zsofie; **Nicknames:** *Zsofika*

ZSUZSANNA Hungarian: Variation of Susan
Zuska

ZSUZSI Hungarian: Variation of Susan

ZUDORA Hindi: Laborer, worker
Zudorah

ZURIA Hebrew: Spelling variation of Tzuria

ZURINA Basque: White, fair-skinned
Nicknames: *Zuri, Zurie*

ZUWENA African: Good (Swahili)
Zwena

ZUZELA Native American: Name of one of Sitting Bull's wives

ZUZU Czech: Lily; familiar form of Zuza and Susan. Fans of *It's a Wonderful Life* will remember the young girl and her glorious flower petals.

ZYLINA Greek: Lives in the forest; variant of Xyleena

ZYMIRAH Hebrew: Spelling variation of Zemirah

ZYTKA Polish: Strong; a familiar form of Brygida

Cypr...
Dakota
Dallas
Dane
Dayton
Denver
Denzel
Darien
Devon
Everest
Eyton
Holland
Housto...
Israel
Ker...
Ke...
L...
...ghton
...ooklyn
...erlin
...airo
Camden
Carlyle
Cayman
Chester
...veland
...on

Boys'
Names

AAGE Norse: Ancestors

AARON Hebrew: The anglicized form of Aharon, meaning high mountain, lofty, or inspired; in the Bible, Moses' brother Aaron was Israel's first high priest and is remembered for his staff which blossomed miraculously. Popular in English-speaking countries since the Protestant Reformation. Arabic: Forest, thicken, strength
(Arabic) *Haroun, Harun;* (Spanish) *Eron;* (Scandinavian) *Aaren;* (Swedish) *Aron;* (Slavic) *Arron;* (Finnish) *Aaro; Ahren, Harun al Rachid;* **Old forms:** *Aharon;* **Star Babies:** *Son of Robert De Niro*

AARRE Finnish: Treasure

AART Anglo-Saxon: Like an eagle

"When I grow up we will have boys."
—Hilda Doolittle

ABALARDO Celtic: Noble

ABALLACH Arthurian Legend: Father of Urien's wife Modron; Aballach is likely a variant of Avallach, a reference to the island of Avalon.

ABASI Egyptian: Stern (Swahili)
Abasy

ABAYOMI African: Brings great joy (Nigeria)

ABBAN Irish: Little abbot; this was the name of a sixth-century Irish saint, the son of King Cormac of Leinster.

ABBAS Hebrew: Father. Arabic: Lion, grim-faced, stern; the name of one of Mohammed's uncles

Abba, Abbe, Abbey, Abbie, Abo; **Nicknames:** *Ab;* **Famous Namesakes:** *Algerian political leader Ferhat Abbas, Khedive of Egypt Abbas Hilmi, Arabic poet Abbas Ibn Al Ahnaf*

ABBEY English: Diminutive variant of Abbas, Abbott, Abelard, and Abner
Abbie, Abby, Aby; **Famous Namesakes:** *Activist Abbie Hoffman*

ABBOT Hebrew, English: Father or head of a monastic community; this surname is likely derived from the Hebrew name Abba and may bring to mind the famed Abbott and Costello comedy team.
(English) *Abbott; Abot, Abott;* **Nicknames:** *Abbey, Abbie, Abby, Abe*

ABDEL Arabic: Servant or slave of Allah; This name rarely stands alone but is generally followed by adjectives that are all attributes of Allah in the Muslim faith, and serve to identify God by one of his ninety-nine names. For example, Hakim means wise, so Abdel Hakim means servant of the wise. To avoid repetition, meanings of those names/adjectives are listed as separate entries.
Abdal, Abdul, Abd El, Abd Al

ABDERUS Greek: A friend of Hercules

ABDULLA Arabic: Servant of God
Abdullah, Abdalla, Abdallah, Abd Allah; **Famous Namesakes:** *Father of the Prophet Mohammed*

ABEJUNDIO Spanish: Like a bee

ABEL Hebrew: Son or breath; in the Bible, Abel was the son of Adam and Eve who was killed by his brother Cain in a fit of jealousy.
(Russian) *Avel;* (Finnish) *Aapeli; Abell*

ABELARD German: Resolute, noble, and steadfast
(Spanish) *Abelardo*

ABHA Hindi: Light, splendor

ABHAINN Scottish: River, from the river

ABHAY Hindi: Fearless

ABIMELECH Hebrew: Anglicized version of Avimelech, meaning father is king
Avimelech

ABIOLA African: Born in wealth

ABIR Hebrew: Strong

ABIRAM Hebrew: Father of heights
Aviram

ABISHA Hebrew: God's gift

ABLENDAN Anglo-Saxon: Dazzling, blinding

ABNER Hebrew: My father is light; in the Bible, Abner was King Saul's cousin and commander of his army.
Avner; **Nicknames:** *Ab, Abbey, Abbie, Abby*

ABRAHAM Hebrew: Father of a multitude; Abraham was the first of the Old Testament patriarchs. God changed his name from Abram when He appointed him to be the father of the Hebrew nation.
(Arabic) *Ibrahim*; (Italian) *Abramo*; (Spanish) *Abran*; (Irish) *Abracham; Avraham*; **Nicknames:** *Abe, Bram*; **Famous Namesakes:** *President Abraham Lincoln*; **Star Babies:** *Son of Matt Groening*

ABRAM Hebrew: Exalted father; the biblical patriarch Abraham's name before God changed it

ABRECAN Anglo-Saxon: To storm, to assault; a warrior's name

ABSALOM Hebrew: Father of peace; the biblical Absalom, favored son of King David, was renowned for his handsome appearance and ability to win loyalty and allegiance.
(Spanish) *Absalon; Avsalom, Avshalom, Axel*

ABU African: Father

ABU BAKR Arabic: Father of a young camel; Abu Bakr was Mohammed the Prophet's companion
Famous Namesakes: *Mohammed's father-in-law, first Caliph to initiate the Islamic conquests*

ACASTUS Greek: Argonaut who exiled Jason and Medea after a trick of Medea's killed his father, King Pelias. Latin: Son of Pelias

ACCALON Arthurian Legend: Morgan le Fay's lover and partner

ACCIUS Latin: Renowned Roman poet and playwright

ACE Latin, English, Anglo-Saxon: Unity; in English, Ace has become a term for one who is superior, one who excels.
Acey, Acer, Acie

ACEL French: Adherent of a nobleman

ACENNAN Anglo-Saxon: Brings forth, gives birth to

ACHAK Native American: Spirit (Algonquin)

ACHATES Greek: Loyal friend; faithful companion of Aeneas whose story is chronicled in Virgil's *Aeneid*

ACHELOUS Greek: A mythological river god, Achelous was the eldest of the many sons of Oceanus and Tethys.

ACHILLES Greek: Achilles was the son of the mortal Peleus and the Nereid Thetis. He was the mightiest of the Greeks who fought in the Trojan War, and was the hero of Homer's *Iliad*.

> *"But sure the eye of Time beholds no name*
> *So blest as thine in all the rolls of fame"*
> —Alexander Pope,
> *The Odyssey of Homer,* referring to Achilles

ACHIM German: Nickname for Joachim

ACIS Latin, Greek: Son of Faunus, a god of the forest similar to Pan; he later became the lover of Galatea, the Nereid

ACKERLEY English: From the oak tree meadow; a possible reference to acre of oak trees
Ackley, Aekerley, Aekley, Oakley, Ackerlea

ACRISIUS Latin, Greek: A mythological king of Argos, Acrisius locked his daughter Danae away in an attempt to avoid a prophecy. Zeus appeared to her as a shower of gold and fathered Perseus.

ACTAEON Greek: From Attica; in mythology, the hunter Actaeon stumbled upon the goddess Artemis while she bathed, so she turned him into a stag. His own hunting dogs then became his killers.
Actaeonis, Acteon

ACTON English: From the town or settlement near the oak trees
Actun

ACWELLEN Anglo-Saxon: Kill, a warrior's name and battle cry
Nicknames: *Acwel*

ADAHY Native American: From in the woods (Cherokee)
Adahi

ADAIAH Hebrew: God's witness, adorned by God; a son of Haman in the Bible
Adaia, Adaya, Adayah

ADAIR Gaelic, Celtic, Scottish: From the oak tree ford; surname. See also *Athdar* (Gaelic) *Athdara*; (Irish) *Adare; Athdair, Athdare*

ADAL German: Noble

ADALARD German: Highborn and courageous. See also *Adel* (English) *Allard; Adalhard, Adelard, Adelhard*; **Old Forms:** *Aethelhard, Alhard*

ADALRICH German: Highborn ruler, noble commander
Adalric, Adalrik, Adelric

ADALSON English: Son of a specific person now unknown, possibly Adam or any of the English names beginning with "Ad"

ADAM Hebrew, English: Son of the red earth; in the Bible, Adam was the first man created by God.
(English) *Addis*; (German) *Adne*; (Spanish) *Adan*; (Gaelic) *Adhamh*; (Czech) *Damek*; (Finnish) *Aatami*; (Hawaiian) *Akamu; Addam, Adem*; **Star Babies:** *Son of Leonard Nimoy, son of Maurice Gibb*

ADAMNAN Irish: Little Adam
Adhamhnan

ADAMSON Hebrew, English: Son of Adam

ADDAI Hebrew: Man of God

ADDIS English: Variation of Adam

ADDISON English: Son of Adam; surname *Addeson, Adison, Adisson;* **Nicknames:** *Ad, Addie, Addy*

ADDY Teutonic: Variant of Adelard and Adam

ADE African: Royal (Nigeria)

ADEBEN African: Twelfth born (Ghana)

ADEL Arabic: Righteous, fair, just; stems from Adl, meaning justice

ADHAMH Gaelic: Variation of Adam

ADIB Arabic: Polite, learned, cultured, honest; stems from Adab, a name meaning manners which is also synonymous with culture and literature; masculine form of Adiba *Adeeb;* **Famous Namesakes:** *Iranian national poet Adib Boroumand*

ADIEL African: Goat

ADIL Arabic: Similar, bundle, equal, like, brother-in-law. Turkish: negotiation

ADIN Hebrew: Pleasure given; Adin was a biblical exile who returned to Israel from Babylon.

ADIR Hebrew: Powerful, mighty

ADISH Persian: Fire

ADIV Hebrew: Delicate, gentle

ADKEN English: Made of oak; strong; variant of Aiken

ADKINS English: Made of oak, strong; son of Aiken *Atkinson, Atkinsone, Attkins*

ADLAI Hebrew: Refuge of God, justice of the Lord; many will associate this name with politician Adlai Stevenson. *Adley;* **Nicknames:** *Ad, Addey*

ADLER German: Eagle *Adlar*

ADMETUS Greek: A king of Pherae who was favored by Apollo, who gave him the gift of allowing another to take his place when it was time to die. His wife Alcestis offered, but the gods intervened and allowed both to continue life together.

ADNAN Arabic: Abiding, stays in one place, pleasurable, he who loves land and makes it similar to Paradise; the latter meaning is derived from *Gannat Adan* (Paradise), the gardens of eternal abode.

ADNE German: Variation of Adam

ADNEY English: Lives on the noble's island; surname *Addaneye, Addney, Adny*

ADOFO Egyptian: Fighter, warrior (Ghana)

ADOLPH German: Noble wolf (French) *Adolphus;* (Spanish) *Adolfo;* (Teutonic) *Adolf;* (Finnish) *Aatu;* **Old Forms:** *Adalwolf;* **Nicknames:** *Dolph, Dolphus*

ADON Hebrew: Lord, master

ADONAI Hebrew: My Lord

ADONIS Greek: Extremely handsome; in Greek mythology, Adonis is a beautiful young man beloved of Aphrodite.

ADRIAN Latin: Dark; from the Adriatic Sea region
(Irish) *Aidrian*; (Russian) *Adrik*; (Polish) *Adok*; (Hungarian) *Adojan*; *Adrien, Adrion, Adron, Andrion, Hadrien*; **Old Forms:** *Hadrian*; **Star Babies:** *Son of Edie Brickell and Paul Simon*

ADRIEL Hebrew: Of the flock of God, a member of God's congregation. Native American: Beaver, symbol of skill
Adriyel

ADRIK Russian: Variation of Adrian

ADVENT French: Born during Advent
Avent

AEGIDIUS Greek: Shield-bearer
(Italian) *Egidio*

AEGIS Greek: Shield; in Greek mythology, Aegis was the goatskin shield of Zeus and his daughter Athena.

AEKERLEY English: From the oak tree meadow; a surname and variant of Ackerley

AEKERMAN English: Man of oak, strong; a surname
Ackerman

AELLE Anglo-Saxon: Name of several Anglo-Saxon kings, including the first king of Deira in northern England
Aella, Aelli

AENEAS Greek: Praiseworthy; the Trojan warrior from Virgil's *Aeneid*
(Spanish) *Eneas*; (Gaelic) *Aneas*

AENEDLEAH English: From the awe-inspiring meadow; variant of Ansley

AENESCUMB English: Lives in the valley of the majestic one

AESON Greek: Mythological father of Jason. When Aeson was very old, Medea gave him the gift of a second youth.

AETHELWULF Anglo-Saxon: King of the West Saxons and father of King Alfred the Great
Ethelwulf

AGENOR Greek: Mythological son of Poseidon, father of Europa and Cadmus

AGER Hebrew: Gathers. Basque: Gatherer

AGIEFAN Anglo-Saxon: Delivers, gives back
Old Forms: *Agyfen*

AGILBERHT Anglo-Saxon: Bishop of the Anglo-Saxon kingdom in Wessex, whose story was told by Bede

AGLAECA Anglo-Saxon: Monster, fighter

AGRICAN French: From the field
Famous Namesakes: *Agrican, king of Tartary*

AHAB Hebrew: Uncle; Ahab was an Old Testament king and the husband of Jezebel, and the name was later given to a sea captain in Herman Melville's novel *Moby-Dick*

AHANU Native American: He laughs
(Algonquin)

AHARON Hebrew: Original form of Aaron

AHEARN Celtic: Lord of the horses
(English) *Hearn, Hearne*; *Aherin, Ahern, Aherne*; **Nicknames:** *Aghy*

AHEAWAN Anglo-Saxon: Cuts, severs

AHEBBAN Anglo-Saxon: Raises, lifts

AHMAD Arabic, Persian: Much praised, laudable; one of the Prophet Mohammed's many names
Amad, Amadi, Emad, Ahmed; **Famous Namesakes:** *Turkish writer Ahmed Mithat, Turkish head of state and writer Ahmed Vefik, Football player and sports announcer Ahmad Rashad*

AHREDDAN Anglo-Saxon: Keep, save, or rescue

AHTI Finnish: God of water, sea, ocean

AIDAN Irish, Gaelic: Little, fiery; Aidan is a modern English spelling of the early medieval Gaelic name Áedán. It was relatively common in early medieval Ireland, and was the name of at least two sixth- and seventh-century Celtic saints. In the late Middle Ages, the saint's name was spelled Aodhán, but the name appears to have dropped out of common use after the tenth century or so. Its modern popularity dates to a revival in the nineteenth or twentieth century.

AIF Norse: Nickname for Alfred

AIKEN Anglo-Saxon: Made of oak, strong; a surname. See also *Adken*
(English) *Adkyn, Aiekin, Akker; Aeker, Aikin, Aitken*

AILBE German: Intelligent or noble

AILILL Gaelic: Sprite; borne in Irish myth by the king of Connaught

AIMO Finnish: Generous amount

AINMIRE Irish: Great lord

AINSLEY Scottish, English: From his own meadow
Ainsleigh, Ainslie, Ansley, Aynsley

AINSWORTH English: From Ann's estate; a surname
Answorth

AKBAR Persian: Big

AKECHETA Native American: Warrior (Sioux)

AKEISHA Anglo-Saxon: Contemporary name combining the letter "A" and the name Keisha.
Akeesha; **Nicknames:** *Keisha*

AKIBA Hebrew: Replaces, supplants; a variant of Akiva. Akiba was a Jewish rabbi, said to have lived in Jerusalem in the time of the Second Temple and to have devoted himself to the study of the law. Many sayings are transmitted in Akiba's name.

AKIL Arabic: Masculine form of Akilah
Akeel

AKIVA Hebrew: Replaces, supplants; variant of Yaakov (see Jacob); Akiva was the name of many renowned Talmudic scholars throughout history.
Akiba, Akavia, Akaviah, Akavya; **Nicknames:** *Kiba, Kiva*

AKKER English: Variation of Aiken

AKRAM Arabic: More generous, more precious, nobler; Akram is the comparative form of the root word and adjective Karam, meaning generosity and nobility.

AKUB Hebrew: Replaces

AL ALIM Arabic: The (Al) Omniscient, informed, knowing, wise, one of the attributes of God; variant of Abd (servant of) Al Alim
El Alim

ALAIR Latin: Happy

ALAN Celtic: Handsome
(French) *Alain*; (Spanish) *Alano*; (Gaelic)
Ailean, Ailin; (Scottish) *Ailein; Ailen, Allan,
Allen*; **Nicknames:** *Al;* **Famous Namesakes:**
*Astronaut Alan Shepard, Actor Alan Alda, Poet
and writer Edgar Allen Poe*

ALARD Teutonic: Resolute

ALARIC German: Noble leader
(Spanish) *Alarico*; (Swedish) *Alrik*; (Danish)
Ulrik; (Czech) *Oldrich; Alarick, Alarik,
Aurick, Aurik, Udo, Ulric*; **Old Forms:** *Ulrich*

ALAWN Welsh: Harmony

ALBA Italian: White; a place name

ALBAN Latin: White; from Alba, a city
on a hill

ALBARIC French: Blond ruler

ALBERN English: Noble warrior, courageous; (Teutonic) noble bear
Alburn; **Old Forms:** *Aethelbeorn*

ALBERT German: Noble, bright; Prince
Albert was Queen Victoria's consort noted
for enthusiastic support of the application of
science to the modern industrial age. Albert
Einstein developed the Theory of Relativity.
(German) *Albrecht, Elbert*; (Italian) *Alberto*;
(Spanish) *Berto*; (Scottish) *Ailbert*; (Hungarian)
*Béla; Aethelbeorht, Aethelberht, Aethelbert,
Alburt, Dalbert, Delbert*; **Old Forms:**
Adalbert, Adelbert; **Nicknames:** *Al, Bertie,
Bert*; **Famous Namesakes:** *Actor/director
Albert Brooks, French philosopher Albert Camus*

ALBIN Latin: White; related to the city Alba
Albinus

ALBINUS Latin: White, pure; the name of
a scholarly monk who encouraged Bede's
creation of the *Ecclesiastical History of the
English People*

ALBRECHT German: Variation of Albert
Famous Namesakes: *German artist Albrecht
Dürer*

ALBUS Latin: White; fictional character
from *Harry Potter* series, Albus Dumbledore
Alcot, Allcot, Allcott, Alkott

ALDEN English: Spelling variation of Alvin

ALDER English: From the alder tree

ALDFRITH Anglo-Saxon: King of
Northumbria known for his love of scholar-
ship

ALDIS English: From the old house
Aldous, Aldus, Aldys, Aldisse

ALDO German, Italian: Old or wise, an
elder; may also be a familiar form of Aldous

ALDRED Anglo-Saxon: Old counsel, old
or wise advisor; a surname. English: Wise
or red-haired man
Eldred, Eldrid, Alldred, Elldred

ALDRICH Anglo-Saxon, English: Old and
wise leader, noble ruler, a surname;
(Teutonic) battle counsel
(French) *Audric; Aldric, Aldrick, Aldrik,
Aldrin, Eldrian, Eldrick, Eldridge*

ALDTUN English: From the old town,
settlement

ALEJANDRO Spanish: Variation of
Alexander

ALEKSEI Russian: Defender, helper; from
the Greek word *alexein*
(Ukrainian) *Alexio; Alexei*; **Old Forms:**
Alexius; **Nicknames:** *Alyosha*; **Diminutive
Forms:** *Alyoshenka*; **Famous Namesakes:**
*Russian author Aleksei Tolstoi, Figure skater
and Olympic champion Alexei Yagudin*

ALERON French: Winged

ALEX English: Nickname for Alexander
Star Babies: *Son of Bob Hoskins*

The Name

What is my name to you? 'T will die:
a wave that has but rolled to reach
with a lone splash a distant beach;
or in the timbered night a cry...

'T will leave a lifeless trace among
names on your tablets: the design
of an entangled gravestone line
in an unfathomable tongue.

What is it then? A long-dead past,
lost in the rush of madder dreams,
upon your soul it will not cast
Mnemosyne's pure tender
beams.

But if some sorrow comes to
you, utter my name with
sighs, and tell the silence:
"Memory is true—there beats
a heart wherein I dwell."

—Alexander Pushkin

ALEXANDER Greek: Defends mankind;
from the Greek word *Alexandros*. Alexander
the Great was the king of Macedon, con-
queror of much of Asia during 356–323 B.C.
See also *Zindel*
(French) *Alexandre*; (Spanish) *Alejandro*;
(Russian) *Aleksandr*; (Czech) *Aleksander*,
Ales; (Polish) *Aleksy, Oles*; (Ukrainian)
Lyaksandro; (Finnish) *Aleksanteri, Aleksi*;
(Hungarian) *Elek, Sandor*; (Persian)
Eskander; (Turkish) *Iskender*; (Hawaiian)
Alekanekelo; Alexandrukas; **Old Forms:**
Alexandras, Alexandros; **Nicknames:** *Alec,
Aleck, Aleko, Alex, Alik, Leksi, Sacha, Sander,
Sandro, Sandy, Santeri, Santtu, Sasha, Shura,
Zander;* **Diminutive Forms:** *Sashenka, Shurik;*
Famous Namesakes: *Inventor Alexander*

*Graham Bell, Russian swimmer Alexander
Popov;* **Star Babies:** *Son of Melanie Griffith
and Steven Bauer, Son of William Hurt*

ALEXANDRE French: Variation of
Alexander
Famous Namesakes: *French author
Alexandre Dumas*

ALF Swedish: Variation of Alfred

ALFRED Anglo-Saxon: Sage, elf wisdom,
implying an almost supernatural under-
standing
(Italian) *Alfredo*; (Swedish) *Aelfraed, Aelfric,
Alfrid, Elfred, Ahlfred, Ailfred, Ailfrid, Ailfryd,
Alfeo, Alfredas, Alfrey, Alfredos, Avery;*
Nicknames: *Alf, Al, Alfey, Alfie, Alfy, Fred,
Freddie, Freddy, Fredo;* **Famous Namesakes:**
*Director Alfred Hitchcock, Poet Alfred Lord
Tennyson*

ALFRID English: Spelling variation of Alfred

ALGAR Anglo-Saxon: Elf spear, spearman;
possible diminutive of Algernon
(German) *Alger*; (Celtic) *Ansgar*; (Norse)
Alfgeir, Elgar; **Famous Namesakes:**
Politician Alger Hiss

ALGERNON French: Moustached
Algrenon

ALI Arabic, Persian: Greatest, Lion of God,
one of the attributes of God; a variant of
Allah. Storybook hero Ali Baba was the main
protagonist in *A Thousand and One Nights:
Ali Baba and the Forty Thieves*. Boxing cham-
pion Muhammad Ali (né Cassius Marcellus
Clay) was named a United Nations Messenger
of Peace by Secretary-General Kofi Annan.
Aly; **Famous Namesakes:** *Viceroy and Ruler
of Egypt, Mohamed Ali (1769-1849), was an
Albanian born in Kavala. He founded the
Mohammed Ali Pasha Dynasty and is some-
times alluded to as the founder of modern
Egypt.*

ALICESON English: Son of Alice; originally one of the few male names to reference a woman, variants of Aliceson are much more widely used for girls today.
Alycesone

ALIM Arabic: Wise, learned, omniscient, informed, knowing; one of the attributes of God. Hebrew: Wise, learned
Abd al Alim, Al Alim, Abdul Alim, Abdel Alim, El Alim

ALISTAIR Gaelic: Defender of mankind; an Anglicized form of Alasdair, a Gaelic variant of Alexander
(Irish) *Alsandair*; (Scottish) *Alastair; Alaster, Alistaire, Alister, Allister*; **Nicknames:** *Alai, Alis*; **Famous Namesakes:** *British broadcaster Alistair Cooke*

ALLARD English: Variation of Adalard

ALLEN Celtic: Spelling variation of Alan

ALOIN French: Noble friend
Aluin

ALON Hebrew: Oak tree
Allon

ALONZO Spanish: Variation of Alphonse
Nicknames: *Lonzo*; **Famous Namesakes:** *Basketball player Alonzo Mourning*

ALPHONSE French: Ready and noble, ready for battle; derived from the Old German name Adelfuns. The variant Alfonso is a royal name in Spain and Portugal.
(German) *Alphonso*; (Italian) *Alanzo, Alonso, Alonzo*; (Spanish) *Alfonso, Foncho, Lonzo*; (Swedish) *Alfons; Alphonsus*; **Old Forms:** *Adelfuns*; **Nicknames**: *Fonsie, Fonso, Fonzell, Fonzie, Fonzo, Alphie, Alfy, Alphy*; **Famous Namesakes:** *French author Alphonse Daudet, Czech poster artist Alphonse Marie Mucha*

ALRIC German: Rules all; the historical Gothic king who plundered Rome in A.D. 410. (English) *Alhrick, Alhrik*

ALSON English: Son of a specific person now unknown, possibly Alice or any of the English names beginning with "Al"

ALSTON English: From the nobleman's town, possibly from the elf's town; surname
Aethelstun, Alsten, Alstin

ALTAIR Arabic: Bird, poultry; Altair is the main star in the constellation Aquila, which is known as Orion in the Western world.

ALTAN Turkish: Dawn

ALVAN Hebrew: Spelling variation of Alvin

ALVAR English: Army of elves
(Spanish) *Alvaro, Alverio*

ALVER Latin: White

A Matter of Fact
Alphonse and Gaston were two courteous comic strip characters created by Frederick Burr Opper, one of the most highly respected cartoonists of late nineteenth- and early twentieth-century America.

ALVIN English: Elf friend, noble friend, implies supernaturally good or wise friend
(German) *Alvaro*; (Spanish) *Aluino*; (Teutonic) *Alcuin, Alwin, Alwyn, Aylmer, Aylwin; Adalwen, Adalwin, Adalwine, Aelfdane, Aelfdene, Alden, Aldin, Aldwin, Aldwyn, Alvan, Alvar, Alvyn, Audwin, Audwine, Aylwyn, Eldwin, Eldwyn, Elvern, Elvin, Elvyn, Elwen, Elwin, Elwyn*;
Nicknames: *Alvy, Elvey, Elvy*; **Famous Namesakes:** *Popular singing chipmunk*

ALVIS English: All-knowing

ALY Arabic: Spelling variation of Ali; Prince Aly Khan was the son of the famously wealthy Aga Khan. The latter was the title of the religious leader and Imam of the Ismaili Nizari sect of Islam, and was originally bestowed by the Persian Shah Fath Ali on Hasan Ali Shah, the forty-sixth Ismaili Imam, in 1818.

AMADEO Spanish: Variation of Amadeus
Star Babies: *Son of John Turturro*

AMADEUS Latin: Loved by God; easily recognized as the name of Wolfgang Amadeus Mozart, an Austrian composer considered one of history's best and most creative musical geniuses
(French) *Amado;* (Italian) *Amadeo, Amedeo; Amadou*

AMASA Hebrew: Burden; the biblical Amasa is King David's nephew.

AMAUD French: Eagle ruler

AMAURY French: Name of a count

AMBROSE Greek: Immortal; Saint Ambrose was a fourth-century bishop of Milan.
(Italian) *Ambrosi;* (Spanish) *Ambrosio;* (Swedish) *Ambrosius;* (Czech) *Ambroz;* (Hungarian) *Ambrus*

AMERY German: Divine. Teutonic: Hard-working. Irish: Ridge, long hill

AMES English: Friend, love; surname adapted to first name use
Aimes, Aymes

AMIN Arabic, Persian: Honest, trustworthy, guardian, faithful, loyal, steadfast, safe; Amin is also a word used in religious celebrations, as in Amen (yes, be it so).
Famous Namesakes: *Afghan political leader Hafizollah Amin, Lebanese President Amin Gemayel, Author Samir Amin*

AMIR Arabic, Persian: Prince, commanding, emir. Hebrew: Strong, powerful
Famous Namesakes: *Indonesian poet Amir Hamzah, Indian poet Amir Khusrau;* **Star Babies:** *Son of Mike Tyson*

AMIRAM Hebrew: My people are mighty

AMITABHA Hindi: One with immeasurable splendor

AMJAD Persian: Most excellent, glorious

AMMA Hindi: Mother

AMMAR Arabic: Builder, constructor
El Ammar, Al Ammar

AMMIEL Hebrew: People of the Lord; several biblical characters carry this name, including one of the spies sent to Canaan by Moses and Bathsheba's father.
Amiel

AMNON Hebrew: Faithful; biblical son of King David
Aminon

AMON Egyptian: The great god of Thebes of uncertain origin; this god is also the Hermopolitian Ogdoad and is represented as a man, sometimes ithyphallic. Identified with Ra (as Amon-Ra) and sacred animals, Amon was part of the Theban Triad, along with Mut and Khonsu. Hebrew: Hidden, possibly builder; name of one of the kings of Judah
Amun, Ammon

AMORY English: Variation of Emery

AMOS Hebrew: Burden carried; the name of one of the twelve minor prophets of the Jewish faith
Star Babies: *Son of Andrea Bocelli*

AMOUR French: Love

Noble Names for Leaders

Certain your baby is destined for greatness?
Peruse this list of names that mean "noble" or "leader."

Boys' Names	Girls' Names
Alaric (German)	Adalina (Teutonic)
Albert (German)	Adena (Hebrew)
Aldrich (Anglo-Saxon)	Alberta (German)
Alphonse (French)	Alfonsa (Spanish)
Barnett (English)	Alice (German)
Baron (Teutonic)	Allyn (Gaelic)
Bryce (Anglo-Saxon)	Aubrey (French)
Caeser (French)	Audrey (Anglo-Saxon)
Cedric (English)	Bricelyn (English)
Coyle (Irish)	Brylee (American)
Derek (English)	Delma (German)
Donald (Scottish)	Dereka (English)
Duke (Latin)	Donelle (Latin)
Earl (English)	Earlene (English)
Eric (Norse)	Edlyn (English)
Errol (German)	Elmira (English)
Eugene (Greek)	Elsa (German)
Herrick (German)	Erica (Norse)
Hiram (Hebrew)	Ethel (Anglo-Saxon)
Howard (English)	Farica (Teutonic)
Lonzo (Spanish)	Freda (German)
Melvin (Celtic)	Frederica (German)
Malloy (Irish)	Freya (Norse)
Nolan (Irish)	Kendra (English)
Patrick (Latin)	Latrice (African)
Quentin (Latin)	Milla (Finnish)
Rajah (Sanskrit)	Patricia (Latin)
Richard (German)	Rikka (Teutonic)
Sherif (Arabic)	Sherifah (Arabic)
Thanos (Greek)	Zalika (African)

AMPHION Greek: Mythological son of the god Zeus and Antiope, he was a king of Thebes known for his supernatural musical abilities

AMREN Welsh: Legendary son of Bedwyr

AMSDEN English: From Ambrose's valley

AMYCUS Greek: Mythical son of Poseidon and the nymph Melia, he was king of the Bebryces and famous for his boxing skills

ANASTASIUS Greek: Resurrection
(Italian) *Anastagio*; (Spanish) *Anastacio, Anastasio*; (Slavic) *Stasio*; *Anstice*

ANATOLE Greek, French: Sunrise, from the east
(Italian) *Anatolio*; (Russian) *Anatoli, Anatoly*; (Polish) *Anatol*; *Anatolius*; **Nicknames:** *Tolya*; **Famous Namesakes:** *French author Anatole France*

ANBESSA Spanish: A Saracen governor of Spain

ANBIDIAN Anglo-Saxon: Awaits, is patient

ANCIL French: Adherent of a nobleman
Ansel, Ansell

ANDERS Scandinavian: Variation of Andrew
Ander, Anderson, Andersson

ANDOR Hungarian: Variation of Andrew. Scandinavian: Eagle thunder

ANDRÉ French: Manly, brave
Famous Namesakes: *André Previn*

ANDRES Spanish: Variation of Andrew

ANDREW Greek, English, Scottish: Manly, brave; from the Greek Andreas; in the Bible, Andrew is the first of the twelve apostles chosen by Jesus and the brother of Peter. Andrew is a patron saint of Greece, Scotland, and Russia.
(Greek) *Andreus, Aniol*; (English) *Andrian, Andric, Andriel*; (German) *Andreas*; (Italian) *Andino*; (Spanish) *Andreo, Andres*; (Portuguese) *Andre*; (Gaelic) *Aindreas*; (Scottish) *Kendrew*; (Welsh) *Andras*; (Scandinavian) *Ander, Anders, Anderson*; (Danish) *Anker*; (Slavic) *Andrei, Andrej, Andrik*; (Russian) *Andrusha*; (Czech) *Ondrej*; (Polish) *Andnej, Jedrej, Jedrek, Jedrick, Jedrik*; (Finnish) *Antero*; (Hungarian) *Andor, Endre*; *Andrea, Andrey, Andries, Androu, Andruw*; **Nicknames:** *Andy, Dru, Tero, Drew*; **Famous Namesakes:** *President Andrew Jackson, President Andrew Johnson, Prince Andrew the Duke of York, Actor Andy Garcia, Actor Andy Griffith, Artist Andy Warhol, Composer, Andrew Lloyd Webber*; **Star Babies:** *Son of Faith Daniels*

ANDSWARIAN Anglo-Saxon: Answers, responds
Andswaru, Andswerian

ANE Anglo-Saxon: One, the first or the only
An

ANGEL Greek, Spanish: Messenger from God
(Italian) *Angelino, Angelo*; *Angell*

ANGUS Scottish, Gaelic: One choice, one strength; the god of love in Celtic mythology
Aengus, Aonghus, Oengus, Ungus, Anghus; **Nicknames:** *Gus*; **Star Babies:** *Son of Gordon Elliott, Son of Amanda Pays and Corbin Bernsen, Son of Donald Sutherland*

ANLON Irish: Champion
Anluan

ANPU Egyptian: Original form of Anubis

ANSCOM English: From the valley of the majestic one; surname
Anscomb, Anscombe

ANSELM Teutonic: God's protection; Saint Anselm was a twelfth-century archbishop of Canterbury and an influential theologian and church leader.
(English) *Ansel, Ansell*; (Spanish) *Anselino, Anselmo, Anzelmo, Chemo, Selmo*; **Famous Namesakes:** *Photographer Ansel Adams*

ANSLEY English: From the awe-inspiring meadow; surname
Aenedleah, Ainslie, Ansleigh, Ainslea, Ainslee, Ainsleigh, Ainsly, Annslea, Annsliegh, Annsley, Anslea, Anslie, Ansly

ANSON English, Anglo-Saxon, German: Anne's son; surname adapted to first name use
Hanson

ANTHONY Latin: Roman clan name of uncertain etymology; popular definitions include highly praiseworthy and priceless
(German) *Anton*; (French) *Antoine, D'anton, Danton*; (Italian) *Antonio*; (Spanish) *Tonio*; (Swedish) *Antonius*; (Basque) *Antton*; (Hungarian) *Antal*; (Hawaiian) *Akoni, Anakoni*; *Antoin, Antonin, Antoniy, Antony*;
Nicknames: *Tony*; **Diminutive Forms:** *Antonino*; **Famous Namesakes:** *Actors Anthony Hopkins, Anthony Perkins, Anthony Quinn, and Antonio Banderas; Composer Antonin Dvorak*; **Star Babies:** *Son of Joan Collins, Jerry Lewis, Gregory Peck, Veronica Lake, Angela Lansbury*

ANTON Russian: Variation of Anthony
Nicknames: *Antosha, Tosha, Toshka*; **Star Babies:** *Son of Beverly D'Angelo and Al Pacino*

ANTRANIG Armenian: First born

ANWAR Arabic: Luminous; President of Egypt Anwar el Sadat presided over Egypt from 1970 until his assassination in 1981. At Camp David, he signed the first peace treaty with Israel in 1978 and obtained the Nobel Peace Prize of the year.

Famous Namesakes: *Actress Gabrielle Anwar, Indonesian poet Chairil Anwar*

AODHFIN Irish: White fire
Aodhfionn

APIS Egyptian: Seen as the bull with a solar disk between its horns, Apis was associated with the gods Osiris and Ptah. See also *Serapis*

APOLLO Greek: Manly beauty; in Greek mythology, Apollo was one of the most important gods. He was the son of Zeus and Leto, and the twin brother of Artemis. Apollo was the god of music, prophecy, colonization, medicine, archery (though not war), poetry, dance, and intellectual inquiry. He was also a god of light and the sun.

AQUILINO Spanish: Eagle

ARAGORN Literature: Central character in J.R.R. Tolkien's *The Lord of the Rings*, Aragorn is the heir of the Numenorean kings, and the one who finally returns to take back the throne.

ARAMIS French: Fictional swordsman from Alexandre Dumas' *The Three Musketeers*

ARASH Persian: Hero

ARCAS Greek: Son of Zeus and the nymph Callisto, whom Hera turned into a bear. When hunting one day, Arcas prepared to kill the bear, not realizing it was his mother. Zeus intervened and transformed the two of them into the constellations Ursa Major and Ursa Minor, forever honoring them.

ARCHARD Anglo-Saxon, German: Sacred. French: Powerful
(German) *Eckerd, Ekhard*; *Archerd, Ekerd, Erkerd*; **Old Forms:** *Erchanhardt*

ARCHER Latin, English: Bowman; an occupational name and English surname adapted to first name use
Archere

ARCHIE English: Nickname for Archibald **Nicknames:** *Arch*

ARDAL Irish: High honor
Ardghal, Artegal, Arthgallo

ARDELL Latin: Eager, industrious. English: From the hare's dell
Ardel

ARDEN Latin: Fervent
Ardin

ARDLEY English: From the home-lover's meadow
Ardaleah, Ardleigh, Ardlea, Ardsley, Ardsly

ARDOLF English: Home-loving wolf
Ardolph, Ardwolf

AREF Persian: Wise

ARGO Greek: Mythological name of Jason's ship

ARI Hebrew: Lion
Arie

ARIBERT French: Variation of Herbert

ARIC Norse: Spelling variation of Eric
Aaric, Arick, Arik, Arrick

ARIEL Hebrew: Lion of God, a biblical name for Jerusalem; Shakespeare's name for a mischievous spirit in *The Tempest*. *Arye, Aryeh, Arel, Aryel, Aryell*; **Famous Namesakes:** *Prime Minister of Israel Ariel Sharon*

ARIF Arabic: Knowing, knowledgeable, acquainted, expert

ARISTO Greek: Best

ARKADI Russian: Native of Arcadia, an ancient pastoral region in Greece

Old Forms: *Arkadios*; **Diminutive Forms:** *Arkasha*

ARLEDGE English: Lake of the hares; a surname and variant of Harlake
Arlidge, Arlledge, Arrledge

ARLEN Irish, Gaelic: Pledge
Arlyn

ARLEY English: From the hare's meadow; variant of Harley
Arlea, Arleigh, Arlie, Arly

ARLO English: Spelling variation of Harlow **Famous Namesakes:** *Folk singer Arlo Guthrie*

ARLYSS Anglo-Saxon: Honorable
Arlys

ARMAN Persian: Ideal

ARMAND French: Variation of Herman **Famous Namesakes:** *Actor Armand Assante*

ARMAS Finnish: Dear

ARMO Finnish: Mercy, grace

ARMON Hebrew: High fortress
(Italian) *Armond, Armondo*; (Teutonic) *Armino, Armonno*; *Armen, Armin*

ARMSTRONG English: Strong-armed

ARNAN Hebrew: Roaring stream

ARNETT English: Little eagle
Arnatt, Arnet, Arnott, Ornet, Ornette

ARNOLD Teutonic: Strong as an eagle (Italian) *Arnaldo*; (Danish) *Arend*; (Finnish) *Aarne, Aarno*; **Nicknames:** *Arnie, Arny*; **Famous Namesakes:** *Actor and politician Arnold Schwarzenegger, Golfer Arnold Palmer*

ARRIGO Italian: Variation of Harry

ARSALAN Persian: Lion
Arzalan

ARSEN Armenian: Variation of Arsenios

ARSENIOS Greek: Strong and virile
(Greek) *Arsenio*; (Russian) *Arseni, Senya*;
(Armenian) *Arsen*; *Arsene*; **Famous
Namesakes:** *Actor and TV personality
Arsenio Hall*

ARSHIA Persian: Throne
Arshya

ART English: Nickname for Arthur

ARTAY Persian: Strong

ARTEMII Russian: Healthy, wholesome
Nicknames: *Artem*

ARTHUR English: Noble, courageous;
possibly related to the obscure Roman family
name Artorius. Other possible sources include
an Irish Gaelic word meaning "stone" and
artos, the Celtic word for "bear." Most
English speakers will associate this name
with legendary King Arthur. Also from the
Icelandic, meaning a follower of Thor, the
Norse god of war.
(French) *Artus*; (Italian) *Arturo*; (Portuguese)
Artur; (Gaelic) *Artuir*; (Finnish) *Arttu, Artturi*;
Nicknames: *Art, Artie, Turi, Arty*; **Famous
Namesakes:** *Musician Art Garfunkel, Tennis
player Arthur Ashe, Playwright Arthur Miller*

ARTIE English: Nickname for Arthur

ARUB Arabic: Eloquent, speaks perfectly
correct grammatical language, close to; Arub
is derived from korb (closeness) and in this
context may mean loves his wife. In colloquial
Egyptian Arabic, this word is sometimes used
to describe someone who is wily.

ARUN Hindi: Sun

ARVAD Hebrew: Wanderer
(Hungarian) *Arpad*

ARVEL Welsh: Cried over
Arvil

ARVIN German, English, Teutonic: Friend
of the people
Arvis, Arvon, Arwin, Arwyn; **Nicknames:**
Arvie

ARVO Finnish: Value, worth

ARWIN English: Spelling variation of Arvin

ARWOOD English: Spelling variation of
Garwood

ARYASB Persian: Possessor of Aryan horses;
name of Kourosh the Great's general and
friend
Ariasb

ARYE Hebrew: Spelling variation of Ariel

ASA Hebrew: Healer, physician; name of one
of the kings of Judah

ASAD Arabic, Hindi, Persian: Form of Abbas
Famous Namesakes: *Former President of
Syria Hafez El Asad*

ASAPH Hebrew: Collector; biblical singer
in King David's choir
Asaf, Asif, Asiph

ASCOT English: From the eastern cottage;
an ascot is commonly known as a broad neck
scarf or tie which is considered sophisticated
and is usually worn with formal wear.
Berkshire, England hosts the famous Ascot
horse races.
(English) *Ascott*; *Estcot, Estcott*

ASH English: Ash tree; the root of several English names and therefore a familiar variant of them, including Ashley and Ashton (Norse) *Ask*; *Ashe*

ASHBURN English: Lives near the ash tree brook; surname
Aesoburne

ASHBY English, Scandinavian: From the ash tree farm; surname
Aescby; **Nicknames:** *Ash*

ASHER Hebrew: Happy, blessed; in the Bible, Jacob blessed his eighth son, Asher, with a life of abundance.
Anschel, Anshel

ASHFORD English: From the ford near the ash trees; surname
Aescford, Aisford, Ashenford; **Nicknames:** *Ash*

ASHKAN Persian: Name of the third dynasty of Persian kings

ASHKII Native American: Boy (Navajo)

ASHLEY English: From the ash tree meadow
Aescleah, Aisley, Ashly, Ashleigh; **Star Babies:** *Son of Barry Gibb, Son of George Hamilton*

ASHLIN English: Lives near the ash tree pool
Aesclin

ASHRAF Arabic: Most honorable, noble; Ashraf is the superlative form of Sherif.

ASHTON English: From the town or settlement near the ash trees; surname
Aesctun, Aiston, Ashtin; **Nicknames:** *Ash*;
Famous Namesakes: *Actor Ashton Kutcher*

ASIM Arabic: Spelling variation of **Kasim**
Asem, Kasim, Kasem

ASLAN Turkish, Persian: Lion; parents and children will recognize Aslan as the majestic golden lion who rules Narnia in the classic C.S. Lewis book *The Lion, the Witch and the Wardrobe*, part of the Chronicles of Narnia.

ASPEN American: Type of tree noted for heart-shaped leaves which flutter in the slightest breeze; place name and ski resort town in Colorado
Aspyn, Aspin

ASWAD Arabic: Black

ASWIN Anglo-Saxon: Spear-friend, implies a close and trusted companion
Aescwine, Aescwyn, Ashwin, Ashwyn, Aswyn, Aswynn, Aswynne

ATA Egyptian: Twin. Turkish: Ancestor

ATASH Persian: Fire

ATEN Egyptian: God of the sun disk, worshipped as the great creator-god by Akhenaten in the eighteenth Dynasty

ATHDAR Gaelic: From the oak tree ford; variant of Adair
Athdair, Athdara, Athdare

ATHELSTAN Anglo-Saxon: First West Saxon king to have effective rule over all England
Aethelstan, Ethelstan

ATHERTON English: From the town or settlement near the spring; surname
Aethretun

ATIF Arabic: Compassionate, affectionate
Ateef, Atef

ATIRA Hebrew: Pray

ATLAS Greek: Carried; in mythology, Atlas was forced by Zeus to carry the heavens on his shoulders forever as a punishment after he and the other Titans fought an unsuccessful war against the Olympian gods.

ATMORE English: From the moor; surname
Attmore

ATTEYA Arabic: Gift, present, allowance; masculine form of Atiya
Atia, Atiya, Ateya, Ateyah

ATUM Egyptian: The original sun-god of Heliopolis who was later identified as Ra (Re); Atum was a primordial god that was represented in the form of a human and a serpent. He was the supreme god in the Heliopolitan Ennead (group of nine gods) and formed with Re to create Re-Atum.

ATWATER English: Near the water; surname
Attewater

ATWELL English: Lives near the well; surname
Attewell, Attwell

ATWOOD English: Lives near or in the woods; surname
Attewode, Atwoode; **Nickname:** *Woody*

ATWORTH English: At the farmstead; surname
Atteworthe

AUBERON English: Rules with elf-wisdom, highborn; possible variant of Aubrey
Auberron, Oberron, Oeberon

AUBREY French, English, Teutonic: Elf ruler, implying leadership with supernatural wisdom
Aubry

AUDEL English: From the ancient valley or dell; surname
Audell

AUDEN English: Old friend; possible variant of Aidan
Audyn

AUDLEY Anglo-Saxon, English: From the ancient meadow; surname
Audie, Audlea, Audlee

AUDRICK German: Variation of Eric

AUDUN Norse: Friend of wealth; Audun the Westfjorder was a central character in Grettir's Saga

AUGUST Latin: Spelling variation of Augustine
Star Babies: Son of Lena Olin

AUGUSTINE Latin: Majestic; Saint Augustine was the first archbishop of Canterbury. (Spanish) *Agustin*; (Irish) *Aguistin*; (Polish) *Augustyn*; (Finnish) *Aukusti*; (Hungarian) *Agoston*; *Agustine, August, Augustin, Austen*; **Nicknames:** *Augusty, Austin*

AUGUSTUS Latin: Majestic dignity, grandeur

AUHERT French: Noble

AULEY Irish: Variation of Olaf

AURA Greek: Soft breeze

AURELIUS Latin: Golden, blond (French) *Aurelien, Aurélien*; (Italian) *Aurelio*; (Spanish) *Aureliano*; (Polish) *Aurek, Aureli*; *Aurelian*; **Famous Namesakes:** *Roman emperor Marcus Aurelius Antoninus*

AURIVILLE French: From the gold town

AUSTIN English: Nickname for Augustine
Austyn; **Star Babies:** *Son of David Lynch, Sela Ward, Tommy Lee Jones, Paula Zahn, Michelle Phillips*

AVALLACH Celtic: Related to the island of Avalon in Arthurian legend and Celtic mythology
Aballach

AVAON Welsh: Legendary son of Talyessin

AVARAIR Armenian: From Avarair

AVEDIS Armenian: Brings good news

AVENELLE French: Lives near the oat field
Avenall, Aveneil

AVERILL Anglo-Saxon, English: Boar or boar warrior; born in April
Averell, Averil, Haverill, Averel, Averyl, Avrel, Avrell, Avrill, Avryll, Haverell; **Nicknames:** *Ave*

AVERY Anglo-Saxon: Elf ruler, implying leadership with supernatural wisdom
Averey

AVI Hebrew: Aramaic variation of Abba, meaning father.

AVIRIT Hebrew: Air

AVISHAI Hebrew: Gift from God
Avisha, Abishai, Avshai

AVITAL Hebrew: Father of dew; one of King David's sons
Abital, Avitul

AVIV Hebrew: Spring, youth

AVONMORE Irish: From the great river

AVRAHAM Hebrew: Spelling variation of Abraham

AVSALOM Hebrew: Spelling variation of Absalom

AXEL German, Scandinavian, Swedish: Father of peace; variant of Absalom
(Finnish) *Akseli*

AXTON English: Surname related to a place, possibly the swordsman's town

AYDIN Turkish: Enlightened

AYERS English: Heir to a fortune; Ayers Rock is an impressive and memorable landmark in Australia.

AYLMER English: Spelling variation of Elmer
Aillmer, Allmer

AYLWARD English, Teutonic: Awesome guardian, noble protector
Old Forms: *Aegelweard, Aethelweard, Athelward*; **Nicknames:** *Ward*

AZAD Persian: Free

AZARIAH Hebrew: Help of God; the name of numerous biblical characters
Azaria, Azaryah, Azaryahu, Azuriah, Azria, Azriah, Azuria, Azariahu, Azorya

AZIBO African: Youth (Nigerian)
Azy

AZIEL Hebrew: God is my strength

AZIM Arabic: Resolute, steady, determined; adjective that stems from Azm or Azima, meaning determination
Azmi, Azem, Azeem

AZIZ Arabic: Cherished, beloved
(Egyptian) *Azizi*

AZRAEL Hebrew: God is my help; in both Muslim and Jewish tradition, Azrael is the angel who parts the soul from the body at death.
Azriel

AZZAM Arabic: Determined, resolved

BABAK Persian: Little father

BAC Scottish: Bank

BACCHUS Latin: Roman mythological god of wine, poetry, and revelry; equated with the Greek god Dionysus
Baccus

BADAN Welsh: From Baddon
Badden, Baddon

BADR Arabic: Full moon; Badr is a site southwest of Medinah, Saudi Arabia, where Mohammed achieved victory over a Quoraychite caravan.

BADRU Egyptian: Born during the full moon

BAGHEL Arabic: Mule driver; derived from Baghl, meaning mule
Baghl

BAHAM Arabic: Lamb, calf, kid, to wean, brave, hero, difficult task

BAHIR Arabic: Dazzling, brilliant, splendid, dazzled by sunlight; masculine form of Bahira
Baheer

BAHRAM Persian: Name of a Persian king; also the planet Mars

BAILEY English: Steward or law enforcer, from occupation of bailiff; surname adapted to first name use
Bayley, Baileigh, Bailie, Bayleigh; **Star Babies:** *Son of Anthony Edwards, son of Tracey Gold*

BAINBRIDGE Gaelic, English: Lives near the pale bridge, a bridge over white water
Bainbrydge, Bainhrydge; **Old Forms:** *Banbrigge;* **Nicknames:** *Bain*

BAIRD English, Celtic, Scottish: Minstrel; a medieval musical entertainer
Bard, Bayrd

BAKARI Egyptian: Noble oath

BAKER English: Spelling variation of Baxter

BAKLI Norse: Son of Blaeng

BALARAMA Hindi: Powerful and blissful

BALASI Greek: Flat-footed

BALDER English: Bold, courageous army. Norse: The mythological son of Odin
Baldr, Baldur; **Old Forms:** *Baldhere*

BALDRIK German: Bold
(Anglo-Saxon) *Baldlice;* (Danish) *Balduin;* *Baldric*

BALE English: Spelling variation of Vail

BALEN Latin: Brave. Arthurian Legend: Brother of Balaan

BALIN Hindi: Mighty warrior.

BALINT Latin: Strong and healthy

BALMORAL Scottish: From the majestic village; Balmoral Castle in Aberdeenshire, Scotland, has been the Scottish home of the Royal Family since it was purchased for Queen Victoria by Prince Albert in 1852.

BALTAZAR Spanish: Protect the king; the name traditionally given to one of the three wise men of the New Testament
(Greek) *Baltsaros;* (German) *Baltasar*

BAMDAD Persian: Early morning

BANA Anglo-Saxon: Killer, slayer, a warrior name

BANAING English: Son of Bana, son of the slayer

BANAN Irish: White

BANBHAN Irish: Piglet

BANCROFT English: From the bean field; surname
Benecroft, Banfield; **Nicknames:** *Ban, Bank, Binky*

BANE Hawaiian: Long-awaited child

BANITI Egyptian: Teacher

BANNING Gaelic: Little blond one. English: Son of the slayer

BAPTISTE Greek, French: Baptizer; named for John the Baptist

BARAK Hebrew: Flash of lightning; in the Bible, the faithful fighter Barak cooperated with Deborah to win victory in battle against overwhelming odds.
Barrak

BARAM Hebrew: Son of the nation

BARAN Teutonic: Noble fighter or ram. Gaelic: Noble warrior

BARCLAY Anglo-Saxon, English, Scottish: From the birch tree meadow; Barclay is the name of one of the largest banks in England. Also a surname; see *Berkeley* and *Bartley*
Bercleah

BARD English: Spelling variation of Baird

BARDEN English: Lives near the boar's den
Bardan

> *"Fortune is Bardolph's foe"*
> Shakespeare's *Henry V*

BARDOLF English: Axe-wielding wolf, ferocious
Bardalph, Bardolph, Bardulf, Barwolf, Bardou, Bardoul, Bardulph; **Old Forms:** *Bardawulf*

BARDON English: Minstrel, a singer-poet

BARI Arabic: Beneficent, reverent, righteous, the godly, the upright, the creator; attributes of Allah

BARIS Turkish: Peace

BARLOW English: Lives on the bare hill

BARNABAS Hebrew: Son of exhortation, from the Aramaic *barnebhu ah*; the biblical Barnabas was the missionary companion of the apostle Paul.
(German) *Bamey*; (French) *Barnabé, Bernabe; Barnabe*; **Nicknames:** *Barnaby, Barney, Barny*

BARNETT English: Nobleman, leader
Barnet

BARNEY English: Nickname for Barnabas

BARNHAM English: From the baron's house

BARNUM English: From the nobleman's home

BARON English, French, Teutonic: Warrior; a title of nobility used as a given name. Hebrew: Derived from phrase Bar Aaron, meaning son of Aaron
Barrin, Barron

BARRA Celtic: Marksman

BARRETT German: Mighty as a bear
or a variant of Barnett
Barret

BARRIC English: From the barley or the
grain farm; surname
Barrick, Beric

BARRINGTON English: A town in England;
refers to a fenced-in place. Irish: Fair-haired
Nicknames: *Barry*

BARRIS Welsh: Son of Harry

BARRY Gaelic: Like a spear
Famous Namesakes: *Actor Barry Pepper,
Baseball player Barry Bonds, Australian actor
Barry Humphries;* **Star Babies:** *Son of Dick
Van Dyke*

BART English: Nickname for Bartholomew
Famous Namesakes: *Football player Bart
Starr*

BARTHOLOMEW Hebrew: Farmer, son of
the earth; one of Christ's twelve apostles
(Hebrew) *Bartel;* (Spanish) *Bartoli, Bartolo,
Bartolome, Toli;* (Gaelic) *Parlan, Parthalan;*
(Swedish) *Bartholomeus;* (Danish) *Bardo;*
(Czech) *Bartolomej;* (Finnish) *Perttu;*
(Hungarian) *Bartalan;* (Aramaic) *Barthelemy;*
Bartley, Bartol; **Nicknames:** *Bart, Barta,
Barth, Bartlett, Batt, Bartlet, Bartlitt*

BARTLETT English: The farmer's son; this
surname is also a variant of Bartholomew.
John Bartlett's *Familiar Quotations* is one of
the most referenced resources for speech
writers and students in the English language.
Bartlet, Bartlitt

BARTLEY English, Scottish: From Bart's
meadow, from the birch-tree meadow;
probable variant of Barclay or Berkeley.
See also *Beartlaidh*
Bartleah, Bartleigh

BARTON English: From the barley town
of settlement; surname
Beretun, Barten, Barrton; **Nicknames:** *Bart*

BARTRAM Danish: Glorious raven; the
raven was consecrated to the Norse war god
Odin and was the emblem of the Danish
royal standard.
(English) *Barthram*

BARUCH Hebrew: Variation of Bennett

BASHIR Arabic: Messenger, brings good
news, herald; Eid el Bishara is the Feast
of the Annunciation
Bashar, Basheer, Bachir; **Famous
Namesakes:** *Lebanese military commander
and politician Bashir Gemayel*

BASIL English: Kingly; Saint Basil the Great
was a fourth-century bishop who was one of
the fathers of the early Christian church.
This was also the name of two Byzantine
emperors.
(Greek) *Basile, Bazyli;* (Spanish) *Basilio;*
(Swedish) *Basmus;* (Dutch) *Basilius;*
(Russian) *Vasily, Vassily;* **Nicknames:** *Vasya;*
Diminutive Forms: *Vasek;* **Star Babies:** *Son
of Dave Foley and Tabitha Southley*

BATUL Arabic: Virgin; masculine form of
Batula
Batoul

BAXTER English: Baker; an occupational
surname transferred to first-name use in the
nineteenth century
Baker; **Old Forms:** *Backstere, Baecere;*
Nicknames: *Bax*

BAYARD French, English: Auburn-haired;
Bayard was a sixteenth-century French
knight and national hero renowned for valor
and purity of heart.
Baylen; **Nicknames:** *Bay*

BEACAN Celtic: Small

BEACHER English: Lives by the beech tree

BEAGEN Gaelic: Little one

BEALE English: Handsome; a variant
of Beau
Beal, Beall

BEARACB Celtic: Marksman

BEARTLAIDH Irish: From Bart's meadow,
from the birch tree meadow; variant of
Bartley

BEATHAN Scottish: Son of the right-handed

BEATTY Gaelic: Blesses
(Gaelic) *Biadhaiche*; *Beatie, Beattie*

BEAU French: Handsome
Famous Namesakes: *Beau Bridges*

BEAUFORT French: From the beautiful
fortress

BEB Egyptian: Osiris' firstborn

BEBHINN Gaelic: Harmony

BECK English: Brook
Bek; **Famous Namesakes:** *Musician Beck*

BECKETT English: Little mouth; a surname
Star Babies: *Son of Melissa Etheridge*

BECKHAM English: Place of the small
stream; well-known surname thanks to
soccer star David Beckham
Beckam

BEECHER English: Lives by the beech tree;
surname

BEHDAD Persian: Given honor

BEHNAM Persian: Reputable

BEHRUZ Persian: A good day
Behrooz

BEHZAD Persian: Of noble family

BELA Hebrew: Destruction; also a
Hungarian variant of Albert

BELDEN English: Lives in the beautiful
glen valley
Beldan, Beldane, Beldene, Beldon

BELLAMY French: Handsome friend
Bellami

BELTRAN Spanish: Variation of Bertram

BEN English: Nickname for Benjamin
Famous Namesakes: *Inventor and states-
man Ben Franklin, Actor Ben Stiller;* **Star
Babies:** *Son of Rowan Atkinson, Jeff Daniels,
Neil Young*

BENECROFT English: From the bean field;
surname and variant of Bancroft
Nicknames: *Ben*

BENEDICT Latin: Blessed; name was borne
by fifteen popes and Saint Benedict, founder
of the monastic Benedictine Order
(German) *Bendix*; (Italian) *Benedetto, Benito*;
(Spanish) *Benedicto*; (Czech) *Benes*; (Polish)
Bendek, Bendyk; **Nicknames:** *Beni*

BENEN Latin, Irish: Kind, well born
(Irish) *Beanon, Beinean, Binean*; **Old Forms:**
Benignus

BENJAMIN Hebrew, Spanish: Son of the
right hand; in the Bible, Benjamin was the
patriarch Jacob's youngest son. His mother
Rachel died giving birth to him and in her
last moments of life named him Benoni,
meaning "son of my sorrow." His father did
not want him to have such an ominous

moniker and renamed him Binyamin.
(Italian) *Beniamino*; (Spanish) *Venjamin*;
(Russian) *Veniamin*; *Venamin*; **Old Forms:**
Benyamin, Binyamin; **Nicknames:** *Ben, Benji,
Benjy, Bennie, Benno, Benny*; **Famous
Namesakes:** *Statesman and inventor Benjamin
Franklin, English composer Benjamin Britten,
Actor Benjamin Bratt*; **Star Babies:** *Son of
Annette Bening and Warren Beatty, son of
Harrison Ford, son of Carly Simon and James
Taylor*

BENNETT Latin: Blessed
(Hebrew) *Baruch*; *Bennet*; **Nicknames:**
Bence, Benci, Benn

BENOIT French: Blessed
Benoist; **Nicknames:** *Ben*; **Famous
Namesakes:** *French director Benoit Jacquot*

BENONI Hebrew: Son of my sorrows

BENROY Hebrew: Royal mountain

BENSON English: Son of Benjamin; surname

BENT Danish: Blessed

BENTLEY English: From the meadow
of coarse or bent grass
Bentleigh, Bentlea

BENTON English: Settlement near the bent
or coarse grass; surname
Bentun; **Nicknames:** *Ben*

BEOLAGH Irish: Foolishly valorous

BEOWULF Anglo-Saxon: Intelligent wolf;
mythical hero whose story is told in one of
the oldest works of English literature, the
epic poem *Beowulf*

BERDE Danish: Glacier

BERG German, Swedish: Mountain

BERGIN Irish: Spear-like

BERGREN Swedish: From the mountain
brook
(English) *Bergen*; (Swedish) *Bergron*;
Berggren, Bergin

BERKELEY Anglo-Saxon, English, Irish:
From the birch tree meadow; also a well-
known university in California. See *Barclay*
and *Bartley*
(Irish) *Berk*; *Berkley*; **Diminutive Forms:**
Berke

BERKER Turkish: Solid man
Berk

BERLIN English: Son of Bert; the capital
of Germany
Berlyn; **Famous Namesakes:** *Composer
Irving Berlin*

BERN Scandinavian: Nickname for Bernard

BERNARD German: Strong and brave as
a bear
(English) *Barnard, Burnell*; (German)
Bernhard; (Italian) *Bernardo*; (Irish)
Beamard; (Dutch) *Barend*; (Basque) *Benat*;
Bearnard, Berinhard, Bernelle, Burnard; **Old
Forms:** *Bernardyn*; **Nicknames:** *Bern, Berne,
Bernie, Bernon, Nardo*

BERNARDO Spanish: Variation of Bernard
Nicknames: *Dino*

BERNIE Scandinavian: Nickname for Bernard

BERT English: Bright; Bert is commonly
given as a nickname for names such as Albert
and Robert
Bertie, Burt, Butch; **Famous Namesakes:**
Actor Burt Lancaster, Actor Burt Reynolds

BERTOLD German: Bright ruler, shines
Berthold; **Nicknames:** *Bert*; **Famous
Namesakes:** *German author Bertolt Brecht*

BERTON English: From the fortified town *Bertin*; **Nicknames:** *Bert*

BERTRAM Teutonic: Bright, shining raven (French) *Bertrand*; (Italian) *Bertrando*; (Spanish) *Beltran*

BERWICK English: From the barley grange *Berwyk*

BES Egyptian: A dwarf-deity with leonine features; Bes is a domestic god, protector against snakes and various terrors. He was venerated as the helper of women in child-birth.

BEVAN Welsh, Celtic: Son of Evan *Beven, Bevin, Bevyn*

BEVERLEY English: From the beaver stream, beaver meadow; traditionally a boy's name, now more popularly used for girls, especially in the U.S. *Beverly, Beverlea*; **Nicknames:** *Bev, Leigh*

BHAGA Hindi: The dispenser, the sun God

BHARAT Hindi: The supporter

BHASKAR Hindi: Sun

BHIMA Hindi: The fear-inspiring

BICKFORD English: From the hewer's ford **Nicknames:** *Bick*

BIENVENIDO Spanish: Welcome

BIJAN Persian: A name from Persian mythology, character in Shahnameh

BILL English: Nickname for William **Famous Namesakes:** *Comedian Bill Cosby, Microsoft founder Bill Gates, Actor Billy Crystal, Musician Billy Joel*

BINAH Hebrew: Understanding

BING German: From the kettle-shaped hollow *Binge*

BIRK English, Scottish: Birch tree, where the birch trees grow; surname *Birch, Birche*

BIRKETT English: From the birch-covered coastland; surname *Birkhead, Birkhed, Burkett, Birket, Birkit, Birkitt, Burkitt*; **Nicknames:** *Birk, Burk*

BIRKEY English: From the island of birch trees; surname *Birkee, Birkie, Birky*

BIRLEY English: From the meadow with the cattle byre (shed); surname *Byreleah, Birlea, Birlie, Birly, Byrlea, Byrlie*

BIRNEY English: From the island with the brook; surname (Irish) *Burney; Bureig, Burneig*

BISHOP English: Overseer

BJORN Scandinavian, Swedish: Bear *Biorn*; **Famous Namesakes:** *Swedish tennis champion Bjorn Borg*

BLAINE Irish, Scottish: Thin *Blainey, Blane, Blaney, Blayne*

BLAIR Gaelic, Irish: Child of the fields

"You know the only people who are always sure about the proper way to raise children? Those who've never had any."
—Bill Cosby

BLAISE Latin, French: Stammerer; Blaise Pascal was a brilliant seventeenth-century

child prodigy, mathematician, scientist, and philosopher who invented the calculating machine and hydraulic press before dying at age thirty-nine.
(French) *Blaisdell*; (Spanish) *Blas*; (Swedish) *Blasius*; (Czech) *Blazej*; *Blais, Blaize, Blase, Blayze, Blaze*

BLAKELY Scandinavian: Black or white, dark-haired; can also mean the reverse: fair, pale
Nicknames: *Blaec, Blake*

BLANCO Spanish: Blond, white

BLISS Anglo-Saxon: Intense joy; a name used since medieval times, but more often for girls

BLYTHE English: Merry

BO Scandinavian: Nickname and abbreviation for Bogart and Beau

BOAZ Hebrew: Swift; an honorable and wealthy man of the Bible who married the loyal Moabite Ruth
Boas

BOB English: Nickname for Robert
Nicknames: *Bobbie, Bobby*; **Famous Namesakes:** *Actor Bob Newhart, Comedian Bob Hope, Musician Bob Dylan, Game show host Bob Barker, Hockey players Bobby Hull and Bobby Orr*

BOBO African: Born on Tuesday

BOCLEY English: Lives at the buck meadow; surname
Bocleah, Boclea, Bocleigh

BODEN Anglo-Saxon: Messenger

BODHI Hindi: Wise or enlightening

BOGART German: Bowstring

BOGDAN Polish, Russian: God's gift (Czech) *Bohdan*; **Nicknames:** *Bogdasha, Danya, Bogdashka*

BOGUMIL Polish: God's love

BOGUSLAW Polish: God's glory
(Czech) *Bohuslav*

BOHUMIR Czech: God is great

BOLDIZSAR Hungarian: God bless the King
Nicknames: *Bodi*

BOLTON English: The specific meaning of this name is unclear, though the ending "ton" likely indicates that it refers to a town or settlement.
Bollton, Bolten, Boltin; **Famous Namesakes:** *Singer Michael Bolton*

BOND English: Tied to the land, farmer; surname; many will associate this name immediately with fictional secret agent James Bond.

BOONE English: Good, a blessing
Famous Namesakes: *American frontier hero Daniel Boone*

BORA Turkish: Hurricane

BORAK Arabic: Lightning; Al Borak was the legendary magical horse that bore Mohammed from earth to the seventh heaven.

BORDEN English, Anglo-Saxon: From the boar valley
Bordan

BOREAS Latin, Greek: North wind

BORG German, Norse, Swedish: From the castle; familiar form of Burkhard

BORIS Russian, Slavic: Fighter; Saint Boris is the patron saint of Moscow.
Nicknames: *Borya, Borka*; **Diminutive Forms:** *Boryenka*; **Famous Namesakes:** *Russian poet Boris Pasternak, author of the novel* Doctor Zhivago; *Tennis star Boris Becker*

BORISLAV Slavic: Glory in battle
(Polish) *Boryslaw*

BORNA Persian: Young

BOTROS Arabic: Variation of Peter
Butrus, Boutros; **Famous Namesakes:** *Secretary-General of the United Nations and Egyptian diplomat Boutros Boutros-Ghali*

BOULUS Arabic: Arabic form of Paul
Famous Namesakes: *Contemporary Arab poet Sargon Boulus*

BOURKE English: Fortified hill.

BOURNE English: From the brook

BOWEN Welsh, Gaelic: Blond, son of Owen
Bow, Bowyn; **Nicknames:** *Bowie*

BOYCE English: Lives near the wood

BOYDEN Anglo-Saxon: Blond or messenger
Nicknames: *Boyd*; **Famous Namesakes:** *Actor Boyd Gaines, Actor Billy Boyd*

BOYNTON Gaelic: From the white river
Nicknames: *Boyne*

BOZIDAR Czech: Divine gift

BRAD English: Broad; a nickname for Bradley and other names beginning with Brad
Famous Namesakes: *Actor Brad Pitt*

BRADAN English: From the broad valley

BRADBURN English: From the broad brook
Bradbourne; **Nicknames:** *Brad*

BRADEN Irish: Salmon; a variant spelling from Gaelic and the surname Ó Bradáin. Folklore tells of Finn MacCool, a well-known Irish hero who burned his thumb while cooking the Salmon of Knowledge. He put the burned thumb in his mouth and acquired the fish's gift of prophecy and wisdom. See also *Bradan*
Braddon, Bradene, Bradon, Bradyn, Braeden, Braedon, Brayden, Braydon; **Nicknames:** *Bradd, Brad*

BRADFORD English: From the broad ford
Nicknames: *Brad, Ford*

BRADLEY English: From the broad meadow; a surname adapted to widespread first-name use
Bradleah, Bradlee, Bradlea, Bradleigh, Bradlie, Bradly, Bradney; **Nicknames:** *Brad, Bradd, Lee*

BRADSHAW English: Broad clearing in the wood
Nicknames: *Brad, Shaw*; **Famous Namesakes:** *Hall of Fame quarterback Terry Bradshaw*

BRADWEN Welsh: Legendary son of Moren

BRADY English: From the wide island; a surname evocative of the popular TV show *The Brady Bunch.* Gaelic, Irish: Spirited; broad
Bradig, Bradee, Bradey, Bradie, Braedy, Braidie, Braidy, Braydie; **Famous Namesakes:** *Baseball player Brady Anderson*

BRAHMA Hindi: The creator; first born of Brahman

BRAHMAN Hindi: Absolute

BRAINARD English, Teutonic: Bold raven
Brainerd

BRAM Irish: Raven, also an abbreviation of Abraham; **Famous Namesakes:** *Bram Stoker, author of* Dracula

BRAN Celtic: Raven

BRANDEIS German: Dwells on a burned clearing

BRANDER Norse: Firebrand

BRANDON English: From the beacon hill or broom hill; sometimes used as a variant of Brendan
(Italian) *Brando; Brandan, Branddun, Branden, Brandin, Brandyn, Brannan, Brannen, Brannon, Branson, Brenden;* **Star Babies:** *Son of Richard Marx, Kenneth Edmonds, Tracy Austin*

BRANDT German: Fiery torch; dweller on land cleared by burning
(Norse) *Brandr; Brantley, Branton, Brantson, Brandy;* **Nicknames:** *Brand, Brant;* **Famous Namesakes:** *Politician Willy Brandt*

BRANIMIR Czech: Great protection

BRANISLAV Czech: Spelling variation of Bronislaw

BRANT English: Proud; variant of Brandt. Mohawk Indian Joseph Brant was a renowned strategist who fought for the British during the American Revolution and a devout scholar who translated Christian religious works into his native Indian tongue.

BRANTON English: Spelling variation of Brandt

BRASIL Celtic: Battle
Breasal

BRAWLEY English: From the meadow at the slope of the hill; surname
Braleah, Brawleigh, Bralea, Brauleigh, Braulie, Brauly, Brawlea, Brawlie, Brawly; **Star Babies:** *Son of Nick Nolte*

BRAXTON English: Brock's town

BRECK Gaelic: Freckled
Brecc, Brec, Brek, Brech

BREDE Norse: Broad

BREN German: Flame

BRENDAN Irish, Gaelic: Prince; the name of Irish saints, one of whom is said to have sailed to North America in the sixth century
Brandan, Breandan, Brenden, Brendon, Brennan, Brennen, Brennon, Brandon; **Nicknames:** *Bran, Brenn;* **Famous Namesakes:** *Irish playwright Brendan Behan, Actor Brendan Fraser*

BRENDIS German: Flame

BRENDON Irish: Spelling variation of Brendan

BRENT English: Hilltop
Brentan, Brenten, Brentley, Brenton; **Nicknames:** *Brendt*

BRETT English, Celtic: Brit, a person from Britain or Brittany; derived from a French surname of that meaning, but co-opted by English as a first name for both girls and boys
(Scottish) *Bretton; Bret, Brittain, Brittan, Britton, Brit, Briton, Britt;* **Famous Namesakes:** *Quarterback Brett Favre, Baseball player Bret Saberhagen*

BRETTON Scottish: Variation of Brett
Brittain, Brittan; **Nicknames:** *Brit, Britt*

BREWSTER English: One who brews ale; may also be a variant of Webster
Brewstere

BRIAN Celtic, Norse: Popular name of uncertain meaning, but generally thought to be of Celtic origin; possible definitions include strength, ascension, or valor. The name is widespread in Ireland, partially due to the renown of Brian Boru, a high king and great national hero who crushed the Vikings' attempts to take his country.
Briant, Brien, Brion, Bryan, Bryant, Bryon; **Famous Namesakes:** *Actor Brian Dennehy, Singer Bryan Adams;* **Star Babies:** *Son of Jim Henson*

BRICE English: Spelling variation of Bryce

BRICK English: Bridge

BRIEUC Celtic: Power, nobility, respect
Brieux

BRIGHAM English: Bridge

BRIGHTON English: From the bright town; a seaside town in Southern England; surname
Bryton

BRITTON English: Brit, a person from Britain; derived from a French surname of that meaning, but co-opted as a first name by English speakers; variant of Brett
Bretton, Briton, Brittain, Brittan

BROCK English: Badger; variant of Brook (Gaelic) *Bhruic; Broc, Brocleah, Brocleigh, Brocly;* **Nicknames:** *Brok*

BRODERICK Welsh: Brother, son of Roderick, or from the broad ridge (Scottish) *Brodric, Brodrick;* (Scandinavian) *Broderic; Broderik, Brodrik;* **Nicknames:** *Brody, Rick*

BRODY Irish, Scottish: From the muddy place; a castle in Scotland
(Scottish) *Brodie*

BROMLEY English: From the broom-covered meadow (broom is a shrub related to heather, with showy yellow flowers); surname
Bromleah, Bromleigh, Bromly, Bromlea, Bromlee, Broomlie

BRONE Irish: Sorrow
Bron

BRONISLAW Polish: Protecting glory
(Czech) *Bronislav; Branislav*

BRONSON English: Brown's son

BROOK English: Near the small stream; a surname originally used for boys that is used often now for girls as well, especially when spelled with the "e" at the end
Brooke, Brooks, Brookes

BRUCE French, English, Scottish: Surname since medieval times; Robert de Bruce, a knight from Normandy, followed William the Conqueror to England. His descendants settled in Scotland and began to give this as a first name.
Famous Namesakes: *Actor Bruce Willis, Singer Bruce Springsteen*

BRUHIER Arabic: Name of a Sultan

BRUNO German, Italian: Brown, dark-haired

BRYANT Celtic: Spelling variation of Brian
Famous Namesakes: *Newsman Bryant Gumbel*

BRYCE Anglo-Saxon: Son of a nobleman; Bryce Canyon in Utah became a national park in 1924 and has formations more than ten thousand years old.
(French) *Brys*; (Scottish) *Brycen, Bryceton, Bryston*; *Brice, Bryson*

BRYNN Welsh: From the hill

BUCK English: Male deer
Boc; **Star Babies:** *Son of Roseanne Barr*

BUCKLEY English: Buck's meadow or meadow of deer; surname. Irish: Boy
Bucklea, Bucklee, Buckleigh, Bucklie; **Nicknames:** *Buck*

BUD English: Short for buddy, or possibly a child's pronunciation of brother; Bud has been used as a nickname since medieval times.
Budd, Buddy; **Famous Namesakes:** *Comedian Bud Abbott, Actor Buddy Ebsen*

BUIRON French: From the cottage; a common family name in France

BULUT Turkish: Cloud

BURCET French: From the little stronghold

BURCH English: Birch tree; variant of Old English Birk
Birch, Birche

BURDETTE English: Bird
Burdett

BUREL French: Coarse hair; a common family name in France sometimes given as a first name in English-speaking countries
Burnell, Burrell

BURGESS English, Celtic: Lives in town
Burgeis; **Famous Namesakes:** *Actor Burgess Meredith*

BURLEY English: From the castle's meadow, from the fortified meadow, from the meadow of knotted wood; surname
Burhleag, Burly, Burlea, Burlee, Byrley

BURNEY English: From the island with the brook; variant of Birney

BURTON English: From the fortified town
Nicknames: *Burt*

BUSBY Norse: Dwells at the village
Nicknames: *Buzz*; **Famous Namesakes:** *Choreographer Busby Berkeley*

BYRNE English: From the brook
Byrnes

BYRON English: The cattle herder or from the cowsheds. Teutonic: From the cottage
Biron, Byram; **Famous Namesakes:** *Golfer Byron Nelson*; **Star Babies:** *Son of Mel Harris*

> *"'Tis pleasant, sure, to see one's name in print; a book's a book, although there's nothing in 't."*
> —Lord Byron

CABLE French: Rope, rope maker; also an English surname
Cabe, Cabell

CADDOCK Welsh: Battle sharp
Caddoc

CADE English: Round or barrel
Caden, Kade; **Star Babies:** *Son of Keith Carradine*

CADELL Welsh: Battle
Cadel

CADMAN Anglo-Saxon, Welsh: Warrior
Cadmon, Caedmon

CADMUS Greek: From the east
Kadmus

CADWALLON Welsh: Battle dissolver
Cadwallen

CAESAR Latin: Long-haired; Julius Caesar was one of ancient Rome's greatest politicians and military leaders, building Rome to be the center of a huge empire. The name Caesar came to be generic for any ruler in the empire and was later translated to Czar in Russian and Kaiser in German.
(French) *Cesar*; (Italian) *Ceasario, Cesare*; (Spanish) *Cesario, Cesaro*; **Famous Namesakes:** *Actor Cesar Romero, Comedian Sid Caesar, Labor union organizer Cesar Chavez*

CAGNEY Irish: Tribute; a surname
Famous Namesakes: *Actor James Cagney*

CAILEAN Gaelic: Child
Caelan, Cailen, Cailin, Caillen, Calan, Caley, Kaelan, Kaelin, Kalan, Kalen, Kalin; **Nicknames:** *Kael*

CAIN Hebrew: Acquired; in the Bible, Cain was the son of Adam and Eve.

CAINE French: French place name unrelated to the biblical Cain

CALDER English: Cold brook; surname
Caldre, Calldwr

CALDWELL English: From the cold spring; surname
Caldwiella

CALEB Hebrew: Bold or dog; an Israelite who joined Moses from Egypt to live long enough to enter the Promised Land
Kaleb; **Nicknames:** *Cale, Kale*; **Star Babies:** *Son of Jack Nicholson, son of Julianne Moore*

CALHOUN Gaelic, Irish: From the narrow forest; a surname

CALIX Latin: Chalice

CALLAGHAN Irish: Strife
Callahan, Ceallach, Ceallachan, Keallach; **Nicknames:** *Cillian*

CALLOUGH Irish: Bald
Calbhach, Calvagh

CALVERT English: Cow herder; surname
Calbert

CALVIN Latin: Bald
(Italian) *Calvino*; **Nicknames:** *Cal, Kal*; **Famous Namesakes:** *President Calvin Coolidge, Baseball player Cal Ripken, Jr., Designer Calvin Klein, Swiss religious reformer John Calvin*

CAMDEN Scottish, Gaelic: From the winding valley; a surname adapted to first-name use and a name of a section of London
(Anglo-Saxon) *Camdene*; *Camdan, Camdin, Camdyn, Kamden*; **Nicknames:** *Cam*

CAMERON Gaelic, Scottish: Crooked nose; the name of a great Highland clan
Camron, Camshron, Kameron, Kamron; **Nicknames:** *Camey, Kam, Cam*; **Star Babies:** *Son of Jimmy Buffett, son of Michael Douglas and Deandra Luker*

CAMILLO Latin: Meaning uncertain, possibly indicates an attendant at a religious ceremony or sacrifice; masculine form of Camilla
Camillus, Camilo

CAMLIN Celtic: Crooked line

CAMPBELL Gaelic, Scottish: Crooked mouth; name of a famous Highland clan
Cambeul; **Nicknames:** *Cam, Camp*; **Famous Namesakes:** *Actor Campbell Scott*

CAN Turkish: Soul

CANAN Turkish: Beloved

CARADOC Welsh: Beloved
Caradog

CARDEN Celtic: From the black fortress

CAREL Polish: Variation of Charles

CAREY Welsh: Near the castle
Cary; **Famous Namesakes:** *Actor Cary Grant*

> *"Cary Grant, born Archie Leach, was a poor boy who could barely spell posh. That's acting for you—or maybe Hollywood."*
> —*Christian Science Monitor*

CARL English: Strong, manly. See also *Karl*
Famous Namesakes: *Actor Carl Reiner, Astronomer Carl Sagan*

CARLETON English: From Charles' town or settlement; surname
Carletun, Charleston, Charleton, Charlton; **Nicknames:** *Carl*

CARLIN Irish: Little champion
Carling, Cearbhallan; **Nicknames:** *Car, Carlie, Carly*; **Famous Namesakes:** *Comedian George Carlin*

CARLISLE English: From the walled city
Carlyle

CARLOS Spanish: Variation of Karl
Nicknames: *Lito, Litos, Carlito, Carlitos*; **Famous Namesakes:** *Musician Carlos Santana, Brazilian musician Antonio Carlos Jobim*

CARLSON English: Carl's son

CARMEL Hebrew: Garden, orchard, vineyard; Mount Carmel in Israel is considered a paradise.
(Italian) *Carmelo, Carmine*; *Karmel*; **Nicknames:** *Carmi*

CARMICHAEL Gaelic, Scottish: Friend or follower of Saint Michael
Caramichil

CARR Scottish: From the marsh or mossy ground
Karr

CARRICK Gaelic: Rocky cliff
Carraig

CARRINGTON English: Origin is not entirely clear, but it refers to a town, possibly Charles' town; English surname
Carington

CARROLL Irish: Champion. German: Manly; variant of Carl
Carol, Carolus, Carrol, Cearbhall; **Famous Namesakes:** *Actor Carroll O'Connor, Author Lewis Carroll*

CARSON English, Scottish: Son of Carr
Carrson; **Famous Namesakes:** *TV personality Carson Daly, Actor and comedian Johnny Carson*

CARSTEN German: Variation of Christian
Carston, Karsten

CARSWELL English: Near the well where the watercress grows; surname
Caersewiella

CARTER English: Drives a cart; from a surname and occupational name
Cartere; **Famous Namesakes:** *President Jimmy Carter*; **Star Babies:** *Son of Alan Thicke*

CARVELL French, English: Spearman's estate or marshy estate

CASEY Irish: Vigilant
Cacey, Kasen, Kasey; **Nicknames:** *Cace*; **Star Babies:** *Son of Beau Bridges*

CASIMIR Slavic, Polish: Announcing peace
(Spanish) *Casimiro*; *Kasimer, Kasimir, Kazimir, Kazmer*; **Nicknames:** *Kazimierz*

CASPAR Persian: Keeper of the treasure; Caspar (sometimes known as Gaspar) is said to be the name of one of the Three Magi who traveled from afar to find the baby Jesus.
(English) *Jasper*; (French) *Gaspar*; (Polish) *Kaspar*; *Gaspard, Casper*

CASPIAN Irish: Borrowed from the sea

CASSIDY Irish, Gaelic: Clever or curly-headed
Caiside; **Nicknames:** *Cass*; **Famous Namesakes:** *Singer David Cassidy, Actor Shaun Cassidy*

CASSIUS Latin: Vain; a name recognized worldwide as belonging to the great boxer Cassius Clay, now known as Muhammad Ali

CAT Scottish: Spelling variation of Chait

CATHAL Irish: Battle strong

CAWLEY Scottish: English cow meadow
Cauley

CECIL Latin: Blind
(Italian) *Cecilio*; *Cecilius*; **Famous Namesakes:** *Director Cecil B. DeMille, Baseball player Cecil Fielder*

CEDRIC English: Battle leader
Cedrick, Cedrik, Keddrick, Kedric, Kedrick, Sedric, Sedrick

CENOBIO Spanish: Spelling variation of Zenobio
Cenovio

CENON Spanish: Variation of Zenon

CHACE English: Huntsman
Chayce, Chaice

CHAD English: Warrior; a medieval given name from abbreviations of surnames Chadwick and Chadwell. Chad is also a seventeenth-century saint and an African country.
Famous Namesakes: *Actor Chad Lowe*

CHADBURN English: From the wildcat brook; originally a surname
Chadburne, Chadbyrne

CHADWICK English: From the warrior's town; originally a surname
Chadwik, Chadwyk

CHAGAI Hebrew: Festive
Chagi

CHAIM Hebrew: Life
Chayim, Hayyim, Hyman

CHAIT Scottish: Catlike
Cat

CHAKRA Hindi: Symbol of the sun

CHALMERS Scottish, Teutonic: Rules the home
Chalmar, Chalmer

CHAN Spanish: Nickname for John

CHANAN Hebrew: Variation of Hanan

CHANCE French: Variation of Chauncy
Star Babies: *Son of Larry King*

CHANCELLOR English: Record keeper
Chaunceler, Chancelor; **Nicknames:** *Chaucer, Chaucor, Chauncory*

CHANDLER French, English: Maker of candles
Chanler

CHANDRA Hindi: Shining moon
Chander

CHANE French: Oak-hearted
Chaney, Chayne, Cheney, Cheyne

CHANNE English: Nickname for Channing

CHANNING English, French: Of uncertain origin, possibly related to French meaning canal or indicating a church official; the spelling is suggestive of a paternal meaning such as Chan's or Cana's child.
Channon; **Nicknames:** *Chann, Channe*

CHANOCH Hebrew: Dedicated

CHAPIN French: Clergyman

CHAPMAN English: Merchant
Nicknames: *Chap*

CHAPPEL French: Chapel
Chappell

CHARLES French: Derived from the Germanic Karl, meaning manly; a royal name borne by ten kings of France and introduced to Great Britain by Mary, Queen of Scots, who named her son Charles James. His son and grandson were also named Charles, furthering the name's popularity. (Gaelic) *Tearlach*; (Irish) *Carlus*; (Welsh) *Siarl*; (Basque) *Xarles*; (Polish) *Carel*; **Nicknames:** *Charley, Charlie, Charlot, Charly, Chas, Chaz, Chick, Chuck*; **Famous Namesakes:** *Prince Charles, English author Charles Dickens*

> *"Every baby born into the world is a finer one than the last."*
> —Charles Dickens

CHARLESON English: Son of Charles

CHARLTON English: From Charles' town or settlement; surname; variant of Carleton
Charleton, Charltun; **Nicknames:** *Carl*;
Famous Namesakes: *Actor Charlton Heston*

CHARRO Spanish: Cowboy

CHASE English: Huntsman
Chayce, Chace, Chayace; **Nicknames:** *Chad*

CHASKA Native American: Firstborn son
(Sioux)

CHATHAM English: From the soldier's land

CHAUNCEY English, Latin: Chancellor,
fortune; a gamble
Choncey

CHAUNCY English: Fortune, luck; from the
French
(French) *Chance*; *Chancey, Chaunce*

CHAVIVI Hebrew: Dearly loved

CHENEY French: Spelling variation of
Chane

CHESS English: Nickname for Chester

CHESTER English: Lives at the camp of the
soldiers; an old Roman (Rochester) settle-
ment in Britain
Cheston; **Nicknames:** *Chess, Chet*; **Famous
Namesakes:** *WWII Admiral Chester Nimitz*;
Star Babies: *Son of Rita Wilson and Tom
Hanks*

CHET English: Nickname for Chester

CHETWIN English: From the small house
on the twisted or winding path
Cetewind, Chetwyn, Chetwynne; **Nicknames:**
Chet

CHEVALIER French: Horseman, knight
(French) *Cheval, Chevell*; **Nicknames:**
Chevy; **Famous Namesakes:** *French actor
Maurice Chevalier*

CHEVY French: Nickname for Chevalier
Famous Namesakes: *Actor and comedian
Chevy Chase*

CHIAMAKA African: God is splendid

CHIBALE African: Kinship

CHICO Spanish: Boy; also abbreviation
of Ezequiel

CHIDI African: God exists

CHIKE African: God's power

CHIKO Japanese: Thousand

CHILTON English: From the town or settle-
ment near the well; surname
Celdtun, Chelton, Chiltun; **Nicknames:** *Chill*;
Famous Namesakes: *Musician Alex Chilton*

CHIRAM Hebrew: Exalted

CHONI Hebrew: Gracious
Honi

CHRIS English: A nickname for Christian
or Christopher, though Chris easily stands
as an independent name
Famous Namesakes: *Actor Chris O'Donnell,
Comedian Chris Rock*

CHRISTIAN Latin: Follower of Christ; in
the middle ages, Christian was more often
used as a girls' name but is now commonly
used for boys.
(Greek) *Christiano*; (German) *Carsten,
Karsten, Krischan*; (French) *Cretien*;
(Spanish) *Cristian, Cristiano*; (Scandinavian)
Kristian; (Swedish) *Krist*; (Danish)
Christiansen; (Dutch) *Kerstan*; *Christiann*;
Nicknames: *Chris*; **Famous Namesakes:**
*Actor Christian Slater, Basketball player
Christian Laettner, Danish author Hans
Christian Andersen, Designer Christian Dior*;
Star Babies: *Son of Mel Gibson, son of Eddie
Murphy*

CHRISTO Slavic: Nickname for Christopher

CHRISTOPHER Greek, Latin: One who carries Christ; a beloved story tells of this name given to a saint that carried the Christ child across a river and is now known as the patron saint of travelers. Others believe Christopher means to carry Christ in one's heart.
(German) *Christoph*; (French) *Christophe*; (Italian) *Cristoforo*; (Spanish) *Cristobal, Cristofer, Cristofor, Criston, Cristos, Cristoval*; (Gaelic) *Crisdean*; (Scottish) *Christie*; (Welsh) *Crist*; (Scandinavian) *Kristof, Kristoffer*; (Danish) *Christoffer, Christofferson*; (Polish) *Krzysztof; Kristofer; Christobel, Christoffel, Christofor, Cristophe, Kristoff, Kristopher*; **Old Forms:** *Christophoros*; **Nicknames:** *Christo, Christy, Cris, Risto, Stoffel, Chris, Topher*; **Famous Namesakes:** *Actor Christopher Walken, Actor Christopher Reeve, Italian explorer Christopher Columbus*; **Star Babies:** *Son of Pierce Brosnan, Gene Hackman, Sean Combs, Maria Shriver and Arnold Schwarzenegger*

CHRISTOS Greek: Familiar form of Christopher
Khristos

CHURCHILL English: Lives near the church by the hill; surname
Churchyll, Circehyll; **Famous Namesakes:** *British Prime Minister Sir Winston Churchill*

CIAN Irish: Ancient. See also *Kian*
Cianan, Kean, Keanan, Keandre, Keane, Keenan, Keene, Keenon, Kenan, Keondre, Kienan

CIAR Irish: Dark

CIARAN Gaelic: Spelling variation of Kieran

CIBOR Polish: Honorable battle

CICERO Latin: Chickpea; best known for the statesman, orator, and author of ancient Rome
(Spanish) *Ciceron*

CIONAODH Irish: Born of fire

CIRO Spanish: Variation of Cyrus

CLARENCE Latin: Bright
Nicknames: *Clare*

CLARK English: Surname and occupational name for a clerk or secretary
Clarke; **Famous Namesakes:** *Superman's alter ego Clark Kent*

CLAUDE French: Lame; derived from an old Roman name
(English) *Claud*; (Spanish) *Claudio; Claudios; Claudion*; **Old Forms:** *Claudius, Klaudius*; **Famous Namesakes:** *Artist Claude Monet, Composer Claude Debussy, Actor Claude Rains*

CLAUDIUS Latin: Original form of Claude
Famous Namesakes: *Roman emperor Claudius Nero Germanicus*

CLAY English: Nickname for Clayton
Famous Namesakes: *Singer Clay Aiken*

CLAYBORNE English: From the brook near the clay
Claiborn, Claybourne, Clayburn; **Nicknames:** *Clay*

CLAYTON English: Mortal; place name and surname
Clayten; **Nicknames:** *Clay*

CLEMENS Latin: Clemency, mercy
(Latin) *Clementius*; (Italian) *Clemente*; (Czech) *Kliment*; (Hungarian) *Kelemen, Kellman, Klemen; Clement, Klemens*; **Nicknames:** *Clem, Klemenis*; **Famous Namesakes:** *German author Clemens Brentano, Author Samuel Langhorne Clemens (pen name Mark Twain), Baseball player Roberto Clemente*

CLEON Greek: Illustrious

CLEVELAND English: Hilly land, from the cliff; a geographical name, most notably in Ohio
Cleavon, Clevon; **Nicknames:** *Cleve*; **Famous Namesakes:** *President Grover Cleveland*

CLIFFORD English: Lives near the ford by the cliff; children will recognize this name of the beloved, canine character Clifford the Big Red Dog
Clyford; **Nicknames:** *Cliff*; **Star Babies:** *Son of Ken Olin*

CLIFFTON English: From the town or settlement near the cliff; surname
Clifton, Cliftun, Clyffton, Clyftun

CLIFLAND English: From the land near the cliffs; surname
Clyfland

CLINT English: Nickname for Clinton

CLINTON English: Surname; from the headland estate or hillside town
Clinttun, Clintt, Klint, Klinton; **Nicknames:** *Clint*; **Famous Namesakes:** *Actor Clint Eastwood, President Bill Clinton*

CLIVE English: Lives near a cliff
Clyve; **Famous Namesakes:** *Music mogul Clive Davis*

CLODOVEO Spanish: Famous warrior

CLOVIS Teutonic, French: Renowned fighter; an early form of Ludwig or Louis

CLUNY Gaelic, Irish: From the meadow
Clunainach

CLYDE Scottish: Place name referring to the River Clyde in Scotland

COALAN Celtic: Slender

COBY English: Uncertain meaning; possibly derived as a nickname for Jacob but is used as an independent name
Kobe, Koby, Cobey, Cobi

COCHISE Native American: Hardwood; renowned chief of the Chiricahua Apache from 1812-1874

CODY English: Pillow
Codey, Codi, Codie, Kodee, Kodie, Kodey, Kody; **Famous Namesakes:** *Frontiersman Buffalo Bill Cody*; **Star Babies:** *Son of Robin Williams, son of Kathie Lee and Frank Gifford*

COHEN Hebrew: Surname, priest

COLBERT French: Dark, dark-haired. English: Seaman
Colbey

COLBY English: Dark-skinned or from a coal town. The name Colby became more prominent following the 1980s television series *The Colbys*.
Kolby

COLE English: Dark; also a nickname for Nicholas
Famous Namesakes: *Composer Cole Porter*

COLIN Gaelic: A child or cub; variant of Coilean. In some languages, Colin is a nickname for Nicholas.
(Irish) *Coilin; Coilean, Collin, Colyn*; **Famous Namesakes:** *British actor Colin Firth, British conductor Sir Colin Davis*; **Star Babies:** *Son of Tom Hanks*

COLLIER English: Coal miner or merchant; surname and occupational name
Colier, Collyer, Colyer

COLTON English: From the coal town or dark town
Coleton, Colten; **Nicknames:** *Colt*

COLUMBA Latin: Dove; Saint Columba was a sixth-century Irish monk who established several monasteries in Ireland and a convent on the Scottish island of Iona.
(English) *Colver, Colvyr, Culver*; (French) *Colombain*; (Italian) *Columbo*; (Gaelic) *Colm, Colum*; (Celtic) *Calum*; (Irish) *Colman*; (Scottish) *Callum*; **Old Forms:** *Columbanus*

CONAN Celtic: Intelligent
Nicknames: *Kyne*

CONNELLY Irish: Love, friendship; surname

CONNOR Irish: Wolf lover
Conner, Conor, Cahner; **Star Babies:** *Son of Patrick Duffy, son of Nicole Kidman and Tom Cruise*

CONRAD German, Slavic: Bold advisor, wise; Joseph Conrad, author of several books including the classic *Heart of Darkness*, was said to spend hours searching for the right word for each sentence in his writing.
(Spanish) *Conrado*; (Swedish) *Konrad*; (Dutch) *Koenraad*; **Nicknames:** *Con, Connie, Koen, Kort, Kuno, Kunz*

CONSTANTINE Latin: Constant, steadfast; Emperor Constantine the Great made Christianity the official religion of the Roman Empire.
(Greek) *Kostas*; (Spanish) *Constantino*; (Russian) *Konstantin*; (Polish) *Konstancji*; **Nicknames:** *Conny, Konstantinus, Kostya*

COOPER English: Barrel maker
Star Babies: *Son of Tim Matheson, son of Hugh Hefner*

CORBIN Latin: Raven-haired
Corben, Corbett, Corbyn, Corvin; **Nicknames:** *Corby*; **Famous Namesakes:** Actor *Corbin Bernsen*

CORBY English: Nickname for Corbin

CORDELL English: Maker or seller of rope or cord; surname
Cordale, Corday, Kordale, Kordell; **Diminutive Forms:** *Cord, Kord*; **Famous Namesakes:** *Football player Kordell Stewart*

COREY Irish: From the hollow
Correy, Cory; **Famous Namesakes:** *Actor Corey Feldman*

CORLISS English: Good hearted, cheery
Nicknames: *Corley*

CORMAC Irish, Gaelic: Charioteer
Cormack, Cormic, Cormick; **Star Babies:** *Son of Tim Roth*

CORNELIUS Latin: Horn
(Spanish) *Cornelio*; (Dutch) *Krelis*; (Czech) *Kornel*

CORT French: Nickname for Curtis

CORTEZ Spanish: A surname, possibly meaning courteous; Spanish explorer and adventurer Hernando Cortes conquered the Aztec civilization of Mexico.

CORVIN English: Raven-haired

CORWIN English: Friend of the heart; close, very dear friend
Corwan, Corwine, Corwyn

COSKUN Turkish: Enthusiastic

COSMO Greek: Universe, order
Cosimo

COURTLAND English: Form of Courtney

COURTNEY French: Courteous or from the court
Courtland Courtnay; Cortland, Courtenay; **Famous Namesakes:** *Actor Courtney B. Vance*

COWAN Irish: Twin
Comhghan

COYAN French: Modest
Coyne

CRAIG Gaelic: Rock

CRANDALL English: From the dell or valley
of the cranes; surname
Crandell

CRANLEY English: From the meadow
of the cranes; surname
Cranleah, Cranly, Cranelea

CREIGHTON English, Scottish: From the
rocky town or settlement; surname
(Scottish) *Crayton; Crichton*

CRISPIN Latin: Curly-haired. The third-
century martyr Saint Crispin is known as
patron of shoemakers.
Famous Namesakes: *Actor Crispin Glover*

CRISTOBAL Spanish: Variation of
Christopher

CRISTOPHE Greek: Spelling variation
of Christopher

CROMPTON English: From the winding
town or settlement

CROSBY Norse: At the cross, at the town
crossroads
Famous Namesakes: *Entertainer Bing
Crosby*

CROSLEY English: From the cross meadow;
surname
*Crosleah, Crosleigh, Crosly, Crosslea, Croslee,
Crossleigh*

CRUZ Spanish, Portuguese: Cross

CUARTO Spanish: Born fourth
Cuartio

CULLEN Irish, Gaelic, Celtic: Handsome
or holly; from an Irish surname MacCuilinn
Cullan, Cullin; **Nicknames:** *Cully*

CULVER English: Variation of Columba

CURRO Spanish: Free; pet form of
Francisco
Currito

CURTIS French, English: Courteous
(English) *Curtiss;* (German) *Kurt, Kurtis;*
(Spanish) *Curcio; Curtice;* **Nicknames:** *Cort,
Court, Curt;* **Famous Namesakes:** *Actor
Tony Curtis*

CYAN English: Greenish-blue color

CYNELEY English: Lives near the royal
meadow; surname
Cyneleah, Cynelea, Cyneleigh

CYPRIAN Greek: From Cyprus
(Italian) *Cipriano*

CYRANO Greek: From Cyrene; Cyrano de
Bergerac was the romantic hero of Edmund
Rostand's play by the same name. The character was based on a French author with this
moniker.

CYRIL Greek: Lordly; Saint Cyril and his
brother Saint Methodius developed the
Cyrillic alphabet.
(Spanish) *Cirilo;* (Russian) *Kiril, Kiryl;*
(Polish) *Cyrek, Cyryl; Cyr, Cyrill;* **Old Forms:**
Kyrillos

CYRUS Persian: Sun or enthroned; Cyrus
the Great conquered Babylon and founded
the Persian Empire.
(Spanish) *Ciro;* **Star Babies:** *Son of Cibyll
Shepherd*

DABIR Arabic: Teacher or manager

DACEY Gaelic: Southerner
(Spanish) *Dacio*; *Dace, Dacian, Dacy, Deasach*

DAEDALUS Greek: Cunning; in Greek mythology, Daedalus was a skilled Athenian craftsman and inventor. King Minos had him imprisoned in his own invention—the labyrinth. Daedalus and his son Icarus tried to escape with wings he created from wax, feathers, and thread, yet Icarus flew too close to the sun and died.

DAEGAN Irish, Gaelic: Black-haired
Dagen, Deegan; **Nicknames:** *Daeg*

DAG Norse, Scandinavian: Day; in Norse mythology, the son of Nott and Dellingr
Famous Namesakes: *Secretary-General of the United Nations Dag Hammarskjold*

DAGAN Hebrew: Grain

DAGOBERT German: Glorious day
(Spanish) *Dagoberto*; *Dagbert*

DAGON Hebrew: Fish; a fish-god of the ancient Philistines

DAGWOOD English: From the shiny forest; a dagwood is a large, multi-layered sandwich with numerous fillings. The sandwich is named after Dagwood Bumstead, the well-known character who eats giant sandwiches in the comic strip *Blondie*.

DAHY Irish: Quick and agile

DAI Japanese: Large

DAIRE Irish: Fruitful or dark oak
Darach, Darragh, Dary

DAKARAI African: Happiness (Zimbabwe)

DAKOTA Native American: To be considered friend, ally; name of a group of tribes more familiarly known as the Sioux
Dakoda, Dakotah; **Star Babies:** *Son of Melanie Griffith and Don Johnson, son of Melissa Gilbert*

DAKSHA Hindi: Brilliant

DALE English: Lives in the dell or valley; originally a surname
Dael, Dayle; **Nicknames:** *Daley*; **Famous Namesakes:** *NASCAR driver Dale Earnhardt*

DALLAS Scottish: From the field with the waterfall; originally a place name in Scotland, but also a major city in Texas
Dalles, Dallis

DALLIN Irish: Unseeing; (English) proud
Dalan, Dalen, Dallan, Dallen, Dallon, Dalon; **Nicknames:** *Dal*

DALTON English: From the town or settlement in the dale; closely related to the name Denton; surname
Daleton, Dallten, Dalten, Daltun; **Nicknames:** *Dale*

DALY Gaelic: Assembly; a common Irish surname
Daley

DALZIEL Scottish: From the little field

DAMAE Greek: Tame

DAMARIO Spanish: Gentle or calf; masculine of the Greek Damaris, a biblical woman who heard Paul speak at the open-air supreme court of Athens
Demario

DAMASKENOS Greek: From Damascus; Damascus is the capital of Syria and one of the world's oldest cities
Damaskinos

DAMEK Czech: Variation of Adam

DAMIAN Greek: One who tames or subdues; Saint Damian is the patron saint of physicians. (English) *Damen, Damion, Damon*; (French) *Damien*; (Italian) *Damiano*; (Irish) *Daman*; *Damone*; **Old Forms:** *Damianos*

DAMON English: Variation of Damian *Daemon, Daman, Damen, Daymon*; **Famous Namesakes:** *Actor Damon Wayans, Actor Matt Damon*

DAN English: Nickname for Daniel **Nicknames:** *Dannie, Danny*; **Famous Namesakes:** *Actor Dan Aykroyd, Newsman Dan Rather*

DANA English: From Denmark *Dain, Daine, Dane*; **Famous Namesakes:** *Actor Dana Carvey, Actor Dane Clark*

DANAUS Greek: According to Greek mythology, Danaus was a father to fifty daughters, known as the Danaides.

DANB Norse: From Denmark

DANIEL Hebrew: God is my judge; the biblical prophet and writer of the Book of Daniel was a teenager when taken to Babylon after the destruction of Jerusalem. He survived two death sentences: a lions' den and a fiery furnace. See also *Danila* (Italian) *Daniele*; (Spanish) *Danilo*; (Irish) *Daineal, Dainial*; (Welsh) *Deiniol*; (Slavic) *Danek*; (Hungarian) *Dani*; (Persian) *Danyal*; *Danell, Danil, Dannel, Dantrell*; **Nicknames:** *Dan, Dannie, Danny, Danya*; **Diminutive Forms:** *Danylko*; **Famous Namesakes:** *Actor Daniel Day-Lewis, Actor Danny DeVito, Frontiersman Daniel Boone*; **Star Babies:** *Son of Dan Rather, son of Natasha Richardson and Liam Neeson*

DANILA Russian: A variant of Daniel; Danila-Craftsman is the hero of Russian tales about a man who made wonderful things out of malachite. *Danya, Danilka, Danilushka*

DANN Hebrew: Judge; biblical fifth son of Jacob and founder of one of the twelve tribes of Israel. An independent name and also an abbreviation of Daniel

DANTE Italian: Enduring; a contracted form of Durante. Italian author Dante Alighieri wrote the epic poem *The Divine Comedy* with its graphic description of medieval Hell known as Dante's Inferno. (English) *Dontae, Donte*; (Spanish) *Dantae, Dantel, Daunte*; *Dontay, Dontaye*; **Famous Namesakes:** *Poet Dante Gabriel Rossetti*

DANTON French: Variation of Anthony **Famous Namesakes:** *Jazz bassist Danton Boller, French revolutionary Georges Jacques Danton*

DAPHNIS Greek: A name of Greek mythology, Daphnis was a shepherd and flute player who was blinded by a lover after being unfaithful to her.

DAR Hebrew: Pearl

DARBY Norse: From the deer estate. Irish: Free man **Famous Namesakes:** *Author Darby Costello*

DARCY French: From the Arcy (Oise River) which flows into the Seine. Irish: Dark *D'arcy, Darce*; **Famous Namesakes:** *Baseball player D'arcy Flowers, Canadian hockey player Darcy Regier*

DARIEN English: A name of uncertain origin, perhaps a variant or blend of names such as Darren, Darius, or Adrian
Darian, Darion, Darrien, Darrion

> *Or like stout Cortez when with eagle eyes*
>
> *He star'd at the Pacific— and all his men*
>
> *Look'd at each other with a wild surmise—*
>
> *Silent, upon a peak in Darien.*
>
> —John Keats, "On First Looking into Chapman's Homer"

DARIUS Persian: Rich; Darius the Mede assumed kingship of Babylon after its conquest by Cyrus.
(Latin) *Dario*; *Darrius*; **Famous Namesakes:** *Singer Darius Rucker*

DARNELL English: From the hidden place
Darnall, Darnel

DARREN Gaelic, English: Great
Daran, Daren, Darin, Daron, Darrin, Darron, Darryn, Daryn, Dearan, Derren, Derrin

DARRENCE English: Uncertain meaning or origin; perhaps a blend of Darryl and Clarence
Darence, Darrance, Derrance

DARROLD English: Uncertain meaning; possibly an invented name, as a blend of Daryl and Harold or Gerald
Darold, Derald, Derrold

DARRYL English: From a French surname and place name D'Arel (from Arielle in Calvados); used as both a surname and given name since the eleventh century
Dareau, Darel, Dariel, Dariell, Darrel, Darrell, Darroll, Darryll, Daryl, Daryle, Daryll, Derell, Derrall, Derrell, Derrill, Derryl; **Nicknames:** *Darry*; **Famous Namesakes:** *Baseball player Daryl Strawberry*

DARSHAN Sanskrit: To perceive

DARTAGNAN French: From Artagnan; one of the main characters in Alexandre Dumas' novel *The Three Musketeers*

DARTON English: From the deer park

DARVIN English: Blend or Darrel and Marvin

DARWIN English: Friend of the deer; the original meaning has taken on the similar-sounding but different meaning of dear friend.
Darwyn, Deorwine, Derwan, Derwin, Derwyn, Durwin, Durwyn; **Famous Namesakes:** *Naturalist Charles Darwin*

DASAN Native American: Ruler

DAVEN Scandinavian: Bright Finn

DAVIAN English: Spelling variation of David

DAVID Hebrew: Dearly loved; the Old Testament has many stories of David's life, including his well-known defeat of Goliath the giant. He went on to become King of Israel and write the Book of Psalms. See also *Havika* (Arabic) *Dawud*; (Italian) *Davide*; (Gaelic) *Daibhid, Daibhidh*; (Irish) *Daithi*; (Welsh) *Dafydd, Dewey, Dewi*; (Persian) *Davood*; *Daveon, Davian, Davidson, Daviel, Davion, Daviot*; **Nicknames:** *Dave, Davey, Davie, Davy*; **Diminutive Forms:** *Dai, Davi*; **Famous Namesakes:** *Rock star David Bowie, TV host David Letterman, Frontiersman Davy Crockett*; **Star Babies:** *Son of Robert Redford*

DAVIS English: David's son; a surname
Famous Namesakes: *Confederate President Jefferson Davis*

DAVU African: The beginning

DAWSON English: David's son; a surname

DAX French: Geographical name; a town in the Gascony region of southwestern France dating from before the Roman occupation
Dack; **Famous Namesakes:** *Indie Actor Dax Shepard*

DAYLAN English: Rhyming variant of Waylon; a historical blacksmith with supernatural powers
Daelan, Dalyn, Daylen, Daylin, Daylon; **Nicknames:** *Dayne*

DAYNE English: Nickname for Daylan

DEACON Greek: Servant; also a church official
Deakin; **Nicknames:** *Deke*; **Famous Namesakes:** *Football player Deacon Jones*; **Star Babies:** *Son of Reese Witherspoon and Ryan Philippe*

DEAN English: From the valley
Deane, Deanne, Dene; **Famous Namesakes:** *Actor Dean Martin, Actor James Dean, Baseball player Dizzy Dean*

DEARBORN English: From the deer brook
Dearbourne

DECLAN Irish: Full of goodness; Saint Declan founded a monastery in Ardmore, County Waterford and is believed to have preached in Ireland before the arrival of Saint Patrick.

DEEMS English: Judge's son

DEERWARD English: Spelling variation of Derward

DEKEL Hebrew: Palm tree

DEL French: Surname prefix meaning *of the*; also used as an independent name and an abbreviation of names beginning with Del

DELANEY Irish: Descendant of the challenger; Delaney could also be derived from the Norman surname De l'aunaie meaning "from the alder grove" in French.

DELANO French: Surname of unclear origin; possibly from *de la nuit* meaning of the night
Famous Namesakes: *President Franklin Delano Roosevelt*

DELBERT English: Spelling variation of Albert

DELLING Norse: Shining

DELMAR Latin: Of the sea
(French) *Delmer, Delmore*

DELMONT French: Spelling variation of Dumont

DELROY French: Of the king
(Spanish) *Delrico*; *Delray, Delron*

DELVIN English: Godly friend
Delvon

DEMBE African: Peace

DEMETRIUS Greek: Of Demeter; Demeter is the mythological Greek goddess of harvest and fertility.
(French) *Dimitri*; (Russian) *Dmitri*; *Demetri, Demetrios, Demitri, Dimitrios*; **Nicknames:** *Dima*; **Diminutive Forms:** *Dimka*

DEMPSEY Gaelic, English: Proud; surname
Dempsy; **Famous Namesakes:** *Boxer Jack Dempsey*

DEMPSTER English: Judicious

DENBY Norse, Anglo-Saxon, Scandinavian: From the Danish settlement; surname

DENHOLM Scottish: A place name

DENIZ Turkish: Sea

DENLEY English: From the valley meadow; surname
Denlie, Denlea, Denleigh, Denly

DENMAN English: Resident of a valley

DENNIS Greek: Follower of Dionysius; Dionysius is the Greek god of wine responsible for growth of the vines, equivalent to the Roman god Bacchus. Saint Denis is the patron saint of France.
(French) Denis; Dennet, Denys; **Nicknames:** Denney, Dennie, Denny, Deon, Dion; **Famous Namesakes:** Actors Dennis Quaid and Dennis Hopper, Sailor Dennis Conner

DENNISON English: Son of Dennis; a surname
Denison, Tennyson; **Nicknames:** Den

"Name is a fence and within it you are nameless."
—Samuli Paronen, Finnish writer

DENTON English: From the town or settlement in the den; a surname closely related to the name Dalton
Denten, Dentin, Dentun; **Nicknames:** Denn, Denny

DENVER English: Variant of the surname Danvers meaning from Anvers; capital of the state of Colorado

DENZEL English: A Cornish place name
Denzell, Denzil; **Famous Namesakes:** Actor Denzel Washington

DEORSA Gaelic: Variation of George

DERBY English: Deertown

DEREK German: People's ruler; a short form of Theodoric commonly used as an independent name
(Dutch) Dirck, Dirk; Darek, Daric, Darick, Darrick, Darroch, Darrock, Dereck, Derick, Derik, Derrek, Derrick, Derrik, Deryck, Deryk; **Famous Namesakes:** Baseball player Derek Jeter

DERMOT Irish: Free man or without envy
Dermod, Diarmad, Diarmaid, Diarmid, Kermit; **Nicknames:** Darby

DERRY Irish: Red-haired or like an oak; name of an Irish city

DERWARD English: Guardian of the deer
Deerward, Deorward

DERWEN Welsh: From the oak tree

DERWENT English: Place name referring to Derwent rivers in England and Australia

DERWIN English: Spelling variation of Darwin
Derwan, Derwyn, Durwin, Durwyn

DERYA Turkish: Ocean

DESIDERIO Italian, Spanish: Desired
Famous Namesakes: Actor and musician Desi Arnaz

DESMOND Irish: From Desmond; an area of South Munster, one of the four provinces of Ireland
Deasmumhan, Desmon, Desmund, Dezmond; **Famous Namesakes:** South African Bishop Desmond Tutu

DESTIN French: Destiny
Destan, Deston

DESTRY French: Variant of a French surname; American classic western film *Destry Rides Again*

DEVEN Hindi: For God

DEVEREL French: Surname derived from place name
(French) *Devereau*; *Deveral, Devere, Devereaux, Deverell, Devery, Devry*

DEVIN Gaelic: Poet, poetic; possibly related to the Latin word for divine. The variant Devon is a county in England noted for beautiful farmland.
Devan, Deveon, Devon, Devyn, Deven;
Nicknames: *Dev*; **Star Babies:** *Son of Denis Leary, son of Vanessa Williams*

DEVLIN Irish, Gaelic: Fierce bravery
Devland, Devlon, Devlyn

DEVRY English: Spelling variation of Deverel

DEWEY Welsh: Variation of David
Dewi

DEWITT Welsh: Blond, white
(English) *Dwight*

DIALLO African: Bold

DIAMOND English: Of high value, brilliant; can refer to the precious stone
Famous Namesakes: *Actor Lou Diamond Phillips*

DICK English: Nickname for Richard
Famous Namesakes: *Actor Dick Van Dyke, TV personality Dick Clark*

DIDIER French: Desired
Famous Namesakes: *French actor Didier Flamand*

DIEGO Spanish: Variation of James

DIETRICH German: Form of Dietrich
Dedric, Dedrik, Dedrick, Dieter

DIGBY Norse: From the settlement or town near the ditch or dike; surname
Dikibyr

DILLON Irish, Gaelic: Faithful; from a different source than the Welsh name Dylan
Dilan, Dillan, Dillen, Dylon

DIMA Russian: Nickname for Demetrius
Nicknames: *Dimka, Dimochka*

DINESH Sanskrit: Sun

DINO English, Spanish: From the dene; (Italian) abbreviation of names such as Bernardino

DION Greek: An abbreviation of Dionysus; more often used as an independent name
Deion, Deon, Dionte, Dondre; **Famous Namesakes:** *Singer Dion (of Dion and the Belmonts), Football player Deion Sanders*

DIONDRE French: Blend of Dion and Andre

DIONYSIUS Greek: The Greek god of wine; the great theater in Athens is dedicated to Dionysius.
(Polish) *Dionizy*; *Dionysios, Dionysus*;
Nicknames: *Deion, Dennis, Deon, Dion*

DIXON English: Son of Dick
Dickson; **Nicknames:** *Dix*

DIYA AL DIN Arabic: Faithful, enlightened by religion

DMITRI Russian: Variation of Demetrius
Dmitrii; **Nicknames:** *Dimochka*; **Famous Namesakes:** *Russian chemist Dmitri Mendeleev discovered the periodic table, Composer Dmitri Shostakovich*

DOANE English: Rolling hills
Doan

DOBRY Polish: Good, kind

DOHASAN Native American: Little bluff (Kiowa); an important Kiowa leader who did much for his tribe, including establishing a peace between the Kiowa and the Osage
Dohosan

DOLAN Irish: Raven-haired

DOMINIC Latin: Of the Lord; a name traditionally given to a child born on Sunday (French) *Dominique*; (Spanish) *Domenico, Domingo*; (Basque) *Txomin*; (Russian) *Dominik*; (Hungarian) *Domo, Domokos*; *Dominick*; **Nicknames:** *Nick*; **Diminutive Forms:** *Dom*; **Famous Namesakes:** *Opera singer Placido Domingo, Basketball player Dominique Wilkins*; **Star Babies:** *Son of Steven Seagal and Kelly LeBrock*

"Babies are such a nice way to start people."
—Don Herold

DON English: Nickname for Donald
Nicknames: *Donnie, Donny*; **Famous Namesakes:** *Actor Don Johnson, Actor Don Rickles*

DONAHUE Irish, Gaelic: Dark warrior
Donaghy, Donnchadh

DONALD Scottish, Gaelic: Ruler of all
Domhnall, Donal, Donall, Donel, Donell, Donnel, Donnell; **Nicknames:** *Don, Donnie, Donny*; **Famous Namesakes:** *Singer Donny Osmond, Business tycoon Donald Trump, Disney character Donald Duck*

DONATIEN Latin: Presence of God

DONATO Latin, Italian: Gift from God
(Italian) *Donatello, Donzel*; (Polish) *Donat*

DONN Irish: Brown; a mythical figure in Irish literature and folklore, Donn was known as king of the underworld.

DONNELLY Irish: Dark
Donnally; **Nicknames:** *Don*

DONOGB Celtic: Strong fighter

DONOVAN Irish: Dark-haired
Donavan, Donavon

DOOLEY Gaelic: Dark hero

DOR Hebrew: Generation

DOREN Hebrew: Gift
Doron

DORIAN Greek: From Doris (region in Greece), descendant of Dorus, also used as a familiar form of Isidore; Dorian was the main character in Oscar Wilde's novel *The Picture of Dorian Gray* who was given his wish that his portrait would age while he remained young and handsome.
Dorien, Dorion; **Star Babies:** *Son of Lindsay Wagner*

DORRAN Celtic: Stranger, exile
Doran, Doron, Dorrance, Dorrel, Dorrell, Dorren, Dorrin

DOUG Scottish: Nickname for Douglas

DOUGAL Scottish: Dark stranger
Doughall, Dugald, Dughall; **Nicknames:** *Dougie*

DOUGLAS Scottish: From the dark river; the Scottish Douglas clan had two historical branches: Black Douglases and Red Douglases. The lords of these clans figure in Sir Walter Scott's writing.
(Celtic) *Doughlas*; *Douglass, Dubhglas*; **Nicknames:** *Doug*; **Famous Namesakes:** *Actor Douglas Fairbanks, Author Douglas Adams, General Douglas MacArthur*

DOVEV Hebrew: Speaks in a whisper

DOW Irish: Black-haired

DOWAN Irish: Black; dimunitive of the Gaelic *Dubh*

DOYLE Irish: Dark stranger
Famous Namesakes: Sherlock Holmes *author Sir Arthur Conan Doyle*

DRAKE English: Dragon
Famous Namesakes: *English explorer Sir Francis Drake*

DREW English: Manly, brave; variant of Andrew
Dru, Drue; **Famous Namesakes:** *Football player Drew Bledsoe*

DRISCOLL Irish: Uncertain meaning, possibly messenger, mediator, or sorrowful
Driscol

DRU American: Nickname for Andrew

DRUMMOND Scottish: At the ridge
Drummand

DRYDEN English: From the dry valley; surname
Dridan, Driden, Drygedene; **Famous Namesakes:** *Poet John Dryden*

DUANE Irish: Small and dark; an Anglicized variant of the Gaelic name *Dubhan*
Dewain, Dewayne, Duayne, Dubhan, Duwayne, Dwain, Dwaine, Dwane, Dwayne

DUBLIN English: Place name for the capital of Ireland

DUDLEY English: From the people's meadow
Famous Namesakes: *Actor Dudley Moore*

DUFF Gaelic, Celtic: Dark
Dubh; **Nicknames:** *Duffy*

DUGAN Gaelic: Swarthy
Duggan

DUKA African: All

DUKE Latin: Leader; a royal title
Famous Namesakes: *Jazz musician Duke Ellington, Actor John "The Duke" Wayne*

DUME African: Bull

DUMI African: Inspirer

DUMONT French: Of the mountain
Delmon, Delmont

DUNCAN Gaelic, Scottish: Brown warrior; an Anglicized variant of Donnchadh and a Scottish royal name. The eleventh-century King Duncan was killed by fellow Scot Macbeth of Moray. Shakespeare portrays a version of Duncan's story in his famous play *Macbeth*.
Donnchadh; **Nicknames:** *Dunn, Dunc, Dunky*; **Famous Namesakes:** *American businessman Duncan Hines, Basketball player Tim Duncan*

DUNHAM Celtic: Dark-skinned man

DUNLEY English: From the hill meadow; surname
Dunleah, Dunleigh, Dunly, Dunlea, Dunlie, Dunnlea, Dunnleigh, Dunnley

DUNMORE Scottish: From the great hill fortress
Dunmor

DUNSTAN English: Hill of stone

DUNTON English: From the town or settlement on the hill

DURANGO Spanish: Strong

DURANT Latin, French: Firm, enduring; more commonly found as a last name (French) *Durante, Dureau; Duran, Durand, Duron, Durrant, Durrell;* **Famous Namesakes:** *Historians Will and Ariel Durant, Entertainer Jimmy Durante, Boxer Roberto Duran*

DURRELL English: Spelling variation of Durant

DURWARD English: Keeper of the gate **Nicknames:** *Ward*

DURWIN English: Spelling variation of Darwin *Durwyn*

DUSTIN English: A fighter *Dustan, Duston, Dustyn;* **Nicknames:** *Dusty;* **Famous Namesakes:** *Actor Dustin Hoffman*

DUVAL French: Of the valley

DUYGU Turkish: Emotion

DWIGHT English: Variation of Dewitt **Famous Namesakes:** *President Dwight D. Eisenhower, Baseball player Dwight Gooden*

DWYER Irish: Dark and wise

DYLAN Welsh: Of the sea; in Welsh mythology, Dylan was the god of the sea. The Welsh name is from a different source than the Irish name Dillon. *Dilan, Dyllan, Dyllon;* **Nicknames:** *Dillie;* **Famous Namesakes:** *Welsh poet Dylan Thomas, Musician Bob Dylan;* **Star Babies:** *Son of Pierce Brosnan, Pamela Anderson and Tommy Lee, Michael Douglas and Catherine Zeta-Jones*

DYSON English: Variant of Dennison

EACHAN Scottish: Brown horse

EAMON Irish: Variation of Edmund *Eamonn*

EARL English: Nobleman; a name based on the English aristocratic title *Earle, Erle, Errol, Erroll;* **Famous Namesakes:** *Actor Errol Flynn, Actor James Earl Jones*

EARNAN Irish: Knowing

EARVIN English: Spelling variation of Irving *Ervin;* **Nicknames:** *Erv;* **Famous Namesakes:** *Basketball player Earvin "Magic" Johnson*

EATON English: Town or settlement by the river; surname *Eatun, Eatton, Eton, Eyton*

EBAN Hebrew: Rock *Eben, Even*

EBENEZER Hebrew: Rock of help; in the Old Testament, Samuel gave this name to a monument he erected to commemorate a victory. Ebenezer Scrooge is a miserly character in the famous story *A Christmas Carol* by Charles Dickens.

EBERHARD German: Brave boar (English) *Everet, Everett;* (Spanish) *Evarado, Everardo;* (Swedish) *Evert; Eberhardt, Eburhardt, Everard, Everhard, Evrard;* **Nicknames:** *Ever*

EBI Persian: Paternal

ED English: Nickname for Edward **Nicknames:** *Eddie, Eddy;* **Famous Namesakes:** *Actor Ed Asner, Jockey Eddie Arcaro*

EDBERT English: Wealthy and bright

EDE Dutch: Variation of Edward

EDEL German: Noble

EDER Hebrew: Flock; Shepherds used the biblical tower of Eder to watch over their sheep.

EDGAR German: Prosperous spearman (French) *Edgard*; (Spanish) *Edgardo*; *Eadger*; **Old Forms:** *Eadgard*; **Nicknames:** *Ed*; **Famous Namesakes:** *Author Edgar Allan Poe, French artist Edgar Degas*

EDISON English: Son of Edward *Eddis, Eddison, Edson*; **Famous Namesakes:** *Inventor Thomas Edison*

EDMUND English: Wealthy protector (French) *Edmond*; (Italian) *Edmondo*; (Spanish) *Edmundo*; (Gaelic) *Eamonn*; (Irish) *Eames, Eamon*; *Eadmund, Edmon, Tedman, Tedmund, Theomund*; **Nicknames:** *Ed, Eddie, Ned, Ted, Teddy*; **Famous Namesakes:** *English poet Edmund Spenser, Senator Edmund Muskie*; **Star Babies:** *Son of Ben Kingsley*

EDRIC Anglo-Saxon: Wealthy ruler *Eddrick, Edrick*

EDSEL English: Rich, wealthy man's estate; most notable as the name of Edsel Ford and the car that bore his name

EDUARDO Spanish: Variation of Edward

EDWARD English: Prosperous, guardian; the name of eight kings of England since the Norman Conquest. See also *Iolo* (Anglo-Saxon) *Edred*; (French) *Eduard*; (Italian) *Edoardo, Eduardo*; (Spanish) *Duardo, Duarte*; (Portuguese) *Edwardo*; (Swedish) *Edvard*; (Dutch) *Ede*; (Basque) *Edorta*; (Finnish) *Eetu*; (Hawaiian) *Ekewaka*; *Edwald*; **Old Forms:** *Eadward*; **Nicknames:** *Ed, Eddie, Eddy, Edik*; **Diminutive Forms:**

Ned; **Famous Namesakes:** *Senator Edward Kennedy, Actor Edward Norton*; **Star Babies:** *Son of Mel Brooks, son of Mel Gibson*

EDWARDSON English: Son of Edward

EDWIN English: Wealthy friend *Edlin, Edwyn*; **Old Forms:** *Eadwine*; **Nicknames:** *Ed, Eddy, Eddie*; **Famous Namesakes:** *Astronaut Edwin (Buzz) Aldrin*

EFIM Russian: Fair speech **Nicknames:** *Fima*

EFRAT Hebrew: Honored

EFREM Russian: Variation of Ephraim

EFRON Hebrew: Bird *Ephron*

EGAN Irish, Gaelic: Fiery *Eagan, Eagon, Eghan, Egon*

EGBERT Anglo-Saxon: Bright edge of a sword

EGIDIO Italian: Variation of Aegidius

EGON German: Strong with a sword. Gaelic, Irish: Fiery

EGOR Russian: Variation of George **Nicknames:** *Egorka, Zhora*

EIMHIN Irish: Swift; a name sometimes Anglicized as Evan and Ewan

EINAR Norse, Scandinavian: Lone warrior (Finnish) *Eino*

EISA Arabic: Arabic form of Jesus as referenced in the Koran *Issa*

EJNAR Danish: Warrior

EKON African: Strong (Nigerian)

EL WASHAK Arabic: Lynx

ELAN Native American: Friendly

ELDEN English: Elf friend, noble friend, implies supernaturally good or wise friend; variant of Alvin or Alden
(English) *Eldan*; *Eldin, Eldon, Eldwin, Eldwyn*

ELDER English: From near the elder tree; has also come to mean older, wiser, and is a governing officer of a church
Aeldra, Eldor

ELDRED Anglo-Saxon: Old counsel, old or wise advisor; variant of Aldred
Eldrid

ELDRIDGE English: Old, wise leader; surname; variant of Aldrich

ELDWIN English: Spelling variation of Alvin

ELEK Polish: Blond

ELEUTHERIOS Greek: Liberator

ELFRED English: Spelling variation of Alfred

ELGAR Anglo-Saxon: Elf-spear, spearman; variant of Algar
Elger, Ellgar, Ellger

ELHANAN Hebrew: He whom God has graciously bestowed

ELI Hebrew: Ascended; this Old Testament figure was a high priest of Israel and instructed the young Samuel.
(French) *Elie*; *Ely*; **Star Babies:** *Son of Sally Field*

ELIAS Greek: Variation of Elijah

ELIEZER Hebrew: God is my helper; in the Old Testament, this name belongs to both a servant of Abraham and one of Moses' sons. (Spanish) *Eliazar*; (Basque) *Elazar*; *Eleazar*

ELIJAH Hebrew: The Lord is my God; a biblical prophet told about in I and II Kings of the Old Testament. See also *Ilias, Ilya* (Greek) *Elias, Ilyas*; (English) *Ellis*; (Spanish) *Elia*; (Persian) *Iliya*; *Elihu, Eliot, Elliott*; **Nicknames:** *Eli, Ely*; **Famous Namesakes:** *Actor Elijah Wood*; **Star Babies:** *Son of Cher, Bono, Wynnona Judd*

ELISHA Hebrew: God is salvation; a prophet and successor to Elijah
(Italian) *Eliseo*

ELKANAH Hebrew: God has created; the Old Testament Elkanah is Samuel's father.

ELLERY English: Island with elder trees; may also be a derivation of Hilary, meaning joyful
Ellary

ELLIOTT Hebrew: The Lord is my God; variant of Elijah
Eliot, Eliott, Elliot; **Famous Namesakes:** *Actor Elliott Gould, Poet T. S. Eliot*

ELLIS English: Variation of Elijah

ELMER English, Anglo-Saxon: Highborn and renowned; (Teutonic) awe inspiring
Almer, Aylmer, Aillmer, Allmer, Eylmer; **Old Forms:** *Aegelmaere, Aethelmaere*

ELMO Italian: Helmet, protection; Saint Elmo is the common name for Saint Erasmus, the patron saint of sailors. Saint Elmo's fire is said to protect sailors and is the glow that accompanies a steady discharge of electricity from objects (such as masts of sailing ships) during thunderstorms or when electrified clouds are present.
Famous Namesakes: *Elmo, the lovable Sesame Street character*

ELMORE English: From the moor with the elm trees; surname
Elmoor

ELOI Latin, French: Chosen one; abbreviation of Eligius
(Spanish) *Eligio, Eloy*; (Czech) *Alois; Elois*;
Old Forms: *Eligius*

ELRAD Hebrew: God is the ruler

ELROY English: Variation of Leroy

ELSDON English: Nobleman's hill; surname
Athelston, Elsden; **Old Forms:** *Aethelisdun, Aetheston*

ELTON English: From the old town
Alton, Eldon; **Famous Namesakes:** *Musician Elton John*

ELVIN English: Elf friend, noble friend; variant of Alvin.
Elveryn, Elvyn

ELVIO Latin, Spanish: Blond, fair

ELVIS English: Elf friend, noble friend; variant of Alvin. Elvis Presley was an early American star of rock and roll and is considered one of the greatest of all time. His popularity has grown well after his death, and his home Graceland is an international tourist attraction.
Alvis, Elvys; **Famous Namesakes:** *Singer Elvis Costello, Skater Elvis Stojko*

ELWIN English: Elf friend, noble friend; variant of Alvin
Elwyn

EMAN Irish: Serious; Irish form of Emest

EMERIL Italian: Meaning unknown
Famous Namesakes: *Popular TV chef Emeril Lagasse*

EMERY German, English: Industrious
(English) *Amory*; (Czech) *Imrich*;
(Hungarian) *Imre*

EMIL Latin: Derived from a Roman clan name meaning industrious
(French) *Emile*; (Italian) *Emiliano*; (Spanish) *Emilio*; (Finnish) *Eemeli*; **Famous Namesakes:** *Actor Emilio Estevez, French writer Emile Zola*

EMMANUEL Hebrew: God is with us; another name for the Messiah, this name is in both the Old and New Testaments
(German) *Immanuel*; (Italian) *Emanuele*;
(Spanish) *Emanuel, Mano, Manolito, Manolo, Manuel, Manuelo*; **Nicknames:** *Iman, Imani, Mannie, Manny*

EMMETT English: Industrious, strong

ENAPAY Native American: Goes forth bravely (Sioux)

ENCELADUS Greek: A giant; in Greek mythology, he fought against the Olympians and Zeus.

ENDYMION Greek: A handsome youth of Greek mythology

> *"A thing of Beauty is a joy forever"*
> –John Keats,
> "Endymion: A Poetic Romance"

ENGELBERT German: Bright angel
Ingelbert, Inglebert; **Famous Namesakes:** *Singer Engelbert Humperdinck*

ENGIN Turkish: Vast

ENOCH Hebrew: Trained and dedicated; Enoch was father of Methuselah, the oldest living man named in the Bible.
(Danish) *Enok*

ENRIQUE Spanish: Variation of Henry

ENZO Italian: Variation of Henry
Star Babies: *Son of Patricia Arquette*

EOGHAN Gaelic: Youth
Eoghann

EPHRAIM Hebrew: Fruitful; in the Old
Testament, a son of Joseph
(Spanish) *Efrain*; (Russian) *Efrem*; *Efraim,
Efran, Efrayim, Efren, Ephram, Ephrem*

ERAN Hebrew: Watchful

ERASMUS Greek: Beloved; Saint Erasmus,
more popularly known as Saint Elmo, is the
patron saint of sailors.
(Spanish) *Erasmo*; *Rasmus*; **Nicknames:**
Elmo

ERDEM Turkish: Virtue

ERI Hebrew: My guardian

ERIC Norse, Scandinavian: Eternal ruler,
forever strong; according to Norse legend,
the Viking Leif Ericson (son of Eric the Red)
landed on the shores of America 500 years
before Christopher Columbus.
(German) *Audrick, Erich*; (Spanish) *Eurico*;
(Scandinavian) *Erik*; (Polish) *Eryk*; (Finnish)
Eero, Erkki; *Aaric, Aric, Arick, Arik, Arrick,
Aurick, Eirik, Erick, Eriq*; **Famous
Namesakes:** *English musician Eric Clapton,
Children's author Eric Carle*; **Star Babies:**
Son of Kirk Douglas, son of Donald Trump

ERICKSON Scandinavian: Son of Eric,
ever kingly
Ericksen, Ericson, Erikson

ERIN Gaelic: Peace; a poetic name for
Ireland, and a name used mostly for girls

ERMANNO Italian: Variation of Herman

ERNEST English: Serious, resolute
(Spanish) *Ernesto*; *Earnest*; **Nicknames:**
Ernie; **Famous Namesakes:** *Author Ernest
Hemingway, Actor Ernest Borgnine*; **Star
Babies:** Son of Loretta Lynn

ERROL Scottish: Spelling variation of Earl
Erroll; **Famous Namesakes:** *Actor Errol Flynn*

ERWIN English: Friend of the wild boar,
friend of the sea; (Welsh) white river; variant
of Irving
(Hungarian) *Ervin*; *Earwin, Earwine,
Earwyn, Erwyn*; **Famous Namesakes:**
Author Irwin Shaw

ESA Finnish: Variation of Isaiah

ESAU Hebrew: Hairy; in the book of
Genesis, Esau is Jacob's older twin brother
and a skilled and adventurous hunter.

ESHKOL Hebrew: Cluster of grapes

ESPEN Scandinavian: Bear god

ESTCOT English: From the eastern cottage;
variant of Ascot

ESTEBAN Spanish: Variation of Stephen
Estefan, Estevan, Estevon; **Nicknames:** *Teb*

ESTON English: From the eastern town;
surname
Easton

ETHAN Hebrew: Strong, firm; an Old
Testament name
Aitan, Ethen; **Old Forms:** *Etan*; **Famous
Namesakes:** *Actor Ethan Hawke*; **Star
Babies:** *Son of John Wayne*

ETHELRED Anglo-Saxon: Noble counsel;
an early Anglo-Saxon king of Wessex and
Kent, son of Aethelwulf, brother of
Aethelbald and Aethelberht
Aethelred

ETHELWULF Anglo-Saxon: Spelling variation of Aethelwulf

ETIENNE French: Variation of Stephen

ETU Native American: Sun

EUGENE Greek: Well born, noble
(Greek) *Jeno*; (Spanish) *Eugenio*; (Swedish) *Eugen*; (Dutch) *Eugenius*; (Russian) *Evgeni, Yevgeny*; (Czech) *Evzen*; (Ukrainian) *Yevhen*; (Hungarian) *Jenci*; **Old Forms:** *Eugenios*; **Nicknames:** *Gene, Zhenechka, Zhenka, Zhenya*; **Famous Namesakes:** *Playwright Eugene O'Neill*

> *"The name we give to something shapes our attitude toward it."*
> —Katherine Paterson

EURUS Greek: Mythological god of the east wind

EUSEBIUS Greek: Pious; the name of several saints
Eusebios

EUSTACE Greek: Fruitful, productive
Eustachy, Eustis; **Nicknames:** *Stacey, Stacy*

EUSTON Irish: Heart

EVAN Scottish: Variant of John; (Celtic) young warrior
(Irish) *Ewan*; *Evann, Evin, Evyn*; **Famous Namesakes:** *Author Evan Thomas*; **Star Babies:** *Son of Diana Ross, son of Bruce Springsteen*

EVANDER Latin: Good man; also a deity of Roman mythology
Famous Namesakes: *Boxer Evander Holyfield*

EVANTON English: God is gracious

EVERARD German: Spelling variation of Eberhard

EVERETT English: Variation of Eberhard
Everet, Evert; **Nicknames:** *Ever*

EVERLEY English: From the boar's meadow; from Ever's meadow; surname; may evoke thoughts of the melodious Everly Brothers singing duo
Eferleah, Everleigh, Everly, Everlie, Everlea

EVIAN English: Variant of Evan; the French town famous for Evian spring water. Evian is also a blend of Evan and Ian meaning John-John.

EWAN Scottish: Young
Euan, Ewen, Ewyn; **Famous Namesakes:** *Actor Ewan McGregor*

EWELL English: Spelling variation of Yule
Euell

EZEKIEL Hebrew: God strengthens; biblical Ezekiel was a prophet among the captives taken to Babylon at the fall of Jerusalem. The Old Testament Book of Ezekiel contains his prophecies.
(English) *Zeke*; (Spanish) *Esequiel, Ezequiel*; *Ezechiel, Haskel*; **Star Babies:** *Son of Beau Bridges*

EZNIK Armenian: Name of a fifth-century philosopher

EZRA Hebrew: Helper; an Old Testament prophet and author of the Book of Ezra
Esdras, Esra, Ezrah; **Famous Namesakes:** *Poet Ezra Pound*; **Star Babies:** *Son of Paul Reiser*

FAAS Dutch: Firm counsel

FABIAN Latin: Bean farmer; derived from the Roman clan name Fabius, a name given several Roman emperors and sixteen saints (English) *Faber*; (French) *Fabien*; (Italian) *Fabiano, Fabio*; (Russian) *Fabi*; *Fabion, Fabiyn, Favian, Favio*; **Famous Namesakes:** *Singer and actor Fabian*

FABRICE French: From the Latin word for craftsman, one who works with his hands (Italian) *Fabrizio*; *Fabrizius*; **Old Forms:** *Fabricius*

FABUMI African: Gift of God

FACHNAN Irish: Meaning unknown; Saint Fachnan became the first bishop of Kilfenora, Ireland, in the twelfth century. *Fachna, Faughnan*

FADEY Russian, Ukrainian: Brave, courageous; also can be a Russian form of Thaddeus *Faddei*; **Diminutive Forms:** *Fadeyka, Fadeyushka, Fadyenka*

FADIL Arabic: Virtuous, excellence, superior, benefit, favor, eminent, grace, distinguished *Fadeel*

FAFNER Norse: A mythical dragon **Old Forms:** *Fafnir*

FAGAN Irish: Ardent *Faegan, Fagen, Fagin, Faodhaghan*

FAHEY Irish: From the green field; surname sometimes used as first name *Fahy*; **Famous Namesakes:** *Actor and dancer Jeff Fahey*

FAHIM African: Learned

FAIION Irish: Ruler; surname sometimes used as first name

FAING Scottish: From the sheep pen

FAIRFAX English: Blond; surname rarely used as a first name

FAISAL Arabic: Decisive, criterion *Faysal*; **Famous Namesakes:** *Iraqi King Faysal the First and the Second, King of Saudi Arabia King Faysal Ibn Abd Al Aziz*

FAKHIR Arabic: Proud, honorary *Fakher*

FALCO Latin: Surname relating to falconry (English) *Falcon, Falkner*; (German) *Falk, Falke*; *Falken, Falko*; **Famous Namesakes:** *Austrian Musician Falco (of "Rock Me Amadeus" fame)*

FALLON Irish: In charge; surname used as a first name

FANE English, Welsh: Joyful, good-natured *Fain, Faine, Fayne*

FAOLAN Gaelic: Little wolf

FARAJI African: Consolation (Swahili)

FARAZ Persian: Above, on the top

FARHAD Persian: Handsome youth; a name from Persian mythology

FARID Arabic, Persian: One of a kind *Fareed*; **Famous Namesakes:** *Egyptian movie star and musician Farid el Atrash*

FARIS Arabic: Knight, horseback rider *Fares*

FARJAD Persian: Excellent

FARLEY English: From the bull's meadow or the sheep's meadow; surname
Faerrleah, Fairlie, Farleigh, Farly, Fairlea, Fairlee, Fairleigh, Fairley, Fairly, Farlea, Farlee, Farlie

FARNELL English: From the fern hill; surname
Farnall, Fearnhealh, Fernald

FARNHAM English: From the fern land or home; surname
Fearnhamm

FARNLEY English: From the fern meadow; surname
Farnly, Fearnleah, Farnlea, Farnleigh

FAROUK Arabic: Wise, one who distinguishes truth from falsehood
Faruk, Faruq; **Famous Namesakes:** *King Farouk of Egypt*

FARQUHAR Gaelic: Very dear; surname used as first name (mainly in Scotland)
Fearchar, Fearcher

FARR English: Traveler, voyager
Faer, Faerwald, Farmon, Farold, Farrs, Fars, Farson, Firman

FARREL Irish, Celtic: Brave, victorious; surname sometimes used as a first name
Farrell, Farry, Ferrell; **Famous Namesakes:** *Irish actor Colin Farrell*

FARREN Irish: Adventurous; some spelling variants are also surnames
Faran, Farrin, Feran, Ferran

FARROKH Persian: Happy, fortunate; Farrokh Bulsara is better known as Freddie Mercury, the flamboyant lead singer of the band Queen.

FARZAD Persian: Splendid birth

FARZAM Persian: Worthy, befitting

FARZAN Persian: Wise

FARZIN Persian: Learned

FASTRED German: Firm counsel

FAUNUS Latin: God of forests

FAUST Latin: Auspicious, lucky; Faust was a legendary German alchemist and astrologer who is said to have sold his soul to the Devil in exchange for knowledge and power.
(French) *Fauste*; (Italian) *Fausto*; **Old Forms:** *Faustus*; **Famous Namesakes:** *Italian soccer star Fausto Rossini*

FAVONIUS Latin: West wind

FAZEL Persian: Learned

FEARGHALL Gaelic: Victorious, highest choice
Fergall, Fergal

FECHIN Irish: Young raven

FEICH Irish: Raven
Fay

FELIPE Spanish: Variation of Philip
Felip, Felipo, Felippe, Filip, Filipe;
Nicknames: *Felo, Lipe, Lipo*

FELIX Latin: Happy or lucky
(French) *Felicien, Félix*; (Italian) *Felicio*;
(Spanish) *Feliciano*; (Polish) *Feliks*; *Felice, Felician*; **Famous Namesakes:** *Boxer Felix Trinidad*

FELTON English: From the settlement in the field; surname
Feldon, Feldtun, Feldun, Feltin

FENTON English: From the settlement or town on the moor (fens)

FEODRAS Greek: Stone

FERDINAND German: Adventurer, traveler (French) *Fernand*; (Italian) *Ferdinando*; (Spanish) *Fernando, Hernan, Hernandez, Hernando*; (Portuguese) *Fernão*; **Nicknames:** *Ferdy, Ferdie*; **Famous Namesakes:** *Portuguese navigator Ferdinand Magellan;* **Star Babies:** *Son of Ben Kingsley*

FERDOWS Persian: Paradise
Firdaus

FERGUS Gaelic, Scottish: Strong man; the name of a warrior prince of Ulster in Irish mythology
Fearghus, Ferghus

FERGUSON Scottish: Son of the first choice, son of Fergus; surname
Fergusson

FERMIN Spanish: Strong

FERNÃO Portuguese: Variation of Ferdinand

FERRIS Celtic: Rock, highest choice; possibly derived from Fergus or may be an Irish variant of Peter. The name Ferris was brought to prominence by the 1986 movie *Ferris Bueller's Day Off*
Faris, Farris

FIACRE Celtic: Eagle; Saint Fiacre was an Irish saint who built a hospice in France.
Fiacra

FIDEL Latin, Spanish: Faithful (Italian) *Fidelio; Fedele, Fidal, Fidello*; **Old Forms:** *Fidelis*; **Diminutive Forms:** *Fido*; **Famous Namesakes:** *Cuban leader Fidel Castro*

FIE Scottish: Dark of peace; MacFie is a Scottish surname
MacFie

FIELDING English: From or lives in the field; surname
Felding

FILBERT German: Brilliant
Felabert, Philbert, Filibert

FILMORE Scottish: Famous; surname
Filmarr, Filmer, Fillmore; **Famous Namesakes:** *President Millard Fillmore*

FINBAR Irish, Celtic: Blond, handsome
Finnbar, Finnobarr, Fionnbarr, Fynbar

FINEEN Irish: Fair at birth
Finghin, Finnin

FINIAN Irish: Fair; Finians were warrior-followers of third-century legendary Irish hero Finn Mac Cumhail.

FINLAY Gaelic: Small blond soldier
Findlay; **Famous Namesakes:** *Scottish actor Finlay Currie*

FINN Irish, English, Gaelic: Fair; in Irish mythology, Finn Mac Cumhail was a legendary hero similar to the English Robin Hood.
Finian, Fionan, Fionn

FINNEEN Irish: Beautiful child

FINNEGAN Irish: Fair; Irish surname given notoriety by James Joyce's novel *Finnegan's Wake*

FIORELLO Italian: Little flower
Famous Namesakes: *New York City Mayor Fiorello LaGuardia*

FIRMAN English: Traveler; more common as a surname

FIROUZ Persian: Victorious

FIRTH Scottish: Narrow inlet of the sea; also a surname
Famous Namesakes: *British actor Colin Firth*

FITCH English: Ermine; surname used as first name
Fitche, Fytch

FITZ English: Surname prefix meaning son of; sometimes a familiar form name for these Fitz- names

FLANN Irish: Ruddy; Flanagan is a common surname derived from Flann
Flainn, Flanagan, Flannagain, Flannagan, Floinn; **Diminutive Forms:** *Flannan*

FLANNERY Irish: Red-haired; a surname

FLAVIAN Latin: Golden or blond; from the Roman family name Flavius
(Italian) *Flavio;* (Polish) *Flawiusz;* **Old Forms:** *Flavius*

FLEMING English, Anglo-Saxon: From Flanders; surname
Famous Namesakes: *British novelist Ian Fleming*

FLETCHER English, Scottish: Profession name, arrow maker
Nicknames: *Fletch;* **Famous Namesakes:** *Sailor Fletcher Christian;* **Star Babies:** *Son of Mia Farrow and Andre Previn*

FLORIAN Latin: Flowering, blooming
(French) *Florien;* (Spanish) *Florentino, Florinio; Floren, Florentin, Florentyn, Florus*

FLOYD English: Gray
Famous Namesakes: *Jamaican musician Floyd Lloyd*

FLYNN Irish: Son of a red-haired man; surname sometimes used as first name
Flynn, Flin, Flinn, Flyn; **Star Babies:** *Son of James Earl Jones*

FONTAINE French: Fountain, water source; surname sometimes given as a first name
(Italian) *Fontana; Fonteine*

FONZO Spanish: Nickname for Alphonse

FORD English: River crossing; familiar form of many names with Ford as their suffix
Famous Namesakes: *President Gerald Ford*

FORREST English: From a surname meaning forest in Old French, originally belonging to a person who lived near a forest. The name now has a strong association with the Tom Hanks character from the 1994 film *Forrest Gump;* (Latin) woodsman, from the woods
Forest, Forester, Forrester, Foster; **Famous Namesakes:** *Actor Forest Whitaker*

FORTUNE French: Luck, fortune
Fortino, Fortun, Fortunato

FOSTER English: Keeps the forest, forest-ranger; more common as a surname

"For my name and memory, I leave it to men's charitable speeches, to foreign nations, and to the next ages."
—Sir Francis Bacon

FRANCIS Latin: Free one, Frenchman; Saint Francis of Assisi was an Italian priest who founded the Franciscan order.
(German) *Frantz, Franz*; (French) *François*; (Italian) *Francesco, Franco*; (Spanish) *Cisco, Farruco, Francisco, Frasco, Frascuelo, Frisco*; (Teutonic) *Franziskus*; (Gaelic) *Frang, Frannsaidh*; (Swedish) *Frans*; (Czech) *Frantisek*; (Polish) *Frandszk*; (Hungarian) *Ferenc, Ferko; Ferke, Frandscus, Franta, Frances*; **Nicknames:** *Feri, Franchot, Frank, Frankie, Franky, Pancho*; **Diminutive Forms:** *Pacho, Paco, Paquito*; **Famous Namesakes:** *Director Francis Ford Coppola, Spanish explorer Francisco Pizarro*

FRANÇOIS French: Variation of Francis
Famous Namesakes: *French President François Mitterand, French director François Truffault*

FRANK English: Free man; a nickname for Francis or Franklin but not uncommon as an independent name
Famous Namesakes: *Singer Frank Sinatra, Architect Frank Lloyd Wright, Musician Frank Zappa*

FRANKLIN English: Free man, landholder
Franklyn; **Nicknames:** *Frank*; **Famous Namesakes:** *President Franklin Delano Roosevelt, President Franklin Pierce*

FRANTISEK Czech: Variation of Francis

FRANZ German: Variation of Francis

FRASER Scottish: Origin unclear, possibly of the forest men or curly-haired; name of a major Scottish clan
Frasier, Frazer, Frazier

FREDERICK German: Peaceful ruler; Numerous royalty from Prussia, Germany, and the Holy Roman Empire have borne this name, including the thirteenth-century patron of the arts Frederick II of Germany, and the eighteenth-century Frederick II of Prussia who was known as *Friedrich der Grosse* (Frederick the Great).(German) *Friedrich*; (French) *Frédéric*; (Italian) *Federico*; (Scandinavian) *Frederik, Fredrik*; (Czech) *Bedrich*; (Polish) *Fryderyk*; (Hungarian) *Fredek; Frederek, Fredi, Fredric, Fredrick, Friedrick*; **Nicknames:** *Fred, Freddie, Freddy, Frici, Frits, Fritz*; **Diminutive Forms:** *Friedel*; **Famous Namesakes:** *Dancer Fred Astaire, Abolitionist Frederick Douglass, Children's entertainer Mr. Fred Rogers*

FREEMAN English, Anglo-Saxon: Free man, a man freed from bound servitude to an overlord; more common as surname
Famous Namesakes: *Actor Morgan Freeman*

FRESCO Spanish: Fresh

FREWIN English: Noble friend
Freowine, Frewen, Frewyn

FREY Norse: He who is foremost; Frey was the god of agriculture and fertility in Norse mythology.
Old Forms: *Freyr*

FREYNE English: Foreigner
Fraine, Frayne

FRIDOLF Scandinavian: Peaceful wolf
Fridolph, Friduwulf, Fridwolf

FRIEDRICH German: Variation of Frederick
Famous Namesakes: *German philosopher Friedrich Nietzsche*

FRITZ German: Nickname for Frederick

GABHAN Gaelic: Variation of Gavin

GABRIEL Hebrew: God is my strength; One of seven archangels, Gabriel appeared to Mary to give her the news of her pregnancy and impending birth of Jesus. He appears in Christian, Jewish, and Muslim texts. (Arabic) *Jabril, Jibril*; (Italian) *Gabriele*; (Spanish) *Gabian, Gabrio*; (Basque) *Gabirel*; (Russian) *Gavriil, Gavrila*; (Czech) *Gabek*; (Finnish) *Kaapo*; (Hungarian) *Gabi, Gabor, Gabrian*; **Old Forms:** *Gavriel*; **Nicknames:** *Gab, Gabbi, Gabby, Gabe, Gabie, Riel*; **Diminutive Forms:** *Gavri*; **Famous Namesakes:** *Columbian author Gabriel Garcia Marquez, Irish actor Gabriel Byrne*; **Star Babies:** *Son of Jerry Hall and Mick Jagger, son of Isabelle Adjani and Daniel Day-Lewis*

GACE French: Pledge
Famous Namesakes: *French troubadour Gace Brulé*

GADIEL Arabic: God is my wealth, twisted rope, way, mood, country, state, tribe, plait of hair

GAETANO Italian: From Gaete
(French) *Gaetane*

GAILLARD French: High-spirited; French surname rarely used as a first name
Famous Namesakes: *Musician Slim Gaillard*

GAIR Scottish, Gaelic: Small one
Gare, Gear

GALAHAD Arthurian Legend: Son of Lancelot, Sir Galahad is best known as the knight who achieves the quest for the Holy Grail.
Galahalt, Galahault

GALE English: Lively; now rarely given as a name for boys
Gail, Gayle, Gaile; **Famous Namesakes:** *Football player Gale Sayers*

GALEN Greek, English: Tranquil; for nearly 1,500 years, accepted medical practices were based on the research of second-century physician Galen.
(Spanish) *Galeno*; (Gaelic) *Gaelan, Galyn*; *Galan, Gaylen*

GALL Celtic, Gaelic: Stranger; Saint Gall was one of the numerous seventh-century Irish monks who brought Christianity and learning back to Europe after the Dark Ages.
Gael, Gale

GALLAGHER Irish, Gaelic: Eager helper; surname
Old Forms: *Galchobhar*; **Famous Namesakes:** *Actor Peter Gallagher, Comedian Gallagher*

GALTON English: Steep, wooded land
Galt, Gallton, Galten

GALWAY Gaelic: Irish place name; surname
Galaway, Galloway; **Famous Namesakes:** *Critic Galway Kinnell, Irish flautist James Galway*

GAMAL Egyptian: Handsome, beautiful; President of Egypt Gamal Abdel Nasser ruled from the time of the revolution in 1952 until his death in 1970.
Jamal, Gimal; **Nicknames:** *Gimi*

GAMBA African: Warrior (Zimbabwe)

GANNON Irish, Gaelic: Fair-skinned
Gannie, Gionnan

GANYMEDE Greek: Cup bearer to the gods, son of King Tros of Troy; according to Greek mythology, this young, beautiful boy became one of Zeus' lovers.

GARCIA Spanish: An old surname of uncertain etymology; possibly means fox **Famous Namesakes:** *Actor Andy Garcia, South American Novelist Gabriel Garcia Marquez*

GARDNER English: Keeper of the garden; surname used as first name (Teutonic) *Gardener; Gardiner;* **Nicknames:** *Gard*

GARETH Welsh: Gentle, modest, and brave; Sir Gareth was a legendary knight of King Arthur's Round Table. **Famous Namesakes:** *British musician Gareth Gates*

GARFIELD English: From the spear field; surname *Garafeld;* **Famous Namesakes:** *President James A. Garfield*

GARLAND English: From a surname meaning triangle land in Old English *Garlan, Garlen, Garlyn;* **Famous Namesakes:** *Musician Garland Jeffreys*

GARNELL English: Spelling variation of Garner

GARNER French: Keeper of grain; surname used as a first name *Garnell, Garnier, Garnar;* **Famous Namesakes:** *Actor James Garner*

GARNET English: Armed with a spear *Garnett;* **Famous Namesakes:** *English military man Sir Garnet Wolseley*

GARNETT English: Spelling variation of Garnet

GARON Hebrew: A threshing floor; also from the Hebrew word for throat *Garan, Garen, Garin, Garion*

GARRETT Anglo-Saxon, English: Rules by the spear; variant of Gerald. See also *Gareth* (English) *Garrick;* (Dutch) *Garritt; Gared, Garet, Garett, Garrad, Garrard, Garred, Garret, Garreth, Jarret, Jarrett;* **Nicknames:** *Garrey, Garry, Gary;* **Famous Namesakes:** *Actor Brad Garrett, Comedian Garrett Morris;* **Star Babies:** *Son of Bo Jackson*

GARRICK English: Variation of Garrett

GARRISON English: Spear-fortified town **Nicknames:** *Gary;* **Famous Namesakes:** *Author and radio host Garrison Keillor*

GARSON English: Son of Gar *Garrson, Garsone;* **Famous Namesakes:** *Playwright Garson Kanin*

GARTH Norse, Scandinavian: Garden; from a surname, indicating someone who lived near or worked in a garden

GARTON English: From the wedge-shaped or three-cornered town or settlement; a surname and probable variant of Gordon *Garatun, Gartin*

GARVEY Gaelic, Irish: Rough peace; surname *Gairbhith, Gairbith, Garbhan, Garvan, Garve, Garvin, Girven, Girvyn;* **Old Forms:** *Garbhach;* **Famous Namesakes:** *Baseball player Steve Garvey, Civil rights activist Marcus Garvey*

GARWOOD English: From the fir forest; surname *Arwood, Ayrwode;* **Nicknames:** *Woody*

GARY English: Nickname for Garrett **Famous Namesakes:** *Cartoonist Gary Larson, British actor Gary Oldman, Actor Gary Sinise;* **Star Babies:** *Son of Jerry Lewis*

GASPAR French: Variation of Caspar

GASTON French: From Gascony *Gascon*; **Famous Namesakes:** *French actor Gaston Modot*; **Star Babies:** *Son of Jaclyn Smith*

GAUTIER French: Variation of Walter **Famous Namesakes:** *French clothing designer Jean-Paul Gaultier*

GAVIN Scottish, Welsh: White hawk (English) *Gawain*; (Italian) *Gavino*; (Gaelic) *Gabhan*, *Galvin*, *Galvyn*, *Gavan*, *Gaven*, *Gavyn*, *Gawen*, *Gawyn*; **Old Forms:** *Gaelbhan*; **Famous Namesakes:** *British musician/actor Gavin Rossdale*

GAWAIN Arthurian Legend: The eldest son of Lot

GAZSI Hungarian: Protects the treasure

GEB Egyptian: Mythical earth god, husband of Nut; Geb was a member of the Heliopolitan Ennead and is represented as a man.

GEDALIAH Hebrew: God has made great *Gedalya*, *Gedalyahu*

GELASIUS Greek: Laughter; name of Pope who decreed February 14th Valentine's Day

GENEROSO Spanish: Generous

GENET African: Eden

GENIUS Latin: Spirit present at one's birth; since a genius is also one with especially high intelligence or talent, this may be a tough name to live up to.

GENNADI Russian: Noble, generous *Genadi*, *Genadiy*; **Nicknames:** *Gena*; **Famous Namesakes:** *Actor Gennadi Vengerov*

GEOFFREY English: Spelling variation of Jeffrey

Nicknames: *Geoff*; **Famous Namesakes:** Author Geoffrey Chaucer

GEORGE Greek: Farmer; in medieval legend, Saint George (the knight who became patron saint of England) slayed a fire-breathing dragon. The name has been borne by numerous heads of state in England, Greece, and the United States. (Greek) *Iorgas*; (German) *Georg*; (Italian) *Giorgio*; (Spanish) *Jorge*; (Gaelic) *Deorsa*; (Welsh) *Sior*; (Scandinavian) *Joran*, *Jorg*, *Jorn*, *Jurgen*; (Swedish) *Goran*, *Gorin*; (Danish) *Joren*, *Jorgen*, *Joris*, *Jory*; (Russian) *Egor*, *Igoryok*, *Yuri*, *Yurik*, *Yurochka*, *Zhorah*; (Czech) *Jiri*; (Polish) *Jerzy*; (Ukrainian) *Yuriy*; (Finnish) *Jorma*, *Yrjö*; (Hungarian) *Gyorgy*, *Gyurgi*, *Gyurka*; (Hawaiian) *Keoki*; *Georges*, *Georget*, *Georgio*, *Jirkar*; **Nicknames:** *Georgie*, *Gorka*; **Famous Namesakes:** *Author George Orwell, Designer Giorgio Armani, First U.S. President George Washington, Presidents George Bush and George W. Bush*; **Star Babies:** *Five sons of George Foreman*

GERALD German: Rules by the spear (English) *Jaryl*; (French) *Geraud*; (Spanish) *Geraldo*, *Jeraldo*; (Gaelic) *Gearald*; (Irish) *Gearoid*; (Scandinavian) *Jarel*, *Jarell*; (Dutch) *Gerrit*; (Polish) *Gerek*; *Geralt*, *Gerold*, *Gerrald*, *Gerrell*, *Gerritt*, *Jerold*, *Jerrald*, *Jerrold*; **Nicknames:** *Jerry*; **Famous Namesakes:** *Journalist Geraldo Rivera, President Gerald Ford*

GERARD German: Spear strength, brave with a spear; introduced to England through the Norman conquest, Gerard has remained popular since the Middle Ages. (German) *Gerhard*; (French) *Gérard*; (Italian) *Gerardo*; (Spanish) *Jerardo*; (Polish) *Gerik*; (Hungarian) *Gellert*; *Geraud*, *Gerrard*, *Girard*, *Jerard*; **Nicknames:** *Gerd*, *Gere*, *Gero*, *Gerry*, *Gert*; **Famous Namesakes:** *French actor Gérard Depardieu*

GERMAIN French: Brotherly; derived from the Latin word *germen* meaning a sprout or bud; Saint Germain was a sixth-century bishop who founded the monastery known today as Saint-Germain-des-Prés in Paris. (English) *Jermaine*; (Spanish) *German*; *Germano, Jermain, Jermane, Jermayne*; **Old Forms:** *Germanus*; **Famous Namesakes:** *Singer Jermaine Jackson*

GERO German: Nickname for Gerard

GERONIMO Greek: Sacred name; variant of the Greek saint's name Jerome. Best known in America as the name of one of the last warriors of the Chiricahua Apache Indians

GERSHOM Hebrew: Exiled; an Old Testament name
Gersham

GERVASE Teutonic: Meaning uncertain, possibly servant of the spear or warrior; Saint Gervasius was an early martyr whose remains were found in Milan. (English) *Jarvis*; (French) *Gervais, Gervaise*; (Spanish) *Gervasio, Gervaso*; (Gaelic) *Gervin*; *Gervasy*; **Old Forms:** *Gervasius*

GHADIR Persian: Sword

GIACOMO Italian: Variation of Jacob **Famous Namesakes:** *Italian composer Giacomo Puccini*; **Star Babies:** *Son of Sting*

GIAN Italian: Variation of John **Nicknames:** *Gianni*; **Star Babies:** *Son of Francis Ford Coppola*

GIANCARLO Italian: Italian double name comprised of John and Charles

GIBSON English: Gilbert's son; surname *Gibbson*; **Nicknames:** *Gib, Gibby*; **Famous Namesakes:** *Australian actor Mel Gibson*

GIDEON Hebrew: Feller of trees (Russian) *Hedeon*; (Ukrainian) *Hadeon*; *Gedeon*; **Star Babies:** *Son of Mandy Patinkin*

GIFFORD English: Brave *Guifford, Giford*; **Famous Namesakes:** *Sports anchor Frank Gifford, Environmental conservation pioneer Gifford Pinchot*

GIL Hebrew: Happiness *Gili, Gilli*; **Famous Namesakes:** *Violinist Gil Shaham, Canadian actor Gil Bellows*

GILBERT German: Trusted oath (Italian) *Gilberto*; *Gilburt, Guilbert, Guillebert*; **Old Forms:** *Giselberht*

GILFRED German: Oath of peace **Old Forms:** *Gilfried*

GILLES Greek: From aigis, meaning shield of Zeus; Saint Gilles was a popular seventh-century saint who worked miracles and healed the lame. *Giles, Ghiles, Gilian, Geli*; **Famous Namesakes:** *Canadian racecar driver Gilles Villeneuve*

GILMORE Celtic, Scottish: Serves Mary; surname *Gilmer*

GILROY Celtic, Scottish: Serves the red-haired lord

GINO Italian: Nickname for John

GIOMAR Italian: Variation of Lothar

GIORGIO Italian: Variation of George **Nicknames:** *Gio*; **Famous Namesakes:** *Italian designer Giorgio Armani*

GIOVANNI Italian: Variation of John *Geovanni, Gian, Gianni*; **Nicknames:** *Giannino, Nino*; **Famous Namesakes:** *Artist Giovanni Bellini*

GIUSEPPE Italian: Variation of Joseph

GLEANN Gaelic: From the glen valley

GLEN Gaelic: From the glen or valley
Glenn, Glyn, Glynn; **Famous Namesakes:**
*Singer Glen Campbell, Bandleader Glenn
Miller, Actor Glenn Ford*

GLENDON Gaelic: From the dark glen valley

GODFREY German, English: Peace of God;
from the Germanic name Gottfried
(German) *Gottfried*; (Italian) *Goffredo*;
(Spanish) *Godofredo*; (Irish) *Gofraidh,
Gothfraidh*; *Godfried, Gofried, Gottfrid*

GOODWIN English: Good friend or friend
of God
*Godewyn, Godwin, Godwine, Godwyn,
Goodwine, Goodwyn, Gowyn*

GORAN Swedish: Variation of George
Famous Namesakes: *Actor Goran Visnjic*

GORDON Anglo-Saxon, Scottish: From the
wedge-shaped or three-cornered town or
settlement; a surname and the name of one
of Scotland's great clans. See also *Garton*
(English) *Garatun, Gorton*; *Gordain, Gordan*;
Nicknames: *Gordie, Gordy*; **Famous
Namesakes:** *Singer Gordon Lightfoot, Hockey
legend Gordie Howe*

GORMAN Gaelic, Irish: Blue-eyed one
Gormain

GOTTFRIED German: Variation of Godfrey

GOVAN Welsh: God of the forge; Govannon
is a son of the goddess Don and the brother
of Gwydion and Amaethon.
Govannon, Goveniayle

GRAHAM Anglo-Saxon: From the grey
or great home; surname
(Scottish) *Graeme; Graeham, Grahem*;
Nicknames: *Gram*; **Famous Namesakes:**
*Author Graham Greene, Inventor Alexander
Graham Bell, Chef Graham Kerr*

GRANGER French, English: Farmer;
surname; Grange organizations have served
U.S. rural agricultural communities for
almost 150 years, providing not only farming
resources, but also social and educational
opportunities.
(English) *Grangere; Grainger*; **Nicknames:**
Grange

GRANT French, Scottish: Great or bestow;
a surname that increased in popularity as a
first name due to Civil War general and
President Ulysses S. Grant
Famous Namesakes: *Basketball player
Grant Hill*

GRANTHAM English: From the great or
grey land or fields; surname; possible variant
of Grantley
Grantland; **Nicknames:** *Grant*

GRANTLEY English: From the large
meadow; from the grey meadow; surname
*Grantlea, Grantleah, Grantlee, Grantleigh,
Grantlie, Grantly*; **Nicknames:** *Grant*

GRANVILLE French: Great or large town;
surname used as a first name
Grenville; **Famous Namesakes:** *English artist
Granville Danny Clarke*

GREELEY English: From the grey meadow;
possibly from the green meadow; surname
Graegleah, Greely, Greelea, Greeleigh

GREGORY Greek: Watchful; the name of
several saints and popes. Pope Gregory I
fostered the development of Gregorian chants.
Pope Gregory XIII established the Gregorian
calendar in 1582 to replace the Julian calendar.

(German) *Gregor*; (French) *Gregoire*; (Italian) *Gregorio*; (Welsh) *Grigor*; (Swedish) *Greger*; (Russian) *Grigory, Grisha*; (Armenian) *Krikor*; *Gergely, Gergor, Greggory, Gregoly, Gregorie, Gregorior*; **Old Forms:** *Gregorios*; **Nicknames:** *Gergo, Greg, Gregg, Gregos*; **Famous Namesakes:** *Actor Gregory Hines, Actor Gregory Peck;* **Star Babies:** *Son of Ray Romano*

GUIDO Italian: Variation of Guy
Famous Namesakes: *Italian musician Guido Deiro*

GUILLAUME French: Variation of William
Famous Namesakes: *French actor Guillaume Depardieu;* **Star Babies:** *Son of Gerard Depardieu*

GUILLERMO Spanish: Variation of William

GULAB Hindi: Rose

GUNNAR Norse: Warrior; in Norse mythology, the husband of Brynhild
(Danish) *Gunder*

GUSTAV Scandinavian: Staff of the Goths; a name borne by several Swedish kings
(French) *Gustave*; (Spanish) *Gustavo*; (Finnish) *Kustaa, Kusti, Kyösti*; (Hungarian) *Gusztav*; *Gustaf, Gustaof, Gustavus*; **Famous Namesakes:** *Austrian painter Gustav Klimt*

GUY French: Guide
(Italian) *Guido*; *Guye, Gye*; **Old Forms:** *Guyon*; **Famous Namesakes:** *French tennis player Guy Forget, Musician Guy Lombardo*

GUYON French: Original form of Guy

GWYN Welsh: Fair, blessed
Gwen, Gwynn

HAAKON Scandinavian: Highborn son; related to the name Hagan
(Gaelic) *Hogan; Hakan, Hakon*

HABIB Arabic, Persian: Beloved, darling, lover, dear; Habib is also used as a term of endearment by adding a letter "i" to the ending for the masculine version *Habibi*, or "ti" for the feminine version *Habibti.*

HACKETT German: Little woodcutter
Hacket; **Famous Namesakes:** *Actor Buddy Hackett*

HACKMAN German: Wood cutter
Famous Namesakes: *Actor Gene Hackman*

HADAR Hebrew: Beautiful, honored

HADDAD Arabic: Smith, ironsmith, blacksmith; Often used as a family name as well as a first name, Haddad was a storm god for the Semites.
Famous Namesakes: *Football player Drew Haddad*

HADDEN English: From the heath, near the hill of heather
Haddon, Haden, Hadon, Haddan, Haddin

HADI Arabic, Persian: Guiding to the light, to follow the true religion

HADLEY English: From the heath or heather-covered meadow; a surname
Heathleah, Heathley, Hadlea, Hadlee, Hadleigh; **Nicknames:** *Leigh*

HADRIAN Latin: Dark; in the second century, Roman Emperor Hadrian built a magnificent wall in Britain. Named for him, the wall still stands as one of the wonders of the world.

HADWIN English: Ally
Hadwyn; **Old Forms:** *Haethowine*

HAEL Welsh: Healthy, well

HAEMON Greek: In Greek mythology, Haemon was the son of Creon and betrothed of Antigone. He is remembered for his defense of Antigone and his arguments about wise leadership.

HAFEZ Persian: Protector

HAFGRIM Norse: Norse mythological character who lived in Southfrey

HAFIZ Arabic: Guardian, committed to memory, one who has memorized the Koran See also *Hafez Mahfouz*; **Famous Namesakes:** *Former President of Syria Hafez el Asad, Sultan of Morocco Moulay Hafiz, Egyptian poet Hafiz Ibrahim*

HAGAN Irish: Youthful (Norse) *Hagen*

HAGAR Hebrew: Stranger *Hager, Hagir, Hagor, Hayger*

HAGLEY English: From the hedged meadow; surname *Hagaleah, Hagalean, Hagly, Haglea, Hagleigh*

HAGOP Armenian: Variation of James

HAGOS African: Happy (Ethiopia)

HAHNEE Native American: Beggar, supplicant

HAIDAR Hindi: Lion

HAIG English: From the hedged enclosure *Hayg*; **Famous Namesakes:** *Statesman Alexander Haig*

HAILAMA Hawaiian: Renowned brother *Hailamah, Hilama, Hilamah*

HAILEY Irish: Spelling variation of Haley

HAINES English: From the vine-covered cottage; surname *Hane, Hanes, Haynes*

HAJI African: Born during the hajj, or pilgrimage to Mecca (Swahili)

HAKAN Native American: Fire

HAKIM Arabic: Wise, learned; colloquially refers to the doctor *Hakeem*; **Famous Namesakes:** *Basketball player Hakeem Olajuwon*

HAKIZIMANA African: God is our savior (Rwanda)

HAL English: A familiar form usually for Henry but also for Halden, Hall, and related names **Famous Namesakes:** *Actor Hal Holbrook, Actor Hal Linden*

> *"Before I knew thee, Hal, I knew nothing"*
> —William Shakespeare, *Henry IV*

HALBERT English: Brilliant hero *Halbart, Halburt*; **Old Forms:** *Halebeorht*; **Nicknames:** *Hal, Bert*

HALCYON Greek: Time of peace, kingfisher (bird); in Greek mythology, Halcyone threw herself into the sea after the death of her husband, and out of pity the gods changed the pair into kingfishers or halcyons. The gods made winds cease blowing during the mating season of the kingfisher. The expression *halcyon days* is derived from this myth and means a time of tranquillity or prosperity.

HALDEN Scandinavian: Half Dane; when this name was coined, Danes were fierce invaders—the name may refer to a child the invaders left behind or to describe someone as formidable. *Haldan, Haldane, Halvdan*

"I only regret that I have but one life to lose for my country."
—Revolutionary War hero Nathan Hale's final words

HALE English: From the remote valley, healthy; an English surname and a Hawaiian variant of Harry
Hayle

HALEN Swedish: Hall, belongs to the hall

HALEY Irish: Ingenious
Hailey, Haleigh, Halley

HALFORD English: From the hall by the ford, from the valley ford
Haleford

HALI Greek: Sea
Halea, Halee, Halie

HALIAN Native American: Youthful, young (Zuni)

HALIFAX English: From the holy or blessed field

HALIG Anglo-Saxon: Variation of Helge

HALIL Turkish: Dear friend
Halill, Halyl

HALIM Arabic: Gentle, patient, indulgent, also means forbearing

HALIRRHOTHIUS Latin: Mythical son of Poseidon, he loved Alcippe, daughter of Ares, for which Ares killed him.

HALITHERSES Greek: A soothsayer on Ithaca who supported Telemachus and Odysseus

HALL English: House, manor; (Norse) in Norse mythology, the son of Helgi the Godless
Haele

HALLAM English: Valley

HALLAN English: Lives at the hall, belongs to the hall
Hallen, Hallin, Hallon

HALLDOR Norse: Thor's rock, the name of a minor character in Norse legend

HALLEY English: From the meadow near the hall (implying large estate home); surname
Healleah

HALLIWELL English: Near or from the holy spring
Hallwell, Halywell; **Old Forms:** *Haligwiella*

HALLWARD English: Guardian of the hall, watchman

HALSEY English: From Hal's island; surname
Halsig, Hallsey, Hallsy, Halsy; **Famous Namesakes:** *Admiral William F. Halsey*

HALSTEAD English: Grounds of the manor, belonging to those grounds; surname
Halsted

HALSTEN Swedish: Rock or stone
Hallstein, Hallsten; **Nicknames:** *Halle*

HALTON English: From the town, estate on the hill
Haltan, Halten, Haltin

HALVOR Norse: Rock, defender; Saint Hallvard is revered as a martyr who died in defense of innocence.
Hallvard, Halvard

HAM Hebrew: Hot; the biblical name of one of Noah's sons

HAMAL Arabic: Lamb, to bear, a cloud containing much water; Hamal is the sign Aries

HAMAR Scandinavian: Hammer
Hammer, Hamer

HAMIDI African: Praised, admired (Kenya)

HAMILL English: Scarred, implying a survivor; surname
Hamel, Hamell, Hamil, Hammill

HAMILTON English, Scottish: From the proud town, estate; surname of one of the great families of Scotland
Old Forms: *Hamelstun*

HAMISH Scottish: Variation of James

HAMISI African: Thursday's child, born on the fifth day of the week (Swahili)

HAMLET French: Little village; Shakespeare's protagonist in *Hamlet* speaks some of the most famous lines ever written for the stage, including, "To be, or not to be."

HAMLIN German: Loves the little home; in fairy tales, the Pied Piper of Hamelin saves the citizens from rats, but when he is not paid for his efforts, he lures the children away as well. *Hamelin*

HAMMER Scandinavian: Spelling variation of Hamar

HAMMETT Scandinavian: From the village

HAMMOND English: From the small town

HAMPTON English: A place name with an unclear original meaning, although it refers to a settlement or town; place name for area outside London and location of Hampton Court Palace; surname
Hampten, Hamptyn

HAMUND Norse: Meaning unclear; the name of Sigmund and Borghild's son in Norse mythology

HAMZA Arabic: Powerful
Hamzah

HANALE Hawaiian: Variation of Henry

HANAN Arabic: Tenderness; (Hebrew) merciful, grace; the name of various biblical men (Hebrew) *Chanan; Hananel, Hannan*

HANANEEL Hebrew: God has graciously given; a tower in the wall at Jerusalem

HANBAL Arabic: Pristine, pure
Hanbel, Hanbil

HANDEL German: Variation of John

HANFORD English: From the high ford; surname

HANIF Arabic: Believes without doubt

HANK Teutonic: Nickname for Henry

HANLEY English: From the high meadow; surname
Hanly, Heanleah, Henley, Handlea, Handleigh, Handley; Hanlea, Hanlee, Hanleigh, Henlea, Henlee, Henleigh

HANNIBAL Phoenician: Grace of God; name of a famous Carthaginian general who fought the Roman Empire and is remembered for his tactical genius and his trek across the Alps on elephants

HANS German, Scandinavian, Dutch: God has been gracious; variant of John (Scandinavian) *Hanz;* (Swedish) *Hansel;* (Finnish) *Hanes, Hannu; Han, Hannah*

HANSEL Swedish: Variation of Hans

HANSON Scandinavian, Dutch: John's son; also a variant of Anson
Hansen

HAOA Hawaiian: Variation of Howard

HAPI Egyptian: The god of the Nile in inundation; in Egyptian mythology, Hapy was represented as a man with full, heavy breasts, a clump of papyrus on his head, and bearing heavily laden offering tables. The name was also used by a different deity, one of the four sons of Horus, representing the north.
Hapy

HARB Arabic: War
Famous Namesakes: *Egyptian economist Mohammad Talaat Harb*

HARBIN German: Little shining warrior

HARCOURT French: From the fortified farm; surname used as first name
Harcort

HARDEN English: From the hare's valley; surname
Hardin, Hardyn, Heardind

HARDING English: Brave, hardy, reliable
Haryng

HARDWIN English: Variation of Baldwin

HARDY German: Daring, strong, bold
Hardie, Harti

HARE English: Rabbit

HAREL Hebrew: Mountain of God
Harrell, Haral, Harell, Hariel

HARFORD English: From the hare's ford; surname
Haraford, Harfurd, Harrford

HARGROVE English: From the hare's grove; surname
Hargrave, Hargreaves

HARI Hindi: Tawny; Hindu deity combining Vishnu and Shiva

HARITH Arabic: Gardener, grower

HARKIN Irish: Deep red color

HARLAKE English: The hare's lake; surname
Harelache, Harlak

HARLAN English: From the land or farm of the hares, from the army land; a surname and possible variant of Harley
Harland, Harlen, Harlon; **Famous Namesakes:** *Colonel Harland Sanders (founder of KFC)*

HARLEY English: From the hare's meadow; Harley is a surname associated with the famous Harley-Davidson motorcycles. Traditionally a boy's name, now increasingly being used for both genders
Arleigh, Arley, Arlie, Hareleah, Harleigh, Arlea, Arly, Harlea, Harlee, Harly

HARLOW English: From the hill of the hares, from the army hill; a surname
Arlo, Harlowe

HARMON English: Form of Herman
Famous Namesakes: *Actor Mark Harmon*

HAROLD Norse, English: Army commander; Harald has been popular since the Vikings and was borne by several kings of Norway
(Spanish) *Haraldo, Heraldo*; (Irish) *Aralt*; (Scottish) *Harailt*; (Scandinavian) *Harald*; *Arild*; **Nicknames:** *Harry*

HAROUN AL RACHID Arabic: Lofty or inspired, a variant of Aaron; the Caliph of Bagdad, Haroun al Rachid, partially inspired Shehrezad's *One Thousand and One Nights.* He was a contemporary of France's

Charlemagne, and in his time Baghdad was the world's largest city and its most prominent cultural seat.
Harun al Rachid

HARPER English: Minstrel; more than just entertainers when this name was created, harpers were a primary source of news and keepers of the historical record.
Old Forms: *Hearpere*; **Star Babies:** *Son of Paul Simon*

HARPOCRATES Greek: Greek form of the Egyptian god Harpa-Khruti (Horus the child), a late form of Horus as son of Isis and Osiris; Harporcrates was represented as a naked child wearing the lock of youth and holding one finger to his mouth. He became the god of silence and secrecy.

HARRINGTON Irish: From Harry's town or settlement; surname
Nicknames: *Harry*

HARRIS English: Son of Harry or diminutive of Harry
Harrison

HARRISON English: Son of Harry; surname
Famous Namesakes: *Actor Harrison Ford*; **Star Babies:** *Son of Jack Wagner*

HARRY English: Familiar form of Herald or Henry; Harry Potter is the young wizard in the extremely popular series of children's books by J. K. Rowling.
(Italian) *Arrigo*; (Hawaiian) *Hale*; **Famous Namesakes:** *President Harry Truman, Actor Harry Hamlin, Musician Harry Connick Jr.*; **Star Babies:** *Son of Billy Bob Thornton, son of Richard Dreyfuss*

HART English: Stag and a familar form of Hartley, Hartford, and similar names. Teutonic: Strong, brave, and a familiar form of Hartman, Hartwig, and similar names
Harte

HARTFORD English: Near the stag or deer's ford

HARTLEY English: From the stag's meadow; surname
Hartlea, Hartlee, Hartleigh, Hartly

HARTMAN German: Strong, brave. English: Surname adapted to first name use
Hardtman, Hartmann

HARTWELL English: From near the deer's well or spring

HARTWIG Teutonic: Strong advisor
Hartwyg

HARTWOOD English: From the stag's forest; surname
Harwood

HARUKO African: First born

HARVEY French: Eager for battle; based on the Old German name Herewig (French) *Hervé*; **Old Forms:** *Herewig*; **Famous Namesakes:** *Actor Harvey Keitel, Playwright and actor Harvey Fierstein*

HASAD Turkish: Harvester, gatherer
Hassad

HASANI African: Handsome (Swahili)
Hasan

HASHIM Arabic: Destroys evil, bountiful, generous
(Persian) *Hashem*

HASIN Hindi: Laughing, smiling
Hazen

HASKEL Hebrew: Spelling variation of Ezekiel

HASLETT English: From the hazel tree land
Haslet, Hazlett, Hazlitt

HASSAN Arabic, Persian: Handsome, good
Famous Namesakes: *Sultan of Morocco*
Hassan the First, Second King of Morocco
Hassan the Second, Arab poet Hasan Ibn
Thabit

HASSEL German: Bewitched place
Hasel, Hassall, Hassell, Hazell

HASTIN Hindi: Elephant
Hastan, Hasten, Haston, Hastyn

HASTINGS English: House counsel; surname
Old Forms: *Haestingas*

HATIM Arabic: Judge
Hateem, Hatem

HAUK Norse: Hawk

HAVELOCK Norse: Sea warrior, sailor
in battle
Haveloc, Haveloch

HAVEN English: Place of safety, shelter.
Dutch: Harbor, port
Havyn; **Old Forms:** *Haefen*

HAVERILL Anglo-Saxon: Spelling variation
of Averill
Haverell

HAVGAN Irish: White, pure
Havgen, Havgin

HAVIKA Hawaiian: Dearly loved; variant
of David

HAWK English: Hunting bird; when this
name was created, hunting with hawks was
considered an aristocratic sport. See also *Hauk*

HAWLEY English: From the hedged meadow;
surname
Hawly, Hawlea, Hawlee, Hawleigh

HAWTHORNE English: Shrub related to the
apple family, known for its pink and white
flowers and its red fruit
Hawthorn

HAYDEN English: From the hedged valley;
surname adapted to given name use
Haydon, Hayes; **Famous Namesakes:** *Actor*
Hayden Christensen

HAYES English: Spelling variation of Hayden.
Irish: Surname

HAYWARD English: Ward or guardian
of the hedged area
Old Forms: *Hagaward*

HAYWOOD English: From the hedged
forest; surname adapted to given name use
Heywood

HAYYIM Hebrew: Spelling variation of
Chaim

HEARNE English: Variation of Ahearn

HEATH English: An open area of land covered
by heather or the heather itself; a familiar
form for Heathcliff and related names
Famous Namesakes: *Actor Heath Ledger*

HEATHCLIFF English: From the heath cliff
or heath-covered cliff; the unforgettable
romantic character from Emily Brontë's
Wuthering Heights
Heathclyf, Hetheclif

HEATON English: From the high town or
settlement; surname

HEBER Hebrew: Partner, ally; biblical
ancestor of Abraham

HECTOR Greek, Spanish: Steadfast; from
Greek legend, a hero of Troy in the Trojan war
(Italian) *Ettore*; **Famous Namesakes:** *Actor*
Hector Elizondo

HEDEON Russian: Variation of Gideon

HEDLEY English: From the heathered meadows; surname
Hedlea, Hedleigh

HEDWIG German: Fighter, strong one

HEDWYN Welsh: Friend of peace

HEIMDAL Norse: White god; in Norse mythology, Heimdal is the son of Odin and one of the Wave Maidens, and he is the guardian of the rainbow bridge.
Heimdall

HEINRICH German: Variation of Henry
Nicknames: *Heiko, Heinz*

HELAKU Native American: Full of sun, sunny day

HELGE Scandinavian: Blessed, holy
(Anglo-Saxon) *Halig*; (Russian) *Oleg*; *Helgi*

HELIOS Greek: Sun; the name of the young Greek sun god who drove a four-horse chariot across the sky each day

HELKI Native American: Touching (Miwok)

HELMER Teutonic: Warrior's wrath

HELMUT German: Brave
Helmutt, Hellmut, Hellmutt, Hellmuth;
Famous Namesakes: *Chancellor Helmut Kohl*

HEMAN Hebrew: Faithful, loyal
Hemen

HEN WYNEB Welsh: Old face

HENDERSON English, Scottish: Henry's son
Henson

HENDRICK Scandinavian: Variation of Henry

HENLEY Irish: Spelling variation of Hanley

HENOCH Hebrew: Leader, initiator; also a variant of Enoch

HENRY German: Rules his household; from the German Heinrich. Introduced by the Normans, the name Henry has belonged to eight English kings and is the name of Prince Charles' younger son.
(German) *Heinrich, Hennings*; (French) *Henri*; (Italian) *Arrighetto, Enrico, Enzo*; (Spanish) *Enrique*; (Portuguese) *Henrique*; (Teutonic) *Henerik, Henning, Hinrich*; (Irish) *Hannraoi, Hanraoi*; (Scandinavian) *Hendrick, Henrick, Henrik*; (Swedish) *Hendrik*; (Russian) *Genry*; (Polish) *Henryk, Honok*; (Finnish) *Heikki*; (Hawaiian) *Hanale*; *Heike, Heinroch, Henrich*; **Nicknames:** *Hank, Harro, Heiko, Heinz*; **Famous Namesakes:** *Philosopher Henry David Thoreau, Automobile pioneer Henry Ford, Actor Henry Fonda*; **Star Babies:** *Son of Julia Louis Dreyfuss and Brad Hall, Meryl Streep, Steve Zahn, Dennis Hopper*

HENSON Scottish: Spelling variation of Henderson

HEPHAESTUS Greek: Greek mythological god of fire and the patron of craftsmen

HERALD English: One who proclaims; also a variant of Harold

HERBERT German: Illustrious warrior; a name introduced to Britain by the Normans
(French) *Aribert*; (Spanish) *Herberto, Heribert, Heriberto; Hurbert*; **Famous Namesakes:** *President Herbert Hoover*

HERCULES Greek: Glory of Hera; the mythological hero was the mortal son of Zeus. After committing a dreadful crime while under a spell of insanity, he was granted a chance to regain honor by completing twelve supposedly impossible tasks, which he did successfully, using both his mighty

physical strength and his cleverness. On his deathbed, he was granted immortality and the status of god.
(Italian) *Ercole*

HERMAN German: Warrior
(French) *Armand*; (Italian) *Armando, Ermanno*; (Swedish) *Hermann; Harman, Harme, Harmen, Harmon*; **Nicknames:** *Harm, Herm*

HERMES Greek: Messenger of the gods; also the name of famous French design label
Hermès

HERMOD Norse: In Norse mythology, Hermod was the son of Odin and Frigg, and welcomed fallen warriors to Valhalla.

HERNANDO Spanish: Variation of Ferdinand

HERRICK German: War leader
Herryk

HERSHEL Hebrew: Deer
Herschel, Hirsch

HERVÉ French: Variation of Harvey

HESPEROS Greek: Evening star
Hespero

HESUTU Native American: Picks up yellow jacket's nest (Miwok)

HEWITT German, French: Smart little one; possibly little Hugh or Hugh's son
Hewett, Hewlett, Hewlitt

HEWSON English: Spelling variation of Hughson
Famous Namesakes: *Singer Paul Hewson (Bono)*

HEZEKIAH Hebrew: God is my strength; an Old Testament name belonging to a king of Judah

HIAMOVI Native American: High chief (Cheyenne)
Hyamovi

HIAWATHA Native American: River creator; historical Iroquois leader (Onodaga tribe) who helped bring about a peace of the five nations of the Iroquois people
Haionwhatha

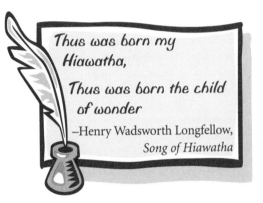

Thus was born my Hiawatha,

Thus was born the child of wonder

—Henry Wadsworth Longfellow,
Song of Hiawatha

HIBAH Arabic: Gift
Hyba, Hybah

HIEREMIAS Greek: God will uplift

HIERONYMUS Latin: Sacred name; famous Roman surname derived from the given name of a second-century B.C. king of Syracuse
Famous Namesakes: *Dutch painter Hieronymus Bosch*

HILAL Arabic: New moon, born at the new moon
Hylal

HILARY English: Cheerful; derived from the Latin Hilarius; Sir Edmund Hillary lead the first expedition to successfully climb Mount Everest. See also *Ilari*
(Greek) *Hilarion*; (Spanish) *Hilario; Hillary, Hillery, Ilarion*; **Old Forms:** *Hilarius*

HILDEBRAND Teutonic: Battle sword
Hildbrand, Hildebrandt

HILDEMAR German: Famous warrior

HILDERIC German: Warrior or fortress

HILLEL Hebrew: Greatly praised; Hillel is the name of the Jewish organization that supports college students. Rabbi Hillel began the Talmud.

HILLIARD Teutonic: Brave defender, brave warrior
Hiliard, Hiller

HILMAR Swedish: Famous, highborn
Hilmer

HILTON English: From the town or settlement on the hill; surname
Hylton

HINTO Native American: Blue (Dakota)
Hynto

HINUN Native American: Storm spirit
Hynun

HIPPOLYTE Greek: Horseman

HIPPOLYTUS Greek: Frees the horses; Greek mythical son of Zeus and Hippolyta, a queen of the Amazons
Hipolit

HIRAM Hebrew: Exalted, noble
Hyrum; **Nicknames:** *Hi*

HIRSCH Yiddish: Spelling variation of Hershel

HOBBARD German: Spelling variation of Hubert

HOBERT German: Bert's hill
Nicknames: *Hobie*

HOBSON English: Robert's son
Hobbs, Hobs, Hobsen

HODGSON English: Spelling variation of Rogerson

HOFFMAN German: Influential, powerful one
Hofman

HOLBROOK English: From the brook in the hollow of the valley
Holbrooke

HOLCOMB English: From the deep valley

HOLDEN English: From the hollow in the valley; Holden Caulfield is the young, disillusioned main character of J. D. Salinger's novel *The Catcher in the Rye*.
Holdin, Holdyn; **Star Babies:** *Son of Dennis Miller, son of Rick Schroder*

HOLIC Czech: Barber

HOLLAND French: Place name as another name for the Netherlands; surname
Hollan

HOLLEB Polish: Dove

HOLLIS English: From the grove of holly trees

HOLMES English: From the river islands; surname of the great fictional detective, Sherlock
Famous Namesakes: *Writer Oliver Wendell Holmes*

HOLT Anglo-Saxon, English: From the woods or forest

HOMAYOUN Persian: Royal, fortunate
Homayoon

HOMER Greek: Security, hostage, promise; the ancient Greek poet responsible for giving the world *The Iliad* and *The Odyssey*
(Spanish) *Homero*; *Homar, Homeros, Homerus*; **Star Babies:** *Son of Bill Murray, son of Carey Lowell and Richard Gere*

HONDO African: Warrior, soldier
(Zimbabwe)

HONON Native American: Bear (Miwok)

HONORÉ French: Honor; derived from the
Latin Honoratus
(Spanish) *Honorato*; **Old Forms:** *Honoratus*;
Famous Namesakes: *French artist Honoré
Daumier*

HONORIUS Latin: Honor; Honorius was
the name of an emperor of the West Roman
Empire and also the name of four popes.

HONOVI Native American: Strong

HONZA Czech: Variation of John

HORACE Latin: Keeper of the hours, time-
keeper; derived from the Roman family clan
name Horatius, and the name of a famous
Roman poet
(Spanish) *Horado*; *Horacio, Horaz*;
Old Forms: *Horatius*

HORATIO Latin: Keeper of the hours;
derived from the same root as Horace and a
Roman surname, Horatio was adapted to
given name use centuries ago. In Shakespeare's
Hamlet, Horatio is the prince's friend; Hamlet
addresses many famous speeches to him.

HOREMHEB Egyptian: Name of a pharaoh
in ancient Egypt

HORST German: Thicket
(English) *Hurst, Hurste*

HORTON English: From the garden town or
estate; Horton is a surname and the name of
the elephant protagonist in the Dr. Seuss
classic *Horton Hears a Who*.

HORUS Egyptian: God of the sky; this earliest royal god was in the shape of a falcon,
with the sun and the moon as his eyes.

Horus was identified with the king during
his lifetime and was regarded as the son of
Isis and Osiris. The many forms of Horus are
Re-Harakhti, Harsiesis, Haroeris, Harendotes,
Khenti-irti, Khentekhtay (the crocodile god),
and Harmakhis (Horus on the horizons).
The Sphinx of Giza is considered to be the
representation of the latter form of Horus.
Harakhty

HOSA Native American: Small crow
(Arapaho)

HOSEA Hebrew: Salvation; the biblical
Hosea was an Israelite prophet, and the Old
Testament Book of Hosea is named after him.
Hoseia, Hoshea, Hoseah

HOTAH Native American: White (Sioux)
Hota

HOTOTO Native American: The whistler
(Hopi)

HOUGHTON English: From the estate
or settlement on the headland

HOUMAN Persian: Possessing a good soul,
good nature
Human

HOUSTON English: From the hill town; a
surname and place name for a major city
in Texas
Huston

HOWARD English: High watchman, noble
watchman; an English surname of a histori-
cally powerful family
(Hawaiian) *Haoa*; **Nicknames:** *Ward*;
Famous Namesakes: *Businessman Howard
Hughes, Actor and director Ron Howard*

HOWE German: High
How

HOWELL Welsh: Eminent, prominent; an Anglicized variation of Hywel
Howel, Hywel

HOWI Native American: Turtledove (Miwok)

HOWIE English: Nickname for Howard, Howland and similar names
Howey; **Famous Namesakes:** *Football player and broadcaster Howie Long*

HOWLAND English: From the hilly land
Howlan

HOYT Irish: Spirit

HRYCHLEAH English: From the meadow's edge; surname
Hrychlea, Hrycleigh

HUARWAR Celtic, Welsh: Son of Avlawn or Halwn, mentioned in Arthurian Legend

HUBERT German: Bright in spirit; Saint Hubert is the patron saint of hunters. (Italian) *Uberto*; (Spanish) *Huberto*; *Hobard, Hobart, Hobbard, Hubbard*; **Nicknames:** *Bert, Hubie, Hugh*; **Famous Namesakes:** *Vice President Hubert Humphrey*

HUD Arabic: Name of a Muslim prophet and used by several Muslim leaders
Star Babies: *Son of John Mellencamp*

HUDSON English: Hugh's son; a surname adapted to given name use and a place name for the Hudson River and famous Hudson Bay in Canada

HUEIL Celtic: Legendary son of Caw, enemy of Arthur

HUEY English: Nickname for Hugh
Famous Namesakes: *Politician Huey Long, Singer Huey Lewis*

HUGH German: Intelligent, thoughtful (German) *Hugo*; (French) *Hugues*; (Italian) *Ugo*; (Welsh) *Hew, Huw*; (Norse) *Hugin*; (Hawaiian) *Hui*; *Hughes*; **Nicknames:** *Huey, Hughie*; **Famous Namesakes:** *English actor Hugh Grant,* Playboy *founder Hugh Hefner*

HUGHSON English: Hugh's son, child; surname
Hewson

HUGI Norse: A minor character in Norse mythology, he was a young giant living in Utgard.

HUGO German: Variation of Hugh
Famous Namesakes: *German fashion designer Hugo Boss*

HULA Native American: Eagle (Osage)

HULBERT German: Brilliant, shining grace
Hulbard, Hulbart; **Old Forms:** *Huldiberaht*

HUMBERT Spanish: Famous warrior; traditional Spanish name from Old German, introduced to Britain by the Normans (Italian) *Umberto*; *Humberto*

> *"Humbert Humbert. What a thrillingly different name."*
> —Vladimir Nabokov, *Lolita*

HUMILITY English: Modesty, a virtue

HUMPHREY German: Peaceful strength (Italian) *Onfrio, Onofredo*; (Welsh) *Wmffre*; (Polish) *Onufry*; *Humfrey, Humfrid, Humfried, Hunfredo, Hunfrid, Hunfried*; **Famous Namesakes:** *Actor Humphrey Bogart*

HUNT English: Pursue; a surname adapted to given name use and a familiar form of Hunter, Huntley, and similar names

HUNTER English: To hunt; an occupational name
Star Babies: *son of Niki Taylor*

HUNTINGTON English: From the hunter's town or settlement; surname
Huntingden, Huntingdon, Huntingtun, Huntingtin; **Nicknames:** *Hunter*

HUNTLEY English: From the hunter's meadow; surname
Huntly, Huntlea, Huntlee, Huntleigh; **Nicknames:** *Hunt, Lee*

HURLBERT English: Strong, shining army; closely related to the name Herbert
Herlbert, Hurlbart; **Old Forms:** *Herlebeorht*

HURLEY Irish: Sea tide
Hurlee, Hurly

HUSAM AL DIN Arabic: Sword of faith or religion

HUSLU Native American: Bear

HUSSEIN Arabic: Good, handsome; the founder of Shiite Islam was named Hussein. (African) *Hasan, Hassain;* (Persian) *Hossein; Husani, Hussain, Husain, Husayn;* **Famous Namesakes:** *King of Jordan Hussein Ibn Talal, Former Iraqi President Saddam Hussein, Sultan of Egypt Hussein Kamal;* **Star Babies:** *Son of the Calif Ali and brother of Hasan*

HUTCHINSON English: Child of the hutch, child of the rural working class

HUTE Native American: Star

HUTTON English: From the town or estate on the ridge; surname

HUXFORD English: From Hugh's ford
Huxeford

HUXLEY English: From Hugh's meadow; surname
Huxly, Huxlea, Huxlee, Huxleigh

HVERGELMIR Norse: In Norse mythology, the wellspring of cold in Niflheim and the source of all cold rivers.

HYACINTH Greek: Flower name, purple; in Greek mythology, Hyacinth was beloved and accidentally killed by Apollo. From his blood sprang the flower that bears his name. (Spanish) *Jacinto, Jax*

HYATT English: From the high gate; surname
Hiatt

HYDE English: A name with several meanings, the oldest is likely deer and from the deer hide, but also may refer to a measure of land, or to the act of concealing
Hid, Hide

HYDER English: Tanner; an occupational name

HYLAS Greek: In Greek mythology, Hylas was the son of Theiodamas and devoted companion of Heracles, joining him on the voyage of the Argo. When fetching water from a spring, a nymph was so entranced by his beauty that she kidnapped him.

HYPERION Greek: He who goes before the sun; the mythological Hyperion is the titan son of Uranus and Gaia and the father of Helios, Selene, and Eos.

HYPNOS Greek: Personification of sleep in Greek mythology; the term "hypnosis" derives from this name.

IAGO Spanish: Spanish and Welsh variant of James; one of literature's famous villains, Shakespeare's Iago is a very clever man.

IAKONA Hawaiian: Healer

IAKOPA Hawaiian: Variation of Jacob

IAKOVOS Greek: Variation of Jacob

IAN Scottish: Variation of John

IAPETUS Greek: In Greek mythology, he is the Titan son Uranus and Gaia, and father of Atlas, Menoetius, Prometheus, and Epimetheus. A moon of Saturn is named for him.

IASION Greek: The mythological Iasion was the son of Zeus and Electra and, by Demeter, the father of Plutus.
Iasius

IB Phoenician: Oath of Baal

IBON Basque: Variation of Ivor

IBRAHIM Arabic: Variation of Abraham

IBSEN German: Archer's son; surname *Ibsan, Ibsin, Ibson*; **Famous Namesakes:** *Norwegian playwright Henrik Ibsen*

IBYCUS Greek: Greek lyric poet; the expression "cranes of Ibycus" derives from a myth that Ibycus' murder was avenged by cranes who saw the crime.

ICARIUS Greek: In Greek mythology, Icarius was an Athenian who so warmly welcomed Dionysus to Attica that the god gave him the gift of wine. He was tragically killed when his shepherds mistook the wine for poison, but the gods honored his spirit by placing him in the stars.

> *"O brave Iago, honest and just,*
> *That hast such noble sense of thy*
> *friend's wrong!"*
> —William Shakespeare, *Othello*

ICARUS Greek: In Greek mythology, he was the son of the inventor Daedalus, and both were imprisoned by King Minos. In an attempt to escape, his father created wings of feathers and wax, but warned his son not to fly too high or the wings would melt. Lost in the joy of flight, Icarus forgot his father's warning. The sea where he died is named for him.

ICELOS Greek: The mythological Icelos was the son of Hypnos responsible for creating the images of humans in dreams.

ICHABOD Hebrew: The glory has gone; an Old Testament name most commonly recognized as the protagonist Ichabod Crane in Washington Irving's *The Legend of Sleepy Hollow*.

IDAL English: From the yew tree valley; a surname and variant of Udell

IDAS Greek: In Greek mythology, Idas was an Argonaut so special that princess Marpessa chose him over the god Apollo.

IDEN Anglo-Saxon: Woody pasture

IDI African: Born during the Id al-Fitr festival, which marks the end of Ramadan

IDOGBE Egyptian: Brother of twins

IDOMENEUS Greek: Grandson of Minos, king of Crete, and leader of the Cretan troops during the Trojan War, Idomeneus was famous for his bravery in battle.

IDRIS Arabic: Name of an important Muslim prophet also called Enoch; (Welsh) eager lord *Idress, Idriss, Idryss*

IESTYN Welsh: Just, lawful, fair; variant of Justin

IGASHO Native American: Wanderer
Igashu

IGGY Latin: Nickname for Ignatius
Famous Namesakes: *Singer Iggy Pop*

IGNATIUS Latin: Fiery; Saint Ignacius of Loyola founded the Catholic Jesuit order. See also *Inigo*
(French) *Ignace*; (Italian) *Ignazio*; (Spanish) *Ignacio, Ignado, Nacho*; (Basque) *Inaki*; (Russian) *Ignat, Ignatiy*; (Czech) *Ignac*;
Nicknames: *Iggy*

IGOR Russian: Variation of Ingvar
Egor; **Nicknames:** *Iggy*; **Famous Namesakes:** *Russian composer Igor Stravinsky*

IKAIA Hawaiian: Variation of Isaiah

IKE English: Nickname for Isaac

IKER Basque: Visit

ILAN Hebrew: Tree
Elan

ILARI Basque: Cheerful; variant of Hilary

ILBERT German: Renowned fighter

ILIAS Greek: The Lord is my God; variant of Elijah

ILIMA Hawaiian: Flower of Oahu
Ilimah

ILLAN Latin, Basque: Young, youthful

ILMARI Finnish: Air

ILYA Russian: The Lord is my God; variant of Elijah

IMAD Arabic: Supportive, relied upon

IMMANUEL Hebrew: God is with us; variant of Emmanuel

IMRAN Arabic: Host

IMRE Hungarian: Variation of Emery

INACHUS Greek: Greek god of the river that bears his name, Inachus was the son of Oceanus and Tethys, and the father of Io.

INAY Hindi: Godlike, supreme

INCE Hungarian: Innocent

INCENCIO Spanish: White, fair

INCENDIO Spanish: Fire

INDER Hindi: Godlike, awe-inspiring
Inderdeep, Inderpeet

INDRA Hindi: In Hindu culture, Indra was the supreme ruler of the gods.

INGEL German: Angel

INGELBERT German: Bright angel; variant of Englebert

INGER Scandinavian: Son's army
Ingharr

INGLISS Scottish: English, from England
Inglys

INGMAR Norse, Swedish: Famous Ing or famous son; refers to Ing, another name for Frey, the handsome Norse fertility god
Ingemar, Inge; **Famous Namesakes:** *Swedish director Ingmar Bergman*

INGRAM English: Angel, angelic

INGVAR Scandinavian: Ing's soldier
(Russian) *Igor*; **Famous Namesakes:**
Swedish singer Ingvar Wixell

INIGO Basque: Fiery, passionate; variant
of Ignatius

INIR Scandinavian: Honorable, good

INNES Scottish, Irish: From the island
or river island
(Celtic) *Inness, Innis*; (Irish) *Inis, Inys*

INNOCENT Latin, English: Innocent; name
of numerous popes
(Italian) *Innocenzio*; (Spanish) *Inocencio,
Inocente, Sencio*

INTEUS Native American: Proud, without
shame

INTO Finnish: Enthusiasm

IOKEPA Hawaiian: May God give increase;
variant of Joseph

IOKIA Hawaiian: Healed by the power
of God
Iokiah

IOLO Welsh: Familiar form of Iowerth,
the Welsh version of Edward

ION Irish: Variation of John

IONAKANA Hawaiian: Gift from God;
variant of Jonathan

IOSIF Russian: Variation of Joseph

IPHIS Greek: In Greek mythology, Iphis
was a shepherd who fell in love with the
maiden Anaxarete, but killed himself when
she refused his love. When she remained
uncaring, Aphrodite turned her to stone.

IRA Hebrew: Watchful
Irah; **Famous Namesakes:** *Composer Ira
Gershwin, Actor Ira Aldridge*

IRAM English: Bright

IRFAN Arabic: Gratitude

IRMIN German: Strong

IRVING English: Friend from the sea or
handsome friend. Irish: Handsome. Welsh:
White or white river
(Welsh) *Inek*; *Earvin, Ervin, Ervine, Irven,
Irvin, Irvine, Irvyn, Irwin, Irwyn*; **Nicknames:**
Irv, Erv; **Famous Namesakes:** *Composer
Irving Berlin*

ISA Arabic: Arabic form of Jesus; (Hebrew)
nickname for Isaiah and Isaac
Isah

ISAAC Hebrew: He laughs; the biblical Issac
was the only son of Abraham by his wife
Sarah. The prediction of his birth was amusing
to the couple because they were very old, so
God gave them the name Isaac for their son,
meaning one who laughs. Isaac later became
a father to the twins Esau and Jacob.
(Greek) *Isaak*; (Arabic) *Ishaq*; (Swedish) *Isak*;
(Dutch) *Issac*; (Basque) *Ixaka*; (Czech) *Izaac,
Izak*; (Armenian) *Sahak*; *Itzhak, Yitzhak*;
Nicknames: *Ike, Isa, Zack, Zak*; **Famous
Namesakes:** *Physicist Sir Isaac Newton,
Author Isaac Asimov, Violinist Itzhak Perlman*;
Star Babies: *Son of Mandy Patinkin, son of
Annie Potts*

ISAIAH Hebrew: God is salvation; the biblical
Book of Isaiah is named for a Hebrew
prophet of the Old Testament.
(Spanish) *Isaias*; (Finnish) *Esa*; (Hawaiian)
Ikaia; *Essaiah, Isiah, Izeyah, Isa, Isai, Isaih*;
Famous Namesakes: *Basketball player Isiah
Thomas*; **Star Babies:** *Son of Mia Farrow*

ISAM Arabic: Safeguard, protection

ISEKEMU Native American: Slow-moving water

ISEN Anglo-Saxon: Iron

ISHAM English: From or belonging to the iron in one's home
Isenham

ISHAN Hindi: Direction
Ishana

ISHMAEL Hebrew: God hears; in the Bible, Ishmael was the elder son of Abraham by Hagar, the Egyptian slave of Abraham's wife Sarah. Ishmael is considered the patriarch of Arabs and forefather of Islam.
(Spanish) *Ismael*

ISIDORE Greek: Gift of Isis; name of several saints
(Spanish) *Cedro, Cidro, Isadoro, Isidoro, Isidro; Esidore, Ixidor, Ysidro*

ISLAM Arabic: Submission (to the will of God); Islam is the name of the religion preached by the Prophet Mohammed.

ISRAEL Hebrew: Prince of God; Israel was the name given to the biblical Jacob after he wrestled the angel of God. It was later taken by the Jewish people as the name of the twelve tribes descended from Jacob's sons and the name of their modern nation.
Isreal, Izreal, Yisreal, Ysrael

ISSA African: God is salvation (Swahili)
Issah

ISTU Native American: Sugar pine tree

ISTVAN Hungarian: Variation of Stephen
Nicknames: *Pista, Pisti*

ITTAMAR Hebrew: Island of palms
Itamar

IULIO Hawaiian: Variation of Julian

IVAN Russian: Variation of John

IVANHOE English: Possible variant of Ivan (John); Ivanhoe is the medieval Saxon protagonist in Sir Walter Scott's work of that name.

IVAR Scandinavian: Spelling variation of Ivor

IVES English: Young archer, a name closely related to Ivor and from the same Norse roots

IVO Teutonic: Yew wood, specifically that which was used for archer's bows

IVOR Scandinavian, English: Archer; a popular Scandinavian name derived from Old Norse elements
(English) *Ivon*; (French) *Yves, Yvet, Yvon*; (Basque) *Ibon*; *Ivar, Iver*

IXIDOR Greek: Spelling variation of Isidore

IXION Greek: A pivotal character in Greek mythology, Ixion was given a second chance after committing a great crime. He was then tricked by Zeus into thinking he was sleeping with Hera, and impregnated a cloud which bore him a son, Centaurus.

IYE Native American: Smoke

IZOD Irish: Fair-haired, blond; famous clothing brand name

IZZY Hebrew: Familiar form of Isaac, Isidore, or Israel

JAAFAN African: Small river

JABARI African, Egyptian: Fearless, brave

JABARL African: Comforter (Swahili)

JABBAR Arabic: Mighty, colossal, omnipotent, oppressor

JABEZ Hebrew: Born in pain, implying a survivor

JABILO African: Medicine man

JABIN Hebrew: Perceptive; the name of two kings of Hazor in the Old Testament

JABIR Arabic: Consoler, one who comforts
Famous Namesakes: *Arab physician, philosopher, and alchimist Jabir Ibn Hayan*

JABULANI African: Happy, jubilant

JACE American: Familiar form of Jason, Jacy, and similar names

JACINTO Spanish: Variation of Hyacinth
Nicknames: *Jax*

JACK English: God has been gracious, has shown favor; derived from Jacques or John but is well established as a name on its own
Famous Namesakes: *Actor Jack Nicholson, Golfer Jack Nicklaus, Comedian Jack Benny;*
Star Babies: *Son of Denis Leary, Luke Perry, Ozzie Osbourne, Meg Ryan and Dennis Quaid, Willem Dafoe, Susan Sarandon and Tim Robbins, Christie Brinkley, Cheryl Tiegs*

JACKSON English: Son of Jack or John; a surname
Jaxon, Jaxson; **Star Babies:** *Son of Maria Bello, Patti Smith, Spike Lee*

JACOB Hebrew: Supplanter or seizing by the heel; Jacob appears in the biblical book of Genesis as the youngest son of Isaac and Rebecca and twin to Esau. Jacob's sons were the founders of the twelve tribes of Israel, and he received the name Israel from God later in life. James is a common variant of this name.
(Hebrew) *Jacobe;* (Greek) *Iakovos;* (Arabic) *Yacoub;* (English) *Jago;* (German) *Jakob;* (French) *Jacquan, Jacquel, Jacquelin, Jacques, Jacquez;* (Italian) *Giacomo;* (Spanish) *Jacobo;* (Dutch) *Jaap;* (Finnish) *Jaakko, Jouko;* (Hawaiian) *Iakopa; Jaccob, Jacobus, Jacoby, Jacque, Yakov;* **Old Forms:** *Yaakov;*
Nicknames: *Jake;* **Star Babies:** *Son of Dustin Hoffman, Albert Brooks, James Caan*

JACOBSON English: Jacob's child

JACOREY English: Modern blend of Jay or possibly Jacob and Corey
Jakari, Jacori, Jacory

JACQUES French: Variation of Jacob

JACY English: Modern name possibly derived from the initials J.C. or as a familiar form of Jason. Native American: Moon

A Matter of Fact

According to UK National Statistics, Jack has been the most popular name for baby boys for nine straight years. It has been one of the most popular choices in recent years for parents in Northern Ireland, Scotland, the Republic of Ireland, and New Zealand; but much less so in the United States and Australia, where it barely makes the top fifty.

JAD Hebrew: Familiar form of Jadon. English: Familiar form of Jadrien and related names

JADON Hebrew: Jehovah has heard; originally a male biblical name now used for both genders
Jaden, Jaiden, Jayden, Jadyn, Jadynn, Jaidyn, Jaidynn, Jaydyn, Jaydynn

JADRIEN Contemporary: Modern blend of Jay and Adrien
Jadrian, Jaydrian, Jaydrien

JAEL Hebrew: Mountain goat
Yael

JAFAR Hindi: Little stream, creek or brook
(African) *Jafaru; Ja'Far*

JAGDEEP Sanskrit: Lamp of the world

JÄGER German: Hunter
Jaegar, Jaeger

JAGGER English: Peddler or carter; for many, the name will bring to mind English musician Mick Jagger, the sometimes controversial and rebellious vocalist of the Rolling Stones.
Jager, Jagar, Jaggar

JAGMEET Sanskrit: Friend of the world

JAHI African: Dignified (Swahili)

JAHNU Hindi: Name of a Hindu legendary sage who played a role in the story of Ganga, the river goddess

JAIDEN Hebrew: Spelling variation of Jadon

JAIME Spanish: Variation of James
Nicknames: *Diego, Yago*

JAIRUS Hebrew: God enlightens; in the New Testament, Jairus is the father of a child brought back to life by Jesus.
(Spanish) *Jair, Jairo*

JAJAUN English: Modern blend of Jay and Juan

JAKEEM Arabic: Raised up, uplifted
Famous Namesakes: *Superhero Jakeem J. Thunder (alias for Jakeem J. Williams)*

JAKOME Basque: Supplanter, variant of James

JAKUB Czech: Form of Jacob

JALAL Arabic, Persian: Glory of the faith, illustrious, majesty
(Hindi) *Jaleel; Jalil;* **Famous Namesakes:** *Persian poet of the thirteenth century Jalal El Din Rumni, Actor Jaleel White*

JALEN American: Modern blend of Jay and Len
Jalan, Jalon, Jaylen, Jaylon; **Famous Namesakes:** *Basketball player Jalen Rose*

JALO Finnish: Noble

JAMAL Arabic: Handsome, beautiful; Jamal was the name of a main character in the movie *Finding Forrester*, starring Sean Connery and Rob Brown. See also *Gamal* (English) *Jamar; Jahmal, Jahmar, Jamael, Jamil, Jemal, Jamaal, Jamahl, Jamall;*
Nicknames: *Jam;* **Famous Namesakes:** *Actor Malcolm-Jamal Warner*

JAMES Hebrew: Supplanter; variant of Jacob. Two of Christ's disciples, son of Zebedee and son of Alphaeus, were named James. In Britain, James is a royal name associated with kings of England and Scotland. See also *Iago, Jakome* (Spanish) *Diego, Jaime, Yago;* (Scottish) *Hamish;* (Armenian) *Hagop;* (Hawaiian)

Kimo; Jayme, Jaymes; **Nicknames:** *Jamie, Jem, Jim, Jimmie, Jimmy;* **Famous Namesakes:** *Poet James Joyce, President Jimmy Carter, Actor Jimmy Stewart;* **Star Babies:** *Son of Art Garfunkel, Jon Voight, Belinda Carlisle, Jerry Hall and Mick Jagger*

JAMESON English: Son of James
(Scottish) *Jamieson; Jamison*

JAMIE Scottish: Nickname for James
Jaimie, Jamey, Jayme; **Famous Namesakes:** *British chef Jamie Oliver*

JAMIL Arabic: Spelling variation of Jamal
Gamil, Gameel, Jamel, Jameel, Jamiel

JAMIN Hebrew: Right hand; in the Old Testament, this is a son of Simeon.
Jamon

JAMSHID Persian: King, a character in Persian mythology (Shahnameh)
Jamsheed

JAN Dutch: Variation of John
Famous Namesakes: *Actor Jan-Michael Vincent, Singer Jan Berry*

JANSEN German: Variation of John

JANUS Latin: Archway; in Roman mythology, Janus is the god of beginnings and endings, and is often shown with a double-faced head looking in opposite directions. The month of January is named after him.
(Polish) *Januarius, Jarek*

JAPHET Hebrew: Handsome or beautiful; used by some as a variant of Japheth

JAPHETH Hebrew: Enlarged, expands; in the Bible, Japheth was a son of Noah and the father of the people of Europe and Asia Minor.
Yaphet

JARAH Hebrew: Honey, he gives sweetness; the biblical Jarah was a descendant of Jonathan.

JARED Hebrew: Descending; a pre-flood biblical name related to Jordan
(English) *Jarrod; Jerad, Jered, Yered, Jarod, Jerod, Jerrod;* **Famous Namesakes:** *Actor Jared Leto;* **Star Babies:** *Son of Richard Harris, son of Paula Zahn*

JARELL Scandinavian: Variation of Gerald

JARETH Contemporary: Modern blend of Jared and Gareth

JARL Scandinavian: Nobleman; royalty title similar to the English Earl

JARLATH Irish: Master, in charge; derived from Iarfhlaith, a name of uncertain origin but with the root *laith* meaning lord

JAROMIR Slavic: Spring
Nicknames: *Jarek;* **Famous Namesakes:** *Hockey player Jaromir Jagr*

JARON Hebrew: He who sings, cry of joy; variant of Yaron

JARRAH Arabic: A vessel, an earthenware jar, emigrating people, tribe

JARRETH Contemporary: Unclear origin, possibly a variant of Gareth, but more likely a modern blend of two names, Jared and Gareth

JARRETT English: Spelling variation of Garrett

JARVIS English: Variation of Gervase
Famous Namesakes: *British singer Jarvis Cocker*

JASON Greek: To heal; in Greek mythology, Jason led a group of warriors called the Argonauts on a search to find the Golden Fleece. The name may also be a variation of Joshua, meaning the Lord is my salvation. (Polish) *Jacek; Jaison, Jasen, Jaysen, Jayson;* **Nicknames:** *Jace, Jase, Jayce;* **Famous Namesakes:** *Actor Jason Alexander, Actor Jason Robards;* **Star Babies:** *Son of Sean Connery*

JASPAR Arabic: Keeper of the treasure; a variant of Caspar or Gaspar. Jaspar was a magic figure in the tale of *Aladdin and the Magical Lamp.* *Jasper;* **Famous Namesakes:** *Musician Bobby Jaspar was a fine bop-oriented soloist equally skilled on his cool-toned tenor and flute;* **Star Babies:** *Son of Wynton Marsalis*

JASPER French: Ornamental stone, brown, beige or red in color; also a variant of Caspar

JAVAD Persian: Liberal

JAVAN Hebrew: Biblical name for son of Japheth *Jahvon, Jaivon*

JAVED Persian: Eternal

JAVIER Spanish: Variation of Xavier *Javiero, Javi*

JAVOR Slavic: Maple tree

JAWHAR Arabic: Jewel, essence, content; Jawhar is the substance as opposed to form. *Jawhara, Gawhara, Gawhar*

JAX English: Nickname for John

JAXON English: Variation of John

JAY English: Originally a familiar form of names such as Jacob, James, and Jason, now a given name in its own right. The name also refers to several species of a large family of birds. Hindi: Various deities in Hindi classical mythological writings are named Jay. *Jae, Jai, Jaye;* **Famous Namesakes:** *Comedian Jay Leno, Author Jay McInerney*

JAYCEE English: Name based on the way the initials J.C. sound, possible variant of Jayce

JAYDEE English: Name based on the way the initials J.D. sound

JAYYED Arabic: Masculine variant of Jaeda, meaning good *Jaied*

JEAN French: Variation of John

JEAN-BAPTISTE French: French combination name honoring Saint John the Baptist

JEAN-PAUL French: Double name composed of Jean (God is gracious) and Paul (little) **Famous Namesakes:** *French fashion designer Jean-Paul Gaultier*

JEDIDIAH Hebrew: Beloved of God; in the Bible, the blessing name Jedidiah was given to King Solomon in infancy. *Jedadiah, Jedaiah, Jedediah, Jediah, Yedidiah, Yedidyah;* **Nicknames:** *Jedd, Jedi*

JEDRICK Polish: Variation of Andrew

JEFF English: Nickname for Jeffrey **Famous Namesakes:** *Racing driver Jeff Gordon, Actor Jeff Bridges, Actor Jeff Daniels*

JEFFERSON English: Son of Geoffrey, a surname adapted to occational given name use **Famous Namesakes:** *President Thomas Jefferson;* **Star Babies:** *Son of Tony Randall*

JEFFORD English: Jeff's ford; surname

JEFFREY French, Anglo-Saxon: Peaceful; a variant of Geoffrey, the three-syllable spelling alternate Jeffery has been used since medieval times.
(French) *Geoffrey*; (Irish) *Sheary, Sheron*; *Geffrey, Jeffery, Jeffry, Jeoffroi*; **Old Forms:** *Geoffroi*; **Nicknames:** *Geoff, Jeff*; **Famous Namesakes:** *English author Jeffrey Archer*

JENO Greek: Variation of Eugene

JENS Scandinavian: Variation of John
Jensen, Jenson

JERARD English: Spelling variation of Gerard
Nicknames: *Jerry*

JEREMIAH Hebrew: The Lord exalts; the name of a major Old Testament prophet
(Greek) *Jeremias*; (Italian) *Geremia*; (Russian) *Yerik*; *Jeramie, Jeramy*; **Nicknames:** *Jere, Jeremy*

JEREMY English: The Lord exalts; variant of Jeremiah
Famous Namesakes: *Actor Jeremy Irons*; **Star Babies:** *Son of Jermaine Jackson*

JERICHO Arabic: City of the moon; in the Bible, Jericho was the City of Canaan that was destroyed when its walls collapsed.
(Spanish) *Jerico*

JERIEL English: Spelling variation of Yeriel

JERMAINE English: Variation of Germain
Famous Namesakes: *Singer Jermaine Jackson*

JEROME Greek: Sacred name; in the fifth century, Saint Jerome created the Vulgate, a Latin translation of the Bible
(French) *Jérome*; (Italian) *Geronimo*; (Spanish) *Jeronimo*; (Polish) *Hieronim*;

Old Forms: *Hieronymus*; **Nicknames:** *Jerry*; **Famous Namesakes:** *Choreographer Jerome Robbins, Comedian Jerry Seinfeld*

JERRETT English: Spear strong; variant of Garrett
Jerett

JERVIS English: Variant of the French name Gervaise spearman

JERZY Polish: Variation of George

JESSE Hebrew: God exists, wealthy; the biblical Jesse was the father of King David. Jesse is also the name of famous American track-and-field star Jesse Owens.
Jessie, Jessy; **Nicknames:** *Jess*; **Famous Namesakes:** *Outlaw Jesse James, Politician Jesse Jackson*; **Star Babies:** *Son of Bob Dylan, son of Jon Bon Jovi*

JESUS Hebrew, Spanish: The Lord is my salvation; Jesus Christ is the central figure of the Bible's New Testament, and Christianity is founded on his life and teachings. The name is most commonly used by Spanish-speaking families and stems from the same Hebrew root as Joshua.

JETHRO Hebrew: Overflowing, abundance; in the Bible, Jethro was Moses' father-in-law.
Famous Namesakes: *Inventor Jethro Tull, Rock group Jethro Tull*

JIM English: Nickname for James
Nicknames: *Jimi, Jimmey, Jimmie, Jimmy*; **Famous Namesakes:** *Actor Jim Carrey, Puppeteer Jim Henson*

JIRAIR Armenian: Industrious

JOACHIM Hebrew: God will judge; Joaquin is a beloved Spanish form of this name
(Spanish) *Joaquin, Quin, Quino, Yoaquin*; (Russian) *Ioakim, Akim*; **Nicknames:** *Achim*; **Famous Namesakes:** *Actor Joaquin Phoenix*

JOB Hebrew: Persecuted; in the Old Testament Book of Job, God allows Satan to test Job's faith through a series of misfortunes.
Old Forms: *Jobe*

JOCELYN French: Transferred surname derived from the Germanic name Gautelen, which comes from the name of a Germanic tribe, the Gauts
Nicknames: *Jos*

JOCK Scottish: Variation of John

JOE English: Nickname for Joseph
Famous Namesakes: Actor Joe Pesci, Boxer Joe Louis, Baseball player Joe DiMaggio, Quarterback Joe Namath; **Star Babies:** *son of Kevin Costner, Christine Lahti*

JOEL Hebrew: Lord is God; a biblical prophet and author of the Book of Joel
Old Forms: *Yoel*; **Famous Namesakes:** *Actor Joel Grey*

JOHANN German: God has been gracious; a variant of John. The German composer Johann Sebastian Bach is considered to be a great genius of Baroque music. He also fathered (and named) thirteen children with his wife Anna.

JOHN Hebrew: God has been gracious; John is the name of one of Christ's disciples, and another biblical John—John the Baptist—baptized Christ in the Jordan River. One of the most popular names in the world, variants of John have been created in almost every language. See also *Johann*
(Greek) *Ioan, Ioannis, Ivan*; (Arabic) *Yahya, Yohanna*; (English) *Jaxon*; (German) *Handel, Jansen, Johan, Johannes*; (French) *Jean, Johnn*; (Italian) *Gian, Giovani, Giovanni, Giovonni*; (Spanish) *Juan, Juancho, Juanito*; (Portuguese) *Joao*; (Teutonic) *Hans*; (Gaelic) *Iain*; (Celtic) *Eoin*; (Irish) *Ion, Keon, Seán*; (Scottish) *Ian, Jock*; (Welsh) *Iwan, Sion*; (Scandinavian) *Jens,*

Jensen, Jenson; (Swedish) *Jan*; (Danish) *Jantzen, Jen, Joen*; (Basque) *Iban*; (Slavic) *Ivano*; (Czech) *Hanus, Honza, Ianos, Jenda*; (Polish) *Janek*; (Finnish) *Hannes, Joni, Jouni, Juha, Juhana, Juhani, Juho, Jukka, Jussi*; (Hungarian) *Jena*; (Hawaiian) *Keoni*; (Estonian) *Jaan; Giannes, Giovanny, Giovany, Jon, Jonn, Jonnie*; **Nicknames:** *Chan, Gino, Jack, Jackie, Jacky, Jax, Johnnie, Johnny, Jonni*;
Famous Namesakes: Actor Johnny Depp, Actor John Wayne, Musician John Lennon, Composer Johannes Bach, President John F. Kennedy; **Star Babies:** *Son of Caroline Kennedy and Ed Schlossberg, Denzel Washington, Michelle Pfeiffer, Rob Lowe*

JOHNSON English: Son of John; most common as a last name
Johnston

JOLYON English: Downy-haired

JON English: Variant of John or abbreviation of Jonathan; Jon is sometimes used in the French fashion, hyphenated with a second name like Jon-Carlo or Jon-Paul.

JONAH Hebrew: Dove; in the Bible, Jonah the prophet was swallowed by a great fish and safely emerged from his belly three days later. Sailors traditionally use this name to personify someone who brings bad luck.
(Greek) *Jonas*; (Finnish) *Joona*; *Yonah*

JONAS Greek: Variation of Jonah
Famous Namesakes: *Research scientist Jonas Salk*

JONATHAN Hebrew: Gift from God; in the Bible, Jonathan was a son of Saul and close friend of King David. See also *Ionakana*
(Finnish) *Joonatan*; *Jonatan, Yehonatan, Jonathon*; **Nicknames:** *Jon*; **Famous Namesakes:** *Actor Jonathan Taylor Thomas, English author Jonathan Swift, Comedian Jonathan Winters*; **Star Babies:** *Son of Paulina Porizkova and Rik Ocasek*

Names That Mean Brains

Looking for an intellectual moniker? Here's a list
of names that have intellectual wisdom in their meanings.

Boys' Names	*Girls' Names*
Ailbe (German)	Alberte (Teutonic)
Akil (Arabic)	Albertyne (German)
Al Alim (Arabic)	Alda (German)
Albert (German)	Aldene (Italian)
Albrecht (German)	Aldred (English)
Alden (Anglo-Saxon)	Alka (Polish)
Aldo (German)	Auberta (Teutonic)
Aldred (English)	Bernardina (Teutonic)
Alfred (Anglo-Saxon)	Channing (English)
Alim (Arabic)	Dana (Persian)
Alvin (English)	Dara (Hebrew)
Aref (Persian)	Darissa (Hebrew)
Bodhi (Hindi)	Eberta (Teutonic)
Conrad (German)	Elberta (Teutonic)
Hewitt (German)	Elda (Anglo-Saxon)
Hugh (English, German)	Ethelda (Teutonic)
Farzan (Persian	Ethelind (Teutonic)
Hakim (Arabic)	Fukayna (Egyptian)
Manu (Hindi)	Gudruna (Swedish)
Quinn (Celtic)	Monica (Latin)
Rambert (German)	Ramona (Spanish)
Raymond (French, German)	Sage (Latin)
Reginald (English)	Salvina (Latin)
Sagan (Slavic)	Shanahan (Irish)
Thaddeus (Hebrew)	Shannon (Irish)
Trevor (Celtic)	Sophronia (Greek)
Zaki (Arabic)	

JOOST Dutch: Variation of Justin
Famous Namesakes: *Dutch author Joost Elfers*

JORAN Scandinavian: Variation of George

JORDAN Hebrew: To flow downward; the river in Palestine where Jesus was baptized has been used as a given name since the Crusades. The name likely had a boost among parents of boys with the popularity of NBA star Michael Jordan.
(French) *Jourdan*; *Jordain, Jordell, Jorden, Jordon, Jourdon, Yarden*; **Nicknames:** *Jordi, Jordy*; **Star Babies:** *Son of Beau Bridges, son of Pia Zadora*

JORDELL Hebrew: Spelling variation of Jordan

JORDY Hebrew: Nickname for Jordan

JORGE Spanish: Variation of George

JORMA Finnish: Variation of George
Famous Namesakes: *Musician Jorma Kaukonen*

JORMUNGAND Norse: In Norse mythology, Jormungand was one of the three children of the god Loki and his wife, the giantess Angrboda. He was a serpent who remained deep in the ocean where he bit his own tail and encircled the world.

JOSE Spanish: Variation of Joseph
Nicknames: *Che, Joselito, Pepe, Pepillo*;
Famous Namesakes: *Actor Jose Ferrer, Spanish opera singer Jose Carreras*

JOSEPH Hebrew: May God give increase; in the Bible, Joseph is the favored son of Jacob. He was sold by his brothers into slavery and later rose to become a supreme power in Egypt. The New Testament carpenter named Joseph was the husband of Mary, the mother of Jesus. See also *Iokepa*

(Arabic) *Yusef, Yusuf*; (German) *Josef*; (French) *Josephe*; (Italian) *Giuseppe*; (Spanish) *Che, Jose, Joselito, Pepe, Pepillo*; (Gaelic) *Ioseph, Seosamh, Seosaph*; (Basque) *Txanton*; (Russian) *Iosif*; (Polish) *Josep*; (Hungarian) *Joska, Jozsef, Jozsi*; (Armenian) *Hovsep*; *Josephus, Yosef*; **Nicknames:** *Joe, Joey*; **Famous Namesakes:** *Actor Joseph Fiennes, Author Joseph Conrad*; **Star Babies:** *Son of Kristin Scott-Thomas*

JOSH Hebrew: Nickname for Joshua
Famous Namesakes: *Actor Josh Hartnett, Actor Josh Charles*

JOSHA Hindi: Satisfied
Joshah

JOSHUA Hebrew: The Lord is my salvation; in the Old Testament, Joshua led his army in the conquest of Jericho and eventually all of Canaan, and was a leader of the Israelites. The Book of Joshua bears his name. According to legend, Mormon pioneers named the rare desert trees in California's Joshua Tree National Park after the biblical figure.
(Spanish) *Josue*; (Hawaiian) *Iokua*; *Jesiah, Josu, Yehoshua*; **Nicknames:** *Josh, Joss*

JOSIAH Hebrew: The Lord supports; the biblical Josiah became king of Judah at age eight after his father was killed and was known for his religious reforms.
(Spanish) *Josias*; *Joziah*

JOTHAM Hebrew: God is upright; a biblical king of Judah during a time of military strife

JOUKO Finnish: Variation of Jacob

JOVAN Latin: Father of the sky, majestic, Jove-like; derived from Jove
Jovani, Jovann, Jovanni, Jovanny, Jovany, Jovi, Jovin, Jovito, Jovon

JOVE Latin: A form of the name Jupiter, the supreme god in Roman mythology

JUAN Spanish: Variation of John
Nicknames: *Chan, Juancho, Juancito, Juanito, Yoni*; **Famous Namesakes:** *Literary hero Don Juan, Spanish King Juan Carlos, Spanish explorer Juan Ponce de Leon*

JUBAL Hebrew: The ram; inventor of the harp and pipes

JUDAH Hebrew: Praised; in the Bible, one of Jacob's twelve sons and the ancestor of the tribe of Judah. The Greek form Judas is associated with the biblical Judas Iscariot who betrayed Jesus.
(Greek) *Judas*; *Yehuda, Yehudi*; **Nicknames:** *Jude, Jud, Judd*

JUDD English: To flow down; originally a familiar form of Jordan, but became more of a name in its own right centuries ago when it was used to refer to children who were baptized with water from the river Jordan. The name is also used as a variant of Judah.
Jud; **Famous Namesakes:** *Actor Judd Hirsch, Actor Judd Nelson*

JUDE Hebrew: Praised; a variant of Judah. The Beatles' smash hit "Hey Jude" was one of the first rock singles to break the standard running time, lasting over seven minutes— yet it still landed in the top spot on the charts in the UK and US.
Famous Namesakes: *Actor Jude Law*

JUDSON American: Son of Judd

JULES French: Variation of Julian
Famous Namesakes: *French author Jules Verne*

JULIAN Latin: Youthful; form of Julius and family clan name of several powerful Roman emperors. In the New Testament, Roman centurion Julius saved Paul's life during a hazardous voyage.
(French) *Jules, Julien*; (Italian) *Giuliano, Giulio*; (Spanish) *Juliano, Julio, Yulius*; (Hungarian) *Gyula, Gyuszi*; (Hawaiian) *Iulio*; *Julen, Jullian, Jullien*; **Old Forms:** *Julius*; **Diminutive Forms:** *Julito*; **Famous Namesakes:** *English actor Julian Sands, English musician Julian Lennon*; **Star Babies:** *Son of Robert De Niro, son of Lisa Kudrow*

JULIO Spanish: Variation of Julian
Nicknames: *Julito, Ulio*; **Famous Namesakes:** *Singer Julio Iglesias*

JULIUS Latin: Youth; an old Roman family name most commonly recognized as the name of Gaius Julius Caesar, one of ancient Rome's greatest generals and leaders
Famous Namesakes: *Basketball player Julius Irving (aka Dr. J)*; **Star Babies:** *Son of Lucy Lawless and Rob Tapert*

JUMOKE Egyptian: Beloved child (Nigeria)

JUNIUS Latin: Young, junior, similar to the name Julius
Junus

JUPITER Latin: Jupiter is the supreme god of Roman mythology, the equivalent to the Greek god, Zeus. Jupiter is also the name of the largest planet in our solar system.

JURGEN Scandinavian: Variation of George
Jorgen

JURO Japanese: Best wishes, long life

JUSTICE English: Variation of Justin
Star Babies: *Son of Steven Seagal*

JUSTIN Latin, English: Just, lawful, fair; a form of the New Testament biblical name Justus. See also *Iestyn*
(English) *Justice*; (French) *Juste*; (Spanish) *Justino*; (Dutch) *Joost*; (Polish) *Justyn*; *Justain, Justis*; **Old Forms:** *Justus*; **Famous Namesakes:** *Singer Justin Timberlake*; **Star Babies:** *Sonof Sean Combs, son of Andie MacDowell*

JUWAN African: True

KACHADA Native American: White man
(Hopi)

KADAR Arabic: Strength, fate, destiny,
predestination, to have power, to be master,
to be capable
Kadir, Qadir, Qadar, Kedar

KAELAN Gaelic: Spelling variation of
Cailean

KAEMON Japanese: Joyful, righthanded;
an old Samurai name

KAFELE Egyptian: Would die for

KAGA Native American: Chronicler

KAGAN Irish: A thinker
Kagen

KAHERDIN Arthurian Legend: Brother
of Isolde

KAHOKU Hawaiian: Star

KAI Welsh, Scottish, Finnish: Keeper of
the keys; (Hawaiian) the sea
(Swedish) *Kaj*

KAIKURA African: Ground squirrel

KAIMANA Hawaiian: Power of the ocean

KAIMI Hawaiian: Seeker

KAINE Gaelic: Spelling variation of Kane

KAIPO Hawaiian: Sweetheart

KAISER German: Emperor; variant
of Caesar

KAISON English: Keeper of the keys;
modern variant of Kai

KAJETAN Italian: From the city of Gaeta

KAJIKA Native American: Walks without
sound

KAKAR Hindi: Grass

KALA Hindi: Black; God of time

KALANI Hawaiian: The sky, chieftain

KALE Hawaiian: Strong and manly

KALEO Hawaiian: One voice

KALEVA Finnish: Hero

KALF Norse: A name from a Norse medieval
saga, the stepson of Asgeir

KALIQ Arabic: Creator (God); also referred
to as Al Khallak
Khaliq, Khalek, Khaleq

KALLE Swedish: Strong, manly; a
Scandinavian variant of Karl

KAMAL Arabic, Persian: Perfection, comple-
tion. Hindi: Lotus
(Turkish) *Kemal*

KAMBIZ Persian: Fortunate

KAMRAN Persian: Successful

KANA Hawaiian: A Maui demigod who
could take the form of a rope and stretch
from Molokai to Hawaii

KANE Gaelic: Battle, warrior; *Citizen Kane*,
starring Orson Welles, is thought by many to
be one of the greatest American movies ever
made. Japanese: Putting together, money
Kaine, Kayne

KANELINQES Arthurian Legend: Father
of Tristan

KANGI Native American: Raven, crow (Sioux)
Kangee

KANIEL Hebrew: Reed

KANNAN Sanskrit: A form of Krishna

KANNON Japanese: A form of Kuan-yin, a Chinese Buddhist deity of mercy

KANO Japanese: One's masculine power; capability

KANOA Hawaiian: Free

KANSBAR Persian: Treasure master

KAPIL Hindi: From Kapila

KAPONO Hawaiian: Righteous one, proper one

KARAM Arabic: Hospitable

KARAYAN Armenian: Dark

KARDEIZ Arthurian Legend: Son of Percival

KARI Norse, Finnish: Gust of wind or curly-haired

KARIM Arabic, Persian: Generous, noble; the Koran lists Al Karim (The Generous) as one of the ninety-nine names of God. *Kareem, Kharim*; **Famous Namesakes:** *Basketball player Kareem Abdul-Jabbar, Indian religious monarch Karim Al Alami*

KARL German: Strong, manly; the writings of Karl Marx helped form the policies for the political and economic system known as communism. See also *Carl, Kalle* (Italian) *Carlo*; (Spanish) *Carlos*; (Slavic) *Karol*; (Russian) *Karolek*; (Czech) *Karel*; (Finnish) *Kaarle, Kaarlo*; (Hungarian) *Karoly*; **Famous Namesakes:** *Actor Karl Malden, Fashion Designer Karl Lagerfeld*

KARLHEINZ German: Strong, manly; a blend of Karl and Heinz

KAROL Slavic: Strong, manly; variant of Karl or Charles

> *"A name? . . . Ah, God, I've been called by a million names all my life. I don't want a name. I'm better off with a grunt or a groan for a name."*
>
> —Bernardo Bertolucci,
> *Last Tango in Paris*

KASEEB Arabic: Fertile

KASEKO African: Mock

KASEY Irish: Spelling variation of Casey

KASIM Arabic: Defender, divider, oath, portion, gift, division, protector; Kasim el Wagh is one who has a handsome face; (African) controller of anger (Egyptian) *Asim*; *Kaseem, Asem, Kasem, Kassem, Kassim, Qaseem, Qassim, Qasim*

KASIYA Egyptian: Departs

KATEB Arabic: Writer, scribe, clerk typist, novelist

KATUNGI African: Rich

KAVEH Persian: A name from Persian mythology, character in Shahnameh

KAVI Hindi: Poet

KAWA Native American: Great (Apache)

KAY Welsh, Arthurian Legend: Uncertain meaning, possibly rejoicing or fiery; in Arthurian Legend, Kay was a knight of the Round Table.

KAYAN Persian: Star

KAYONGA African: Ash

KAZI African: Work

KEAHI Hawaiian: Fiery one

KEALY Irish: Handsome

KEANAN Irish: Spelling variation of Cian

KEANU Hawaiian: Cool breeze over the mountains
Famous Namesakes: *Keanu Reeves*

KEARNEY Irish: Victorious
Carney, Karney

KEARY Celtic: Dark

KEATON English: Surname derived from a place name meaning "shed town" in Old English
Famous Namesakes: *Actor Buster Keaton, Actor Michael Keaton*

KEDRIC English: Battle or war leader; variant of Cedric
Cedric, Kedrick, Keddrick

KEEFE Irish, Gaelic: Handsome, cherished

KEEGAN Irish, Gaelic: Small and fiery
Aodhagan, Keagan, Keaghan, Kegan

KEELAN Gaelic: Slender. See also *Kellan Caolan, Kealan, Keilan, Keillan, Kelan, Kellen*;
Nicknames: *Caley, Caly*

KEENAN Irish: Spelling variation of Cian
Famous Namesakes: *Actor Keenan Ivory Wayans, Actor Keenan Wynn*

KEI Arthurian Legend: Arthur's brother
Ke

KEIJI Japanese: Joyours; Governs peacefully.

KEIR Gaelic: Dusky, dark-haired
Famous Namesakes: *Actor Keir Dullea*

KEITARO Japanese: Blessed

KEITH Irish: Forest; originally a Scottish place name, Keith was also the surname of a long line of Scottish earls.
Famous Namesakes: *English musician Keith Richards, Actor Keith Carradine, Baseball player Keith Hernandez*

KEKOA Hawaiian: The brave one

KELBY Norse: Farm near the spring

KELE Native American: Sparrow hawk (Hopi)
Kelle

KELL Norse: From the spring

KELLACH Irish: Strife

KELLAN Gaelic: Spelling variation of Keelan. African: Powerful

KELLMAN Hungarian: Variation of Clemens

KELLY Irish: Warrior or bright-minded (Gaelic) *Kellye; Kelle, Kelley, Kellee*; **Famous Namesakes:** *Dancer and actor Gene Kelly*

KELSEY English: From the island, possibly from the island of ships; (Irish) warrior (Norse) *Kelsig, Kiollsig*; **Famous Namesakes:** *Actor Kelsey Grammer*

KELVIN Gaelic, English, Celtic: From the narrow river; possibly a place name for the River Kelvin in Scotland
Kelvan, Kelven, Kelvyn, Kelwin, Kelwyn;
Famous Namesakes: *British physicist Lord Kelvin*

KEME Native American: Thunder (Algonquin)

KEMEN Basque, Spanish: Strong

KEMP English: Warrior, champion

KEMUEL Hebrew: God has raised up; Kemuel is a biblical figure and relative of Abraham.

KEN English: Nickname of Kenneth and an abbreviation of names beginning with Ken; Ken is also known as the main squeeze of the world-famous Barbie doll. Japanese: Healthy, strong
Kenn, Kennan; **Nicknames:** *Kennie, Kenny*;
Famous Namesakes: *Baseball player Ken Griffey Jr., Producer Ken Burns, Singer Kenny Rogers*

KENDALL English: Valley of the Kent; this surname has become a unisex name and likely refers to a river in England.
Kendal, Kendale, Kendel, Kendell, Kendhal;
Nicknames: *Ken, Kenny*

KENDI African: Loved one

KENDRICK Anglo-Saxon: This is a name with a disputed meaning, and there are several possibilities: royal power from the Old English name Cyneric, bold power from Old English Ceneric, high hill from the Welsh Cynwrig, or son of Henry from the Gaelic surname Mac Eanraig.
Kendric; **Nicknames:** *Kendrix*

KENELM English: Bold defender; Saint Kenelm was a ninth-century prince (or perhaps king) of Mercia.

KENJI Japanese: Intelligent second son, strong and vigorous
Nicknames: *Kenjiro*

KENLEY English: From the king's meadow; a surname and variant of Kingsley

KENNARD English: Royal guard, chieftain

KENNEDY Gaelic: Helmet-head or mis-shapen head
Famous Namesakes: *President John F. Kennedy*

KENNELLY Irish: Pledge

KENNER Gaelic: Brave chieftain

KENNETH Scottish, English: Born of fire, handsome
Nicknames: *Kenney, Kenny, Ken, Kennie*;
Famous Namesakes: *Actor Kenneth Branagh, Composer Kenneth "Babyface" Edmonds*

KENT English: Border, coast, bright white; Kent is a county in England known for its lovely countryside.

KENTARO Japanese: Sharp; big boy

KENTON English: From the royal settlement or town, likely related to the county Kent in England; surname
Kentan, Kentin, Kentun

KENTRELL English: Royal chieftain

KENWARD English: Bold guardian

KENWAY English: Bold warrior
Nicknames: *Ken*

KENYON Gaelic: Blond

KEREM Turkish: Kindness

KERMICHAEL Gaelic: From Michael's fortress

KERMIT Gaelic: Free man or without envy; a variant of Dermot. Kermit is a name made famous by Jim Henson's lovable green muppet Kermit the Frog who stars on *Sesame Street.*

KERR Gaelic: Marshland

KERRY Gaelic: Dark, dusky; refers to the county that lies along the southwestern coast of Ireland
Kerrigan; **Famous Namesakes:** *Football player Kerry Collins*

KERWIN Irish: Little dark one
Kerwen, Kerwyn

KESIN Hindi: Long-haired beggar

KESTER Latin: From the Roman camp

KETIL Norse: Sacrificial kettle
Kjell

KEVIN Irish: Handsome; name of a famous Irish hermit-saint
Cavan, Kavan, Kaven, Kevan, Keven, Keveon, Kevinn, Kevion, Kevon, Kevyn; **Nicknames:** *Kevis, Kev*; **Famous Namesakes:** *Actors Kevin Costner, Kevin Bacon, Kevin Spacey, Kevin Kline*; **Star Babies:** *Son of Tatum O'Neal and John McEnroe*

KEVORK Armenian: Farmer

KEYVAN Persian: World, universe
Kayvan

KHACHIG Armenian: Small cross

KHAJAG Armenian: Blue-eyed

KHALFANI Egyptian: Shall rule

KHALID Arabic: Eternal, immortal, glorious
Kalid; **Old Forms:** *Khaldun*; **Star Babies:** *King of Saudi Arabia Khalid Ibn Abdel Aziz*

KHALIL Arabic: Companion, friend, lover; the writings of Lebanese poet Khalil Gibran in *The Prophet* have been translated worldwide.
Kahliel, Kahlil, Kalil; **Famous Namesakes:** *Arab philologist Al Khalil Ibn Ahmad*

KHAN Arabic, Turkish: Prince; a title used by central Asian tribal chieftains and ruling princes. Khan is also an inn built around a courtyard where caravans may rest.
(Turkish) *Khanh*; *Kan*; **Famous Namesakes:** *Indian singer Ustad Salamat Ali Khan*

KHARIF Arabic: Autumn, fall; born during autumn
Karif, Kareef

KHASIB Arabic: Fertile
Khaseb, Kaseeb

KHAYRI Arabic: Generous, charitable, benevolent (act or organization); derived from Kheir, meaning goodness
Famous Namesakes: *Egyptian playwright Badie Khayri*

KHAYYAT Arabic: Tailor
Famous Namesakes: *Artist and singer Isaac Khayat*

KHONS Egyptian: God of the moon represented as a man; with Amon and Mut as father and mother, these three gods form the Theban triad.

KHOURY Arabic: Priest; this name is very popular in Lebanon, both as a first name and as a family name.
Koury; **Famous Namesakes:** *Lebanese head of state Bichara Khalil El Khoury, Egyptian author and photographer Ayman Khoury*

KHRISTOS Greek: Spelling variation of Christos

KIAN Irish: Spelling variation of Cian; (Persian) surname of the second dynasty of Persian kings

KIEFER German: Barrel maker; possibly a variation of Cooper
Keefer, Keifer, Kieffer; **Famous Namesakes:** *Actor Kiefer Sutherland*

KIERAN Gaelic, Celtic, Irish: Dark-haired; an Anglicized form of Ciaran, a popular Irish name
Ciaran, Kearn, Keiran, Kern, Kiernan, Kieron, Kyran; **Nicknames:** *Kearne, Kierce*; **Famous Namesakes:** *Actor Kieran Culkin*

KIERCE Irish: Dark-haired one; a surname and variant of Kieran

KILBY Teutonic: From the farm by the spring

KILDARE Irish: Church of the oak; a place name from County Kildare in the Irish province of Leinster
Kildaire

KIMBALL Welsh: Warrior chief; this name gained in popularity through Rudyard Kipling's novel *Kim*, a story about an orphan Irish boy growing up in India.
Kimble; **Nicknames:** *Kim*

KIMONI African: Great man

KINDIN Latin: Born fifth

KING English: King is one of several titles occasionally used as given names.

KINGDON English: From the king's hall

KINGSLEY English: From the king's meadow; surname
Kenley, Kenly, Kinsley, Rexley, Kenlea, Kenlee, Kenleigh, Kenlie, Kingslea, Kingslie, Kingsly, Kinsey, Kinslea, Kinslee, Kinslie, Kinsly;
Famous Namesakes: *Actor Ben Kingsley, English novelist Kingsley Amis*

KINGSTON English: From the king's village or estate; the Kingston Trio was a popular folk group from the San Francisco Bay area in the late 1950s and early 1960s.

KINNELL Gaelic: From the head of the cliff

KINNEY Scottish: The fire-sprung; possibly derived from Cionaodh, a compound of the elements cion meaning respect or affection and Aodh, the name of a pagan god of fire.

KINNON Scottish: Fair-born

KINNY Scottish: From the top of the cliff

KINSEY English: Victorious

KIP English: From the pointed hill
Kipp, Kippar; **Nicknames:** *Kippie*

KIRABO African: Gift from God

KIRBY English, Teutonic, Norse: Church village, Teutonic residence
Kerbie, Kerbey, Kirbey, Kirkbie, Kirkby;
Famous Namesakes: *Baseball player Kirby Puckett, Actor Bruno Kirby*

KIRK English, Scandinavian: From the church; a nickname for many male English names related to churches, such as Kirkland and Kirkwood
(Scottish) *Kerk, Kyrk; Kirke*; **Famous Namesakes:** *Actor Kirk Douglas, Actor Kirk Cameron*

KIRKAN Armenian: Watchful
Nicknames: *Kirk*

KIRKLAND English, Scottish: From the
church land; surname
(Scottish) *Kirklin, Kirklyn*; **Nicknames:** *Kirk*

KIRKLEY English: From the church's
meadow
Kirkly, Kirklea, Kirklee, Kirkleigh, Kirklie;
Nicknames: *Kirk*

KIRKWOOD English: From the forest near
the church; surname
Kyrkwode; **Nicknames:** *Kirk*

KIRYL Russian: Variation of Cyril

KIVA Hebrew: Replaces, supplants; variant
of Akiva
Kiba

KLAS Swedish: Victorious; a short form
of Nicholas and Nikolaus

KLAUS German: Nickname for Nicholas
Famous Namesakes: *German actor Klaus
Kinski*

KNIGHT English: Noble, soldier
Famous Namesakes: *Basketball coach Bobby
Knight*

KNOX English: From the hills
Knocks

KNUT Norse: Knot; a name most likely
recognized in America for the legendary
football coach Knute Rockne
Canute, Cnut, Cnute, Knud, Knute

KOHANA Native American: Swift (Sioux)

KOI Hawaiian: Urge, implore; the Hawaiian
equivalent of Troy. Native American: Panther
(Choctaw)

KOJO African: Born on Monday

KOLB Armenian: From Kolb

KOLINKAR Danish: Born to the conquering
people

KONALA Hawaiian: World ruler

KONANE Hawaiian: Bright

KONRAD German: Bold advisor, wise;
a spelling variation of Conrad
Nicknames: *Kord, Kort, Kunz*

KOREN Hebrew: Shining, beaming

KORNEL Czech: Variation of Cornelius

KORT German: Bold advisor, wise; a nickname for Conrad and Konrad

KOUROSH Persian: The first Persian king

KRATOS Greek: Strength, power

KRIKOR Armenian: Variation of Gregory

KRISTIAN Scandinavian: Variation of Christian

KRISTOFF Scandinavian: Spelling variation
of Christopher

KUDRET Turkish: Power

KULBERT German: Calm, bright

KUMAR Hindi: Prince

KURON African: Thanks

KURT German: Variation of Curtis
Famous Namesakes: *Actor Kurt Russell,
Author Kurt Vonnegut*

KURUK Native American: Bear (Pawnee)

KYLE Gaelic, Irish: A narrow strait or channel
Kile, Kylan, Kylar, Kylen, Kyler, Kyrell;
Nicknames: *Kiley, Kye;* **Famous
Namesakes:** *Actor Kyle MacLachlan, Actor
Kyle Chandler;* **Star Babies:** *Son of Clint
Eastwood*

KYLER Gaelic: A narrow strait or channel;
this variant of Kyle could also be derived
from a Dutch surname meaning archer.

KYNE English: Intelligent; variant of Conan

KYRKSEN Scottish: Dweller by the church

KYROS Greek: Master

LABAN Hebrew: White; the Old Testament
father of Rachel and Leah
Lavan

LACHLAN Scottish: Land of lakes, land of
lochs; originally a Scottish nickname for
someone from Norway
(Gaelic) *Lachlann;* (Irish) *Lochlain, Lochlann,
Loughlin; Lakeland, Laochailan;* **Nicknames:**
Lach, Lache, Laec, Laughlin

LACKO Slavic: Famous ruler

LADBROC English: Lives by the path by
the brook

LADD English: Young boy
Lad, Ladde, Laddey, Laddie, Laddy; **Famous
Namesakes:** *Actor Alan Ladd*

LADON Greek: Dragon of Hera

LAEFERTUN English: Spelling variation
of Leverton

LAERTES Greek: A character in Greek
mythology, father of Odysseus and king of
Ithaca

LAFAYETTE French: This is a surname
used as first name; at the age of twenty, the
French nobleman Marquis de Lafayette
fought for four years in the American
Revolution.

LAGMANN Norse: Lawyer

LAIDLEY English: From the meadow near
the creek; surname
Laidly, Laidlea, Laidlee, Laidleigh, Laidlie

LAILOKEN Arthurian Legend: A name
from Celtic mythology of a Scottish lord and
madman with prophetic abilities. Lailoken
may have been the source for the character
of Merlin.

LAINE English: Spelling variation of Lane

LAIRGNEN Celtic: Of Connaught

LAIS Hindi: Lion

LAIUS Greek: The mythological father of Oedipus

LAJCSI Teutonic: Famous holiness *Laji*; **Nicknames:** *Lajos*

LAL Hindi: Beloved

LAMAR French: Of the sea *Lamarr*; **Famous Namesakes:** *Senator Lamar Alexander*

LAMBERT German, French: Light of land *Lambart, Lambrecht*; **Famous Namesakes:** *Actor Christopher Lambert*

LAMBI Norse: A name from Medieval Norse saga, son of Thorbjorn the Feeble

LAMONT Scandinavian, Scottish: Man of law; a clan name *Lamond, Lemond*; **Famous Namesakes:** *Cyclist Greg LeMond*

LAMORAT Arthurian Legend: The brother of Percival

LANCE French: Assistant (Italian) *Lanzo*; **Old Forms:** *Lancelin, Lancelot, Launcelot*; **Famous Namesakes:** *Cyclist Lance Armstrong*

LANCELOT French: Assistant; Sir Lancelot was one of King Arthur's greatest and bravest knights in the legends of the Round Table. The scandal that followed his love affair with Queen Guinevere, the king's wife, led to his downfall. *Launcelot*

LANDER German: Landowner

LANDON Anglo-Saxon, English: Grassy plain

Landis, Landan, Landen, Landin; **Famous Namesakes:** *Actor Michael Landon*

LANDRY Anglo-Saxon: Ruler of the place **Famous Namesakes:** *Football coach Tom Landry*

LANE English: Path or small roadway (Scottish) *Lean, Leane*; *Laine, Layne*

LANG Anglo-Saxon: Long, tall **Nicknames:** *Lange*

LANGDON English: Ridge, long hill *Lancdon*

LANGFORD English: Lives near the long ford

LANGLEY English: From the long meadow; Langley, Virginia is well known as the home of the Central Intelligence Agency *Langleah*

LANGSTON English: From the farm of the tall man, town of the giant *Lankston, Lanston, Langsden, Langsdon, and Langton*; **Famous Namesakes:** *Poet Langston Hughes*

LANGUNDO Native American: Peaceful

LANNY English: Nickname for Roland

LANSA Native American: Lance (Hopi)

LANSTON English: From the long estate

LANTZ Yiddish: Lancer

LANY Irish: Servant

LAOCOON Greek: In Greek mythology, Laocoon was the Trojan priest who warned his countrymen against the wooden horse left by the Greeks.

LAOIDHIGH Irish: Poet, poetic

LAOMEDON Greek, Latin: The mythological father of Priam, King of Troy

LAPIDOS Hebrew: Torch
Nicknames: *Lapidoth*

LAPU Native American: Cedar bark (Hopi)

LARAMIE French: A place name and transferred surname; Laramie is a town in Wyoming named for the nineteenth-century French fur trapper Jacques Laramie.

LARCWIDE Anglo-Saxon: Counsel

LAREN Scottish: Laurel; variant of Lawrence

LARES Latin: The Lares were friendly mythological guardian spirits of households and fields.

LARGO Italian: Wide, broad; in music, *largo* indicates a very slow tempo

LARNELL English: Modern blend of the English names Larry and Darnell

LARRY English: Nickname for Lawrence
Famous Namesakes: *Basketball player Larry Bird*

LARS Scandinavian: Variation of Lawrence
Larsen, Larson, Larz

LARTIUS Latin: Lartius and his companion Herminius were legendary heroes who saved Rome.

LARUE French: Street; surname used as first name

LASALLE French: The hall; surname used as a first name

LASZLO Hungarian: Nickname for Vladislav

LATHAM Teutonic: Dwells by the barn

LATHAN English: A contemporary rhyming variant of Nathan

LATHROP English: From the farmstead with the barn; surname

LATIF Arabic, Egyptian: Gentle, kind, pleasant, nice; spelling variant of Lutfi

LATIMER English: Intepreter

LATINUS Latin: King of Latium, the kingdom from which the Roman Empire gradually emerged

LAUDALINO Latin: Praise

LAUDEGRANCE Arthurian Legend: The father of Guinevere

LAUGHLIN Irish: Nickname for Lachlan

LAUNDER English: From the grassy plain

LAUNFAL Arthurian Legend: A knight in Arthurian Legend

LAUREN English: Variation of Lawrence

LAURENZ German: Laurel. Variant of Lawrence

LAURIANO Latin: Laurel. Variant of Lawrence

LAWFORD English: From the ford at the hill

LAWLER Gaelic: Soft-spoken

LAWLEY English: From the hill meadow; surname
Lawly, Lawlea, Lawleigh, Lawlie; **Diminutive Forms:** *Law, Lawe*

LAWRENCE Latin, English: Laurel; the laurel tree is symbolic of honor and victory. The name is also considered to mean *from Laurentium*, a city in ancient Italy known for its laurel trees. Saint Lawrence was a Roman deacon and martyr. See also *Laurenz, Laren* (Latin) *Laurencho*; (English) *Loran, Loren, Lorin*; (German) *Lorenz*; (French) *Laurent*; (Italian) *Lauro, Lorenzo, Renzo*; (Gaelic) *Labhras*; (Scottish) *Labhrainn, Lorne*; (Scandinavian) *Lars, Lorens*; (Swedish) *Larz*; (Danish) *Lauritz*; (Dutch) *Laurens*; (Czech) *Vavrinec*; (Polish) *Laiurenty*; (Finnish) *Lasse, Lauri*; (Hungarian) *Lenci, Lorant, Loreca, Lorenc, Lorencz*; *Laureano, Laurente, Laurian, Lawron*; **Old Forms:** *Laurentius*; **Nicknames:** *Larry, Lauriano, Laurie, Lawrie, Lawson, Lorry*; **Famous Namesakes:** *Actor Laurence Olivier, Actor Laurence Fishburne, Musician Lawrence Welk*

LAWSON English: Laurel. Variant of Lawrence; surname meaning son of Lawrence

LAWTON English: From the hill town or settlement, possibly the town near the lake or Lawrence's town; surname *Laughton, Loughton*; **Nicknames:** *Law*

LAYNE English: Spelling variation of Lane

LAYTON English: From the meadow town or settlement; a surname and variant of Leighton

LAZARUS Hebrew: Help of God; in the Bible, Lazarus, Martha and Mary's brother, was brought back to life by Jesus Christ. The religious order of Saint Lazaro was established during the time of the Crusades. (Italian) *Lazzaro*; (Spanish) *Lazaro*; **Nicknames:** *Lazar*; **Famous Namesakes:** *Greek Lazarus the Painter*

LEAL English: Loyal, faithful

LEANDER Greek: Lion-man; a figure from Greek mythology and also the name of a sixth-century saint who became the bishop of Seville

(French) *Leandre*; (Spanish) *Leandro*; (Contemporary) *Leandrew; Liander, Liandro*; **Old Forms:** *Leandros*

LEANNAN Gaelic: Lover
(Irish) *Lennon*

LEAR English: The story of King Lear existed up to four centuries before Shakespeare's play *King Lear*. Lear was a British king who reigned before the birth of Christ. Predated by references in British mythology to Lyr or Ler, Geoffrey of Monmouth recorded a story of King Lear and his daughters in his *Historia Regum Britanniae* of 1137.

LEARY Irish: Shepherd
Laoghaire; **Famous Namesakes:** *Comedian Denis Leary*

LEAX Anglo-Saxon: Salmon

LEE English: Meadow
Lay, Leigh

LÉGER French: Name of a French saint and several French villages
Famous Namesakes: *French artist Fernand Léger*

LEGOLAS Literature: Character in *The Lord of the Rings* trilogy by J.R.R. Tolkien. Legolas is the son of the elf lord Thranduil and is an incredibly accurate archer. Legolas means green leaf in his language.

LEIB Yiddish: Lion

LEICESTER Latin: Name of the city in England founded in Roman times
Lester

LEIDOLF Norse: Wolf descendant

LEIF Scandinavian: Son, descendant; according to Norse legend, Viking Leif Ericson landed his longboat on North

American shores some 500 years before Columbus arrived in the Caribbean.
Famous Namesakes: *Actor Leif Garrett*

LEIGH English: Spelling variation of Lee
Lee

LEIGHTON English: From the meadow town or settlement; surname
Layton, Leyton

LEITH Celtic: Broad ridge
Leathan

LELAND English: From the meadow land; surname
Leeland, Leighland, Leyland

LEMAN English: From the valley

LEMUEL Hebrew: Dedicated to God; an Old Testament name

LEN Native American: Flute (Hopi). English: Bold as a lion; an abbreviation of Leonard

LENNO Native American: Man

LENNON Irish: Variation of Leannan
Famous Namesakes: *John Lennon;* **Star Babies:** *Son of Patsy Kensit and Liam Gallagher*

LENNOX Scottish, Gaelic: Surname and clan name, which was derived from the name of a district in Scotland, the Levenach. Lennox, a Scottish nobleman, appears in Shakespeare's *Macbeth.*
Lenox

LEO Latin: Lion; a popular name in ancient Rome and the name of thirteen popes; the lion is a figure in art and religious symbolism of many cultures symbolizing royalty, grandeur, and courage.
(English) *Lion;* (French) *Léon, Léonce;* (Italian) *Leone;* (Spanish) *Leon;* (Russian)
Lev; (Armenian) *Levon;* **Nicknames:** *Levka, Lewa;* **Famous Namesakes:** *Russian author Leo Tolstoy*

LEON Spanish: Variation of Leo

LEONARD German: Bold as a lion; name of a medieval saint
(German) *Leonhard;* (Italian) *Leonardo;* (Swedish) *Lennart; Leonaldo;* **Nicknames:** *Lenny, Leo;* **Famous Namesakes:** *Composer and conductor Leonard Bernstein, Artist Leonardo da Vinci, Musician Lenny Kravitz*

LEONIDAS Greek: Lion; Leonidas was a Spartan king from the fifth century B.C. who sacrificed his life defending the pass of Thermopylae from the Persians; also the name of a saint and martyr from Alexandria
(Spanish) *Leonides;* (Russian) *Leonid, Lyonya; Leonide, Leontis*

LEOPOLD German: A bold man, prince of the people
(Italian) *Leopoldo; Luitpold*

LEORAD Teutonic: Bold for his people

LERON Hebrew: The song is mine; (French) the circle; derived from le rond

LEROUX French: The red-haired one; surname sometimes used as a first name

A hare, upon meeting a lioness one day, said reproachfully, "I have always a great number of children while you have only one or two now and then."

The lioness replied, "That is true, but my one child is a lion."

–Ethiopian fable written by Lokman (c. 1100 B.C.)

LEROY French: The king
(English) *Elroy*; (French) *Leroi*; *Learoyd*,
Leeroy; **Famous Namesakes:** *Artist Leroy
Nieman*

LESLIE Scottish, Gaelic: From the gray
fortress, smaller meadow, or garden of
hollies; Leslie was derived from a Scottish
place name, became a surname, and is now
used as a first name for both sexes.
Lesley; **Famous Namesakes:** *Actor Leslie
Howard, Actor Leslie Nielsen*; **Star Babies:**
Son of Gene Hackman

LESTER English: Phonetic form of
Leicester, originally denoting a person who
was from that place

LEVERTON English: From the rush farm;
surname
Laefertun, Levertun; **Nicknames:** *Lev*

LEVI Hebrew: Joined; in the Bible, Jacob's
third son and father of the tribe of priests
(Finnish) *Leevi*; *Levey*; **Nicknames:** *Lev*

LEVKA Russian: Nickname for Leo

LEVON Armenian: Variation of Leo

LEWIS English: Renowned fighter; a form
of Louis
Nicknames: *Lew*; **Famous Namesakes:**
Author Lewis Carroll

LIAM Irish: Diminutive form of William
Famous Namesakes: *Irish actor Liam
Neeson*; **Star Babies:** *Son of Kevin Costner,
Faye Dunaway, Calista Flockhart, Rachel
Hunter and Rod Stewart*

LIANDRO Latin: Spelling variation of
Leander

LIBBY English: My God is bountiful, God of
plenty; masculine form of Elizabeth, can be
used as a surname

LIBER Latin: Free

LICHAS Greek: In Greek mythology, Lichas
was Heracles' servant. He brought the poisoned
shirt from Deianira to Heracles, killing him.

LIDMANN Anglo-Saxon: Sailor

LIFTON English: From the hillside town

LINCOLN English: Lakeside colony; this
name of an early Roman settlement in England
is widely recognized in the United States as
the surname of President Abraham Lincoln.
Nicknames: *Linc, Link*

LINDELL English: Lives in the linden tree
dell or valley; surname
*Lendall, Lendell, Lindael, Lindel, Lyndell,
Lyndale*; **Nicknames:** *Linn*; **Diminutive
Forms:** *Lin*

LINDEN English: The linden tree; this name
describes a variety of popular ornamental
shade trees
Lindon, Lyndon; **Nicknames:** *Lind, Lin,
Lindy, Lyn*; **Diminutive Forms:** *Lynd*;
Famous Namesakes: *President Lyndon
Baines Johnson*

LINDLEY English: From the linden tree
meadow; surname
Lindleigh, Lindly, Lindlea, Lindlee, Lindlie

LINDSAY English, Scottish: Island of linden
trees
Lyndsie, Lindsey

LINFORD English: Linden tree ford

LINLEY English: From the meadow of flax;
surname
Linleah, Linly, Lindlea, Lindleigh, Lindlee

LINN Anglo-Saxon: A short form of several
names beginning with Linn-; not common
as an independent name for boys

LINUS Latin: Flax; Linus is the Latin form of the Greek name Linos. In Greek legend, Linos was the son of the god Apollo and a music teacher to Heracles. Today, parents and kids will recognize Linus as the blanket-carrying *Peanuts* character.
Lino; **Famous Namesakes:** *Chemist Linus Pauling*

LINWOOD English: Lives in the linden tree grove or forest; surname
Lynwood

LIONEL Latin: Young lion
(Spanish) *Leonel*; *Lionell, Lonell*; **Famous Namesakes:** *Actor Lionel Barrymore, Musician Lionel Richie*

LISIMBA Egyptian: Lion

LIST Anglo-Saxon: Cunning

LIVINGSTON English: From Lyfing's town
Old Forms: *Lyfing*

LIWANU Native American: Growling bear (Miwok)

LLACHEU Arthurian Legend: Name of one of King Arthur's illegitimate sons

LLEWELYN Welsh: Lionlike
Lewellyn, Llewellyn

LLOYD Welsh: Gray
Floyd; **Famous Namesakes:** *Actor Lloyd Bridges*

LLYR Welsh: God of the sea
(Irish) *Lir*

LOCKE English: Lives by the stronghold; a surname referring to a lock or locksmith
Famous Namesakes: *John Locke*

LOGAN Gaelic: From the hollow
Logen, Loghan; **Star Babies:** *Son of Robert Plant*

LOHENGRIN Arthurian Legend: The son of Percival; Lohengrin is also a romantic opera by Richard Wagner.

LOIC French: Variation of Louis

LOMAN Irish: Bare

LOMBARD Latin: Long beard

LON Gaelic: Fierce; blackbird

LONATO Native American: Flint

LOOTAH Native American: Red (Sioux)

LORAN English: Variation of Lawrence

LORCAN Irish: Little fierce one
Star Babies: *Son of Peter O'Toole*

LORENZO Italian: Variation of Lawrence

LORIMAR English: Saddle maker

LORNE Scottish: Variation of Lawrence
Famous Namesakes: *Canadian actor Lorne Greene, Producer Lorne Michaels*

LORNE Scottish: Variation of Lawrence
Lauren, Loren, Lorren; **Famous Namesakes:** *Canadian actor Lorne Greene, Actor Loren Dean,* Saturday Night Live *producer Lorne Michaels*

LORNELL Scottish: Form of Lawrence

LORREN English: Form of Lauren

LOT Hebrew: A covering, veil; the biblical nephew of Abraham, Lot was miraculously delivered from the destruction of Sodom and Gomorrah.

LOTHAR German: Famous in battle
(German) *Luther*; (Italian) *Geomar, Giomar*; *Loring, Lothair, Lotharing*

LOUGHLIN Irish: Variation of Lachlan

LOUIS German, French: Famous warrior; popular French spelling of Ludwig. See also *Ludwig*
(French) *Loic, Ludovic*; (Italian) *Ludovico, Luigi*; (Irish) *Lughaidh*; (Scottish) *Luthais*; (Swedish) *Ludvik*; (Polish) *Ludwik*; *Lewis*; **Nicknames:** *Lutz, Lou, Louie, Louey*; **Famous Namesakes:** *Musician Louis Armstrong, Writer and director Louis Malle*; **Star Babies:** *Son of Mel Gibson, son of Bill Pullman*

LOUKAS Latin: Spelling variation of Luke

LOUP French: Wolf; often used in combined names like Jean-Loup
Famous Namesakes: *French author Paul-Loup Sulitzer*

LOWELL French: Young wolf
Lovell, Lowel, Lovel; **Famous Namesakes:** *Actor Lowell Sherman*

LOXIAS Greek: Oracle; one of the titles of Apollo

LOYAL French: True, faithful, unswerving

LUBOMIR Polish: Loves peace

LUBOSLAW Polish: Loves glory
Ludoslaw

LUC French: Variation of Luke

LUCAS English: Spelling variation of Luke
Lukas; **Star Babies:** *Son of Richard Marx, Willie Nelson, Mick Jagger*

LUCKY English: Fortunate; Lucky is also used as a nickname for Lucas and its variants.
Famous Namesakes: *Actor and model Lucky Vanous*

LUDLOW English: Surname derived from the name of the ancient town of Ludlow, in North Wales. Llud, in Welsh, signifies whatever connects or keeps together. Llud was also a prince of the Britons.

LUDWIG German: Famous fighter; Ludwig van Beethoven is one of the most famous composers in history. He broke the norm of composing solely for social, religious, or teaching purposes, and earned a new freedom in music composition for others.

LUFIAN Anglo-Saxon: Love

LUGHAIDH Irish: Variation of Louis

LUKA Russian: Light; the Russian form of Lucas, and Luke

LUKAS German: Variation of Luke

LUKE Greek: Light giving; Luke was a first-century Christian who wrote one of the four Gospel accounts of the life of Christ and the book of Acts. He was known as the beloved physician. See also *Luka*
(Anglo-Saxon) *Lucan*; (German) *Lukas*; (French) *Luc, Lucas, Lucien*; (Italian) *Lucca, Luciano, Lucio*; (Spanish) *Lucero*; (Polish) *Lucaas, Lucjusz, Lukasz*; (Hungarian) *Lukacs*; (Armenian) *Ghoukas*; *Loukas, Lucian, Lucious, Lucius, Luk, Luken, Lukyan*; **Famous Namesakes:** *Actor Luke Perry, Actor Luke Wilson*; **Star Babies:** *Son of Rick Schroder*

LUKMAN Egyptian: A prophet

LUNAIRE French: Moon-like, related to the moon

LUNDEN Anglo-Saxon: From London

LUNDY Scottish: Lundy Island sits off the Bristol Channel off the north coast of Devon in the United Kingdom, and many puffin live there.

LUTFI Arabic: Gentle, kind, pleasant, nice; can also be used as a family name
Loutfy, Loutfi, Lutfy

LUTHAIS Scottish: Variation of Louis

LUTHER German: Variation of Lothar
Famous Namesakes: *Civil rights activist Martin Luther King, Jr., Musician Luther Vandross*

LUTZ German: Famous fighter; a variation of Louis. A lutz is also a jump in figure skating, named after Austrian skater Alois Lutz.

LUXOVIOUS Celtic: Mythical god of Luxeuil

LYCAON Greek: A king of Arcadia

LYCOMEDES Greek: A king in the island of Scyros, to whose court Achilles, disguised as a maiden, was sent by his mother who was anxious to prevent her son from going to the Trojan War.

LYDELL English: From the open dell

LYEL Scottish: Loyal

LYFING English: Dearly loved

LYLE French: From the island *Lisle*; **Famous Namesakes:** *Musician Lyle Lovett*

LYMAN English: From the meadow

LYNN Anglo-Saxon: Lake

LYOVA Russian: Lion; a pet form of Lev
Nicknames: *Lewa*

LYSANDER Greek: Liberator; Lysander is a main character in Shakespeare's *A Midsummer Night's Dream.*
(Spanish) *Lisandro*

LYTING Norse: A name from medieval Norse saga, Lyting is the brother of Thorstein Torfi.

MAALIK African: Experience

MABLEVI African: Do not deceive

MABON Welsh, Celtic: Legendary son of Modron

MACARIO Spanish: Blessed; derived from ancient Greek and the name of several saints

MACAULEY Scottish: Righteous
Famous Namesakes: *Actor Macaulay Culkin*

MACE English: Heavy staff; a medieval weapon used by knights in the Middle Ages (Spanish) *Macerio*

MACK Scottish: Son of; nickname often used for people with surnames like McGregor, McAllister, McAndrews, etc. *Mac*

MACKAY Scottish: Son of fire

MACKENZIE Scottish: Child of the fair or wise one
Nicknames: *Kenzie, Mac*

MACKLIN Celtic: Son of Flann or form of Mack *Macklyn*

MACNAB Gaelic, Scottish: Son of the abbot *McNab, McNabb*; **Famous Namesakes:** *Quarterback Donovan McNabb*

MACON English: To make; a variant of Mason and the name of cities in France and the state of Georgia

MACSEN Welsh: Greatest

MADDOCK Welsh, Celtic: Beneficent *Maddoc, Maddog, Madoc, Madog*; **Old Forms:** *Madawc*

MADDOX English, Welsh: Son of Maddock.
Celtic: Beneficent
Madox

MADU Egyptian: Of the people

MAGNUS Latin: Great; the name of several
kings of Norway and Sweden
(Gaelic) *Maghnus, Manus*; (Finnish) *Mauno*

MAHDI Arabic: Guided to the right path;
Mahdi is the Muslim messiah, expected by some
to return and restore the true religion. This is
the title used for Mohammed's successor.
(Persian) *Mehdi*

MAHER Arabic: Skilled, skillful
Mahir; **Famous Namesakes:** *Comedian Bill
Maher*

MAHFOUZ Arabic: One who is protected;
the passive voice variant of Hafiz, which
means custodian or guardian
Mahfooz

MAHKAH Native American: Earth (Sioux)

MAHMOUD Arabic: Praised, glorified; this
variant is often used for Mohammed, the
founder of the Islamic religion.
Mahmood, Mahmud; **Famous Namesakes:**
*Ottoman sultans, Turkish Sultan Mahmud
Bigara*

MAHPEE Native American: Sky (Sioux)

MAIMUN Arabic: Lucky
Maamun

MAITLAND English: From the meadow
land, possibly from Matthew's land; surname

MAJID Persian: Great, superior
Majeed

MAKANI Hawaiian: Wind, breeze

MAKIN Arabic: Strong, firm, solid
Makeen

MALACHI Hebrew: Messenger of God;
a minor prophet in the Old Testament and
author of the biblical Book of Malachi
Malachy

MALCOLM Scottish, Gaelic: Servant of
Saint Columba; a royal name in Scotland. A
Shakespearean tragedy is based on the true
story of Prince Malcolm who became king
after Macbeth killed his father Duncan.
Nicknames: *Colm*; **Famous Namesakes:**
*British actor Malcolm McDowell, Civil rights
activist Malcolm X (né Little);* **Star Babies:**
*Son of Harrison Ford, son of Denzel
Washington*

MALEK Arabic: King, owner
Malik; **Famous Namesakes:** *Eighth-century
Arab musician Malek Ibn Abu Samah Al Tai*

MALLOGAN English: My small cove

MALLORY German: War counselor;
(French) misfortune

MALLOY Irish: Noble chief

MALONEY Irish: Serves Saint John; (Gaelic)
devoted to God

MANASSEH Hebrew: Forgetful; the Greek
variant Manasses is a Civil War battlefield in
Virginia.

MANFRED German: Man of peace
(English) *Manfrid; Manfried*; **Old Forms:**
Manfrit; **Nicknames:** *Mani, Mann*; **Famous
Namesakes:** *German chemist Manfred Eigen,
Musician Manfred Mann*

MANKATO Native American: Blue earth
(Sioux)
Mahecate, Monecato

MANLEY English: From the man's meadow; a name with connotations of masculinity
Manly, Mannleah, Manlea, Manleigh

MANNING English: Son of a hero

MANNIS Gaelic: Great

MANO Hawaiian: Shark

MANSFIELD English: From the field by the small river; surname
Maunfeld

MANSOUR Arabic: Triumphant, supported by God
Mansoor; **Famous Namesakes:** *Persian musician Mansour, Iranian tennis player Mansour Bahrami*

MANTON Anglo-Saxon, English: From the man's (or possibly Mann's) town or settlement, from the hero's settlement; surname
Manten, Mannton; **Nicknames:** *Man*

MANU Hindi: Wise; a ruler of the earth

MANUEL Spanish: Variation of Emmanuel
Nicknames: *Manny, Mano, Manolito, Manolo, Manuelo;* **Famous Namesakes:** *Shoe designer Manolo Blahnik*

MANVILLE French: From the great town
Mandeville, Manneville, Manvel, Manvil

MANZO Japanese: Ten thousand-fold-strong third son

MARCEL French: Warlike, hammer; a variant of Mark
(French) *Marceau;* (Italian) *Marcello, Marcelo; Marcell, Marcellin, Marcely;* **Old Forms:** *Marcellus;* **Diminutive Forms:** *Marcelino;* **Famous Namesakes:** *French mime Marcel Marceau;* **Star Babies:** *Son of Dr. Dre*

MARCUS Latin: Hammer; a popular name in Roman times, as evidenced by the naming two famous Romans: emperor and philosopher Marcus Aurelius and statesman Marcus Tullius Cicero.
Famous Namesakes: *Football player Marcus Allen, Civil rights activist Marcus Garvey;* **Star Babies:** *Son of Michael Jordan*

MARDEN English: From the valley with the pool; surname used as a given name
Mardon

MAREO Japanese: Rare

MARIKA Slavic: A nymph; also a variant of Mary or Maria

MARINO Latin: Of the sea
Famous Namesakes: *Quarterback Dan Marino*

MARIO Latin, Italian, Spanish: A name of uncertain meaning, possibly derived from a Roman family name Marius indicating the Roman war god Mars; derived from the Latin root mas, meaning manly; or used as a masculine variation of Mary, meaning bitter and most often given in honor of the Virgin Mary.
(Spanish) *Mariano;* **Old Forms:** *Marius;* **Famous Namesakes:** *Politician Mario Cuomo, Racing driver Mario Andretti, Hockey player Mario Lemieux*

MARK Latin: Warlike, of Mars (the god of war); the biblical Mark, sometimes called John Mark, was a missionary companion to Peter and Paul and writer of one of the four Gospel accounts of the life of Jesus; (Arthurian Legend) Tristan's uncle
(Latin) *Markel;* (German) *Markell, Marx;* (French) *Marc;* (Italian) *Marciano, Marcio, Marco, Marquise;* (Spanish) *Marcos;* (Irish) *Marcas;* (Welsh) *Mawrth;* (Scandinavian) *Marten;* (Dutch) *Markos, Markus;* (Czech) *Marek;* (Finnish) *Markku;* (Hungarian)

Marton; (Hawaiian) *Maleko*; *Marq, Marque, Martel, Martell, Martyn*; **Nicknames:** *Markey, Marty*; **Famous Namesakes:** *Actor Mark Wahlberg, Swimmer Mark Spitz, Baseball player Mark McGwire, Roman general and statesman Mark Antony*

MARLEY English: Near the meadow by the lake; surname
Marleigh, Marly, Marlea; **Famous Namesakes:** *Musician Bob Marley*

MARLOWE English: Marshy; from the hill by the lake
Famous Namesakes: *Christopher Marlowe*

MARMION French: Small one; also title of popular narrative poem by Sir Walter Scott
Marmeon, Marmyon

MARQUIS French: A title name ranking below duke and above earl
(Spanish) *Marquez*; (Portuguese) *Marques*; **Famous Namesakes:** *Baseball player Marquis Grissom*

MARSH English: From the marsh

MARSHALL French: Horse-keeper, steward; an occupational name and a common family name in Scotland
Marshal; **Famous Namesakes:** *Department store founder Marshall Field, Football player Marshall Faulk, Media theorist Marshall McLuhan*

MARSTON English: From the town or settlement near the marsh; surname
Marsden, Marsten, Merestun; **Star Babies:** *Son of Hugh Hefner*

MARTIN Latin: Warlike; another name originating from Mars, the Roman god of war
(Italian) *Martino*; (Spanish) *Martinez*; (Gaelic) *Mairtin, Martainn*; (Polish) *Marcinek*; (Finnish) *Martti*; *Martel, Martial, Martinien, Morten*; **Old Forms:** *Martinus*; **Nicknames:**

Marton; **Famous Namesakes:** *Civil rights leader Martin Luther King, Jr., Director Martin Scorsese, Theologian Martin Luther*

MARVIN English: Friend of the sea
Marven, Marvyn, Marwin, Marwyn; **Famous Namesakes:** *Composer Marvin Hamlisch, Singer Marvin Gaye*

MASAO Japanese: Righteous

MASLIN French: Little Thomas
Masselin

MASON French: Stone worker; from French word *maçon*
Macon, Masson; **Famous Namesakes:** *Actor Mason Adams*; **Star Babies:** *Son of Cuba Gooding Jr., son of Josie Bissett and Rob Estes*

MASOUD Arabic: Fortunate, lucky
(Egyptian) *Masud*; *Massoud*

MASSIMO Italian: Variation of Maximilian

MATHER English: Powerful army

MATIN Arabic: Strong, solid, firm, hard

MATOSKAH Native American: White bear
(Sioux)

MATTHEW Hebrew: Gift of God; the biblical Matthew was one of Christ's apostles and author of the first gospel in the New Testament.
(Hebrew) *Machau, Matyas, Misi, Miska*; (German) *Matthias*; (French) *Mathieu, Matthieu*; (Italian) *Matteo*; (Spanish) *Matias*; (Portuguese) *Mateus*; (Welsh) *Mathias*; (Swedish) *Mats, Matteus, Mattias*; (Russian) *Matvey*; (Ukrainian) *Matviyko*; (Finnish) *Matti*; (Hawaiian) *Makaio*; *Mathew, Mayhew*; **Nicknames:** *Mate, Matej, Mateo, Mathe, Matro, Matt, Matusha, Matz*; **Famous Namesakes:** *Actors Matthew Broderick, Matthew McConaughey, and Matt Damon*;

writer and producer Matt Groening;
Star Babies: *Son of Elvis Costello,*
Christopher Reeve, Rob Lowe, Connie Chung
and Maury Povich

MAURICE French: Moorish; dark skinned
(Latin) *Mauritins*; (Greek) *Maur*; (English)
Morse; (German) *Moritz*; (Italian) *Maurio*,
Maurizio; (Spanish) *Maricio, Mauricio,*
Mauritio; (Welsh) *Myrick*; (Russian) *Moriz*;
(Finnish) *Mauri*; (Hungarian) *Moricz*;
Mauro, Merek, Moor, Moore, Morell; **Old**
Forms: *Mauricius*; **Nicknames:** *Maury,*
Morie, Morrey, Morrie; **Famous Namesakes:**
French actor and singer Maurice Chevalier,
Children's book author Maurice Sendak,
Musician Maurice Gibb

MAVERICK Contemporary: Independent;
when a nineteenth-century American named
Maverick refused to brand his calves as other
ranchers did, his name came to signify an
independent man who avoids conformity.
Mavrick

MAX Latin: Greatest; a nickname for names
such as Maximilian and Maxwell, but also an
independent name
Star Babies: *Son of Dustin Hoffman*

MAXFIELD English: From Mack or Max's
field; surname
Maxfeld; **Nicknames:** *Max*; **Famous**
Namesakes: *Painter Maxfield Parrish*

MAXIMILIAN Latin: Greatest; Maximilian I
reigned as the Holy Roman Emperor from
1493 to 1519, while the Vienna-born
Ferdinand Maximilian Joseph ruled as
emperor of Mexico from 1864 to 1867.
(English) *Maxton*; (German) *Maximillian*;
(French) *Maxence, Maxime*; (Italian)
Massimo, Maximiliano, Maximino, Maximo;
(Russian) *Maxim*; (Polish) *Maksym,*
Maksymilian; *Maximos*; **Old Forms:**
Maximus; **Nicknames:** *Mac, Mack, Max*;
Famous Namesakes: *Austrian actor*

Maximilian Schell; **Star Babies:** *Son of*
Jeremy Irons

MAXWELL Anglo-Saxon, Scottish: From
Marcus' pool or well; a surname
Nicknames: *Max*; **Star Babies:** *Son of*
Andrew Dice Clay

MAYER Latin, German: Great or mayor
Mayor; **Famous Namesakes:** Businessman
Oscar Mayer

MAYFIELD English: From the strong man's
field; surname
Mayfeld

MAYNARD Anglo-Saxon: Powerful, brave
Mayne, Maynor; **Famous Namesakes:** *Jazz*
musician Maynard Ferguson, Economist John
Maynard Keynes

MAYO Gaelic: Lives near the yew trees; this
name of a county in Ireland is likely more
recognized in the United States as that of
Mayo Clinic, one of the world's largest
medical centers.

MEAD English: From the meadow; a surname
possibly related to the rich honey wine
(Irish) *Meade*; *Maed*

MECCUS Anglo-Saxon: Son of Gus

MEDUS Greek: Son of Medea by Aegeus;
Medus conquered barbarians after having
come to Colchis with his mother, and called
his kingdom Media after himself.

MEDWIN Teutonic: Powerful friend
Medwine, Medwyn

MEHRDAD Persian: Gift from the sun

MEINHARD German: Firm; see also
Maynard
Meinke, Meinrad, Meinyard; **Nicknames:**
Meino

MEIR Hebrew: Enlightens
Meyer

MEL English: A nickname for Melvin and other names beginning with Mel.
Famous Namesakes: *Actor and director Mel Gibson, Actor and filmmaker Mel Brooks, Voice specialist Mel Blanc*

MELBOURNE English: From the mill stream
Melborn, Melburn, Melbyrne; **Nicknames:** *Mel*

MELCHIOR Persian: King; according to tradition, Melchior was one of the three wise men who traveled a long distance to see the baby Jesus.
Melchoir, Melker

MELDON English: From the hillside mill

MELDRICK English: From the powerful mill
Meldrik

MELICERTES Greek: In Greek legend, the son of the Boeotian prince Athamas

MELRONE Irish: Servant of Saint Ruadhan

MELVILLE French, Anglo-Saxon: Busy, industrious town; surname used as first name
Mellville; **Nicknames:** *Mel*; **Famous Namesakes:** *Author Herman Melville*

MELVIN English: Mill friend; (Celtic) leader or chief
Malvin, Malvyn, Melvon, Melvyn; **Nicknames:** *Mel*

MEMPHIS Contemporary: A city in Tennessee; Memphis was also the first capital of ancient Egypt.

MENACHEM Hebrew: Comfort

MENASHE Hebrew: Forgetful

MENDEL German: One who repairs

MENELAUS Greek: In Greek legend, Menelaus was the son of Atreus and the brother of Agamemnon. He was married to Helen, and became the ruler of Helen's homeland, Lacedaemon.

MERCER English: Merchant
Mercher; **Nicknames:** *Merce*; **Famous Namesakes:** *Jazz musician Mercer Ellington (son of Duke Ellington), choreographer Merce Cunningham*

MEREDITH Welsh: Magnificient chief or protector
Meridith

MERLE French: Blackbird
Merla; **Famous Namesakes:** *Singer Merle Haggard*

MERLIN Anglo-Saxon, French: Falcon; in Arthurian Legend, the wizard Merlin was King Arthur's mentor.
Marlan, Marlin, Marlon, Merlion, Merlyn; **Famous Namesakes:** *Football player Merlin Olsen*

MERLOW English: From the hill by the lake
Merlo, Merloe

MERRICK Welsh: Dark-skinned, a Moor; variant of Maurice
Merrik

MERRILL English: Shining sea. Teutonic: Famous
Merril

MERRITT English: Little famous one

MERTON English, Anglo-Saxon: From the estate by the lake

MERVIN English: Hill by the sea or a famous friend; sometimes used as a form of Merlin *Merwin, Merwyn*; **Old Forms:** *Mervyn*

MEYER Hebrew: Spelling variation of Meir

MICAH Hebrew: Who is like the Lord; a variant of Michael. Micah was a prophet and writer of the biblical book that bears his name. *Mycah*; **Star Babies:** *Son of Neil Diamond*

MICHAEL Hebrew: Who is like the Lord; an archangel of Jewish and Christian scripture, Michael is portrayed as a warrior and leader of heaven's armies who defeats and casts out the dragon in the Book of Revelation. Michael has been such a popular name throughout history that a list of famous Michaels would contain hundreds of individuals, including emperors, politicians, writers, poets, actors, sports heroes, and more. See also *Miguel, Misha* (Hebrew) *Mika, Mikel*; (Latin) *Mikelle*; (Greek) *Mikhalis, Mikhos*; (French) *Michel*; (Italian) *Michele*; (Spanish) *Migel, Migueo*; (Gaelic) *Micheil*; (Irish) *Mícheál*; (Welsh) *Mihangel*; (Scandinavian) *Mikael, Mikell, Mikkel*; (Basque) *Miquel*; (Slavic) *Miko*; (Russian) *Mikhail, Mischa*; (Polish) *Michal*; (Ukrainian) *Mychajlo*; (Finnish) *Mikko*; (Hungarian) *Mihaly; Maichail, Micah, Michail, Micael, Mical, Michiel, Mihail, Mikol, Mycah, Mychal, Mykal, Mykell*; **Nicknames:** *Mick, Mickey, Miikka, Mike, Micky, Mikey, Miky*; **Diminutive Forms:** *Mishenka*; **Famous Namesakes:** *Singer Michael Jackson, Actors Michael Douglas and Michael Caine, Basketball player Michael Jordan, Russian President Mikhail Gorbachev*; **Star Babies:** *Son of Julio Iglesias, Kelly Ripa, Natasha Richardson and Liam Neeson*

MICHELANGELO Italian: A blend of Michael and Angelo; Italian artist Michelangelo Buonarroti is one of history's greatest painters and sculptors. His works are famous throughout the world, including *David, The Pieta,* and the Sistine Chapel.

MICHIO Japanese: Road, husband

MIDAS Greek: In Greek mythology, everything King Midas touched turned to gold.

MIGUEL Spanish: Who is like the Lord; a variant of Michael *Migel, Migueo*; **Nicknames:** *Mico*

MIKI Japanese: Trunk of tree

MIKLOS Czech: Variation of Nicholas

MIKSA Latin: Greatest

MILAD Persian: Birth

MILAN Czech: The favored one or beloved one; also the name of Italy's second largest city
Famous Namesakes: *Czech author Milan Kundera*

MILAP Native American: Charitable

MILBURN English: From the mill stream

MILES Latin, Greek, English: Soldier; sometimes used as a variant of Michael *Myles*; **Famous Namesakes:** *Jazz musician Miles Davis*; **Star Babies:** *Son of Lionel Richie, son of Susan Sarandon and Tim Robbins*

MILFORD English: From the mill's ford

MILLARD English: Miller, one who grinds grain; occupational surname used as first name
Famous Namesakes: *President Millard Fillmore*

MILLER English: One who grinds grain; an occupational name *Millen*; **Famous Namesakes:** *Playwright Arthur Miller, Bandleader and musician Glenn Miller*

MILO English, Greek: Soldier; form of Miles *Mylo*; **Star Babies:** *Son of Mel Gibson, Camryn Manheim, Ricki Lake*

MILOS Slavic, Czech: Pleasant

MILOSLAV Slavic: Lover of glory

MILTON English: From the mill town or settlement, possibly from the middle town or settlement; surname *Millton, Milten, Miltin, Miltun, Mylton*; **Nicknames:** *Milt, Milty*; **Famous Namesakes:** *Comedian Milton Berle*

MINNINNEWAH Native American: Whirlwind (Cheyenne)

MINORU Japanese: Bear fruit, ripen

MINOS Greek, Latin: In Greek mythology, Minos is the son of Zeus and the King of Crete.

MIRO Finnish: Variation of Miroslav

MIRON Polish: Peace

MIROSLAV Russian: Peaceful (Finnish) *Miro*; *Miroslaw*

MISHA Russian: Who is like the Lord; a familiar form of Michael, also meaning bear cub in Russian
Nicknames: *Mishka*; **Diminutive Forms:** *Mishenka*

MISU Native American: Rippling brook (Miwok)

MITCHELL Hebrew: Who is like the Lord; a variant of Michael *Mitchel*; **Nicknames:** *Mitch*

MOCHNI Native American: Talking bird (Hopi)

MODESTUS Latin: Modest *Modeste, Modesto*

MOGENS Danish, Dutch: Powerful

MOHAMMAD Arabic: Praiseworthy, glorified; Mohammad was the founder of the Islamic religion. Derived from hamd, meaning giving thanks (usually to God). (Persian) *Hamed*; *Hamden, Hamdun, Hamid, Hammad, Humayd, Mahmoud, Muhammad*; **Nicknames:** *Hamada, Hammouda*

MOHAN Hindi: The deluder

MOHSEN Persian: One who does good

MOJAG Native American: Never silent

MOKETAVATO Native American: Black kettle (Cheyenne)

MOLIMO Native American: Bear walking into shade (Miwok)

MONGWAU Native American: Owl (Hopi)

MONROE Gaelic, Scottish: From the mount on the river Row *Munro, Munroe*; **Famous Namesakes:** *President James Monroe*

MONTAGUE French: Pointed mountain; Romeo's surname in Shakespeare's *Romeo and Juliet* (Italian) *Montae*; *Montagew, Montaigu*

MONTANA Latin: Mountain; a northwestern US state (French) *Montagne*; **Famous Namesakes:** *Quarterback Joe Montana*; **Star Babies** *Son of Laurence Fishburne, son of Richard Thomas*

MONTGOMERY English: From the wealthy man's mountain; Montgomery is also the state capital of Alabama. (Italian) *Montay, Montes, Montez*;

Nicknames: *Monte, Montie, Monty*; **Famous Namesakes:** *Actor Montgomery Clift*

MONTREAL French: Royal mountain; a city in Quebec
Montrell, Montrelle

MONTY English: Nickname for Montgomery
Famous Namesakes: *Game show host Monty Hall*

MOORE Irish: Marshland; a moor

MORAD Persian: Desire, wish

MORDECAI Hebrew: Servant of Marduk; in the Old Testament, Mordecai was the cousin and caretaker of Esther.

MORELEY English: From the meadow on the moor; surname
Morlee, Morly, Moorley, Moorly, Morleigh, Morrley; **Famous Namesakes:** *Newsman Morley Safer*

MOREN Welsh: Legendary son of Iaen

MORGAN Welsh: Circling sea; originally a surname and given name for boys, Morgan has become frequently used for girls also.
Famous Namesakes: *Actor Morgan Freeman*

MORIO Japanese: Actively vigorous

MORITZ German: Variation of Maurice

MORRELL Latin: Swarthy

MORRIS Latin: Dark-skinned, a Moor; an English form of Maurice

MORTEZA Persian: Chosen

MORTIMER Latin: Dwells by the still water
Mortemer; **Nicknames:** *Mort*; **Famous Namesakes:** *Author Mortimer J. Adler*

MORTON English: From the town or settlement near the moors; surname
Morten, Mortin, Mortun

MORVAN Gaelic: The big gap or big peak

MORVEN Welsh: Lives by the sea; a district in North Argyll Scotland. See also *Morvan Morvin, Morvyn, Moryn*

MOSES Hebrew: Saved from the water; Moses was the biblical prophet who received the ten commandments, led the oppressed Jewish people out of Egypt, and founded the state of Israel. He was born in ancient Egypt in the town of Goshen. Just before his birth, Pharaoh had ordered that all male Hebrew infants be put to death. Moses' mother placed him in a basket made of papyrus and set it floating on the Nile, where it was found by Pharaoh's daughter, who raised Moses as her own child.
(Arabic) *Musa*; (Spanish) *Moises*; *Mozes*; **Old Forms:** *Mosheh*; **Nicknames:** *Moshe, Moss*; **Famous Namesakes:** *Basketball player Moses Malone, Baseball player Moises Alou*

MOSI African: Born first

MOSWEN African: Light-colored skin

MOTEGA Native American: New arrow

MOUKIB Arabic: Last of the prophets

MUATA Native American: Yellow jackets inside a nest (Miwok)

MUDAWAR Arabic: Round

MUHUNNAD Arabic: Sword

MUIR Scottish: From the moor

MUKHTAR Arabic: Chosen

MUKKI Native American: Child
(Algonquin)

MUNA Arabic: Desire, aspiration
Omneya

MUNDY Irish: From Reamonn

MUNI Hindi: One who teaches the truth

MURACO Native American: White moon

MURDOCK Scottish: Protector of the sea
Murdoc, Murdoch; **Famous Namesakes:**
Media magnate Rupert Murdoch

MURPHY Irish: Sea warrior
Murphey, Murfee; **Nicknames:** *Murph*

MURRAY Celtic: Protects the sea; children
may recognize this name as belonging to
Murray, the red-shirted musician of The
Wiggles. Scottish: Ancient Scottish clan
surname and a place name now called Moray
Murry; **Old Forms:** *Murtagh*; **Famous
Namesakes:** *Actor Bill Murray, Actor F.
Murray Abraham*

MYLES Latin: Spelling variation of Miles
Star Babies: *Son of Eddie Murphy*

MYRON Greek: Derived from myrrh;
myrrh, an aromatic gum resin obtained from
several Asian or African trees and shrubs, is
used in making perfume and incense. Arabic:
The name Myron (accent on the second syllable) is the Arabic name of the
Confirmation Sacrament in Christianity.

NAAMAN Hebrew: Pleasant, sweet, beautiful;
in the Bible, Naaman was the general of the
army of Aram.

NAASIR African: Defender

NAB Scottish: Abbot

NABIL Arabic: Noble
Nabeel

NACHMAN Hebrew: Compassionate

NADAV Hebrew: Noble, generous; the biblical
Nadav was the oldest son of Aaron, the high
priest.
Nadiv

NADIM Arabic: Friend, companion, someone
to confide in
Nadeem

NADIR Arabic: Rare, precious
Nader; **Famous Namesakes:** *Persian King
Nadir Shah*

NAFTALI Hebrew: To wrestle or be crafty or
a comparison; in the Bible, the sixth son of
Jacob
Naftalie; **Nicknames:** *Naf*

NAHUM Hebrew: Compassionate; a biblical
tribesman of Judah

NAISER African: Founder of clans

NAJIB Arabic: Generous, noble-born,
excellent; Egyptian Naguib Mohammad
was one of the Free Officers who planned
and executed the overthrow of the British
occupation of Egypt.
(Egyptian) *Naguib; Nagib, Nageeb, Najeeb*;
Famous Namesakes: *Egyptian novelist
Naguib Mahfouz*

NAJJAR Arabic: Carpenter
(Egyptian) *Naggar*

NAMIR Hebrew: Leopard

NANSEN Swedish: Nancy's son

NAOIS Celtic: Mythical warrior

NAPOLEON Italian: Man from Naples; Napoleon will likely always be linked with French emperor Napoleon Bonaparte, a great military genius who created an enormous empire.

NARAYAN Hindi: The house of beings

NARCISSUS Greek: Daffodil; in Greek mythology, Narcissus fell in love with his own reflection—giving us the term Narcissism. *Narcisse*; **Nicknames:** *Narkis*

NARDO German: Nickname for Bernard

NARIUS Latin: Cheerful
(Italian) *Nario*; **Nicknames:** *Nari*

NARMER Egyptian: Name of a king

NASH English: Cliff

NASIM Arabic, Persian: Breeze, fresh air; Sham el Nasim, or smell the breeze, is an Egyptian spring festival that takes place the day after Easter in commemoration of Pharaonic spring and Nile festivals, and is celebrated by Muslims and Christians alike. *Nassim, Naseem*

NASSER Arabic: Victorious, supporting, protector; President Gamal Abdel Nasser was the first president of Egypt.

NASSOR Egyptian: Victor

NASTAS Native American: Curve like foxtail grass (Navajo)

NAT Hebrew: Gift from God; a short form of Nathan and Nathaniel
Famous Namesakes: *Singer Nat King Cole*

NATAL Spanish: Born at Christmas

NATHAN Hebrew: Gift from God; the biblical Nathan was a prophet during the reigns of David and Solomon. Nathan Hale was a courageous American patriot and spy of the Revolutionary War, and one of America's earliest heroes.
Nicknames: *Nate*; **Famous Namesakes:** *Actor Nathan Lane*; **Star Babies:** *Son of Mark Hamill, son of Leeza Gibbons*

NATHANIEL Hebrew: Gift from God or born on Christmas; one of Christ's twelve disciples
(French) *Nathanael*; *Natanael, Nataniel, Nathanial, Nethanel*; **Nicknames:** *Nat, Nate, Nathan*; **Star Babies:** *Son of Jonathan and Renee Davis*

NAVID Persian: Good news
Naveed

NAZAIRE French: Blessed; based on Hebrew name

NEALON Celtic: Spelling variation of Neil

NEB Welsh: Legendary son of Caw

NECHEMYA Hebrew: Comforted by the Lord
Nechemia, Nechemiah

NED English: Diminutive form of Edward
Star Babies: *Son of Dave Foley and Tabitha Southley*

NEFEN German: Nephew
Nefin; **Nicknames:** *Nef, Neff*

NEHEMIAH Hebrew: Comforted by God; an Old Testament leader of the Jews responsible for numerous political and religious reforms
Nicknames: *Nemo, Nemos*

NEIL Gaelic: Champion; a dynasty of Irish kings was founded by Niall of the Nine Hostages.
(English) *Neal, Niles*; (Spanish) *Niguel*; (Scandinavian) *Nils*; *Neale, Neall, Nealon, Neill, Nigel*; **Famous Namesakes:** *Astronaut Neil Armstrong, Singer Neil Diamond, Singer Neil Young*

NEKA Native American: Wild goose

NELEUS Greek: Mythic son of Poseidon and Tyro, twin brother of Pelias, and father of Nestor, Neleus became king of Pylos but angered Heracles, who killed him.

NELS Celtic: Nickname for Nelson

NELSON English: Son of Neil
Nicknames: *Nels*

NEMESIO Spanish: Justice

NEPTUNE Latin: The mythological god of water; Neptune is also is one of the two planets in our solar system that cannot be seen from Earth with the naked eye.

NEREUS Greek: A mythological name of uncertain meaning; god of the sea and the nereids

NESTOR Greek: Traveler; ruler of Pylos and a great warrior of Greek mythology, Nestor was known for his wisdom and longevity.
(Spanish) *Nestorio*

NEVILLE French, English: From the new town
Old Forms: *Neuveville*; **Famous Namesakes:** *British Prime Minister Neville Chamberlain*

NEVIN Gaelic, Teutonic: Worships the saints
Nevan, Nevins, Nevyn

NEWTON Anglo-Saxon, English: From the new town or settlement; surname; evocative of scientist Sir Isaac Newton
Newtun; **Nicknames:** *Newt*

NIALL Irish: Champion or passionate; variant of Neil
(Scandinavian) *Nijel*; *Nigel*

NICHOLAS Greek: Victorious; this New Testament name grew in popularity through Saint Nicholas, a fourth-century bishop known as the patron saint of sailors, travelers, bakers, merchants, and especially children. Saint Nicholas is now best known in the United States as Santa Claus, a name that comes from Sinterklaas, which is Dutch for Saint Nicholas.
(Greek) *Nicolaus, Niklaus, Nikolos*; (English) *Colson, Nickson*; (German) *Nickolaus, Nikolaus*; (French) *Nicolas*; (Italian) *Niccolo*; (Spanish) *Nicanor*; (Gaelic) *Neacal, Niocol*; (Scottish) *Neakail*; (Scandinavian) *Neilson, Nielsson, Nilsen*; (Swedish) *Niklas, Nils*; (Danish) *Niels*; (Dutch) *Nicolaas*; (Slavic) *Miklas, Mikolas, Nicholai*; (Russian) *Nicolai, Nikolai*; (Czech) *Miklos*; (Polish) *Mikolaj*; (Finnish) *Niilo, Teemu*; *Nicholaus, Nickolas, Nikolajis, Nikolas*; **Nicknames:** *Cole, Coley, Colin, Klas, Klaus, Kolya, Nick, Nicky, Nico, Nicol, Nicoli, Nicolo, Nik, Nikki, Nikko, Niklos, Niko, Nikos, Nilo, Nilos*; **Famous Namesakes:** *Actor Nicolas Cage, Actor Nicholas Brendon*; **Star Babies:** *Son of Vanna White, Gene Simmons, Phil Collins*

NICK English: Nickname for Nicholas
Famous Namesakes: *Actor Nick Nolte*

NICODEMUS Greek: Victory of the people; in the Bible, Nicodemus was a Pharisee and a member of the Jewish court in Jerusalem. He later helped entomb Christ's body.
(Polish) *Nikodem*

NIGAN Native American: Ahead

NIGEL Gaelic: Champion; from the Irish Gaelic name Niall
Nijel; **Famous Namesakes:** *Actor Nigel Hawthorne*

NIK Persian: Good

NIKITA Russian: Unconquered
Old Forms: *Aniketos*; **Famous Namesakes:** *Soviet premier Nikita Kruschev*

NIKITI Native American: Round or smooth

NILES Scandinavian: Son of Neil

NISSIM Hebrew: Miracle

NITIS Native American: Friend (Delaware)

NIXON English: Abbreviation of Nicholas, possibly meaning Nick's son; the mythological Nike was the Greek goddess of victory and root origin of Nicholas.
Nixen; **Famous Namesakes:** *President Richard Nixon*

NIYOL Native American: Wind (Navajo)

NOAH Hebrew: To comfort; in the Old Testament, God chose Noah to build a great ark that kept him, his family, and enough animals to repopulate the earth alive during the Great Flood which lasted forty days and forty nights.
(Spanish) *Noe*; (Dutch) *Noach*; **Famous Namesakes:** *Actor Noah Wyle*; **Star Babies:** *Son of Jason Alexander, Thom Yorke, Kim Alexis*

NODIN Native American: Wind

NOEL French: Born on Christmas or Christ's birth
Natalio, Noell, Nohle; **Famous Namesakes:** *Singer Noel Gallagher*

NOLAN Irish: Noble and renowned
Noland, Nolen, Nolyn

NORBERT German, English: Shining one from the north; (Norse) hero
(Spanish) *Norberto*

NORCROSS English: From the northern crossroads; surname
Northcross; **Nicknames:** *North*

NORMAN English, German, French: From the north, northerner; the name Norman appeared before the French Norman Conquest, and therefore while both names may come from the same root, they are not as directly linked as may first appear.
(German) *Normand*; (Spanish) *Normando*; **Nicknames:** *Norm*; **Famous Namesakes:** *Artist Norman Rockwell, Author Norman Mailer*

NORRIS French, English: From the north, northerner; based on Old French surname
Famous Namesakes: *Author Frank Norris*

NORTHCLIFF English: From the northern cliff; surname
Northclif, Northcliffe, Northclyf

NORTHROP English: From the northern farm; surname
Northrup

NORTON Anglo-Saxon, English: From the northern town or settlement; surname
Northtun, Nortin; **Famous Namesakes:** *Actor Edward Norton*

NORVILLE Anglo-Saxon: From the north village or estate; surname
(Scottish) *Norval*; *Norvel*

NORVIN English: Friend from the north; surname
Norwin, Norwyn

NORWARD English: Northern guardian; surname. Teutonic: Guardian of the north road
Northward

NORWELL English: From the northern well or spring; surname
Norwel, Northwell

NORWOOD English: From the northern woods; surname
Northwode, Northwood; **Nicknames:** *North*

NOSHI Native American: Father (Algonquin)

NOUR Egyptian: Light, luminous
Nur; **Famous Namesakes:** *Egyptian actor Nour el Sherif*

NUDAR Arabic: Pure gold or silver

NUNCIO Latin: Messenger
Nunzio

NURI Hebrew: My fire

NYLE English: Island; (Celtic) champion. Anglo-Saxon: Desire

OAKDEN English: From the oak tree valley

OAKES English: Near the oaks
Okes

OAKLEY English: From the oak tree meadow; a surname and variant of Ackerley
Oaklea, Oaklee, Oakleigh, Oaklie, Oakly

OBADIAH Hebrew: Servant of God; a minor Old Testament prophet
Obediah, Ovadiah, Oved

OBERON German: Highborn and bear-like; the most famous Oberon is Shakespeare's king of the fairies in *A Midsummer's Night Dream*. (French) *Obéron; Auberon, Oberron, Oeberon*

OCEANUS Greek: Father of the Oceanids; in Greek mythology, Oceanus was a Titan father of rivers and water nymphs.

OCHEN African: Twin

OCTAVIUS Latin: Eighth
(French) *Octave*; (Spanish) *Octavio, Tavio; Octavian*; **Nicknames:** *Tavey*; **Famous Namesakes:** *Mexican poet Octavio Paz*

ODAKOTA Native American: A friend (Sioux); variant of Dakota

ODDVAR Norse: The spear's point

ODED Hebrew: To restore

ODELL English: Of the valley, or an old English place name and surname meaning woad hill; woad is an Old World plant formerly grown for its leaves that yield a blue dye.
Odale, Odayle, Odel

ODILO Teutonic: Rich in battle

ODIN Norse: A chief deity of Norse mythology, Odin is the god of war and death, poetry and culture.

ODION African: First child of the twins

ODON Anglo-Saxon: Wealthy defender; variant of Edmund
Odin; **Nicknames:** *Odi, Ody*

ODRAN Irish, Gaelic: Little pale green one
Odhran, Oran

ODYSSEUS Greek: Wrathful; the clever and resourceful mythological hero of Homer's epic *The Odyssey*.
Ulysses

OEDIPUS Greek: Swollen foot; Oedipus was the king of Thebes in Greek mythology who unknowingly killed his father and married his mother. The story led to the term "Oedipus complex," first used by Sigmund Freud.

OFER Hebrew: Fawn
Ofar

OGALEESHA Native American: Red shirt wearer (Sioux)

OGDEN English: From the oak tree valley; surname
Ogdon, Ogdan; **Famous Namesakes:** *Poet Ogden Nash*

OHANZEE Native American: Shadow (Sioux)

OHIN African: Chief

OKAL African: To cross

OLAF Scandinavian: Ancestral heritage; in use since the Viking age, this name was borne by several Norwegian kings, including Saint Olaf, the patron saint of Norway. See also *Olen*

(Irish) *Auley, Auliffe*; (Finnish) *Olavi, Olli; Ola, Olav, Olave, Olin, Olof*; **Nicknames:** *Ole*

OLDRICH Czech: Variation of Alaric

OLEG Russian: Variation of Helge
Olezka; **Famous Namesakes:** *Russian fashion designer Oleg Cassini*

OLEN Russian: Deer
Olian, Oliene, Olyan

OLIVER Latin: Peaceful or the olive tree, which symbolizes fruitfulness, beauty, and dignity; extending an olive branch signifies an offer of peace. Norse: Affectionate
(French) *Olivier*; (Spanish) *Oliverio*; (Portuguese) *Olivieros*; (Irish) *Oilibhear; Olliver*; **Nicknames:** *Ollie*; **Star Babies:** *Son of Goldie Hawn and Bill Hudson, Amanda Pays and Corbin Bernsen, Martin Short*

> *"I find the great thing in this world is not so much where we stand, as in what direction we are moving—we must sail sometimes against it—but we must sail, and not drift, nor lie at anchor."*
> —Oliver Wendell Holmes

OLLIE Latin: Peaceful

OMAR Arabic: Life or thriving, long-living
(African) *Omarr; Ommar, Omer*; **Famous Namesakes:** *Arab poet Omar Abi Rabeiah, Actor Omar Sharif, Actor Omar Epps*

OMER Hebrew: Sheaf

OMID Persian: Hope

OMRI Hebrew: Sheaves of grain

ONAN Turkish: Prosperous

ONNI Finnish: Happiness

ONOFREDO Italian: Variation of Humphrey
Onfrio, Onofrio

ONSLOW English: From the zealous one's hill
Onslowe

ONURIS Egyptian: God of This in Upper Egypt; the divine huntsman is represented as a man.

ORANG Persian: Wisdom
Aurang

OREL Russian: Eagle
Oral, Orrel

OREN Hebrew: Pine tree; (Gaelic) pale-skinned
Orin, Orren, Orrin; **Famous Namesakes:** *Senator Orrin Hatch*

ORESTES Greek: From the mountain
Oreste

ORETA Greek: Virtue, the Greek concept of striving for excellence in all aspects of one's life; variant of Arete
Oretha, Oretta, Orette

ORFORD English: From the cattle ford

ORI Hebrew: My light

ORINGO African: He who likes to hunt

ORION Greek: Son of fire, dawning; the mythological Orion was a mighty hunter and son of Poseidon. The constellation Orion contains three conspicuous stars.
(Basque) *Zorian, Zorion*

ORLANDO Spanish, Italian: Renowned in the land; variant of Roland
Orlan, Orland, Orlondo; **Nicknames:** *Lando, Olo*; **Famous Namesakes:** *Actor Orlando Bloom*

ORMAN English: Spearman

ORO Spanish: Gold

ORPHEUS Greek: A great musician and poet of Greek myth, Orpheus was greatly in love with his wife Eurydice, whom he lost twice to death.

ORRICK English: From the ancient oak tree
Orik

ORSON Latin, English: Little bear, like a bear (Italian) *Orsino*; *Ourson*; **Famous Namesakes:** *Actor and director Orson Welles*

ORTON English: From the shore settlement or town; a surname
Oratun, Ortun; **Famous Namesakes:** *Playwright Joe Orton*

ORVILLE French: Gold town
Orvelle, Orvil; **Famous Namesakes:** *Aviation pioneer Orville Wright, Popcorn icon Orville Redenbacher*

ORVIN English: Spear friend
Orvyn

OSBERT English: Divinely brilliant

OSBORN English: Divine bear
Osbourne, Osburn, Usbeorn; **Nicknames:** *Oz, Ozzie, Ozzy*; **Famous Namesakes:** *Singer Ozzy Osbourne*

OSCAR English: God's spear; (Irish) deer friend
(Finnish) *Oskari*; (Hungarian) *Oszkar*; *Osckar, Oskar, Osker*; **Famous Namesakes:** *Writer Oscar Wilde*

"When I like people immensely, I never tell their names to anyone. It is like surrendering a part of them."
—Oscar Wilde

OSIRIS Egyptian: God of the dead and the underworld; Osiris is regarded as the king who watches over the netherworld and is rejuvenated in his son, Horus. As the symbol of eternal life he was worshipped at Abydos and Philae. As a god of inundation and vegetation, he is also represented as a mummified king.

OSMAN Arabic: Young of bustard, young of snake, Abu (father of) Osman means serpent; Othmani refers to someone of Ottoman descent. This name can be used as a first or last name. *Othman;* **Famous Namesakes:** *Turkish Prince Osman the First was responsible for establishing the Ottoman Empire.*

OSMAR English: Divinely glorious

OSMOND English: Divine protector *Osman, Osmont, Osmund;* **Famous Namesakes:** *Singer Donny Osmond*

OSRED English: Divine counselor

OSRIC English: Divine ruler *Osrick*

OSWALD English: Divine power (Spanish) *Osvaldo;* (Scandinavian) *Osvald; Oswell;* **Nicknames:** *Ossie, Waldo;* **Famous Namesakes:** *British author Oswald Chambers*

OSWIN English: God's friend

OTHMAN German: Wealthy

OTIENO African: Born at night

OTIS German: Wealthy; derivation of Otto **Famous Namesakes:** *Singer Otis Redding*

OTTO German: Wealthy; a modern form of Odo used in numerous countries (Czech) *Ota, Otik; Odo, Otho, Oto*

OURAY Native American: Arrow (Ute); renowned leader of the Uncomaghre Ute

OVADYA Hebrew: Serves God

OWEN Celtic, Welsh: Young warrior (French) *Ouen; Owin, Owyn;* **Old Forms:** *Owain;* **Famous Namesakes:** *Actor Owen Wilson;* **Star Babies:** *Son of Christopher Reeve, Stephen King, Phoebe Cates and Kevin Kline*

OXFORD English: A place name, meaning from the ox ford; the prestigious Oxford University is the oldest university in the United Kingdom.

OXTON English: From the oxen town or settlement; surname *Oxtun;* **Nicknames:** *Ox*

OZ Hebrew: Powerful, courageous **Nicknames:** *Ozi, Ozzi, Ozzie, Ozzy;* **Famous Namesakes:** *Baseball player Ozzie Smith, Singer Ozzy Osbourne*

OZGUR Turkish: Free

PABLO Spanish: Variation of Paul
Famous Namesakes: *Artist Pablo Picasso,*
Poet Pablo Neruda

PACE English: Peace
Paice

PACO Spanish: Free one; a nickname for
Francisco, a popular Spanish form of Francis

PAGE French: Attendant
Padgett, Paget, Paige

PALAEMON Greek: A sea god of Greek
mythology

PALBEN Basque: Blond

PALINURUS Latin: The helmsman for
Aeneas

PALMER English: Pilgrim bearing a palm
branch
Palmere

PALTI Hebrew: My deliverance

PAN Greek: The mythological god of shepherds and flocks, Pan is often depicted with
a reed pipe and chasing nymphs through the
forests while in the shape of a goat. Parents
and children will both recognize the name as
also belonging to Peter Pan, the flying boy
who journeyed to Never-Never Land to
escape adulthood.

PANCHO Spanish: Free; a variant of
Francisco. Pancho Villa was a rebel general
during the Mexican Revolution.

PARIS Greek, French: Original meaning
uncertain, though the modern meaning
refers to the French capital; as a man's name,
Paris is most recognized for a well-known
character of Greek mythology. Paris fell in
love with and abducted Helen of Troy, the
beautiful wife of King Menelaus. This led to

the Trojan War, during which Paris killed the
Greek hero Achilles with a bow and arrow.
Star Babies: *Son of Blair Underwood, son*
of Pierce Brosnan

PARKER English: Park keeper
Parke; **Nicknames:** *Park*; **Famous**
Namesakes: *Actor Parker Stevenson;* **Star**
Babies: *Son of Rosie O'Donnell*

PARKIN English: Little rock

PARNELL French: Little Peter
Parnall, Parnel, Pernel, Pernell; **Famous**
Namesakes: *Nineteenth-century Irish*
Nationalist Charles Parnell

PAROUNAG Armenian: Grateful

PARR English: Castle park

PARRISH English: Lives near the church
Parisch, Parish

PARTHENIOS Greek: Virgin

PASCAL French, Hebrew: Born at Passover
or Easter; this name derives from both
Hebrew and Latin, and is appropriate to
celebrate the birth of a child born during
either spring holiday.
(Italian) *Pasquale*; (Spanish) *Pascual, Pasqual*;
Pascale; **Famous Namesakes:** *French*
philosopher and inventor Blaise Pascal

PATRICK Latin, Irish: Noble, patrician;
Saint Patrick (whose original name was
Sucat), adopted his name when he became a
missionary to Ireland. He is now the patron
saint of Ireland, and there are numerous
legends about him. Of course his feast day of
March 17 is commonly known as the holiday
of shamrocks and wearing o' the green.
(French) *Patrice*; (Italian) *Patrizio*; (Spanish)
Patricio, Patrico; (Gaelic) *Padhra, Padruig*;
(Irish) *Paddy, Padhraig, Padraic, Padraig,*
Padriac, Paidi; (Polish) *Patryk*; **Nicknames:**

Pat; **Famous Namesakes:** *Actor Patrick Stewart, Actor Patrick Swayze, Basketball player Patrick Ewing*; **Star Babies:** *Son of Tom Berenger, John Wayne, Arnold Schwarzenegger*

PATROCLUS Greek: In Greek mythology, Patroclus was Achilles' best friend, slain by Hector the great warrior during the Trojan War.

PATTON English: From the fighters' town or settlement; a surname and possibly a variant of Peyton or Patrick
Patten, Pattin; **Famous Namesakes:** *General George S. Patton*

PAUL Latin: Little; the biblical apostle and evangelist Paul was an important leader in the church. His letters to early Christians comprise many New Testament books. (Greek) *Pavlos*; (Italian) *Paolo*; (Spanish) *Pablo, Paulino, Paulo*; (Gaelic) *Pol*; (Welsh) *Pewlin*; (Scandinavian) *Pal*; (Danish) *Poul*; (Dutch) *Pauel*; (Slavic) *Pavel*; (Russian) *Pavlo*; (Czech) *Havel*; (Polish) *Pawel, Pawelek, Pawl*; (Finnish) *Paavali, Paavo*; (Hungarian) *Palko*; (Armenian) *Boghos*; **Old Forms:** *Paulus*; **Nicknames:** *Paulie*; **Famous Namesakes:** *Artist Paul Cezanne, Actor Paul Newman, Musicians Paul McCartney and Paul Simon*

PAX Latin: Peace

PAXTON English: From the peaceful town or settlement
Paxon, Paxtun; **Nicknames:** *Pax*; **Famous Namesakes:** *Actor Bill Paxton*

PAYAM Persian: Message

PAYDEN English: From the fighter's den or valley; surname

PAZ Hebrew: Gold; (Spanish) peace

PEDRO Spanish: Variation of Peter
Famous Namesakes: *Spanish conqueror Pedro de Alvarado, Pitcher Pedro Martinez*; **Star Babies:** *Son of Frances McDormand and Joel Coen*

PEGASUS Greek: The offspring of Medusa and Poseidon, Pegasus was the winged horse of Greek mythology

PELLTUN English: From the town or settlement near the pool

PEMBROKE Welsh: Lives in the headland

PENATES Latin: The inner ones; in Roman mythology, the Penates were the gods of the household.

PENLEY English: From the enclosed pasture meadow; surname
Penleigh, Pennleah, Penlea, Penly, Pennlea, Pennleigh, Pennley

PENTON English: From the enclosed town or settlement; surname
Pentin, Pentun

PERCIVAL French: Pierce the valley; in Arthurian Legend, Percival was a knight of the Round Table who glimpsed the Holy Grail.
(German) *Parsifal*; *Parsefal, Perceval*; **Nicknames:** *Percy*

PERCY French: From Percy; also a nickname for Percival
Famous Namesakes: *English Poet Percy Bysshe Shelley*

PERKIN English: Little Peter
Perkins

PERRY English, Latin: Pear tree; also a nickname for the Latin Peregrine
Famous Namesakes: *Singer Perry Como, Actor Matthew Perry*

PERUN Slavic: Thunder

PESACH Hebrew: To pass over; the Hebrew name of the Passover holiday commemorating the sparing of the Hebrews in Egypt
Pessach

PETER Greek: Rock; Peter was a biblical fisherman and one of Christ's twelve disciples. In Catholic tradition he is the first pope. See also *Takis*
(Greek) *Panos, Petros*; (Arabic) *Botros*; (French) *Pierre*; (Italian) *Pero, Piero, Pietro*; (Spanish) *Pedro*; (Gaelic) *Peadair, Peadar*; (Welsh) *Pedr*; (Scandinavian) *Pedar, Petter*; (Dutch) *Pieter*; (Slavic) *Pyotr*; (Czech) *Petr*; (Polish) *Pietrek, Piotr*; (Finnish) *Pekka, Pietari*; (Armenian) *Bedros*; **Nicknames:** *Pete, Petya*; **Famous Namesakes:** *English actor Peter Sellers, English musician Peter Gabriel, English musician Pete Townshend;* **Star Babies:** *Son of Mikhail Baryshnikov and Lisa Rinehart, Princess Anne and Mark Phillips, Stephanie Seymour, Jack Wagner*

PEVERELL French: Piper

PEYMAN Persian: Promise
Payman

PEYTON English: Warrior's village; *Peyton Place* was the name of a popular TV show from the 1960s. Irish: A variant of Patrick. Latin: Regal or royal
Paden, Paegastun, Paton, Payton; **Famous Namesakes:** *Football player Peyton Manning*

PHAETON Greek: Shining one; the son of the sun-god Helios in Greek mythology

PHANTASOS Greek: Apparition; a son of Hypnos in Greek mythology and a personification of dreams

PHELAN Gaelic, Irish: Little wolf
Faolan, Felan

PHELPS English: Son of Philip

PHERSON Scottish: Parson

PHILBERT German: Spelling variation of Filbert
Philibert

PHILEMON Greek: Affectionate; one of Paul's epistles in the New Testament is addressed to Philemon.

PHILIP Greek: Lover of horses; Philip was one of Christ's twelve apostles. This name has also been borne by numerous kings of Spain, France, and Macedonia.
(French) *Philippe*; (Italian) *Filippio, Filippo*; (Spanish) *Felipe, Filipo*; (Gaelic) *Pilib*; (Scandinavian) *Filip*; (Hungarian) *Fulop*; *Philipp, Phillip*; **Nicknames:** *Flip, Phil*; **Famous Namesakes:** *Britain's Prince Philip, Painter Filippo Lippi, TV host Phil Donahue, Football player Phil Simms*

PHILO Greek: To love

PHINEAS Hebrew: Meaning uncertain; suggested definitions include oracle, dark-skinned, mouth of brass, and a serpent's mouth
Phinees, Phineus, Pinchas, Pinchos, Pincus, Pinhas, Pinkas, Pinkus; **Nicknames:** *Pini*; **Famous Namesakes:** *Showman Phineas Taylor (P.T.) Barnum*

PHOEBUS Greek: Shining one; Phoebus was an epithet of Apollo in Greek mythology.

PHOENIX Greek: Dark red; in mythology, the phoenix was a beautiful bird that built its own pyre and then was reborn from the ashes.
Famous Namesakes: *Actor Joaquin Phoenix and his late brother River Phoenix*

PHORCYS Greek: A sea god in Greek mythology

PICKFORD English: From the woodcutter's ford

PIERCE English: Rock; a variant of Piers, an older form of Peter
Pearce, Pearson, Peirce, Piers, Pierson;
Famous Namesakes: *Actor Pierce Brosnan*

PIERPONT French: Lives by the stone bridge; surname made famous by American banker J. Pierpont Morgan
Pierrepont

PIERRE French: Variation of Peter
Famous Namesakes: *Canadian Prime Minister Pierre Trudeau, French fashion designer Pierre Cardin*

PIO Latin: Pious; a name of numerous popes
Pious, Pius

PIPPIN French: Eighth-century king of the Franks, father of Charlemagne, Emperor of the Holy Roman Empire
Peppin

PITNEY English: From the stubborn island; surname
Pittney; **Nicknames:** *Pitt*

PLACIDO Spanish: Tranquil
Famous Namesakes: *Opera singer Placido Domingo*

PLATO Greek: Broad-shouldered; Plato was a renowned philosopher of Greece, a student of Socrates, and a teacher of Aristotle. (Spanish) *Platon*

PLATT French: The flat land

PLUTO Latin: Wealth; a mythological Roman god of the underworld whose Greek name is Hades. Pluto is also the name of a planet and Mickey Mouse's dog.

PLUTUS Greek: Wealth; in Greek mythology, Plutus was the god of wealth, said to be blinded by Zeus so he could bestow gifts freely regardless of merit.

POLDI Hungarian: Patriotic

POLLARD Teutonic: Short-haired

POLLUX Latin: In Greek mythology, Pollux was the brother of Helen of Troy and a twin of Castor, with whom he forms the constellation Gemini.

POLYPHEMUS Greek: Mythic son of Poseidon and Thoosa, Polyphemus was a Cyclops, a giant semi-human monster with a single eye in the center of his forehead. He's best known for capturing Odysseus in Homer's epic *Odyssey*.

POMEROY French: An apple orchard

PONCE Spanish: Fifth
Famous Namesakes: *Spanish explorer Ponce de Leon*

PONTIFEX Latin: Priest; in ancient Rome, the pontifex was an official that supervised religious activities.

PORFIRIO Greek: Purple stone
Porfiro, Prophyrios; **Famous Namesakes:** *Mexican President Porfirio Diaz*

PORTER Latin: Gatekeeper

POSEIDON Greek: The Greek mythological god of the sea, earthquakes, and horses

POUYAN Persian: Searcher

POWELL Welsh: A contraction of Ap Howell, meaning son of Howell; a surname
Powel, Pouel, Pauwel

PRENTICE English: Apprentice

PRESCOTT English: From the priest's cottage; surname
Prescot, Priestcot

PRESLEY English: From the priest's meadow; a surname evocative of Elvis Presley
Preslea, Preslee, Presleigh, Preslie, Priestley, Priestlea, Priestleigh; **Nicknames:** *Pres*; **Star Babies:** *Son of Cindy Crawford and Rande Gerber*

PRESTON English: From the priest's estate
Pfeostun, Prestin; **Nicknames:** *Pres*

PREWITT French: Brave
Pruitt

PRIAM Greek: In Greek mythology, Priam was king and ruler of Troy during the Trojan War.

PRIAPUS Greek: A mythological god of fertility

PRIESTLY English: From the priest's meadow; a surname and variant of Presley
Priestley, Priestlea, Priestleigh; **Famous Namesakes:** *Actor Jason Priestley*

PRIMO Italian: Firstborn

PRINCE Latin: Prince
Famous Namesakes: *Musician Prince*; **Star Babies:** *Two sons of Michael Jackson*

PRINCETON English: From the town or place belonging to the prince or the royal family; an Ivy League university in New Jersey

PROCTOR Latin: Administrator; an occupational name

PROMETHEUS Greek: A mythological deity, Prometheus stole fire from the gods and gave it to men.

PROSPERO Spanish: Successful

PROTESILAUS Greek: In Greek mythology, Protesilaus was the Thessalian king and the first to die in the Trojan War. Even though it had been foretold that the first Greek who touched Trojan ground would die, Protesilaus did not hesitate.

PROTEUS Greek: A prophetic sea god of Greek mythology

PRYOR Latin: Servant of the priory, though as a title it refers to the head of a monastery
Prior

PTAH Egyptian: Creator god of Memphis; this god coalesced with Sokaris and Osiris and is represented as a man in mummy form, possibly originally as a statue. He was the patron god of craftsmen and was equated by the Greeks with Hephaestus. See also *Hephaestus*

PUCK English: Elf; mischievous character in Shakespeare's *Midsummer's Night Dream*

PUNDARIK Hindi: White

PUTNAM English: Dwells by the pond

PYGMALION Greek: A sculptor and king of Cyprus; according to Greek legend, Pygmalion carved a statue of a beautiful woman from ivory and adored it so much he named her Galatea and prayed for a wife like her. The goddess Aphrodite brought the sculpture to life for Pygmalion, and he and his bride shared a happy life together.

PYRY Finnish: Snowstorm, blizzard

QABIC Arabic: Able, capable
Quabic

QABIL Arabic: Capable
Qabill

QADIM Arabic: Ancient
Quadim

QAMAR Arabic: Moon
Quamar, Quamir

QASIM Arabic: Divides
Quasim

QEB Egyptian: Father of the earth

QIMAT Hindi: Of value
Quimat

QUADARIUS English: Modern blend name of Quan (possibly as a variant of Juan) and Darius
Quadarias, Qudarius

QUADE Latin: Fourth, born fourth (English) *Quaid*; *Quartus, Quaden, Quadin, Quadre, Qwade*

QUAIN French: Clever, quick

QUANAH Native American: Fragrance, specific odor (Comanche)

QUANDRE English: Modern blend of Quan (possibly as a variant of Juan) and Andre
Quandray, Qudre

QUANMAINE English: Modern blend of Quan (possibly as a variant of Juan) and Jermaine
Quanmain, Quanmane

QUANTAVIUS English: Modern blend of Quan (possibly as a variant of Juan) and Octavius
Quantavious

QUASHAWN English: Modern blend of Quan and Shawn
Quashan, Quashen, Quashon

QUENNEL French: From the little oak tree
Quenal, Quenall, Quenel, Quenell

> *"The children despise their parents until the age of forty, when they suddenly become just like them— thus preserving the system."*
>
> —Author Quentin Crewe in a 1962 *Saturday Evening Post* piece about the British upper class

QUENTIN Latin, French: Born fifth; Quentin is the name of numerous religious and political leaders throughout history. The famous prison in San Francisco derives its name from the martyred Saint Quintin. English: From the Queen's place, town *Quenton, Quinton, Quenten, Quentyn*; **Old Forms:** *Quintus*; **Nicknames:** *Quent, Quint*; **Famous Namesakes:** *Filmmaker Quentin Tarantino*

QUENTRELL English, French: A modern name of unclear origins, but probably related to Quentin

QUIGLEY Gaelic, Irish: From the mother, the maternal side; may have been related at some point specifically to land belonging to the mother's side
Quiglea, Quiglee, Quigleigh

QUILLAN Gaelic: Cub, small one
Quilan, Quilen, Quilin, Quillen

QUILLON Latin: Sword, long knife
Quilon

QUIMBY Norse: From the man's estate
Quinby, Quenby, Quenbey, Quemby

QUINCEY French: From the fifth child's
estate
Quincy; **Famous Namesakes:** *President John
Quincy Adams, Music icon Quincy Jones*

QUINDARIUS English: Modern blend of
Quin and Darius

QUINLAN Gaelic: Graceful, strong, well
made; also a variant of Quinn

QUINN Gaelic, Scottish: Wisdom, intelli-
gence; Quinn is derived from O'Cuinn, a
Gaelic surname and is also a familiar form of
Quincey and similar names
Quin; **Famous Namesakes:** *Actor Aidan
Quinn, Actor Anthony Quinn;* **Star Babies:**
Son of Sean Young

QUINSHAWN English: Modern blend of
Quin and Shawn

QUINT French: Nickname for Quentin

QUINTAVIUS English: Modern blend of
Quin and Octavius

QUINTRELL English: Unclear origin, but a
variant of Quentin, Quincey, and Quinn

RA Egyptian: Sun god of Heliopolis; From
the fifth dynasty onwards, Ra became a
national god and combined with the
supreme deity Amon. As head of the great
ennead and supreme judge, this god was
represented as falcon-headed and was often
linked with other gods aspiring to universality,
such as Amon, Amon-Ra, and Sobk-Ra.
Re

RAAMAH Hebrew: Thunderclap
Rama, Ramah

RAANAN Hebrew: Fresh, beautiful

RABI Arabic: Spring; also means my lord if
pronounced with accent on the first syllable

RACER English: One who races, loves to
run or compete
Rayce; **Nicknames:** *Race*

RACHAM Hebrew: Sympathetic, filled with
compassion
Rachaman, Rachamin

RADAMES Egyptian: An Egyptian prince
and the name of the hero in Puccini's opera
Aida

RADBERT English: Red-haired or brilliant
counselor
Radburt

RADBURN English: Lives by the red stream
*Radbourne, Radbyrne, Raedburne, Radborn,
Radborne, Radbourn, Radburne*

RADCLIFF English: Near the red cliff;
surname
Radclyf, Radeliffe, Raedclyf, Ratcliff, Ratcliffe

RADFORD English: From the red or reedy
ford; a variant of Redford
Radferd, Radfurd, Raeford

RADLEY English: From or near the red meadow; surname
Raedleah, Redley, Ridley

RADMAN Slavic: Happy
Radmon

RADNOR English: From the red shore or the reedy shore

RADOLF English: Red wolf
Radolph

RADOMIL Slavic: Peaceful bliss

RADORM Norse: In Norse mythology, the brother of Jolgeir

RADOSLAW Polish: Contented, at peace

RADWAN Hebrew, Arabic: Delightful

RAED Arabic: Leader, scout, explorer, major (military title)
Raiid

RAFE English: Nickname for Rafferty or Ralph

RAFFERTY Irish: Rich, prospering
Rafertey, Raferti, Raferty; **Nicknames:** *Rafer, Rafe, Raffer*; **Star Babies:** Son of Sadie Frost and Jude Law

RAFI Arabic: Exalted. Hebrew: Nickname for Raphael

RAFIK Arabic: Companion, friend
Rafeek, Rafiq

RAGHIB Arabic: Desires, wants

RAGNAROK Norse: The final battle of the gods in Norse mythology, the end of the world, the beginning of a new one

RAI Japanese: Thunder

RAIDON Japanese: Mythological thunder god
Raiden, Rayden, Raydon

RAINE English: Rule, also wise
Rane, Rayne, Rain, Raines

RAINIER French: Variation of Raynor
Famous Namesakes: *Prince Rainier of Monaco*

RAJABU African: Born in the seventh month of the Islamic calendar (Swahili)

RAJAH Sanskrit: King, prince, the ruler
Raja, Rajan; **Nicknames:** *Raj, Raji*

RAJNISH Hindi: Hindu god of the night

RAKIN Arabic: Respectful, firm, steady, confident

RAKTIM Hindi: Bright red

RALEIGH English: From the roe deer meadow; surname and the capital city of North Carolina
Raleah, Raley, Rally, Rawley, Ralea, Rawlea, Rawleigh, Rawlee; **Famous Namesakes:** *English explorer Sir Walter Raleigh*

"We find a delight in the beauty and happiness of children that makes the heart too big for the body."
—Ralph Waldo Emerson

RALPH English: Wolf counsel; an old name from Scandinavian and Germanic elements, Ralph is pronounced "Rafe" in many areas outside the United States. See also *Rolfe* (French) *Raoul*; (Spanish) *Raul*; (Scandinavian) *Rolf, Raff, Ralf, Rolph*; **Famous Namesakes:** *Actor Ralph Fiennes, Activist Ralph Nader, Fashion designer Ralph Lauren*

RALSTON English: Ralph's town or wolf's town
Ralsten

RAM English: Male sheep; Ram is also a nickname for Ramsden, Ramsey, and related names.
Ramm

RAMA Sanskrit: Awesome, godlike; Rama was the mythological seventh incarnation of Vishnu.
Ram, Ramanan

RAMBERT German: Mighty or intelligent
Rambart

RAMI Arabic, Persian: Loving, thrower, rifleman
Ramy, Ramey

RAMIRO Spanish: Highest judge
Ramario, Ramires, Ramos

RAMON Spanish: Variation of Raymond
Ramone; **Famous Namesakes:** *Spanish poet Juan Ramon Jimenez*

RAMSDEN English: From the ram's valley
Ramsdin

RAMSES Egyptian: Begotten by or belonging to Ra, the sun god; the name of several powerful Pharaohs of ancient Egypt

RAMSEY English, Teutonic: Ram's island or raven's island; surname adapted to popular first name use
Ramsay, Ramzey, Ramzi

RANCE English: Familiar form of Laurence and Ransom

RAND English: Shield, defender

RANDALL English: Shield wolf; variant of Randolph
Randahl, Randal, Randale, Randel, Randell, Rendall, Rendell; **Nicknames:** *Randy*; **Famous Namesakes:** *Actor Tony Randall, Quarterback Randall Cunningham*

RANDOLPH English: Shield wolf, defender and protector; the wolf is revered for its strength, cunning, and fearlessness. Quite possibly this name was derived as an identifier for a family which used the emblem of the wolf as part of its coat of arms.
Randolf, Ranolf; **Nicknames:** *Rando*

RANDON English: Possibly from the shielded town or valley, possibly a form of Randolph

RANDSON English: Rand or Randolph's son, possibly child of the shield as a reference to a young man in training for battle

RANDY English: A nickname of Randolph, Randall, Rand and related names
Famous Namesakes: *Actor Randy Quaid, Composer Randy Newman, Pitcher Randy Johnson, Singer Randy Travis*

RANEN Hebrew: To sing, to be joyful
Ranon

RANG English: Raven

RANGER French: Ward of the forest
Rainger

RANGEY English: From raven's island

RANGFORD English: From the raven's ford

RANI Hebrew: My song, my joy

RANJAN Hindi: Delighted

RANKIN English: Little shield, child of the shield
Randkin, Ransom

RANSLEY English: From the raven's meadow; surname
Ranslea, Ranslee, Ransleigh, Ransly

RANSOM Latin: Redeem. English: Shield child, Rand's son

RAPHAEL Hebrew: God has healed; the name of one of the archangels and of one of the greatest painters of the Renaissance (Italian) *Rafaele, Rafaello*; (Spanish) *Rafael*; (Polish) *Rafal; Raphale, Rapheal, Raphello*; **Famous Namesakes:** *Composer Raphael Mostel, Painter Raphael Sanzio*; **Star Babies:** *Son of Juliette Binoche, son of Robert De Niro*

RASHAD Arabic: Thinker, counselor; one who shows reason, good sense, integrity and maturity, also means nastartium (flower); a spelling variation of Rashid
Reshad, Rashaad

RASHAWN Contemporary: Modern blend of Ray or Ra and Shawn
Rashae, Rashane, Rashaun, Rayshaun, Rayshawn, Reshawn, Rishawn

RASHID Arabic: Counselor, thinker, spiritual instructor; Rashid is also the name of Rosetta, a large town in Egypt. See also *Rashidi*
Rasheed, Rashed; **Famous Namesakes:** *Journalist Ahmed Rashid, Basketball player Rasheed Wallace*

RASHIDA African: Righteous

RASHIDI African: Thinker; counselor (Swahili)

RASMUS Greek: Spelling variation of Erasmus

RATMIR Russian: Peace protector

RAUL Spanish: Variation of Ralph
Raol, Raoul, Raulio; **Nicknames:** *Rulo*; **Famous Namesakes:** *Actor Raul Julia*

RAVEN English: Raven, black bird
Ravenel, Ravin

RAVI Sanskrit: Sun; also the name of the mythological Hindi sun god Ravi
Famous Namesakes: *Sitar player and composer Ravi Shankar*

RAVID Hebrew: Ornament; also a form of Arvid

RAVIV Hebrew: Rain, dew, reviving waters
Ravyv

RAWDON English: From the rough hill

RAWLEY English: From the roe deer meadow; a surname and variant of Raleigh
Rawlea, Rawleigh, Rawlee

RAWLING English: Raleigh's son, small Raleigh

RAWLINS French: Roland's child or diminutive for Roland

RAWLS English: Raleigh's son or a short form of Raleigh
Famous Namesakes: *Singer and actor Lou Rawls*

RAY Latin: Radiant. English: Familiar form of Rayburn, Raymond, and related names. French: Regal, royal

RAYCE English: Spelling variation of Racer

RAYFORD English: Deer's ford

RAYHAN Arabic: God favors

RAYI Hebrew: Friend of mine

RAYMOND German: Wise protector
(English) *Redmund*; (German) *Raimund*;
(Italian) *Raimondo*; (Spanish) *Rai*,
*Raimundo, Ramon, Ramone, Rayman,
Raymon, Reymundo*; (Gaelic) *Reamonn*;
(Irish) *Redmond*; (Polish) *Rajmund*;
Radmund, Raimond, Ramond, Raymund;
Famous Namesakes: *Actor Ray Romano,
Actor Raymond Burr;* **Star Babies:** *Son of
Jack Nicholson, son of Tina Turner*

RAYNE English: Spelling variation of Raine

RAYNOR Norse: Warrior of judgment; the
origin of this name seems to stem from both
the Germanic name Reginar and the Norse
name Ragnar.
(German) *Rainer, Reiner*; (French) *Rainier,
Ranier*; (Scandinavian) *Ragnar, Regner*;
Rainor, Rayner, Raynord

RAYSHAWN Contemporary: Spelling variation of Rashawn

RAZI Aramaic: Secret
Raziel

READ English: Redhead; variant of Reid

READING English: Reid's son, diminutive of
Reid, or the wandering redhead
Redding

REAGAN Irish: Little king
*Reaghan, Regan, Riagan, Raegan, Raegin,
Raegon, Raegyn, Raugan, Raigen, Raigin,
Raygan, Reagen, Reigan, Reigen, Reighan,
Rheagan;* **Famous Namesakes:** *President
Ronald Reagan*

REBEL English: Modern name reflecting an
independent personality

RED English: Color name and a variant for
Redman, Redley, and related names

Redd; **Famous Namesakes:** *Actor Red
Skelton, Actor Redd Foxx*

REDA Arabic: Fulfilled, contented
Ridah, Ridha

REDFORD English: From the red or reedy
ford
Old Forms: *Raedford;* **Famous Namesakes:**
Actor Robert Redford

REDLEY English: From or near the red
meadow; variant of Radley

REDMAN English: Red-haired advisor,
companion
Old Forms: *Redamann*

REECE Welsh, English: Passionate, enthusi-
astic
Rees, Reese, Reyes, Rhett, Rhys, Rice;
Nicknames: *Rhy*

REEVE English: Steward, an occupational
name referring to a caretaker; when this
name was coined in medieval times, the
reeve was very important and oversaw the
running of the entire estate, including the
lives of feudal serfs.
Reave, Reve

REEVES English: Reeve's son, belonging
to Reeve
Reaves

REGIN Norse: A mythical blacksmith god,
Regin was the son of Rodmar and the foster
father of Sigurd.

REGINALD English: Powerful, wise counsel.
Teutonic: Strong judgment
(French) *Renaud*; (Italian) *Rinaldo*; (Spanish)
Reynaldo, Reynardo; (Gaelic) *Raghnall*;
Ragnol, Reynold, Reynolds; **Old Forms:**
Regenweald; **Nicknames:** *Reggie, Reg;* **Famous
Namesakes:** *Baseball player Reggie Jackson*

REID English: Redhead; a surname adapted a long time ago for given name use
Read, Reade, Redd, Reed

REIDAR Norse: Nest fighter
Reider

REIJO Finnish: Vigilant, watchful

REINHARD German: Strong and courageous counselor
(French) *Raynard*; *Rainart, Rainhard, Renke, Reynard, Reinhart*

REINHOLD Teutonic: Variant of Reynard or Reinhart; the various roots of this name have the general meaning of stong, wise advisor, or advice. Swedish: Variant of Ragnar. English: Variant of Reynold
Famous Namesakes: *Actor Judge Reinhold*

REKU Finnish: Variation of Richard

REMINGTON English: From the raven family settlement or town; this name will remind art lovers of Frederick Remington who specialized in scenes of western life.
Famous Namesakes: *Fictional detective Remington Steele*

REMUS Latin: Quick; in Roman mythology, Remus and Romulus were the twin brothers who founded Rome.

REMY French: From Rheims, France. English: Familiar form of Remington
Remi

RENDOR Hungarian: Peacekeeper, policeman

RENÉ French: Reborn, to rise again
(Spanish) *Renato*; *Rene*; **Old Forms:** *Renatus*;
Nicknames: *Rennie, Renny*; **Famous Namesakes:** *French philosopher and scientist René Descartes*

RENFIELD English: From the raven's field, possibly from the roe deer field; surname
Ranfield

RENFRED English: Enduring peace; possibly a derivation from peaceful raven
Renfrid, Rinfred

RENFREW Welsh: From the raven woods

RENJIRO Japanese: Honest, true

RENNY Irish: Small but powerful. French: Form of Rene
Renne, Rennie

RENSHAW English: From the raven forest

RENTON English: From the roe deer town or settlement; surname
Rentin, Renten

RENWICK Teutonic: Place where the ravens nest
Renwyk

REUBEN Hebrew: Behold a son; in the Old Testament, the firstborn of Jacob and Leah, and patriarch of one of the twelve tribes of Israel
(Greek) *Rouvin*; (Spanish) *Ruben*; *Reuven, Rubin, Rueban*; **Nicknames:** *Rube, Ruby*;
Famous Namesakes: *Cartoonist Rube Goldberg*

REX Latin: King

REXFORD English: From the king's ford

REXLEY English: From the king's meadow; variant of Kingsley
Rex

REXTON English: From the king's town, settlement

REY French: Regal, kingly; a variant of Roy. Spanish: Familiar form of Reynaldo

REYES English: Spelling variation of Reece

REYNALD English, German: King's advisor, closely related to Reginald

REZ Hungarian: Redhead, copper-haired

REZA Persian: Will, consent

REZIN Hebrew: Delightful, a joy

RHADAMANTHUS Greek: A judge in the underworld of Greek mythology

RHEGED Anglo-Saxon, Welsh: From Rheged, a northern kingdom of England; name of Uriens, one of the most famous of kings in Arthurian legend and a historical figure who was one of the earliest Christian kings

RHESUS Latin: A mythical king of Thrace and the name of a species of monkeys

RHETT Welsh: Passionate, enthusiastic; a variant of Reece. Rhett Butler is the dashing hero of Margaret Mitchell's *Gone With the Wind*.

RHODES Greek: Where the roses grow; an island in Greece
(Spanish) *Rodas*; *Rodes*

RHYS Welsh: Spelling variation of Reece
Famous Namesakes: *British actor Rhys Ifans*

RICE Welsh, English: Variant of Reece
Ryce

RICHARD German, English: Powerful, strong ruler; this Old German name was introduced to England by the Normans and borne by three kings of England. King Richard the Lion-hearted was the first of them.
(Italian) *Ricardo, Ricco*; (Spanish) *Cardo, Richi, Rico, Riqui*; (Welsh) *Rhisiart*; (Scandinavian) *Rikkard, Rikki*; (Swedish) *Rikard*; (Dutch) *Rikke*; (Polish) *Ryszard*;

(Finnish) *Reku, Riku*; *Ricard, Riccardo, Ricciardo, Rickard, Rickey, Rickie, Rickward, Ricman, Ricweard, Riocard*; **Old Forms:** *Richart, Rikward*; **Nicknames:** *Dick, Ric, Rich, Rick, Ricky*; **Famous Namesakes:** *President Richard Nixon, Actor Richard Dreyfuss, Actor Richard Gere*

"*I had a math teacher in junior high school named Richard Dick. Yes, he went by the name Dick Dick. Poor, poor man...*"
—from BabyZone.com's Message Boards

RICHMAN English: Powerful
Rickman, Richmen, Richmun, Rychman;
Famous Namesakes: *Actor Alan Rickman*

RICHMOND German, English: Strong protector, powerful defender; Richmond is the capital city of Virginia and a town in Yorkshire, England.

RICK English: Familiar form of Cedric, Frederick, and Richard
Nicknames: *Ricky*; **Famous Namesakes:** *Actor Rick Moranis, Entertainers Rick Springfield and Ricky Martin*

RICKER English: Strong army

RIDDOCK Irish: From the smooth field
Reidhachadh, Riddoc, Riddick; **Famous Namesakes:** *Boxer Riddick Bowe*

RIDER English: Horseman, knight
Ridere, Ryder, Ridder, Rydder

RIDGE English: From the ridge or cliff's edge
Rigg, Rydge

RIDGELY English: From the meadow's ridge or from the meadow near the ridge; surname
Ridgeley, Ridgelea, Ridgeleigh

RIDLEY English: From or near the red meadow; variant of Radley
Famous Namesakes: *Film director Ridley Scott*

RIEL Spanish: Nickname for Gabriel

RIGBY English: From the ruling valley; surname
Rigbee, Rigbie, Rygby

RIGEL Arabic: Foot; Rigel is a blue star of the first magnitude that marks the hunter's left foot in the Orion constellation.
Rigl, Regl

RIGGS English: Son of Ridge, belonging to Ridge
Famous Namesakes: *Tennis player Bobby Riggs*

RIGOBERT German: Wealthy, wonderful

RILEY Irish: Brave. English: Rye meadow (Irish) *Ryleigh*; *Reilley, Reilly, Ryley*; **Star Babies:** *Son of David Lynch*

RING English: Ring, circle
Nicknames: *Ringo*

RINGO English: Nickname for Ring
Famous Namesakes: *Beatle Ringo Starr*

RIO Spanish: Variant of River; a familiar form of Spanish names ending with -rio. The Rio Grande is one of the longest rivers in North America, and Rio de Janeiro is the second largest city in Brazil.
Star Babies: *Son of Sean Young*

RIORDAN Irish, Gaelic: Royal bard
Riordain; **Old Forms:** *Rioghbhardan*

RIPLEY Anglo-Saxon, English: From the shouter's meadow; surname
Hrapenly, Hrypanleah

RISHI Hindi: Sage, wise man

RISLEY English: From the meadow of brushwood or shrubs; surname
Rislea, Rislee, Risleigh, Rislie

RISTO Greek: Nickname for Christopher

RISTON English: From the town or settlement near the shrubs; surname
Risten, Ristun, Whriston, Wriston

RITTER German: Knight, abiding by the knight's code of ethics, chivalrous
Famous Namesakes: *Actor John Ritter*

RIVER English: Body of water. See also *Rio*
Famous Namesakes: *Actor River Phoenix*

RIYAD Arabic: Garden; stems from rayy, meaning rain, abundant or copious water; Riyadh is the capital of Saudi Arabia.
Riyadh

ROALD Swedish: Variation of Ronald
Famous Namesakes: *British author Roald Dahl, Norwegian explorer Roald Amundsen*

ROAR Norse: Praised warrior

ROB English: Nickname for Robert
Robb; **Famous Namesakes:** *Actor Rob Lowe*

ROBERT English: Bright with fame; an all-time favorite boys' name since the Middle Ages and popular worldwide (German) *Rupert, Ruprecht*; (Italian) *Roberto*; (Gaelic) *Riobart*; (Irish) *Riobard, Roibeard, Roibin*; (Scottish) *Rab*; (Finnish) *Pertti, Roope*; **Nicknames:** *Bob, Bobbie, Bobby, Rob, Robb, Robbie, Robbin, Robby, Robinet, Robin*; **Famous Namesakes:** *Actors Robert DeNiro, Robert Duvall, Robert Redford; Scottish author Robert Louis Stevenson; Confederate General Robert E. Lee; Poet Robert Frost; Senator Robert Kennedy*

A name with meaning
could bring up a child,

Taking the child out of the
parents' hands.

Better a meaningless
name, I should say,

As leaving more to nature
and happy chance.

Name children some
names and see what you
do.

—Robert Frost,
from "Maple"

ROBERTSON English: Robert's son, belonging to Robert
Roberts, Robinson

ROBIN English: Bright with fame; abbreviation of Robert popular since the medieval days of Robin Hood. Robin is well known to children as the name of Winnie the Pooh's boy companion Christopher Robin.
Robbin, Roibin, Robyn; **Famous Namesakes:** *Actor Robin Williams, Musician Robin Gibb*

ROBINSON English: Variant of Robertson and name of the adventurous protagonist in Daniel Defoe's *Robinson Crusoe*

ROCCO Italian: Rock
Star Babies: *Son of Madonna*

ROCK English: Rock, solid
Roch, Rocke; **Nicknames:** *Rocky*; **Famous Namesakes:** *Actor Rock Hudson*

ROCKFORD English: From the rocky ford; surname

ROCKLAND English: From the rocky land; surname

ROCKLEDGE English: From the rocky ledge; surname

ROCKLEY English: From the rocky meadow, fields; surname

ROCKWELL English: From the rocky well; surname
Famous Namesakes: *Artist Norman Rockwell, Artist and author Rockwell Kent*

ROCKY English: Familiar form of Rock; the well-known fictional prizefighter Rocky Balboa fought his way to the top.

ROD English: Staff, also a familiar form for several names, including Roderick and Rodney
Rodd

RODDY German: Nickname for Roderick

RODEN English: From the red or deer valley
Rodan, Rodin, Roedan; **Famous Namesakes:** *Artist Auguste Rodin*

RODERICK German: Famous ruler (French) *Rodrigue*; (Spanish) *Roderigo, Rodrigo*; (Czech) *Radek*; *Roddric, Roderic, Roderik, Rodric, Rodrick, Rodrik*; **Nicknames:** *Rodd, Roddy, Rod*

RODION Russian: Rosy; Rodion Raskolnikov is the main character in Dostoyevsky's novel *Crime and Punishment*.
Nicknames: *Rodya, Rodenka, Rodka*; **Famous Namesakes:** *Russian composer Rodion Shchedrin*

RODMAN German: Famous man

RODNEY English: From the famous one's island
Nicknames: *Rod, Rodd*

RODWELL English: Lives by the red spring

ROE English: Deer
Row, Rowe

ROGAN Irish: Spelling variation of Rohan

ROGER Teutonic: Famous spearman
(Italian) *Ruggero, Ruggiero*; (Spanish)
Rogelio, Rogerio, Rogerios; (Scandinavian)
*Rutger, Ruttger; Rogir, Rotger, Rudger,
Rudiger, Rodger*; **Nicknames:** *Rog*

ROGERSON English: Roger's son, child;
surname
Hodgson; **Old Forms:** *Hodsone*; **Nicknames:**
Hod

ROHAN Gaelic, Irish: Redheaded. Sanskrit:
Ascending. Persian: Learned, scholarly
Rowen; Rogan, Rowin, Rowyn; **Old Forms:**
Ruadhagan; **Nicknames:** *Row, Rowe*

ROI French: Spelling variation of Roy

ROLAND German, French: Renowned in the
land; Roland was a great legendary knight
who served the medieval king Charlemagne.
(English) *Rolando, Rollins*; (Spanish) *Roldan;
Orlin, Rollan, Rolland, Rollin, Rowland,
Orlando, Orlondo*; **Nicknames:** *Lannie,
Lanny, Rollie, Rollo, Lando, Olo*

ROLFE German: Familiar form for either
Ralph or Rudolph
Rolph

ROLLINS English: Variation of Roland

ROLON Spanish: Famous wolf
Rollon

ROMAN Latin: One from Rome
(French) *Romain*; (Italian) *Romano*;
(Portuguese) *Romao*; **Nicknames:** *Mancho,
Roma*; **Star Babies:** *Son of Francis Ford
Coppola*

> *"What's in a name? That which we
> call a rose
> By any other name would smell
> as sweet.
> So Romeo would, were not he
> Romeo called"*
> —William Shakespeare, *Romeo and Juliet*

ROMEO Latin: Pilgrim to Rome; the most
famous Romeo is likely the protagonist of
Shakespeare's *Romeo and Juliet*, the tragic
story of a young couple that falls in love
despite the violent feud between their
families, and whose death ends that feud.
One of the most famous scenes in literature
is the balcony scene, which begins with Juliet
wishing Romeo is not who he is.

ROMNEY Welsh: From the winding river
Old Forms: *Rumenea*

ROMULUS Latin: Twin brother of Remus
and the mythical founder of Rome, after
whom the city derives its name

RONALD English, Scottish: Powerful, rules
with counsel; from the same root as Reynold
(Spanish) *Naldo, Renaldo*; (Swedish) *Roald;
Ranald, Ronal*; **Nicknames:** *Ron, Ronn,
Ronnie, Ronny*; **Famous Namesakes:**
*President Ronald Reagan, Clown Ronald
McDonald*; **Star Babies:** *Son of Tina Turner*

RONAN Irish: Little seal

RONDEL French: Short poem of fourteen
lines containing only two rhyming sounds

RONEL Hebrew: Song of the Lord
Ronell; **Nicknames:** *Roni*

RONSON English: Son of Ronald
Ronaldson, Ronsen

ROOK English: Raven
Ruck

ROONEY Irish, Gaelic: Red-haired
Famous Namesakes: *Actor Mickey Rooney,*
Newsman Andy Rooney

ROOSEVELT Scandinavian: Rose field
Famous Namesakes: *President Theodore*
Roosevelt, President Franklin Delano Roosevelt

ROPER English: Rope maker; an occupational name
Rapere

RORY Irish: Red; the last high king of
Ireland was Rory O'Connor, who died in
1198. Irish rebel chief Rory O'More is
celebrated in poetry, drink, and music.
Rorey, Rorry, Ruairi; **Star Babies:** *Son of Bill*
Gates

ROSARIO Spanish, Portuguese: Rosary;
refers to devotional prayers honoring the
Virgin Mary

ROSCOE Scandinavian, English: Land
or forest of the roe deer
Rosco

ROSS Scottish, Latin: From the headlands.
German: Variant of Roswald. English:
Variant of Roswell, Russell
Ros

ROSTISLAV Slavic: Seize glory

ROSWALD English: Rose field

ROSWELL English: From the horse well
or spring

ROTH German, Scottish: Red, redhead; used
as a surname and given name
Famous Namesakes: *Author Philip Roth*

ROTHWELL Norse: Dwells near the red
spring

ROURKE Irish, Gaelic: Famous king; an
ancient given name adopted as an Irish clan
name
Roark, Rorke, Ruarc, Ruark; **Famous**
Namesakes: *Actor Mickey Rourke*

ROVER English: Wanderer
Old Forms: *Rovere*

ROWAN Irish, English: Little red-haired one;
can also refer to the flowering Rowan tree
Roan, Roane, Ruadhan; **Nicknames:** *Row*

ROWDY English: Boisterous, loud; Many
parents would consider this a perfect
description of an excited young boy.

ROWE Irish: Nickname for Rohan

ROWELL English: From the roe deer's
spring

ROWLEY English: From the rough or
roughly cleared meadow; surname
Ruhleah, Rowlea, Rowlee, Rowleigh, Rowly

ROWSON Anglo-Saxon: Rowe's son, the
redhead's son
Roweson; **Old Forms:** *Ruadson*

ROXBURY English: From the raven's town
or estate

ROY French: Regal, kingly; (Gaelic)
red-haired
Roi, Royal, Royall, Rui

ROYAL French: Spelling variation of Roy

ROYCE English, French: Roy's son or variant of
Reece. German: Famous. Latin: Regal
(English) *Royse*; **Star Babies:** *Son of Sinbad*

ROYDEN English: From the rye or royal valley

RUDD English: Familiar form of several names including Rudolph and Rudyard

RUDOLPH Teutonic: Famous wolf; well known by children for the fabled red-nosed reindeer
(Spanish) *Rodolfo, Rolo, Rudi, Rudolfo, Rudy*; (Scandinavian) *Rudolf*; (Swedish) *Rolf, Rolfe*; **Nicknames:** *Rolphe*; **Famous Namesakes:** *Actor Rudolph Valentino, Dancer Rudolf Nureyev*

RUDY German: Nickname for Rudolph
Famous Namesakes: *Politician Rudy Giuliani, Figure skater Rudy Galindo*

RUDYARD English: From the rough enclosure
Nicknames: *Rudy*; **Famous Namesakes:** *Author Rudyard Kipling*

RUFORD English: From the red ford
Rufford

RUFUS Latin: Red-haired; several early saints had this name
(French) *Ruff, Ruffe*; (Spanish) *Rufio, Rufo*; (Polish) *Rufin*; *Rufeo*

RUGBY English: From the raven's estate, fortress; the popular sport of rugby was named after a school bearing this name.

RULE Latin: Command
(French) *Ruelle*

RUMFORD English: From the wide ford

RUNE German, Swedish: Secret. English: Puzzle, pictograph

RUPERT German: Variation of Robert
Ruprecht; **Famous Namesakes:** *British actor Rupert Everett, Media magnate Rupert Murdoch*

RUSH French: Nickname for Russell
Famous Namesakes: *Conservative political pundit Rush Limbaugh*

RUSHFORD English: Lives near the rush ford
Old Forms: *Ryscford*

RUSHKIN French: Nickname for Russell

RUSLAN Russian: This name was used by Aleksandr Pushkin in his poem "Ruslan and Ludmila."

RUSSELL French, English: Redhead; (Anglo-Saxon) fox, color of the fox (red)
Roselyn, Roslyn, Roslin, Rosselin, Rosselyn, Rousse, Roussel, Rousset, Rousskin, Russel; **Nicknames:** *Rush, Rushe, Rushkin, Russ, Rust, Rusty*; **Famous Namesakes:** *Actor Russell Crowe*

RUSTY English: Nickname for Russell

RUTHERFORD English: From the cattle ford
Rutherfurd; **Famous Namesakes:** *President Rutherford Hayes*

RUTLAND Norse: From the red or root land
Rotland

RUTLEDGE English: From the red ledge or cliff; surname
Routledge

RUTLEY English: From the root meadow or red meadow; surname
Rutlea, Rutleigh, Rutlee, Rutlie

RYAN Irish, Gaelic: Kingly
Rayan, Rian, Rion, Ryen, Ryon, Rien, Ryne;
Famous Namesakes: *Actor Ryan O'Neal,*
Baseball player Ryne Sandberg

RYCE English: Spelling variation of Rice

RYCROFT English: From the rye field;
surname
Ryecroft

RYDER English: Spelling variation of Rider

RYDGE English: Spelling variation of Ridge

RYE English: A specific grain used in breads,
cereals, and whiskey; also a familiar form of
many English names which contain the root
ry or rye

RYLAND English, Irish: From the land
or fields of rye; surname
(Irish) *Rylan*

RYMAN English: Rye merchant

RYTON English: From the rye town or settlement; surname

SAA Egyptian: A nature god

SAADYA Hebrew: God's helper

SAAM Persian: A name from Persian
mythology, a character in Shahnameh
Sam

SAAMAN Persian: Home, welfare
Saman

SAAR Hebrew: Wind

SABIH Arabic: Handsome
Sobhi

SABIN Latin: A Sabine; the Sabines were a
rival tribe living in central Italy near the time
that Rome was established by Romulus and
Remus.
(Italian) *Savino;* (Spanish) *Sabino;*
Old Forms: *Sabinus*

SABIR Arabic: Patient, enduring, persevering
Saber; **Famous Namesakes:** *Kurdish poet*
Refiq Sabir, Swimmer Sabir Muhammad

SABOLA Egyptian: Pepper

SABRA Egyptian: Patient

SABRE French: Sword

SABURO Japanese: Third son

SACHI Hindi: Descended from the sun god

SACHIN Sanskrit: Pure

SACHIO Japanese: Fortunately born

SADEGH Persian: Sincere

SADIKI Egyptian: Faithful

SADIQ Arabic: Friend
Sadeeq

SAGE English, French: Wise one
Sagan, Sagar, Saige, Sayge; **Star Babies:** *Son of Tracey Gold and Roby Marshall, Sylvester Stallone*

SAGHIR Arabic: Short, small

SAHALE Native American: Falcon

SAHEN Hindi: Above

SAHIR Arabic: Wakeful. Hindi: Friend

SAID Arabic, Persian: Happy, fortunate; Port Said is a large city on the Suez Canal in Egypt.
Saeed

SAJAG Hindi: Watchful

SAKA Hindi: From the Shaka

SAKERI Hebrew: Remembered by God

SAKIMA Native American: King

SALAH Arabic: Righteous, righteousness, goodness

SALEEM African: Peaceful (Swahili)

SALEM Hebrew: Peace; in the Psalms, Salem is used as an abbreviated name for Jerusalem.
Old Forms: *Shalom*

SALIH Egyptian: Upright

SALIM Arabic, African: Peaceful, safe
Salam, Selim

SALMALIN Hindi: Claw

SALMONEUS Greek, Latin: King of Elis who pretended to be equal to Zeus by driving around in a bronze chariot and imitating Zeus' thunder and lightning.

SALTON English: From the willow tree town or settlement; surname
Salhtun, Saltin, Salten

SALVADOR Latin, Spanish: Savior; given in reference to Jesus Christ
(Italian) *Salvatore, Salvatorio*; (Spanish) *Salbatore, Salvadore, Salvino, Xabat, Xalbador, Xalvador*; *Salvator*; Nicknames: *Sal*;
Famous Namesakes: *Artist Salvador Dali*

SAMI Arabic, Persian: Elevated, exalted. Finnish: Asked of God; short form of Samuli

A Matter of Fact

First Ayyubid Sultan of Egypt, Salah al-Din Yusuf Ibn Ayyub (1138–1193) became renowned in the western world under the name of Saladin. Despite his fierce opposition to the Christian powers, Saladin achieved a great reputation in Europe as a chivalrous knight, so much so that there existed by the fourteenth century an epic poem about his exploits, and Dante included him among the virtuous pagan souls in Limbo.

SAMMAN Arabic: Grocer, butter merchant

SAMSON Hebrew: Sun; the biblical Samson was an Israelite judge given superhuman strength by God. His power diminished when Delilah, his Philistine mistress, learned his strength was in his long hair and had his locks shorn.
(English) *Sampson*; *Sanson*

SAMU Finnish: Asked of God; short form of Samuli

SAMUEL Hebrew: Told by God; the biblical Samuel was a judge and prophet in early Israel who anointed Saul and David as kings. Two Old Testament books are named for him. See also *Samu* (Finnish) *Samuli*; (Hungarian) *Samuka*; (Yiddish) *Schmuel*; *Samoel, Schmaiah, Samual, Samuell, Samualle*; **Nicknames:** *Sam, Sammy, Sami*; **Famous Namesakes:** *Irish playwright Samuel Beckett, Actor Samuel Jackson, Opera singer Samuel Ramey, Actor Sammy Davis Jr., Baseball player Sammy Sosa*; **Star Babies:** *Son of Bob Dylan, Sally Field, Jessica Lange and Sam Shepard*

SANAT Hindi: Ancient

SANDERS English: Alexander's son; surname

SANDERSON English: Alexander's son

SANDY English: Defender of man; abbreviation of Alexander
Famous Namesakes: *Pitcher Sandy Koufax*

SANI Native American: The old one, age implying wisdom (Navajo)

SANIIRO Japanese: Praiseworthy, admirable

SANJAR Persian: Emperor, king

SANJIV Hindi: Long life

SANTIAGO Spanish: Saint James; Santiago is the capital and largest city of Chile.

SANTO Italian: Sacred, holy, saint (Spanish) *Sancho, Santos*; **Diminutive Forms:** *Santino*

SAQR Arabic: Falcon

SARAD Hindi: Bom during the fall

SARKIS Armenian: Protector, shepherd

SARSOUR Arabic: Bug; masculine version of Sarsoura

SASHA Russian: Nickname for Alexander

SASSON Hebrew: Joy

SATCHEL American: Small bag, sack **Nicknames:** *Satch*; **Famous Namesakes:** *Baseball player Satchel Paige*; **Star Babies:** *Son of Woody Allen and Mia Farrow*

SATIVOLA English: Name of an eighth-century saint

SATURN Latin: Saturn was the god of the harvest in early Roman mythology. Saturn is also the second largest planet in our solar system and has seven rings around it. (Spanish) *Saturnin*; (Welsh) *Sadwm*; (Basque) *Satordi*

SAUL Hebrew: Inquired of God; name of the first king of Israel and the Hebrew name of the apostle Paul before his conversion to Christianity
Famous Namesakes: *Author Saul Bellow*

SAVILLE French: From the willow farm; surname
Sauville, Savill, Savile; **Famous Namesakes:** *Designer Peter Saville*

SAVION Contemporary: Possibly derived from Xavier
Famous Namesakes: *Tap dancer Savion Glover*

SAWYER English, Celtic: Woodcutter; This surname is familiar to many as the main character of Mark Twain's classic novel *The Adventures of Tom Sawyer*.
Sawyere, Sawyers; **Star Babies:** *Son of Kate Capshaw and Steven Spielberg*

SAXON English, Teutonic: Swordsman, knife; Saxons were among the Germanic tribes who invaded and settled fifth-century England.
Saxan, Saxton

SAYER Welsh: Carpenter; surname
Saer, Sayers, Sayre, Sayres; **Famous Namesakes:** *British musician Leo Sayer*

SAYYID Arabic: Master

SCHUYLER Dutch: Shelter, scholar
Schylar, Schyler, Skyelar, Skylar, Skyler, Skylor

SCOTT English, Scottish: From Scotland, a Gael; also a surname
Scot, Scottas; **Nicknames:** *Scottie, Scotty*; **Famous Namesakes:** *Basketball player Scottie Pippen, Musician Scott Joplin*

SCULLY Irish, Gaelic: Herald; surname
Old Forms: *Scolaighe*

SEABERT English: Glory at sea
Saebeorht, Seabright, Seaburt, Sebert

SEAGHDA Irish: Majestic

SEAMUS Gaelic: Supplanter; variant of James
Seumas, Shamus, Shemus

SEAN Irish: God has been gracious; a very popular variant of John
Seanan, Shaan, Shain, Shaine, Shan, Shandon, Shandy, Shane, Shann, Shauden, Shaughn, Shaun, Shaundre, Shawn, Shayne, Shonn;
Famous Namesakes: *Actors Sean Astin, Sean Connery, Sean Penn*; **Star Babies:** *Son of John Lennon, Oliver Stone, Pierce Brosnan*

SEARLE English, Teutonic: Armed, manly
Searlas, Searlus

SEATON Anglo-Saxon, English: The town or settlement near the sea; surname
Seeton, Seton

SEB Egyptian: God of the earth

SEBASTIAN Latin: Revered or the Roman term for a person from the ancient city of Sebastia; a third-century martyred centurion became Saint Sebastian, patron saint of soldiers.
(French) *Sebastien*; (Italian) *Sebastiano*; (Spanish) *Bastian, Sevastian*; (Hungarian) *Sebestyen, Sebo*; *Sabastian, Sebasten*; **Old Forms:** *Sebastianus*; **Famous Namesakes:** *British track star Sebastian Coe*; **Star Babies:** *Son of James Spader*

SEDGELEY English: From the sword meadow, referring possibly to a sharp vegetation in the meadow, possibly to a meadow owned by a swordsman, possibly a training meadow for swordsmen; surname
Sedgley, Sedgely, Sedgelea, Sedgleigh

SEEGER English: Seaman; surname
Seager, Segar, Seger; **Famous Namesakes:** *Musician Pete Seeger, Musician Bob Seger*

SEFU Egyptian: Sword

SEGENAM Native American: Idle (Algonquin)

SEGUNDO Spanish: Born second

SEIGNEUR French: Lord
Senior

SEIJI Japanese: Lawful, manages affairs of state
Famous Namesakes: *Japanese conductor Seiji Ozawa*

SEIREADAN Irish: Untamed

SEITH Welsh: Seven

SEKANI Egyptian: Full of laughter

SELBY English: From the manor village or estate; a surname and possible variant of Shelby

SELIG German: Blessed, happy in life *Saelig, Sealey, Seeley, Seely, Selik, Zelig, Zelik, Zeligman, Zelyg*; **Old Forms:** *Seelig*; **Famous Namesakes:** *Baseball Commissioner Bud Selig*

SENUSNET Egyptian: Name of a pharaoh

SEPPO Finnish: Smith

SEPTIMUS Latin: Born seventh

SERAPHIM Hebrew: Fiery; Seraphim are angels of heaven, each with three pairs of wings and known for their strong love. (Spanish) *Serafin*; *Serafim, Serafino, Sarafino*

SERAPIS Egyptian: Variant for the god Apis; Serapis was mainly worshipped in Alexandria, and was later worshipped by the Greeks as Zeus. He was never fully accepted by the Egyptians in the Ptolemaic period.

SERENO Latin: Calm **Old Forms:** *Serenus*

SERGIO Latin, Italian: Attendant, servant (French) *Serge*; (Russian) *Sergei, Seriozha, Seriozhenka*; (Polish) *Sergiusz, Serjuisz*; *Sergeo*; **Old Forms:** *Sergios, Sergius*; **Famous Namesakes:** *Film director Sergio Leone*

SETH Hebrew: Compensation; Seth was the third child of Adam and Eve, so named because God gave Eve another son after Abel had been killed. Egyptian: The god of storms and the desert, son of Geb and Nut, and brother of Osiris (and later, his murderer); in the Heliopolitan Ennead, this god was in the form of an animal with no zoological equivalent and is hence identified with many animals. The Greeks equated him with Typhon.

Set, Sutekh; **Star Babies:** *Son of Sylvester Stallone*

SETHOS Egyptian: Name of a prince

SEVAN Armenian: Name of a lake, meaning unknown

SEVRIN Latin: Strict, restrained; a saint's name
(French) *Severin*; (Spanish) *Severo*; (Polish) *Seweryn*; *Severn, Severne*; **Old Forms:** *Severus*

SEWARD English: Sea guardian; a surname. William Henry Seward was the secretary of state during the American Civil War. While in office, he oversaw the purchase of Alaska from Russia. At the time, Alaska did not seem valuable to the United States, and the purchase was called "Seward's Folly." **Old Forms:** *Saeweard*

SEXTUS Latin: Bom sixth *Sixtus*

SEYMOUR English: Marshy land near the sea

SHABAKA Egyptian: Name of a king

SHAHAB Persian: Shooting star, meteor

SHAHAM Persian: The exact meaning of this name is unknown, though it is derived from the Persian word shah, meaning king.

SHAHIN Persian: Falcon *Shaheen*

SHAKA African: The name of the Zulu tribal leader sometimes compared to Attila the Hun. Shaka shaped an amalgamation of tribes into the great Zulu nation in the early nineteenth century. Hindi: From the Shaka

SHAKIR Arabic: Grateful; masculine form of Shakira *Shakeer*

SHAKOUR Arabic: Grateful
Shakur, Shakoor

SHAKTAR Hindi: Name of a hermit

SHALYA Hindi: Throne

SHAMBA Hindi: Son of Krishna

SHAMI Hindi: Husband

SHAMIL Persian: The north wind

SHAN Gaelic: Old, wise

SHANDLEY English: From the loud or bois-
terous meadow; surname
Scandleah, Shandlea, Shandlee, Shandleigh;
Nicknames: *Shandy*

SHANE Irish: Variant of Sean, a popular
Irish cognate of John; *Shane* was a successful
Western motion picture of the 1950s.

SHANKARA Hindi: Grand

SHANNON Irish: Old and wise; from the
Shannon, a river of Ireland
Shannen; **Famous Namesakes:** *Football
player Shannon Sharpe*

SHARIF Arabic: Spelling variation of Sherif
Sherif, Charif, Cherif, Shereef, Shareef;
Famous Namesakes: *Egyptian actor Omar
Sharif*

SHASHIDA Hindi: Ocean

SHAW English: From the shady grove. Irish:
Surname

SHEA Irish: Hawklike or majestic; an Irish
family name and the name of New York's
Shea Stadium
Shae, Shai, Shay, Shaye, Shey; **Star Babies:**
Son of John Grisham

SHEARY Irish: Variation of Jeffrey

SHEFFIELD English: From the crooked
field; surname
Scaffeld

SHELBY English: From the village or estate
on the ledge; though appropriate for boys or
girls, use for boys has declined while use for
girls has risen in recent history.
(Anglo-Saxon) *Shelny*; *Selby, Selbey*; **Star
Babies:** *Son of Reba McEntire*

SHELDON English, Anglo-Saxon: A farm
in a deep valley
Shelden

SHELLEY Anglo-Saxon, English: From the
ledge meadow; a surname evocative of the
poet Percy Bysshe Shelley
Shelly

SHELTON English: From the ledge town
or settlement; surname
Scelftun

SHEM Hebrew: Renown, name, as in one
of note; the biblical Shem was the eldest of
Noah's three sons and therefore, according
to lore, an ancestor of the human race.

SHEPHERD English: Shepherd
Shepard, Shephard; **Nicknames:** *Shep*; **Famous
Namesakes:** *Newsman Shepard Smith*

SHEPLY Anglo-Saxon, English: From the
sheep meadow (sheep being extremely
important to the English economy and
culture); surname
(English) *Sceapleigh*; *Shepley, Shipley*

SHERIDAN Irish: Untamed
Sheriden, Sheridon

SHERIF Arabic: Illustrious, noble, honorable, respectable, honest; Sharif is a term used to describe Mohammed's descendants.
Ashraf, Sharif, Shereef, Shareef, Cherif, Charif; **Famous Namesakes:** *Egyptian actor Nour el Sherif*

SHERLOCK English: Blond; made famous by the Sherlock Holmes detective stories by Sir Arthur Conan Doyle

SHERMAN English: Cuts the nap of woolen cloth; in medieval times, the shireman served as governor-judge of an English shire or county.
(German) *Shermon*

SHERWIN English: Swift, quick as the wind
Sherwyn

SHERWOOD English: From the bright forest; Sherwood Forest in England has long been associated with the legendary hero Robin Hood.

SHESHA Hindi: King of serpents

SHILAH Native American: Brother (Navajo)

SHILOH Hebrew: The peaceful one, he who is to be sent; in the Bible, Shiloh is a prophetic name for the Messiah. Shiloh is also significant as the site of a crucial battle in the American Civil War.
Shilo

SHIMON Hebrew: Son of Simon
Old Forms: *Shim'on;* **Famous Namesakes:** *Israeli Prime Minister Shimon Peres*

SHIMSHON Hebrew: Bright sun

SHIRIKI Native American: Coyote (Pawnee)

SHIRON Hebrew: Songfest

SHIVA Hindi: God of the moon

SHIYE Native American: Son (Navajo)

SHIZHE'E Native American: Father (Navajo)

SHODA Japanese: Flat and level field

SHU Egyptian: The god of air and the bearer of heaven; Shu was an ancient cosmic power who, with Tefnut, formed the first pair of gods in the Heliopolitan Ennead. He is represented as a man separating the sky from the earth.

SHUNNAR Arabic: Bird

SIAMAK Persian: Black-haired man

SIARL Welsh: Variation of Charles

SIBLEY Latin: Prophetic

SICHEII Native American: Grandfather (Navajo)

SIDNEY French, English: Uncertain meaning; Sidney may be from a French place name, Saint Denis. Another theory states that this name stems from Old English meaning wide island. Sidney is favored for boys, while Sydney is used almost entirely for girls.
Sydney; **Nicknames:** *Sid, Syd;* **Famous Namesakes:** *Actor Sidney Poitier*

SIDONUS Latin: Follower of Saint Denis, the martyred Bishop of Paris
(Czech) *Zdenek*

SIEGFRIED German: Victorious peace
Siegfred, Sigfrid, Sigfried, Sigifrid, Sigifrith

SIGMUND German: Victorious protection
(Norse) *Sigurd, Sigvard;* (Polish) *Zygmunt; Sigismondo, Sigismund, Sigmond, Zsigmond;* **Nicknames:** *Zsiga, Siggy, Ziggy;* **Famous Namesakes:** *Austrian psychiatrist Sigmund Freud*

SIGWALT German: Victorious ruler
Sigiwald, Sigwald

SIJUR Norse: Victorious defender

SIKE Native American: He sits at home
(Navajo)

SILAS English: Variation of Silvain

SILVAIN Latin: Of the forest; referring to
the mythological Roman god of trees
(English) *Selvyn, Silas, Sylvester*; (German)
Silvan, Silvester; (French) *Silvestre*; (Italian)
Silvio; (Spanish) *Silvanio, Silvano*;
(Portuguese) *Silverio*; *Silio, Silos, Silvanos,
Sylvan, Sylvanus*; **Old Forms:** *Silvanus,
Silvius*; **Nicknames:** *Sil, Sill*; **Famous Name-
sakes:** *French animator Sylvain Chomet*

SILVESTER German: Variation of Silvain
Sylvester, Sly; **Famous Namesakes:** *Actor
Sylvester Stallone*

SIMAO Hebrew: Obedient

SIMCHA Hebrew: Joy

SIMON Hebrew: Hearkening, listening;
there were several men named Simon in the
Bible, including Simon Peter, one of Christ's
twelve disciples. See also *Ximenes*
(Hebrew) *Siomon*; (Greek) *Symeon*; (French)
Simeon; (Gaelic) *Sim*; (Russian) *Semyon*;
(Finnish) *Simo*; *Simen, Simpson, Symon,
Ximen, Ximon, Ximun*; **Famous Namesakes:**
*British director Simon West, Musician Paul
Simon, Playwright Neil Simon*; **Star Babies:**
Son of Phil Collins

SINCLAIR French, English, Scottish: Saint
Clair
Sinclaire; **Famous Namesakes:** *Author
Sinclair Lewis*

SINDRI Norse: A mythical dwarf
Star Babies: *Son of Björk*

SINJON English: Holy, sanctified; a name
honoring Saint John
Sinjin, Sinjun

SINON Greek: A Greek spy who gained the
trust of the Trojans during the Trojan War
by pretending to be on their side

SIODHACHAN Irish: Little peaceful one

SIOR Welsh: Variation of George

SISYPHUS Greek: Son of Aelous

SIV Norse: Victorious defender

SIWILI Native American: Tail of the fox

SKAH Native American: White (Sioux)

SKANDA Hindi: God of war

SKEET English: Swift
Skeat, Skete, Sketes; **Famous Namesakes:**
Actor Skeet Ulrich

SKIPPER English: Captain
Skippere; **Nicknames:** *Skip, Skippy*

SKYE English: Refers to the Scottish Isle
of Skye; a nature name referring to the sky

SLADE English: From the valley; surname
Slaed, Slayde; **Star Babies:** *Son of David
Brenner*

SLAVIN Gaelic: Mountain; surname
Sleven, Slevin, Slevyn

SLAVOCHKA Slavic: Glory

SLOAN Gaelic, Scottish: Warrior, fighter;
surname
Sloane

SMEDLEY English: From the flat meadow
Smetheleah, Smedlea, Smedleigh, Smedly

SMITH English: Tradesman, blacksmith; surname
Smyth, Smythe; **Famous Namesakes:** *Actor Will Smith*

SNEFERU Egyptian: Name of a pharaoh

SOBHI Arabic: Spelling variation of Sabih
Sobhy; **Famous Namesakes:** *Egyptian comedian Mohammed Sobhy, Egyptian artist and painter Magdi Sobhy*

SOBK Egyptian: The crocodile god worshipped throughout Egypt, but especially in the Faiyum, and at Gebelein and Kom Ombo in Upper Egypt

SOCRATES Greek: Meaning unknown; Socrates was an ancient and influential Greek philosopher and teacher.

SOHRAB Persian: A name from Persian mythology and character in Shahnameh

SOL Spanish: Sun

SOLOMON Hebrew: Peace; variant of Salem. Solomon (son of David and Bathsheba) succeeded his father as King of Israel. The Old Testament's Proverbs and Ecclesiastes are ascribed to him.
(Arabic) *Sulaiman*; (Spanish) *Salomon*; (Yiddish) *Schlomo*; *Salamon*; **Nicknames:** *Sol*; **Famous Namesakes:** *Artist and writer Solomon Charles Levine*

SOMNUS Latin: Sleep

SONGAA Native American: Strong

SONNY English: Son; a nickname and given name
Sonnie; **Famous Namesakes:** *Actor and politician Sonny Bono*

SOREN Danish: Strict; possibly a variant of Severin, Soren is the Danish form of Thor

Famous Namesakes: *Danish philosopher Soren Kierkegaard*

SOROUSH Persian: Messenger

SORRELL French: Reddish-brown hair
Sorel

SOTERIOS Greek: Savior

SOUTHWELL English: From the southern well; surname

SOWI'NGWA Native American: Black-tailed deer (Hopi)

SPALDING English: From the split or divided field; a surname and well-known brand of sporting goods
Spelding, Spaulding; **Famous Namesakes:** *Humorist and author Spalding Gray*

SPENCER English: Keeper of provisions
Spenser; **Nicknames:** *Spence*; **Famous Namesakes:** *Actor Spencer Tracy*; **Star Babies:** *Son of Cuba Gooding Jr.*

SQUIRE English: Shieldbearer
Squier; **Famous Namesakes:** *Actor Squire Fridell*

STACY English: Productive; familiar form of Eustace
Famous Namesakes: *Actor Stacy Keach*

STAMITOS Greek: Enduring
Stamatis

STANBURY English: From the stone fortress; surname adapted to first name use
Stanbeny; **Old Forms:** *Stanburgh*

STANDISH English: From the stony park; a surname evocative of Pilgrim leader Miles Standish
Standisch

STANFIELD English: From the stony field; surname
Stanfeld, Stansfeld, Stansfield

STANFORD English: From the stony ford; a surname and the name of the prestigious Stanford University in California
Stamford, Standford

STANHOPE English: From the stony hollow; surname
Stanhop

STANISLAUS Slavic: Camp of glory, military glory; a name borne by Slavic kings and Saint Stanislaus, the patron saint of Poland (Spanish) *Estanislao*; (Russian) *Stanislav*; *Stanislas, Stanislaw*; **Nicknames:** *Stannes, Stas, Stan*; **Famous Namesakes:** *Wrestler Stanislaus Zbyszko*

STANLEY English: From near the stony meadow; a surname commonly used as a first name
Stanly; **Nicknames:** *Lee*; **Diminutive Forms:** *Stan*; **Famous Namesakes:** *Director Stanley Kubrick*; **Star Babies:** *Son of MC Hammer*

STANTON English: Stony town or village; surname
Stantun, Staunton, Stanten

STANWAY English: Stony road or path; surname
Stanweg

STANWICK English: Lives in or near the stony village; surname
Stanwic, Stanwik, Stanwyk

STANWOOD English: From the stony wood or forest; surname
Stanwode; **Nicknames:** *Stan, Woody*

STARBUCK English: Star deer, a prized deer; for many, this name likely conjures up images of piping hot java from the Starbucks coffee chain.

STAS Slavic: Nickname for Stanislaus

STAVROS Greek: Victorious

STEELE English: Hard or durable (as steel)
Steel

> *"Groucho is not my real name. I'm breaking it in for a friend."*
> —Groucho Marx

STEIN German: Stone; surname (Swedish) *Sten*; *Steen, Steiner*; **Famous Namesakes:** *Actor Sten Eirik, Actor Ben Stein*

STEPHANOS Greek: Original form of Stephen

STEPHEN Greek: Crowned in victory; the New Testament portrays Stephen as an inspired leader of the church. A speech of his stirred an angry mob and he was stoned, becoming Christianity's first martyr.
(German) *Stefan*; (French) *Etienne, Stéphane*; (Italian) *Stefano, Stephano*; (Spanish) *Esteban, Estebe, Estefan, Estevan, Estevon*; (Portuguese) *Estevao*; (Gaelic) *Steaphan, Stiabhan*; (Welsh) *Steffan, Steffen*; (Swedish) *Staffan*; (Russian) *Stepan, Stepka*; (Hungarian) *Istvan, Pista, Pisti*; *Steafan, Steffon, Stefon, Stephon, Stevan, Steven, Stevon, Stevyn*; **Old Forms:** *Stefanos, Stephanos*; **Nicknames:** *Steve, Stevie*; **Famous Namesakes:** *Actors Stephen Baldwin and Steve Martin, Author Stephen King, Filmmaker Steven Spielberg*

STERLING English, German: Of high quality, pure; refers to sterling silver, and may come from the star emblem found on early coins
Staerling, Starling, Sterlyn, Stirling, Styrling;
Famous Namesakes: *Football player Sterling Sharpe*

STETSON American: Cowboy hat

STEWART Scottish, English: Steward; a medieval steward was charged with the care of castle and estate affairs. Stuart and Stewart are clan names of the royal house of Scotland.
(English) *Stuart; Steward, Stewert;*
Nicknames: *Stew;* **Famous Namesakes:**
Musician Stewart Copeland

STIG Swedish: From the mount

STOCKLEY English: From the meadow of tree stumps; surname
Stocleah, Stocklea, Stockleigh

STORM English: Tempest, storm; nature name
Storme; **Famous Namesakes:** *Meteorologist Storm Field*

STROM Czech: Stream, tree
Famous Namesakes: *Senator Strom Thurmond*

STUART English: Variation of Stewart

SUFFIELD English: From the south field; surname
Suthfeld

SULAIMAN Arabic: Variation of Solomon

SULEYMAN Turkish: Peace

SULLIVAN Irish: Dark eyes; surname
Sulliven; **Old Forms:** *Suileabhan;*
Nicknames: *Sully*

SULLY English: From the south meadow; Sully is the beloved monster from the animated movie *Monsters, Inc.* Sully is also a nickname for Sullivan.

SULO Finnish: Sweet

SULYA Hindi: God of the sun

SUMMER Contemporary: Born in summer
Sommer

SUNREET Hindi: Pure

SUNUKKUHKAU Native American: He crushes (Algonquin)

SURTR Norse: A mythical giant

SUTCLIFF English: From the southern cliff; surname
Sutclyf, Suthclif, Suttecliff

SUTHLEY English: From the south meadow; surname
Suthleah

SUTTON English: From the southern settlement or town; surname

SUZU Japanese: Long-lived, crane

SVEN Scandinavian: Youth
Svein, Svend, Svens, Svewn, Sveyn;
Famous Namesakes: *Director Sven Nykvist*

SWAIN English: Knight's attendant
Swayn

TABBART German: Brilliant
Nicknames: *Tab*

TABER Irish: Well

TABIB Arabic: Physician
Tabeeb

TABOR Hebrew: Drum; in the Bible, Mount
Tabor is a landmark mountain near
Nazareth; (Hungarian) camp
Nicknames: *Tab*

TADD English: Nickname for Thaddeus

TADEO Spanish: Praise

TADLEIGH Irish: Bard

TAFT English: River
Nicknames: *Taffy*; **Famous Namesakes:**
President William Howard Taft

TAG Teutonic: Day; (Irish) handsome;
a variant of Teague
Tage

TAGGART Gaelic: Son of a priest

TAHIR Arabic: Pure, purify
(Persian) *Taher*; *Tahu*

TAHKEOME Native American: Little robe
(Cheyenne)

TAIMA Native American: Thunderclap
Taiomah, Tama, Tamah

TAJ African: Exalted (Urdu); (Sanskrit)
crown
Star Babies: *Son of Tito Jackson*

TAJO Spanish: Day

TAKEO Japanese: Take

TAKIS Greek: Contemporary Greek variant
of Peter

TAKODA Native American: Friend to everyone (Sioux)

TAKSHAKA Hindi: Carpenter

TAL Hebrew, English: Dew

TALBOT English: To destroy bad messages;
the surname of an aristocratic Irish family
who gave this name to their bloodhound,
thus creating a breed of dogs name Talbot
Talbert, Talbott, Talford; **Nicknames:** *Tally*

TALEB Arabic: Seeker
Talib

TALIESIN Welsh: Brow; in Welsh mythology,
Taliesin was a wizard and bard who acquired
the gift of prophecy.

TALON French, English: Claw
Tallon

TALUS Greek: In Greek legend, Talus was
the son of Perdix and twelve-year-old
nephew and apprentice of Daedalus. He
surpassed his uncle in skill, however, by
inventing the saw, potter's wheel, and
compass for drawing circles.

TAMAR Hebrew: Palm tree
(Russian) *Tamryn*; *Tamarr*

TAMIR Arabic: Owns palm trees, date dealer,
full of dates

TANGUY French: Warrior

TANISHIA African: Born on Monday

TANJIRO Japanese: High-valued second son

TANNER English: Leather worker; occupational surname
Tannere

TANTON English: From the quiet river farm

TAPIO Finnish: Finnish god of the forest, hunting, and animals

TARAFAH Arabic: Twinkling of an eye, sight, glance, to blink; can be used to imply nobility of birth from both parents

TAREK Arabic: This name has several meanings including morning star, nocturnal visitor, and to knock at a door. In the year 711, a former slave, a Berber by the name of Tariq Ibn-Ziyad, led an army of about 7,000 Moors ashore at a point close to the huge rock which dominates the entrance to the Mediterranean. They called the rock Jabal Tariq, or Tariq's Mount, and eventually western tongues changed the name to Gibraltar.
Tareq, Tarik, Tariq, Tareeq, Tarique, Tarick, Tareck; **Famous Namesakes:** *Egyptian writer Tarek Ali Hassan, Director and producer Tarek El Khashef*

TARIF Arabic: Unique, novel, rare, exquisite; often used to describe an interesting story

TARIK Egyptian: Form of Tariq

TARIQ Arabic: Spelling variation of Tarek; if emphasis is placed on the second syllable, Tariq additionally means way, road, or path.
Tarik; Tareeq

TARMO Finnish: Energy

TARO Japanese: Big boy or first son

TARRANT Welsh: Thunder
Tarant, Tarynt

TASUNKE Native American: Horse (Dakota)

TATANKA PTECILA Native American: Short bull (Sioux)

TATE English: Cheerful. Native American: He who talks too much. Irish: Measure of land
Tait, Tayt, Tayte

TAU African: Lion

TAURUS Latin: Bull; Taurus is a constellation picturing the forequarters of a bull and is a sign of the zodiac.
(Spanish) *Taurino, Tauro, Toro; Taurean*

TAVEON Irish, Scottish: Twin; variant of Thomas
(Italian) *Tavio*

TAVEY Latin: Nickname for Octavius

TAVIS Scottish, Irish: Twin; possibly a variant of Thomas
Tavish, Tavon, Tevin, Tevis

TAVORIAN African: Misfortune

TAWEEL Arabic: Tall
Tawil, El Tawil, Al Taweel; **Famous Namesakes:** *Egyptian composer Kamal El-Tawil*

TAYEB Arabic: Good, kind
Tayib, Tayyeb, Tayyheb

TAYLOR English: Tailor
Taylan, Tayler, Taylon, Tylor; **Famous Namesakes:** *President Zachary Taylor*

TEAGUE Celtic: A poet or philosopher
(Greek) *Tiege*; (Irish) *Tighe; Teaghue, Teauge*; **Nicknames:** *Tag*

TEARLACH Scottish: Variation of Charles

TEARLE English: Stern
Nicknames: *Tearley, Tearly*

TED English: Nickname for Theodore

TEDMUND English: National protector
Tedman

TEDRICK English: Variation of Theodore

TEETONKA Native American: Talks too much (Sioux)

TELAMON Greek: In Greek mythology, Telamon was the son of Aeacus, King of Aegina. He was one of the Argonauts who accompanied Jason on the quest for the Golden Fleece, and was present at the hunt for the Calydonian boar.

TELFORD French: Ironworker
(Polish) *Telek*; *Telfer, Telfor, Telfour*

TELUTCI Native American: Bear making dust (Miwok)

TEMPLETON English: Town near the temple, very possibly related to strongholds of the Knights-Templars; Templeton will be recognized by children as the name of Wilbur's rat friend in the classic book *Charlotte's Web*. *Tempeltun, Templeten*; **Nicknames:** *Temple, Temp*

TERENCE Latin, English: Tender, good and gracious; a Roman clan name
Tarrence, Terrance, Terrence; **Nicknames:** *Teris, Terry*

TERIKA English: Masculine form of Teresa

TERO Finnish: Manly; short form of Antero

TERRELL English: Powerful, thunder ruler; may be alluding to Thor, the Norse god of thunder
Terell, Terrall, Terrel, Terrelle, Terrill, Tirell, Teral, Terryl, Teryl, Tarel, Tarrell, Terall; **Famous Namesakes:** *Football player Terrell Davis*

TERRIS English: Son of Terrell or Terry
Terriss, Terrys

TERRON English: Earthman; contemporary rhyming blends of "Ter" plus Darin
Taren, Taron, Tarran, Tarrin, Terran, Terrin

TERRY English: Abbreviation of Terrance and Terrell; Terry is also an Anglicized phonetic form of the French given name Thierry, from an older Germanic name meaning powerful ruler.

TESHI African: Bright

TEVIN Irish: Twin; possibly a variant of Thomas

THAD Greek: Nickname for Thaddeus

THADDEUS Greek: Meaning uncertain, possibly brave or wise; Thaddeus was one of the twelve apostles described in the New Testament of the Bible.
Thaddius, Thadeus; **Nicknames:** *Tad, Tadd, Thad*

THAMYRIS Greek: In Greek mythology, Thamyris was a poet who loved the beautiful youth Hyacinthus.

THANE English, Scottish: Follower; Shakespeare's Macbeth was Thane of Cawdor.
Thayne

THANOS Greek: Nobleman

THATCHER English: Roofer; an occupational name
Thacher, Thacker, Thackere, Thaxter

THAW English: Melting ice

THAYER Teutonic: Nation's army

THEO Greek: Nickname for Theodore
Star Babies: *Son of Kate Capshaw and Steven Spielberg*

THEOBALD Teutonic: People's prince
(Irish) *Tibbot*; *Thibaud*; **Nicknames:** *Thilo*

THEODORE Greek: Gift of God; the name of saints, popes, and American president Theodore Roosevelt, for whom the teddy bear was originally named
(English) *Tedric, Tedrick*; (Italian) *Teodoro*; (Gaelic) *Teadoir*; (Welsh) *Tewdwr*; (Norse) *Theodrekr*; (Russian) *Fedor, Fedyenka, Feodor, Fyodor*; (Polish) *Teodor, Teos, Tolek*; (Hungarian) *Tivadar*; *Teodors, Theodon*; **Old Forms:** *Theodoros*; **Nicknames:** *Fedya, Ted, Tedd, Teddie, Teddy, Teo, Teyo, Theo, Tuder*; **Famous Namesakes:** *President Theodore Roosevelt, Singer and actor Theodore Bikel, Russian author Fyodor Dostoyevsky*

> *"The boy who is going to make a great man must not make up his mind merely to overcome a thousand obstacles, but to win in spite of a thousand repulses and defeats."*
> —Theodore Roosevelt

THEODRIC German: People's ruler; the original form of the more common names Derek and Dirk
Theodrik; **Old Forms:** *Theodoric*; **Nicknames:** *Dedrick, Dieter, Thieny, Thierry*

THEOPHILE Greek: Divinely loved

THERON Greek, French: Hunter, untamed
Therron

THILO German: Medieval short form of all German male names beginning with the prefix "Diet" (as in Dietrich)

THOMAS Aramaic, Greek: Twin; in the New Testament, Thomas the apostle doubted the resurrection of Jesus. This name is also borne by several saints, including philosopher and theologian Saint Thomas Aquinas.
(French) *Thomé*; (Italian) *Tommaso*; (Spanish) *Tomas*; (Irish) *Tomaisin*; (Welsh) *Tomos*; (Polish) *Tomasz, Tomek, Tomislaw*; (Finnish) *Tomi, Tommi*; (Hungarian) *Tamas*; *Thompson*; **Nicknames:** *Thom, Tom, Tommy*; **Famous Namesakes:** *Inventor Thomas Edison, President Thomas Jefferson*; **Star Babies:** *Son of Dana Carvey, son of Jamie Lee Curtis and Christopher Guest*

THOMÉ French: Variation of Thomas

THOMKINS English: Little Tom

THOR Norse: Thunder; Mythological Thor was the Norse god of thunder and a son of Odin. His main weapon was a hammer named Mjollnir. The day Thursday was named for Thor. See also *Thorbert*
(Scandinavian) *Thoren, Thorian*; *Thorin, Tor*

THORALD Norse: Thor ruler

THORBERT Teutonic: Glorious as Thor

THORLEY English, Teutonic: From Thor's meadow; surname
Thurleah, Thurleigh, Torley, Thorlea, Thorlee, Thorleigh, Thorly

THORMOND English: Thor's protection
Thormod, Thormund

THORNLEY English: From the thorny meadow; surname
Thornly, Thornlea, Thornleigh

THORNTON Gaelic: Town of thorns
Thorntun; **Nicknames:** *Thorn*

THOROLF Norse: Thor's wolf

THORPE English, Teutonic: From the village
Thorp; **Famous Namesakes:** *Athlete Jim Thorpe, Australian swimmer Ian Thorpe*

THOTH Egyptian: Moon god; associated with wisdom and sacred writing

THUNDER English: Stormy tempered

THURLOW English: From Thor's hill
Nicknames: *Thurl, Thurle*

THURMAN Scandinavian: Thunder; a surname and variant of Thor

THURMOND English: Thor's protection

THURSTON Scandinavian, English, Teutonic: Thor's stone, thunder; surname adapted to first name use
(Teutonic) *Thorsten*; (Norse) *Thorstein*; (Swedish) *Torsten*; *Thurstan, Thurstun*

TIASSALE African: It is forgotten

TIBBOT Irish: Variation of Theobald

TIBERIO Italian: From the Tibet River

TIBOR Slavic: Holy place

TIERNAN Celtic: Lord, chief
Tiernay; **Nicknames:** *Tier*

TIERNAY Celtic: Spelling variation of Tiernan
Tierney

TIHKOOSUE Native American: Short (Algonquin)

TILDEN English: From the fertile valley; surname
Tiladene, Tillden, Tildon

TILFORD English: From the fertile ford

TILL German: Medieval pet form of all German male names beginning with the prefix Diet- (as in Dietrich)

TILLMAN English: Virile. German: Mighty
Tilman; **Nicknames:** *Till*

TILTON English: From the fertile town or estate; surname
Tillton

TIMOTHY Greek: One who honors God; the biblical Timothy was a young Christian friend of Paul in the New Testament.
(Greek) *Timotheos, Timun*; (English) *Timon*; (Spanish) *Timo, Timoteo*; (Irish) *Tiomoid*; (Welsh) *Timotheus*; (Polish) *Tymek, Tymon, Tymoteusz*; **Nicknames:** *Tim, Timmy*;
Famous Namesakes: *Actor Timothy Hutton, Actor Tim Robbins, Comedian Tim Allen*;
Star Babies: *Son of Tim Roth*

TITOS Greek: Of the giants

TITUS Latin, Greek: Hero; an early Christian missionary and companion to Paul. See also *Titos*
(Italian) *Tito*; *Tityus*; **Famous Namesakes:** *Tito Jackson*

TOBIAS Greek: God is good; a form of Tobiah, an Old Testament Hebrew name
(Hebrew) *Tobiah*; (English) *Tobin, Tobyn*; (Finnish) *Topias*; **Nicknames:** *Tobey, Tobie, Toby, Topi*

TOBY English: Nickname for Tobias
Tobey, Tobie; **Famous Namesakes:** *Actor Tobey Maguire*

TOCHO Native American: Mountain lion (Hopi)

TODD English, Scottish: Fox; a clever or wily person.
Tod; **Famous Namesakes:** *Designer Todd Oldham, Skater Todd Eldredge*

TOGQUOS Native American: Twin (Algonquin)

TOHOPKA Native American: Wild beast (Hopi)

TOIVO Finnish: Hope

TOKALA Native American: Fox (Sioux)

TOLAND Anglo-Saxon, English: From the toll or taxed lands; surname
Tolan, Tolland

TOLMAN English: Collects taxes

TOM English: Nickname for Thomas
Thom; **Nicknames:** *Tommie, Tommy*;
Famous Namesakes: *Actor Tom Cruise, Actor Tom Hanks, Designer Tommy Hilfiger*

TOMKIN English: Little Tom

TOMLIN English: Little twin

TOOANTUH Native American: Spring frog (Cherokee)

TORIN Irish, Scottish: Chief; also a variant of Torrance

TORMEY Irish: Thunder spirit
Tormaigh

TORMOD Gaelic, Teutonic: From the north

TORQUIL Teutonic: From Thor's cauldron (Swedish) *Torkel*

TORRANCE Gaelic, Scottish: From the knolls; Torr is a name for a craggy hilltop and also may refer to a watchtower.
Toran, Torean, Torence, Torion, Torran, Torrans, Torrence, Torrian; **Nicknames:** *Tor, Toren, Torey, Torr, Torrey, Torrie, Torry, Tory, Toryn*

TORSTEN Teutonic: Spelling variation of Thurston

TORU Japanese: To deify or pass, absorb

TORYN Irish: Nickname for Torrance

TOSHI Japanese: Superior, fast, has advantage or is auspicious

TOSHIRO Japanese: Talented, intelligent, or fast

TOVI Hebrew: My goodness
Tohy

TOWLEY English: From the town meadow; surname
Townly, Tunleah, Townlea

TRACY French: From Thracia; a surname taken from a Norman French place name.
Tracey; **Nicknames:** *Trace*; **Star Babies:** Son of Ice T

TRAHERN Celtic, Welsh: Strong as iron

TRAUGOTT Teutonic: God's truth

TRAVIS French: Crossing or crossroads (French) *Travers*; **Star Babies:** *Son of Kyra Sedgwick and Kevin Bacon*

TREASACH Irish: Warlike
Treacy, Treasigh

TREMAINE English: House made of stone
Tramaine, Tremain, Tremayne

TRENTON English: Rapid river or stream; the capital of New Jersey
Trenten, Trentin

TREVELYAN Welsh: From Elian's home or a fair town
Traveon, Travion, Travon, Trevan, Trevelian, Treven, Trevian, Trevion, Trevon, Trevonn, Trevyn

TREVES French: A place name and surname

TREVOR Celtic: Wise, prudent; (Welsh) goodly town
Trevin; **Star Babies:** *Son of Wayne Gretzky and Janet Jones*

TREY English: Three; a variant of Traigh
Traigh; **Star Babies:** *Son of Will Smith and Sheree Zampino*

TRIPPER English: Traveler
Nicknames: *Trip, Tripp, Tryp, Trypp*

TRISTAN Celtic: Full of sorrows; a variant of Tristam. In Arthurian Legend, Tristan was a knight of the Round Table and tragic hero of the medieval tale Tristan and Isolde. (Welsh) *Trystan*; *Tristen, Tristian, Tristin, Tristyn*; **Old Forms:** *Tristam, Tristram*; **Star Babies:** *Son of Wayne Gretzky and Janet Jones, son of Natasha Henstridge*

TRISTRAM Arthurian Legend: Original form of Tristan

TRITON Latin, Greek: In Greek mythology, Triton is the son of Poseidon and Amphitrite and lived with them in a golden palace under the sea. Triton was represented as having the body of a man with the tail of a fish.

Literary Lore

The character of Walter Shandy in Laurence Sterne's novel *Tristram Shandy* believes that names are as important to a person's character as noses are to a person's appearance. Walter's solution to the problem of his new child's crushed nose is to name him Trismegistus, the name of the greatest king, lawgiver, philosopher, priest, and engineer of all time. Walter's rationale is that if one does not have a sizable nose, he still has a chance in life if he has a significant name, and this is one of the best. In the end, however, his child is accidentally christened with the name Tristram, which Walter considers the worst name in the world.

TROY Irish: A foot soldier; the ancient city of Troy was made famous in Greek legends.
Troi, Troye, Troyes; **Famous Namesakes:** *Football player Troy Aikman*; **Star Babies:** *Son of Jane Fonda and Tom Hayden*

TRUESDALE English: From the beloved one's farm
Truesdell, Truitestall

TRUMAN English: Loyal, honest
Trumen; **Nicknames:** *True, Tru*; **Famous Namesakes:** *Author Truman Capote, President Harry S Truman*; **Star Babies:** *Son of Rita Wilson and Tom Hanks*

TRUMBLE English: Strong or bold
Trumbald, Trumhall

TUBANSI African: Enduring

TUCKER English: Tucker of cloth
Tuckere

TUDER Greek: Nickname for Theodore

TUKETU Native American: Bear making dust (Miwok)

TULIO Latin, Spanish: Lively

TULLIS Latin: Rank
Nicknames: *Tulley, Tully*

TULLIUS Latin: Name of a king

TULLY Irish: Peaceful

TUPI Native American: To pull up (Miwok)

TUPPER English: Ram herder
Tuppere

TURNER Latin: One who turns bone, wood, or metal on the lathe. French: Champion in a tournament

TUTANKHAMUN Egyptian: Name of a pharaoh; King Nebkheperura Tutankhamun (King Tut) remains the most famous of all the Pharaohs of Ancient Egypt, but in fact he was a short-lived and fairly insignificant ruler during a transitional period in history. Little was known of him prior to Howard Carter's methodical detective work, but the discovery of his tomb and the amazing contents it held ultimately ensured this boy king of the immortality he sought.
Tutankhamon, Tutankhamoun; **Nicknames:** *King Tut*

TUVIYA Hebrew: The biblical Tuviya was a Levite during the reign of Jehoshaphat.
Tuvya

TYLER English: Tile layer or a variant of Taylor, an English surname frequently used as a given name.
Taylar

TYR Scandinavian: Warrior; Tyr was a daring and brave god of war in Norse mythology.

TYRE Latin: From Tyre

TYREE Scottish: Island dweller

TYREECE English: Form of Terrence

TYREL English: Powerful, thunder ruler; a form of Terrell
Tyrell, Tyrelle; **Star Babies:** *Son of Jesse Ventura*

TYRONE Irish: From Owen's territory; the name of a county in Ireland; (Greek) sovereign
Tyronne; **Nicknames:** *Ty*; **Famous Namesakes:** *Actor Tyrone Power*

TYRUS English: Modern blend of Tyrone and Cyrus; may also be a reference to the ancient Phoenician city of Tyre. See also *Tyre*

TYSON French: Hot tempered, firebrand. English: The son of Ty, which is a form of the Greek God of wine, Dionysus (English) *Tyvan; Tyeson, Tyesone*; **Nicknames:** *Ty, Tyce, Tye, Tyeis*

TZURIEL Hebrew: God is my rock, rock of Jehovah
Zuriel

UBERTO Italian: Variation of Hubert

UDELL English: From the yew tree valley; surname
Idal, Iwdael, Udale, Udall, Udayle, Yudell

UDOLF English: Prosperous or wealthy wolf
Udolph

UGO Italian: Variation of Hugh
Famous Namesakes: *Venezuelan President Ugo Chavez*

ULF Scandinavian: Wolf

ULFRED English: Peaceful wolf

ULGER English: Warring or fighting wolf

ULL Norse: Glory; in Norse mythology, the god of winter and skiers

ULLOCK English: Sporting wolf
Ullok

ULMER English: Famous wolf
(Norse) *Ulfmaerr; Ulmar, Ulmarr*

ULRICH German: Noble leader

ULYSSES Latin: Wrathful; variant of the Greek *Odysseus*, best known as a main character of the poet Homer's two great epics. Ulysses S. Grant commanded the Union armies during the Civil War and became President of the United States in 1868. (Spanish) *Ulises*

UMBERTO Italian: Variation of Humberto
Famous Namesakes: *Italian author Umberto Eco*

UMI African: Life

UNWIN English: Not a friend, implies stranger
Unwine, Unwyn

UPCHURCH English: From the upper church

UPTON Anglo-Saxon, English: From the upper town or settlement; surname
Uptun; **Famous Namesakes:** *Author Upton Sinclair*

UPWOOD English: From the upper forest
Upwode

URBAN Latin: Of the city
(Spanish) *Urbano; Urbain*

URI Hebrew: Light, flame; an Old Testament name that is also a short form of Uriah and Uriel

URIAH Hebrew: Light, flame
Urian, Uriel; **Nicknames:** *Uri*

UZIAH Hebrew: God is my strength; an Old Testament name
Uziel, Uzziah, Uzziel

VACLAV Czech: More glory; a form of Wenceslas
Famous Namesakes: *Czech President Václav Havel*

VADDON Welsh: From Bath

VADIM Russian: Attractive *Wadim;* **Famous Namesakes:** *French Director Roger Vadim (né Roger Vadim Plemiannikov)*

VADIN Hindi: Speaker

VAHAN Armenian: Shield

VAHID Persian: The only one

VAIL English: Lives in the valley; familar to many as the name of a ski resort town in Colorado
Bale, Vale, Vayle

VAL Latin: Nickname for Valerian
Famous Namesakes: *Actor Val Kilmer*

VALDEMAR Swedish: Variation of Walter

VALENTINE Latin, English: Valiant, strong; variant of Valentinus and the name of more than fifty saints and three Roman emperors (English) *Valen;* (Italian) *Valentino;* (Spanish) *Valentin; Valentyn;* **Nicknames:** *Val*

VALERIAN Latin: Valiant, brave, healthy; Valerian has a similar origin and meaning as Valentine but are not from the same name. See also *Valiant*
(Latin) *Valerius;* (Italian) *Valerio;* (Russian) *Valerik, Valery; Valera, Valerijs, Vallen;* **Nicknames:** *Val*

VALFRID Swedish: Variation of Walfried

VALI Norse: Uncertain meaning; Vali was a son of Odin in Norse mythology.

VALIANT English: Brave, strong, and healthy; main character of the historical adventure comic strip *Prince Valiant*

VALO Finnish: Light

VANCE English: Marshland; surname
Famous Namesakes: *Secretary of State Cyrus Vance*

VARDON French: From the green hill; surname
Varden

VARICK Teutonic: Defending ruler (English) *Warrick; Vareck, Varek, Varik, Varrick*

VARTAN Armenian: Giver of roses
Famous Namesakes: *Armenian musician Vartan Gevorkian*

VAVRIN Czech: Laurel

VELI Finnish: Brother

VERGE Anglo-Saxon: Owns four acres of land

VERN English: This surname is also used as an abbreviation of Vernon or Lavern.

VERYL French: True
Verel, Verrall, Verrell, Verrill

VESA Finnish: Sprout, young tree

VICTOR Latin, Spanish: To conquer (Italian) *Vittorio;* (Spanish) *Victoriano, Victorino, Victorio, Victoro;* (Russian) *Viktor;* (Polish) *Wictor;* (Hungarian) *Vidor;* **Nicknames:** *Vic, Vick, Victorien;* **Famous Namesakes:** *French author Victor Hugo*

VICTORIO Spanish: Variation of Victor

VIDAL French: Variation of Vito
Famous Namesakes: *Hair stylist Vidal Sassoon*

VINCE Latin: Nickname for Vincent
Famous Namesakes: *Musician Vince Gill*

VINCENT Latin: To conquer; the name of several early saints in France
(Italian) *Vincenzio, Vincenzo;* (Spanish) *Vicente;* (Hungarian) *Vencel, Vincze; Vincens, Vinci, Vincien, Vinzenz;* **Nicknames:** *Vince, Vinnie;* **Famous Namesakes:** *Artist Vincent Van Gogh;* **Star Babies:** *Son of Sophie Marceau*

> "If one feels the need of something grand, something infinite, something that makes one feel aware of God, one need not go far to find it. I think that I see something deeper, more infinite, more eternal than the ocean in the expression of the eyes of a little baby when it wakes in the morning and coos or laughs because it sees the sun shining on its cradle."
> —Vincent Van Gogh

VINSON English: Vincent's son, Vinn's son
Vinsone

VIRGIL Latin: Flourishing; most commonly recognized as the name of the Roman poet-philosopher and author of the time-honored epic *The Aeneid*
(Latin) *Verdell, Vernell;* (Spanish) *Virgilio*

VITALY Russian: Variation of Vito
Vitaliy; **Nicknames:** *Vitalik, Vytya, Vitia;* **Famous Namesakes:** *Gymnast Vitaly Scherbo*

VITO Latin, Italian: Life; also a surname
(French) *Vidal;* (Spanish) *Videl;* (Russian) *Vitaly;* (Polish) *Wit, Vital, Vitale;* **Old Forms:** *Vitus;* **Famous Namesakes:** *Actor Danny DeVito*

VLAD Russian: To rule
Diminutive Forms: *Vladik*

VLADIMIR Slavic, Russian: To rule the land
Nicknames: *Volodya;* **Famous Namesakes:** *Russian President Vladimir Putin*

VLADISLAV Russian, Slavic: Rules with glory
(Slavic) *Ladislas;* **Nicknames:** *Laszlo*

VLAS Russian: Slow

VOITTO Finnish: Victory

VOLGA Russian: Name of a river in Russia

VOLKER German: People's guard, defender
Famous Namesakes: *German director Volker Schlondorff*

VUKAN Romanian: Possibly a variant of Vulcan, the Roman smith god; the historical Vukan was son of Stephen, the founder of the Nemanyid dynasty in Serbia.

WACIAN Anglo-Saxon: To keep watch, alert

WADE Anglo-Saxon: River ford; also a name from Scandinavian mythology
Waed, Wayde; **Famous Namesakes:** *Baseball player Wade Boggs*

WADLEY English: From Wade's meadow, from the ford meadow; surname
Wadeley, Wadelea, Wadlea, Wadleigh

WADSWORTH English: From Wade's estate; surname
Famous Namesakes: *Poet Henry Wadsworth Longfellow*

WAFIYY Arabic: Loyal, faithful; masculine variant of Wafaa

WAGNER German: Wagon maker; an occupational surname
Famous Namesakes: *Composer Richard Wagner*

WAINWRIGHT English: Wagon maker; an occupational name and surname
Famous Namesakes: *Folk musician Loudon Wainwright*

WAITE English: Guard, watchman; surname
Wait, Wayte

WAKEFIELD English: From Wake's field, from the damp field; surname
Wacfeld

WAKELEY English: From Wake's meadow, from the damp meadow; surname
Wacleah, Wakelea, Wakeleigh

WAKEMAN English: Watchman; an occupational name and surname
Wacuman; **Diminutive Forms:** *Wake*

WALCOTT English: Cottage by the wall, possibly a Welshman's cottage; surname
Walcot, Wallcot, Wallcott, Wolcott

WALDEN English: From the wooded valley; for many, this name is associated with *Walden*, a classic piece of American literature from Henry David Thoreau.
Waldon

WALDO English: Nickname for Oswald
Famous Namesakes: *Author and poet Ralph Waldo Emerson*

WALFORD English: From the Welshman's ford

WALFRED German: Spelling variation of Walfried

WALKER English: Worker in cloth; a surname and occupational name
Famous Namesakes: *Author Walker Percy*; **Star Babies:** *Son of Adrienne Barbeau and Billy Van Zandt*

WALLACE English, Scottish: Welshman; Sir William Wallace was a Scottish hero who led a revolt against King Edward I of England.
Wallis, Walsh, Welch, Welsh; **Nicknames:** *Wally*; **Famous Namesakes:** *Poet Wallace Stevens*

WALT German: Nickname for Walter
Famous Namesakes: *Poet Walt Whitman*

WALTER German: Powerful warrior, ruler of an army
(French) *Gauthier, Gautier*; (Italian) *Galterio*; (Spanish) *Galtero, Gualterio*; (Irish) *Ualtar*; (Swedish) *Valdemar*; (Dutch) *Wouter*; (Finnish) *Valtteri*; *Walten, Walthari, Walther*; **Nicknames:** *Walt*; **Famous Namesakes:** *English author Sir Walter Scott, News anchorman Walter Cronkite*

WALTON English: From the Welshman's town or settlement

WALWYN English: Welsh friend

WAMBLEESHA Native American: White eagle (Sioux)

WARD English: Guard, watchman; an occupational name and surname
Warde, Warden, Weard, Worden; **Famous Namesakes:** *Fictional TV dad Ward Cleaver, Actor Ward Bond*

WARDLEY English: From the watchman's or guardian's meadow; surname
Weardleah, Wardlea, Wardleigh; **Nicknames:** *Ward, Lee*

WARFIELD English: From the field by the weir (trap for catching fish); surname
Weifield; **Famous Namesakes:** Football player Paul Warfield

WARFORD English: From the ford near the weir (a trap for catching fish)
Weiford

WARLEY English: From the meadow near the weir (a trap for catching fish)
Warleigh, Weirley

WARNER German, English: Defending warrior
Famous Namesakes: *Actor Warner Baxter*

WARREN English: Warrior; surname or place name
Famous Namesakes: *President Warren Harding, Actor Warren Beatty*

WASHBURN English: From the flooding brook
Washbourne, Washburne, Washborn

WASHINGTON English: From the intelligent one's town or settlement; surname
Famous Namesakes: *Author Washington Irving, Educator Booker T. Washington*

WASIM Arabic: Handsome

WATSON English: Son of Walter, son of Watt
Watkins, Wattekinson, Wattesone, Wattikinson, Wattkins, Watts, Wattson; **Famous Namesakes:** *Golfer Tom Watson*

WAVERLEY English: From the meadow of quaking aspen trees; evocative of Sir Walter Scott's Waverly novels
Waefreleah, Waverly, Waverlea, Waverlee, Waverleigh; **Famous Namesakes:** *Cookbook author Waverly Root*

WAYLAND English, Scandinavian: The land by the path or road; the mythological Scandinavian Wayland was a blacksmith with supernatural powers similar to Vulcan.
Waylan, Waylin, Waylon, Wegland, Weyland, Waylen, Weylan, Weylin, Weylon; **Nicknames:** *Way*; **Famous Namesakes:** *Singer Waylon Jennings*

WAYNE English: One who makes or drives wagons
Wain; **Famous Namesakes:** *Hockey star Wayne Gretzky, Entertainer Wayne Newton*

WEATHERLY English: From the wether sheep meadow; a surname and variant of Wetherly

WEBBER German: Weaver
Webb, Webbe, Weber; **Famous Namesakes:** *British theatrical composer Andrew Lloyd Webber, Jazz drummer Chick Webb*

WEBLEY English: From the weaver's meadow; surname
Webbeleah, Webbley, Weblea, Webbly, Webly

WEIRLEY English: Spelling variation of Warley

WELBORNE English: From the spring brook; no connection to aristocratic birth *Welborn, Welburn*

WELBY English, German: Well-farm; name of a popular TV doctor Marcus Welby, MD

WELTON English: Place of the well, town near the well; surname

WENCESLAS Slavic: More glory; Saint Wenceslas was a tenth-century duke of Bohemia murdered by his brother. He is the patron saint of the Czech Republic. This was also the name of several Bohemian kings. *Wenceslaus*; **Nicknames:** *Vaclav*; **Famous Namesakes:** *Czech President Václav Havel*

WENDELL German: Wanderer *Wendale, Wendall, Wendel*; **Famous Namesakes:** *Attorney and presidential candidate Wendell Willkie*

WERNER German: Defending warrior (Finnish) *Verneri*

WESLEY English: From the western meadow; surname *Wessley, Westleah, Westley, Weslie, Weslea, Wesleigh, Weslee*; **Diminutive Forms:** *Wes*; **Famous Namesakes:** *Actor Wesley Snipes, General Wesley Clark*

WESTBROOK English: From the western brook; surname *Westbroc, Wesbrook, Westbrooke*; **Nicknames:** *Brook, Brooke, Wes, West*

WESTBY English: From the western farm; surname *Wesby, Westbee, Westbie,*

WESTCOTT English: From the western cottage; surname *Westcot, Wescot, Wescott*; **Nicknames:** *Wes*

WESTON English: From the western town or settlement; surname *Westen, Westin, Westun*; **Nicknames:** *West, Wes*; **Star Babies:** *Son of Nicolas Cage*

WETHERLY English: From the wether sheep meadow (sheep being extremely important to the English culture and economy); surname *Weatherby, Weatherly, Wetherby, Wethrby, Wethrleah, Wetherlea*

WHARTON English: From the town or settlement near the weir (a trap for catching fish); this variant of Warton is recognized as the name of Ivy League Wharton School of Business. *Warton, Wartun*

WHEATLEY English: From the wheat meadow; surname *Wheatlea*; **Old Forms:** *Hwaeteleah*

WHEELER English: Wheel maker **Old Forms:** *Hweolere*

WHITBY English, Scandinavian: From the white farm; surname *Hwitby, Whitley, Whitbey, Whitbee, Whitbie*; **Nicknames:** *Whit*

WHITCOMB English: From the white valley; surname *Whitcumb, Whitcombe*; **Nicknames:** *Whit*

WHITFIELD English: From the white field; surname

WHITFORD English: From the white ford *Hwitford*

WHITLAW English: From the small white hill; surname **Old Forms:** *Hwithloew*

> *"Heaven lies about us in our infancy!"*
> —William Wordsworth

WHITLOCK English: Blond, white locks of hair
Old Forms: *Hwitloc*

WHITMORE English: From the white moor
Whitmoor, Whittemore, Witmore, Wittemore

WHITNEY English, Anglo-Saxon: From the white island; in recent years, Whitney has been used more for girls than boys.

WHITTAKER English: From the white acre

WICKHAM English: From the village paddocks; surname
Wiccum, Wickam; **Famous Namesakes:** *British actor Jeffrey Wickham*

WICKLEY English: From the village meadow; surname
Wicleah, Wichlea

WILBUR German: Resolute, brilliant
(German) *Wilbart; Wilber, Wilbert, Wilburn, Wilburt*; **Famous Namesakes:** *Aviation pioneer Wilbur Wright*

WILEY English: Spelling variation of Wylie
Wylie; **Famous Namesakes:** *Actor Wiley Wiggins*

WILFRED English, Teutonic: Desires peace
(German) *Wilfredo; Wilford, Wilfrid*

WILL English: Nickname for William
Famous Namesakes: *Actor Will Smith*; **Star Babies:** *Son of Colin Firth and Meg Tilly*

WILLIAM German: Resolute protector; *will* meaning strong and *helm* meaning helmet. For centuries after the Norman conquest in 1066, large numbers of English boys were given the name William in tribute to William the Conqueror. The firstborn son of Prince Charles is named William.
(German) *Wilhelm*; (French) *Guillaume*; (Italian) *Guglielmo, Guillermo*; (Gaelic) *Uilleam, Uilliam*; (Welsh) *Gwilym*; (Swedish) *Vilhelm*; (Dutch) *Willem*; (Czech) *Vilem*; (Finnish) *Viljami; Guilerme*; **Nicknames:** *Bill, Billie, Billy, Pim, Will, Willie, Willy, Wim*; **Diminutive Forms:** *Liam, Lyam*; **Famous Namesakes:** *President William Jefferson Clinton, Playwright William Shakespeare, Actor William Hurt*

WILLY English: Nickname for William

WILSON English: William's son; a surname often used as first name
Willesone, Williams, Williamson, Wilsyn, Willsyn, Wilsen, Wylson; **Nicknames:** *Will, Willie, Willy*; **Famous Namesakes:** *Musician Wilson Pickett*; **Star Babies:** *Son of Christine Lahti and Thomas Schlamme*

WIM German: Nickname for William
Famous Namesakes: *German film director Wim Wenders*

WINDSOR English: Riverbank with a winch; surname of the British royal family

WINFIELD English: Friend's field; surname
Winefeld, Winefield, Wynfield, Winnfield, Wynfeld; **Famous Namesakes:** *Baseball player Dave Winfield*

WINFRED English, Teutonic: Friend of peace; This surname is rarely used, perhaps because it sounds so similar to Winifred. *Winefrith, Winfrid, Winfrith, Winfryd, Wylfrid, Wynfred, Wynfrith*

WINSLOW English: Friend's hill, friend's place; surname
Winslowe; **Famous Namesakes:** *Painter Winslow Homer*

WINSTON English: From the friend's (or friendly) town or settlement, or from Wine's town or settlement; surname
Winton, Wynston, Wynton, Winsten, Winstonn, Wynstan; **Famous Namesakes:** *British Prime Minister Winston Churchill, Jazz musician Wynton Marsalis*

WINTER English: Seasonal name, born in the winter
Wynter, Winters, Wynters

WOLCOTT English: Lives in Wolf's cottage (Wolf is a person's name, not the animal); surname
Woolcott, Wulfcot

WOODLEY English: From the wooded meadow; surname
Wodeleah

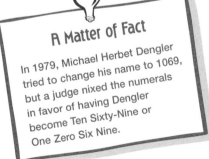

A Matter of Fact

In 1979, Michael Herbet Dengler tried to change his name to 1069, but a judge nixed the numerals in favor of having Dengler become Ten Sixty-Nine or One Zero Six Nine.

WOODROW English: From the cottages in the wood; woody
Woodroe, Woodrowe; **Nicknames:** *Woody*;
Famous Namesakes: *President Woodrow Wilson, Filmmaker Woody Allen*

WOODWARD English: Forester
Nicknames: *Woody*

WULFHERE Anglo-Saxon: An early king of the Mercia

WYATT English: Guide
Wiatt; **Famous Namesakes:** *American frontiersman Wyatt Earp*; **Star Babies:** *Son of Goldie Hawn and Kurt Russell*

WYCLIFF English: From the white cliff; surname
Wyclyf, Wyclyffe, Wyclef; **Nicknames:** *Cliff, Wyc, Wake*; **Famous Namesakes:** *Musician Wyclef Jean*

WYLIE English: Well-watered meadow; sounds like wily, meaning beguiling or clever. Anglo-Saxon: Enchanting
Wiley

WYMAN Anglo-Saxon, English: Fair-haired man, possibly fair-haired warrior

WYNDHAM English: From the windy village, hamlet; surname adapted to first name use
Windham

WYNN English, Welsh: Friend, fair; the root *wynn* is part of many English given names and surnames, emphasizing the importance of a good friend in life.
(Welsh) *Winn*; *Wyne*

WYNONO Native American: Firstborn, eldest (Sioux)

WYTHE English: Near the willow tree; surname adapted to first name use
Wyth

XALVADOR Spanish: Variation of Salvador

XANTHIPPUS Greek: Fair horse
Zanthippus, Xanthyppus

XANTHUS Greek, Latin: Golden-haired; in
Greek mythology, an immortal horse belonging to Achilles, given the power of speech by
Hera so that he could warn Achilles that he
was about to die

XANTI Basque: Named for Saint James

XARLES Basque: Variation of Charles

XAVIER Basque: The new house; popular-
ized by the sixteenth-century Jesuit mission-
ary Saint Francis Xavier
(Spanish) *Javier, Javiero, Xever;* (Basque)
Xaiver; Xabief, Zavier; **Famous Namesakes:**
Cuban musician Xavier Cugat

XENOS Greek: Stranger; also a common
variant of Xenophon
Xeno

XERXES Persian: Ruler over heroes,
monarch; name of a fifth-century B.C. king
of Persia. He attempted an invasion of
Greece that ended unsuccessfully at the battle
of Salamis.

XIMENES Spanish: Hearkening, listening;
variant of Simon

XIMON Hebrew: Spelling variation
of Simon

XIOMAR German: Famous in battle; variant
of Geomar

XUTHUS Greek: Son of Helen

XYLON Greek: From the forest

YAEL Hebrew: Spelling variation of Jael

YAFEU African: Bold

YAGIL Hebrew: He will rejoice
Yagel, Yagyl

YAHTO Native American: Blue (Sioux)

YAHYA Arabic: Variation of John
Yehya, Yehia

YAIR Hebrew: Enlighten

YAKOV Hebrew: Spelling variation of Jacob

YALE Welsh: From the fertile hill; associated
with Ivy League Yale University

YAMA Hindi: God of death and time in
Brahmanism

YANCY Native American: Englishman,
derived possibly from yankee
Yancey, Yansey, Yauncey, Yanci

YAPHET Hebrew: Enlarge, expand; variant
of Japheth

YARDEN Hebrew: Spelling variation
of Jordan
Yardeni

YARDLEY English: From the enclosed
meadow
*Yardly, Yardlee, Yardlea, Yardleigh, Yarley,
Yeardley*

YARON Hebrew: He who sings, cry of joy
Jaran, Jaren, Jaron, Jarren, Jarron, Yairon

YASHA Russian: Russian familar form
for Jacob or James
Yashka, Yashko

YASIN Arabic: Rich, prophet

YASIR Arabic: Easy, simple, homely, small; masculine version of Taysir

YATES English: Lives near the gates, gate keeper
Yeats; **Famous Namesakes:** *Irish poet and dramatist William Butler Yeats, Irish painter and writer John Butler Yeats*

YAVIN Hebrew: He understands
Javin, Yabin

YEDIDIAH Hebrew: Spelling variation of Jedidiah
Yedidyah

YEHUDI Hebrew: Praised; variant of Judah
Yehuda; **Famous Namesakes:** *British violinist and conductor Yehudi Menuhin*

YEOMAN English: Retainer, attendant; a man born free; in England a yeoman is considered next in order to gentry.
Yoman, Youman

YERIEL Hebrew: Established by God
Jeriel

YESHAYA Hebrew: Gift

YEVGENY Russian: Variation of Eugene
Famous Namesakes: *Russian conductor Yevgeny Svetlanov, Russian conductor Yevgeny Mravinsky*

YIFTACH Hebrew: He will open

YIGAL Hebrew: He shall redeem, be redeemed
Yigel

YISREAL Hebrew: Wrestles with God; variant of Israel

YOHANNA Arabic: Variation of John

YORK English: From the boar estate; from the yew town; place name, York in England, New York in the US; Duke of York is a title held by the English royal family (usually a younger son of king or queen)
Yorke, Yorick, Yoricke; **Famous Namesakes:** *Actor Dick York*

YOSEF Hebrew: Spelling variation of Joseph

YSBADDADEN Celtic: In Celtic mythology, Ysbaddaden was a fierce giant who would die if separated from his daughter, Olwen.
Yspaddaden

YSIDRO Greek: Spelling variation of Isidore

YSRAEL Hebrew: Wrestles with God; variant of Israel

YUDELL English: From the yew tree valley; surname; variant of Udell

YULE English: Born at Yuletide or winter's soltice, late December, now taken to mean born at Christmas
Ewell, Yul, Euell; **Famous Namesakes:** *Actor Yul Brenner*

YULI Basque: Youthful, young

YUMA Native American: Chief's son

YURI Russian: Variation of George
Yurii; **Nicknames:** *Yurochka, Yura, Yore, Yorii, Yurick*; **Famous Namesakes:** *Russian Cosmonaut Yuri Gagarin*

YUSUF Arabic: Variation of Joseph
Yousef, Youssef, Yousuf, Yusef

YUVAL Hebrew: Rejoice, be happy

YVES French: Variation of Ivor
Yvon; **Famous Namesakes:** *French singer Yves Montand, French fashion designer Yves Saint Laurent*

ZABDIEL Hebrew: Gift, present
Zabdil, Zabdyl; **Nicknames:** *Zabdi, Zabdy, Zabi, Zavdi, Zebdy*

ZACCHAEUS Hebrew: Clean, pure; the biblical Zacchaeus was a wealthy tax collector who became a disciple of Jesus.

ZACHARIAH Hebrew: Original form of Zachary

ZACHARY Hebrew: God remembers, remembrance of the Lord; derived from the name Zechariah; there are over thirty men with this name mentioned in the Bible, including the author of the Book of Zechariah.
(Hebrew) *Zachaios;* (German) *Zacharia;* (Spanish) *Zacarias;* (Finnish) *Sakari, Sakarias, Saku;* (Persian) *Zakaria; Zacharias, Zachely, Zackary, Zackery, Zakari, Zakary, Zechariah;* **Old Forms:** *Zachariah;* **Nicknames:** *Zach, Zack, Zak;* **Famous Namesakes:** *Actor Zachary Scott, President Zachary Taylor, Actor Zachery Ty Bryan;* **Star Babies:** *Son of Cheryl Tiegs*

ZADOK Hebrew: Just, righteous
Zadoc

ZADORNIN Basque: Saturn

ZAFIR Arabic: Victorious, successful
(Hindi) *Zafar, Zafeer;* **Famous Namesakes:** *Bosnian journalist Zafir Behlic*

ZAHID Arabic: Self-denying, ascetic, abstemious; if accent is placed on the second syllable, means moderate, little, trifling, insignificant
Zahed

ZAHIR Arabic: Sparkling, bright
Zuhayr, Zaher; **Famous Namesakes:** *Afghan singer Ahmed Zahir, King of Afghanistan Mohammed Zahir Shah*

ZAHUR African: Flower, from the Arabic word for flourishing (Swahili)

ZAID Arabic: Increases, grows
Zaied, Zaiid, Zayd

ZAIDE Hebrew: Elder
Zayde

ZAIM Arabic: General, title of authority

ZAKAI Hebrew: Pure, sinless, innocent

ZAKI Arabic: Smart, intelligent, compassionate
Famous Namesakes: *Egyptian musician Zaki*

ZALE Greek: Power of the sea
Zail, Zaile, Zayl, Zayle

ZANDER English: Nickname for Alexander

ZANE Hebrew, English: Everything that is good and beautiful; also ornament or decoration
Zain, Zaine, Zayne; **Nicknames:** *Zani;* **Famous Namesakes:** *Author Zane Gray*

ZANTHIPPUS Greek: Spelling variation of Xanthippus

ZARAD Hebrew: Ambush, trap
Zared

ZAREK Polish, Greek, Slavic: God protect the king; biblical king of Babylon who learned of his impending defeat by literally reading the writing on the wall
Zarec, Zareck, Zaric, Zarik, Zaryk, Zereck, Zerick

ZAVIER Arabic: Spelling variation of Xavier

ZAYIT Hebrew: Olive

ZBIGNIEW Polish: Do away with anger, be content

ZE'EV Hebrew: Wolf; in the Bible, when Jacob blesses his son Benjamin, he compares him to a wolf with this name.

ZEBEDIAH Hebrew: God's gift; biblical father of the apostles James and John
Zebadiah, Zebadia, Zebadya, Zebadyah, Zebedia, Zebedya, Zebedyah, Zebidia, Zebidiah; **Nicknames:** *Zeb, Zebedee, Zebad*

ZEBULON Hebrew: From the high house, the honored one; biblical son of Jacob
Zebulun, Zevulun, Zabulan, Zebulan, Zebulen, Zebulin, Zebulyn, Zevulon, Zhebule

ZEDEKIAH Hebrew: The Lord is mighty and just; biblical king of Judah
Zedechiah, Zedekiahs; **Nicknames:** *Zed*

ZEKE Hebrew: Nickname for Ezekiel
Star Babies: *Son of Neil Young*

ZEKI Turkish: Clever
Zekie, Zeky

ZELENY Czech: Green, fresh
Nicknames: *Zel*

ZELOTES Latin: Name given to Simon, one of the apostles, probably in association with the sect of Zealots

ZEMARIAH Hebrew: Song
Zemaria

ZENAS Greek: Welcoming
Zenios

ZENOBIO Greek, Spanish: Life of Zeus
Cenobio, Cenovio, Senobio, Senovio, Zenobios, Zenovio

ZENON Greek: Derived from the name Zeus, ruler of the gods in Greek mythology. Greek philosopher Zeno was the founder of stoicism.
(Spanish) *Cenon, Senon; Zeno*

ZEPHANIAH Hebrew: Treasured by the Lord; a minor Old Testament prophet and author of the Book of Zephaniah
Nicknames: *Zephan, Zeph*

ZEROUN Armenian: Respected, honored for wisdom

ZESIRO African: Older twin (Uganda)

ZETES Greek: Son of Boreas, brother of Calais, one of the famous argonauts of Greek mythology

ZETHUS Greek: Mythical son of Zeus and Antiope, and twin brother of Amphion

ZEUXIPPUS Latin: Mythical son of Syllis the nymph and the god Apollo

ZEV Hebrew: Familar form of Zebediah, Zebulon and other similar Hebrew names

ZEVID Hebrew: Given a gift

ZIGOR Basque: Punishes, punishment

ZIKOMO African: Gratitude

ZIMRAN Hebrew: Sacred, holy; one of Abraham's sons

ZIMRI Hebrew: Worthy, to be praised

ZINDEL Yiddish: Defends mankind; variant of Alexander

ZION Hebrew: Name of an ancient citadel located in the center of Jerusalem. Zion is also used to refer to a Jewish homeland and to heaven.

ZIPKIYAH Native American: Hunter with the big bow (Kiowa)

ZITOMIR Czech: Live well
Zitek

ZIVEN Slavic, Polish: Full of life, vigorous
Zivon

ZIYA Arabic: Shining light
Zia

ZIYAD African: Increasing, adding to

ZOHAR Hebrew: Shines brightly
Zohair, Zohare; **Nicknames:** *Ziv*

ZOLTAN Hungarian: Life, energy, from the Greek *zoe*, meaning life
Zoltar; **Famous Namesakes:** *Hungarian composer Zoltán Kodály*

ZORION Basque: Variation of Orion
Zorian

ZUHAYR Arabic: Sparkling; Zuhayr is also the masculine, diminutive form of Zahra, changing the meaning to small flower or blossom.

ZURIEL Hebrew: Spelling variation of Tzuriel

ZVI Hebrew: Deer, gazelle
(Dutch) *Zwi*

ZYGMUNT Polish: Variation of Sigmund

The Top 100 Names of 2004

As reported by the Social Security Administration

 Boys' Names

1	Jacob	35	Austin	69	Ian
2	Michael	36	Robert	70	Jesus
3	Joshua	37	Thomas	71	Carlos
4	Matthew	38	Connor	72	Adrian
5	Ethan	39	Evan	73	Diego
6	Andrew	40	Aidan	74	Julian
7	Daniel	41	Jack	75	Cole
8	William	42	Luke	76	Ashton
9	Joseph	43	Jordan	77	Steven
10	Christopher	44	Angel	78	Jeremiah
11	Anthony	45	Isaiah	79	Timothy
12	Ryan	46	Isaac	80	Chase
13	Nicholas	47	Jason	81	Devin
14	David	48	Jackson	82	Seth
15	Alexander	49	Hunter	83	Jaden
16	Tyler	50	Cameron	84	Colin
17	James	51	Gavin	85	Cody
18	John	52	Mason	86	Landon
19	Dylan	53	Aaron	87	Carter
20	Nathan	54	Juan	88	Hayden
21	Jonathan	55	Kyle	89	Xavier
22	Brandon	56	Charles	90	Wyatt
23	Samuel	57	Luis	91	Dominic
24	Christian	58	Adam	92	Richard
25	Benjamin	59	Brian	93	Antonio
26	Zachary	60	Aiden	94	Jesse
27	Logan	61	Eric	95	Blake
28	Jose	62	Jayden	96	Sebastian
29	Noah	63	Alex	97	Miguel
30	Justin	64	Bryan	98	Jake
31	Elijah	65	Sean	99	Alejandro
32	Gabriel	66	Owen	100	Patrick
33	Caleb	67	Lucas		
34	Kevin	68	Nathaniel		

Girls' Names

1	Emily	35	Katherine	69	Sofia
2	Emma	36	Megan	70	Jordan
3	Madison	37	Alexandra	71	Alexa
4	Olivia	38	Jennifer	72	Rebecca
5	Hannah	39	Destiny	73	Gabrielle
6	Abigail	40	Allison	74	Caroline
7	Isabella	41	Savannah	75	Vanessa
8	Ashley	42	Haley	76	Gabriella
9	Samantha	43	Mackenzie	77	Avery
10	Elizabeth	44	Brooke	78	Marissa
11	Alexis	45	Maria	79	Ariana
12	Sarah	46	Nicole	80	Audrey
13	Grace	47	Makayla	81	Jada
14	Alyssa	48	Trinity	82	Autumn
15	Sophia	49	Kylie	83	Evelyn
16	Lauren	50	Kaylee	84	Jocelyn
17	Brianna	51	Paige	85	Maya
18	Kayla	52	Lily	86	Arianna
19	Natalie	53	Faith	87	Isabel
20	Anna	54	Zoe	88	Amber
21	Jessica	55	Stephanie	89	Melanie
22	Taylor	56	Jenna	90	Diana
23	Chloe	57	Andrea	91	Danielle
24	Hailey	58	Riley	92	Sierra
25	Ava	59	Katelyn	93	Leslie
26	Jasmine	60	Angelina	94	Aaliyah
27	Sydney	61	Kimberly	95	Erin
28	Victoria	62	Madeline	96	Amelia
29	Ella	63	Mary	97	Molly
30	Mia	64	Leah	98	Claire
31	Morgan	65	Lillian	99	Bailey
32	Julia	66	Michelle	100	Melissa
33	Kaitlyn	67	Amanda		
34	Rachel	68	Sara		

Baby Name Workbook

It's time to name your baby! The following ten exercises correspond with those found in chapters one through five. (Brief recaps of the instructions are provided for your convenience). Pencils only, please, as we encourage you to add or erase names at any time throughout the process.

Exercise One: Visualization (see page 15)

*Throughout your pregnancy visualize who your child might be and what she might look like. Now visualize the same person as a young adult, and then imagine her in a career or family setting. Begin thinking of names for this person, and as these names come to you, record them below. **This is your primary ongoing collection**; you may add to this list throughout the process and refer to it as you complete the other exercises. You're just brainstorming at this point, so be as creative as you'd like!*

GIRLS' NAMES	BOYS' NAMES

🖉 Exercise Two: "A" Is for Alliteration (see page 18)

Flip through the alphabetical listings of names with a similar initial sound as your last name,
as well as similar sounds within your name. (Middle names are optional at this stage.)
For example, Smith should look at S and C.
If any names in these sections appeal to you, add them to your list.

GIRLS' NAMES		
First	Middle (optional)	Last
Example: Susan		Smith

BOYS' NAMES		
First	Middle (optional)	Last

Exercise Three: The Acronym Game (see page 18)

Use the first letter of your last name: ___ (example: P for Peters)

What desirable three-letter words can it spell?

(Feel free to use phonetic, rather than actual spellings.)

P O P ___ ___ ___ ___ ___ ___ ___ ___ ___

Now choose first and middle combinations that achieve the desired acronyms.

GIRLS' NAMES				
Example: Pamela	Olivia	Peters	=	P O P
_____	_____	_____	=	_____
_____	_____	_____	=	_____
_____	_____	_____	=	_____
_____	_____	_____	=	_____
_____	_____	_____	=	_____
_____	_____	_____	=	_____
_____	_____	_____	=	_____

BOYS' NAMES				
_____	_____	_____	=	_____
_____	_____	_____	=	_____
_____	_____	_____	=	_____
_____	_____	_____	=	_____
_____	_____	_____	=	_____
_____	_____	_____	=	_____
_____	_____	_____	=	_____
_____	_____	_____	=	_____

✎ Exercise Four: Get Descriptive (see page 22)

Write down adjectives that define personal characteristics most important to you.
Then look through the book for names with those meanings, or check synonyms
in a thesaurus for possible name options.
(See pages 89, 171, 236, and 311 for lists of virtue names.)

GIRLS' NAMES

Adjective	*Name*
Example: Honest	Candid

BOYS' NAMES

Adjective	*Name*

Exercise Five: The Family Name Quiz (see page 23)

Try answering the following questions about your family for inspiration:

(1) Which relative(s) has inspired you the most throughout life?

(2) What is your mother's maiden name?

(3) Is there a relative that has passed away that should be remembered?

(4) Any other special family names? Add them to your list.

GIRLS' NAMES	
Adjective	*Name*
_____	_____
_____	_____
_____	_____
_____	_____
_____	_____
_____	_____

BOYS' NAMES	
Adjective	*Name*
_____	_____
_____	_____
_____	_____
_____	_____
_____	_____
_____	_____

🖊 *Exercise Six: Place Names (see page 25)*

Is there a special place in your lives that could be the perfect name? Try answering these questions:

1) Where did you meet your partner?

2) Where were you when you got engaged?

3) Where did you go on your honeymoon?

4) Where were you when you conceived your child?

5) What do you think is the most beautiful place on earth?

6) Do any special places or moments come to mind?

GIRLS' NAMES	BOYS' NAMES
Example: Georgia	Troy

Exercise Seven: The Ethnic Challenge (see page 27)

Peruse the name dictionary for names specific to your or your partner's ethnic background.
(These names could even be contenders for your baby's middle name.)

Mom's Ethnicity: _____

Dad's Ethnicity: _____

GIRLS' NAMES	BOYS' NAMES

🖉 Exercise Eight: Choose Your Lists (see page 35)

Do any of the following categories of names have special meaning for you:
Biblical, Nature, New Age, Shakespearean, Musical, Place, or Surnames as First Names?
If so, peruse the various lists in chapter four, and write down any names that appeal to you.
If a category doesn't interest you, leave it blank.

GIRLS' NAMES	BOYS' NAMES

Biblical

_____	_____
_____	_____
_____	_____
_____	_____
_____	_____

Nature

_____	_____
_____	_____
_____	_____
_____	_____
_____	_____

New Age

_____	_____
_____	_____
_____	_____
_____	_____
_____	_____

GIRLS' NAMES	BOYS' NAMES

Shakespearean

_____   _____
_____   _____
_____   _____
_____   _____
_____   _____

Place Names

_____   _____
_____   _____
_____   _____
_____   _____
_____   _____

Musical

_____   _____
_____   _____
_____   _____
_____   _____
_____   _____

Surnames as First Names

_____   _____
_____   _____
_____   _____
_____   _____
_____   _____

Exercise Nine: Mom and Dad's Lists of Favorites (see page 50)

Now it's time to start narrowing down your choices. Mom and Dad, separately go through
the lists you created in the previous exercises—or look up new names, if you think the
perfect one is still out there—and write your favorite names below (*first* names only at
this stage). Include your reason for choosing each one. Then rate each name from one to ten.

MOM'S LIST		
Girls' Names	*Reason*	*Rating*
Boys' Names	*Reason*	*Rating*

DAD'S LIST		
Girls' Names	*Reason*	*Rating*
_____	_____	____
_____	_____	____
_____	_____	____
_____	_____	____
_____	_____	____
_____	_____	____
_____	_____	____
_____	_____	____
_____	_____	____
_____	_____	____

Boys' Names	*Reason*	*Rating*
_____	_____	____
_____	_____	____
_____	_____	____
_____	_____	____
_____	_____	____
_____	_____	____
_____	_____	____
_____	_____	____
_____	_____	____
_____	_____	____

🖊 Exercise Ten: The Final Cut (see page 51)

Now, Mom and Dad, work together again. First, write down any first name appearing on both of your lists from the previous exercise. Then, put your heads together to choose a complementary middle name. (See page 19 for important factors to consider when selecting a middle name.)

GIRLS' NAMES

Any name appearing on **both** lists   Favorite complementary **middle** name

_____   _____

_____   _____

BOYS' NAMES

Any name appearing on **both** lists   Favorite complementary **middle** name

_____   _____

_____   _____

Note: If you're doing this exercise on your own,
simply choose your favorite two names from your
boys' and girls' lists and write them above.

Next, compare your individual lists and select your favorite first names from your partner's lists. For each first name that Dad chooses, Mom gets to choose her favorite complementary middle name and vice versa.

GIRLS' NAMES

Dad's favorite first name from **Mom's** list

Mom's favorite complementary **middle** name

_____

_____

Mom's favorite first name from **Dad's** list

Dad's favorite complementary **middle** name

_____

_____

BOYS' NAMES

Dad's favorite first name from **Mom's** list

Mom's favorite complementary **middle** name

_____

_____

Mom's favorite first name from **Dad's** list

Dad's favorite complementary **middle** name

_____

_____

Now that you've chosen the final contenders, it's time to pick the winner. Spend as much time as you need with the above lists of names.
For tips on making your final selection, see pages 51-52.

Baby's Name

Name:

Meaning: